lonely planet

Austria

Upper Austria p162
VIENNA p50
Lower Austria & Burgenland p123
The Salzkammergut p214
Tyrol & Vorarlberg p323
Salzburg & Salzburgerland p245
Styria p187
Carinthia p294

Rudolf Abraham, Becki Enright, Anthony Haywood, Samantha Priestley, Kerry Walker

Stadtturm (p334), Innsbruck

CONTENTS

Plan Your Trip

The Journey Begins Here 4
Austria Map 6
Our Picks 8
Regions & Cities 20
Itineraries 22
When to Go 30
Get Prepared 32
The Food Scene 34
Skiing & Snowboarding 37
The Outdoors 40

The Guide

Vienna 50
- Historic Centre: Innere Stadt 56
- Prater & Around: Leopoldstadt 81
- Belvedere & Beyond: Landstrasse 87
- Naschmarkt & Around: Wieden & Mariahilf 93
- Neubau, Josefstadt & Alsergrund 99
- Schloss Schönbrunn: Hietzing 110
- Outer Districts 116

Skiing, Mayrhofen (p343)

Lower Austria & Burgenland 123
- The Wachau Valley 126
- Waldviertel & Weinviertel 144
- Neusiedler See 151

Upper Austria 162
- Linz 166
- Nationalpark Kalkalpen 176

Styria 187
- Graz 190

The Salzkammergut 214
- Bad Ischl 220
- Hallstätter See 224
- Wolfgangsee & Mondsee 230
- Bad Aussee & Around 235
- Traunsee & Attersee 239

Salzburg & Salzburgerland 245
- Salzburg 248
- Zell am See 273
- Hohe Tauern National Park 279

Carinthia 294
- Klagenfurt & Wörthersee 298
- Villach 303
- Central Carinthia 307
- Millstätter See 310
- Lienz & the Dolomites 318

Tyrol & Vorarlberg 323
- Innsbruck 328
- The Zillertal 340
- Kitzbühel 348
- The Ötztal 356
- St Anton Am Arlberg 362
- Bregenz 369

Christmas market (p78), Vienna

Toolkit

Arriving 382
Getting Around 383
Train Travel 384
Money 385
Accommodation 386
Family Travel 387
Food, Drink & Nightlife 388
Responsible Travel 390
Health & Safe Travel 392
LGBTIQ+ Travellers 393
Accessible Travel 394
Nuts & Bolts 395
Language 396

Storybook

A History of Austria in 15 Places 400
Meet the Austrians 404
The Green City: Capital of a Green Nation 406
Austria's Coffee House Culture 408
From Falco to Mozart 412
Mountain Highs: Hiking in Austria 414
Mountains of the Mind 417

Pinzgauer Spaziergang (p275)

AUSTRIA
THE JOURNEY BEGINS HERE

Austria looks deceptively small on a map, but as most of it is vertical, there's always a mountain pass, alpine view or hidden hamlet to discover. As a hiker, I'm happiest when breaking a sweat hoofing up a 3000m precipice on a trail in Tyrol or Salzburgerland as the last light makes the summits blush. *Alpenglühen*, they call it. Ever since I first set foot in real snow in the Austrian Alps more than 20 years ago, these mountains have instilled a childlike wonder in me. Then there are Vienna's grand coffee houses, palaces and peerless art collections, the vine-laced Wachau (and its summer-in-a-glass white wines), the Salzkammergut's stained-glass blue lakes and Carinthia's medieval villages, not to mention castles and abbeys that send spirits soaring on every beautiful bend. What's not to love?

Kerry Walker
@kerryawalker; kerryawalker.com

A lifelong Austria lover, Kerry divides her time between the Alps and home in England. Kerry wrote the Salzburg & Salzburgerland and Tyrol & Vorarlberg chapters.

My favourite experience is hiking the **Pinzgauer Spaziergang** (p275) above Zell am See on a cloudless summer day, with uplifting views of Austria's highest peaks on the horizon.

WHO GOES WHERE

Our writers and experts choose the places, which for them, define Austria.

Neusiedler See (p161) in the north of Burgenland is a strangely magical place. It's unlike any preconceived idea of what Austria looks like, or the Austria I fell in love with so many years ago – surrounded by a landscape as flat as a pancake, with not a mountain in sight – but with stacks of laid-back charm, and home to an incredible amount of wildlife and ridiculously good wines.

Rudolf Abraham

@rudolfphoto

Rudolf is an award-winning travel writer and author specialising in central and southeast Europe. He wrote the Lower Austria & Burgenland and Styria chapters.

Vienna (p50) captivates with glorious architecture and masterpiece museums. But its quieter corridors of time reveal more about the city's earlier history: in old market squares, hidden courtyards, overlooked alleyways, and in the subterranean passages and ruin stacks beneath it all. Vienna's history from the Roman, Medieval and Imperial to now is as stacked as its layers.

Becki Enright

@bordersofadventure

Becki is a travel writer penning guidebooks and articles. She has called Vienna home for 10 years. Becki wrote the Vienna chapter.

Having spent my early years on the water around Perth, Western Australia, I love Austria's lakes. The **Weissensee** (p316) is a favourite. I love swimming in its cool waters and hiking to meadow huts in the mountains above the lake to enjoy a cold platter and a wine or beer. And if the sun's shining, everything tastes better.

Anthony Haywood

anthonyjhaywood.com

Anthony is a writer and editor based in southern Germany who has been researching and writing about Austria for over a decade. Anthony wrote the Salzkammergut and Carinthia chapters.

The streets of **Linz** (p166) tell us stories of an industrial past that lingers in the air, but they are also pathways to creativity, community and cake. As the Danube wanders right through the city like smoke, so too do the memories of music and the forging of festivals that take art in all its forms and usher it forward into the future.

Samantha Priestley

@sampriestleywriter

Samantha writes about travel, and food and drink from her home in Sheffield. Samantha wrote the Upper Austria chapter.

Salzburg
Unleash your inner Maria in cinematic Salzburg (p248)

Kitzbühel
Ride slopes of Olympic legend at this glam town in the Tyrolean Alps (p348)

The Zillertal
Watch cows come home from summer pastures (p340)

Hohe Tauern National Park
Scale sky-high peaks in Austria's alpine heartland (p279)

Grossglockner Road
Buckle up for an epic alpine drive (p284)

Werfen
Explore the world's largest accessible ice caves (p269)

PLAN YOUR TRIP

Linz
Tune into cutting-edge art and new-wave technology (p166)

The Wachau
Quaff wine among romantic vines (p126)

Stift Melk
Marvel at this abbey's golden glory (p128)

Vienna
Admire Austrian art in revamped imperial stables (p50)

Hallstätter See
Take in soaring alpine scenery peaks on crazily pretty lake shores (p224)

Klagenfurt
Chill out in Carinthia's relaxed capital and on the shores of nearby Wörthersee (p298)

Graz
Immerse yourself in art and slow food in Austria's UNESCO-listed second city (p190)

Neusiedler See
Enjoy fine wines, birdlife and watersports at this wetland wonderland (p151)

INSPIRED BY AUSTRIA

With its palace-bejewelled cities, castle-crested hills, looking-glass lakes and soaring, snowcapped Alps, Austria does backdrops like nowhere else on Earth. Over centuries, artists, poets, novelists, composers and Hollywood filmmakers have found inspiration in its grand designs and wondrous nature. Whether with pen, paintbrush, composer's baton or camera, they have captured and immortalised Austria's beauty, catapulted it onto the world stage, inspired generations of people to visit and forever defined their travel aspirations.

Problems Like Maria

Salzburg birthed *The Sound of Music*, where a yodelling nun taught the world to sing. But you'll also find film locations in the sublime, lake-spattered Salzkammergut.

Take a Bow

Austria's classical music heritage runs deep: Mozart, Beethoven, Strauss, Schubert, Haydn and Bruckner are all on the podium, and concert halls still resonate with their symphonies.

Silent Night

The origins of the world's best-loved carol can be found in **Salzburg** (p248), Hallein and the Oberndorf chapel where it was first performed in 1818.

Wiener Riesenrad (p84), Prater Park, Vienna

BEST INSPIRED EXPERIENCES

Sing your gleeful heart out as you pedal from abbey to garden, lake and pavilion, ticking off *The Sound of Music* film locations in ❶ **Salzburg** (p248) by bike.

Seek out the shadowy world of film noir on a *The Third Man* tour in ❷ **Vienna** (p50), dipping into the Prater where the Riesenrad twirls.

Hurtle down the powdery slopes of the ❸ **Montafon** (p375) in the shadow of the pointy Silvretta Alps, just as Hemingway did in *A Moveable Feast*.

Waltz along the most beautiful stretch of the Danube, the ❹ **Wachau** (p126), to the tune of Strauss' 1866 'An der schönen blauen Donau', commonly known in English as *The Blue Danube*.

Lift your gaze to the heavens in the resplendent ❺ **Stift St Florian** (p175), the abbey where composer Anton Bruckner was organist and composed his first motets and a requiem.

Danube Cycle Path (p132), Wachau Valley

RIDES TO REMEMBER

With the Alps ripping across half the country, Austria has a lot of altitude. With its lyrical landscapes, journeys here are about more than getting from A to B – whether whizzing along a lakefront by e-bike, unzipping a ravishing mountain valley by train or corkscrewing up to a wind-buffeted pass by car.

Drive Time

The Austrian Alps are laced through with sensational road trips, but many toll roads over mountain passes disappear with the snow (opening roughly from May to October).

Renting Wheels

Road, mountain and e-bikes are available in most towns and resorts. ÖBB stations rent out bikes (download the app) or try the local Intersport.

BEST RIDE EXPERIENCES

Buckle up for the 48km sky-high ❶ **Grossglockner Road** (p284), helter-skeltering into the glaciated realms of Hohe Tauern.

Slip into a saddle on the 380km ❷ **Danube Cycle Path** (p132), passing the Wachau's spirit-lifting castles, abbeys and wine country.

Chug through tunnels and across bridges on the nostalgic 19th-century ❸ **Semmeringbahn** (p142).

Swing over the mountains from Mayrhofen to the thunderous Krimmler Wasserfälle on the 37km ❹ **Gerlos Alpine Road** (p345).

Take a twilight tram spin around Vienna's monu-mental ❺ **Ringstrasse** (p76), an architectural tour de force.

IN HIGH SPIRITS

There's no need to choose between grape and grain in Austria, a country where glasses are always half full. From *Weingut* (winery) tastings in the Wachau and South Styria, to apple ciders in the Mostviertel, monastic brews in Salzburg and fiery schnapps in Tyrol, one of the main words you'll need to know here is *Prost!* Cheers!

BEST TASTING EXPERIENCES

Drink a perfect pint at the *Brauhaus* in ❶ **Freistadt** (p172) – this community-run brewery has been going strong since 1383.

Taste zesty Grüner Veltliner and Riesling wines among vines ribbing the banks of the Danube in the ❷ **Wachau DAC wine region** (p127).

Beer Gardens

A fine excuse to take a break on a balmy day, Austria's *Biergärten* (beer gardens) really come into their own in summer. Besides local brews, many also serve traditional grub like sausages and pork roast.

Autumn Harvest

Gold-tinged harvest days in September are the best time to try *Most* (usually cider), *Sturm* (pictured; fizzy, semi-fermented juice) and young cider.

Quaff plum schnapps made from the surrounding orchards in the plateau-perched distillery village ❸ **Stanz** (p361).

Have a cold one under chestnut trees in the 1400-seat beer garden of Salzburg's 400-year-old ❹ **Augustiner Bräustübl** (p265).

Heurigen

Sprinkled among the vines in the capital's fringes, Vienna's *Heurigen* (wine taverns) are a proper slice of Austrian life. Most open from spring to autumn – look out for the sprig of pine and *Ausg'steckt* sign.

Hop from vineyard to *Heuriger* as the harvest gets underway on Vienna's annual wine hike, the ❺ **Wiener Weinwandertag** (p119).

FROM LEFT: JONATHON STOKES/LONELY PLANET, IAN PATRICK/ALAMY

GRAND DESIGNS

You can't point a finger at a map of Austria without knocking over a palace, castle or abbey. Over centuries, margraves and dukes, Benedictine and Cistercian monks, prince-archbishops and Habsburg emperors have drained the country's coffers to build designs ever grander, leaving the most impressive legacy for generations to come. Beyond their ornate trappings, these magnificent edifices capture the spirit and soul of Austria, as centres of worship and pilgrimage, and repositories of history and art.

Choose Your Palace

Nowhere can rival Vienna for Habsburg pomp and splendour, but avoid *Schloss* fatigue by homing in on just one or two palaces. You can't see them all.

Pilgrimage Trails

Driving across Austria you'll tick off abbeys like rosary beads, but for a more profound experience, walk in the blistered footsteps of pilgrims on long-distance trails like the Jakobsweg.

Counting Castles

Plonked on high crags and backdropped by the Alps, Austria's castles are Grimm fairy-tale stuff especially in Salzburgerland and Tyrol.

Stift Melk (p128), Wachau Valley

BEST GRAND DESIGN EXPERIENCES

Delve into 900 years of rip-roaring history at hilltop ❶ **Festung Hohensalzburg** (p250), one of Europe's best-preserved fortresses.

Whizz back to the age of empires at Vienna's graceful ❷ **Hofburg** (p64), Habsburg HQ for 640 years and host to the treasury's imperial crowns and lavish state apartments.

Gasp at the golden glory of twin-spired ❸ **Stift Melk** (p128). Rising like a vision above the Danube, this Benedictine abbey-fortress is a baroque tour de force.

Venture deep into the soaring peaks of the Gesäuse mountains in Styria for a glimpse of the baroque-in-overdrive Benedictine abbey in ❹ **Admont** (p209).

Saunter in the dainty footsteps of Empress Elisabeth around the opulent state apartments and gardens of UNESCO World Heritage summer palace ❺ **Schloss Schönbrunn** (p112).

Hallstätter See (p224)

ON THE WATER

The sea might be miles away but, trust us, you won't miss it. This ravishing little country is sprinkled with thousands of lakes, woven with mighty rivers – the Danube, Inn and Drava – and splashed with turbulent falls. Under the surface, hot springs bubble. Embrace them with a swim, raft, bath or paddle.

Spa Time

Austria's spas tap into healing thermal waters. Take a dip in the likes of belle-époque Bad Gastein (Tyrol), Roman-rooted Baden bei Wien (near Vienna) and Villach (Carinthia).

Lake District

A lake, you say? Make a beeline for the Salzkammergut, glittering with 76 lakes – from mountain tarns to greats like Wolfgangsee, Attersee, Mondsee and Hallstätter See.

BEST WATER EXPERIENCES

Windsurf reed-fringed ❶ **Neusiedler See** (p151), Europe's second-largest steppe lake and the lowest point in Austria.

Brave the foaming rapids of the Inn and Ötztaler Ache rivers on a white-water rafting trip from ❷ **St Anton am Arlberg** (p362).

Marvel over alpine scenery while stand-up paddleboarding on ❸ **Hallstätter See** (p224), evading crowds in one of Austria's prettiest towns.

Dive into the crystal-clear waters of mountain-rimmed ❹ **Millstätter See** (p310), a fine spot for swimming and kayaking.

Take a refreshing dip in Carinthia's highest swimmable glacial lake – the turquoise, 930m-high ❺ **Weissensee** (p316).

LAND OF ART & MUSIC

For such a small country, Austria's impact on the arts has been off the charts. The Habsburgs left a legacy of historic paintings, sculptures, concert halls and the Vienna Philharmonic – one of the world's finest orchestras. And this is where child prodigy Mozart dazzled, Strauss taught the world to waltz and Klimt created the ultimate kiss.

BEST ART & MUSIC EXPERIENCES

Marvel at Klimt and Kokoschka masterpieces in Vienna's ❶ **MuseumsQuartier** (p102), former imperial stables reborn as one of the world's biggest art spaces.

Hear world-class opera reverberate over Lake Constance during the summertime ❷ **Bregenz Festival** (p370).

Zoom in on edgy contemporary arts at spacey ❸ **Kunsthaus Graz** (p190), nicknamed the 'friendly alien'.

Catch top-drawer opera, music and drama all over the city at the mammoth ❹ **Salzburger Festspiele** (p262).

Tune into forward-thinking museums, galleries and festivals at ❺ **Kunstmeile Krems** (Art Mile Krems; p126) in the Wachau.

Klimt Fever

Vienna's where it's at. Start your gold-kissed Klimt journey at Schloss Belvedere and continue it at the Leopold Museum, *Beethoven Frieze*-bedecked Secession and Kunsthistorisches Museum (pictured).

Linz Street Art

Industrial buildings have been revived at the Mural Harbor gallery in Linz, a pop-up urban gallery with 300 murals. Anyone is welcome to add to it.

Scoring Tickets

If you want to score concert and opera tickets for a song, look out for inexpensive standing-room tickets (most are sold around 80 minutes before the performance).

THE REALLY WILD SHOW

Mother Nature pulled out all the stops in Austria. Over millennia, elemental forces have dramatically shaped its landscapes, etched with forests, rippled through with lofty peaks and riven with deep valleys. Then there are the natural wonders that force you to gaze up in wide-eyed wonder: great glaciers and waterfalls, ice caves and soaring rock formations that fire the imagination and make you feel like a tiny speck on the face of the planet.

Wildlife Watch

National parks pulse with wildlife. Grab binoculars for Hohe Tauern (eagles, ibex – pictured, chamois, marmots), Neusiedler See-Seewinkel (migratory birds) and Kalkalpen (the elusive lynx).

Ranger Hikes

Many national parks offer ranger hikes (sometimes free or discounted with a guest card), which give the inside scoop on landscape, geology and wildlife.

Photo Ops

Make the most of early-morning and evening light. Wildlife close-ups are best with a telephoto zoom lens; moving too close unnerves animals.

Krimmler Wasserfälle (p285), Salzburgerland

BEST NATURE EXPERIENCES

Join twitchers on the reedy shores of ❶ **Neusiedler See** (p151) to spot spoonbills, herons, sea eagles and bee-eaters.

Wrap up warm for a frosty welcome at ❷ **Eisriesenwelt** (p269), the world's largest accessible ice caves, high above Werfen in the Tennengebirge.

Feel the spray of the mist-dashed, rainbow-kissed ❸ **Krimmler Wasserfälle** (p285), plummeting 380m over forested cliffs in Hohe Tauern National Park.

Hike to the edge of the deeply crevassed ❹ **Pasterze Glacier** (p282), the longest stream of eternal ice in the eastern Alps.

Climb to the cavernous ❺ **Dachstein Caves** (p228) and find yourself in a strange world of eerily lit ice and subterranean hollows.

Cows, the Zillertal (p340)

ROOTED IN TRADITION

Austria's age-old folk heritage is woven deep into its cultural fabric. From time-lost villages to timber-clad taverns dishing up traditional food, Vienna's grand coffee-house culture to yodelling festivals in the Alps and riotous pre-Lenten parades, the country keeps a tight grip on its traditions.

Folk Music

You'll hear it up and down the Alps, but Tyrol's Zillertal is numero uno for *Alpenländische Volksmusik* (alpine folk music), with 200 thigh-slapping bands and groups in the valley.

Rock the Tracht

Tracht (traditional costume) isn't just for special occasions. In hotels and restaurants in the Alps, you'll often see women dressed in embroidered Dirndl and men in Lederhosen and woollen jackets.

BEST TRADITIONAL EXPERIENCES

Watch the cows come home from high summer pastures, adorned with bells and floral wreaths, during the Almabtrieb in ❶ the **Zillertal** (p340).

Get an insight into traditional *Blaudruck* (indigo printing) in a family workshop in ❷ **Burgenland** (p122).

Dash away from the whip-cracking demon Krampus, who tears through Tyrolean towns like ❸ **Igls** (p336) near Innsbruck on 5 December.

Live it up with costume parades, folk music, arts and crafts at Villacher Kirchtag in ❹ **Villach** (p303).

Make merry with ❺ **Weinviertel** (p144) locals on Easter Monday's *'in d'Grean gehen'* ('outing in the green').

SKY-HIGH ADVENTURES

Any Austrian will confess that the only way to really get under the skin of their lovely little land is to hoof it up a whopping great mountain – or tear down one on skis. Whether it's to be a peak-bagging day hike, a forest snowshoe shuffle or a heart-pumping downhill dash, this land has outrageous beauty to knock your socks (and skis) off.

Prep Your Walk

High-level trails (above 2000m) in the Alps are best tackled in summer. Regardless of signposting, invest in a compass and topographical 1:25,000 map. Kompass and Freytag & Berndt are good bets.

Get a Hut

Austria has an extraordinary network of alpine huts (many run by the ÖAV; Austrian Alpine Club), which open roughly from mid-June to September. Book your backcountry bed well ahead.

Glacier Skiing

Fancy an above-the-clouds summer ski instead? Head above 3000m for skiing at the likes of the Stubai, Hintertux, Sölden and Kitzsteinhorn glaciers.

BEST SKY-HIGH EXPERIENCES

Feel your heart thud and stomach drop as you dive into white wilderness on the Harakiri black run in ❶ **Mayrhofen** (p343).

Peer giddily into the void on the cliff-hugging ❷ **Five Fingers viewing platform** (p229) in the Dachstein mountains above Obertraun.

Climb Austria's highest peak, ❸ **Grossglockner** (p280) at 3798m, in the rugged heart of Hohe Tauern National Park.

Strike out on the ❹ **Pinzgauer Spaziergang** (p275) hike above Zell am See, full of alpine splendour.

Walk where eagles soar on the 300km ❺ **Adlerweg** (p365) in Tyrol, an epic unravelling of falls, gorges, forests, rivers and dizzying peaks.

REGIONS & CITIES

Find the places that tick all your boxes.

The Salzkammergut

MOUNTAINS, LAKES AND SALT MINES

With towering peaks and glassy alpine lakes, the Salzkammergut's looks send filmmakers and Instagrammers into raptures. The region is richly historic: salt was mined here as early as 5000 BCE. Today, swim or sail across Wolfgangsee, Hallstätter See and Mondsee, or dodge the day-trippers and slip into remote wilderness.

Salzburg & Salzburgerland

BAROQUE BRILLIANCE AND ALPINE HIGHS

Cue fantasy Austria. Beyond Salzburg, with its high-on-a-hill castle, UNESCO-listed baroque Altstadt, and culture whirling from Mozart to Maria von Trapp, there are landscapes to make you yodel out loud, with ravines, crashing waterfalls and colossal ice caves. And it's all just the drumroll for the country's highest peaks in Hohe Tauern National Park.

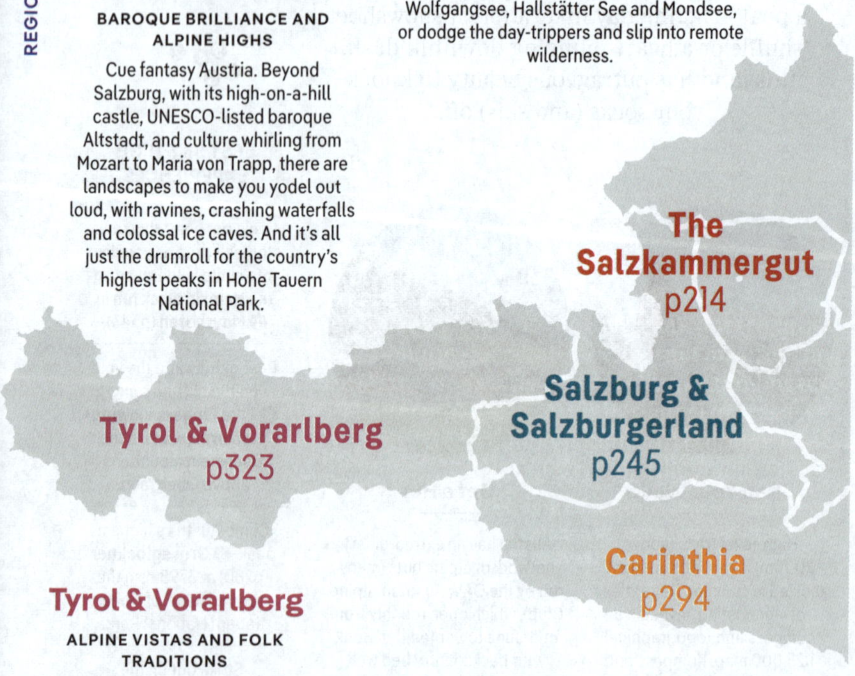

The Salzkammergut p214

Salzburg & Salzburgerland p245

Tyrol & Vorarlberg p323

Carinthia p294

Tyrol & Vorarlberg

ALPINE VISTAS AND FOLK TRADITIONS

In this deeply traditional area of the country, alpine traditions from folk music to cattle drives and pre-Lenten parades are fiercely preserved. Some of the country's finest hiking, skiing and rafting happens in this outdoor-obsessed region, and resorts such as Mayrhofen, Kitzbühel and St Anton am Arlberg live to thrill.

Carinthia

DRAMATIC LANDSCAPES AND MEDIEVAL HISTORY

If you've never heard of Carinthia, you're missing a trick. Here, deep carved valleys and high peaks give way to glittering, palm-rimmed, hot-spring-warmed lakes (the most popular being Wörthersee), walled medieval villages and vibrant, sunny cities such as Klagenfurt that have a whisper of nearby Slovenia and Italy about them.

Upper Austria

A LAND OF CONTRADICTIONS

Happy to hover under the radar, Upper Austria keeps it real with authentic alpine villages, historic towns, quiet mountains and national parks where tourists rarely venture, and backcountry farmstays where you can enjoy a slice of country life and glass of *Most* (cider). Industrial-cool media-arts hub Linz pings you into the future with on-the-pulse technology and art.

Vienna

THE CLASSICAL CITY IN CONTEMPORARY REVIVAL

Habsburg pomp and glory reverberates through the palaces, coffee houses and galleries of ever-so-grand Vienna to this day. But there's more to the Austrian capital than Sisi and *Wiener Schnitzel*. Dive into the modern-day city and its bohemian *Bezirke* (districts) to find out why the Austrian capital is constantly a chart-topper in quality of living surveys.

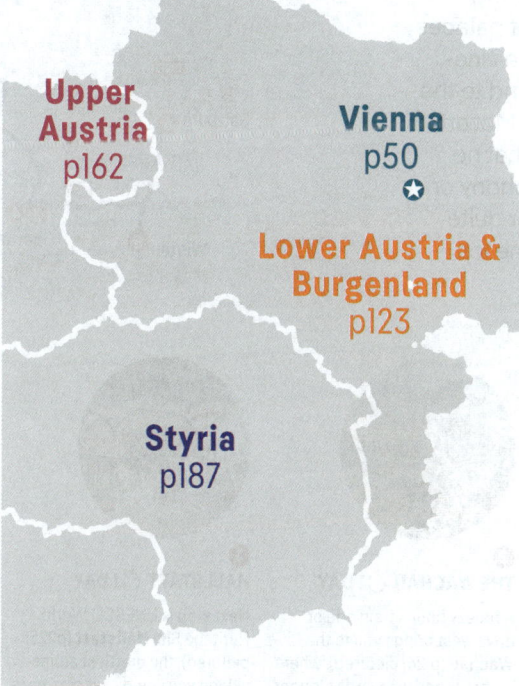

Upper Austria p162

Vienna p50

Lower Austria & Burgenland p123

Styria p187

Lower Austria & Burgenland

VINEYARDS, CULTURE AND NATIONAL PARKS

Inhabited since the Ice Age, Lower Austria has history that runs deeper than the waters of its famous blue Danube (Donau). Though much of its beauty is unsung, you'll be smitten by the vine-swaddled Wachau's abbeys, romantically ruined castles and *Heurigen* (wine taverns). Or go off-piste on foot or by bike into the Waldviertel's rolling hills and Burgenland's wetlands.

Styria

THE GREEN HEART OF AUSTRIA

Nudging the Slovenian border, little-explored Styria is astoundingly diverse, winging you from culture-packed, food-loving, castle-topped capital, Graz, to a rich tapestry of landscapes from snow-iced peaks and limestone plateaus to the vineyards and pumpkin fields of Südsteiermark. Pin-drop peaceful national parks, uncrowded ski pistes, wine tasting at backcountry *Buschenschenken* (wine taverns) – it's all here.

ITINERARIES

Vienna to Salzburg

Allow: 7 days **Distance**: 460km

Unravelling from east to west, this itinerary wings you from Vienna's whirl of opulent palaces and coffee houses to the vine-ribbed Wachau Valley and to the Alps of Salzburgerland. Mozart, Maria and landscapes that no well-orchestrated symphony or yodelling nun could ever quite capture – this one has the lot.

❶ VIENNA ⏱ 2 DAYS

Oh, **Vienna** (p50)! There's nowhere like it for imperial pomp, rococo palaces, cake-filled coffee houses, world-famous concert halls, and more art than you could ever hope to enjoy in a lifetime. Marvel at Klimt masterpieces at Schloss Belvedere, treasures amassed by the Habsburgs at the Hofburg and edgy creations in the MuseumsQuartier (pictured). Then, detour to the cooler 2nd, 7th and 9th districts.

❷ THE WACHAU ⏱ 1 DAY

A breezy hour's train ride or drive west brings you to the **Wachau** (p126; pictured), where orchards and vineyards stagger down terraced slopes to the River Danube, and trails waltz through field and forest to medieval hillside castles. Seek out cultural stunners like Stift Melk, a twin-spired, onion-domed wonder of a baroque abbey, or Dürnstein's ruined medieval castle, where King Richard the Lionheart was once banged up.

❸ HALLSTATT ⏱ 1 DAY

Next stop is UNESCO World Heritage Site **Hallstatt** (p225; pictured), the prettiest alpine village you could ever clap eyes on, snuggling on the shores of a glass-green lake and with the Dachstein Mountains rising sheer and rugged above. Be warned: selfie-seeking crowds flock here en masse. Come in low season or before day-trippers rock up to appreciate its backdrop and Bronze Age salt mine, Salzwelten.

PLAN YOUR TRIP ITINERARIES

④ OBERTRAUN ⏱ 1 DAY

A short hop from Hallstatt brings you to **Obertraun** (p228), the springboard for the wondrous Dachstein caves (pictured) – the surreally illuminated Rieseneishöhle ice caves and the Mammuthöhle, one of the longest caves in the world. While here, cable car to Krippenstein (2109m), and the glass-bottomed Five Fingers viewing platform, which juts out over the Salzkammergut's tapestry of mountains and lakes.

⑤ WERFEN ⏱ 1 DAY

Crazily pretty **Werfen** (p269) in the Salzach Valley peers up to the jagged limestone Tennengebirge. For such a tiny village, there's tons to see: enter a Narnia-like world at Eisriesenwelt (pictured), the world's largest accessible ice caves, get a medieval castle fix at cliff-hugging Burg Hohenwerfen, or sing your heart out skipping through meadows on The Sound of Music trail.

⑥ SALZBURG ⏱ 1 DAY

With its cake-topper of a medieval fortress, alpine backdrop and UNESCO-listed baroque centre straddling the Salzach River, **Salzburg** (p248; pictured) is an instant heart-stealer. As the home town of Mozart and the place where Maria taught the world to sing in *The Sound of Music*, this city has music in its DNA. Try to catch a performance in one of its palaces, churches or concert halls.

FROM LEFT: BRENDAN RILEY/SHUTTERSTOCK, FOTOFEELING/GETTY IMAGES, JAKOBRADLGRUBER/GETTY IMAGES

Schlegeisspeicher (p342), Zillertal

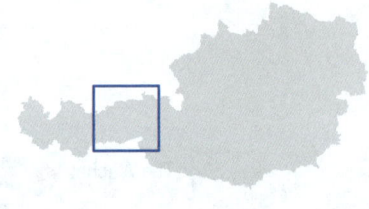

ITINERARIES

Into the Tyrolean Alps

Allow: 5 days **Distance**: 175km

One word: mountains. Wherever you go in Tyrol – even in the bijou capital Innsbruck – you'll be confronted by big, in-your-face, often snow-dusted summits. Grab your hiking boots or skis and dive into these incredible alpine valleys.

❶ INNSBRUCK ⏱ 1 DAY

Kick off in Tyrol's charismatic capital, **Innsbruck** (p328), where the Nordkette Alps rise up like a theatre curtain. Breeze up to the highest point, Hafelekar (2334m), in the space-age funicular (pictured) designed by Zaha Hadid, or linger in the medieval lanes of the Altstadt (old town). It's well stocked with opulent Habsburg palaces, Gothic churches, cafes and restaurants.

❷ HALL ⏱ ½ DAY

A 10-minute hop east of Innsbruck, **Hall** (p336) is a beautifully preserved slice of medieval Austria, with cobbled, lantern-lit lanes to stroll and a salt-mining heritage reaching back to the 13th century. Roam Oberer Stadtplatz to see the Gothic Pfarrkirche St Nikolaus (pictured) and nip into Burg Hasegg, a castle with a 300-year history as a mint for silver thalers.

❸ WATTENS ⏱ ½ DAY

One village over in the valley is **Wattens** (p338), which sparkles with Swarovski crystals. You'll need at least half a day at the crystal fantasy world of Swarovski Kristallwelten (pictured). You'll be dazzled by the Crystal Cloud, Alexander McQueen's wintry *Silent Light* and a black-and-white carousel glittering with 15 million crystals by Spanish designer Jaime Hayon.

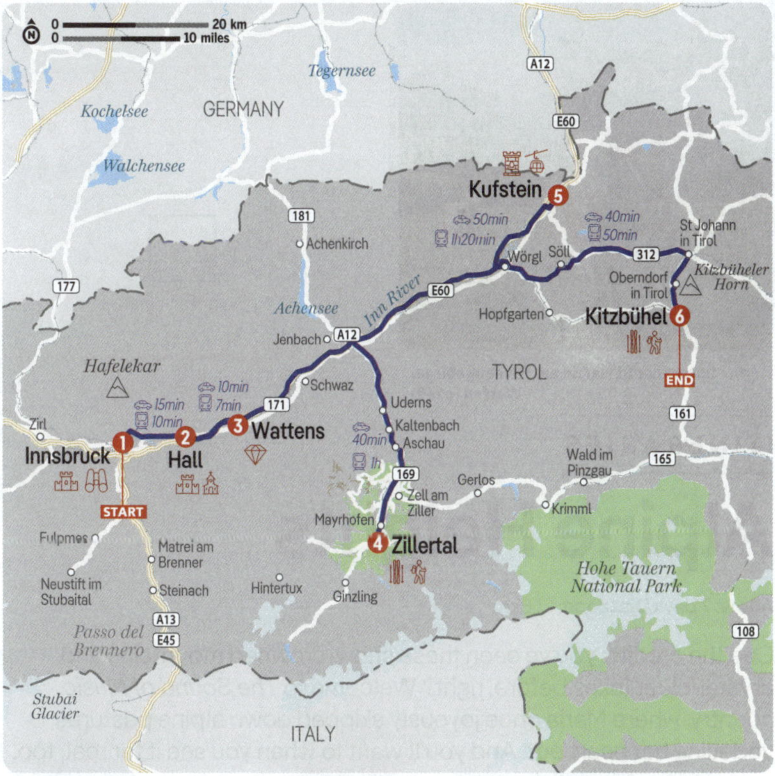

④ THE ZILLERTAL ⏱ 1 DAY

Detouring south, the **Zillertal** (p340; pictured) turns up the alpine glory to max. This valley is a riot of snow-encrusted peaks, roaring waters and flower-freckled meadows. Ski Mayrhofen's heart-racing slopes in winter, or swing over to Zell am Ziller for mountain biking, paragliding, hiking and white-water rafting. In summer, the valley reverberates with the folksy melodies of *Volksmusik*.

⑤ KUFSTEIN ⏱ 1 DAY

Snuggling up against the Bavarian Alps, **Kufstein** (p353; pictured) has gingerbread looks, with its cobbled alleys stacked with frescoed houses, lantern-lit taverns and medieval fortress, Festung Kufstein, lifting the gaze above the Inn River to forests and meadows. Take the retro Kaiserlift chairlift up to the rugged peaks of the Kaisergebirge.

⑥ KITZBÜHEL ⏱ 1 DAY

Its ski pistes are the stuff of Olympic legend, but there's more to the ritzy town of **Kitzbühel** (p348; pictured) than downhill thrills. In summer, the slopes hum with hikers and a cable car swings up to the alpine flower garden at Kitzbüheler Horn. Paragliding, and mountain- and e-bike tours ramp up the action.

FROM LEFT: EVA BOCEK/SHUTTERSTOCK, INA MEER SOMMER/SHUTTERSTOCK, BBA PHOTOGRAPHY/SHUTTERSTOCK

Cows near St Martin am Tennengebirge, Werfen (p269)

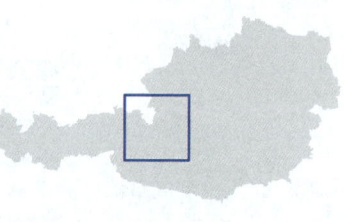

ITINERARIES

Alpine Heights

Allow: 7 days **Distance**: 268km

Cue the credits: you've seen these snow-crowned mountains and crystal-clear lakes before, right? Welcome to *The Sound of Music* country, where Maria once joyously skipped down alpine pastures, yodelling her heart out. And you'll want to when you see it for real, too.

❶ SALZBURG ⏱ 2 DAYS

Begin on a baroque high in the World Heritage heart of **Salzburg** (p248; pictured), where the dome-encrusted Altstadt pulses year-round with cultural life. Once you've ticked off big-hitters like the Residenz palace, high-on-a-hill Hohensalzburg fortress and Mozart's former abodes, linger for park life, riverside bike rides, concerts and spins of *The Sound of Music* film locations.

❷ WERFEN ⏱ 1 DAY

Werfen (p269) is a visual feast with the spiky limestone peaks of the Tennengebirge towering above the river-woven valley. Arrive early to take a bus and cable car up to Eisriesenwelt, the world's largest accessible ice caves. Then make for 900-year-old Hohenwerfen fortress (pictured) for views of the Salzach Valley and a walk in Maria's footsteps on *The Sound of Music* trail.

❸ FILZMOOS ⏱ 1 DAY

Bischofsmütze (Bishop's Mitre) pops up dramatically above **Filzmoos** (p271; pictured), southeast of Werfen. The pull of the ragged limestone Dachstein peaks is strong here, whether you stop off to ski in winter, drift above the Alps in a hot-air balloon or embark on epic long-distance, hut-to-hut hikes like the Dachstein Circuit or two-day, ridge-hugging Gosaukamm Circuit.

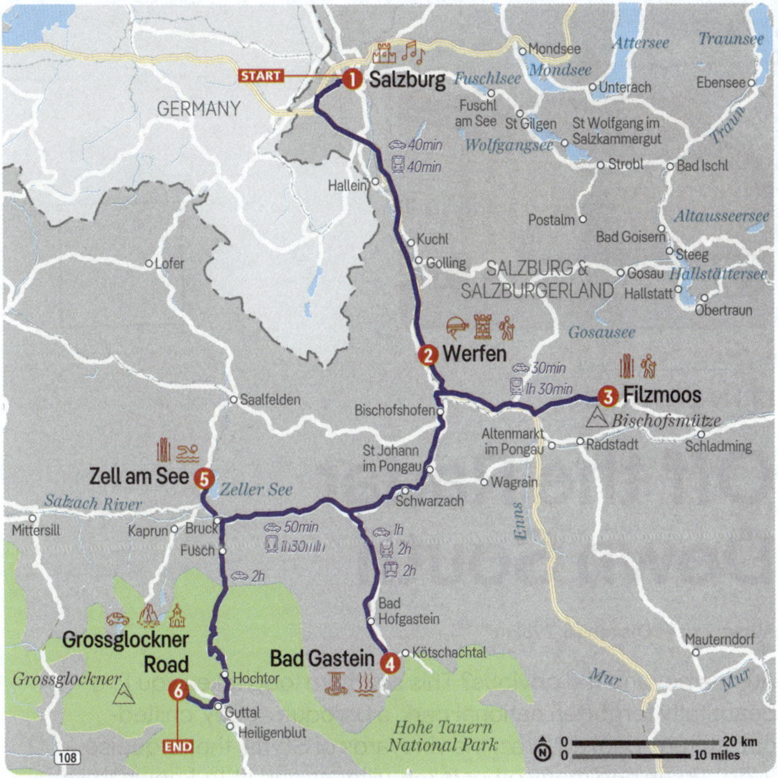

④ BAD GASTEIN ⏱ 1 DAY

Head south to **Bad Gastein** (p286; pictured), in a romantic valley at the foot of the glacier-capped Hohe Tauern mountains. With a waterfall crashing through its heart, belle-époque villas pasted to its forested slopes and radon-laced thermal waters (bathe in them at Felsentherme and Alpentherme), the town has won fans from Klimt to Empress Elisabeth over the years.

⑤ ZELL AM SEE ⏱ 1 DAY

Surrounded by sky-high peaks, including glacier-capped 3203m Kitzsteinhorn, lakeside **Zell am See** (p273; pictured) is a cracking base for Hohe Tauern National Park, either for winter skiing or summer swimming, boating and SUP on the lake. Take the cable car up to Schmittenhöhe to trek the five-hour Pinzgauer Spaziergang for views of Austria's highest peak, 3798m Grossglockner.

⑥ GROSSGLOCKNER ROAD ⏱ 1 DAY

End on the **Grossglockner Road** (p284), unwrapping Hohe Tauern's off-the-scale beauty. Brace yourself for 48km of hairpin bends, glaciers, thundering falls, lakes and mountains (pictured). Highs include Heiligenblut, where the needle-thin spire of a 15th-century church reaches for the heavens, and Pasterze Glacier hikes at Kaiser-Franz-Josefs-Höhe.

FROM LEFT: NAUMENKO ALEKSANDR/SHUTTERSTOCK, NIKOLPETR/SHUTTERSTOCK, FOOTTOO/SHUTTERSTOCK

Graz (p190)

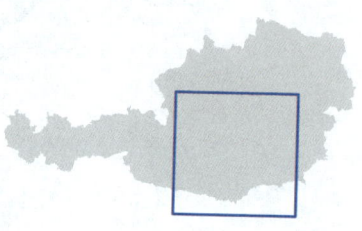

ITINERARIES

Off the Radar Down South

Allow: 7 days **Distance**: 295km

Austria beyond the obvious? This southern loop takes you to a beautifully forgotten national park, a baroque abbey, chilled-out, culture-packed Graz, the vineyards of Styria, the turquoise Wörthersee and many other lakes, villages and little-known trails.

❶ NATIONALPARK GESÄUSE ⏱ 1 DAY

For full-on nature and few crowds, visit the forgotten wilderness of Styria's **Nationalpark Gesäuse** (p209; pictured), with its jagged mountain ridges, rock towers, deep valleys, alpine pastures and forests. Hike 2369m Hocktor, raft the Enns River and dig into game in rustic huts. By night, spot stars and planets in some of Austria's darkest night skies.

❷ ADMONT ⏱ 1 DAY

West is **Admont** (p209), dwarfed by one of Austria's most opulent baroque abbeys. It brings together museums, religion, and modern art and architecture into an award-winning cultural ensemble. Its star attraction is its lavishly frescoed Stiftsbibliothek (pictured), the largest abbey library in the world, while its Kunsthistorisches Museum is a trove of religious treasures.

❸ GRAZ ⏱ 2 DAYS

With a castle high on a bluff, an Altstadt that's a jumble of Renaissance courtyards, baroque palaces nodding at nearby Italy, and avant-garde galleries, **Graz** (p190) is a laid-back city for dipping deeper into this oft-overlooked region. Factor in sights like the space-age Kunsthaus Graz (pictured) and gracious Schloss Eggenberg along with the superb food and nightlife.

FROM LEFT: MARTA KIA/SHUTTERSTOCK, T.DZ/SHUTTERSTOCK, DEYMOS/GETTY IMAGES

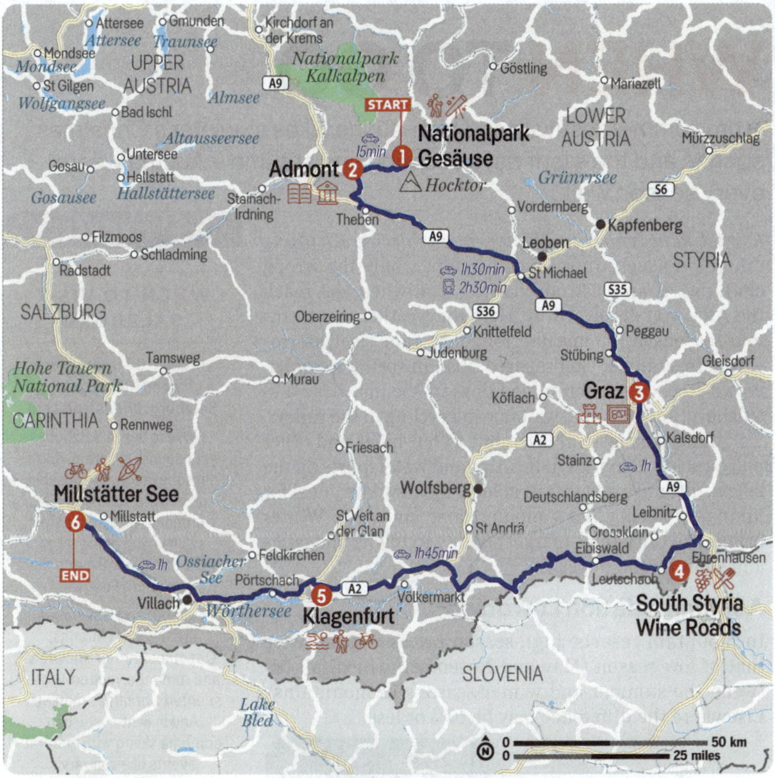

④ SOUTH STYRIA WINE ROADS ⏱ 1 DAY

Road trip it along the **Südsteirische Weinstrasse** (p206; pictured), corkscrewing south of Graz through a Tuscan-like landscape hugging the Slovenian border with vineyards at every bend. Weaving through villages like Leutschach, Ehrenhausen, Gamlitz and Berghausen, you'll find wineries offering tastings and farmhouses for rustic respite.

⑤ KLAGENFURT ⏱ 1 DAY

Rest for a spell in the upbeat, university city of **Klagenfurt** (p298; pictured), with strolls in the Inner Stadt, and refreshing lido swims and easy cycling around the shore of beautiful Wörthersee. This green-blue, drinking-water-quality lake is a sight to behold, with action on and around the water from hiking, running and biking to wakeboarding and SUP.

⑥ MILLSTÄTTER SEE ⏱ 1 DAY

Round out your trip at mountain-clasped **Millstätter See** (p310), with the Romanesque Benedictine abbey in Millstatt (pictured) and the chance to spend the day cycling, kayaking or SUPing around or on the lake. Or head for **Gmünd** (p316) for the day, with its Kunsthaus. Whichever you choose, Spittal an der Drau is your seductive springboard, with its fountains and colourful flowerbeds.

FROM LEFT: LUNGHAMMER/SHUTTERSTOCK, AKO PHOTOGRAPHY/SHUTTERSTOCK, HANSENN/GETTY IMAGES

WHEN TO GO

From summer festivals and high-alpine hikes to winter's Christmas sparkle and the silent days of spring and autumn – Austria wears every season well.

Es gibt kein schlechtes Wetter, nur schlechte Kleidung ('there's no such thing as bad weather, only the wrong clothing') is an Austrian mantra. And when you reach the Alps, you discover why. Here the weather can throw four seasons at you in a day: fog, snow, rain, sleet, storms – even in summer. Go prepared. Visit in spring for quiet, crowd-free, culture-crammed days in Vienna, Graz and Salzburg, and blossom, walking and cycling in the valleys.

Summer has festival fever, hut-to-hut hikes and other pulse-racing activities in the Alps and watersports on the lakes. Autumn often means golden, mellow days, ideal for hiking, exploring and sampling game and wine. Winter brings the Christmas market sparkle to towns and cities and snow on the slopes.

Accommodation Lowdown

In mountain resorts, high-season prices can be twice that of low season (May and November, which fall between the summer and winter seasons in mountains). Elsewhere the difference may be 10% or less.

> ### ⓘ I LIVE HERE
>
> ### WHEN TO VISIT SALZBURG
>
> **Hildegard Strohmeyer is a city and hiking guide in Salzburg.** *hildastroh.com*
>
> I love to live in Salzburg year-round. In spring, don't miss the magnolia blossom on Makartplatz. Come in summer to hike in the Alps, swim in one of the lakes near the city and catch the Salzburg Festival.
>
> October and November are the quiet months. December brings snowfall and romantic, mulled-wine-scented Christmas markets. And in winter, you can combine skiing with cultural events like January's Mozart Week.

FROM LEFT: TATIANA POPOVA/SHUTTERSTOCK, ALESSANDRA SARTI/ALAMY

Obergurgl, the Ötztal (p356)

FÖHN EFFECT

You'll often hear Austrians talking about the *Föhn:* hot, dry, downward winds that roar down from the Alps at speeds of up to 150km/h, causing snow to melt and bringing warmer weather. When they blow, conditions are perfect for windsurfing.

Weather Through the Year: Vienna

JANUARY	FEBRUARY	MARCH	APRIL	MAY	JUNE
Avg daytime max: **3°C**	Avg daytime max: **5°C**	Avg daytime max: **9°C**	Avg daytime max: **15°C**	Avg daytime max: **20°C**	Avg daytime max: **25°C**
Days of rainfall: 9	Days of rainfall: 7	Days of rainfall: 9	Days of rainfall: 7	Days of rainfall: 9	Days of rainfall: 8

I HEAR THUNDER

Sunny in the Alps? Perhaps, but the weather can change at the drop of a hat, bringing fog, sleet, snow – you name it. Rising temperatures mean that thunderstorms often bubble up in the Alps on summer afternoons, so start hikes early in the day.

Opera, Music & Christmas Markets

Europe's biggest free open-air music festival rocks Vienna's Danube Island at the **Donauinselfest** (p75) – three days of rock, pop, hardcore, folk and country music.
🌞 **June**

World-class opera, classical music and drama take the stage by storm in Salzburg's baroque Altstadt at summer's unmissable **Salzburger Festspiele** (p262). Tickets are gold dust – book months ahead.
🌞 **July to August**

Vorarlberg's top-class cultural event brings dramatically choreographed opera, orchestral works and other imaginative productions to a floating, open-air stage on Bodensee (Lake Constance) at the **Bregenzer Festspiele** (p370). 🌞 **July to August**

During Advent, Vienna glitters brighter than ever at its **Christkindlmärkte** (p78), with gingerbready huts, beautifully lit trees, carols, concerts and ice skating.
❄️ **November to December**

Parades, Street Theatre & Edgy Arts

It only happens every four years, but the World Heritage **Schemenlaufen** (p360) carnival in Imst, Tyrol, is worth the wait, with jumping, bell-jangling masked characters, bears and witches hitting the streets. 🌞 **February**

Slide on south to Styria's cultured capital, Graz, for **Elevate** (p191), a high-spirited, feel-good arts festival mixing up art, film, electronic music, DJ sets, workshops and political discourse.
🌞 **February to March**

Electric lights are extinguished and lit by torches and flares as Friesach rewinds to the Middle Ages at **Spectaculum** (p309). Jesters, princesses and armoured knights stroll around juggling, fire-eating and staging jousting tournaments. 🌞 **July**

Held in Graz each autumn, the avant-garde **Steirischer Herbst** (p191) festival has a bold line-up of new music, theatre, film, edgy exhibitions and art installations and more.
🌞 **September to October**

🌐 I LIVE HERE

HOHE TAUERN ALPS

Ekkehard Heider is a park ranger in the Hohe Tauern National Park. *@nationalpark_hohetauern*

Every season is special in Hohe Tauern National Park. In spring, there's still snow, but everything is gearing up for summer. In summer, the alpine flowers are in full bloom. In autumn, all the animals are preparing for winter. Many areas are now totally covered with snow and with a bit of luck you can spot red deer, chamois, ibex, snow rabbit and ptarmigan.

Alpine flowers, Hohe Tauern National Park (p279)

SNOW FALLS

The flakes fall on high peaks from November, and from December to March (prime ski season) snow is pretty much guaranteed in the Austrian Alps, especially above the magic 2000m mark.

JULY	AUGUST	SEPTEMBER	OCTOBER	NOVEMBER	DECEMBER
Avg daytime max: **27°C**	Avg daytime max: **27°C**	Avg daytime max: **15°C**	Avg daytime max: **11°C**	Avg daytime max: **9°C**	Avg daytime max: **2°C**
Days of rainfall: 9	Days of rainfall: 8	Days of rainfall: 7	Days of rainfall: 7	Days of rainfall: 8	Days of rainfall: 9

PLAN YOUR TRIP — WHEN TO GO

Hiking, Tannheimer Tal, Tyrol (p323)

GET PREPARED FOR AUSTRIA

Useful things to load in your bag, your ears and your brain.

Clothes

Layers Winter can be cold and the ground icy, so several layers of warm clothing and flat shoes (for slippery cobbles) are essential, along with gloves, scarf and a woollen hat. In summer, wear layers you can peel off.

Waterproofs Pack waterproofs for occasional rain showers year-round.

Dressy clothes Especially in larger cities, Austrians tend to dress up in the evenings for high-end restaurants, but jeans are fine even for upmarket clubs and restaurants if teamed with a good shirt or blouse and a blazer (*Sakko*) or summer jacket.

Alpine gear For the Alps, pack solid walking boots (and possibly walking poles), sunscreen and hat for high-alpine rays, waterproof, thermal layers and a daypack. In winter, you'll need full-on ski gear and snow-boots.

Manners

Bon appétit! When dining with Austrians, it's polite to wish *Guten Appetit* or *Mahlzeit* before digging in.

Asking for tap water (*Leitungswasser*) isn't the done thing, especially in upmarket places.

Every drink deserves a *Prost* (cheers) and eye contact with fellow drinkers; not doing so is thought of as rude. Even worse, it's believed to result in bad sex for seven years.

📖 READ

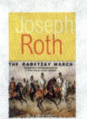   

Radetzky March (Joseph Roth; 1932) Chronicles the decline of the Austro-Hungarian Empire.

The World of Yesterday (Stefan Zweig; 1942) Zweig's moving memoir as a Jew in exile is set against the rise of Nazi power.

A Death in Vienna (Daniel Silva; 2005) This page-turning spy thriller digs up the ghosts of WWII.

The Painted Kiss (Elizabeth Hickey; 2005) Gustav Klimt's relationship with his pupil and muse in early 20th-century Vienna.

Words

Moagn (mwah-gen) The Austrian abbreviated form of the German *Guten Morgen* (good morning).

Servus (ser-vus) A cheery, informal way to say 'hello' or 'goodbye' in the Austrian dialect, similar to the Italian 'ciao'. Alternatively, say **Griass di** (grias-di), or 'hello there'.

Grüss Gott (grias-got) A more formal greeting, literally translating as 'may God bless you'.

Wie geht's? (vee gehts) A common way to ask 'how are you?', but there are regional variations. A common reply is *Gut, danke* (guht, dahn-keh), which means 'I'm fine, thanks'.

Saying thank you in Austria depends on how polite and/or effusive you wish to be. *Danke* (dahn-keh) is a casual 'thanks', while *Danke schön* (dahn-keh sch-oen) and *vielen Dank* (fee-len dahnk) mean 'thank you very much'.

Jause (yeow-ze) Austrian for 'snack', which can be anything from coffee and cake to a *Brettljause* (bre-tel yeow-ze), which is a sharing platter of cold meats, cheese, bread and pickles often served at mountain huts in the Alps.

Sackerl (sak-erl) Austrian for a 'bag' and you'll often hear it at shop checkouts.

Verlängerter (fer-leng-er-ter) A word you'll often hear in a coffee house. It's basically an espresso lengthened with hot water, similar to an Americano.

Oida (oi-da) Exclamation that can be used in pretty much any situation. It translates as 'old one', but can mean 'hey', 'wow', 'dude' or 'mate'.

Bussi, Baba! (buh-si ba-ba) That most Austrian of goodbyes, basically meaning 'kisses, see you later'.

🎬 WATCH

The Third Man (Carol Reed; 1949) Classic film noir set in shadowy, postwar Vienna.

The Piano Teacher (Michael Haneke; 2001) A young man falls for a masochistic piano teacher in this psychological masterpiece.

Metropolis (Fritz Lang; 1927) Industry and prescient futuristic grunge in a silent sci-fi film.

Woman in Gold (Simon Curtis; 2015) This true story drama zooms in on Maria Altmann's legal campaign to reclaim Klimt's *Portrait of Adele Bloch-Bauer*.

Corsage (Marie Kreutzer; 2022) A historical drama providing a fictional account of the latter years of Empress Elisabeth of Austria.

🎧 LISTEN

Falco 3 (Falco; 1985) Falco's third album features mega hits like *Vienna Calling* and *Rock Me Amadeus*.

Eine kleine Nacht Musik, K 525, (Wolfgang Amadeus Mozart; 1787) The most uplifting and recognisable composition for a chamber ensemble.

This Atom Heart of Ours (Naked Lunch; 2007) Edgy pop-rock rhythms from this alternative indie band hailing from Klagenfurt, Carinthia.

The Princess (Parov Stelar; 2012) Electric swing courtesy of this musician, producer and DJ from Linz. His clubby tracks blend jazz, house, electro and breakbeat.

Wiener Schnitzel **(breaded veal cutlet)**

THE FOOD SCENE

Schnitzel with noodles and crisp apple strudel are just for starters. Dive into Austria's culinary waters for menus that sing of seasons and regions.

Austria's food scene is more exciting than ever thanks to new-wave chefs riffing creatively on local ingredients in farm-to-fork menus. Worldly markets, biodynamic wineries and a rising taste for organic, foraged flavours are making this a culinary destination to watch like never before. Food is lighter, brighter and more imaginative than ever. Global flavours and vegan bistros sit alongside kitchens dabbling in gastronomic waters – the country now shines with over 80 Michelin-starred restaurants.

Here innovation is rooted in responsible sourcing. The mountain valleys of Carinthia wear the Slow Food crown since it became the world's first Slow Food Destination in 2019, while in 2025 Austria glittered with 33 Michelin green stars. Sustainability matters.

Gone are the days when Austria couldn't rival France or Italy in the kitchen. Today, food is an integral part of the travel experience, be it tangy cider in Mostviertel orchards, Wachau wines and *Marillen* (apricots), Waldviertel poppy-seed specialities, Styrian pumpkins, Tyrolean Alpine cheeses or fish plucked from the Salzkammergut's looking-glass lakes.

Regional & Seasonal

Locals take genuine pride in homegrown produce. On Saturday morning, they're combing farmers markets, baskets and jute bags in hand, for whatever is seasonal. It's as much a matter of ethics as taste: Austrians believe in supporting their farmers, cheesemakers and vintners, many going out of their way to buy organic, regional goods. Chefs often make the most of seasonal, regional ingredients, too, and many have piggybacked on the Slow Food trend (look for

Best Austrian Dishes	WIENER SCHNITZEL	TAFELSPITZ MIT KREN	GRÖSTL	KÄSESPÄTZLE
	Breaded veal cutlet, often as big as a boot and fried to golden perfection.	Boiled beef with root veg, *Kren* (horseradish) and dumplings.	Tyrolean leftover-fry-up, usually potato, pork and onions, topped with a fried egg.	Stubby egg noodles served with loads of gooey cheese and fried onions.

the snail symbol). Bregenzerwald's piquant *Bergkäse* (mountain cheese), Neusiedler See fish, Styria's dark, nutty pumpkinseed oil, and the Wachau's zesty Riesling never taste better than at the source.

Through the Grapevine

Many vintners open their doors for tastings, and rustic *Heurigen* (wine taverns) pair wine with hearty grub like roast pork, blood sausage and pickled vegetables. Often identified by a *Busch'n* (green wreath or branch) hanging over the door, these taverns date to the Middle Ages and can sell their wine directly from the premises. They're seasonal and open on a roster so it's easiest to pick up the *Heurigenkalendar (Heurigen* calendar) from the tourist office. New wines are sold September to mid-October, after the harvest. This is the time to indulge in *Sturm* ('storm' for its cloudy appearance and chaotic effects on drinkers).

Coffee House Culture

Like many good fairy tales, the coffee-house culture in Vienna began with magic beans. In 1683, the Ottoman Turks dumped sacks of coffee at the city gates when fleeing the Battle of Vienna – soon after the Austrian capital's first coffee house was born. Swing open the heavy wooden door of a Vienna *Kaffeehaus* and it's like the clocks stopped in 1910. The waiters are just as aloof, the menu still baffles and newspapers outnumber smartphones. Outside life rushes ahead, but the *Kaffeehaus* is immune to time and trends. Coffee really is rocket science here and you'll need to know your *Mokka* (black coffee) from your *Melange* (cappuccino), *Brauner* (macchiato) and *Verlängerter* (Americano) to order Viennese-style.

Heuriger (wine tavern; p138)

FOOD & DRINK FESTIVALS

Aufsteiren (p191) Sample a feast of seasonal Styrian goodies at this September event in Graz, from pumpkin noodles and soup to *Backhendl* (breaded, crunchy fried chicken).

Wiener Weinwandertag (p119) Take a culinary stroll through the *Weinberge* (vineyards) on Vienna's fringes, ticking off wineries and *Heurigen* (wine taverns; pictured).

Stanz Brennt (p361) A speck of a Tyrolean village, Stanz is famous for its schnapps distilleries. Juicy local plums shine in food, chutneys and brandies at this September fest.

Steirischer Apfelfeste (p207) Bite into crisp, juicy apples, roam the orchards and crack open cider in early September in Styria.

Ottakringer Bierfest (p118) At the cavernous Ottakringer Brauerei in Vienna's 16th district, this beer fest delivers classic and craft brews, live music, street food and yoga from late June to early September.

Café Central (p72), Vienna

STEIRISCHER BACKHENDLSALAT	PINZGAUER KASNOCKEN	KÄRNTNER NUDEL	ERDÄPFELSALAT
Breaded chicken in *Kürbisöl* (pumpkinseed oil) served with salad.	Mini dumplings with cheese, chives and onions, hailing from Tyrol.	Ravioli-like pasta pockets filled with potato, cheese, mint, wild chervil and mushrooms.	Potato salad with waxy potatoes, fried onions, mustard dressing and parsley.

Local Specialities

Meaty Street Snacks

Käsekrainer This fat, cheese-filled sausage is a popular wee-hour, beer-mopping snack.
Bosna bratwurst The spicy king of Vienna's *Würstelstände* (sausage stands).
Leberkässemmel Crunchy roll stuffed with meatloaf. Pin down a *Metzgerei* (butcher's) for a good one.
Schnitzelsemmel A schnitzel in a bun for a meal on the run.
Döner Turkish import of pitta kebab stuffed with cabbage and lamb mince. For added spice, order it *'mit scharf'*.

Dare to Try

Graukäse The Zillertal's grey, mouldy, sour-milk cheese is tastier than it sounds, honest!
Leberknödelsuppe Liver dumpling soup is the starter that gets meals off to a hearty kick all over Austria.
Rindfleischsulz Jellied beef brawn, often drizzled in pumpkinseed-oil vinaigrette.
Schnecken Escargots to the French, snails to English speakers, these gastropods are slithering onto many top menus.
Zillertaler Bauernschmaus A farmer's feast of cold cuts, sauerkraut and dumplings.

Apfelstrudel

Sweet Treats

Krapfen Grab oven-fresh doughnuts, filled with apricot, chocolate or vanilla cream, from a *Konditorei*.
Marillenknödel Sweet dumplings, wrapped in cream-cheese dough, filled with apricots and rolled in breadcrumbs, cinnamon and icing sugar.
Apfelstrudel Indulgent classic with sugar-dusted layers of flaky pastry, diced apple and cinnamon.
Kaiserschmarrn These fluffy, raisin-studded pancakes, shredded and dusted with icing sugar, are fit for an emperor.
Sacher Torte The ultimate chocolate cake – rich, iced and with a layer of tangy apricot jam.

MEALS OF A LIFETIME

Meierei im Stadtpark (p88) Head to the Meierei for fine cheese and Stadtpark views, or book a table for Michelin-star dining by the Wien River.
Esszimmer (p260) Andreas Kaiblinger works culinary magic with market-fresh ingredients at this Michelin-starred number in Salzburg.
Restaurant Bootshaus (p241) Lukas Nagl and team marry tradition and natural flavours on the Traunsee.
Gasthof Prankl (p130) Dine in a 500-year-old former ship-owner's house in the Wachau Valley.
Verdi (p169) The freshest seasonal flavours at a chic Linz address.
Obauer (p269) The Obauer brothers make regional fare shine at this two Michelin-starred stunner in the Alps.
Die Wilderin (p329) This Innsbruck number is a love letter to Tyrol, with foraged flavours and a bistro buzz.

THE YEAR IN FOOD

SPRING
Chefs add springtime oomph to dishes with *Spargel* (asparagus) and *Bärlauch* (wild garlic). *Maibock* (strong beer) is rolled out for beer festivals in May.

SUMMER
It's time for *Marille* (apricot) madness in the Wachau, touring dairies in Tyrol and the Bregenzerwald, and eating freshwater fish by lake shores. Villages get into summer with beer festivals and folk music.

AUTUMN
Autumn sees a feast of mushrooms and game. *Sturm* (young wine) brings fizz to *Heurigen*. Sip new *Most* (perry and cider) in the Mostviertel's orchards. Goose is served for St Martin's Day (11 November).

WINTER
Try *Vanillekipferl* (crescent-shaped biscuits) and *Glühwein* at twinkling Christmas markets. Vienna's coffee houses and huts high in the Alps serving gooey fondue are the perfect winter warmer.

Skiing, Mayrhofen (p343)

TRIP PLANNER

SKIING & SNOWBOARDING

No matter whether you're a slalom expert, a fearless freerider or a beginner, there's a slope for you in Austria. And oh, what slopes! You'll find intermediate cruising, knee-trembling black runs and summertime glacier skiing – in short, powdery perfection for every taste and ability.

PICK A PISTE

Piste maps are available on most tourist office websites and at the valley stations of ski lifts; runs are colour-coded according to difficulty as follows. Blue runs are easy, well-groomed and suitable for beginners. Red runs for intermediates are groomed but often steeper and narrower than blue runs. Skiers should have a medium level of ability. Black runs are for expert skiers with polished technique and skills. The runs are mostly steep, not always groomed and may have moguls and steep vertical drops.

EQUIPMENT HIRE

Skis (downhill, cross-country, telemark), snowboards, boots, poles and helmets can be rented at sport shops such as Intersport (*intersport.at*) in every resort. Ski, snowboard or cross-country ski rental costs from €30/165 per day/week, or €35/250 for top-of-the-range gear. Boot hire starts at around €12/75 per day/week. Airlines will charge you between €40 and €80 if you want to bring your own skis.

SKI TUITION

Most ski resorts have one or more ski schools; for a list of regional ski schools, visit the **Snowsport Austria** (*snowsport austria.at*) website. Group lessons for both adults and children typically cost from €120 per day (two hours in the morning, two hours in the afternoon), from €330 for

RESOURCES

Bergfex *(bergfex.com)*
A great website with piste maps, snow forecasts for the Alps and details of every ski resort in Austria.

If You Ski *(ifyouski.com)* Resort guides, ski deals and info on ski hire and schools.

On the Snow *(onthesnow.co.uk)*
Reviews of Austria's ski resorts, plus snow reports, webcams and lift-pass details.

Austria.info *(austria.info)*
Tons of info on everything from resorts to family-friendly skiing, freeriding, off-piste and activities beyond the slopes.

Sno.co.uk *(sno.co.uk)*
A handy Top 10 resort guide ranked according to theme and level, plus deals on holidays and hotels.

TOP FIVE REGIONS

Ski Amadé *(skiamade.com)*
In Salzburgerland (p245), Austria's biggest ski area covers a whopping 760km of pistes. Its 25 resorts are divided into five snow-sure regions that channel every level from gentle cruising on tree-lined runs to off-piste touring. Bad Gastein (p286) and Filzmoos (p271) are headline resorts.

Ski Arlberg *(skiarlberg.at)*
Tyrol's (p323) famous skiing region has 300km of signposted pistes. Its star is St Anton am Arlberg (p362), beloved of expert skiers and boarders, with an impeccable snow record, challenging terrain, terrific off-piste and pumping après-ski. Its neighbours are celeb-magnet resorts Lech (p367) and Zürs (p367).

Kitzbühel *(kitzbuehel.com)*
The legendary Hahnenkamm (p348), 233km of groomed slopes and upbeat nightlife make Kitzbühel as popular as ever. Critics grumble about unreliable snow – with a base elevation of 762m, Kitzbühel isn't high by alpine standards – but skiers still come for the varied downhill, snowboarding and off-piste.

The Zillertal 3000 *(zillertal.at)*
Mayrhofen (p343) is the showpiece of the Zillertal 3000 (p343), which covers 202km of slopes. Besides being intermediate heaven, Mayrhofen has Austria's steepest black run, the kamikaze-like Harakiri with a 78% gradient, and appeals to freestylers with its terrain park. Snow's thin on the ground? It's guaranteed at the Hintertux Glacier (p343).

Zell am See-Kaprun *(zellamsee-kaprun.com)*
At the foot of the glacier-capped Hohe Tauern range, Zell am See-Kaprun (p273) has 408km of pistes, covered by a single ski pass, and ultra-modern lifts powered by green energy. There's fresh powder and a terrain park at the Kitzsteinhorn Glacier (p277).
Turn to our **Help Me Pick: Snow Sports** feature (p376) for more details on resorts.

four days and from €430 for six days. Usually, the more days you take, the cheaper the per day rate gets. Private instruction and off-piste guiding are available on request. Kids can start learning from the age of three.

LIFT PASSES

Costing roughly €400 for six days, lift passes are a big chunk out of your budget. The passes give access to one or more ski sectors and nearly always include ski buses between the different areas.

Lift passes for lesser-known places may be as little as half that charged in the jet-set resorts. Count on around €50 to €75 for a one-day ski pass, with substantial reductions for longer-term passes. Kids are usually charged half-price, while children under five or six ski for free (bring a passport as proof of age).

Most lift passes are now 'hands-free', with a built-in chip that barriers detect automatically, and many can be prebooked online.

SAFETY ON THE SLOPES

Get in good shape before hitting the slopes and build up gradually.

Avalanches are a serious danger in snowbound areas and can be fatal. If you're skiing

Snowshoeing, Altenmarkt-Zauchensee, Salzburgerland (p245)

off-piste, never go alone and always take an avalanche pole (a collapsible pole used to determine the location of an avalanche victim), a transceiver, a shovel and – most importantly – a professional guide. See lawine.at for the avalanche risk and snow coverage by region.

UV rays are stronger at high altitudes and intensified by snow glare; always wear ski goggles and sunscreen.

Wear layers to adapt to the constant change in body temperature; make sure your head, wrists and knees are protected (preferably padded).

Skiing, Kitzbühel (p348)

SLOPE SAVERS

It's worth checking websites such as **Iglu Ski** (igluski.com), Sno (sno.co.uk), **IfYou Ski.com** (ifyouski.com) and **J2Ski** (j2ski.com) for last-minute ski deals and packages. Local tourist offices and austria.info might also have offers.

You can save time and euros by pre-booking ski and snowboard hire online at **Snowbrainer** (snowbrainer.com) or **Ski Set** (skiset.co.uk), which give discounts of 10% to 50% on shop rental prices.

INSURANCE

Before you hurtle down the black run, make sure you're properly insured and read the small print: mountain-rescue costs, medical treatment and repatriation can soon amount to four figures.

SUMMER SNOW

If the thought of pounding the powder in summer appeals, hightail it to glaciers such as the **Stubai Glacier** (p339), **Hintertux Glacier** (p343) and **Kitzsteinhorn Glacier** (p277), where, weather permitting, there's fine downhill skiing year-round.

CROSS-COUNTRY SKIING

Fancy sidestepping the crowds to glide or skate through silent, snowy forests and along twinkling tracks? Cue *Langlauf*, or cross-country skiing, a cleaner, greener, cheaper and less-crowded alternative to downhill skiing. A day/week pass costs around €10/45. The two main techniques are the classic lift-and-glide method on prepared tracks (*Loipen*) and the more energetic 'skating' technique. The basics are easy to master at a cross-country school and tracks are graded from blue to black according to difficulty.

Seefeld in Tyrol (p338) features among Austria's top cross-country skiing destinations, with 245km of *Loipen* crisscrossing the region, including a floodlit track. **Zell am See–Kaprun** (p273) is another hot spot, with 107km of groomed trails providing panoramic views of the Hohe Tauern mountains.

Other great resorts to test your stamina and stride include the **Bad Gastein** (p286) region, with 45km of well-marked cross-country trails. To search for cross-country regions and packages, visit langlauf-urlaub.at.

BIG FOOT

Tired of the jam-packed pistes? Snowshoeing is a great alternative for non-skiers.

On a sunny day, there's little that beats making enormous tracks through deep powder and glittering forests in quiet exhilaration. If you imagine snowshoes as old-fashioned, tennis-racquet-like contraptions, think again: the new ones are lightweight and pretty easy to get the hang of.

Many resorts in the Austrian Alps have marked trails and some offer guided tours for a small charge.

It costs about €12 to €20 to hire a set of snowshoes and poles for the day.

Rock climbing

THE OUTDOORS

With rivers deep, mountains high and looking-glass lakes, Austria is ripe for just about every adventurous pursuit you care to mention.

One look at a map of Austria says it all: jagged peaks, glacier-gouged valleys, and mighty rivers and lakes cover almost every last inch of the country.

Be it hiking through wildflower-strewn pastures jangling with cowbells to a remote mountain hut, schussing down Tyrol's mythical slopes with the Alps tearing across the horizon, SUP-ing across a jewel-blue lake or freewheeling along the Danube (Donau), Austria's great outdoors will elevate, invigorate and amaze you.

Walking & Hiking

For Austrians, *Wandern* (walking) is second nature. Kids frolicking in alpine pastures, nuns Nordic-walking in the hills, super-fit 70-somethings trekking over windswept 2000m passes – such wanderlust is bound to rub off on you. Walking opportunities are endless – Austria is crisscrossed with well-maintained and graded *Wanderwege* (walking trails), waymarked with red-white-red stripes. In summer, lots of towns run themed guided hikes, sometimes

---

More Outdoor Thrills

ROCK CLIMBING
Test your mountaineering mettle scampering up the country's highest peaks in **Hohe Tauern National Park** (p279).

YOGA
Perform sun salutations on an alpine plateau in mountain-yoga mecca **St Anton am Arlberg** (p362).

PARAGLIDING
Catch thermals to float as free as a bird above the peaks tandem paragliding in **Zell am Ziller** (p340).

FAMILY ADVENTURES

Keep an eye out for marmots, ibex and golden eagles in wildly mountainous **Hohe Tauern National Park** (p279).

Take active kids white-water rafting, canyoning and river-bugging in the gorgeous mountains of the **Zillertal** (p340).

Explore the glittering ice empire of **Eisriesenwelt** (p269), the world's largest accessible ice caves, in Werfen.

Whizz down miners' slides into the salty depths of **Salzwelten** (p268) in Hallstatt and swoon over the ravishing village.

Get little hearts pumping with a waterpark, flying fox, high-rope course and canyoning at **Area 47** (p358) in the Ötztaler Alpen.

Dive deep into a fairy-tale gorge, glimpse mythical caves and tear down slopes on an alpine roller coaster at the **Rosengartenschlucht** (p358) in Tyrol's Imst.

---

free with a guest card such as in Innsbruck and Kitzbühel. Regions like **Hohe Tauern National Park** (p279) and **Naturpark Zillertaler Alpen** (p346) charge a nominal fee for ranger-led rambles.

Rock Climbing & Via Ferrata

Synonymous with mountaineering legends like Peter Habeler and South Tyrolean Reinhold Messner, Austria is a summertime paradise for ardent *Kletterer* (rock climbers). In the Alps there's a multitude of climbs ranking all grades of difficulty. Equipment rental (around €10) and guided tours are widely available.

If you're not quite ready to tackle the three-thousanders yet, nearly every major resort in the Austrian Alps now has a *Klettersteig* (via ferrata). These fixed-rope routes – often involving vertical ladders, ziplines and bridges – are great for getting a feel for climbing; all you'll need is a harness, helmet and a head for heights.

Watersports

Austria may be landlocked but it has plenty of watery action. Rafting, canoeing and kayaking the foaming alpine rivers are beloved summer escapades. Big rivers supporting these sports include the Enns and Salza in Styria; the Inn, Sanna and Ötztaler Ache in Tyrol; and the Isel in East Tyrol.

Sailing, windsurfing and kitesurfing are popular on Austria's lakes. Near Vienna, **Neusiedler See** (p151) is one of Central Europe's few steppe lakes and the number-one place for windsurfing and kitesurfing thanks to its stiff winds. It hosts a Surf World Cup heat late April to early May.

HIT THE SLOPES
Find your ideal slope for skiing and snowboarding. See p376

Windsurfing, Neusiedler See (p151)

VIA FERRATA
Flirt with mountaineering by clipping onto Hafelekar's dizzying *Klettersteig* (via ferrata) in **Innsbruck** (p328).

GLACIER SNOWSHOEING
Slip away from the crowds and survey a parade of 3000m peaks glacier snowshoeing at **Kitzsteinhorn** (p277).

STAND-UP PADDLEBOARDING
Grab a board and paddle to head across reed-fringed **Neusiedler See** (p151), Europe's biggest steppe lake.

CANYONING
Cliff jump, abseil and swim among dramatic rock formations canyoning in the **Ötztaler Alpen** (p356).

Cycling & Mountain Biking

Bike-friendly Austria is interlaced with well-marked cycling trails that showcase the mountains, valleys and cities. You can test your stamina on hairpin bends and leg-aching mountain passes, blaze downhill on a mountain bike in the Alps or freewheel leisurely around the glorious lakes.

Nearly every town has road, mountain and e-bikes for hire. **Intersport** *(intersport.at)* and train stations (download the ÖBB bike app) are good bets.

Hut-to-Hut Hiking

One of the joys of hiking in Austria is spending the night in a mountain hut. These trailside refuges give you the freedom to tackle multiday treks in the Alps with no more than a daypack. The highly evolved system means you're hardly ever further than a five- to six-hour walk from the next hut, so there's no need to lug a tent, camping stove and other weighty gear.

Huts generally open from mid-June to mid-September, when the trails are free of snow; the busiest months are July and August, when advance bookings are highly recommended. Consult the **ÖAV** *(alpenverein.at)* for details and dates.

Accommodation is in multi-bed dorms called *Matratzenlager,* or in the *Notlager* (emergency shelter – wherever there's space) if all beds have been taken. Blankets and pillows are provided but you might need to bring your own sleeping sheet. In popular areas, huts are more like mountain inns, with drying rooms and even hot showers (normally at an extra charge).

Most huts have a convivial *Gaststube* (common room), where you can socialise and compare trekking tales over drinks and a bite to eat. ÖAV members can order the *Bergsteigeressen* – literally 'mountaineer's meal' – which is low in price but high in calories, though not necessarily a gastronomic treat. It's worth bringing your own tea or coffee, as *Teewasser* (boiled water) can be purchased from the hut warden.

Mountain biking, the Zillertal (p340)

Alpine hiking

HOW TO... Plan an Alpine Hike

Der Berg ruft ('the mountain calls') is what Austrians say as they gallivant off to the hills at the weekend, and what shopkeepers post on closed doors in summer. And what more excuse do you need? With its towering peaks, forest-cloaked slopes and luxuriantly green valleys, the country's landscapes are perfectly etched and the walking opportunities are endless. Strike into Austria's spectacularly rugged backyard, listen closely and you too will hear those mountains calling...

When to Go

Hiking in the Austrian Alps goes roughly with the (melting) snow. The season runs from around late June to mid-September, when the huts open. At slightly lower elevations (below 2000m), you can often hike from May right through to October. Spring and autumn can be quiet and incredibly beautiful, with flowers and foliage respectively.

Route Planning

Like ski runs, trails are colour-coded according to difficulty. Blue means well-marked, mostly flat and easy to follow; red routes can be steeper and more exposed, and require a good level of fitness and basic mountain experience; while black routes are for experienced mountain hikers, require proper equipment and can be dangerous in bad weather.

Guided Hikes

Tourist offices are usually well-armed with maps and information on accredited guides, who know the mountains like the back of their hand and can help you get off the beaten track, negotiate tougher hikes, via ferrata and climbs, and provide valuable insight into what you're seeing.

In summer, lots of places run themed guided hikes, which are sometimes free with a guest card; for instance in **Innsbruck** (p334) and **Kitzbühel** (p349). Other regions such as **Hohe Tauern National Park** (p282) charge a nominal fee. The walks can range from herb trails and wildlife spotting, to half-day and family-friendly hikes and photo excursions.

MODERN-DAY SHERPAS

If you love long-distance hiking but find carrying a rucksack a drag, you might want to consider *Wandern ohne Gepäck* (literally 'walking without luggage'). Many regions in Austria now offer this clever scheme, where hotels transport your luggage to the next hotel for a small extra charge.

Visit **Austria. info** *(austria.info)* or **Wanderhotels** *(wanderhotels.com)* for details.

A family favourite is llama trekking. Nothing motivates kids to walk quite like these hikes, which reach from two-hour forest strolls to two-week treks on pilgrimage routes. The llamas carry your luggage and leave you free to enjoy the scenery.

Walk Descriptions

Distances should be read in conjunction with altitudes – significant elevation can make a greater difference to your walking time than lateral distance. Times given are often based on the actual walking time and do not include stops for snacks, taking photos, rests or side trips. Be sure to factor these in when planning your walk.

Mountain Hotels

Gone are the days when hiking meant a clammy tent and week-old socks. Austria has upped the comfort ante with **Wanderhotels** (wanderhotels.com), which can help organise hikes and have equipment for hire. There's something to suit every taste and pocket, from farmstays to plush spa hotels.

Going a step further are Austria's **Wanderdörfe** (wanderdoerfer.at), a countrywide network of 42 hiker-friendly regions. Here, you can expect well-marked short- and long-distance walks, beautiful scenery and Alpine huts, good infrastructure and hosts geared up for walkers.

Mountain Safety

On high-alpine routes, avalanches and rock falls can be a problem. Always stick to the marked and/or signposted route, particularly in foggy conditions when you should wait by the path until visibility is clear enough to proceed.

ÖAV MEMBERSHIP

Before you hit the trail in the Austrian Alps, consider becoming a member of the **Österreichischer Alpenverein** (ÖAV, Austrian Alpine Club; alpenverein.at).

Adult membership costs €69 per year, with reductions for students and people aged under 25 or over 61. Membership gets you discounts of up to 50% at Austrian (ÖAV) and German (DAV) alpine huts, plus other benefits including insurance, workshops, access to climbing walls countrywide and discounts on maps.

You should allow at least two months for your application to be processed.

Increase the length and elevation of your walks gradually to help prevent altitude sickness and fatigue.

Never take the weather for granted (conditions can change at the drop of a hat). Check the forecast before embarking on long hikes at wetter.at, snow-forecast.at or alpenverein.at. Where possible, don't walk in the mountains alone (two is considered the minimum number for safe walking), and inform a responsible person, such as a hut warden or hotel receptionist, of your plans, and let them know when you return.

Mountain hiking, Dachstein (p271)

Hiking, Niederer-Gernkogel (p275)

HIKING EQUIPMENT CHECKLIST

Clothes & Shoes

- ✓ Windproof and waterproof jacket
- ✓ Walking boots with a good grip
- ✓ Trekking sandals or thongs
- ✓ Breathable fleece
- ✓ Loose-fitting walking trousers, preferably with zip-off legs
- ✓ Hiking shorts
- ✓ T-shirts or long-sleeved shirts
- ✓ Socks (polypropylene)
- ✓ Sun hat and glasses
- ✓ Thermal underwear

Other Essentials

- ✓ Map
- ✓ Compass
- ✓ First-aid kit
- ✓ Torch (flashlight) with batteries and bulbs
- ✓ Insect repellent
- ✓ Sunscreen (SPF30+)
- ✓ At least 1L of water per person per day
- ✓ Backpack or daypack
- ✓ Sleeping bag
- ✓ Water bottle

📅 RESOURCES

Waymarking is no substitute for a decent map and/or compass in the Alps.

Federal Office of Metrology and Surveying (BEV) *(maps.bev.gv.at)*
Visit this site for a zoomable topographic country map.

Freytag & Berndt *(freytagberndt.com)*, **Kompass** *(kompass.de)* & **ÖAV** *(alpenverein.at)*
They produce excellent and reliable topographic maps at scales of 1:25,000 and 1:50,000. Some come with details on mountain huts and background information on the trails.

Walking in Austria: 101 Routes *(Kev Reynolds, Cicerone)*
A useful guide, listing more than 101 walks in many regions (mostly in the Alps).

ACTION AREAS

Where to find Austria's best outdoor activities.

Watersports

1. Area 47, the Zillertal (p358)
2. St Anton am Arlberg (p362)
3. Neusiedler See (p151)
4. Hallstatt (p224)
5. Millstätter See (p310)

Skiing/Snowboarding

1. St Anton am Arlberg (p362)
2. Mayrhofen (p343)
3. Zell am See-Kaprun (p273)
4. Kitzbühel (p348)
5. Schladming-Dachstein (p211)

Walking/Hiking

1. Dachstein Rundweg (p212)
2. Mariazell Pilgrimage Trail (p206)
3. Berliner Höhenweg (p346)
4. Salzburger Almenweg (p271)
5. Pinzgauer Spaziergang (p275)

Cycling/Mountain Biking

1. Danube Cycle Path (p132)
2. Murradweg (p211)
3. Bodensee Radweg (p371)
4. Zillertal Radweg (p340)
5. Lackenradweg (p154)

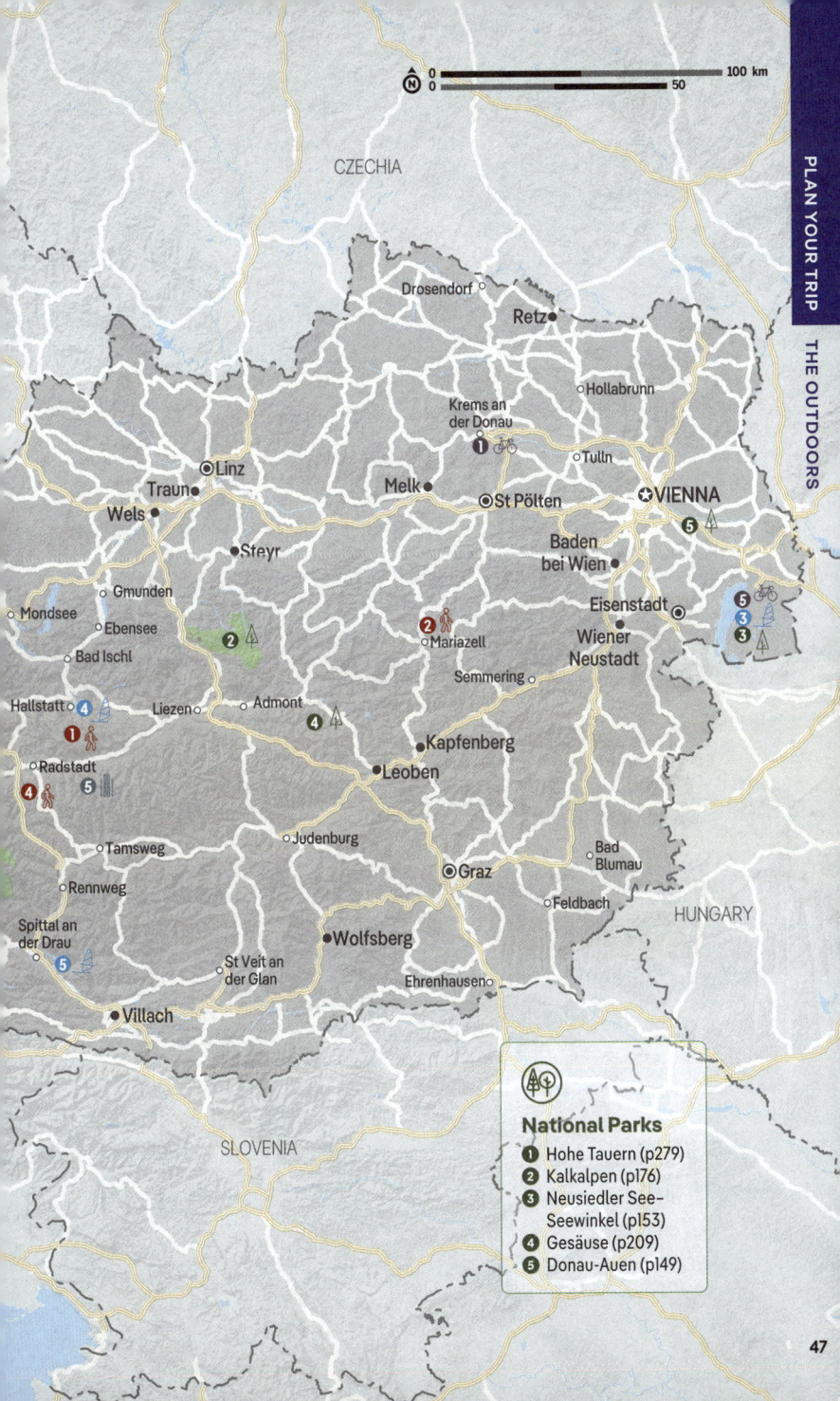

THE GUIDE

AUSTRIA
THE GUIDE

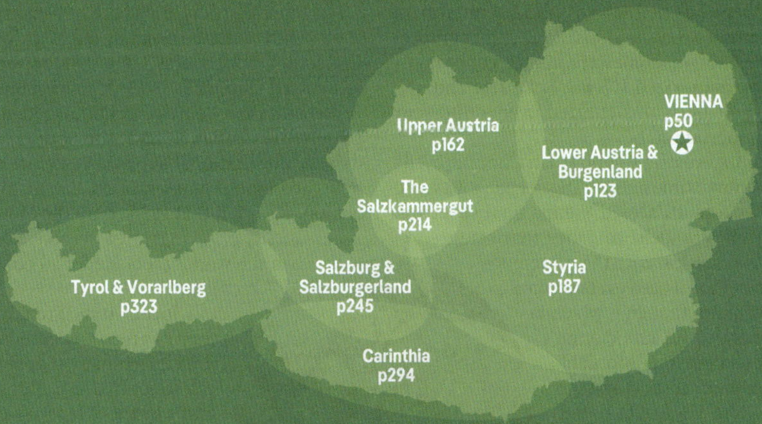

VIENNA p50

Upper Austria p162

Lower Austria & Burgenland p123

The Salzkammergut p214

Salzburg & Salzburgerland p245

Styria p187

Tyrol & Vorarlberg p323

Carinthia p294

Chapters in this section are organised by hubs and their surrounding areas. We see the hub as your base in the destination, where you'll find unique experiences, local insights, insider tips and expert recommendations. It's also your gateway to the surrounding area, where you'll see what and how much you can do from there.

Salzburgerland (p245)
BLUEJAYPHOTO/SHUTTERSTOCK

Researched by Becki Enright

Vienna

THE CLASSICAL CITY IN CONTEMPORARY REVIVAL

More than its monarchal pomp and Habsburg heritage splendour, Vienna's modern metropolis has melded its heady historic sites with the bohemian *Bezirke* (districts).

Vienna is defined by grand remnants of Empire days and Sisi fame, the composing of symphonies, traditional coffee houses, plate-sized *Wiener Schnitzel* and art-vault museums curated over a 600-year imperial reign.

But Austria's capital isn't bound by its vintage time bubble. Dig deeper, and you'll see a multifaceted Vienna on a spectrum from grandeur to gritty that bridges the classical with the contemporary. You'll need to cover some ground, though – which is easy to do via Vienna's excellent and affordable public transport system.

The UNESCO-listed Innere Stadt (inner city) layers the Roman, medieval and Habsburg reserves within cobblestoned streets, laneways and courtyards. It's circled by the Ringstrasse – an architectural icon built upon the razed old city walls to bring the suburbs and the city together. Whirling from the centre, architect Otto Wagner's snail spiral design of 23 districts stumps most visitors on where to begin outside the outer 'burb big hitters, Schönbrunn and Belvedere.

The inner districts are where modernity intertwines with the ornately old. A growing contemporary-arts scene has driven a street-art movement, modern coffee joints jostle with their bentwood chair, wooden-panelled ancestors, and the student-driven, international subcultures craft a new face for this understated European capital. A capital that clocked up the Mercer Quality of Living 'most liveable city in the world' accolade for 10 consecutive years.

Join locals indulging in the city's green credentials, from the climate-adapted city streets to the walking trails in the Wienerwald (Vienna Woods), sipping the local harvest in the *Heurigen* (wine taverns) of the vineyards that surround the city basin, taking a dip in the calm waters of the Alte Donau (Old Danube) or relaxing at the riverside 'beach' bars in the warmer months. A chaotic metropolis it is not. Vienna has a pace more leisurely than its European capital neighbours and a *'Passt scho'* (everything is okay) attitude that adds to its mellow vibe. To enjoy it all, you simply need to take your time.

THE MAIN AREAS

HISTORIC CENTRE: INNERE STADT
Monumental heirlooms and timeless charm.
p56

PRATER & AROUND: LEOPOLDSTADT
The hip, green heart of Vienna.
p81

BELVEDERE & BEYOND: LANDSTRASSE
The meld of art and architecture. **p87**

NASCHMARKT & AROUND: WIEDEN & MARIAHILF
Viennese microcosm of cool. **p93**

> For places to stay in Vienna, see p120

THE GUIDE

VIENNA

Left: *Wiener Schnitzel*; Above: Stephansdom (p56)

NEUBAU, JOSEFSTADT & ALSERGRUND
The bohemian, bourgeois and bon vivant.
p99

SCHLOSS SCHÖNBRUNN: HIETZING
The high-class, palatial past.
p110

OUTER DISTRICTS
The bold and the beautiful.
p116

Find Your Way

Vienna's historic centre and inner districts are easy to explore on foot, including the Hofburg, museum complexes, modern neighbourhoods with landmarks and low-key nightlife. Schloss Schönbrunn is a little further but can be easily reached by tram or metro from the centre. Get information at wienerlinien.at.

Neubau, Josefstadt & Alsergrund
p99

FROM THE AIRPORT
Vienna International Airport is 18km southeast of the centre. S-Bahn trains connect to Wien Mitte/Landstrasse and ÖBB RJ and RJX trains to Hauptbahnhof within 30 minutes – budget alternatives to the fast City Airport Train (CAT); buses go to Schwedenplatz (22 minutes) and Westbahnhof (45 minutes); taxis charge a flat fare.

Outer Districts
p116

Schloss Schönbrunn: Hietzing
p110

WALK
Compact central Vienna is perfect for strolling the sites, from grand palaces to pretty stone streets. You can walk from the Danube Canal to the Hofburg in around 20 minutes, and easily navigate from the Ringstrasse into neighbouring districts.

Prater & Around: Leopoldstadt
p81

Historic Centre: Innere Stadt
p56

Belvedere & Beyond: Landstrasse
p87

chmarkt & Around: ieden & Mariahilf
p93

METRO

Vienna's five U-Bahn (metro) lines run from 5am to midnight and 24 hours on Friday and Saturday. A sixth line is due for completion in 2026. Maps are easy to read, and station announcements are also in English. All stations have wheelchair access.

TRAM & BUS

Vienna's trams are a slower but visually rewarding journey, especially on the Ringstrasse and the approach to Schönbrunn. Buses link to all corners of the city. Both can be trickier to navigate than the metro. Download the WienMobil app for ticket purchase and route planning.

Plan Your Days

From the ruins of Roman Vindobona to its rise as a cultural bastion of Europe, Vienna's millennia of history presents itself in a myriad of experiences.

Fruit and veg stalls, Naschmarkt (p96)

DAY 1

Morning
● Begin in the historic centre, using **Stephansdom** (p56) as your waypoint. Wander old byways between palace grounds, parks and traditional pit stops, and stroll along the **Ringstrasse** (p76).

Afternoon
● Take a break in a Viennese coffee house. **Prückel** (p72), **Schwarzenberg** (p72) and **Landtmann** (p72) are the last of the 27 cafes that once lined the ring road. Then marvel at the **Hofburg** (p64), starting with the Imperial Apartments.

Evening
● Feast at **Figlmüller** (p61), said to be the original home of the schnitzel, or dine in **Griechenbeisl** (p71), the city's oldest restaurant. Catch a performance at the **Wiener Staatsoper** (p80) or have a nightcap in the art deco **Loos American Bar** (p74).

You'll Also Want to...
Delve into Vienna's cultural foundations and discover what makes the city tick beyond its historic centre and palaces.

ATTEND THE SUMMER NIGHT CONCERT
Lounge on the lawns of Schönbrunn to the classical sounds of the Summer Night Concert (p114) of the Vienna Philharmonic.

SEE STREET ART IN ACTION
Artists paint murals and tours explore urban artwork displays during the annual **Calle Libre festival** (p104).

TASTE VIENNESE WINES
Sample local grapes like Grüner Veltliner and Riesling at **10er Marie**, Vienna's oldest *Heuriger*, dating to 1740.

DAY 2

Morning
- Beat the crowds and tour the imperial family's summer residence, **Schönbrunn** (p112), when it opens, ending with a stroll through its gardens. Or visit **Belvedere** (p90), the princely palace turned art museum and home to Gustav Klimt's *Der Kuss* (The Kiss).

Afternoon
- Circuit the trendy **Freihausviertel** (p96) and enjoy a lunch at the inviting, age-inclusive **Vollpension** (p95). Walk to neighbouring **Karlsplatz** (p95) and admire the baroque **Karlskirche** (p95).

Evening
- Walk to the buzzing outdoor **Naschmarkt** (p96), where restaurants carry the vibe into the evening. Finish with cocktails at Mariahilf's **Miranda Bar** (p97) or Neubau's **Die Parfümerie** (p104).

DAY 3

Morning
- View the vast art collections of the imperial family, collated over 600 years, at the **Kunsthistorisches Museum Vienna** (p68). Contemporary art lovers can opt for **MuseumsQuartier** (p102) (MQ), for mumok and Austrian Modernism in the Leopold Museum.

Afternoon
- Take a walking tour through the trendiest of **inner districts** (p99), starting in bohemian Neubau (7th), through stunning Josefstadt (8th) and ending at Alsergrund (9th), home to the **Sigmund Freud Museum** (p106).

Evening
- Enjoy some of the 250 attractions at **Prater Park** (p36). Grab a bite in the hip **Karmeliterviertel** (p83) or at **Danube Canal** (p83) spots like **Motto am Fluss** (p71) and **Strandbar Herrmann** (p89).

FIND VIENNA'S BEST VIEWPOINT
Lofty 150m **Donau Turm** (Danube Tower), Austria's tallest building, gets you the best view of the city and beyond.

HIKE THE WOODLAND TRAILS
Walk 14 city trails, from urban parks to the Vienna hills and the Kahlenberg and Leopoldsberg 'mountains'.

ANCHOR ON THE ALTE DONAU
Boat, pedalo or kayak – renting a skiff and taking to the Alte Donau (Old Danube) waters is a Viennese summer pastime.

THE LONG NIGHT OF MUSEUMS
For one night in October, you can pack in as many of the city's 100 or more museums, from 6pm until midnight, with a single ticket.

Historic Centre: Innere Stadt

MONUMENTAL HEIRLOOMS AND TIMELESS CHARM

GETTING AROUND

The historic core is easy to get around on foot and well connected by the U-Bahn (metro), particularly the U3 line that runs through it. Herrengasse station is located next to the Hofburg, Stephansplatz is directly outside the Cathedral, and Stubentor is opposite the Stadtpark.

Schwedenplatz, on the U1 line, sits on the northern fringe of the 1st district adjacent to the Danube Canal; the line connects to Wien Hauptbahnhof, Vienna's main train station, 3km south, passing Stephansplatz. Karlsplatz (U1, U2, U4) is closest to the Wiener Staatsoper. Trams 1 and 2 circle the Ringstrasse.

Book a clip-clopping tour of the city via the Fiaker horse-drawn carriage at Stephansplatz and Michaelerplatz.

The oldest of the 23 *Bezirke,* Vienna's 1st district is the cobbled-street, pastel-hued, boulevard-ringed, historical heart. It's a layering of centuries and splendour compacted in an open-air museum, filled with the clopping echoes of *Fiaker* – horse-drawn carriages. Here Roman ruins reveal the foundations of the military encampment of Vindobona; the noble thread of the Middle Ages runs through the Gothic thoroughfares; the palatial complexes and art arsenals of the former Austro-Hungarian Empire powerhouse still stand; and the coffee house culture continues. At its core, soaring 136m above, is the Gothic masterpiece and city symbol, Stephansdom. Below is a labyrinth of crypts, catacombs and cellars. So much significance is layered in its near 3-sq-km frame that the historic centre of Vienna is designated a UNESCO World Heritage Site. It all started here, so why shouldn't you?

Seeking Out Stephansdom

MAP P58

Vienna's symbolic landmark cathedral

Vienna's Gothic masterpiece **Stephansdom** *(stephanskirche.at; all-inclusive ticket adult/child €25/7)* soars above. The cathedral's three-centennial-long Gothic glow-up peaked with its 136.4m South Tower and was cut short in its half-finished domed North Tower. A mosaic of 230,000 glazed roof tiles crests in between, stamped with the imperial double-headed eagle. It's free to venture into the vaulted, prismatic glass site, though it is a bit of a scrum. You have to pay to enter the central nave *(adult/child €7/3, cash only)* for a closer look at the 16th-century Gothic sandstone masterwork on the **Pilgramkanzel** (Pilgrim pulpit) and the commanding baroque black marble **High Altar** consecrating the holy space some 100 years later.

Ticketed entry grants more access. Austria's largest bell, the 21-tonne **Pummerin**, which only rings in the New Year, is accessible via an elevator journey to the **North Tower** *(adult/child €7/3)* platform overlooking Stephansplatz. Sweeping city

SIGHTS
1. Haydnhaus
2. House of Strauss
3. Johann Strauss Wohnung
4. Schubert Geburtshaus
5. Schubert Sterbewohnung
6. Shoah Wall of Names Memorial
7. Wiener Stadthalle

DRINKING & NIGHTLIFE
8. Café Sperl
9. Flex

ENTERTAINMENT
10. Arena Wien
11. Art Advent am Karlsplatz
12. Mittelalterlicher Adventmarkt
13. Schloss Schönbrunn Christmas Market
14. Weihnachtsdorf Altes AKH
15. Weihnachtsdorf Schloss Belvedere
16. Wintermarkt Prater

views from the **South Tower** (*entrance outside at Stephansplatz 1; adult/child €6.50/2.50*) require enough stamina to climb 343 precarious, winding steps to access the peering Türmerstube (tower room). In the depths of the **Catacombs** (*adult/child €7/3*), move from the noble burial chambers and imperial Ducal Crypt into the sombre, bone-stacked ossuary caverns, the resting place for the more than 10,000 people who perished during the Plague.

If you plan to visit all the cathedral sites, consider the all-inclusive ticket, which also includes entry to the **Treasury of the Teutonic Order**, filled with altarpiece art and ecclesiastical antiquities.

Remembering Jewish Vienna   MAP P58
Museums and memorials

Vienna's Jewish history spans back to the Middle Ages, but by 1945 only 5000 of its 180,000 members had survived the Holocaust. The **Jüdisches Museum** (*jmw.at; adult/child €15/free*) encourages dialogue about the road to reconciliation. Its split collection – 1945 to the present day and the Middle Ages to the Shoah – elucidates varied perspectives on identity, persecution and present-day Judaism in Vienna, while temporary exhibitions often tackle more controversial topics. Its second branch on **Judenplatz**, built around the on-show excavations of the destroyed synagogue of 1421, is a visual tour of the city's medieval Jewry. Tickets allow entry to both museums.

The old Jewish Quarter, **Judenplatz**, has been a place of remembrance since 2000. The striking and interpretive concrete Holocaust memorial, designed by Rachel Whiteread, presents

continues on p61

> ### ☑ TOP TIP
> The circular centre is far from sprawling, but there's an easy way to know when you've left it. The grandiose architectural loop of the Ringstrasse surrounding the Innere Stadt, completed on one side of the Danube Canal, is a great orientation point. Beyond this boulevard border, you enter the inner districts.

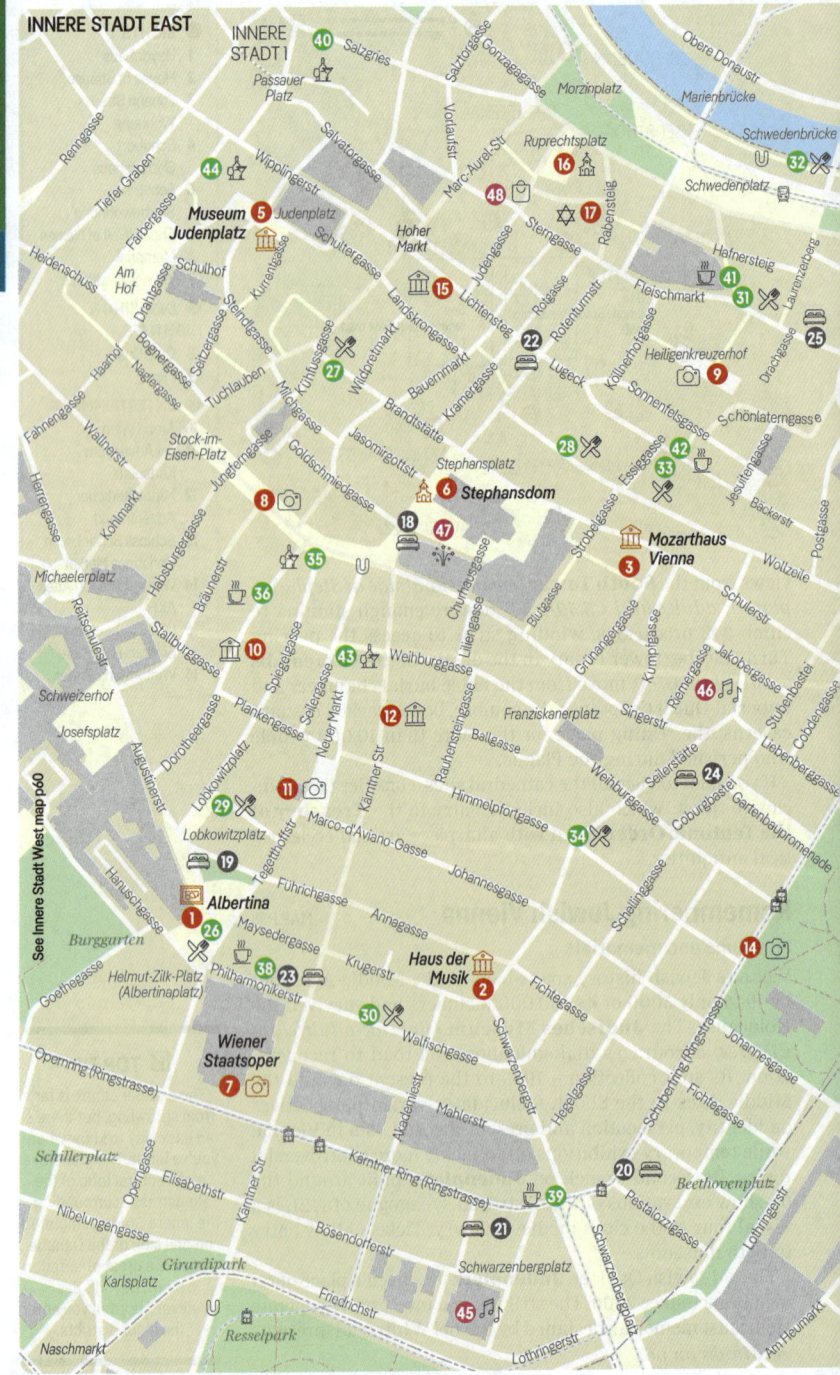

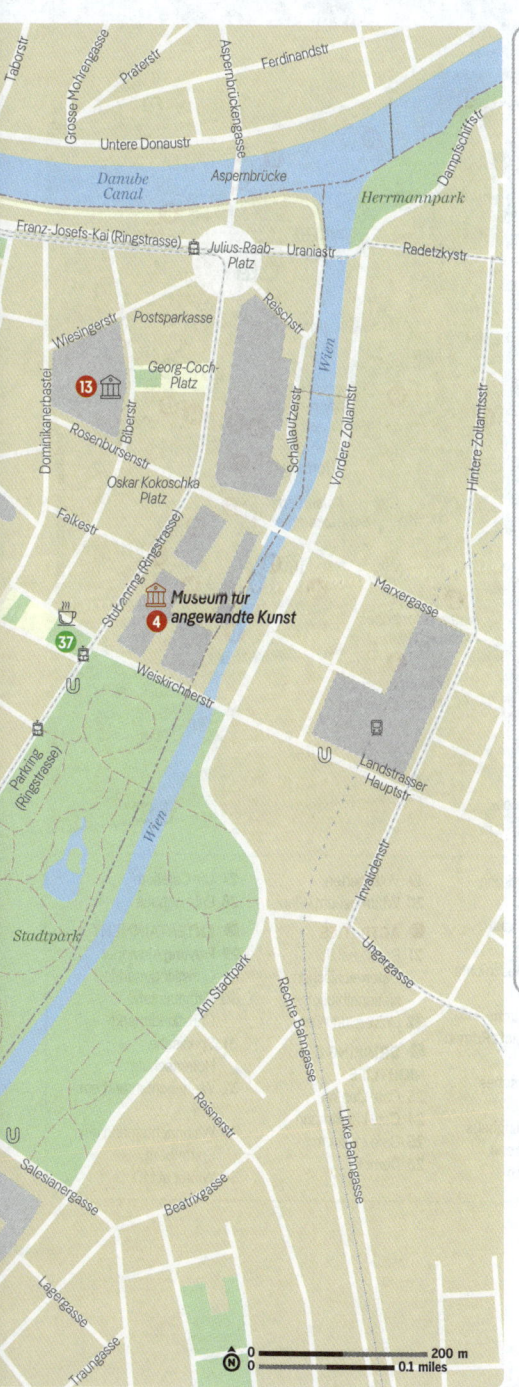

★ HIGHLIGHTS
1. Albertina
2. Haus der Musik
3. Mozarthaus Vienna
4. Museum für angewandte Kunst
5. Museum Judenplatz
6. Stephansdom
7. Wiener Staatsoper

● SIGHTS
8. Graben
9. Heiligenkreuzerhof
10. Jüdisches Museum
11. Kapuzinergruft
12. Mythos Mozart
13. Österreichische Pootspaikasse
14. Ringstrasse
15. Römer Museum
16. Ruprechtskirche
17. Stadttempel

● SLEEPING
18. DO & CO
19. Guest House
20. Hotel Grand Ferdinand
21. Hotel Imperial
22. Hotel Lamée
23. Hotel Sacher
24. Palais Coburg
25. Ruby Lissi

● EATING
26. Bitzinger Würstelstand am Albertinaplatz
27. Café Korb
28. Figlmüller
29. Gasthaus Reinthaler
30. Gasthaus zur Oper
31. Griechenbeisl
see 20 Meissl & Schadn
32. Motto am Fluss
33. Parémi
34. Tian

● DRINKING & NIGHTLIFE
35. Cabaret Fledermaus
36. Café Hawelka
37. Café Prückel
38. Café Sacher
39. Café Schwarzenberg
40. Dino's Apothecary Bar
41. Fenster Café
42. Kaffee Alt Wien
43. Loos American Bar
44. Needle Vinyl Bar

● ENTERTAINMENT
45. Musikverein
46. Porgy & Bess
47. Weihnachtsmarkt Stephansplatz

● SHOPPING
48. Shakespeare & Company

HISTORIC CENTRE: INNERE STADT VIENNA

INNERE STADT WEST

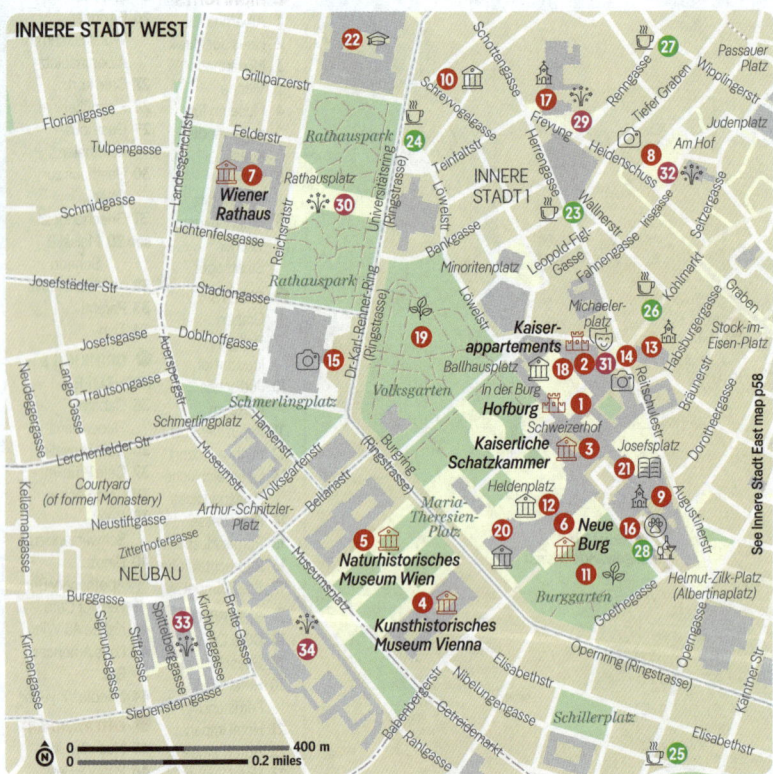

⭐ HIGHLIGHTS
1. Hofburg
2. Kaiserappartements
3. Kaiserliche Schatzkammer
4. Kunsthistorisches Museum Vienna
5. Naturhistorisches Museum Wien
6. Neue Burg
7. Wiener Rathaus

🔴 SIGHTS
8. Am Hof
9. Augustinerkirche
10. Beethoven Pasqualatihaus
11. Burggarten
12. Haus der Geschichte Österreich
13. Michaelerkirche
14. Michaelerplatz Roman Ruins
15. Österreichisches Parlament
16. Schmetterlinghaus
17. Schottenkirche
18. Sisi Museum
19. Volksgarten
20. Weltmuseum Wien

🔴 ACTIVITIES
21. Prunksaal der Österreichischen Nationalbibliothek
22. Universität Wien

🟢 DRINKING & NIGHTLIFE
23. Café Central
24. Café Landtmann
25. Café Museum
26. Demel
27. Die Cafetière
28. Palmenhaus

🔴 ENTERTAINMENT
29. Freyung Altwiener Christkindlmarkt
30. Rathausplatz Christkindlmarkt
31. Spanische Hofreitschule
32. Weihnachtsmarkt am Hof
33. Weihnachtsmarkt am Spittelberg
34. Winter at MQ

continued from p57

an inverted library in a sealed room, alluding to untold stories. The **Shoah Wall of Names Memorial** in Alsergrund (9th district) was inaugurated in 2021. Across 16 districts, vertical **Lichtzeichen** *(lichtzeichen.wien)* installations of an inverted Star of David are markers for where synagogues once stood; the **Stadttempel** (City Temple) is the only survivor of Vienna's 94 synagogues destroyed during the November Kristallnacht pogroms of 1938 because of its coveted construction within a block of apartments.

Finding Hidden History
Roman ruins and medieval walls

MAPS P58 & P60

The exposed Roman relics on **Michaelerplatz** are a sneak peek of Vienna's ancient foundations; the best-preserved excavation basement ruins and some 300 of the 150,000 uncovered artefacts from the legion of Vindobona are housed below Hoher Markt in the **Römermuseum** *(Roman Museum; wienmuseum.at/roemermuseum; adult/child €8/free)*.

Fragments of Vienna's medieval city walls can be found in obscure spaces. Enter the U3 metro station **Stubentor** and find a ticket hall straddled by exposed stone bulks. The luxurious hotel **Palais Coburg** *(palais-coburg.com)* incorporated the foundational relics of the site into its modern reconstruction. The noble family home, built in 1845 upon a bastion, survived the fortification destruction; visitors are free to enter the ground-floor exhibit.

Step into the Middle Ages
Medieval squares and backstreets

MAP P60

Narrow trader alleys, age-old market squares and courtyards – pockets of the Innere Stadt are a window into medieval Vienna. Start in **Blutgasse**, **Franziskanerplatz** and **Ballgasse**, some of the city's most beautiful streets hidden behind Stephansdom.

Palatial **Am Hof** stands upon the grand designs of 1154, when the Duke of Bavaria, Heinrich II, retreated to Vienna and built the palatinate compound of structures around a square. He commissioned Vienna's oldest monastery church **Schottenkirche** (Scottish Church) on neighbouring **Freyung** in 1170. Some 100 years later, Am Hof turned vendor and festival square, continued today by weekend antique dealers and annual festive markets, while luxury hotel Park Hyatt revives the grandeur.

EXCAVATING VIENNA'S ORIGINS

A new chapter in the history of Vindobona was unearthed during an archaeological excavation in 2025 in the 11th district, Simmering, southeast of the centre. Human bones, alongside dagger, helmet, armour and hobnail fragments, found during the renovation of a sports field, date to the 1st-century Roman Empire.

Archaeologists believe the skeletal remains of 129 young men to be those of Roman soldiers who were hastily buried following a disastrous defeat during Emperor Domitian's Danube campaigns.

The discovery adds a new layer to the expansion of Vindobona from a small military encampment into a fortified settlement, thereby shedding new light on the origins of modern Vienna.

 EATING IN INNERE STADT: WIENER SCHNITZEL — MAP P58

| **Figlmüller at Wollzeile:** The establishment that popularised the schnitzel has been serving it since 1905; the pork version is their speciality. *11am–10.30pm* €€ | **Meissl & Schadn:** Before feasting, watch how the schnitzel is perfectly beaten and baked through the open salon kitchen in front of the restaurant. *11.30am–11pm* €€€ | **Gasthaus Reinthaler:** It's like time stopped still in this 1977 *Beisl*, one of the historic district's last remaining authentic taverns. *11am–11pm Mon-Fri* €€ | **Gasthaus zur Oper:** The contemporary venue of the classic culinary institution Plachutta serves a lovely house recipe *Wiener Schnitzel*. *11.30am–midnight* €€ |

HISTORY SURROUNDING STEPHANSPLATZ

START	END	LENGTH
Stephansplatz	Hoher Markt	3km; 45mins

From the cathedral on ❶ **Stephansplatz**, turn right onto ❷ **Graben** (p74), passing the ❸ **Wiener Pestsäule** (Plague Column). Left onto ❹ **Kohlmarkt** brings you to historic ❺ **Café Demel** (p72). At Michaelerplatz, turn right onto Herrengasse, passing Art Nouveau ❻ **Looshaus**, to reach the grand ❼ **Café Central** (p72). Ahead, pink flags advertise the ❽ **Ferstel Passage**. Walk through the arcade to Freyung, looking out for the ❾ **Schottenkirche** (p61) and Bank Austria Kunstforum (art forum) opposite.

Towards Am Hof, loop right onto pretty Naglergasse and left into Irisgasse, which leads to Park Hyatt Vienna. Follow Drahtgasse to ❿ **Judenplatz**. Walk along Jordangasse, turning right onto Wipplingerstrasse, passing the ⓫ **Altes Rathaus** (old town hall), owned by the city since 1316. Then left on Marc-Aurel-Strasse and right on Sterngasse. Beautiful ⓬ **Shakespeare & Company** has been selling English books here since 1982. Turn left for ⓭ **Ruprechtskirche** to marvel at Vienna's oldest church. Walk down the Ruprechtsstiege (stairs) and right towards Schwedenplatz. After 150m, turn right into Rotenturmstrasse and left onto ⓮ **Griechengasse** – it curves past Fenster Café to the city's oldest restaurant, ⓯ **Griechenbeisl** (p71). Right onto Fleischmarkt, left onto Köllnerhofgasse and left to Grashofgasse brings you to the secluded ⓰ **Heiligenkreuzerhof** courtyard; exit at stunning Schönlaterngasse.

Cut through the buildings and turn right onto Bäckerstrasse, passing French pâtisserie Parémi, vintage Kaffee Alt Wien and *Beisl* legend Figlmüller at Wollzeile. Continue through Lugeck and onto Lichtensteg to ⓱ **Hoher Markt**, where the Art Nouveau Ankeruhr (Anker clock) figures move at noon. Stephansdom is around the corner.

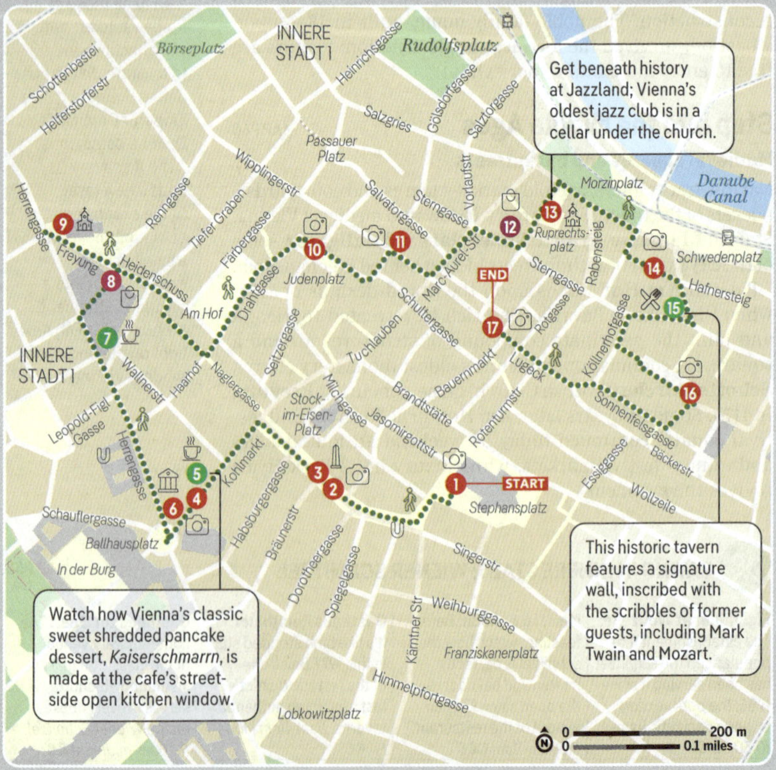

> Get beneath history at Jazzland; Vienna's oldest jazz club is in a cellar under the church.

> Watch how Vienna's classic sweet shredded pancake dessert, *Kaiserschmarrn*, is made at the cafe's street-side open kitchen window.

> This historic tavern features a signature wall, inscribed with the scribbles of former guests, including Mark Twain and Mozart.

The courtyard curiosity of **Heiligenkreuzerhof** has its foundations in the 1135-founded Heiligenkreuz Abbey. A time-warp passage between Schönlaterngasse and Grashofgasse, today's courtyard was added in 1771 after multiple adaptations. Neighbouring **Ruprechtskirche** (St Rupert's Church), from 1200, is the oldest in Vienna, overlooking Schwedenplatz and perched on an elevated weave of cobbled alleys that chart the prettiest route down to the Danube Canal.

Alternative Walking Tours
Hear it from the locals

Relatively short but historically rich, a walking tour with a local guide can help crunch the millennia of stories into understandable morsels or set you on the path to seeing the city from an entirely different perspective.

Rebel Tours (rebeltoursvienna.com; adult/child €35/15) offers an alternative introduction to the historic centre – with no stately stuffiness – on their Hidden Vienna walk, during which you'll hear about the lesser-known legends behind the city's centuries-old hidden courtyards and cobblestoned laneways.

Meanwhile, **Hidden Vienna Tours** (hiddenvienna.guide, adult/child €35/27) reveals Vienna's Cold War–era secrets on their I Spy Vienna tour. In 1945, the 1st district was divided into a quadrant Inter-Allied Zone. Listen to stories of espionage and how Vienna came to be known as the city of spies. And if you thought the city was steeped only in palatial splendour, learn all about the struggle for survival on its streets and slums during imperial times on the Gangs of Vienna tour.

Vienna is known for its boundless beauty, but Eugene Quinn from **Whoosh** (whoosh.wien; adult/child €10/free) shows the controversial and rebellious architectural misfits on his Vienna Ugly Tour – a tongue-in-cheek look at the city's worst buildings.

You'll learn about the polarising, often unseen sides of the city with **Shades Tours** (shades-tours.com; up to 15 people €234) – city walks led by those affected by homelessness and addiction, and for whom a job as a guide is a chance to rebuild their lives. Only private tours in English.

Circle the City on Wheels
Speedy sightseeing

Those with a need for speed can set off in a single-seater pocket-rocket motor car on a **Hot Rod City Tour** (hotrod-tour-wien.com; €150), circuiting the city in convoy on a 1½-hour adrenaline ride around the architectural conveyor belt Ringstrasse and through historic centre alleys. A valid class B driving licence is required. Or cycle the boulevards on a Classic Vienna Bike Tour with **Pedal Power** (pedalpower.at; €47) – a leisurely three-hour wheel through the city's break-and-behold monuments.

continues on p71

RUN THE CITY

Gabi and **Basti** – the Austrian-Brazilian sibling duo behind Rebel Tours Vienna – talk about a unique way to experience the city.
@rebeltoursvienna

Combining sport and history presents the city in a new light. Early mornings in the 1st district, where you usually wouldn't think to run, has a different vibe.

We start outside the museums on Maria-Theresien-Platz, head to the top of the Albertina, back down to the Ringstrasse and its beautiful buildings like the Opera, then to the Belvedere gardens, learning along the way. It's 6.5km and takes around 1½ hours, moving from the centre and through green Vienna.

When running, you get to the bottom of what this city is about. The pace is far from a sprint; it's possible for everyone. Even the locals join in.

Alte Burg (Old Castle) at sunrise

TOP EXPERIENCE

Hofburg

Nothing epitomises the extravagant reign of the Habsburgs more than the humongous 240,000-sq-metre **Hofburg**. The sovereign home and seven-century-long power base of the imperial family up until 1918 is a tapestry of heritage across its 18 wings and 19 courtyards, showcasing a staggering collection of cultural artefacts and art masterpieces in grand museums and preserving a classical equestrian art form in its Spanish Riding School.

DON'T MISS

- Sisi Museum and Kaiserappartements
- Prunksaal der Österreichischen Nationalbibliothek
- Spanische Hofreitschule
- Kaiserliche Schatzkammer Wien
- Weltmuseum

Alte Burg – Imperial Resplendence Revisited

Roll back the times in the Alte Burg (Old Castle) gilded Imperial Chancellery Wing and Amalia Residence. Enter the **Sisi Museum** and **Kaiserappartements** (*Imperial Apartments; sisimuseum-hofburg.at; adult/child €20/12*) via the marbled Emperor's Staircase – as visitors seeking an audience with Emperor Franz Joseph I once did – and meander through 17 resplendent rooms of court life accompanied by a 75-minute audio guide. The misunderstood life and final days of Empress Elisabeth are sensitively showcased in an upfront exhibit of 300 personal items, from childhood trinkets to beauty items, gloves and replica gowns. Move to the bedazzling belt of living spaces, including bedrooms and bathrooms, studies and saloons, preserved with their chandeliered ceilings, decked walls, regal red silk upholstery and royal gold embellishments.

Burrowed within the wings of the Schweizerhof (Swiss Courtyard) in the oldest part of the Hofburg are the coveted crown jewels of Austria. The **Kaiserliche Schatzkammer Wien** *(Imperial Treasury Vienna; kaiserliche-schatzkammer.at; adult/child €18/free)* is a chambered millennia of majesty with its Holy Roman and Habsburg Empire heirloom displays. Those seeking the illuminated masterpieces of imperial regalia should beeline to the bejewelled Crown and Holy Lance of Emperor Rudolf II (Room 2), the precious stone- and pearl-adorned Imperial Crown of the Holy Roman Empire of the German Nation (Room 11), and the distinguished insignia of the Order of the Golden Fleece (Room 15).

The Hofburg residents today are the world-famous white Lipizzaner stallions. The classical skills of horse-riding art and equestrianship have been practised at the **Spanische Hofreitschule** *(Spanish Riding School; srs.at; adult/child from €26/reduced)* since 1565. This unique preservation of equestrianism only exists here, and has topped both the Intangible Cultural Heritage and Intangible Heritage of Humanity UNESCO lists. Every rider is responsible for the daily training of their small group of horses to perfect the graceful skills proudly demonstrated in the famed musical performances in the baroque Winter Riding School arena.

Palace Gardens – Sumptuous Strolls

Vienna's manicured green spaces started here; the **Volksgarten** (public garden) was the first garden built by the Habsburgs for the people. You'll know it by its Greek Theseus Temple or the smell of its 3000 rose bushes. It's not uncommon to see locals lounging on the **Burggarten** (Palace Garden) lawn. Emperor Franz Joseph's verdant enclosure opened to the public in 1919, and his Jugendstil glasshouse jungle, later turned into a classy cafe-bar **Palmenhaus** *(Palm House; palmenhaus.at)*, shared with the tropical **Schmetterlinghaus** (Butterfly House), with hundreds of colourful flitters.

Neue Burg – World Culture Curated

The arc wing of the Neue Burg (New Castle) and the forecourt Heldenplatz (Heroes' Sq) is the new kid of the grand expansion of the Hofburg in the late 19th century. An imperial guesthouse was planned for the Corps de Logis wing but instead has been home to one of the world's most important ethnographic collections since 1928 – the personal 'souvenirs' amassed from the continental expeditions of the three Habsburg Archdukes, Ferdinand Max, Crown Prince Rudolf and Franz Ferdinand throughout the 1800s.

Following his 10-month world voyage in 1892, Franz Ferdinand envisioned what is now the **Weltmuseum** *(World Museum; weltmuseumwien.at; adult/child €16/free)*. Across 14 halls on the middle floor is a permanent exhibit of a mind-blowing 250,000 anthropological objects from outside Europe, accompanied by objects, drawings, photographs and scientific notes from other explorers, including British seafarer James

> **STRONGHOLD TO SPLENDOUR**
>
> Extravagant expansions ravaged the foundational four-towered medieval castle of 1246. Well, not all. In the oldest segment, the Swiss Wing, see remains of the old moat when you enter the **Renaissance Schweizertor** *(Swiss Gate)*, added around 1550 as part of the first imperial residence upgrades and incorporating part of the drawbridge ball chains.
>
> The 15th-century Gothic elements of the Hofburg Chapel have also been preserved.

LIPIZZANER MORNING MAGIC

In the vaulted corridor on Reitschulgasse, you might be lucky to glimpse the Lipizzaner stallions resting in the **Stallburg** (Stable Palace) after their workout routine.

During training hours (7am to 12.55pm), they cross the street to the Winter Riding School approximately every 30 minutes. While not guaranteed, the most majestic setting for a sighting is in the Burggarten, between 8.30am and 10am from spring to autumn. Mondays are their day off.

Cook and German naturalist Otto Finsch. Notably, an exhibit examines the modern-day debate about the cause and consequence of Europe's colonial expansion and the plundered, given or exchanged context of acquiring archaeological and cultural relics.

A continuation of worldly acquisition, the neighbouring **Ephesos Museum** *(khm.at/exhibitions/ephesos-museum; incl in House of Austrian History ticket)* is a collation of the work of Austrian archaeologists who have been excavating the ancient Greek city of Ephesos since 1895. Important statues and friezes from the site, now located in present-day Turkey, were relocated to Vienna; its prized masterpieces include the cherished carved-stone panel reliefs of the Parthian Monument and the Amazon relief from the Temple of Artemis, one of the original seven wonders of the world.

Those looking for a detailed timeline and debate on the past 100 years of political events in Austrian history can untangle it all in 57 interactive stations in the thought-provoking **Haus der Geschichte Österreich** *(House of Austrian History; hdgoe.at; adult/child €10/free)* covering the move from Monarchy to Republic, the annexation of Austria to the Third Reich before WWII and Austria's place in the European Union.

The Other Neue Burg

One part of the complex leaves something to the imagination. The Habsburgs loved to flex political prowess with architecture, and no mightier show was planned than with the 1869 blueprint for the gigantic Kaiserforum (Emperor's Forum)

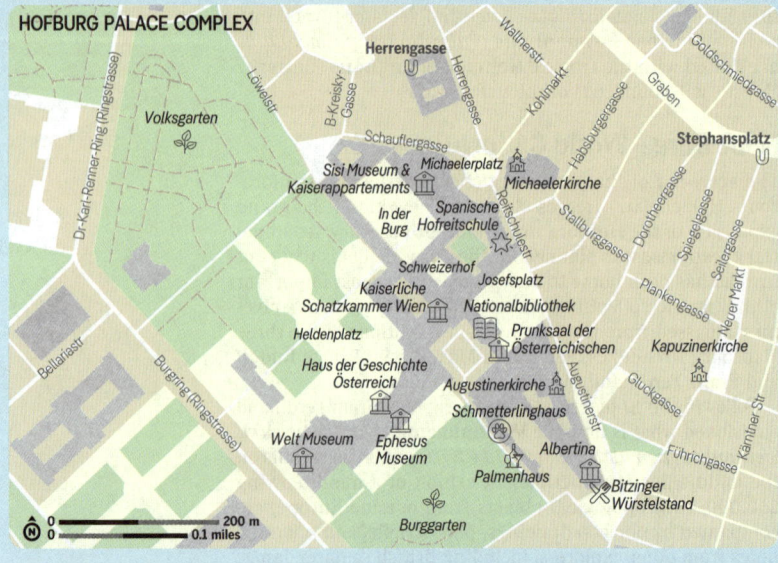

– two symmetrical arc buildings to stand alongside the Kunsthistorische and Naturhistorische Museums. The lofty aspirations were abandoned, leaving just half of it: the Neue Burg.

Prunksaal – Baroque Bibliotheca

So grand is the nearly 80m-long court library of Habsburg Emperor Karl VI that it is stationed in its own dedicated wing. The 18th-century baroque beauty of the **Prunksaal der Österreichischen Nationalbibliothek** *(State Hall of the Austrian National Library; onb.ac.at/museen/prunksaal; adult/child €11/free)*, built to elaborate imperial taste, is one of the most important libraries in the world. Marble-columned archways open to circular rooms of dark-walnut-wood shelves with gilded motifs, overarched by magnificent ceiling dome frescoes. A statue of the emperor stands in the middle, surrounded by 200,000 leather-bound books, the earliest dating to 1501.

Michaelerplatz & Around

Members of the Habsburg family were not entombed in one place; their body parts were split in three and spread across the city. The Herzgruft (heart burial vault) is in the Loreto Chapel of **Augustinerkirche** *(Augustinian Church; guided tours only on Sunday after High Mass; €10)*, the intestines in Stephansdom's Ducal Crypt and the rest of the body in the imperial crypt, **Kapuzinergruft** *(Capuchin's Crypt; kapuzinergruft.com; adult/child €13/7)*, where 150 Habsburg family members have been laid to rest (English tours: Monday, Wednesday and Saturday).

Not for the faint-hearted, the baroque Habsburg royal parish of **Michaelerkirche** *(St Michael's Church; michaelerkirche.at; adult/child €8/4; private tours in English up to six people €48)* on Michaelerplatz is a mesh of catacombs filled with the bones of over 4000 buried here from 1631 to 1784, and the cold rooms of noble crypts whose temperature conditions have partially preserved the now mummified bodies. Guided tours are currently only in German.

Continue along Augustinerstrasse for the **Albertina** *(albertina.at; adult/child €19.90/free)* and browse an art bundle of drawings and prints that's become the world's largest. Housing the works of master sketchers, including Monet and Picasso, its most famed work is the 1502 watercolour *Young Hare* by Albrecht Dürer. The green rabbit sculpture on top of the **Bitzinger Würstelstand** is a nod to this precious work of art. Or continue the imperial gazing and visit the 20 restored luxurious Habsburg State Rooms of this former royal palace (included in the admission ticket).

TOP TIPS

- The closest metro is Herrengasse (U3), or it's a 12-minute walk from Stephansplatz.

- Entry to the Alte Burg for the Sisi Museum, Imperial Apartments and Spanish Riding School is at St Michael's Gate on Michaelerplatz. The Outer Gate on the Ringstrasse opens onto the Neue Burg complex. A walkway connects the gates passing by the Swiss Gate – the entrance to the Imperial Treasury. Access to the Prunksaal is from Josefsplatz.

- Winter Riding School performances are only at weekends; watch training on weekday mornings. Guided tours of the Spanish Riding School run daily; architecture tours on Saturday afternoons.

- It's a multi-museum complex; get discounted entry with the **Vienna City Card** *(wien.info/en/travel-info/vienna-city-card)* from the tourist office opposite Albertina or online.

Kunsthistorisches Museum Vienna

TOP EXPERIENCE

Kunsthistorisches Museum Vienna

The Kunsthistorisches Museum Vienna (Art History Museum), home to the city's most impressive art assemblage, has been open to the public since 1891, yet the neo-baroque magnificence and size can still bewilder even the most discerning of art aficionados. This half-day roam of the halls will guide you through this Habsburg treasure house.

> **DID YOU KNOW**
>
> The rooms of imperial coffers extend beyond these walls. Other notable collections include the **Collection of Historical Instruments** and the **Imperial Armoury** displays in the complex of the **Weltmuseum** (p65).

Egyptian & Near Eastern Collection

From the Cupola Hall entrance, ascend the stairs immediately to the right for a 5000-year dynastic dive into the Egyptian and Near Eastern Collection (Level 0.5), covering the Predynastic Period to the Christian Era. Enter the first hall with paintings created by Ernst Weidenbach in 1873, recreating scenes from the Beni Hasan tomb of Chnumhotep II.

Offering Chapel of Ka-ni-nisut

Take a left to Room II and stand within the **1. Offering Chapel of Ka-ni-nisut** – the recreated funerary cult of the early 5th-century Dynastic official, discovered in Giza in 1913. Continue to Room V for the symbolic statuette of the **2. Blue**

Hippopotamus and muse the mysteries behind the displays of Egyptian sarcophagi and canopic jars (organ urns), burial offerings and stone-carved reliefs.

Greek & Roman Antiquities

Skip millennia to Room X and enter the Collection of Greek and Roman Antiquities. Admire the carved marble masterwork of the **3. Amazon Sarcophagus** relief and the mythological scene setting floor **Mosaik of Theseus** in Room XI and the captivating gem-carved **4. Gemma Augustea Cameo** in Room XVI, glorifying the reign of Emperor Augustus.

Kunstkammer Wien

The adjacent wing is devoted to the Kunstkammer Wien (cabinet of art and curiosities) – a window into the royal fashion of collecting all that was peculiar and precious, such as Benvenuto Cellini's golden **5. Saliera tableware** in Room XXIX, clockmaker Hans Schlottheim's magnificently mechanised **6. Automaton in the form of a ship** in XXVII and the ivory-carved **7. Apollo and Daphne statuette** in Room XX.

TOP TIPS

● Bypass the long queues and pre-book admission tickets online via shop.khm.at/tickets.

● It's best to tackle the museum one floor at a time; start on the ground floor and work your way up, ending with the elevated lounge viewpoint.

● Take advantage of Thursday late openings (6–9pm) for fewer crowds.

● One-hour guided tours in English take place every Sunday, focusing on the highlights of one collection. An admission ticket is required; tours are extra.

KUNSTHISTORICHES MUSEUM VIENNA

First Floor: Gemäldegalerie (Picture Gallery)

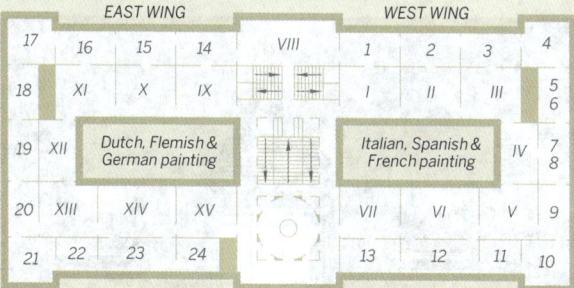

Ground Floor

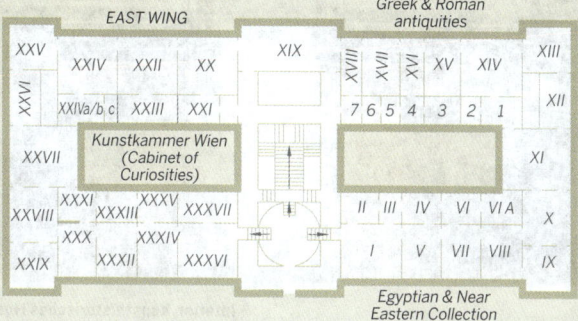

FINDING KLIMT

View Gustav Klimt's **The Spandrels** – the wall murals above the arches and between the columns of the Main Staircase at Level 1 encapsulating the museum's collections.

The centre figures represent Ancient Egypt and Ancient Greece. Above the left arch, the Roman and Venetian Quattrocento, and from the right, Early Italian Painting.

Picture Gallery

Ascend the grand marble staircase to Level 1, where you'll pass Antonio Canova's marble **8. Theseus Slaying the Centaur** before entering the colossal compilation of Renaissance and baroque paintings in the Picture Gallery.

Italian, Spanish & French Paintings

Turn right into the halls for Italian, Spanish and French painting masterpieces, including Raphael's bucolic **9. Madonna of the Meadow** in Room III, Caravaggio's devoted **10. Madonna of the Rosary** in Room VI and Velázquez's defining portrait **11. Infanta Margarita in a Blue Dress** in Room 10.

Dutch, Flemish & German Paintings

Continue past the Lounge to the opposite wing for the Dutch, Flemish and German painting rooms. Take in Vermeer's muse in **12. The Art of Painting** in Room XII en route to Dürer's altarpiece **13. Adoration of the Trinity** in Room XI, and end on a high with Pieter Bruegel the Elder's entrancing **14. The Tower of Babel** in Room X.

Lounge Views

Before you leave, don't miss the enchanting views over the circular **15. Lounge** from the alcoves on Level 2, next to the Imperial Coin Collection money cabinet spanning three millennia.

Interior, Kunsthistorisches Museum Vienna

continued from p63

Musical Genius in the Golden Hall MAP P58
Musikverein magnificence

The Viennese live classical music; it's in their DNA. Composing geniuses like Haydn, Mozart and Beethoven and their successors, Strauss, Schubert and Mahler, built their legacy here. Centuries on, 10,000 people listen to live performances of their scores every evening.

The prestigious **Musikverein** *(musikverein.at)* opened the doors of its two main halls in 1870, of which its gilded cuboid Goldener Saal (Golden Hall) is most famed – it's the permanent home of the **Wiener Philharmoniker** *(Vienna Philharmonic Orchestra; wienerphilharmoniker.at)*, whose sell-out New Year's Concert is broadcast globally from here. The architectural acoustic wonder holds an audience of 2000, overlooked by Apollo and the Nine Muses on its frescoed ceiling. Take a 45-minute tour *(€10; Mon-Sat)* to go behind the scenes of this remarkable building.

Conduct an Orchestra at Haus der Musik MAP P58
The house of sound

The four-floored **Haus der Musik** *(hdm.at; adult/child €17/7)* is a multisensory classical-music schooling, starting with a melodic staircase entrance. The archive-filled 1st floor is dedicated to the Wiener Philharmoniker – its founder, conductor and composer Otto Nicolai lived here from 1841 to 1847. Before moving between the visual thwack of rooms resounding the symphonic scores of each of the six Great Masters, understand the science of sounds on the 2nd-floor interactive Sonotopia laboratory. By the end, you'll pick up a conducting baton and test your skills on the Virtual Conductor, cueing the Philharmonic Orchestra in the Golden Hall of the Vienna Musikverein.

Inside the Figaro House MAP P58
Mozart's last remaining apartment

The image of the world's most famous composer is ubiquitous in Vienna. By age 25, he was residing here, working as an independent musician. Mozart changed addresses 13 times; his most successful years were spent at Domgasse 5 – the only apartment still standing. Navigate three exhibit floors

continues on p74

COFFEE IN THE 1ST DISTRICT

Michael Prem, owner of sustainable coffee roastery Prem Frischkaffee *(frischkaffee.at)*, shares his favourite third-wave espresso bars and coffee spots.
Café Exchange: A special place inside the Österreichische Postsparkasse where you can breathe in the atmosphere of architect Otto Wagner while enjoying a daily lunch menu, homemade cakes and coffee brews crafted by award-winning baristas.
Parémi: Heaven-on-earth French bakery combining impeccable coffee with Vienna's best croissants. With its selection of high-quality products, you'll be impressed with whatever you choose.
Fenster Café: This hole-in-the-wall cafe near Schwedenplatz serves its own roast. Get a speciality brew when passing by.

 EATING IN THE HISTORIC CENTRE: OUR PICKS — MAPS P57 & 58

Motto am Fluss: Canal-anchored boat with cafe and restaurant serving contemporary Austrian cuisine. *6-11pm Mon-Sat, to 10.30pm Sun, bar to midnight* €€

Griechenbeisl: Feast on *Wiener Schnitzel* and *Kaiserschmarrn* (sweet pancake) in the city's oldest *Beisl* (inn). *noon-11pm* €€

Tian: This Michelin-star gourmet vegetarian restaurant is rooted in rare ingredients and experimental cooking. Book well ahead. *6pm-11pm Tue-Sat* €€€

Die Cafetière: Revived mid-century modern cafe and purveyors of the tastiest Viennese cheese and ham toastie. *7.20am-6pm Mon-Fri, 9am-4pm Sat* €€

HELP ME PICK:

Traditional Coffee Houses of Vienna

Vienna's first *Kaffeehaus* (coffee house) opened in 1683, with origins linked to the Ottoman Siege of Vienna. So profoundly ingrained is this legacy that UNESCO granted it Intangible Cultural Heritage status in 2011, which the Innere Stadt protects in its historic cache of cafes. These plush institutions – featuring wood-panelled and chandelier-lit rooms with bentwood Thonet chairs and banquettes, newspaper stacks and waiters in formal attire – have long been an extended living room for writers, artists and thinkers.

Where to Go For...

The Refined

The vaulted, marble, gilded **Café Central** *(Herrengasse 14)* was the elite meeting place of poets, philosophers and revolutionaries, though it now commands the longest queues for entry for today's storytellers.

Elegant **Demel** *(Kohlmarkt 14)* has also served artisanal delicacies since 1786. Its graceful window displays will lure you in, but the rococo-regency salon cafe upstairs is where to sample its Demel Sachertorte, which compares with the original at the regal, red-upholstered **Café Sacher** *(Philharmonikerstrasse 4)*.

Timestamped 1880 **Café Sperl** *(Gumpendorfer Strasse 11)* is the living room for artists, and where the founders of the Secessionist art movement met. Its chocolate, vanilla and almond *Sperl Torte* is also a secret recipe heirloom.

The Redefined

Art history enthusiasts will marvel at the interior of **Café Museum** *(Operngasse 7)*, which has changed three times, reverting to the 1931 Josef Zotti redesign of the 1899 Adolf Loos original, complete with silver-sphere light fixtures and some original furniture.

Pops of colour and hanging portraits give 1904-established **Café Korb** *(Brandstätte 7/9)* a modern art touch, blending with its 1960s-era remodelling with red-velvet booths and glass light shades.

The Bohemian

Family-run **Café Hawelka** *(Dorotheergasse 6)* has been a city institution since 1939, known for its late-night servings of sweet, doughy, jam-filled *Buchteln*, made to a family recipe; the poster-plastered walls and dusky-lit **Kaffee Alt Wien** *(Bäckerstrasse 9)* is the predecessor – Leopold Hawelka and his wife Josefine taking it over in 1936 before moving to Dorotheergasse. With their 1am late-night opening hours, the melded vibes of coffee house and pub are a hip blend.

The Ringstrasse Greats

The Ringstrasse era of the mid-1800s spawned cafe construction, and 27 cafes once lined the show road of the Nouveau Riche; today, just three remain. The pastel-hued 1903 **Café Prückel** *(Stubenring 24)* is an icon of Art Nouveau style. Freud's favourite, the polished **Café Landtmann** *(Universitätsring 4)*, continues to serve Viennese coffee house culture to international patrons as it did when it opened in 1873 for the Vienna World's Fair. And the step-back-in-time, wood-bound, marble-mirrored **Café Schwarzenberg** *(Kärntner Ring 17)*, is the oldest Ringstrasse cafe from 1861.

Café Prückel

Café Central

HOW TO

When to Go
Average opening hours are between 8am and 11pm. The sacred *Kaffee und Kuchen* (coffee and cake) hour is typically 4pm.

Before You Go
It's not only sweet treats; most coffee houses serve *Wiener Küche* (Viennese cuisine), from *Frühstuck* (breakfast) to hearty *Hauptspeisen* (mains).

Ordering
Never ask for 'a coffee' but choose specifically from the menu. It limits the 'grumpy waiter' intimidation; it's not personal, just part of the Viennese experience.

Budget
Plan on paying in cash. Expect to pay between €4 and €7 for a coffee, €5 and €8 for a slice of cake, and €10 and €25 for a main.

The Kaffeehaus Experience

Traditional joints may jostle with their new-gen caffeine-kick counterparts, but the truth is, you don't come to a *Kaffeehaus* for the quality of the brew, but the beauty of the atmosphere. Yet it's not as simple as asking only for a coffee, either; you'll be choosing from a specialist, often mind-boggling list of options.

For a classical plunge, order a *Wiener Melange* (half coffee, half milk foam, similar to a cappuccino), though you'll find the familiar in a *kleiner Schwarzer* (a single espresso), a *kleiner Brauner* (espresso with a side of milk or cream) and a *Verlängerte* (an espresso lengthened with hot water).

The Viennese are sweet-toothed, with menus dedicated to satiny *Schlagobers* (whipped cream), like the *Einspänner* (espresso topped with cream and served in a glass), a *Kapuziner* (a double shot of espresso with a whipped topping) or an *Eiskaffee* (cold coffee and vanilla ice cream with lashings of cream). You might also find some boozy whipped-cream-topper options on the menu, including the *Maria Theresia* (double espresso with orange liquor) and the *Fiaker* (double espresso and rum).

Coffee houses remain bastions of cultural inspiration. Linger over a coffee to the sounds of live piano music; Café Central hosts daily performances from 4.30pm to 9.30pm. Every Sunday, Café Schwarzenberg hosts live jazz music sessions from 11am to 1pm, while Café Korb's schedule includes evening music concerts and readings almost daily.

SHOPPING STREET SPLENDOUR

Vienna's iconic shopping streets were built for strolling.
Graben: Roman ditch turned Vienna's most ornate axis, where traditional Viennese stores occupy magnificent mansions.
Kärntner Strasse: The shopping mile from Sacher to Stephansplatz, with Steffl department store's view-worthy Sky & Roofgarden.
Ferstel Passage: Chic stores line the exquisite Venetian trecento-style arcade of the historic 1860 Palais Ferstel.
Kohlmarkt: The haute-couture highway stretching to Tuchlauben is lined with luxury flagship stores.
Tuchlauben: Boutique design stores and jewellery ateliers dazzle on this more than 100m-long fashion avenue.

continued from p71

of **Mozarthaus Vienna** *(mozarthausvienna.at; adult/child €14/4.50)* with the free one-hour audio guide, starting with the composer's arrival in Vienna in 1781, moving through his musical repertoire, notably *The Marriage of Figaro*, which he wrote here, and ending at the apartment on the 1st floor where he lived for 2½ years. Special attention is given to highlighting original decor and placing a period object in each of the seven rooms to bring the 18th-century grandeur to life.

When Mozart died in 1791, aged 35, he was living at Rauhensteingasse 8, where the Steffl Department Store now stands. In its lower level, the **Mythos Mozart** *(mythos-mozart.com; adult/child €23/€12/under 6 free)* exhibition presents a timeline of his life through a multimedia melody across five fantastical rooms.

The Legacy of Johann Strauss II   MAP P57

Waltzing Vienna

The city waltzes at more than 400 balls across its winter season between November and February. The Opera and Vienna Philharmonic soirees are the most prestigious, although there is a ball for every profession, a tradition dating back to the Viennese Biedermeier period (1815–48), when dance halls thrived in the post-Napoleon era. It was 'Waltz King' Johann Strauss II who made the seasonally celebrated *Blue Danube*

DRINKING IN THE HISTORIC CENTRE: BARS   MAP P58

Dino's Apothecary Bar: A dark wood-panelled, low-lit classic cocktail bar with an extensive experimental menu. *5pm-2am Tue-Thu, to 3am Fri & Sat*

Loos American Bar: Celeb magnet and cult-status bar designed by Viennese modernism architect Adolf Loos. *noon-4am*

Lamée Rooftop Bar: The chic and colourful rooftop bar of Hotel Topazz Lamee, with one of the best views of Stephansdom. *11am-1am Sun-Thu, to 2am Fri & Sat*

Needle Vinyl Bar: A trendy, retro-styled, record-spinning bar lounge, mixing music and signature cocktails. *5pm-2am*

Ferstel Passage

Waltz and the dance genre a global icon. He is immortalised in gold in the Stadtpark, and his legacy lives on at the **House of Strauss** (*houseofstrauss.at; adult/child €23/9.50*) exhibition, a multi-dimensional delve into the Strauss dynasty in the historic Casino Zögernitz, where all four Strauss musicians once played. Its preserved performance hall hosts evening orchestral performances; a timeline of Strauss II's life through his music, enhanced with audio-visual projections.

At Home with the Master Composers MAPS P57 & P60
Waltz around six composer abodes

Beethoven changed his address more than any other composer, but the Pasqualati family kept the 4th-floor apartment for him. The **Beethoven Pasqualatihaus** (*Mölker Bastei 8; adult/child €5/free*) museum focuses on his eight years here, where he composed three of his nine symphonies and his only opera, *Fidelio*. The 19th district's **Beethoven Museum** (*Probusgasse 6; adult/child €8/free*) is a broader account of his life's work, and among the displays are his piano and a lock of hair.

The last 12 years of Haydn's life were spent in the now 6th district **Haydnhaus** (*Haydngasse 19; adult/child €5/free*), composing his notable works *The Creation* and *The Seasons*. In the 2nd district **Johann Strauss Wohnung** (*Praterstrasse 54; adult/child €5/free*), the composer created the exalted anthem of Vienna, the *Blue Danube Waltz*, in 1867. The homely **Schubert Geburtshaus** (*Nussdorfer Strasse 54; adult/child €5/free*) in the 9th district details his formative years and exhibits a pair of the composer's spectacles. Enthusiasts can picture where he composed his last musical drafts at the 4th district **Schubert Sterbewohnung** apartment (*Kettenbrückengasse 6; adult/child €5/free*), where he died in 1828.

Pay per site or get a discounted combined ticket, **Musikus** (*shop.wienmuseum.at/en/tickets; adult/child €21/16*).

FREE MUSIC FESTIVALS & EVENTS IN VIENNA

The city of music brings music, film and performance to its streets, squares and green park stages throughout the year, though summer to autumn is when festivities abound.

Film Festival Rathausplatz: Open-air music films from concert and stage greats, plus pop-up eats at the City Hall square. *Jul-Sep*

Kultursommer Wien: Music, theatre and dance performances are staged in parks, squares and gardens across the city. *Jun-Aug*

Gürtel Night Walk: Up-and-coming artists and local bands perform outside the Gürtel (belt) road of bars. *last weekend in Aug*

Donauinselfest: Europe's biggest free open-air music festival brings the party to the Donauinsel (Danube Island). *last weekend in Jun*

ROAD TRIP

Ringstrasse Highlights

When Emperor Franz Joseph called for the band of medieval walls to be demolished in 1850 to unite the city and the suburbs, it set in motion the most revolutionary urban design project of its time. The 5.3km **Ringstrasse** (Ring Rd) ignited a societal shift towards liberalism and new wealth, expressed through the historicism style of combining various architectural types. Walk or combine trams 1 and 2 to circle the ring road in either direction.

❶ Österreichische Postsparkasse

Otto Wagner's first building commission gave the public **Austrian Postal Savings Bank** *(ottowagner.com/oesterreichische-postsparkasse)* a makeover in Viennese modernism, switching extravagance for practicality. The sleek steel and glass Art Nouveau bank hall was realised between 1904–12. Inside this functionalist space, some of the original ticket counters are repurposed by vendors and creative areas.

❷ MAK – Museum of Applied Arts

The impressive red-brick building with Italian Early Renaissance facade features and a columned arcade hall was the Ringstrasse's first museum, built in 1871 for the **Museum für angewandte Kunst** *(MAK, Museum of Applied Arts; mak.at)*. Exhibits of furniture and other arts and design materials from the Middle Ages to the present detail a sociohistorical deep dive into the search for Viennese modern style.

❸ Wiener Staatsoper

A capsule of Vienna's classical-music heritage, the **Vienna State Opera** (p80) *(wiener-staatsoper.at)* opened in 1869 to Mozart's *Don Giovanni* and has since continued the legacy of the great composers who wrote scores for the stage. The world's largest repertoire of classical music is performed on a daily rotation.

❹ Neue Burg of the Hofburg Complex

If the Hofburg wasn't staggering enough, the Neue Burg (p65) was a deliberate architectural plan to assert power by taking a front row seat on the Ringstrasse. Even today, it remains one of the most prominent and dazzling structures to stroll past.

Österreichisches Parlament

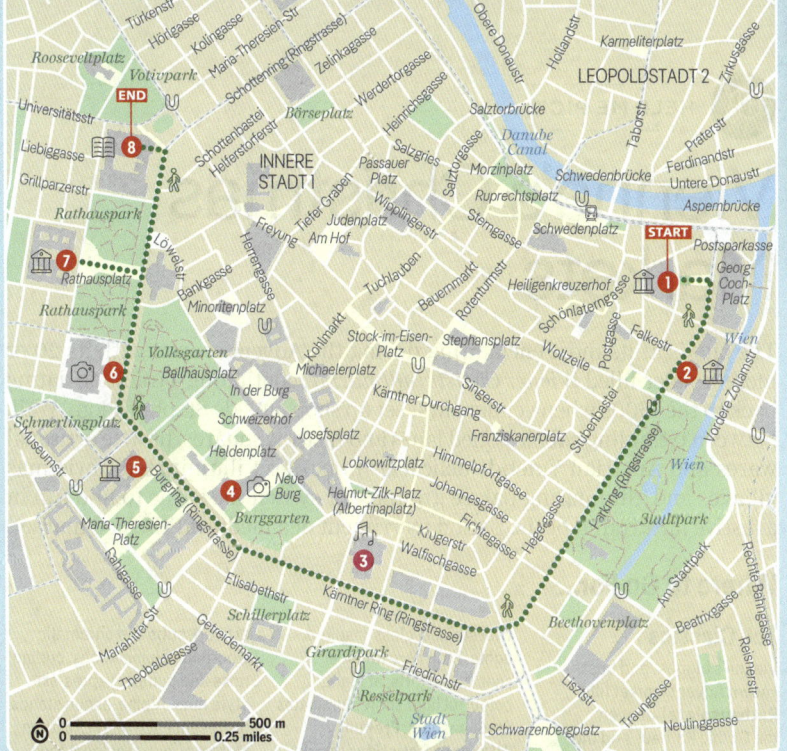

❺ Palatial Museums on Maria-Theresien-Platz

The magnum opus of museum complexes, the construction of the **Naturhistorisches Museum** *(Natural History Museum; nhm-wien.ac.at)* in 1889, followed by the symmetrical **Kunsthistorisches Museum** (p68) two years later, was the exalted stage for the Habsburgs' extensive treasury of finds including meteorites and minerals, ancient antiquities and world-famous paintings.

❻ Österreichisches Parlament

With its Greek temple facade, the **Austrian Parliament** *(parlament.gv.at)* by prominent Ringstrasse architect Theophil von Hansen was emblematic of the political shift from imperial to republic, built in the time of monarchy between 1874 and 1883. Reopened in 2023 after a five-year renovation, today interactive exhibits and building tours give an insight into the living democracy of Austrian politics.

❼ Wiener Rathaus

The dominating neo-Gothic–style **City Hall** *(wien.gv.at/english/cityhall)* built between 1872 and 1883 was representative of a newly enlarged population. It's a community pillar, with people gathering on the square opposite the distinguished Burgtheater (Imperial Theatre) for seasonal event highlights including the Vienna Film Festival, the famed Christmas market (Wiener Christkindlmärkte) and Vienna's Pride Parade.

❽ Universität Wien

A study in style, the Italian High Renaissance–designed **University of Vienna** *(univie.ac.at)* opened in 1884 – home to the oldest university in the German-speaking world, founded in 1365. See the masterwork of Ringstrasse architect Heinrich von Ferstel up close on a guided tour through the Main Ceremonial Chamber and Great Reading Room.

HELP ME PICK:

Vienna's Christmas Markets

The city is at its most enchanting during the Advent season with its 20 or more wonder-filled *Wiener Christkindlmärkte*, continuing a tradition dating back to the 1600s when vendors first set up shop outside Stephansdom. Walk between twinkling cobblestoned lanes and historic squares, browse artisanal wares and Austrian Yuletide delicacies in park-set illuminated Christmas villages and glimmering palace grounds, or switch the scene to find fun in a festive fairground or the period merriment of a medieval-themed market.

Where to Go For...

The Classics

Vienna's biggest and best-known Advent market fills **Rathausplatz** between the Gothic Rathaus and the neo-baroque Burgtheater with a 'Christmas Dream' themed wonderland. Ride a vintage carousel, saunter through 120 huts and visit the gardens with dazzling tree light displays, illuminated pathways and a loop-lane ice rink. The cobbled lanes of **Spittelberg** (p99) dial up the idyllic when hemmed with over 100 festive and eco-focused booths with woodwork, textiles and metalwares, alongside vegan and organic food. Stroll and skate to the most iconic imperial backdrop at **Schloss Schönbrunn** when its Parade Court turns majestically festive with a traditional ice rink and 90 booths brimming with regional crafts and delectable treats.

Historic Backdrops

Stephansplatz is pocketed with a cluster of booths topped with stained-glass-inspired lights. Stop here for local snacks and gifts; at night, colourful light show illuminates Stephansdom. **Freyung Altwiener Christkindlmarkt** packs a compact space with 50 crafts and food stalls, and hosts daily brass and choir performances; **Weihnachtsmarkt am Hof** adds 70 more exhibitors to the neighbouring historic square. The rear of **Upper Belvedere** is an elegant baroque lakeside stage for the small but stately market, featuring over 40 stalls selling unique, traditional gifts.

Artistry & Modern Takes

The creative display of the **Art Advent am Karlsplatz** unfurls in front of the illuminated baroque Karlskirche. Shop from handpicked makers of leather, metal, wood, ceramic, glass and visual arts, and stay for the live music. The **Weihnachtsdorf Altes AKH** at the Universität Wien campus courtyard is packed with artwork cribs and chromatic woodland illuminations, curling rinks and pumping après-ski style huts. Alpine-esque stands represent each of the Austrian states, offering regional food and drink specialities. At **MuseumsQuartier**, box booths line the courtyard as light projections create new forms upon former imperial walls and DJs spin beats.

The Different

Across four days in early December, the **Mittelalterlicher Adventmarkt** *(Medieval Market)* at the Military History Museum is a period spectacle featuring costumed vendors, Middle Ages–inspired cuisine and crafts, fencing and fire shows. **Wintermarkt Prater** turns Riesenradplatz into a dedicated festival playground, with street food and music concerts. The devilishly Krampus procession typically takes place on the first Sunday of December.

Rathausplatz Christmas market

---- **HOW TO** ----

When to Go
The markets open in mid-November and run until 23 December; Rathausplatz and Stephanplatz continue until 26 December, Schönbrunn into early January.

Before You Go
All markets are outdoors and exposed to the elements. Layer up and absolutely pack a thick winter jacket, warm shoes, a hat and gloves.

When You Are There
You'll need to pay a deposit for the mug (up to €5). Return and refund at the end, or keep as a souvenir.

Budget
Plan on paying in cash. *Glühwein* and *Punsch* cost up to €6, snacks around €5 and hot food plates from €10. Markets are free to enter.

Visiting the Christmas Markets

Market hopping is a marathon, though public transport circles all sites. Route through four of the best markets on a one-hour walking tour (minus meandering time), following an anti-clockwise run of the Ringstrasse: start in Altes AKH, then to Rathausplatz, Spittelberg and continue to Karlsplatz.

At every market, you'll get your 'deposit' mug from any drink-selling stall. *Glühwein* (mulled wine) and *Glühmost* (hot apple cider) are the spicy old-timers, while the sweeter *Punsch* (a hot fruit and spirit blend) moves from traditional *Beeren* (berry), *Orangen* (orange) and *Apfel* (apple) to flavour-cranking and experimental liqueur and tropical fruit concoctions. The fiery upgrade to *Glühwein* is a *Feuerzangenbowle*, which has a rum-soaked sugar cube topper, set alight in a blue flame to add caramelised sweetness.

Find black barrel grills piled with *Maroni* (roasted chestnuts) and *Kartoffelpuffer* (grated potato pancakes). *Käsespätzle* (cheesy dumplings with fried onions), sausages, soup in bread bowls and *Langos* (Hungarian deep-fried flatbread) are heartier staples at almost every market, as are sweet servings of *Kaiserschmarrn* (fluffy, caramelised pancakes) and *Lebkuchen* (gingerbread).

Austrian-made products abound, but it pays to question the origin of classic wooden crafts and blown-glass baubles if in doubt. Vienna invented the snowglobe in 1900, and spotting an original is easy – 'Vienna Snowglobe Austria' is marked on the base. Markets proudly platform their handpicked vendors: Schönbrunn values its offering of traditional craftsmanship, while the Karlsplatz and Spittelberg markets champion their design artisans of wearables and wares.

CONTEMPORARY MUSIC VENUES IN VIENNA

Beyond classical performances, Vienna's ensemble of arenas, halls and clubs resound year-round with all music genres.
Porgy & Bess: Creative basement jazz and music club staging European and international talent.
Cabaret Fledermaus: The 1st district's legendary home of the Viennese cabaret scene since 1907.
Arena Wien: This edgy venue for alternative music acts is on the site of a former slaughterhouse.
Wiener Stadthalle: Vienna's largest music hall with a year-round line-up of world-famous artists.
Flex: Live music club on the banks of the Danube Canal hosting concerts and DJ sets.

Wiener Staatsoper

Step into the Vienna State Opera   MAP P58

Inside the crescendo of music halls

Experience a 19th-century ambience in the world-renowned **Wiener Staatsoper** *(Vienna State Opera; wiener-staatsoper.at)*. With the largest repertoire, daily rotating performances, and around 50 operas and Vienna State Ballet productions per season, an evening at the Wiener Staatsoper is a quintessential Viennese experience. Buy tickets online or wait a couple of hours in line to bag cheaper tickets for €18 or less at the standing-room box office on Operngasse (available 80 minutes before the performance).

Beyond performances, you can tour the house and find details you might otherwise miss with all eyes on the stage. Daily guided tours *(adult/child €15/9)* wind from the grandiose foyer and staircase, through the plush auditorium levels and into the opulent state rooms that survived wartime damage. Book online or at the ticket office 30 minutes before the tour.

Prater & Around: Leopoldstadt

THE HIP GREEN HEART OF VIENNA

The vibrant urban wedge between the waters of the bar-lined Danube Canal (Donaukanal) and the Danube (Donau) River is the 2nd district. The former Jewish quarter, multicultural at its heart, has become a hip spot while remaining the heart of the community with kosher stores and bakeries. At its core, though, is nature. Prater Park's greenery stretches 3000 acres through the district, almost close enough to reach either end. This city oasis is home to the amusement park of the same name, with the big wheel of the Wiener Riesenrad as its icon. The palace-set baroque gardens of Augarten, juxtaposed with the wartime concrete Flakturm towers and the trendy Karmelitermarkt culinary market, complete the trio of highlights.

Taborstrasse and Praterstrasse are the main arteries connecting the green spaces to the centre, teeming with international eats, trendy bars and cafes. It's all happening here.

Park Life in Augarten
Historical baroque gardens

The tip of the triangle of parks above Stadtpark and Prater, **Augarten** (augarten.com; museum adult/child €8/free, guided tours €21/free) is often overlooked. If you come here, you'll find yourself in the manicured hedgerow maze of Vienna's oldest baroque garden, though not without its dark history looming. The park is punctuated by two of Vienna's six concrete **Flaktürme** (flak towers) – the above-ground air-raid-defence bunkers from 1944. Fortunately, the Augarten survived destruction.

The former imperial hunting ground from 1614 was expanded by Habsburg rulers over the century, with Emperor Joseph II allowing public access in 1775. Of its musical lineage, Mozart, Schubert and Strauss performed here; today the acclaimed Vienna Boys' Choir has its concert-hall home, **Das MuTh**, on the Augarten's southern tip.

GETTING AROUND

The 2nd district's Danube Canal stretch is reachable by a short bridge from Schwedenplatz U-Bahn (U1 and U4 lines) on the 1st district side.

Karmelitermarkt is a five-minute walk south from Taborstrasse (U2) or a 10-minute walk from the canal; altogether, a compact, walkable district. The heart of Augarten is a 10-minute walk north of the station. You can't miss the main entrance to Wurstelprater from Praterstern (U1 and U2) or take tram lines O and 5.

☑ **TOP TIP**

Vienna's low-cost public bike-rental service, **WienMobil Rad** (wienerlinien.at/wienmobil/rad), covers all districts with 185 pick-up stations. Download the app and grab a bike at Schwedenplatz station.

PRATER & AROUND: LEOPOLDSTADT

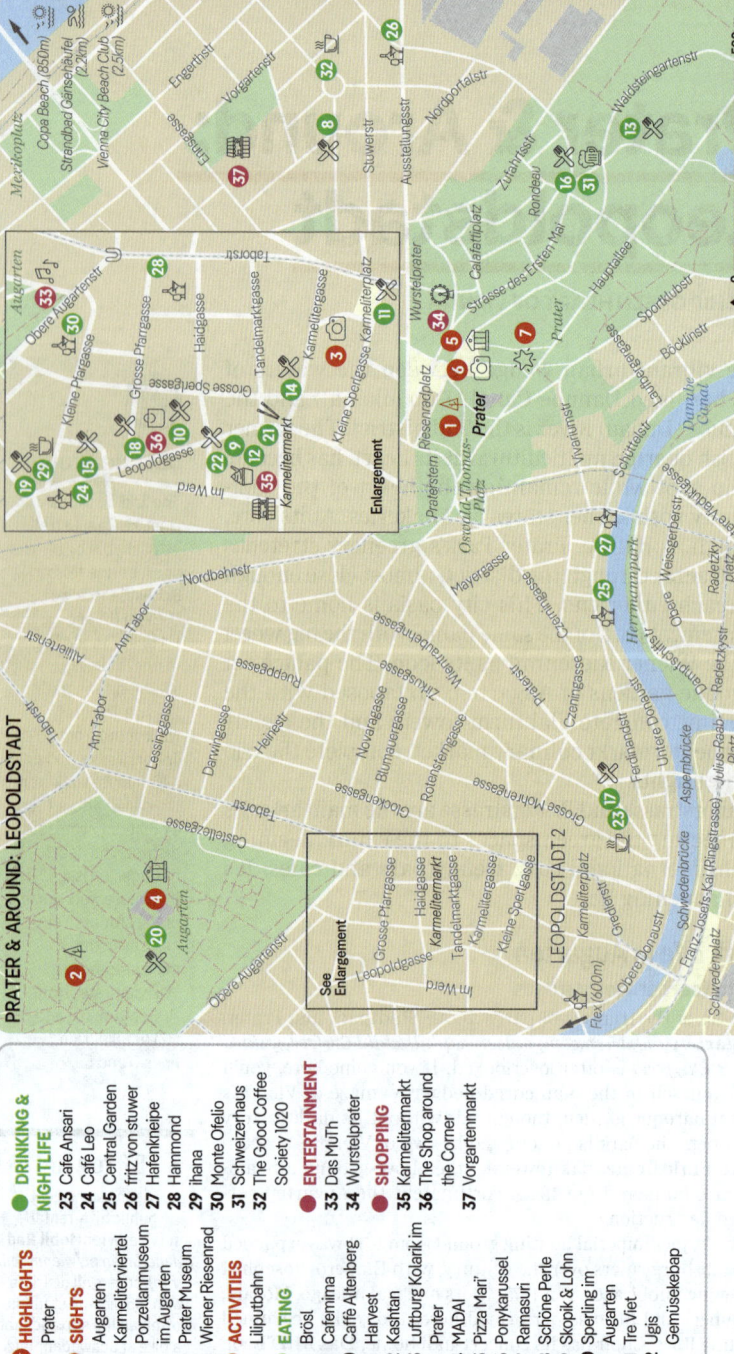

★ HIGHLIGHTS
1 Prater

● SIGHTS
2 Augarten
3 Karmeliterviertel
4 Porzellanmuseum im Augarten
5 Prater Museum
6 Wiener Riesenrad

● ACTIVITIES
7 Liliputbahn

● EATING
8 Brösl
9 Cafemima
10 Caffè Altenberg
11 Harvest
12 Kashtan
13 Luftburg Kolarik im Prater
14 MADAI
15 Pizza Mari'
16 Ponykarussel
17 Ramasuri
18 Schöne Perle
19 Skopik & Lohn
20 Sperling im Augarten
21 Tre Viet
22 Ugis Gemüsekebap

● DRINKING & NIGHTLIFE
23 Cafe Ansari
24 Café Leo
25 Central Garden
26 fritz von stuwer
27 Hafenkneipe
28 Hammond
29 Ihana
30 Monte Ofelio
31 Schweizerhaus
32 The Good Coffee Society 1020

● ENTERTAINMENT
33 Das MuTh
34 Wurstelprater

● SHOPPING
35 Karmelitermarkt
36 The Shop around the Corner
37 Vorgartenmarkt

The palace isn't a residential relic but houses the **Augarten Porcelain Manufactory** *(Porzellanmuseum im Augarten)* – the second-oldest porcelain factory in Europe, which still produces Habsburg classics, the candy-striped Josef Hoffmann collection from 1929, alongside contemporary collaborations, such as that with Italian fashion designer Giambattista Valli. You can trace Vienna's decorative pottery-art history, dating to its inception in 1718, in the small but beautifully presented two-floored museum, or browse the shop for free. You'll need deep pockets for this precious and prized porcelain.

Meandering the Karmeliterviertel
The trendsetting quarter

Between Hollandstrasse/Leopoldsgasse and Taborstrasse, and spreading a little outside this street ladder, is the **Karmeliterviertel** (Carmelite Quarter), the happening subdistrict of Leopoldstadt.

There are boutique and secondhand clothing stores like **The Shop around the Corner**, cool cocktail bars including the longstanding **Hammond**, the bohemian vegan bedrock **Harvest Cafe-Bistrot**, Italian aperitivo spots **Caffè Altenberg**, **MADAI** and **Monte Ofelio**, indie-cool **Café Leo** and cubby-hole cafes like Finnish **ihana**.

By the weekend, however, the humming weekday corner of the **Karmelitermarkt** (Carmelite Market) is a beatnik magnet. Come here on Fridays and Saturdays for the farmers market and join the ranks of locals packing out the grid of gastronomy stalls from Vietnamese to vegetarian bites.

The area merges with the end of Praterstrasse and its trendy triangle of establishments close to the Danube Canal; you'll see a buzz around the Nestroy Denkmal statue, with peppy bistros such as **Cafe Ansari** and **Ramasuri** leading the charge.

Chill Out on the Danube Canal
The waterside hangout

One side of the art-graffiti-covered **Danube Canal** is claimed by the 2nd-district borders – and it's jam-packed full of bars and buzz. Between Augartenbrücke and Franzensbrücke is a promenade smattered with restaurants and waterside dens, community gardens and sculpture artworks, as well as

continues on p86

HISTORY OF LEOPOLDSTADT

The history of how Leopoldstadt came to be is solemn. Before Vienna's city walls were demolished, this outlying suburb grew to have a substantial Jewish population by way of persecution; Jews were expelled from the centre of Vienna in 1670 and resettled here, just a little over 100 years before the opening of Prater. It's named after Emperor Leopold I, who commanded this order. This Jewish enclave thrived over the centuries, though its Jewish population once again faced expulsion and deportation during the Holocaust.

Today, you'll find a (primarily) Orthodox community continuing the district's Jewish heritage; most notably around the Karmeliterviertel, Vienna's archetype neighbourhood of coexistence.

EATING IN LEOPOLDSTADT: OUR PICKS

Skopik & Lohn: *Beisl* turned trendy bistro in the Karmeliterviertel with contemporary dishes and one of the city's best schnitzels. *6pm-midnight Tue-Sun* €€

Pizza Mari': The best authentic Neapolitan pizza this side of the canal, best served on the outdoor terrace. Pizza serving hours vary. *noon-midnight Tue-Sat, to 11pm Sun* €

Schöne Perle: Modern joint with *Beisl* nostalgia, serving regional fare and Austrian wines, as well as vegetarian and fish mains. *11am-11pm Mon-Fri, 10am-midnight Sat & Sun* €€

Sperling im Augarten: Beautiful palace-set restaurant whose terrace overlooks the park. Modern Austrian fare and seasonal menu. *9am-10pm Tue-Sat, to 6pm Sun* €€

TOP EXPERIENCE

Prater Park

Vienna's green spaces go beyond palace gardens and city parks, and the 2nd district delivers. **Prater** is typically referenced as two parts; the recreational city escape of Green Prater, formed when Emperor Joseph II opened the imperial hunting grounds to the public in 1766, and the supercharged **Wurstelprater** fairground with over 200 attractions.

> **DID YOU KNOW**
>
> Prater was the site for the Vienna World's Fair in 1873. Aside from countless country pavilions, its showpiece Rotunda was the largest domed construction in the world; it burned down in 1937. The **Prater Museum** revives the history of the amusement park.

Iconic Wurstelprater Attractions

Take a Turn on the Wiener Riesenrad

The Rotunda may no longer stand, but the **Wiener Riesenrad** (*Vienna Giant Ferris Wheel*; wienerriesenrad.com; adult/child €14.50/6.50) remains a firm fixture. The landmark of the park since 1897, the 30-gondola attraction was built in celebration of the Golden Jubilee of Emperor Franz Joseph I and was the largest of its time. A turn in one of its 15 iconic red wagons circles you 64.75m above Vienna for a Danube-side view over the city and its green basin – a 15-minute journey with audio commentary. Eight cabins were turned into exhibits in the **Wheel of History** audiovisual panorama museum; the wheel ticket includes entry.

Swing High on the Prater Turm

There are high-speed spinners and hair-raising coasters, but **Prater Turm** (*Prater Tower*; €10) is an old-time metal swing carousel sensation twirling 117m up the axis. You don't get expansive city views, but you get a terrific look at the span of Prater from its highest attraction.

Ride the Lilliputian Locomotive

The **Lilliputian Locomotive** *(liliswelt.at; round trip adult/ child €6/€3.50)* has been trundling a 4km loop between the Ferris Wheel and the Green Prater forests since 1928 and it's a rite of passage for all visitors. The nearly 60-year-old diesel locomotive is today's main runner while the 90-year-old mini historic steam locomotive is pulled out for the big events. In 20 minutes, you get a scenic introduction – and easier access across four stations – to a large swathe of the park. It operates from March to November.

Into Green Prater Nature

Walk the Green Highway Hauptallee

Covering 6 million sq metres, exploring the blanket of Prater can seem daunting, but the 4.5km-long tree-lined Hauptallee (Main Ave) cutting straight through it is the best way to enjoy it without getting lost. Walk from Wurstelprater to the path's end at the former imperial hunting lodge turned classic Lusthaus restaurant in around one hour. You'll pass the Republic of Kugelmugel, declared a 'micronation' by its artist creator to save it from demolition. It's now a (sporadically opened) gallery space in the park. If you want to step out of Vienna for a short while at the end of the route, the Japanese Buddhist temple and **Vienna Peace Pagoda** are 20 minutes away, a white stupa tranquilly sitting on the banks of the Danube.

Get Off Track on the Prater Hiking Trail

Ramblers can get off the main path. The **Wien Stadtwanderwege**, Vienna city walking trails, has a well-marked 13km round-loop through the woodland, getting you into more dense and serene pockets, but without being completely isolated. Look for the wooden signposts etched with 'Stadtwanderwege 9'.

Wiener Riesenrad

WHERE TO EAT AND DRINK

Schweizerhaus
Prater's traditional beer garden since 1766 is known for having the best pork knuckle. €€

Luftburg Kolarik im Prater
The world's largest fully certified organic restaurant, in an urban garden setting. €€

Ponykarussel
A floral-clad breakfast and sweet treats cafe within the old pony riding stables pavilion. €€

TOP TIPS

● The entrance to Prater is closest to the Praterstern U-Bahn station on lines U1 and U2.

● The park is busiest at weekends and on public holidays when locals make the most of it. Consider visiting on weekdays to avoid the crowds.

● Wear comfortable clothing and footwear; you'll cover a lot of ground.

● Architecture enthusiasts can admire the Zaha Hadid–designed Library & Learning Center of the neighbouring Wirtschaftsuniversität (Business University) campus, accessible from the U2 Messe-Prater station.

BEACHES IN THE 22ND DISTRICT

There's no real beach in Vienna, but some of the banks of the Danube's tributaries have been transformed into sandy shores.

Copa Beach: Exit the U-Bahn station at Donauinsel (U1) to reach this recreational beach on the Neue Donau (New Danube) riverfront, with lounging sandbanks and hut bars.

Vienna City Beach Club: The cool 'coastline' den on the Neue Donau is a bougie beach complex (with deckchairs, volleyball court, DJ sets and a cocktail bar.

Strandbad Gänsehäufel: The Alte Donau (Old Danube) has its own island with a self-contained swimming-pool complex complete with a beach, restaurants and kayak hire.

Danube Canal (p83)

continued from p83

easygoing watering holes such as **Central Garden**, **Hafenkneipe** and **Flex** (p79), the drum 'n' bass club. On warmer days, this strip is packed and the hot spot for sundowners. But you don't even have to enter an establishment for a drink – join locals sitting along the canal banks and bring your own.

New Quarter Rising
Hip hangouts in the Stuwerviertel

Shedding its former sketchy persona through slow gentrification, the **Stuwerviertel** is the latest area of Leopoldstadt gaining ground in its hip hangout offering. **Vorgartenmarkt** (though overshadowed by Karmelitermarkt) has always been a market-hub mainstay, but a growth of reformed places are giving new life to this lesser-known district quarter including **Brösl**, an old Beisl turned modern pub with seasonal grub; mellow cocktail-bar **fritz von stuwer**; and the second branch of quality brew stars, **The Good Coffee Society**.

EATING AT KARMELITERMARKT: OUR PICKS

Cafemima: Cafe with outdoor seating, serving healthy breakfast bowls and homemade lemonades. *8.30am-10pm Tue-Fri, 8am-2pm Sat, 9.30am-5pm Sun* €

Ugis Gemüsekebap: Not your ordinary kebab; this joint specialises in vegetable-loaded and plant-based meat doner and wraps. *11am-9pm Mon-Fri, 10am-6pm Sat* €

Tre Viet: Vietnamese bistro with pho, banh mi, bao and rolls, and weekly noodle and curry specials. Also has a small shop. *10am-8.30pm Mon-Fri, 8am-6pm Sat* €

Kashtan: The sweet tooth spot with handmade fruit moose desserts, cakes, tarts, croissants and matcha drinks. *9am-8pm Mon-Thu, 8am-8pm Fri, 8am-6pm Sat* €

Belvedere & Beyond: Landstrasse

A MELD OF ART AND ARCHITECTURE

Landstrasse is far from bustling but exudes a quiet elegance in boulevards, parks and landmarks; the splashy 18th-century baroque palace and UNESCO World Heritage Site, Belvedere, its centrepiece. Wander the grounds and halls of the twin-set stately home of Prince Eugene of Savoy which is now an art museum of masterpieces, and join the pilgrimage to *The Kiss* by Gustav Klimt. The heart of the 3rd district can be found between here and the canal. There's the city's Stadtpark, half of which is claimed by the district's borders, and Hauptstrasse and Ungargasse, old-time avenues of opulent architecture, leading right to it. In its residential corner is the second art abode of a very different kind, the Hundertwasserhaus – transformed to be untypical with modern architectural styles to harmonise with nature. You don't come to Landstrasse for the action but for the Austrian art avant-garde.

GETTING AROUND

For those who do not wish to see it all on foot, Stubentor is your anchor for the main sites. Tram line 1 gets you to the Hundertwasser House in 10 minutes, and Tram D heads south to Belvedere Palace in less than 15. Schlachthausgasse U-Bahn (U3) is closest to Marx Halle, Erdberg (U3) to the Arena music venue.

Art of the Hundertwasserhaus
Designing green living

Eccentric artist and eco-activist Friedensreich Hundertwasser's design ethos was to create spaces where human beings and nature coexist harmoniously. Deliberately visually deviant from its conventionally classical neighbours with its motley paintwork, curvy lines and forest sprouting balconies and rooftop, the Hundertwasserhaus achieves its goal of getting people to stop and think about city planning and ecological living.

The famed viewing point of the eclectic facade is on Kegelgasse, where the small crowds gather. As it's a functioning living space, you can't enter this private apartment building, although the elevated terrace cafe allows you to stay longer and linger over the questions it poses. Opposite is the **Hundertwasser Village**, a touristic hub but valuable for a closer glimpse at the bright bulbous ceramic columns, mosaics and undulating levelling styles that define the artist's signature style. Another facade view is on Löwengasse, with a small shop and indoor cafe playing an aged documentary-style film about the building design – the only chance you'll get to curb your curiosity about what's on the inside.

☑ TOP TIP

Don't let the map fool you – Landstrasse points of interest are closer than they look and easy to navigate on foot. It takes around 30 minutes to get from the Belvedere museums to the Hundertwasserhaus, taking in the architecturally beautiful areas and avenues, and from there, a 12-minute walk to Landstrasse U-Bahn station.

Curating Museum Hundertwasser
Consciousness of nature

Five minutes on foot to Untere Weissgerberstrasse brings you to a monochrome mosaic house with technicolour windows. A furniture factory turned arthouse founded by the artist, **KunstHausWien (Art House Vienna) Museum Hundertwasser** *(kunsthauswien.com; adult/child €16/7)* is a multi-level ode to, and permanent gallery of, the artist's graphic and paint works, scale models and blueprints of his other structural works in Austria, including the Spittelau incinerator in Vienna's 9th district, and projects never realised. The uneven floors create an experience Hundertwasser saw as 'a melody of the feet'; more often than not, they stop you in your tracks to admire more of his work on display.

Other gallery space is dedicated to temporary exhibitions on social-environmental topics, ecology exhibits and topical features. Even if you don't enter the building, don't miss the tranquil tree-enclosed garden cafe at the back.

Sip & Shop at Rochusmarkt
Butchers, *Blumen* and beyond

You'll rarely find a district without a fresh produce supply – an Austrian market, crammed with stands, is a way of life. On a cobblestoned, church-facing fountain square on Landstrasse Hauptstrasse, compact Rochusmarkt has everything from butchers to *Blumen* (flowers), its many floral stalls continuing the trade from when it was exclusively a flower market. Stop to sip on Viennese vino at the **Arrigo** wine bar, or order an Aperol spritz and snack at Italian joint **Pappa e Ciccia** – both are top spots with outdoor seating to revel in the market atmosphere.

Historical Green Escapes
Beyond the baroque

Landstrasse's green spaces are plenty if you want to explore beyond the princely baroque grounds. The southernly **Schweizergarten** *(Swiss Garden)* occupies a space in front of the imposing red-brick former-military-arsenal building (part of which is now the Museum of Military History), constructed after the revolution against imperial troops in 1848. The old training grounds and wasteland between two railway stations were turned into an English garden in 1904 when the city expanded. Sporadic art sculptures create interaction, almost in extension to its Belvedere 21 neighbour, and a history walk via information

A BUZZING CITY

Aside from the Hundertwasser apartment, thousands of eco-residents have always lived on Landstrasse.

Bees were first introduced to the city when Empress Maria Theresia founded the first beekeeping school in Augarten in 1769; today, some 2 million are abuzz in the modern metropolis.

Out of the 456 species, 130 call the Botanical Garden of the University of Vienna in the Belvedere Garden home. Next door, Hotel Daniel hosts the mighty buzzers; one of a slew of hotels with rooftops open to special guests, as does KunstHausWien.

Continuing the imperial fashion for apiculture, around 350,000 bees reside on the rooftop of the Kunsthistorisches Museum; in keeping with tradition, its beekeepers still fill jars of Imperial Honey.

 EATING ON LANDSTRASSE

Meierei im Stadtpark (Steirereck): Cafe-restaurant of Austria's top fine-dining venue on the Vienna River promenade. *8am-11pm Mon-Fri, 9am-7pm Sat* €€€

Joseph Brot: Sourdough reigns at one of Vienna's finest bio bakeries. It's a super spot for a wholesome breakfast or brunch. *7.30am-7pm Mon-Fri, to 6pm Sat, to 4pm Sun* €€

Stöckl im Park: Ambient dining in a Belvedere garden, serving regional specialities and snacks to complement the in-house brewery offering. *11.30am-11.30pm* €€€

Das Suess'kind: Cosy bistro and takeout with an organic, plant-based daily menu, including snacks and sweets. *11am-3pm Mon-Fri* €€

BELVEDERE & BEYOND: LANDSTRASSE

⭐ HIGHLIGHTS
1. Oberes Belvedere
2. Schloss Belvedere

⬤ SIGHTS
3. Arenbergpark
4. Belvedere Gardens
5. Hundertwasserhaus
6. KunstHausWien
7. Stadtpark

⬤ EATING
8. Das Suess'kind
9. Joseph Brot
10. Meierei im Stadtpark
11. Rochusmarkt
12. Stöckl im Park

⬤ DRINKING & NIGHTLIFE
13. Strandbar Herrmann

⬤ ENTERTAINMENT
14. Marx Halle

CITY BEACH

The 3rd district is home to the inner city's only beach, **Strandbar Herrmann** (strandbarherrmann.at), where you can soak up some holiday vibes in this bar and hangout aptly named after the inventor of the postcard. Grab a deckchair and umbrella, order a *Hugo Spritz* (a Prosecco, elderflower, lime and mint cocktail), feel the sand under your feet and see the Danube Canal as your ocean.

Come here also for the tasty street-food bites, the beats of the DJ sets, the chills of beach yoga and the alternative silent beach-disco parties that hum canal-side until late.

boards provides more insight into its development. One block from Landstrasse Hauptstrasse to the east is **Arenbergpark**, whose large trees enclose the peaceful park and reclaim the space taken by two other wartime Flaktürme (flak towers). On the district's northern fringes is the **Stadtpark** – Vienna's first municipal park, opened in 1862. While typically considered a 1st-district darling with its golden statue of Johann Strauss, half of it falls into Landstrasse's boundaries – a promenaded, woodland link between the city and the inner district.

The Entertainment Core
Urbanite community beats

Hip locale and pop-up entertainment hub **Wild im West** (instagram.com/wildimwest) has a home in Landstrasse, on the undeveloped grounds next to the former cattle market turned industrial clad theatre and events space **Marx Halle**. The urban bar and lounge space, with DJs and flash retailing, describes itself as a 'cultural oasis', with events from community kitchens to concerts. At the weekend *Flohmarkt* (flea market), browse trendy clothing and vinyl, and stay for evening music sets from hip-hop beats to punky sessions.

Oberes Belvedere

TOP EXPERIENCE

Belvedere

Prince Eugene of Savoy's baroque palace from 1723 is a masterpiece; the art connoisseur filled it with his collections, which Empress Maria Theresia turned into the Imperial Picture Gallery in 1777, opening Vienna's first public museum. This assemblage of art and architecture is the legacy of **Belvedere** three centuries on; the dual complex is a trove of Austrian art from the Middle Ages to the present day and displays the world's largest collection of Klimt works.

DID YOU KNOW

From a state function room to a historic venue, Upper Belvedere's Marble Hall was the location for the milestone signing of the Austrian State Treaty in 1955 between the Allied powers, reestablishing Austria's independence.

Oberes Belvedere – Permanent Collection

It's a dizzying display of grandeur entering **Oberes Belvedere** *(Upper Belvedere)*. From the white vaulted sculptured **Sala Terrena**, ascend the **Grand Staircase** with its stucco reliefs into the gilded, columned ochre **Marble Hall**. Prince Eugene brought Italian fresco artists Carlone, Chiarini and Fanti to Vienna to paint the ceilings. That famous view of the city? It's from the balcony right here. The halls may be ordered by an 800-year chronological style timeline, but they go beyond a display of artisanship. With mood-changing multi-hued halls,

PRACTICALITIES
- belvedere.at
- Oberes Belvedere 9am-7pm; adult/child €21/free
- Unteres Belvedere 10am-6pm; adult/child €18/free
- Combi ticket adult/child from €31.50/free

it presents the collection in the context of the era it was made, spotlighting the social, political and cultural periods and events that shaped the artist and their work, including war and migration, ideal environments and subjective inner worlds.

The halls left of the Marble Hall house the extravagant Austrian Baroque (1600–1800), alongside Neoclassicism, Romanticism and highlights of realism-based Viennese Biedermeier (1880–65). Franz Xaver Messerschmidt's *Character Heads* depicting human emotions in portrait busts is a highlight. The seven halls to its right house the revered **Vienna 1900** collection. An expressive display of progression from avant-garde artists of the Klimt-led Viennese Secession, alongside their international Impressionist contemporaries like Monet, Renoir and Van Gogh and expressionist successors, including Munch and Schiele. It climaxes in Gustav Klimt's most famous work, *Der Kuss* (The Kiss), which, of his 22 paintings here, never leaves the gallery. If you're beelining for this, it's at the end of the wing close to the preserved octagonal Palace Chapel.

The 2nd floor continues the art journey through Emerging Modernism (1900–20) and postwar Avant-Gardes (1920s–50s). On the ground floor is the dynamic Avant-Gardes of the 1960s & 1970s. Despite the dash to the Marble Hall, chronologically, the collection starts down here with Middle Ages to the Renaissance (1200–1600) – its preserved frescoed Carlone Hall entrance is an astonishing picture.

Unteres Belvedere – Home of Prince Eugene

Temporary exhibitions continue the lineage of the Moderne Galerie established in Unteres (Lower) Belvedere in 1903, but really, this is a ticket to Prince Eugene's illustrious world. For this esteemed military general to the Habsburgs, the construction of Belvedere was a show of his power, commissioning

BEST ARTWORKS OF UPPER BELVEDERE

Klimt's *The Kiss* is a standout masterpiece, but these paintings are some of the best of the vast collection of 24,000 works.

- Jacques-Louis David, *Napoleon at the Great St Bernhard*, 1801
- Ferdinand Georg Waldmüller, *Self-portrait as a Young Man*, 1828
- Claude Monet, *The Cook*, 1882
- Vincent van Gogh, *The Plain of Auvers*, 1890
- Gustav Klimt, *Judith*, 1901
- Helen Funke, *Dreams*, 1913
- Egon Schiele, *The Family*, 1918
- Marie-Louise von Motesiczky, *Self-Portrait with Comb*, 1926
- Hundertwasser, *224 The Big Way*, 1955

TOP TIPS

- Belvedere is split into three galleries: Upper Belvedere, Lower Belvedere and Belvedere 21.

- Purchase discounted timed entry tickets online to avoid queues and save money.

- Audio guides are available at the ticket counter or as a smartphone download, both for an extra cost.

- You'll need at least half a day to visit the art collections and the grounds. All gardens, except the Kammergarten (Privy Garden) and Alpine Garden, are free to enter.

famous baroque architect Johann Lucas von Hildebrandt to design the opulent summer residence.

Lower Belvedere is the extravagant residential wing. Another **Marmorsaal** (Marbled Hall) entrance dazzles, but look back for a prime view of Upper Belvedere, moving to the fanciful floor-to-ceiling painting display in the **Groteskensaal** (Hall of Grotesques) and the white-stuccoed red **Marmorgalerie** (Marble Gallery) built to display figurine sculptures.

The gilt- and porcelain-plated, mirrored **Goldkabinett** (Gold Cabinet) is the gaudy showstopper, a refurnished design of Maria Theresia that has been displayed in its original condition since 1765.

The **Orangerie** modern exhibition space connects to the medieval-art-filled **Prunkstall** (Palace Stables) and the tranquil **Kammergarten** (Privy Garden), hidden from view of the public palace gardens.

Belvedere Gardens – Strolling this Baroque Beauty

Both visitors and locals come to freely stroll the terraced, **baroque gardens**; Parisian-born Prince Eugene was reportedly inspired by the designs of Versailles. The entrance to Upper Belvedere on its south side has a large pond to intentionally reflect the image of the palace, and temporary exhibitions often incorporate art on the water.

It takes around 10 minutes to walk the symmetrical parterres and guarding Sphinx statues between the twinned Belvederes, passing the Lower Cascade fountain trickling Vienna's spring water. The seated nooks within the topiary rows closer to Lower Belvedere are ambient hidden corners, as is the Upper Belvedere's elusive Botanical Garden, added by Maria Theresia in 1754.

OBERES BELVEDERE

Second Floor
- Interwar Period
- Realism & Impressionism

First Floor
- Early-19th-Century Art
- Neoclassicism, Romanticism & Biedermeier Art
- Marmorsaal

Ground Floor
- Temporary Exhibition
- Sala Terrena
- Medieval Art
- Main Entrance

Naschmarkt & Around: Wieden & Mariahilf

VIENNESE MICROCOSM OF COOL

Southwest of the Ringstrasse spills the 4th (Wieden) and 6th (Mariahilf), the edgy inner districts mixing urban grunge with historical grand. They meld with village-like compactness but remain distinguishable by their anchor landmark and cranny of streets where their character sparks in street art, creative stores, multicultural cafes, restaurants and trendy bars. At Wieden's core is architectural Karlsplatz, a lively garden-flanked square and festival pad with its namesake baroque church that's both a casual summer hangout and home to the judge-picked crafts stalls of the Art Advent Christmas market. In Mariahilf, Naschmarkt – a bustling open-air food paradise and Vienna's most famous market – is a whirl of street-food vendors rubbing shoulders with trendy dining rooms. Head here to dip your toes into downtown Viennese life.

Charting City History
Vienna's timeline retold

The **Wien Museum** *(wienmuseum.at; permanent exhibition free)* chronicles the urban history of Vienna across three floors, featuring an ensemble of 1700 objects and scale models intricately detailing its evolution.

The ground floor digs into Vienna's Palaeolithic era and beyond, where you'll find a mammoth tusk, a Roman stone relief from the eastern gate of the Vindobona fortress, and medieval sculptures from Stephansdom among its relics. The art, attire and architecture showcased on the 1st floor spans the period from 1700 to 1900, timelining the rise of the Empire, the aftermath of the Napoleonic Wars and the Industrial Age. 'Since 1900' on the 2nd floor charts Vienna's acceleration to becoming a European cultural centre; its displays include Klimt's 1902 portrait of Emilie Flöge and his blue smock, the only surviving garment of the artist.

It moves to more provocative social discourse, starting with the cultural achievements of social democratic 'Red Vienna'

GETTING AROUND

Once there, the 4th and 6th districts are easily connected on foot. Reach the 6th district, Mariahilf, from MuseumsQuartier U-Bahn (U2 line); Gumpendorferstrasse is a two-minute walk away. Naschmarkt is wedged in between; south of it lies the 4th district, Wieden, accessible by Kettenbrückengasse U-Bahn (U4) at the market's western end and Karlsplatz (U1, U2 and U4) on its eastern tip, closest to the Freihausviertel.

☑ TOP TIP

Head to Karlsplatz during the day for the highlights, but if you want to experience the authentic vibes of these districts, join the after-work crowd in the bars and hip foodie spots in the Freihausviertel and around Gumpendorfer Strasse, and join the throng of hagglers at Naschmarkt's lively Saturday flea market.

NASCHMARKT & AROUND: WIEDEN & MARIAHILF

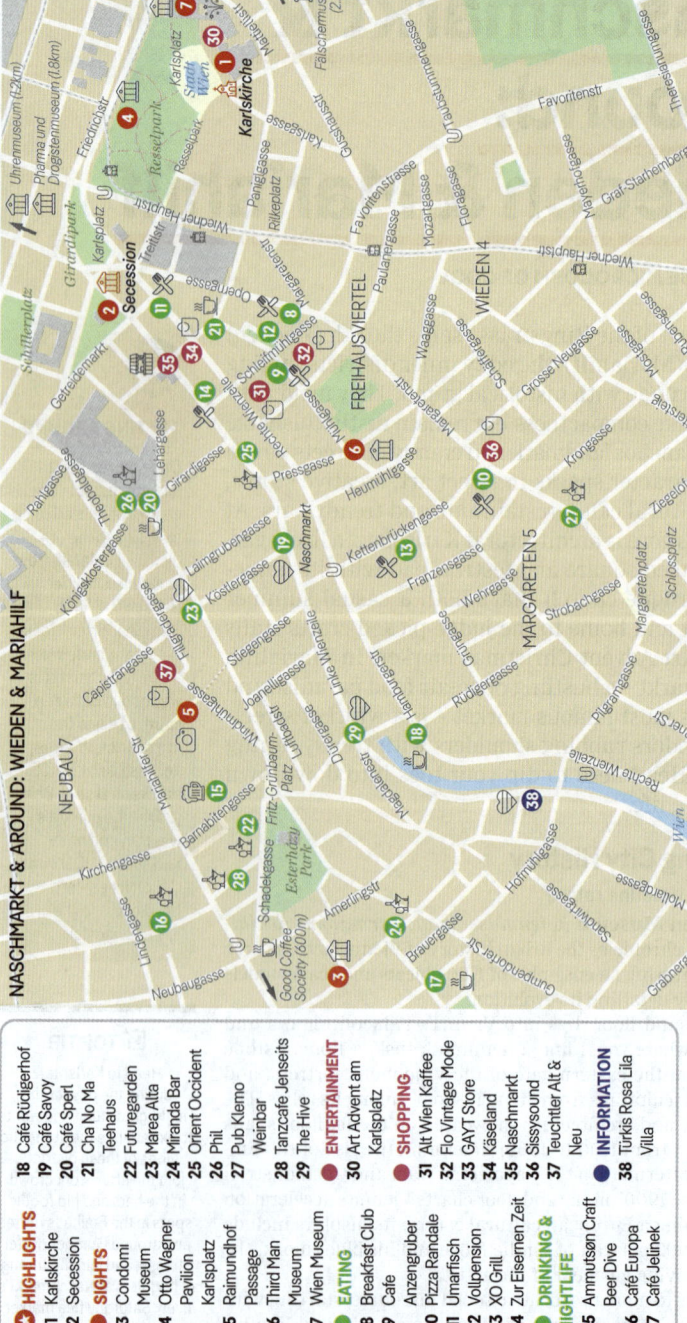

NASCHMARKT & AROUND: WIEDEN & MARIAHILF

★ HIGHLIGHTS
1. Karlskirche
2. Secession

● SIGHTS
3. Condomi Museum
4. Otto Wagner Pavilion Karlsplatz
5. Raimundhof Passage
6. Third Man Museum
7. Wien Museum

● EATING
8. Breakfast Club
9. Cafe Anzengruber
10. Pizza Randale
11. Umarfisch
12. Vollpension
13. XO Grill
14. Zur Eisernen Zeit

● DRINKING & NIGHTLIFE
15. Ammutsøn Craft Beer Dive
16. Café Europa
17. Café Jelinek
18. Café Rüdigerhof
19. Café Savoy
20. Café Sperl
21. Cha No Ma Teehaus
22. Futuregarden
23. Marea Alta
24. Miranda Bar
25. Orient Occident
26. Phil
27. Pub Klemo Weinbar
28. Tanzcafe Jenseits
29. The Hive

● ENTERTAINMENT
30. Art Advent am Karlsplatz

● SHOPPING
31. Alt Wien Kaffee
32. Flo Vintage Mode
33. GAYT Store
34. Käseland
35. Naschmarkt
36. Sissysound
37. Teuchtler Alt & Neu

● INFORMATION
38. Türkis Rosa Lila Villa

THE GUIDE

94

after WWI, Austria's annexation into the German Reich in 1938 and Vienna's postwar urban transformation to the present day. The 3rd-floor terrace has an elevated side view of Karlskirche and features a revolving artist showcase on its muralled rooftop.

Baroque Karlskirche
Symbolic Karlsplatz inside and out

Karlsplatz is named after Emperor Karl VI and the baroque **Karlskirche** *(St Charles Church; karlskirche.eu; adult/child €9.50/5)* after the plague saint Charles Borromeo. The church was constructed from 1716–37 on the emperor's solemn vow after the 1713 plague in Vienna. Designed by Schloss Schönbrunn architect Johann Bernhard Fischer von Erlach, it's an architectural world pick 'n' mix of Greek temple, Roman arch and Byzantine elements, with a marbled pilaster nave and baroque frescoed interior (ticketed entry). Climb a level for a closer balcony view of the dome frescoes by Johann Michael Rottmayr, depicting God answering the saint's prayers to end the plague.

The panoramic terrace is the closest you'll get to the 72m-high dome; it overlooks Karlsplatz with views of Stephansdom's south spire.

Otto Wagner Pavillon
Tracking urban design

Otto Wagner, the urban-architect pioneer of 20th-century Viennese modernism, trailblazed Vienna's landscape with his functionalist-high aesthetic designs. A significant project was construction of the Stadtbahn (Vienna metropolitan railway). The Pavilion at Karlsplatz, dating to 1898, served as a station alongside Emperor Franz Joseph's Court Pavilion at Hietzing and the converted U-Bahn stations Schönbrunn and Stadtpark (U4), Währinger Strasse-Volksoper and Josefstädterstrasse (U6), some of the best preserved. The **Otto Wagner Pavillon Karlsplatz** *(wienmuseum.at; adult/child €5/4)* is a signature green-and-gold-accented exhibition space dedicated to Wagner's life and work. Its twin portal is a cafe and home of music Club U.

Coffee & Cake with Meaning
Vienna's generational cafe

Vollpension *(full board; vollpension.wien)* is the city's only generational cafe concept where you can experience Austrian *Jause* (break time over food) with the warmth of its Oma and Opa (grandma and grandpa) hosts. Find a space in the at-home vintage-decorated, brick-painted living room, order snacks, drinks and homemade cakes prepared by the city's favourite grandparents, and engage in heartwarming conversation. This is a meaningful initiative to combat loneliness and poverty in old age, and it's a place baked in love and nostalgia.

VIENNA BEFORE SUNRISE

Film buffs will recognise the interior of the **Teuchtler Alt & Neu** *(Windmühlgasse 10)* record shop in the 6th district. Inside this 1948-established music staple, not everyone is flicking through stacks of vinyl. The shop is better known as one of the backdrops of Richard Linklater's 1995 film *Before Sunrise,* where American Jesse and French Céline take a romantic romp through Vienna after meeting on a train, though the listening booth here used by the love-struck pair no longer exists.

You can relive other scenes at Westbahnhof, the Ringstrasse tram, Zollamtssteg bridge, the Danube Canal, Café Sperl, Kleines Café, Arena, the Roxy Club, Spittelberg, Albertina, Prater's Giant Ferris Wheel and the Cemetery of the Nameless.

COLLECTION OF CURIOSITY

The Habsburgs may have been ardent collectors, but the Viennese penchant for it continues; whether weird and wacky, unconventional or unique, the city's museum count exceeds 100.
Fälschermuseum: *(Museum of Art Fakes; faelschermuseum.com)* Swap masterpieces for maven copies and forgeries.
Funeral Museum: *(bestattungsmuseum.at)* Bury yourself in the Viennese morbid fascination with death at the Central Cemetery's museum.
Pharma und Drogistenmuseum: *(Pharmacy and Druggist Museum; drogistenmuseum.at)* At a reconstructed wood panelled pharmacy from 1908, learn about centuries-old remedies.
Condomi Museum: *(Condom Museum; liebens-wert.at)* Muse the evolution of the prophylactic.
Uhrenmuseum: *(Clock Museum; wienmuseum.at/uhrenmuseum)* Admire over 700 time-ticking crafts.

Naschmarkt Flea Market
Super Saturday thrifting

With bursts of colour, tantalising samples and a bustle of restaurants, a walk through the 120 food stalls of **Naschmarkt** *(Naschen,* meaning the joy of eating something sweet) is a chance to sample diverse flavours. Vienna's biggest market started as a fruit and veg market at Freyung, relocating to its current home and expanding as the Wien Fluss (Vienna River) was covered (it's still there underneath it). Its trio of pavilion laneways remain largely unchanged since 1902. The bazaar switches gears at the weekend. Join bargain hunters and antique hawkers at the Saturday *Flohmarkt* (flea market) to sift through clothing, rummage through boxes and peruse trinkets to the sounds of energetic price-calling and the hum of haggling.

Legendary Viennese Nightlife
Boudoir bars and beats

There's one boudoir bar here that is a very Viennese institution. At kitsch and eccentric **Tanzcafe Jenseits** (Dance Cafe Jenseits), the patronage is a wild mix, the dance floor small and the setting dimly lit with scarlet-velvet textiles and wallpaper. Living up to its name, it's a Wednesday to Sunday late-night-DJ mixed afterparty until the early hours. Nearby **Café Europa** is the chilled nocturne counterpart.

Time-capsule Alleyway
The highstreet loophole

Take a trip through the 18th century between Windmühlgasse 20 (near Naschmarkt) and the shopping strip of Mariahilfer Strasse 45. The **Raimundhof Passage** – named after thespian and playwright Ferdinand Raimund since it charts a route through his birth house – is a tucked-away cobblestoned connection of staircases and courtyards filled with modish artisanal stores and teeny cafes. The Secret Garden's courtyard hideaway is a retreat from the high street.

Shopping Freihausviertel
The creative quarter

There are no definitive boundaries of the **Freihausviertel**, but navigate the grid lanes between Paniglgasse and Pressgasse, and you'll find yourself in the thick of this uber-creative cluster of stores and stomping grounds.

Schaurhofergasse houses the Japanese supermarket **Nippon-Ya** and neighbouring **Cha No Ma Teehaus**. Schleifmühlgasse brings in everything retro. The **Breakfast Club** morning cafe neighbours the **Vollpension** (p95) cafe. Unassuming but legendary **Cafe Anzengruber** keeps traditional fare hip, **FLO Vintage Mode** makes secondhand timeless and **Alt Wien Kaffee** brews top blends at its inner-city roastery.

Kettenbrückengasse may take you into the 5th district, but its absorption into the Freihausviertel's funk is seamless. Smash hamburger joint **XO Grill** is always chock-full, **Pizza Randale**

Naschmarkt

turns out top-rated Neapolitan pizza, and **Sissysound** racks up secondhand records and CDs. Walk further along Margaretenstrasse and find a spot in **Pub Klemo Weinbar**, serving European vintage, fine and rare wines by the glass.

Around Gumpendorfer Strasse

Mariahilf's artery of cool

Gumpendorfer Strasse is a grungy strip above Naschmarkt with vintage-design stores and a conveyor of cafes stretching from the historic 1880 wood-panelled **Café Sperl** (p72) to vibrant bookshop-cafe **Phil** and cosy, old-time **Café Jelinek**. Sample third-wave brews of European roasters at the **Good Coffee Society** nearby. This side of the market is where you'll find the bar corner that spills around the Haus des Meeres aquarium site, including the alternative **Futuregarden** barroom on Schadekgasse, arty cocktail bar **Miranda** on Esterhazygasse and craft-beer-tap bar **Ammutsøn** on Barnabitengasse.

The Art Nouveau Trail

Modernism in construction

The design movement around 1900 has left structural artworks across the city. Less than a 10-minute walk from the Otto Wagner Pavilion (p94) is the **Secession** (secession.at; adult/child €12/free) exhibition space, founded in 1897 by the Klimt-led

LGBTIQ+ SCENE

Denise Van De Cruze, founder of Villa Vida Café (villavida.at) and producer of Queer Mode (queermode.com) shares her picks for queer Vienna.
Villa Vida Café: A vibrant community hub in the historic **Türkis Rosa Lila Villa**. Its signature Dragalicious Brunch features international queens and an all-you-can-drink mimosa buffet.
Marea Alta: Cosy, no-frills queer bar with strong drinks, good conversation and regular DJ sets.
Café Savoy: The institution in Vienna's gay scene – elegant, historic and unapologetically itself.
GAYT Store: Vienna's only queer superstore is a wonderland of leather, lace, lube and liberation. Don't miss the fetish art gallery downstairs.
The Hive: An edgy bar on Vienna's gay male scene known for its alternative vibe and themed nights.

EATING AT NASCHMARKT

| Käseland: Specialist cheese shop, best sampled with a platter and wine-tasting session. *9am-6.30pm Mon-Fri, 8am-6pm Sat* €€ | Umarfisch am Naschmarkt: Upmarket fish and seafood restaurant serving dishes from soup to signature mussel. *11.30am-10pm Mon-Sat* €€€ | Zur Eisernen Zelt: Naschmarkt's oldest *Beisl* from 1916 serves hearty *Gulasch* and *Wiener Schnitzel*. *11am-11pm Mon-Sat, to 5pm Sun* €€ | Orient Occident: 'East meets West' restaurant and bar. Expect kebab bowls to burgers, and daily lunch menus. *7am-midnight Mon-Sat, 10am-9pm Sun* €€ |

FESTIVALS IN KARLSPLATZ

More than its baroque backdrop, Karlsplatz and the surrounding Resselpark transform into the grounds and stages of some of Vienna's most artistic event showcases.

Popfest: This four-day experimental music festival in July sees a mega line-up of Austrian acts playing multiple locations around Karlsplatz; its main stage is set around the artificial lake in front of Karlskirche.

Buskers Festival: Over three days, a performance-art festival in September featuring circus acts, daring acrobatics, fire shows, dance, stilt performers and more.

Art Advent: In November and December, Karlsplatz continues its artistic theme with its Christmas market featuring jury-voted creative wares, workshops and music acts.

Secession (p97)

visual artist collective. The white-cubed building topped by a gold dome of 3000 gold-plated laurel leaves is Vienna's *Jugendstil* symbol and the world's oldest independent exhibition hall dedicated to contemporary art. Its permanent display is from the art movement's 14th exhibition in 1901 in tribute to Beethoven on the 75th anniversary of his death – the monumental work of Klimt's *Beethoven Frieze* depicting the search for happiness. Today's viewing is a multisensory experience, observing the painted wall while the composer's *Symphony No 9 in D Minor* plays through headphones.

At Naschmarkt, you can admire another of Otto Wagner's designs at the decorative plant-motif-tiled **Majolikahaus** *(Linke Wienzeile 40)*, just not without the signature gold and green finishes. Nearby Secessionist building **Rüdigerhof** *(Hamburgerstraße 20)* with its plaster swirl facade was built in 1902 by Wagner student Oskar Marmorek; get a closer look from its in-house **Café Rüdigerhof**.

Follow the Third Man
Go subterranean on a sewer tour

Film history was made when postwar Vienna was the setting for the 1949 Carol Reed film-noir classic *The Third Man*. You can retrace the scenes of protagonist Harry Lime (Orson Welles) from Prater's Giant Ferris Wheel and in the historic centre on the **Third Man Walking Tour** *(viennawalks.com; €26)*. However, for a radical kind of exploration come to **Karlsplatz Girardipark**. Helmet up and get into an older part of Vienna's waste-water system on a guided **Sewer Tour** *(drittemanntour.at; adult/child €10/5)*; reserve online. It's far from grim; instead, a tunnelled light-projection show along a walkway looks at subterranean Vienna while reliving the famous chase scene. Thousands of items from film props, photos, scripts and documents are also exhibited in the **Third Man Museum** *(3mpc.net; adult/child €12/8, audioguide download free)* in the 4th district.

Neubau, Josefstadt & Alsergrund

THE BOHEMIAN, BOURGEOIS AND BON VIVANT

Bordering the west side of the Ringstrasse on a curve north and contained by the outer Gürtel (belt) road are the inner districts of the 7th (Neubau), 8th (Josefstadt) and 9th (Alsergrund). Start in the Museums-Quartier (MQ) art and culture complex, Neubau's creative nucleus. From here a hub of upmarket hip unfolds, with concept stores, fashion boutiques and urban high-end drinking and dining.

While the bourgeois 8th isn't laden with core sights, the residential historical pocket makes for a charming architectural add-on as you move towards the bon-vivant 9th. The 9th has a residential archive including Sigmund Freud's flat and the baroque Palais Liechtenstein; thriving creative corners of the haute-culture hamlet Servitenviertel; and the gritty, mural waterside Spittelau and its Hundertwasser-designed waste incinerator. In this trio of districts, creative style meets classic sublime.

The Preserved Suburb of Spittelberg

Historical laneways of the 7th

Directly behind the MuseumsQuartier, you can step back centuries in the adjacent historic area. On a four-lane stretch behind Kirchberggasse, wander a narrow alley system that has preserved some of the original baroque builds of the suburb of **Spittelberg** that sat outside Vienna's city walls. Settlement here dates to 1584, but by 1720 it was a district of 120 houses; the structures that were not replaced centuries later by classicist and historic buildings still bear date plaques from that time.

The historical laneways of **Stiftgasse**, **Schrankgasse**, **Spittelberg** and **Gutenberggasse** are not just timeworn paths; the area is a thriving creative hub full of stores, studios and dining establishments, many filling the streets, and the **Amerlingbeisl** restaurant retaining its beautiful courtyard. The performing-arts showcase **Theatre am Spittelberg** also has its home here, and in winter, the area transforms into one of Vienna's most beautiful Christmas markets, the **Weihnachtsmarkt am Spittelberg**, with over 100 artisans' stalls.

continues on p104

GETTING AROUND

It's a 10-minute walk from the Hofburg to the MuseumsQuartier, Spittelberg and Burggasse, Volkstheater (U3) and MuseumsQuartier (U2) are the closest U-Bahn stations.

The 8th district spills out behind the Rathaus (U2) and exits onto the central thoroughfare, Josefstädter Strasse. The 9th district's Servitenviertel, Palais Liechtenstein and waterfront are within a 10-minute walk from Rossauer Lände U-Bahn (U4). The 13A bus runs from Alser Strasse in the 8th to the Hauptbahnhof.

☑ TOP TIP

You'll need half a day for the MuseumsQuartier and the 7th before venturing to the 8th and 9th – you'll know when you've crossed over by the street signs, which start with the district number followed by a full stop and comma.

NEUBAU, JOSEFSTADT & ALSERGRUND

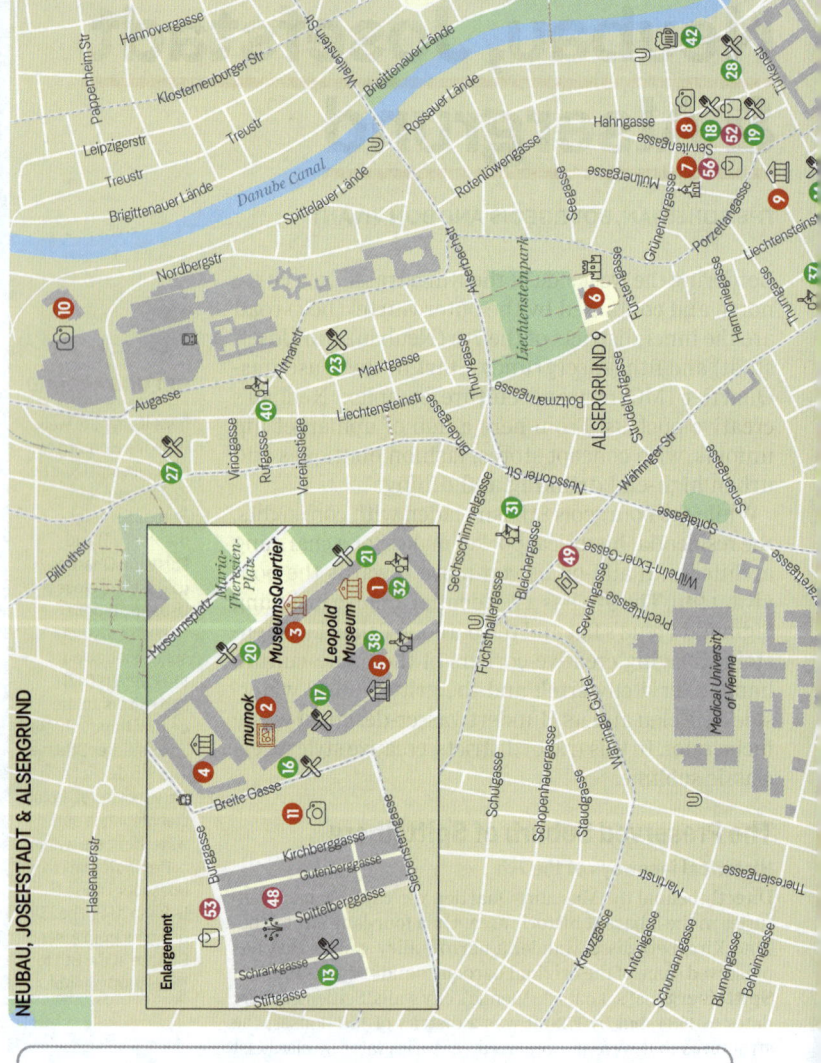

★ HIGHLIGHTS
1. Leopold Museum
2. mumok
3. MuseumsQuartier

● SIGHTS
4. Architekturzentrum Wien
5. Kunsthalle Wien
6. Palais Liechtenstein
7. Servitenkirche
8. Servitenviertel
9. Sigmund Freud Museum
10. Spittelau Incinerator
11. Spittelberg
12. WestLicht

● EATING
13. Amerlingbeisl
14. Der Wiener Deewan
15. Gastwirtschaft Schilling
16. Glacis Beisl
17. Halle
18. König
19. La Mercerie
20. MQ Kantine
21. MQDaily
22. Pizza Bussi Ciao
23. Reznicek
24. Schnitzelwirt
25. Speisekammer
26. Wiener Würstelstand
27. Würstelstand LEO
28. Zum Roten Bären

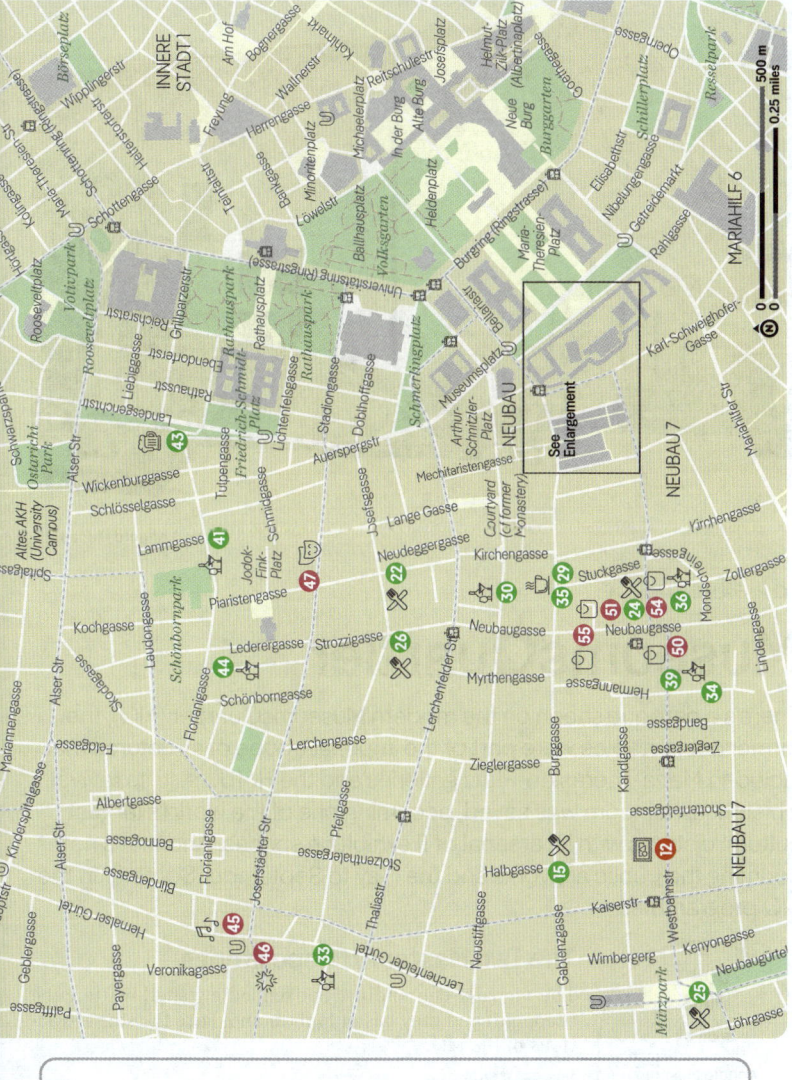

VIENNA NEUBAU, JOSEFSTADT & ALSERGRUND

● DRINKING & NIGHTLIFE
29 Adlerhof
30 Atlas
31 Café Clash
32 Café Leopold
33 Chelsea
34 Die Parfümerie
35 Espresso
36 Fitzcarraldo
37 Krypt
38 Mango Sky Bar
39 Plus43
40 Sign Lounge
41 Sipsong Bar
42 Summer Stage
43 The Long Hall
44 Tunnel Vienna Live

● ENTERTAINMENT
45 Café Carina
46 Kramladen
47 Theater in der Josefstadt
48 Weihnachtsmarkt am Spittelberg
49 WUK

● SHOPPING
50 Art Point
51 Bootik 54
52 Caffè a Casa
53 Das Cafe
54 Kitsch Bitch Sight Store
55 Ramsch und Rosen
56 Xocolat

101

Leopold Museum

TOP EXPERIENCE

MuseumsQuartier

There's a baroque sheen on the modern MuseumsQuartier (MQ); the former court stables were part of the imperial troupe of structures that included Maria-Theresien-Platz galleries and the Hofburg. In its revival, a historical heirloom was saved, becoming one of the world's largest cultural districts with its arsenal of 11 exhibition spaces. And that's not counting the public artworks and the May to September Sommer in the MQ programme.

DON'T MISS

mumok

Leopold Museum

MQ Libelle Terrasse

Kunsthalle Wien

Architekturzentrum

Art Passages

MQ Schauräume

The Two Master Art Repositories

The visually contending, bookended eggshell-white cube (Leopold) and grey basalt hull (mumok) are the star attractions of the MQ.

Leopold Museum

If Belvedere was your introduction to modernist art, **Leopold** (*leopoldmuseum.org*) is your graduation. More than 8300 works across five exhibition floors compile one of the most important collections of Austrian art of early modernism;

PRACTICALITIES
- mqw.at
- courtyard open 24/7, museum entry times vary. On-site bars typically close between 10pm and midnight
- Save on individual entry with the MQ Fab 5 ticket (€39); discounted or free entry for children across all museums

its pride and joy *Vienna 1900* package covers three. Moving through Leopold's brightly lit marble interior is an awakening, much like modernist art was an innovation. Between the world's most comprehensive Egon Schiele collection that includes 40 paintings, Gustav Klimt's *Death and Life* masterwork, and exhibits detailing the Viennese Secession movement and *Jugendstil* design, you get to understand the birth of modernism and its socio-political context.

The **MQ Libelle** (admission free) glass-fronted terrace is on Leopold's rooftop, overlooking the museum complex towards the Hofburg.

mumok

A journey through **mumok** *(Museum of Modern Art, Ludwig Foundation Vienna; mumok.at)* is meant to stir your senses, ignite discourse and challenge perceptions. There's a galaxy of contemporary-art forms as you transition from sparky exhibits to the darkened centriole bathed in natural light: expressionist classical modernism; experimental pop and conceptual art of the 1960s and 1970s avant-gardes; the radical exposé of the taboo and the tragic in 20th-century Viennese actionism to the reality-based, institutionally provocative contemporary evolution. The museum's acquired bank of film and photography works expands the collection.

The Modern Trio with More Time

If you plan to hang around longer in the converted stable halls, three other exhibitions wrap the five-strong art package.

Vienna is a European epicentre for art, but **MQ Freiraum** hands the floor over to international artists. **Kunsthalle Wien** showcases contemporary-art museum exchanges from places typically overshadowed by dominant European-art capitals. Baroque remnants from the former Winter Riding Hall are incorporated into the exhibition infrastructure on its ground floor.

If you've wandered Vienna and noticed a layered multi-structural design, the **Architekturzentrum Wien** (Architecture Centre) 'Hot Questions – Cold Storage' unravels it. The industrial-clad, multi-coloured, socially themed hall features sketches, scale models, videos and images of Vienna's urban planning as well as Austrian architecture of the 20th and 21st centuries, from the revolutionary to the unrealised.

Public Micro Museums & Showrooms

MQ's public baroque art-vault passages take you through worlds of imagination before you've even hit the courtyard. Sound art echoes in the **Tonspur passage**; world fonts are scripted in **Typopassage**; enter a visual reading room of baroque books in the **Literaturpassage**; walk beneath a comic display in **Kabinettpassage**; and see starry-light phenomena in the **Sternenpassage**. The front-of-house corridors host the **Schauräume** – a free-to-roam ribbon of artist studios and offices interspersed with installations, getting you closer to resident creativity as it happens.

VIENNA'S LIVING ROOM

People don't visit MQ just for its exhibition halls. As symbolic as the art behind the walls, the furniture of the MQ courtyard creates its own canvas. The bold, geometric Enzi chairs were designed to entice people to lounge – all day, in all seasons. With good weather, you'll rarely see the inside of MQ empty – an atmosphere you won't find anywhere else.

TOP TIPS

● You'll need half a day for just one main museum. If you plan to visit both the Leopold and mumok, save money with the Duo Ticket.

● mumok and Kunsthalle Wien are closed on Monday; Leopold Museum on Tuesday.

● Kunsthalle Wien has free entry 5pm to 9pm Thursday.

● Dig deeper into the world's largest cultural district on the one-hour Secret MQ tour *(mqw.at/ programm/secret-mq-tour-1-1; English tours Sat 3pm)*.

● Refuel with organic plates at **MQ Kantine**, takeout bites and beverages from **MQDaily**, Italian cuisine at **Halle** and Southeast Asian fare at **Café Leopold**.

WÜRSTELSTAND CULTURE

The unassuming booth of the *Würstelstand* (sausage stand) is a street-food staple and part of the local psyche; it's a quick fix, after-dark, post-concert snack.

Move beyond the 1st district and come here for some of the city's best. Taste the legendary *Käsekrainer*, filled with cheese cubes, or a *Burenwurst* – a salty, spiced Viennese old-timer.

Würstelstand LEO: Vienna's oldest institution has been passed down through generations since 1928. It serves a half-kilo 'Big Mama' *Käsekrainer*.

Wiener Würstelstand: Offerings at this trendy joint include *Bio-Würstel*, *Bosna* (a hot-dog-sandwich meld) and Salzburger Augustiner beer.

Speisekammer: Get smash burgers and locally sourced sausages at this hip interpretation, with homemade sauerkraut.

continued from p99

Shopping Burgasse to Neubaugasse
The hipster highways

Something creative brews in nearly every street in the 7th district, but the standout thoroughfares make for good navigation into this bougie bubble. Running from MuseumsQuartier and above the Spittelberg village is one of the oldest streets in Neubau.

Burggasse is so named for being a parallel highway to the Hofburg, and on the stretch to the cross-section of Neubaugasse. The road is a braid of cafes interspersed with design outlets, but you come here to sit and people-watch. Long-standing institutions include urban **Das Cafe**, the historically revived **Adlerhof** cafe, casual-cool **Cafe Espresso** and 1950s rustic tavern **Gastwirtschaft Schilling**.

Neubaugasse, meanwhile, is almost entirely crammed with artisanal design and fashion stores, including local brands **Kitsch Bitch** and **Art Point**, and vintage boltholes like **Ramsch und Rosen** for homeware and clothing crib **Bootik 54**. As for making all that is traditional cool, you'll always see long queues at the 50-year-old family-run **Schnitzelwirt** next door. The small grid of four streets west of Neubaugasse continues the creative spirit, home to the notable **WestLicht** photography museum and camera-store corner.

Gürtel Road Nightlife
Live music belt

The peaceful 8th revs up a gear on its district edges. On the Gürtel (belt) road is a near half-mile strip of bars and clubs built within the bricked metro rail arches, pumping until the early hours, but its cluster of live-music venues around the Josefstädter Strasse U-Bahn station are the alternative epicentre. Long-established music venues include the large concert space and DJ spot **Chelsea**, known for its club nights that rave until 4am, the intimate stage space of **Kramladen**, home to the English stand-up comedy community, and the grungy **Café Carina**, where you can catch homegrown musical talent.

Neubau's Street-Art Styling
Creativity reaches new heights

The Danube Canal became the legalised area for graffiti in the '90s, keeping the Innere Stadt polished, but the inner districts are where street art is popping (outside of unsightly

EATING & DRINKING IN THE 7TH

Atlas: Brunch and browse in this long-standing *Beisl*-turned-gastropub and art-gallery space. *4pm-1am Mon-Thu, to 2am Fri & Sat, kitchen to10.30pm* €€

Glacis Beisl: Bohemian *Beisl* between MuseumsQuartier and Spittelberg with mod-classic Viennese cuisine. *noon-midnight* €€

Die Parfümerie: This small but swank, unpretentious and hip cocktail bar has a wittily creative menu. *6pm-1am Tue-Thu, to 2am Fri & Sat*

Mango Sky Bar: Sip in Vienna's first queer rooftop bar above the MuseumsQuartier's Leopold Museum. *4pm-midnight Mon & Tue, 2pm-midnight Fri-Sun*

tagging). The **Calle Libre festival** *(callelibre.at)* has played a part in transforming the urban landscape of Vienna – many of the expressive building murals are a result of inviting local and international artists to come and paint the walls every August. Live painting allows the public to come and watch the work in action.

Between Naschmarkt and Burgasse, you'll catch a considerable cluster of works bringing life and colour to bare walls; Neubau is an excellent place to start. Behind **mumok** (p103) is a **street-art passage**; monochrome mural *The Mother* covers the firewall of the house standing in **Gutenbergpark**; a classical figure on **Siebensterngasse** adorns a strip of a building under a modern rooftop; a mother and child abstract work can be found at **Kirchengasse**; a bird mural covers the side of classic house at **Karl-Farkas-Park**; a sketch comic scene overlooks **Andreaspark**; yellow figures dominate an apartment facade on **Kandlgasse**, and the **WestLicht courtyard** hosts an extinct species masterwork.

Pretty Palais Liechtenstein
The home of aristocrats

The ruling family of the Principality of Liechtenstein were descendants of Austrian aristocracy, simultaneously residing here and making their mark with two palaces in the city: the renovated-to-historical-glory Stadtpalais (City Palace) in the Innere Stadt and the **Gartenpalais** *(palaisliechtenstein.com; tours per person €24)* summer residence here in the 9th. Built between 1691 and 1711, the three-storey ornate work of art is typically admired from the outside.

Monuments, including the Golden Chariot in the Sala Terrena, the frescoes of Vienna's largest baroque hall, the Herkulessaal (Hercules Hall), and the 100,000-book-stacked marble library, can only be seen on one-hour guided tours. English tours are limited, though audio guides are available on German tours. However, the gardens are open and free to enter, granting a closer look at this landmark.

Step into Servitenviertel
Lifestyle by design

The set-stone street of Servitengasse is the vein of the cultural corner of the **Servitenviertel** (Serviten Quarter), a thread of lanes surrounding **Servitenkirche** (Serviten Church). It's known for its high concentration of speciality cuisine outlets

---

WHY I LOVE VIENNA

Becki Enright, Lonely Planet writer

I love how Vienna doesn't try to impress you, but still does. Masterpiece halls jostle with avant-garde galleries; time-warp coffee houses brew alongside artisanal roasters; and classical concerts share the same evening calendar with contemporary gigs. Traditional, imperial-fringed fare meets Michelin-starred cuisine; and the metropolis straddles nature, on the grassy banks of the Alte Donau for a skyscrapper-backed swim or a tram ride to the start of a woodland trail.

Once you crack the city's grandiose shell, revel in its contradictions, go with the *Passt scho'* flow and click with the sarcastic wisdom of *Wiener Schmäh* humour that holds it all together, it's hard to leave.

 EATING & DRINKING IN THE 8TH

The Long Hall: Former beer tavern turned gastropub, with Kozel beer, bottomless brunch and sports viewing. *10am-1am Mon-Thu, to 2am Fri & Sat, to 1am Sun* €€

Pizza Bussi Ciao: A nostalgic ode to an Austrian family holiday in Italy, with Neapolitan pizzas. *5-10pm Mon-Wed, to 11pm Thu & Fri, 12.30-11pm Sat, to 10pm Sun* €€

Sipsong Bar: Flamboyant bar of legendary Thai eatery Mamamon, with signature bites and drinks, and special-brewed sato. *5.30-11.30pm Wed-Sat*

Tunnel Vienna Live: Youthful, grungy pub with a cellar hosting daily jazz, comedy and open-mic nights. *9am-2am Mon-Sat, to midnight Sun*

Spittelau Incinerator

CREATIVE MIXES: SECRET BARS

With the slew of creativity in these districts comes some of the city's best secret and experimental cocktail bars.

Fitzcarraldo: This art deco speakeasy bar serving a dozen signature cocktails is hidden behind an inconspicuous vending machine on Neubaugasse.

Plus43: You have to call for a space and the coveted door code for entry to this chic hideaway. If you feel experimental, the bartender will whip up a tailored creation.

Krypt bar: There's no door sign for this craft-cocktail bar at Wasagasse 17, but that's part of the fun of getting down into this old cellar that is now a stylish speakeasy.

The Sign Lounge: The creations at this experimental cocktail lounge have incorporated items like popcorn buckets, baby bottles, paint palettes and mini bubble baths.

and indie-owned stores on its 350m, two-block stretch. Its quaint buildings and fancy Franco-style lamppost-dotted, tree-lined avenues have also given it the nickname 'Little Paris'.

The **Caffè a Casa** coffee roasters, fine chocolate makers **Xocolat**, the **König** European deli and French cafe-bakery **La Mercerie** are top choices to get acquainted with in the area.

The Gourmet Waterfront
Drinking and dining on the riverside

In the warmer months, locals gather at waterside **Summer Stage** (*summerstage.at*) – a culinary cluster of terraced bars and restaurants overlooking the 9th district stretch of the Danube Canal. After a day of sightseeing, take your pick from European, Asian or Latino cuisine, or sample a glass or two in the wine pavilion.

Sigmund Freud at Berggasse 19
The birthplace of psychoanalysis

Sigmund Freud Museum (*freud-museum.at; adult/child €15/free*) is found at Berggasse 19, the famous address of the father of psychoanalysis. This was Sigmund Freud's family home and workplace for 47 years before having to flee from

EATING & DRINKING IN THE 9TH

Wiener Deewan: An all-you-can-eat Pakistani buffet in a community-driven restaurant where you pay as much as you wish. *11am-11pm Mon-Sat* €

Café Clash: Edgy, arty *Beisl*-bar with a weekly music programme that attracts the cool district dwellers. *6pm-2am* €

Zum Roten Bären: Arty bohemian meets Viennese charm. Come for Austrian classics and regional beer and wine. *5pm-midnight Mon-Fri, 11am-midnight Sat & Sun* €€

Reznicek: Upscaled Viennese tavern charm with a regional, seasonal mod-traditional Austrian menu and handpicked wine pairings. *5pm-1am Tue-Sat* €€

persecution due to the Nazi takeover in 1938. The museum's multi-floor renovation in 2020 opened all the apartment rooms and the practice spaces of Sigmund and his therapist-teacher daughter, Anna Freud. The original entrance hallway and waiting-room area remain relatively untouched, a step into the home as visitors in treatment once did.

The remainder of the presentation is through monochrome-designed displays that compile a window into Freud as a father and the development of his life's work through letters, published manuscripts, photos, furniture and private objects, including his signature spectacles. The rooms have not been re-created to their original styling; exhibits and panels are sparsely placed like the void left. Almost all of Freud's methods were developed and written up here. But don't expect to see the famous couch; that remains in London.

Hundertwasser Incinerator
The alternative city landmark

There are not many places where you travel to look at a waste incineration plant. Beyond the artist's residential project in the district of Landstrasse, painter and environmentalist Hundertwasser was commissioned to turn the rebuilt heat-production plant in Spittelau into a work of art. He adorned it with his signature kaleidoscopic, checkered facade, added tree-planted terraces and topped the vivid, blue-panelled chimney with a gold sphere.

Free guided tours of the **Spittelau Incinerator** *(events. xres.at; tours in English available)* take you through the facility and onto its rooftop. The alternative city skyline landmark stands outside the U-Bahn station and complements the street-art-covered canal arches beneath it.

The Culture House
Former factory turned performance centre

The imposing red-brick **WUK** *(Werkstätten und Kulturhaus, Workshop and Culture House; wuk.at)* is a former locomotive factory that is now a bastion of cultural events promoting inclusive and interdisciplinary arts. A pillar of Vienna's creative scene, there's a regular programme of performance, DJ and live music across its stage, exhibition and music concert halls, plus a 12,000-sq-metre entertainment and participation space that makes it one of largest socio-cultural centres in Europe.

If you can't make it to an event, feel inspired by the cafe-restaurant **Statt-Beisl** serving a small menu of vegan, vegetarian and organic meat-based dishes, or kick back with a drink in the cosy courtyard area, part of an artistic repurposing of the old industrial structures fostering a sense of community.

LITTLE ITALY

Italian influence abounds, given that Italy neighbours Austria, but the abundance of la dolce vita in these districts has formed a 'Little Italy' of Vienna.
CiaoContessa: Grocery store stocking the delights of 'Italy's food capital' Bologna, including off-the-block Parmigiano Reggiano.
Cibaria: The street-view hand-crafted pasta nods to Genoese cuisine.
Fratelli Valentino: The Pugliese brothers run a mozzarella (and more) fromagerie and bar.
Diego's Street Food Napoletano: Authentic flaky sfogliatelle pastry, arancini and fritti (fried) Neapolitan favourites.
SicilEat: Sicilian fruits, cheeses, nuts and savoury snacks.
Barbarella: Espresso bar specialising in Sicilian sweets and wine.

WALKING TOUR

Neubau to Alsergrund

This one-hour walking tour takes you from Burgasse in the 7th to Berggasse in the 9th, through the three inner districts' most beautiful streets and architectural corners.

Laneways & Passages

Start at Schmollgruber at ❶ **Burggasse 3** – the smallest house in Vienna. With the MuseumsQuartier behind you, walk down Burggasse until you reach ❷ **Spittelberggasse**, the 4th street on the left. Explore this grid of quaint old streets, exiting onto Siebensterngasse and turning right. Walk this strip of design stores and international outlets like Casa Mexico and Finnshop, passing the street's institutional cafe and bar, 7Stern Bräu. Continue to Siebensterngasse 46, reaching the ❸ **Adlerhof**. Walk through this beautiful hidden arcade from 1874, crossing its five mesmerising courtyards and arcades. Emerging back onto Burgasse, continue straight up Kirchengasse to Neustiftgasse, turn right and reach another archway at No 16, the historic ❹ **Freiwilliger Durchgang** (voluntary passage) – a 19th-century bypass invention where people opened their courtyards to connect parallel streets. Exit onto Lerchenfelder Strasse (border of the 8th district).

Architectural Lodestars

Continue straight to Lange Gasse. On a Saturday, you'll find one of the city's trendiest farmers markets here. Take a left onto Josefstädter Strasse 14 passing ❺ **Theater in der Josefstadt** – Vienna's oldest theatre in operation was opened by Beethoven in 1788. A right onto Piaristengasse opens onto Jodok-Fink-Platz dominated by the mammoth baroque ❻ **Maria Treu Kirche** – the foundation stone was laid by Emperor Leopold I in 1698. Continue until you reach

Strudlhofstiege

Alser Strasse (the border of the 9th district), passing the park that backs onto the block-street-wide Palais Schönborn, which today houses the ⑦ **Austrian Folk Museum**.

The Palatial Stretch

Enter the main entrance of the **Campus der Universität Wien** (Campus of the University of Vienna), a lively student hub with restaurants and outdoor eateries. It's still called by its former name, Altes AKH (Altes Allgemeines Krankenhaus; Old General Hospital), part of Emperor Joseph II's societal reforms, which included this mega hospital complex in 1784. Cut through its centre, Hof 1 (courtyard 1), heading northeast to Hof 7 and straight to the brick rotunda ⑧ **Narrenturm** (Fool's Tower). The five-storey cell complex opened the same year as the hospital as a treatment centre for the mentally ill; today it's the Pathological-Anatomical Museum. Head eastward to Strudlhofgasse and walk 11 stepped metres down the district's zigzagging limestone Art Nouveau staircase, ⑨ **Strudlhofstiege**. The original on this spot from 1690 belonged to baroque sculptor and painter Peter Strudel. Walk past the grand entrance of ⑩ **Gartenpalais Liechtenstein** (p105), rounding to Grünentorgasse. You'll eventually come to the landmark Servitenkirche for the Franco-feel laneways of the ⑪ **Servitenviertel** (p105), which connects to Berggasse for the ⑫ **Sigmund Freud Museum** (p106) at No 19.

The Masterpiece Finish

To continue to the centre, walk to the nearby neo-Gothic masterpiece of ⑬ **Votivkirche** (Votive Church) on the fringes of the 1st district old town. The second-highest church after Stephansdom was built as a symbol of gratitude after the failed assassination attempt on Emperor Franz Joseph.

Schloss Schönbrunn: Hietzing

HIGH-CLASS, PALATIAL PAST

GETTING AROUND

The Schönbrunn palace and gardens complex has a dedicated U-Bahn station on the U4 line. For a picturesque arrival, take trams 10 or 60 from Westbahnhof and get off at the Schloss Schönbrunn stop.

Hietzing U-Bahn (U4) opens out onto the heart of the district, or exit Schönbrunn Gardens behind the Palmenhaus via the Hietzinger Tor path.

For Hietzing Cemetery, take the 56 or 58 buses outside the U-Bahn. The 56 A and B buses continue to Lainzer Tor for the Hermes Villa and Lainzer Tiergarten.

The well-to-do reside in Hietzing (13th district), just as they always have historically. It's known as the noble district, half covered by the forest meadows of the former imperial hunting ground, Lainzer Tiergarten on one side and cradled by the Habsburg summer hideaway of Schloss Schönbrunn on the other. The residential wedge in between is a modicum of the middle-high class in tree belts of historical villas filling the once-imperial court cadastral of nobles and officials.

Really, you come here to look inside and around two houses – Klimt's last studio and the district's palatial 18th-century star. Cornering Schloss Schönbrunn Park is Hietzing's centre, a pocket-sized taste of the enduring stately character beyond the sumptuous as you venture from a classy old imperial guesthouse to classic Viennese culinary institutions. When you're here, you'll walk among the well-heeled.

Imperial Trails of Lainzer Tiergarten
Vienna's biodiverse corner

Within the vast swathe of the eastern Wienerwald (Vienna Woods), covering almost half of Hietzing, is the former imperial hunting ground that is now a public nature reserve and protected biosphere park, **Lainzer Tiergarten** (Lainzer Zoo). Of its almost 25-sq-km habitat, around 80% is forest and grass meadows harbouring a zoological and botanical intermix including 400-year-old beech and oak trees, nearly 100 bird species, and stag and boar among its wild animal residents.

A shortcut to get here from Schönbrunn is the historic **Hermesvilla** *(wienmuseum.at/hermesvilla; adult/child €8/free)* lodge, where you can continue the imperial living curiosity. The 56B bus from Heitzing U-Bahn stops at Lainzer Tor (Lainzer Gate) – a primary entrance to the park. It takes around

SCHLOSS SCHÖNBRUNN: HIETZING

Kunsthistorisches Museum Vienna (3.2km)

★ HIGHLIGHTS
1 Schloss Schönbrunn

● SIGHTS
2 Gloriette
3 Hietzinger Friedhof
4 Schloss Schönbrunn Gardens

● SLEEPING
5 Parkhotel Schönbrunn

● EATING
6 Café Donmayer
7 Plachutta Stammhaus Hietzing
8 Waldemar-Tagesbar

30 minutes. It's a short walk to Empress Elisabeth's summer palace, a villa within verdant land created by the architect of the **Naturhistorisches** (p77) and **Kunsthistorisches Museum** (p68), Carl von Hasenauer, at the request of Emperor Franz Joseph. Ticketed entry grants a look inside the private imperial getaway, an interweave of stately decor and original furniture, and the pièce de résistance of Elisabeth's bedroom with artwork of Austrian painters Franz Matsch, Hugo Charlemont, Gustav Klimt and his brother Ernst, each adding their brushstroke to the *A Midsummer Night's Dream* murals. Guided tours and exhibits are in German only.

The park's longer marked trails are more suited to experienced walkers used to wilderness. For an introduction, take the 40-minute track above Hermesvilla via St Veiter Tor (gate) to the elevated Vienna vantage point of the **Wienerblick**. Exit at the gate, walking to Ghelengasse/Stock im Weg for bus 54A or B back to Hietzing U-Bahn. However, make sure you note when the gates close before you set off, which can be as early as 5pm in winter.

☑ TOP TIP

If you are travelling to Schloss Schönbrunn by metro, don't miss Otto Wagner's Hofpavillion (Imperial Pavilion) at the end of Hietzing Station. It was Emperor Franz Joseph's private access to the metropolitan railway, although he only used it twice. Ticketed entry gets you inside to view the octagonal waiting-salon artwork.

EATING & DRINKING AROUND SCHÖNBRUNN: OUR PICKS

Gloriette Bar im Parkhotel Schönbrunn: The restored guesthouse of Emperor Franz Joseph is now a bar looking into the hedgerow green of Schönbrunn. *5pm-1am Tue-Sat*

Plachutta Stammhaus: Viennese institution with signature *Tafelspitz* (boiled beef, roasted potatoes, vegetables and horseradish). *11.30am-3pm & 6-11pm Mon-Fri, 11.30am-11pm Sat & Sun* €€€

Café Donmayer: Hietzing's coffee house with red banquette seating, chandeliers, and pastries and cakes from Viennese confectioner Oberlaa. *7.30am-8.30pm* €€

Waldemar-Tagesbar: Casual, stylish cafe-bar with a hearty breakfast menu and brunch cocktails, sandwiches and smoothies. *8am-10pm Mon-Fri, 9am-3pm Sat & Sun* €€

Schloss Schönbrunn

TOP EXPERIENCE

Schloss Schönbrunn

No other site in Vienna is more entrenched in imperial legacy than Schloss Schönbrunn – the city's most iconic Habsburg residence packs a four-century-long timeline of imperial history into its rococo state rooms, ceremonial halls, private apartments and opulent gardens. The UNESCO World Heritage Site is so remarkable in size you'll want to give yourself at least half a day to experience its majestic heritage.

DON'T MISS

Private Apartments of Franz Joseph & Elisabeth

Schönbrunn Ceremonial Rooms

Apartments of Maria Theresia

Gloriette

Privy Garden (Crown Prince Garden)

Orangery Garden

Inside Schloss Schönbrunn

Schönbrunn's size is arresting, but the site that came into the Habsburg fold back in 1569 grew over centuries into a layer cake of palatial personal stamping. First was the 1642 Château de Plaisance (Pleasure Palace) of Emperor Ferdinand II's wife, Eleonore von Gonzaga, then the imperial hunting lodge that Emperor Leopold had baroque architect Johann Bernhard Fischer von Erlach build for his son, Crown Prince Joseph. Much of the resplendent overhaul was the work of

PRACTICALITIES

- schoenbrunn.at
- The park opens from 6.30am, closing times vary by season. Nov-Mar: 8.30am-5pm, Apr-Jun & Sep-Nov: to 5.30pm, Jul & Aug: to 6pm.
- Vienna's most-visited attraction has a bewildering array of ticket options. The Classic Pass *(adult/child €40/31)* covers the main highlights.
- Skip the queue and book your time-allocated tickets before you arrive.

palace matriarch Empress Maria Theresia during her reign from 1740-80. The grandiose gardens were her last extravagant touch. Schönbrunn remained the favoured Habsburg summer abode, the pinnacle of court life and centre of diplomacy, and in its final years, the home of Empress Elisabeth and Emperor Franz Joseph, who died here in 1916.

There's an exhaustive complex of 1441 rooms, but enough in the open 40 to indulge in the tastes of the times – more so in the palace centrum and Maria Theresia's apartments, unveiling some of the finest examples of rococo art. The visual apex is the 10m-wide ball and banquet room of the **Great Gallery** (Room 21), with its crystal-glass mirror, stucco work and ceiling frescoes. It was the prestigious venue for the Congress of Vienna in 1814-15, reshaping Europe in the Napoleonic aftermath.

Move to the **Oval Chinese Cabinet** (24), where exquisite gold-dissolved, black-lacquered panels strike on white panelled walls. The **Blue Chinese Salon** (28), decked in 18th-century rice-paper wall hangings, is where the 1918 renunciation of Emperor Karl I ended the Austro-Hungarian monarchy. Phenomenal gilded black lacquer cloaks the **Vieux Laque Room** (29), Maria Theresia's devoted memorial room to her husband, Emperor Franz I Stephan von Lothringen.

The **Napoleon Room** (30) was the operational quarters of the French commander in Schloss Schönbrunn during his dual occupation of Vienna in 1805 and 1809. Be bamboozled in the **Porcelain Room** (31), whose three-dimensional garlands and frames are wood-made ceramic imitations. The priceless **Millions Room** (32) is embellished with rare rosewood panelling, while the ceremonial state bed remains preserved in a humidity-controlled chamber in the **Rich Room** (37).

> **40 ROOMS, TWO ROUTES**
>
> The 40 halls of state apartments and imperial chambers are accessible on two audio-guided routes with varying access levels.
>
> The 25-minute **State Apartments tour** covers central rooms 19-26, including the Great Gallery.
>
> The one-hour **Palace Ticket tour** encompasses all 40; this is the best-value tour that includes the private apartments of Franz and Elisabeth (rooms 1-18) and the sumptuous bundle of Maria Theresia's apartments.

The Park at Schloss Schönbrunn

Outside the regal digs is the expanse of **Schloss Schönbrunn Park**, stretching from the Great Parterre symmetrical horticultural gardens to the Schönbrunn hill and cresting at the triumphant arch of the Gloriette. It opened to the public in 1779 and remains a city sanctuary for ramblers and runners, and a drawing card for visitors wanting to wander the historical and cultural enclosure.

Notable features are the lavish palatial toppers by early classicist architect Johann Ferdinand Hetzendorf von Hohenberg, commissioned by Maria Theresia. The foothill **Neptune Fountain** with its marbled plinthed staging of Neptune and his entourage being pulled across the seas is the centrepiece; the grotto basin **Obelisk Fountain**, adorned with river gods and a golden-sphere-topped obelisk; and the crumbling colonnade archway of the **Roman Ruins**, an effigy of the Ancient Roman temple of Vespasian and Titus. On the other side, the tranquil spaces of the **Rose Garden** and **Japanese Garden** are backed by **Schönbrunn Zoo** – the oldest in the world, founded in 1752 by Maria Theresia's husband.

Ticketed entry gets you into unique attractions like the multi-climatic-zoned **Palm House** *(adult/child €9/7)* and the former imperial succulent-growing hothouse, which is now a

GLORIETTE VIEWPOINT

The crowning viewpoint of Schönbrunn is on the eagle-capped, arcaded archway of the **Gloriette** on Schönbrunn hill.

While the glass base houses Café Gloriette, climbing to its balustrade roof provides commanding views of the palace with Vienna rising above it in the background.

You need a ticket to enter.

re-created exhibition of the **Desert House** *(adult/child €9/7)*. The secluded **Privy Garden** (Crown Prince Garden) is a highlight; its elevated Garden on the Cellar parterre from around 1700 was wrapped with a tunnelling, trellised pergola, with a halfway viewing platform.

The vaulted longhouse of the **Schönbrunn Orangery** details its 1754 beginnings when it was built as a temperature-controlled environment for the overwintering of citrus trees and the stage for grand banquets. Measuring 189m by 10m, it remains one of the two largest baroque orangeries in the world, alongside Versailles, still blooming exotic fruit. The modern reconstruction of the original **Maze** from 1720 is a 2700-sq-metre circuit. It splits into a dead-end-dotted labyrinth that leads to a viewing platform and a 10-minute strolling course with mirrored and musical interactive stations.

If you don't purchase a Classic Pass, the Exclusive Gardens at Schönbrunn combo ticket *(adult/child €15/10)* includes entrance to the Privy and Orangery gardens, the Maze and the Gloriette terrace.

Schönbrunn Summer Night Concert

Tickets for the worldwide broadcast of the Wiener Philharmoniker (Vienna Philharmonic) New Year's concert *(wienerphilharmoniker.at/en/summernightconcert)* are like gold dust, but if you find yourself in Vienna in June, you'll catch the midyear classical-music highlight. The Summer Night Concert at Schloss Schönbrunn is a free open-air concert staged on the baroque lawn between the iconic palace and its elevated Gloriette monument. If you can't snag a chair in front of the orchestra podium, no problem. Join the tens of thousands of locals setting down a blanket and picnicking on the slopes. The symphony of sounds typically begins at 8.30pm.

Klimt Villa

At Home with Gustav Klimt
Klimt in life and death

The two-storey neo-baroque **Klimt Villa** *(klimtvilla.at; adult/child €10/free)* in residential Hietzing isn't the exact property he lived in – it was extended by the owners some five years after his death. Yet the renovations in 2012 saw the original ground floor of the summer house restored, preserving Gustav Klimt's reception room and final studio space where he worked on 50 paintings between 1911 and his death in 1918. A permanent exhibition focuses on the Klimt works lost and stolen, and the stories of patrons and perpetrators.

The Klimt grave is in **Hietzinger Friedhof** (Hietzing Cemetery) just outside the Schloss Schönbrunn Park – a modest gravestone bearing only his name.

HIETZING'S HIDDEN HISTORY

Jascha Novak, Viennese local and licensed tour guide, reveals Hietzing's secrets on his 13th district walking tour. *@hiddenvienna.guide*

Few visitors venture into the peaceful streets of Hietzing that still whisper secrets of the imperial past.

Next to the palace's western entrance stands a post office, once home to the Empress' physician who was later famed as history's first vampire hunter.

Pass the statue of Mexico's ill-fated Emperor Maximilian and slip into old Hietzing's narrow lanes.

On Altgasse, enjoy the weekly Saturday market (9am–4pm) and imagine the village it once was before it became a fashionable summer retreat for Vienna's elite in the 19th century.

Stroll Wattmanngasse and Gloriettgasse for a glimpse of the elegant summer villas, and spot an art deco treasure or two.

Outer Districts

THE BOLD AND THE BEAUTIFUL

GETTING AROUND

Mariahilfer Strasse high street, which cuts through the 6th district, continues through the 15th; places of interest spill into the streets on its western side.

Yppenplatz and the Brunnenmarkt in the 16th are a 5-minute walk from Josefstädter Strasse U-Bahn (U6) on the Gürtel belt road; residential Ottakring and the brewery are better accessed by Ottakring U-Bahn (U3).

The wine village of Grinzing in the 19th district is accessible by the 38A bus from Heiligenstadt U-Bahn station (U4).

Vienna's urban snail spiral layout has some worthy outer districts bordering the inner-city stars. From the 7th, you can cross to the 15th (Rudolfsheim-Fünfhaus). At first glance, it might be hard to muster a reason why, but look around – this gritty residential district is undergoing a transformation. A weave of pop-ups and lesser-known joints are kickstarting and spreading from Mariahilfer Strasse – the road continuing from its shopping-street spine.

From the 8th, cross the belt road to the multicultural 16th (Ottakring) and get into the thriving square of Yppenplatz, surrounded by watering holes and restaurants, and upping the vibrant ante at weekends with the bustling Brunnenmarkt.

From the 9th, venture into the hills of the pretty 19th (Döbling), where the culture of *Heurigen* (wine taverns) spotlights Vienna as a city surrounded by vineyards. This is an insight into many a local pastime...if you have time.

Extend the Trend in the 15th

The district in transformation

The 15th district is rarely spoken of, overshadowed by the forerunner trendsetting 6th and the 7th districts in front of it. A district seen as more socially disadvantaged, it's brushing off its rundown atmosphere, an understated transformation with a gritty-creative edge. Walk past Westbahnhof station along Mariahilfer Strasse, and it's all laid out in a tempting mantle of cafes, bars and restaurants that stretch all the way down to the Schwendermarkt local market pavilion. For more district vibes, head down to Reindorfgasse, where book, bike and eco-fashion stores jostle with old-timer institutions like the **Gasthaus Quell** restaurant and **Pizzeria Mafiosi**.

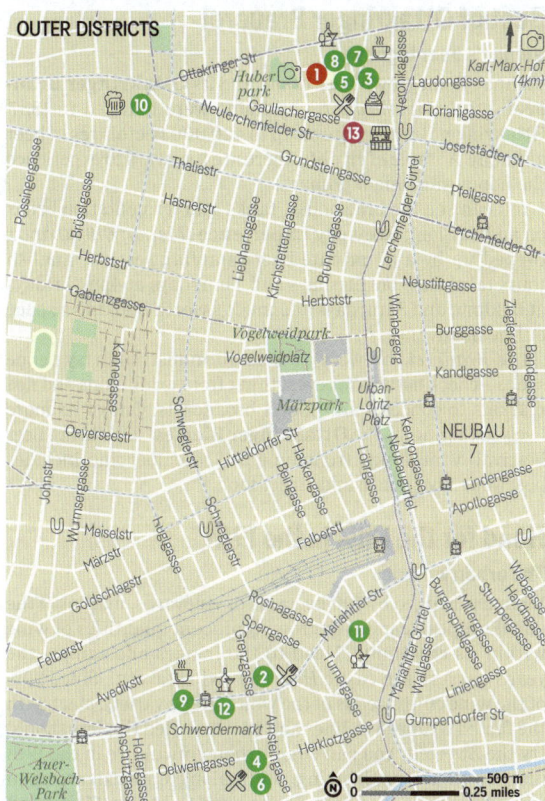

- **SIGHTS**
  1 Yppenplatz
- **EATING**
  2 Beats & Beans
  3 Eisbazar
  4 Gasthaus Quell
  5 Mani
  6 Pizzeria Mafiosi
- **DRINKING & NIGHTLIFE**
  7 Cafe C.I – Club International
  8 Fania Bar
  9 GOTA Coffee Experts
  10 Ottakringer Brauerei
  11 The Chapel
  12 Zum Schwarzen Flamingo
- **SHOPPING**
  13 Brunnenmarkt

World Fare & Flair in the 16th
Multicultural market square

Residential Ottakring (the 16th) is a large and stretched district, but its spirited soul is Yppenplatz (Yppen Sq), the multicultural kernel where everything happens. Its daily **Brunnenmarkt** is Vienna's biggest and most boisterous street market with 170 stalls, pumped at weekends when more people gather to find bargains at one of the city's cheapest markets. Across nearly 1000m of vendor displays on Brunnengasse between Ottakringer Strasse and Thaliastrasse are a spark of colour and a trailing incense of spices and vegetable stacks, flower bundles and cheese barrels, fresh meat and cooked eats. This multicultural flair and walk through of the world has granted it the nickname 'Orient around the corner'.

When the buzz is over, continue to the permanent store-and-gallery-hugged and pavilion-filed **Yppenplatz**, just as deliciously mixed in its offerings from the Middle East to Latin America.

☑ TOP TIP

These areas come alive at weekends when markets and squares are in full vendor throttle. While visiting a *Heuriger* is a pleasure at any time, there's more life in the Vienna Hills when the locals decamp to the woodland green after the working week.

Best of Ottakringer Brauerei
Vienna's beer legacy

Vienna's homegrown beer brand and its **Ottakringer Brauerei** *(ottakringerbrauerei.at)* home were founded in 1837. Ottakringer Brauerei brews up to 420,000 hectolitres of beer annually. A staple of city life, there are two ways to experience the hoppy-smelling landmark.

You can see the brewhouse, tanks and fermentation cellar on an hour-long **Brewery Experience** *(bier.at; €19.90)* tour, topped up by a 30-minute beer-sampling session. English tours take place on Tuesdays and Thursdays at 4pm, Fridays at 6.30pm, and Saturdays at 5pm. It's worth booking a space online in advance.

The *Brauerei* (brewery) is also an industrial-artsy venue space – check listings for everything from exhibitions and flea markets to concerts and sports broadcasts. One of its more lively gatherings is the **Ottakringer Bierfest** (Ottakring Beer Festival) which runs from June to September and includes beer yoga, live music and street food.

Head for the Hills in the 19th
The urban wineries

Vienna is hedged by 700 hectares of vineyards, making it the only European capital to grow significant quantities of wine within its city limits. Head to the fringes and sample the year's harvest at a rustic *Heuriger* (wine tavern). Since 80% of the wine cultivated is of the white-grape variety, start with the famed Grüner Veltliner and Riesling. Red tipplers should try the Zweigelt. You can enjoy urban viniculture in the 19th district village of Grinzing. Walk along Cobenzlgasse and sporadically dip into wineries or head to nearby **Hans und Fritz Buschenschank** for the vineyard city views. Actively sip on the **Stadtwanderweg 1** (city hiking trail 1), through the vineyards of **Nussdorf** and the mountain vantage point of **Kahlenberg** or hail an rideshare and head into the quaint village of **Neustift am Walde**. **Fuhrgassl-Huber** *(buschenschank-fuhrgassl-huber.at)* – the family behind the city's oldest *Heuriger* in Ottakring, 10-er Marie – has a tavern here with a beautiful courtyard garden.

Neighbouring **Das Schreiberhaus** *(dasschreiberhaus.at)* is a 200-year-old house with classic-haute cuisine. If you summon the sounds of the table-side *Schrammelmusik* (Viennese folk music), you'll experience a wine tavern in its centuries-old glory.

OTTO WAGNER REIMAGINED

The gilded dome of **Kirche am Steinhof** glistens upon the foot of Gallitzinberg hill in the 14th district, just west of the 16th.

It bears the hallmarks of Otto Wagner's modernist visions, with a copper-detailed and marble-clad exterior and a functional interior. Europe's first modern church was crafted to meet the needs of the patients of the psychiatric hospital below; on the path up, visitors walk past the 1907-built clinical complex Wagner conceptualised. The 60 Art Nouveau pavilions underwent numerous infirmary iterations over time.

Today the area designated as the Otto Wagner Areal *(owa-wien.at)* is helping to preserve a catalogue of listed buildings that form part of Vienna's architectural heritage, reimagined through a cultural programme of events and exhibitions.

 EATING & DRINKING IN THE 15TH DISTRICT: OUR PICKS

GOTA Coffee Experts: One of Vienna's top speciality coffee shops, home to award-winning baristas. Tasty breakfasts. *7am-6pm Mon-Fri, 8am-6pm Sat & Sun* €

Beats & Beans: Wood-panelled tavern revitalised by the chef and DJ owner into a vinyl store and eatery with seasonal menu. *5-10pm Mon-Fri* €€

Zum Schwarzen Flamingo: Chilled, retro-fitted den with arty vibes, bar snacks and a large drinks selection. *6pm-midnight Tue-Thu, to 2am Fri & Sat, 5-11pm Sun*

The Chapel: This dimly lit speakeasy is an altar of experimental, scripture-themed cocktails. Follow the image of the whispering nun for entry. *6pm-1am Tue-Thu, to 3am Fri & Sat*

Vineyards, Kahlenberg

Vienna's Wine Hiking Day
Active vineyard ambling

On the last weekend of September, the Viennese, in their quest to taste the season's wine harvest, enjoy a hike through the hills on a multi-stop sampling of the city's vintners and vineyards – the two-day celebration of wine growing known as **Wiener Weinwandertag** (Vienna Wine Hiking Day).

There are four hiking routes, but two are accessible in this area. Route 1, through the 19th district, from Neustift to Nussdorf (passing through Grinzing) combines more than a dozen sampling stops with unbeatable vantage points. Route 3, in the 16th district, is a smaller loop and perfect taster, starting and ending at the former imperial hunting retreat which is now a hotel, Schloss Wilhelminenberg (Wilhelminenberg Castle).

RED VIENNA

The aftermath of the monarchy's collapse and postwar impoverishment fuelled the ruling Social Democratic Workers' Party's reforms centred around urban communal living.

The period from 1919 to 1934, known as 'Red Vienna', saw the construction of around 400 *Gemeindebauten* – mega-apartment estates with all-encompassing social infrastructure including clinics, kindergartens, green space and amenities. These recognisable buildings pocket almost every district. It's a legacy still in operation, with around one in four Viennese citizens living in social housing. The largest of these red landmarks is the 1930-built **Karl-Marx-Hof** in the 19th district. It's the longest continuous residential building in the world, stretching over 1100m through Heiligenstadt.

EATING & DRINKING ON YPPENPLATZ

Eisbazar: Artisanal ice cream with oriental flavours, including saffron, tahini, pomegranate and mango lassi. *2-8.30pm Mon-Fri, noon-6pm Sat* €

Mani: Shakshuka breakfasts and delicious hummus among mezze and mains at this modern Middle Eastern bistro. *5-11pm Mon-Fri, 9am-11pm Sat* €

Fania Bar: Step out of Vienna and into this cosy Latin American bar bringing salsa beats and Colombian vibes. *6-11.30pm Mon & Tue, to 4am Wed-Sat*

Cafe C.I: Social hot spot where outdoor seating spills between the main building cafe and the square-side pavilion. *8am-2am Mon-Sat, 9am-2am Sun* €

Places We Love to Stay

€ Budget €€ Midrange €€€ Top End

Innere Stadt   MAP p58

Hotel Imperial €€€ The grandest and most decadent hotel of them all, retaining its majestic palace features, from the royal staircase to the sumptuous rooms.

Hotel Sacher €€€ Distinguished luxury and historical ambience at Vienna's most prestigious address, with two restaurants, a bar and a small spa.

The Guest House €€€ Boutique hotel and brasserie opposite Albertina with the timeless stamp of British designer Sir Terence Conran. Price includes a fabulous minibar.

Hotel Grand Ferdinand €€ Pick from stylish mahogany bunks and designer suites with chandeliers. Dine at the panoramic rooftop terrace with an open-air infinity pool.

Hotel Lamée (p74) **€€** Glamorous art deco styled hotel a short stroll from Stephansplatz. With king-sized beds, Penhaligon toiletries and chic city-view rooftop bar.

DO & CO €€€ Plush design hotel with 43 rooms and suites; some have a front-row view to Stephansdom, also seen from the 6th- and 7th-floor bar-restaurants.

Ruby Lissi €€ Franz and Sisi travel-themed hotel with a 24-hour bar in lieu of a restaurant. Modern-classic rooms with Marshall speakers and guitars for hire.

2nd District

Superbude Wien Prater €€ Culture space and hipster hotel on the fringe of Prater with themed and artist-decorated rooms. Hosts flea markets and live music events.

Social Hub Vienna €€ Vibrant hybrid hotel and student accommodation with bar, playroom, auditorium and coworking space. Between Augarten and Prater.

SO/Vienna €€€ Canal-side hotel with minimalist-monochrome rooms facing the city or Prater Park. With a hammam spa, panoramic glass rooftop restaurant, and bar Das Loft.

Grätzlhotel €€ Former artisan trade stores reworked by local architects into design-forward self-check-in suites. A local living experience located on the fringe of Karmelitermarkt.

3rd District

Hotel Daniel €€ Smart-luxury, minimalist-style hotel next to Belvedere, with one of the best brunches in town. Has vespas and bikes for hire.

Hoxton Vienna €€ Retro outfitted 1950s building with 196 mid-century modern rooms and a Havana-inspired rooftop bar and pool overlooking Stadtpark.

Magdas €€ Social business hotel with on-site restaurant integrating people from a refugee background. The sustainable, upcycled design supports NGOs and local artists.

Ruby Sofie €€ Boutique 'lean luxury' hotel in the revived historic Sofiensäle concert hall where Johann Strauss II once played. Bar hosts live-music gigs.

4th & 6th Districts

Die Josefine Hotel €€ Boutique 49-room hotel with *Great Gatsby* vibes and home of the stylish Barfly's speakeasy.

Jaz in the City €€ Music-themed design hotel from floor to rooftop bar. Every room has a vinyl player; choose your records at reception.

Hotel Motto €€ The Paris of the 1920s meets the Vienna of the 2020s. Chic rooms, art deco restaurant and grill-bar rooftop with city views.

Hotel Beethoven Wien €€ Family-run, characterful boutique hotel with 47 individually designed rooms across six Viennese themed floors. Its Lvdwig Bar is a highlight.

Wombat's City Hostel Naschmarkt € Modern, trendy traveller's hub next to the Naschmarkt, with private rooms and dorms, on-site cafe and a lively bar hosting weekly concert nights.

7th District

Altstadt €€€ Feel-at-home hotel and gallery. The 62 bespoke-designed rooms, deco lounge, and sculpture- and portrait-filled passageways display the collections of its art aficionado owner.

Hotel am Brillantengrund €€ This lemon-yellow building conceals 34 vintage-stamped rooms surrounding a palm-strewn courtyard which hosts community events and a tasty Filipino kitchen.

Max Brown 7th District €€ Retro, industrial chic meets mid-century-modern in this trendy hotel with pool table lounge and movie theatre.

Hotel Gilbert €€ A stylish green space with a trellis facade, plant-filled atrium restaurant-bar, and 57 sleek rooms in marine blue and warm wood.

Sans Souci Wien €€€ Boutique base with a brasserie, champagne bar and basement spa, opposite the Volkstheater. Elegantly stylish rooms feature designer furniture and pop art.

25hours Hotel €€ Boutique circus-inspired hotel with the Dachboden bar and rooftop terrace overlooking its MuseumsQuartier neighbour. Also has a small basement spa and Italian restaurant.

JO&JOE Vienna € Funky meld of hostel and hotel with expansive city-view garden terrace atop an eco-building shared with IKEA. Hosts regular evening events.

8th & 9th Districts

Harmonie Vienna €€ Elegant-modern, eco-conscious hotel within an Otto Wagner–designed building in the Servitenviertel. Has a gym, bar and bistro with an organic menu.

Hotel Rathaus Wein & Design €€ Boutique hotel and wine bar with rooms dedicated to Austrian winemakers. Minibars are stocked with the grower's vintage.

Boutiquehotel Stadthalle €€ The greenest of all, having achieved a zero-energy balance. Rooms with upcycled furniture, an oasis courtyard garden and a lavender rooftop with bees.

Artist Boutique Hotel €€ Chic 56-bed art hotel in the heart of the residential 8th with bespoke design rooms named after artists and a stylish bar-lounge.

Hotel Sacher

Above: Stift Dürnstein (p134); Right: Vineyard, Wachau Valley (p126)

Researched by
Rudolf Abraham

Lower Austria & Burgenland

VINEYARDS, CULTURE AND NATIONAL PARKS

From the Wachau and Waldviertel's rolling hills to Burgenland's extraordinary wetlands and the mountainous ripple of the Viennese Alps – plus some of Austria's best wines.

It's easy to overlook Austria's northeast, save for the cultural and artistic seat of Vienna, and the beautiful sweep of the blue, blue Danube (Donau) that defines the Wachau Valley. But Lower Austria and Burgenland contain some of the country's greatest treasures, from superb architecture and excellent museums to UNESCO-listed landscapes.

Three of Austria's six national parks are here, along with magnificent monasteries, romantic castle ruins, baroque palaces and sizeable feats of 19th-century engineering, not to mention some of the country's best spots for wildlife watching and cycling. You can also indulge in some of Austria's best wines, and local and seasonal dishes at a low-key but enormously welcoming *Heuriger* (wine tavern).

Much of the region is easily accessible via day trips from Vienna, but it's worth staying longer and looking beyond the main tourist sites. Spend a couple of days cycling around Neusiedler See, stop and enjoy top-notch Grüner Veltliner along the Wachau Valley, relax at a historic spa in Baden bei Wien, immerse yourself in the music of Haydn, Liszt and Beethoven (all of whom have ties with the region), or lace up those hiking boots and set off to explore some of the walking trails of the Wiener Alpen.

Though largely unsung, Lower Austria and Burgenland most definitely do not disappoint.

THE MAIN AREAS

THE WACHAU VALLEY
The Danube, culture and wine.
p126

WALDVIERTEL & WEINVIERTEL
Rolling hills and vineyards.
p144

NEUSIEDLER SEE
Nature, wildlife and wine.
p151

Find Your Way

Lower Austria is the largest of the country's nine states; however, given Vienna's proximity, transport links are very good. Northern Burgenland is well connected by rail to Vienna; its central and southern areas, like northern Waldviertel, require more careful planning.

Waldviertel & Weinviertel, p144
The hills of Waldviertel are home to castles and Nationalpark Thayatal, while Weinviertel is Austria's largest wine-growing region.

Neusiedler See, p151
The unique landscape of Neusiedler See is one of Austria's greatest bird-watching areas, and it also produces some of the country's best wines.

The Wachau Valley, p126
This UNESCO-listed stretch of the Danube between Melk and Krems is famous for its well-preserved mix of historic towns, monasteries and vineyards.

TRAIN & BUS
Good rail connections between Vienna and Krems via St Pölten, between Vienna and Neusiedler See, and via Wiener Neustadt and the Semmeringbahn to Graz. Jennersdorf can be reached by train from Graz. Buses cover central and southern Burgenland.

CYCLING
Along with the famous Danube Cycle Path, many areas of Lower Austria and Burgenland are fantastic for cycling – in particular Neusiedler See and the wine country of Weinviertel, central and southern Burgenland.

Spitz an der Donau (p130)

Plan Your Time

Lower Austria and Burgenland pack a lot in, from national parks to UNESCO sites to exceptionally good wines – allow yourself time to explore.

One Week

● Base yourself in **Krems** (p126) and explore the **Wachau Valley** (p126) – easily done by bicycle – making sure you see **Melk** (p128), **Spitz** (p130) and **Dürnstein** (p133). Head up into Waldviertel to visit **Nationalpark Thayatal** (p144), then to **Schneeberg** (p142) for hiking. Finally, spend a couple of days around **Neusiedler See** (p151), with its excellent wines and birdlife.

Two Weeks

● You can see a lot of Lower Austria and Burgenland in two weeks. Spend a little more time in **Waldviertel** (p144), head over to **Weinviertel's wine country** (p148), then visit the floodplain landscape of **Nationalpark Donau-Auen** (p149), east of Vienna. Head down to **Burgenland** (p151) for yet more excellent wines in an area that sees comparatively few visitors.

SEASONAL HIGHLIGHTS

SPRING
Wildflowers are in bloom on the Wiener Alpen and there's excellent cycling on the Danube Cycle Path.

SUMMER
Excellent hiking on Rax-Schneeberg, swimming in Neusiedler See, and large open-air opera and operetta festivals in Burgenland.

AUTUMN
The wine harvest means local festivals, vineyard tours and tastings in the Wachau Valley, Weinviertel, Neusiedler See and other areas.

WINTER
Skiing at Rax-Schneeberg and Semmering, and winter bird migration at Neusiedler See.

The Wachau Valley

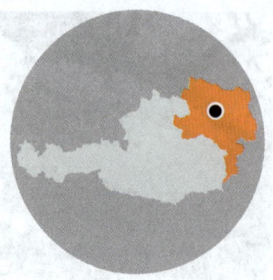

ANCIENT VINEYARDS | HISTORIC ABBEYS | RIVER DANUBE

Places
Krems an der Donau p126
Willendorf p128
Melk p128
Aggsbach p129
Spitz an der Donau p130
Weissenkirchen p133
Dürnstein p133

GETTING AROUND

Between Krems and Melk, you can take a river cruise (a little over three hours) or travel by train on the Wachau Bahn (50 minutes; other rail tickets not valid), in both cases calling at Spitz and Dürnstein, and there are rail connections between Krems and Vienna via St Pölten. Regional buses ply the route too.

The Danube Cycle Path runs along both banks of the river. If you're travelling one way by boat/train and cycling back along the Danube Cycle Path, reserve a place for your bike when you book your ticket.

Between the historic abbey in Melk and the beautifully preserved and wonderfully agreeable riverside town of Krems stretches one of the most attractive parts of the Danube. This is the Wachau Valley – a landscape packed with history and culture, pretty towns, romantic castle ruins and renowned sites such as the abbeys of Dürnstein and Melk set among ancient vineyards, many steeply terraced with dry-stone walling.

Enjoy a cruise on the Danube, cycle alongside the river or between vineyards following some of the excellent Danube Cycle Path, visit top-notch museums in Krems, discover the area's close connection with the English King Richard the Lionheart, and while away the time at a *Heuriger* – the Grüner Veltliner here really is first class. Its unique balance of culture and carefully preserved land management earned the Wachau the status of a UNESCO World Heritage Site in 2000.

Krems an der Donau

Krems is one of the prettiest towns sitting beside the Danube, with an intact historic centre, top-quality Grüner Veltliner from local vineyards, a region-driven food scene and high-calibre museums. The town can be divided into three areas: Krems in the east, where you'll find yourself if arriving by rail; Stein in the west, formerly a separate port town and where Danube cruises arrive and depart; and Und in the middle.

Cultural hot spot & Wachau gateway

The main concentration of museums lies along the so-called **Kunstmeile** (Art Mile), which stretches between Minoritenkirche and Dominikanerkirche.

Krems' excellent **Karikaturmuseum** *(Caricature Museum; karikaturmuseum.at; €12)*, opened in 2001, is the only museum of its kind in Austria – a 780-sq-metre gallery dedicated entirely to caricatures, cartoons, comics and satirical art. Along

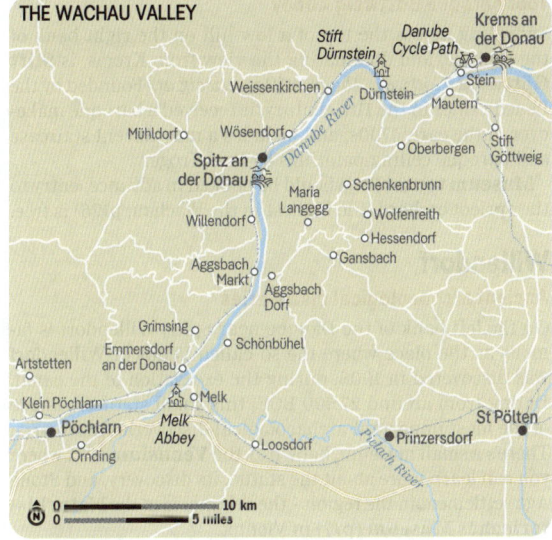

with temporary exhibitions, there is a permanent exhibition of Manfred Deix's work on the 1st floor, and a permanent display of the work of Austrian architect and caricaturist Gustav Peichl (Ironimus). One of Austria's most famous cartoonists, Deix was born in St Pölten – two of his works, *Mr and Mrs Austria*, greet you in the forecourt. It was Peichl, whose other works include Bonn's Bundeskunsthalle and Vienna's Millennium Tower, who designed the museum itself.

Next door, the **Landesgalerie Niederösterreich** *(State Gallery of Lower Austria; landesgalerie-noe.at; €12)* is a major collection of around 100,000 objects, housed in a striking modern building. It spans the Middle Ages, the baroque, the 19th century and contemporary works. Directly opposite is the **Kunsthalle Krems** *(kunsthalle.at; €12)*, set in a former 19th-century tobacco factory, which was transformed in the 1990s into a major exhibition space for modern and contemporary art. It showcases the work of established and emerging artists, and in the summer, the Dominican Church is used as an additional venue.

If you're visiting more than one museum in Krems, it's well worth getting a **Super-Kombiticket** *(€18)* which includes entry to the Karikaturmuseum, Landesgalerie Niederösterreich, Kunsthalle Krems, Dominikanerkirche and Forum Frohner.

Stein's old town centre is a wonderfully atmospheric succession of cobbled streets, presided over by the 13th-century **Minoritenkirche**. The Minorites founded the adjacent monastery, now used an exhibition and cultural space – **Forum Frohner** *(forum-frohner.at; €6)*, named after artist Adolf Frohner. Steiner Tor in Und is the last surviving part of the former defensive walls.

THE WACHAU BY BOAT

Taking a cruise along the Danube is almost part and parcel with spending time in the Wachau Valley. It's a nice, lazy way to spend half a day, and the views from the upper deck, enhanced and unobstructed, are very enjoyable – so order yourself a cool spritzer from the onboard bar, sit back and watch the world go by. Tables on the upper deck tend to fill up fast.

You can easily combine a boat cruise with a return journey by train or bicycle (p129; don't forget to reserve a place for your bike when you book).

DDSG Blue Danube *(ddsg-blue-danube.at)* offers cruises on the river between Krems and Melk, calling at Dürnstein and Spitz.

☑ TOP TIP

The best way to explore the region's beautiful towns, castle ruins, abbeys and vineyards is via a combination of cycling, taking a river cruise and using the Wachau Bahn.

KREMSER SCHMIDT

Krems was the home of the great painter and draughtsman Martin Johann Schmidt (also known as Kremser Schmidt), one of leading figures of the high baroque and rococo styles in Austria, whose work clearly shows the influence of Rembrandt.

The son of a sculptor, Schmidt was born in the Wachau Valley in 1718, and is thought to have refined his technique in Venice. Later he became a member of the Academy in Vienna. He painted numerous altarpieces, portraits, and historical and mythological scenes for churches and monasteries along the Danube and beyond, including in Slovenia and Hungary.

Many of his paintings can be seen in the **Belvedere** (p90) in Vienna.

Tour baroque Göttweig Abbey

Sprawling across the top of a low hill on the right bank of the Danube, and dominating the view from Krems, is **Stift Göttweig** (Göttweig Abbey; stiftgoettweig.at). Founded by the Benedictines in the 11th century, it received a baroque makeover in the early 1700s, and includes a magnificent staircase and baroque ceiling paintings by Paul Troger.

Museum tours (€14) should be booked in advance; entry to the apricot orchard (the highest in the Wachau; p126) is free.

Willendorf

Ancient archaeological discoveries

On the left bank of the Danube near Spitz, Willendorf is famous as the place where the so-called Venus of Willendorf was discovered in 1908, during the excavation of the canal. Dating from around 27,500 BCE, this small statuette is one of the most important archaeological discoveries in Austria. There's a small museum, known as the **Venusium** (€3), where you can learn more about the statue, its discovery, and Stone Age settlement in the region – the original is in the **Naturhistorisches Museum** (p77) in Vienna.

Melk

The Wachau's baroque masterpiece

Perched on a granite outcrop overlooking the Danube, the Benedictine abbey **Stift Melk** (stiftmelk.at; €16) is one of the finest ensembles of baroque architecture anywhere in Europe. The abbey was built on the site of a castle, which Leopold II of Babenberg gave to Benedictine monks from Lambach in Upper Austria. It's a huge and imposing place, founded in 1089 but owing its current style to an 18th-century reconstruction, having burnt down a couple of times before then.

The abbey church has frescos by the baroque master Johann Michael Rottmayr and Paul Troger, a highly influential painter who rejected the characteristic dark palette of baroque painting

WALDVIERTEL

As well as the gateway to Wachau, Krems is a natural springboard to the region of **Waldviertel** (p144), to which it belongs.

EATING & DRINKING IN KREMS AN DER DONAU: OUR PICKS

MOYOme: Cool eatery serving tasty cakes and all-day breakfasts. Good vegetarian and vegan options. 8am-7pm Mon-Fri, 8.30am-6pm Sat, 9am-5pm Sun €

Café-Konditorei Hagmann: Landmark cafe and confectionary shop founded in 1836, with fabulous cakes and chocolates. 8am-6pm Mon-Sat

Weinhimmel: Hip wine bar with regional, international and natural wines, plus platters of local cheese and cold cuts. 4-10pm Mon, Wed & Thu, from 2pm Fri, from 10am Sat

Gasthaus Jell: Traditional, family-run restaurant with seasonal ingredients and down-to-earth cuisine. 11.30am-2.30pm & 6-10.30pm Tue-Sat €€

Stift Melk

in favour of lighter, more vibrant colours, which foreshadowed the emergence of the rococo style. His huge, illusionistic ceiling painting is in the abbey's so-called Marble Hall. The church itself is the work of the baroque master architect Jakob Prandtauer.

Around two dozen monks reside in the abbey and surrounding parishes, and the abbey school, which opened in the 12th century, is Austria's oldest continuously operating school. English-language **guided tours** of the abbey take place two or three times a day and last around 50 minutes. If you're in Melk on 13 October, you can catch the big annual fair held here since 1451 in honour of St Colman, patron saint of the town and the abbey.

Aggsbach

Visit a Carthusian abbey

Around 12km downstream from Melk on the right bank of the Danube, **Kartause Aggsbach** *(Aggsbach Charterhouse; kartause.net)* is a former Carthusian monastery, founded in 1380 and dissolved in 1780, after which it was converted into a castle. The **Carthusuan Museum** *(adult/child €3/free)* and the abbey church can both be visited by prior arrangement; find contact details on the website.

BOAT, TRAIN & BICYCLE: PRACTICAL TIPS

One thing to note if you're planning to combine a river cruise or the Wachau Bahn with cycling some of the Danube Cycle Path: by boat it's over three hours from Krems to Melk, which realistically doesn't give you enough time to cycle back to Krems and actually visit places on the way (the last entry to Dürnstein Abbey is at 4.30pm).

However, Krems to Spitz is only 1½ hours. The Wachau Bahn takes just 50 minutes from Krems to Emmersdorf, and leaves earlier than the boat. Our advice? Take the train from Krems if you want to start cycling back from Emmersdorf/Melk, or take the boat if you want to start cycling back from Spitz.

 EATING & DRINKING IN KREMS AN DER DONAU: OUR PICKS

Heuriger Hamböck: Lovely *Heuriger* on a terrace above Stein (Krems) overlooking the Wachau Valley, with excellent food and wine. *2.30-11.30pm Apr-Dec* €

Wellen Spiel: Waterfront location beside the Danube cruise pier, with coffee and cakes, salads, steaks, pizzas and more. *8am-11pm* €€

Schmid's: Popular place with burgers and craft beers, plus salads and cakes. Vegetarian and vegan options. *11am-11pm Tue & Wed, to midnight Thu-Sat* €€

Salzstadl: Traditional restaurant and Wirtshaus, with live music some nights. *11am-3pm & 6-11pm Mon-Fri, closed Wed in winter* €€

SHOPPING IN THE WACHAU: LOCAL PRODUCTS

VIWE: Wine shop in Mautern, well stocked with local Wachau wines.
Vinothek Hubert Fohringer: Huge wine shop in Spitz, with wines from the Wachau and other regions.
Bauernmarkt Krems: Friday market on Dreifaltigkeitplatz in Krems, with local cured meats, cheeses and honey.
Vinotake Dürnstein-Loiben: Cute wine shop in Dürnstein, which is also a great place to stop for a glass of wine.
Vinothek Thal Wachau: Seasonal wine shop in Weissenkirchen, with local winemakers on site to talk you through their wines.
Café-Konditorei Hagmann: Artisanal chocolate maker and cafe serving delicious cakes in Krems.

The story behind Aggstein Castle

Also downstream from Melk on the Danube's right bank lie the ruins of **Burg Aggstein** *(Aggstein Castle; ruineaggstein.at; adult/child €9.50/free)*. Dating back to at least the 12th century, at which time it was owned by the Kuenrings, a powerful local family, it was given to Jörg Scheck vom Wald in 1429, who rebuilt the castle in Gothic style, and gained the right to impose taxes on ships travelling upriver.

According to legend, vom Wald became infamous for imprisoning anyone who failed to pay his toll on a small, high ledge, where they were left to either starve or leap to their death. There's a hiking trail (allow one hour) from Aggstein up to the castle ruins – which are quite extensive – as well as a road there.

Spitz an der Donau

Home of top-notch Grüner Veltliner

The pretty market town of Spitz an der Donau lies at the centre of the Wachau's wine-producing region, and locals will tell you Spitz's wines are the best in the Wachau – and they certainly are rather good, so tasting some local Grüner Veltliner or Riesling is definitely in order.

EATING & DRINKING IN THE WACHAU: OUR PICKS

Gasthof Prankl: Deservedly popular, with delicious food and local wines, in a 500-year-old former ship owner's house in Spitz. *8am-10pm Fri-Tue* €€

Landgasthaus Essl: Refined dining on the Danube's right bank between Spitz and Dürnstein. Awarded 15/20 by Gault Millau. *hours vary* €€€

Gasthof Goldenes Schiff: Family-run traditional restaurant and guesthouse, right in the centre of town, with a nice big terrace. *11.30am-8pm Thu-Tue* €€

Klosterhof Spitz: Set in a vineyard on the east side of Spitz, with tables in an atmospheric brick-vaulted interior. *11.30am-7pm Wed-Sun* €€

Burg Aggstein

The late-Gothic parish church, **Pfarrkirche**, here has close links with Bavaria, since it was part of the Niederaltaich Abbey near Regensburg for several centuries. Originally dedicated to St Godehard (whose sculpture can be seen in a niche) it was later rededicated to St Maurice.

A cable ferry runs across the river between Spitz and Arnsdorf, carrying passengers, bikes and vehicles, which makes a cheap and fun way to explore both banks of the Danube (there's another one between Weissenkirchen and St Lorenz).

Learn about shipping on the Danube

While in Spitz an der Donau, be sure to visit the **Schifffahrts Museum** *(schifffahrtsmuseum-spitz.at; adult/child €7/5)*, which is the best place to learn about the history of river traffic on the Danube and its sheer scale in the era before railways (eg 70 horses pulling a fleet of more than half a dozen cargo boats).

Legends at the Church of St Michael

Just over 1km east of Spitz lies the fortified **Wehrkirche St Michael** (Church of St Michael). Its origins lie in a shrine founded here by Charlemagne sometime in the early 9th century, dedicated to St Michael, and built on a Celtic sacrificial

BICYCLE HIRE IN THE WACHAU

Bikes/e-bikes cost from €15 to €35 per day.
Wachau Explorer: One of the largest bike rental outfits in the Wachau Valley, with e-bikes, trekking bikes and kids' bikes. Based in Krems.
Rent a Wachau Bike: E-bikes, trekking, kids' and city bikes. Branches in Mautern an der Donau and Furth-Palt.
Gartenhotel Pfeffel: Guesthouse north of Dürnstein with bikes and e-bikes available to rent.
Wachau Turistik Bernhardt: Based in Spitz and Melk, with e-bikes, city bikes and trek bikes.
Nextbike: One of the most convenient ways to hire a bike in the Wachau Valley and beyond. Set up an account online, then pick up or drop off at any rental point within Lower Austria.

 EATING & DRINKING IN THE WACHAU: OUR PICKS

Gasthof Weisses Rössl: In Mühldorf, west of Spitz, with an emphasis on local, seasonal and organic produce. *10am-11pm Wed-Fri, 9am-11pm Sat & Sun* €€

Hofmeisterei Hirtzberger: Michelin-listed dining in a historic tavern near Weissenkirchen. *noon-2pm & 6-9pm Mon & Sat, 6-9pm Thu & Fri, noon-9pm Sun* €€€

Weingut & Heuriger Pomassl: Authentic rural *Heuriger* between Weissenkirchen and Dürnstein. Seasonal hours. *May, Jun & mid-Sep-mid Oct* €€

Landhaus Bacher: Two-Michelin-starred venue, across the river from Krems. *6.30pm-midnight Wed, noon-4.30pm & 6.30pm-midnight Thu-Sat, 11.30am-11.30pm Sun* €€€

THE WACHAU BY BICYCLE

Cycle through the Wachau Valley, following a stretch of the Danube Cycle Path. Head upriver on the Wachau Bahn to Emmersdorf and Melk, then back to Krems.

START	END	LENGTH
Emmersdorf an der Donau	Krems an der Donau	35km

Take the train from Krems to start your cycling route at ❶ **Emmersdorf an der Donau**, or if you want a shorter ride, take a boat (departing from near the Kunsthalle) to Spitz. From Emmersdorf you'll need to cross to the right (south) bank of the river via the road bridge to reach Melk. Visit the baroque Benedictine abbey masterpiece that is the ❷ **Stift Melk** (p128) then cross back to the left (north) bank of the Danube and cycle towards Spitz.

At ❸ **Aggsbach Markt** you'll be able to see the ruins of Burg Aggstein on the opposite bank. At ❹ **Willendorf**, stop at the small museum known as the Venusium; this is the place to find out more about the famous Venus of Willendorf, now in the Naturhistorisches Museum in Vienna. Continue to ❺ **Spitz**, where you can visit the Schifffahrtsmuseum and take a lunch break.

From here, continue along the left bank, passing steeply terraced vineyards and the ❻ **Wehrkirche St Michael** (p131), with its enigmatic sculptures of 'hares' along its roof. Continue through ❼ **Weissenkirchen** with its fortified church to reach ❽ **Dürnstein** (p134), where a visit to the famous abbey is essential. You can also lock your bicycle in town and hike up to the ruins of Dürnstein Castle. Continue along the left bank back to ❾ **Krems** (p126).

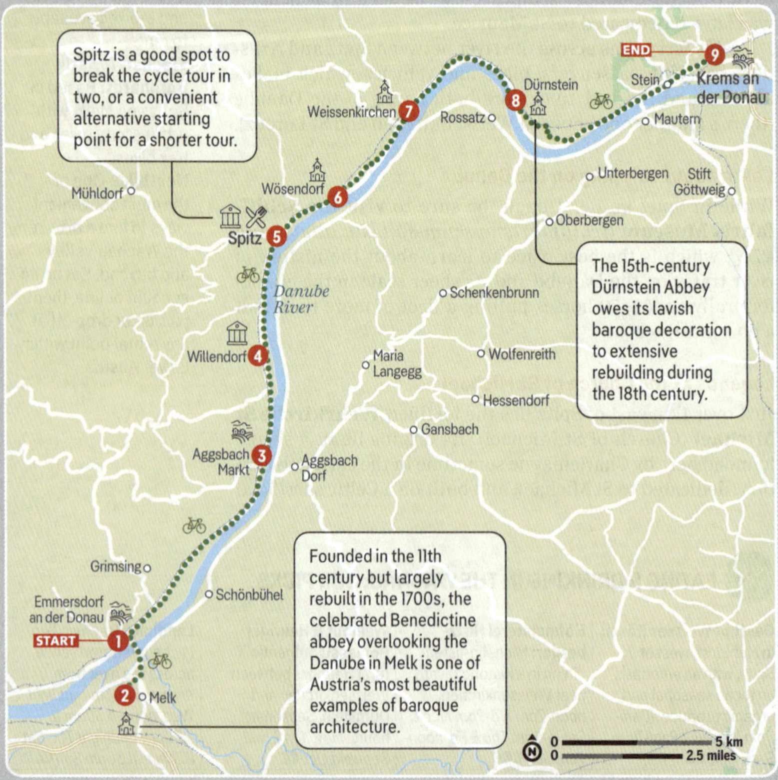

Spitz is a good spot to break the cycle tour in two, or a convenient alternative starting point for a shorter tour.

The 15th-century Dürnstein Abbey owes its lavish baroque decoration to extensive rebuilding during the 18th century.

Founded in the 11th century but largely rebuilt in the 1700s, the celebrated Benedictine abbey overlooking the Danube in Melk is one of Austria's most beautiful examples of baroque architecture.

site. The adjacent round tower is a late 14th-century Gothic charnel house (ossuary). The church was transformed in Late Gothic style in the first half of the 16th century, shortly before the construction of its defensive walls which were originally up to 7m high.

Look for the row of small animals on the ridge of the church roof – usually described as 'hares' (though they possibly represent deer or horses). According to legend they were confined to this spot after they climbed up here during a particularly severe winter and were unable to get down again.

You can walk or cycle here from Spitz, or take a local bus.

Weissenkirchen

Fortified parish church

Further downstream towards Dürnstein, Weissenkirchen has a particularly impressive 14th-century fortified **parish church** that towers above the market square in the town centre. Below it stands Teisenhoferhof, a Gothic fortress also dating from the 1300s which was enlarged in the 15th century by Heinrich Teisenhofer (whose coat of arms you can see above the gate), then remodelled in Renaissance style in the 1540s. It now houses the **Teisenhoferhof Wachaumuseum** and Gallery. Next to the church is the oldest primary school in Austria, which was first mentioned in 1385 – it's still in use.

Dürnstein

Castle ruins

The pretty little town of Dürnstein stands on an impossibly photogenic curve in the Danube, backed by low hills. An essential stop on any tour of the Wachau Valley is Dürnstein's famous **Kuenringerburg** (Dürnstein Castle) above the town. This is the castle where Richard I of England – yes, the Lionheart – was once imprisoned. He ended up here due to a dispute with Leopold V, Duke of Austria, during the Third Crusade – Richard removed Leopold's banner following the Siege of Acre (and refused an equal share of the booty

ART NOUVEAU IN ST PÖLTEN

If baroque isn't your thing, visit the **Stadtmuseum** (p135) (City Museum) in St Pölten to see its Art Nouveau collection instead.

WACHAU APRICOTS

The Wachau Valley is famous not only for its excellent wines, but also for its delicious apricots, which have PDO (Protected Designation of Origin) status. You'll find Wachauer Marillen on most menus, in many guises ranging from *Marillenkuchen* to *Marillenpalatschinken* to apricot tiramisu.

They're also made into a rather exquisite fruit brandy, Marillen brand (which comes in at a volatile 40%).

A good place to see apricots growing is the 11th-century **Göttweig Abbey** (p128), which sprawls across the top of a low hill on the right bank of the Danube, dominating the view from Krems – the apricot orchard here is the highest in the Wachau.

EATING & DRINKING IN THE WACHAU: OUR PICKS

Rathauskeller Der Melker Gasthof: Atmospheric old tavern, around since 1669, in Melk's old town hall. Traditional Austrian dishes. *9am-11pm* €€

Landgasthof Hinterleithner: Michelin Bib Gourmand-awarded restaurant serving regional Austrian and Asian dishes. *5.30-9pm Tue, 11am-3pm & 5.30-10pm Wed-Sat* €€€

Weingut Alfred Schwaiger: *Heuriger* in Wösendorf, midway between Spitz and Weissenkirchen. Seasonal opening hours. €

Buschenschank Strawanzer: *Heuriger* in Spitz, not far from the Schifffartsmuseum. Seasonal opening hours. *from 4pm Mon-Fri, from 3pm Sat & Sun* €

Kuenringerburg (p133)

FOLLOW EUROPE'S GREATEST RIVER

The Danube Cycle Path (p132) is one of Europe's greatest long-distance cycle routes – and one of its most beautiful sections is between Krems and Melk, through the UNESCO-listed Wachau Valley. The path follows both banks of the Danube, so you can cycle along one bank and return along the other. Even better, you can take your bike on a boat from Krems to Melk, visiting Dürnstein and Spitz – or on a train from Krems to Emmersdorf (the town opposite Melk), stopping at Dürnstein, Spitz and other places.

This makes it nice and easy to combine a river cruise or train ride through the area's legendary vineyards, stopping to soak up some of the Wachau's celebrated cultural sites while sampling its excellent wines.

with England and France). This infuriated Leopold and he had Richard incarcerated on his way back from the Holy Land. Leopold was excommunicated for imprisoning a fellow Crusader, and was obliged to have Richard released (following the payment of a sizeable ransom – 35 tonnes of silver). Only ruins of the castle remain, but they can still be visited, and the view is lovely. It takes 20 minutes to walk up from town following a clearly marked trail.

Historic abbey with a blue tower

Stift Dürnstein *(Dürnstein Abbey; stiftduernstein.at; €12)*, with its distinctive blue tower, stands beside the river in Dürnstein. Founded in 1410, the abbey received its current baroque makeover in the 18th century – the entrance portal and courtyard were designed by Jakob Prandtauer, the tower's lower portion and the church portal and interior were designed by Matthias Steinl, while much of the rest of the work fell to Prandtauer's nephew, Josef Munggenast. The decoration of the abbey church is particularly rich, and along with all the stucco and flamboyant sculpture, includes a rather impressive altar with a tabernacle in the shape of a globe. There are daily **guided tours** of the abbey in German, and there's an English-language audio guide available.

Pleasing aesthetics aside, there's a reason that the famous tower at Dürnstein Abbey is painted such a distinctive shade of blue. Its colour, known as smalt blue, was chosen as it's extremely close to the colour of porcelain, and like fine porcelain the blue is offset by areas of white. At the time of the tower's construction, porcelain was a luxury item only available to the very wealthy, so here it was used as a way to project on a grand scale the abbey's considerable importance and prosperity. This was just one of the many layers of meaning, carefully planned and chosen by Provost Hieronymus Übelbacher, who oversaw the abbey's baroque transformation.

Beyond The Wachau Valley

From the Vienna Woods to the ripple of mountains of the Wiener Alpen.

Southeast of the Wachau lie the rolling, wooded hills of the Wienerwald and Austria's most famous spa town, Baden bei Wien. Meanwhile the Wiener Alpen (Viennese Alps) in the southern corner of Lower Austria feature some of the province's most spectacular landscapes. Here the hills rise to meet the Alps, peaking at Schneeberg (2076m), a mountain popular among the Viennese for its skiing and hiking possibilities. Nearby Semmering has long been a favourite of the capital's burghers, due mainly to its crisp alpine air, while Wiener Neustadt maintains a nice, authentic feel.

One of the greatest highlights of the area, though, is the journey here; the winding railway over the Semmering Pass has been designated a UNESCO World Heritage Site. Mostviertel forms the westernmost part of the region, its name deriving from this area's history of perry- and cider-making.

St Pölten

TIME FROM VIENNA: **25MINS**

The Lower Austrian capital

South of the Danube on the train line and motorway between Vienna and Salzburg is Lower Austria's administrative capital of St Pölten. Many people whizz past St Pölten – and Mostviertel as a whole, come to that – on their way elsewhere. However, it's worth a stop here, if only to see the **cathedral**, the work of baroque master Jakob Prandtauer – he of the great church and abbey at Melk (p128) – who lived and died here. The cathedral's frescoes were created by Habsburg court painter Daniel Gran.

The **Stadtmuseum** (City Museum) also warrants a visit, with its Art Nouveau collection, and **Rathausplatz** (town hall square) – fronted on one side by the 18th-century Rathaus (town hall) and awash with pastel facades – makes a good place to stop for *Kaffee und Kuchen*. The tall, white-marble **Dreifaltigkeitssäule** (Trinity Column) dates from 1782, and was installed to mark the passing of the Plague.

Places

St Pölten p135
Tulln p136
Ötscher Tormäuer Nature Park p136
The Wienerwald p137
Baden bei Wien p139
Wiener Neustadt p140
Semmering p142
Puchberg am Schneeberg p143
Payerbach p143

GETTING AROUND

There are direct trains from Vienna to Wiener Neustadt (30 minutes) and Baden bei Wien (27 minutes). Mödling, gateway to the Wienerwald, is 25 minutes from Wien Hauptbahnhof on the S-Bahn. Puchberg am Schneeberg is 45 minutes by train from Wiener Neustadt, and is the starting point of the Schneebergbahn cog railway.

Trains from Vienna to Graz take you over the Semmering Pass, on the route of the historic Semmeringbahn.

135

TOP CYCLE ROUTES

Ybbstal Cycle Path: From the Danube to Lake Lunz (107km), following the River Ybbs through a succession of spectacular landscapes.

Traisental Cycle Path: From Traismauer on the southern bank of the Danube to the pilgrimage site of Mariazell (111km). Relatively flat, good for families.

Perry Road Cycle Tour: Circular route (110km) through the Mostviertel, starting and finishing in Amstetten.

Triesting-Gölsental Cycle Route: From Leobersdorf in the southern part of the Vienna Woods, to the Traisental Cycle Path in Traisen (60km).

EuroVelo 9: Wiener Neustadt to Mönichkirchen: A 55km section of this megaroute from the Baltic to the Adriatic, taking in the Bucklige Welt region (aka the land of a thousand hills).

Ride the Mariazellerbahn

St Pölten is the northern terminus of the **Mariazellerbahn** *(mariazellerbahn.at; single from €22)* – Austria's longest narrow-gauge railway, running south for around 85km by way of 19 viaducts and 21 tunnels, to the Mariazell pilgrimage centre in Styria (p206). Construction of the line lasted from 1898 and 1907, and the gauge – 760mm, also known as the Bosnian Gauge – followed that used widely in Habsburg realms. The original U-type steam locomotives were replaced when the line was electrified shortly before WWI – although one of them is still in use on the remaining section of the Steyr Valley Railway – then by diesel locomotives in the 1930s. The current, low-floor trains (known as the Himmelstreppe) were designed and introduced in 2013.

Trains depart hourly from St Pölten, and the very scenic journey lasts around 2½ hours. Services with panorama wagons sporting huge windows run on Saturdays and Sundays from 1 May to early November, and during Advent, as do trains pulled by the original 100-year old diesel locomotives. Trains pulled by Mh 6 steam locomotives depart every second Sunday of the month from September to October, and every Sunday during Advent.

Tulln
Birthplace of Egon Schiele

TIME FROM VIENNA: 30MINS

Halfway between Krems and Vienna, Tulln is best known as the birthplace of Egon Schiele – one of the 20th century's greatest artists and a leading figure in Vienna's modernist movement. Don't miss Tulln's **Egon Schiele Museum** *(schielemuseum.at; €6)*, which has an important collection of the artist's works and temporary exhibitions that change annually. The museum is housed in the former city prison, which was converted into a museum in 1990 on the 100th anniversary of Schiele's birth. You can also visit the **Egon Schiele Birthplace** *(€2)*, where Schiele was born and lived for the first 10 years of his life. He died of the Spanish flu, aged 28, shortly after his pregnant wife had also succumbed to it.

Ötscher Tormäuer Nature Park
Austria's Grand Canyon

TIME FROM VIENNA: 3HRS

On the southern edge of Mostviertel, Ötscher Tormäuer Nature Park, the largest nature park in Lower Austria, is a sprawling area of wilderness which – especially if you've arrived from

EATING & DRINKING IN THE MOSTVIERTEL: OUR PICKS

Zur Palme: Chef Theresia Palmetzhofer in Neuhofen an der Ybbs serves regional dishes with a modern twist. *11am-midnight Thu-Sat, 9am-9pm Sun* €€€

Hueber der Wirt in Bründl: Family-run since 1892, this restaurant champions Mostviertel produce. *lunch 11.30am-2pm Fri-Sun, dinner 5.30-9pm Wed-Sat* €€

Rendl Keller: Atmospheric brick-vaulted tavern in St Pölten with traditional food and plenty of wines. *4-11pm Thu-Sun, kitchen closes 8pm Sun* €€

Mostheuriger Familie Lettner: Traditional cider tavern near the confluence of the Danube and the River Enns. The orchard has about 180 trees – local cider varieties. *hours vary* €

Mariazellerbahn

the bucolic setting of the Wachau Valley – you'll find surprisingly wild and rugged in places.

At the heart of Ötscher Tormäuer lies Ötschergräben – a staggeringly impressive gorge, along the course of the Ötscherbach stream, the almost sheer, 40m-high walls of which have earned it the nickname 'Austria's Grand Canyon'.

The Mariazellerbahn stops at half a dozen stations within the nature park (Puchenstuben, Gösing, Annaberg, Wienerbruck, Erlaufklause and Mitterbach), making it easy to get around and enjoy some of the many hiking trails in the area without a car. You can also buy a combination ticket covering the entrance fee to the nature park and a journey within the park on the Mariazellerbahn.

The Wienerwald

TIME FROM VIENNA: **20-40MINS**

Hike Vienna's wooded hills

The Wienerwald – the Vienna Woods – are the rolling, wooded hills dotted with meadows and pastures to the west and southwest of Vienna, as well as the wine-growing region directly south of the capital. Declared a UNESCO Biosphere Reserve in 2005, the Wienerwald is the city's green lungs, a favourite place for walking, picnicking, climbing and mountain biking – and, despite its close proximity to a city of nearly

MOSTVIERTEL

South of the Danube, Mostviertel forms the southwestern chunk of Lower Austria – one of the state's four historical regions or 'quarters' along Waldviertel and Weinviertel to the north, and the Industrieviertel to the east, from which it is divided by the Wienerwald (Vienna Woods). It includes the cities of St Polten and Amstetten, the valley of the River Ybbs – and technically at least, the town of Melk, though that is much more logically visited as part of exploring the Wachau Valley.

The name Mostviertel derives from the tradition of perry- and cider-making in the region – and the best way of acquainting yourself with this is of course by visiting one or more of the local *Mostheurige* or cider taverns.

The Mostviertel is particularly beautiful in April, when the pear trees are in blossom.

EATING & DRINKING IN THE WIENERWALD: OUR PICKS

Babenbergerhof: Long-standing, family-run traditional restaurant in Mödling serving a well-priced two-course set menu. *11.30am-2.30pm & 6-9pm Mon-Fri* €€

Stockerwirt: Excellent and deservedly popular restaurant on the western flanks of Naturpark Föhrenberge. *11.30am-midnight Mon-Sat, to 7pm Sun* €€

Klostergasthof Heiligenkreuz: Traditional inn at the historic abbey. The setting is more of a drawcard than the food. *10am-10pm Mon-Fri, 9am-10pm Sat & Sun* €€

Heuriger Spaetrot: *Heuriger* with an emphasis on Slow Food and local organic fare. Owner Johanna has twice won Heuriger Innkeeper of the Year. *11am-11pm Thu-Mon* €

Stift Heiligenkreuz

AUSG'STECKT IS

A *Heuriger* (plural *Heurigen)* is a traditional wine tavern, licensed to serve that year's wine with food on the premises.

Heurigen are synonymous with excellent local wine, and simple but great food – think cold platters of delicious local cured meats and cheeses, crunchy pickles and the like – not to mention a lovely ambience. Eating and drinking at a *Heuriger* is an integral part of local culture in the wine regions of Austria, in particular Lower Austria and Burgenland.

Heuriger are open seasonally – usually a week or so each month from April to October; always check ahead before visiting. The words you're looking for are *'Ausg'steckt is'* – literally meaning, open. Traditionally a wreath or cluster of pine or spruce twigs outside shows it's open.

two million inhabitants, a place of remarkable biodiversity. It was here in the Wienerwald that the Ural owl (a species that had disappeared from Austria by the 1950s) was successfully reintroduced, in 2008.

The best way to explore here is on foot. There are plenty of hikes to choose from – try one of the following. The **Hoher Lindkogel** can be included in a 19km circular route starting from Pottenstein, with a 650m ascent. Hike through the **Hagenbachklamm** gorge, on a 17.5km circular route with a 350m ascent, starting in Wördern. Or starting from Kahlenbergerdorf, there's a 14km circular route which includes the Habsburgwarte tower on **Hermannskogel**, with a 580m ascent.

For a via ferrata, head for the **Peilstein Klettersteig** on Peilstein (716m), an easy route which is good for beginners and older kids. Peilstein itself offers dozens of much more challenging climbing routes, and is near the Peilsteinhaus mountain hut. If you're driving, there's a car park at Holzschlag. There are two information centres for the biosphere reserve on the southwestern edge of the city – one in the Steinhofgründe and the other off Kalksburger Strasse.

EATING & DRINKING IN & AROUND BADEN BEI WIEN: OUR PICKS

Doblhoff: Lakeside cafe-restaurant near the rose gardens in Baden bei Wien. *10am-9pm* €€

Heuriger Zierer: Good *Heuriger* in a pretty, cobbled lane in Baden bei Wien, with a nice garden. *seasonal hours 3-11pm Mon-Fri, 11am-11pm Sat & Sun* €

Heuriger Drexler-Leeb: Family-run *Heuriger* and winery in Perchtoldsdorf. A tavern was recorded here from the 15th century. *hours vary. from 9.30am during Ausg'steckt* €

Heuriger Kernbichler: Popular *Heuriger* on the northeast side of town. *from 10am Wed-Mon during Ausg'steckt* €

In the footsteps of Beethoven & Schoenberg

The natural gateway to the Wienerwald, the picturesque town of **Mödling**, just 15km south of Vienna, was once favoured by the musically inclined – Beethoven sojourned here, and the Austrian composer Arnold Schoenberg lived in the town for several years following WWI, during which time he developed his version of the 12-tone technique, a method of composing based on 12 notes that was to prove hugely influential among later composers.

The town had suffered miserably during the two Ottoman sieges of Vienna and from the Plague, with much of it being rebuilt after the late 17th century. Mödling was also one terminus of the Mödling-Hinterbrüel tram, which ran from 1883 to 1932 – this was the first electric tram or railway in Austria, and the first in the world to operate from overhead power lines.

The well-preserved old town is partly pedestrianised, and centred around the old **Rathaus** (popular for wedding ceremonies), with the large **Church of St Othmar** lying west of this. Don't miss the atmospheric castle ruins, **Burgruine Mödling**, which stand on a hill above the town.

Ancient Cistercian abbey

Just off the A21, **Stift Heiligenkreuz** is the second-oldest surviving Cistercian abbey in the world, founded in 1133 by Leopold III (the oldest is at Rein near Graz). Along with some standout architectural features – the earliest ribbed vaulting in Austria, dating from the 13th century, plus an impressive Gothic choir hall – the abbey contains the tombs of four Brabenberg rulers: Friedrich I and II, and Leopold IV and V (the latter ruler is generally known as the one who had English King Richard the Lionheart locked up in **Dürnstein Castle** (p133)). Leopold III himself was buried at the abbey of Klosterneuburg, which he also founded, on the outskirts of Vienna.

Baden bei Wien

TIME FROM VIENNA: **30-50MINS**

Historic thermal springs

Baden's history as Austria's most illustrious spa town stretches back around two millennia – the Romans founded a bath here to luxuriate in its sulphurous mineral springs in about 50 CE. But it was really from the beginning of the 19th century that the town rose to fame, after Emperor Franz I had visited a few years earlier. He went on to name it his official summer residence, spending almost every summer here until 1834. This prompted a spectacular influx of the rich and famous to the little town, and the building of houses, palaces and gardens on a suitably grand scale, by the likes of the great architect and designer Otto Wagner, a leading figure of the Vienna Secession movement.

The **Römertherme** *(roemertherme.at; day ticket from €24)* and the **Thermalstrandbad** *(€11)* are the two main places to take to the town's celebrated spa waters, which well up at a temperature of between 32°C and 36°C from 14 natural sulphur thermal springs. The Römertherme has views of

---

THE GREAT COMPOSERS & BADEN BEI WIEN

Among the impressive list of composers and other luminaries who flocked to Baden bei Wien are Beethoven, Mozart, Schubert and Strauss. Schubert wrote his *'Fugue in E Minor'* over the course of one night in Baden, while Beethoven composed *'Ode to Joy'* and other parts of his famous Symphony No 9 while sojourning here – he spent several summers in Baden in the early 1820s.

The house where Beethoven stayed is on Rathausgasse – it's now called (perhaps not surprisingly) the **Beethovenhaus**, though back then it was owned by a coppersmith. It's open as a museum and an audio experience, and in 2014 the original wall paintings on the upper floor where Beethoven stayed were uncovered.

AEIOU

The popular translation for Friedrich III's symbolic device 'AEIOU' is 'Alles Erdreich Ist Österreich Untertan' ('Everything in the world is subservient to Austria').

However, while it was obviously very appealing to the Habsburgs, this interpretation has more recently been called into question, since it is based on an inscription in a notebook which predates Frederich's time as ruler, and is in a different hand from the rest of the notebook.

More plausibly, it might refer to a couplet in the same notebook, which translates roughly as 'Loved by the elect, avenger of the unjust'. But in the end, it still remains something of an enigma.

the Weinerwald thanks to a vast glass roof while the Thermalstrandbad features a beach in the form of a sizeable strip of imported sand. In 2021 Baden bei Wien was named a UNESCO World Heritage Site, along with 10 other spa towns scattered across Germany, Czechia and beyond, which together make up the Great Spa Towns of Europe.

Arnulf Rainer Museum & Rollett Museum

Beyond the spas, the **Arnulf Rainer Museum** *(arnulf-rainer-museum.at; €10)* is also well worth a visit. Located inside the former Frauenbad (Women's Bathhouse) near the tram terminus, this interesting museum showcases the work of its namesake Arnulf Rainer, who was born in Baden in 1929 and known for his abstract paintings.

For more on Baden bei Wien's history, head for the **Rollett Museum** *(rollettmuseum.at; €6)*. The most unusual exhibit here is the collection of skulls, busts and death masks amassed by the founder of phrenology, Josef Gall, who sparked the unpleasant craze of inferring criminal characteristics from the shape of a person's cranium.

Outdoors in Baden

Baden's historic **Kurpark** makes a lovely setting for a stroll or as a place to repose on the benches in front of the late-19th-century bandstand, where free concerts are held in the summer months. For a picnic, head to **Doblhoff Park**, which has well-maintained picnic areas surrounded by masses of rose beds. If you're curious to know where the emperor spent his summers, the house is at Hauptplatz 17.

Wiener Neustadt

TIME FROM VIENNA: **35MINS**

Former Habsburg residence

Though slightly off the tourist trail, Wiener Neustadt is worth a stop for its cathedral and main square, plus its low-key, authentic feel. The town used to be known simply as Neustadt (New Town) or Nova Civitas and was built by the Babenbergs in 1194 with the help of King Richard the Lionheart's ransom payment. It became a Habsburg residence in the 15th century during the reign of Friedrich III, whose famous symbolic device 'AEIOU' can be found engraved at the castle and elsewhere in the city. The town was severely damaged in WWII (only 18 homes were left unscathed), so what you see today is mainly a postwar rebuild.

EATING & DRINKING IN & AROUND WIENER NEUSTADT: OUR PICKS

Alten Backhaus: Traditional Austrian dishes with contemporary flair. *11.30am-1.30pm Tue-Fri, 5.30-9pm Tue-Sat* €€

Alter Stadtheuriger Fucik: Popular fourth-generation *Heuriger* opened in 1919 and now one of the last traditional *Heurigern* in the old town. *seasonal hours* €

Heuriger Fingerlos: *Heuriger* south of the city, with meat from their own butchery. *seasonal hours* €

Triad: Michelin-listed restaurant in Bad Schonau, south of Wiener Neustadt. *noon-2pm & 6pm-midnight Wed-Sat* €€€

Cathedral, Wiener Neustadt

Construction on the **cathedral** began in the 13th century, in Romanesque style, but it gained Gothic elements in the 14th century, and the interior received a complete baroque makeover in the 17th and 18th centuries. The bust on the tomb of Cardinal Melchior Klesl is attributed to the great Italian sculptor Gian Lorenzo Bernini and his assistants. The two towers – among the town's main landmarks – were demolished and rebuilt following an earthquake in the late 19th century. The **Reckturm**, a 15th-century reconstructed tower framed by a portion of the old city walls, contains a small private arms collection (ask at the tourist office about arranging a visit). The **Oldtimer Museum** *(€8)* contains an extensive collection of classic cars, amassed over a period of 30 years by Friedrich and Ronald Fehr.

Wiener Neustadt's Militärakademie

Occupying the site of the former castle, the **Militärakademie** *(Military Academy; €10)* is one of the oldest in the world, established by Empress Maria Theresia in 1751. The conversion from medieval castle to military academy involved substantial alterations to the older building, and further changes were required after it was damaged by an earthquake in 1768. It was bombed to bits in WWII, after which it had to be almost completely rebuilt.

The highlight of the academy is the **Cathedral of St George**, built in the mid 1400s, with a fine late-Gothic interior (though like the rest of the academy, it was completely rebuilt after WWII). It was rededicated to St George in 1479, after the Order of the Knights of St George moved their headquarters to Wiener Neustadt. Maximilian I, who was born in the castle, is buried under the altar, while on the exterior of the church you'll find the Wappenwand – a collection of heraldic coats of arms dating from 1453. Only 14 of the heraldic arms are real – the rest were invented by Peter von Pusica, the church's architect.

AUSTRO-HUNGARIAN STRIKE OF JANUARY 1918

The Austro-Hungarian strike of January 1918 – in which workers demanded improved working and living conditions and an end to WWI, and which spread like wildfire across Austria – began in Wiener Neustadt.

Inspired by the October Revolution in Russia the previous year, workers at the Daimler Motor factory (which like most factories was involved in production for the war), most of them women, walked out following a reduction in flour rations, and marched on the town hall, where they were joined by workers from other major factories.

NATURE PARKS IN LOWER AUSTRIA: OUR PICKS

Lower Austria has 20 nature parks, ranging from alpine peaks and pastures to low-lying wetland areas.

Heidenreichstein Nature Park: Beautiful wetland area with raised peat bog in northwest Waldviertel.

Hohe Wand Nature Park: Between Schneeberg and Wiener Neustadt, with great views from its skywalk and cliff walkway, plus llama and alpaca trekking for kids.

Kamptal-Schönberg Nature Park: Where the southeast corner of the Waldviertel merges into the landscape of Kamptal, with its quiet villages and vineyards.

Nordwald Nature Park: West of Waldviertel, with rare plant life, and forests reminiscent of Scandinavia.

Ötscher-Tormäuer Nature Park: Rugged area between the Wachau Valley and Mariazell, with some stupendous gorges.

Semmeringbahn

Semmering

TIME FROM VIENNA: 1¼HRS

Europe's first alpine railway

The **Semmeringbahn** *(semmeringbahn.at)* is a historic railway line, completed in 1854 by the Venetian-born engineer Karl Ritter von Ghega. It runs 41km between Gloggnitz and Mürzzuschlag, rising some 457m to its highest point of 896m at Semmering Bahnhof. The Semmering line was Europe's first true alpine railway, built with standard rather than narrow-gauge tracks, and for its time it was an incredible feat of engineering – it took more than 20,000 workers almost six years to complete. Due to its engineering genius, the Semmeringbahn gained UNESCO World Heritage status in 1998.

Today, it continues to impresses with its scenic mountain views, including precipitous cliffs and forested hills, and succession of tunnels and viaducts (15 of the former, 16 of the latter, some of them two-storeyed). The most scenic section is the 30-minute stretch between Semmering and Payerbach *(single €4.20)*. From Vienna, most express services heading to Graz stop at Mürzzuschlag, from where you take a regional train to Semmering; some express services also stop at Semmering.

Hikes around Semmering

Semmering itself is a popular but low-key resort, still favoured for its proximity to Vienna (a direct train takes just 1¼ hours) and for family skiing. There are plenty of hiking trails in the area: one of these goes from the town centre up over 1292m Pinkenkogel, 1403m Ochnerhöhe and 1535m Kampalpe, to finish in Spital am Semmering, from where you can take the train back to Semmering – the trail is 14.5km and takes around five hours. Another circular trail heads southeast from the town centre to 1523m Sonnwendstein, where you can stop for a bite at Pollereshütte, before returning via 1504m Erzkogel and 1340m Hirschkogel (11.5km, 4½ hours).

Puchberg am Schneeberg TIME FROM VIENNA: 1½HRS
Historic mountain railway & hiking

To the north of Semmering are two of Lower Austria's highest peaks: **Schneeberg** (2076m) and **Raxalpe** (2007m), part of the Rax-Schneeberg group. The area is easily reached by train from Vienna, making it a popular hiking destination. The Schneebergbahn cog railway, which was completed in 1897, leaves from Puchberg am Schneeberg and takes about 40 minutes to reach the station at Hochschneeberg, at an elevation of 1800m. It's a modern diesel train – named after and painted something like a salamander for some reason – though a vintage steam train makes the run a couple of times a month, and takes a more sedate 1½ hours. Puchberg is just 45 minutes by train from Wiener Neustadt.

From the upper station, a straightforward 7.5km circular hiking route heads past the super-homely Damböckhaus mountain hut, and takes in the 2076m Hochschneeberg/Klosterwappen before looping past the well-placed Fischerhütte on the way back to the station (allow three hours' walking time).

On the southern side of Schneeberg is the scenic **Höllental** (Hell's Valley), a deep, narrow gorge created by the Schwarza River. From Hirschwang an der Rax, a small village in Höllental, the Rax-Seilbahn cable car ascends to 1547m, from where there are plenty of hiking trails, and there are more than half a dozen mountain huts in the area. The Rax-Seilbahn is the site of Austria's first cable car, built in 1926.

Payerbach TIME FROM VIENNA: 1HR
Modernist Architecture

On the south side of the Höllental, above Payerbach, is the **Looshaus**. This small mountain hotel is also something of an architectural pilgrimage site for anyone interested in 20th-century design. It's a late work by Austrian modernist architect Adolf Loos: a private country home that was completed in 1930 for Viennese industrialist Paul Khuner (whose fortune arose from inventing an early form of margarine). The home was bought and renovated by the present owners' grandmother in 1959, and has been run as a hotel and restaurant ever since. In keeping with Loos' style, the rooms have a simple, functional aesthetic – very different to the decorative style that characterises the art and architecture of the Viennese Secession.

KOKOSCHKA IN PÖCHLARN

Oskar Kokoschka, one of the great towering figures of modern art and the forerunner of the Viennese Expressionist movement, was born in Pöchlarn, a small town just a few kilometres west of Melk.

The house where he was born and spent the first few years of his life, before being accepted into the Kunstgewerbeschule (now the University of Applied Arts) in Vienna, is now open as the **Kokoschka Museum** *(oskarkokoschka.at; €8)*. During the summer months, it stages themed exhibitions centred on various aspects of Kokoschka's oeuvre.

THE MARIAZELLERBAHN

For another scenic railway, ride the Mariazellerbahn (p136), which connects St Pölten with the pilgrimage site of Mariazell in Styria.

Waldviertel & Weinviertel

PRISTINE NATURE | FALCONRY & CASTLES | ROLLING VINEYARDS

Places
Nationalpark Thayatal p144
Kamptal Reservoirs p145
Zwettl p146
Waldreichs p146
Rosenburg am Kamp p146
Drosendorf p147
Langenlois p147
Weinviertel p148

GETTING AROUND

With a little planning, it's easy enough to reach the far north of Waldviertel by public transport. You can travel between Drosendorf and Retz on a vintage train, the **Reblaus Express** *(reblausexpress.at)*, which runs at weekends and on Fridays during the summer months. It goes through a landscape of gentle hills and vineyards, and takes you within walking or cycling distance of Thayatal. The train's Heurigenwaggon serves local wines, and you can take bicycles onboard for free.

North of the Danube, the rolling hills of Waldviertel stretch up to the Czech border. It's here that you'll find the small but perfectly formed Nationalpark Thayatal, centred on a beautiful valley of the River Thaya – a great place for hiking and cycling, with plenty of wildlife. Also in the north is the little town of Drosendorf, with its well-preserved medieval walls. Across the centre of Waldviertel, Kamptal has vineyards and a series of large, idyllic reservoirs, while Schloss Waldreichs and Schloss Rosenburg are famous for their amazing falconry displays, easily among the best in Austria.

East of Waldviertel lies Austria's largest wine region, Weinviertel, a gently undulating landscape with vineyards stretching to the horizon. It's dotted with villages, good for exploring by bike – and it goes without saying that this is a region where you should stop at as many vineyards and *Heurigen* as you possibly can.

Nationalpark Thayatal

Home of the wildcat

In the Weinviertel's northwestern reaches, hugging the border between Austria and Czechia, lies the 13.6-sq-km **Nationalpark Thayatal** *(np-thayatal.at)*, Austria's smallest national park. Despite this, Thayatal has extraordinary bio-diversity and 44% of Austria's native flora is found here. The rich wildlife here includes the highly elusive feline, the European wildcat, once thought to have disappeared from Austria long ago, but was recorded here in 2007. You can also see otters, black storks and white-tailed eagles.

It's a beautiful landscape – one of Central Europe's last natural river valleys, with most of the park made up of scattered meadows and mixed forest, through which the River Thaya meanders. There are several hiking trails – the walk to the **Überstieg viewpoint** has excellent views. There's also a cycle route, the **Nationalpark Thayatal Radweg**, which makes

TASTING WINE IN KAMPTAL

Weingut Bründlmayer: Award-winning Grüner Veltliner, Riesling, sparkling wine and more from prestigious vineyards around Langenlois. *bruendlmayer.at*

Weingut Hirsch: Top-notch Grüner Veltliner and Riesling produced on a 500-year-old farmstead. *weingut-hirsch.at*

Weingut Schloss Gobelsburg: Award-winning wines from outside Langenlois, with vineyards arranged around a castle, each with its own distinctive terroir.

Weingut Brandl: Vineyard on the prestigious conglomerate sandstone of Heiligenstein, near Zöbing.

Ursin Haus: Large wine shop in Langenlois, with around 300 wines from 60 Kamptal winemakers. *ursinhaus.at*

a 40km loop from Hardegg, heading through Niederfladnitz before switching to the Czech side of the border and returning though Lukov.

You can find more information on hikes and cycle routes at the **National Park Office**, located between Merkersdorf and Hardegg. E-bikes can also be hired here.

Kamptal Reservoirs

Swim, SUP & sail

The **Ottenstein**, **Dobra** and **Thurnberg reservoirs** stretch along the River Kamp, at the heart of the Waldviertel. Surrounded by forests and meadows, their shores dotted with castle ruins, the three reservoirs were formed in the 1950s when the Kamp was dammed to provide electricity – Ottenstein (in the west) is the largest, Thurnberg (in the east) is the smallest. Together they offer gentle hiking and cycling trails, along with kayaking, stand-up paddleboarding and sailing, or refreshing swimming off the usual tourist trail. There's a campground on Dobra's northern shore, and places to rent SUPs and other watercraft.

EATING & DRINKING IN WALDVIERTEL: OUR PICKS

Esslokal: Michelin-starred dining in Hadersdorf, just outside Langenlois. *6-8.30pm Tue-Thu, noon-1.30pm & 6-8.30pm Fri & Sat* €€€

Landgasthof Mann: Restaurant and guesthouse run by the same family for five generations, across the river from Schloss Rosenburg. *7am-10pm Wed-Sat, 7am-3pm Sun* €€

Waldschenke Schreiber: On the edge of the forest northwest of Zwettl, championing regional dishes and seasonal ingredients. *from 11am Fri & Sat, from 9am Sun* €€

Cafe und Wein: It's in the name – good coffee, local wines and a short but well-priced menu, set in Langenlois' main square. *9am-11pm Tue-Sat, to 6pm Sun & Mon* €

☑ TOP TIP

Weinviertel is a fantastic cycling destination, with plenty of cycle-friendly restaurants and hotels – look for places certified as RADfreundliche Betriebe. With its easy terrain, quiet roads and greenways it's particularly well suited to families cycling with kids.

FALCONRY

Austria has a long history of falconry, which is inscribed on the UNESCO list of Intangible Cultural Heritage. The falconry displays at **Schloss Rosenburg** and **Schloss Waldreichs** are up there with those at Burg Hohenwerfen as the best in Austria – including, at Schloss Rosenburg, historical falconry displays on horseback.

'Falconry' is not restricted to falcons and hawks – a wide range of other birds of prey, including eagles, kites and kestrels, are all used to hunt, and they all hunt in different ways.

The best place to learn more about the history of falconry is the **Falconry Museum** at the Lower Austrian Falconry & Bird of Prey Centre, founded by Austria's leading falconry expert, Josef Hiebeler.

Seecamp Ottenstein *(campingottenstein.at)* on the north shore of Stausee Ottenstein has SUPs, kayaks, rowing boats and paddle boats to rent; and **Enjoy4Elements** rents SUPs from several locations in the area including **Camping Dobra** *(camping-dobra.at)*.

Zwettl
From medieval to Hundertwasser

The little town of Zwettl, located on the River Kamp and home of the Zwettler Brewery since 1708, features 900m of unexpectedly impressive **medieval walls**, which include six surviving towers. There's a **Hundertwasser fountain** on the pretty main square too.

Zwettl is also the starting point for an easy 13km marked hiking trail, the **Wasserwunderweg 55a** *(Water Wonders Trail)*, which takes in peaceful woodland, riverbanks and towering blocks of granite, along with two more works by Hundertwasser – a water mill, and the museum in Roiten where the trail finishes.

A 12th-century Cistercian abbey

The rather splendid **Stift Zwettl** *(Zwettl Abbey)* lies around 3km northeast of the town centre, near the western end of the Ottenstein Reservoir. Founded in 1138 by monks from Heiligenkreuz, this Cistercian abbey has a particularly beautiful 13th-century cloister, a Romanesque chapter house (the oldest surviving Cistercian chapter), while the abbey church has a late Gothic hall choir. There are audio guides for the abbey available in English.

You can reach the abbey easily enough on foot, following part of the Thayaquellenwanderweg – cross the River Kamp on the northern side of town, then cross the river again at Neumühle.

Waldreichs
Austria's pre-eminent falconry centre

Schloss Waldreichs, which lies on the road to nowhere near the Ottenstein and Dobra reservoirs, is home to the excellent **Lower Austrian Falconry & Bird of Prey Centre** *(greifvogelzentrum.at; €12)*. There are about 60 birds at the centre – including various eagles, falcons and several species of owl. The falconry displays are held at 11am and 3pm Friday to Sunday during summer.

Rosenburg am Kamp
Falconry displays at a Renaissance castle

This huge and beautifully preserved Renaissance castle and its setting are quintessential Waldviertel – perched on a crag above Kamptal, bristling with towers and overlooking rolling, wooded hills. The big drawcard for most visitors are the historical falconry displays, which take place in the huge medieval tilting (jousting) ground at **Schloss Rosenburg** *(rosenburg.at; €17)*, at 11am and 3pm. The castle also hosts

Schloss Rosenburg

opera and other performances. It's a 20-minute walk from the train station to the castle – cross the footbridge over the River Kamp and follow the marked footpath uphill.

Drosendorf

Waldviertel's walled town

On the northern fringe of the Waldviertel, above a prominent bend in the River Thaya near the Czech border, the lovely little fortressed town of Drosendorf is often overlooked – it's simply too far flung. Yet, with completely intact town walls, it's a beautiful, unique place and well worth the trouble it takes to reach it. A fortress walk passes the **castle** and exits through the **Hornertor**, the main gate in the southeast, dating from the 13th to 15th centuries. Cross the moat and follow the wall clockwise. To reach Drosendorf from Vienna, take a train to Retz, then bus 875 – or better still, the Reblaus Express (p144).

Langenlois

Gateway to Kamptal

The pretty but hard-working town of Langenlois lies at the centre of the wine-growing Kamptal. Lush lowlands meet gently rolling hills and vines stretch as far as the eye can see. White wines – Grüner Veltliner, Riesling, Welschriesling and Weissburgunder in particular – reach stellar heights here, and the town square is full of *Vinothek* (wine merchants) and seemingly every lane and road is lined with *Heurigen* or cellar doors.

LOISIUM WeinWelt *(loisium.at; €17.50)* is a paean to Langenlois' long history of wine growing. Audio tours last 1½ hours and lead you through a 1.5km network of ancient and deep tunnels where wine is stored, and finish with a wine tasting. Head southeast to Grafenegg for top-notch classical concerts in the castle grounds.

GREY GOLD

Along with its stellar wines, there is another, less widely known product for which the Waldviertel is celebrated – poppy seeds.

The climate of the Waldviertel is particularly well suited to growing poppies – plenty of warm sunny days, cool nights and heavy dews – and between 200 and 700 hectares are given over to their cultivation, mostly in the area around Armschlag. Ottenschlag is renowned for producing poppy-seed oil. The 'Waldland' grey poppy seeds from the Waldviertel have PDO (protected designation of origin) status, and are even traded on the London Stock Exchange.

The dish you need to taste while you're here is obviously *Mohnstrudel,* a delicious strudel filled with poppy seed paste – although you'll find many other culinary specialities concocted around poppy seeds.

Weinviertel

A Trip into the Green

East of Waldviertel lies the Weinviertel, Austria's largest wine-growing region, with 130 sq km of vineyards. Grüner Veltliner is the main grape variety, with other varieties grown including Riesling, Pinot blanc, Traminer, Zweigelt and Blauer Portugieser. The Grüner Veltliners from the Weinviertel is characterised by their peppery notes, and the region was the first in Austria to obtain protected Designation of Origin status (Weinviertel DAC). Traditional cellar lanes, *Kellergasse*, are a characteristic of the region. These white-painted cellar buildings, once used to produce and store wine, are a distinctive part of the landscape, and are now used for festive occasions. The **Weinviertel Weinstrasse** stretches some 400km, starting from Heldenberg and taking in the Schmidatal and Pulkautal valleys, Retz, Falkenstein, Poysdorf, Mistelbach, the hilly landscape of the Matzner Hügel and Wolkersdorf.

There is plenty of scope for cycling – including from one end of the 423km Kamp-Thaya-March Cycle Route. The **Weinviertel tourist office** *(weinviertel.at/radfahren)* website has a good selection of cycle routes in the region. One of these is the **Weinviertel DAC Radtour**, a 56km circular route starting in Retz, and taking in several villages including Zellendorf, Roseldorf, Röschitz and Pulkau, with plenty of places to stop for wine along the way.

IN D'GREAN GEHEN

A popular custom in Weinviertel is *'in d'Grean gehen'* ('taking an outing into the greenery'). This derives from an old tradition where winemakers would invite their workers to their cellars on Easter Monday to try the new vintage, as an expression of thanks after all the hard winter's work.

Going for a relaxed walk 'into the green' of the vineyards, and enjoying a glass of wine in the cellar lanes – these days with family and friends – is still an important custom in the Weinviertel.

The good news is you can experience *'in d'Grean gehen'* between the end of March and the end of May; many vineyards offer this as a seasonal activity for visitors.

NATIONAL PARKS IN LOWER AUSTRIA & BURGENLAND

Along with Thayatal, there are two other national parks in the low-lying states of Lower Austria and Burgenland: **Donau-Auen** and **Neusiedler See-Seewinkel** (p153).

EATING & DRINKING IN WEINVIERTEL: OUR PICKS

Landgasthaus Winkelhofer: Family-run spot with meat and veg from their farm. Between Langenlois and Eggendorf. *11am-10pm Sat & 11am-6pm Sun* €€	**Buschenschank Humer:** *Heuriger* and winery on the outskirts of Maissau, with views across the landscape from the terrace. *seasonal hours. Wed-Sat, 7am-3pm Sun* €	**Gasthaus mit Gästehaus Bsteh:** 200-year-old inn near Laa an der Thaya. *9am-2.30pm & 5-10pm Mon & Fri, 9am-2.30pm Thu, 9am-10pm Sat, 9am-3pm Sun* €€	**Franz Joseph Wirtshaus:** Set on the main square in Obermarkersdorf, 5km from Retz. Traditional dishes with contemporary flair. *10am-10pm Wed-Sun, 9am-4pm Sun* €€
Pollak's Wirtshaus – Der Retzbacherhof: Super place near Retz, with local wine. *10am-3pm & 5-11pm Thu & Fri, 10am- 11pm Sat, 10am-4pm Sun* €€	**Gasthaus Herbst:** Old inn near Laa an der Thaya, serving traditional Weinviertel dishes. *10am-9.30pm Wed-Sat, to 2.30pm Sun* €€	**Gastwirtschaft Neunläuf:** Award-winning traditional restaurant in Hobersdorf, serving local cuisine. *9am-11pm Wed-Sat, 10am-6pm Sun* €€	**Gasthaus Zum alten Zollhaus:** Family-run restaurant in Korneuburg near the Danube. *9am-10pm Mon, Wed-Fri, 9.30am-3pm Sat & Sun* €€

Beyond Waldviertel & Weinviertel

Europe's greatest river in all its unspoilt splendour.

Stretching from the eastern city limits of Vienna to the border with Slovakia, the March-Donauland is dominated by the Danube and its natural flood plains – a flat area at the heart of which lies Nationalpark Donau-Auen. The Danube as you'll see and experience it in Nationalpark Donau-Auen is very different to the more familiar Danube of river cruises, fine wines and tourist brochures – despite its proximity to the Austrian capital, this is as close to untamed as you'll find it in Austria. The surrounding, level countryside is dotted with industry, but is still quite pretty. The town of Carnuntum is worth visiting for its Roman history. The main drawcard, however, is Donau-Auen National Park, centred along a 38km stretch of the Danube – a place of riparian forests, wet and dry meadows, oxbow lakes and extraordinary wildlife.

The easiest way to visit these areas is as day trips from Vienna – it's easy to reach both Donau-Auen National Park and Carnuntum by train.

Nationalpark Donau-Auen

TIME FROM VIENNA: 40MINS

Europe's last great floodplain landscape

The Danube east of Vienna is protected as far as the Slovak border as the Nationalpark Donau-Auen. It was founded in 1996, although the initial drive towards protecting this area goes back to the 1970s. Covering some 96 sq km, the national park is home to a whole host of wildlife, including Eurasian beavers, European pond turtles, elk and white-tailed eagles – magnificent birds, formerly extinct in Austria, which have been breeding here in these Danube wetlands since 2005.

The gateway to the national park is the **schlossORTH National Park Centre**, housed in a medieval moated castle in Orth an der Donau, and another visitor centre close to Vienna, the **wien-lobAU National Park House**. There are plenty of interactive displays, making it fun to visit with kids, plus an observation tower (one of the castle turrets) with sweeping views of the surrounding landscape and a walk-in underwater observation area. A Renaissance spiral staircase, spanning three floors of the castle and dating from the 16th century, was restored in 2022 and is also now accessible to the public.

Places
Nationalpark Donau-Auen p149
Carnuntum p150

GETTING AROUND

Reaching Nationalpark Donau-Auen from Vienna is straightforward by bus – the 550 runs from Wien Aspernstrasse to Orth/Donau, the main gateway to the park. The river landscapes of the park itself are best explored on foot, or on a guided boat trip with a park ranger.

On the south bank of the Danube, Petronell-Carnuntum is 45 minutes by S-Bahn from Wien Rennweg.

Both Nationalpark Donau-Auen and Petronell-Carnuntum lie on the Danube Cycle Path, via the Orth-Haslau ferry.

THE RIVER RUNS WILD

Along with the Wachau, Nationalpark Donau-Auen has the last free-flowing stretch of the Danube in Austria – the rest of its course has been canalised and tamed since the 19th century to improve navigation, with fixed embankments and dredging. From the 1950s it has been compartmentalised by the building of hydroelectric power plants.

In the national park the river is free to flood, ensuring the survival of crucial habitats like riparian forest – wetland forest, which is flooded several times a year and where otherwise rare and endangered tree species are common.

Along with these wetland forests, there's a patchwork of steppe-like dry meadows rich in wildflowers, along with floodplain meadows, and a network of water channels and oxbow lakes.

Danube bicycle ride

One of the best ways to experience this watery wilderness is on a boat trip or a guided walk with a national-park guide. There are also plenty of hiking trails to explore under your own steam (though you should pay particular attention to flood warnings in this area – don't try walking a trail if it's marked as closed). Some of these start from the schlossORTH National Park Centre, including the 5km **Orth Circular Trail** (Orther Rundwanderweg), which explores a wedge between two water channels, Fadenbach and Klein Binn, where you have a good chance of seeing beavers. Or from Schönau an der Donau, the 2km **Schönau Danube Trail** (Schönauer Donaurunde) makes its way to the Danube Towpath, through stretches of riparian forest and with footbridges across a swift-flowing branch of the river, with plenty of birdlife including herons and kingfishers.

Carnuntum

TIME FROM VIENNA: **45MINS**

Traces of Rome

The Roman settlement of Carnuntum, located 45km east of Vienna (45 minutes by S-Bahn), was the most important political and military centre in the empire's northeast, once known as Upper Pannonia. Founded in the 1st century CE, it grew and thrived over the next 400 years or so, becoming a major civilian as well as military city. With a population of 50,000 at its peak, it made Vienna look like a village in comparison. It was abandoned to the Huns in the 5th century.

A visit to Carnuntum encompasses several sites including a reconstructed Roman city quarter and the remains of an amphitheatre and a triumphal arch (the so-called Heathen's Gate). The **Museum Carnuntinum** (carnuntum.at; €14) is also worth seeing – it was built in the style of a Roman villa and opened in 1904, with exhibits from various collections across Lower Austria. One ticket covers entry to all the sites.

Neusiedler See

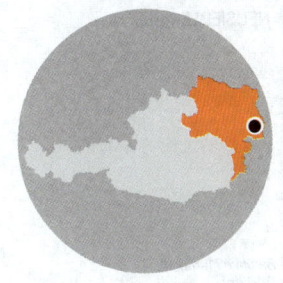

STEPPE LAKE | BIRD-WATCHING | SUPERB WINES

In the far-flung, easternmost state of Burgenland, on the edge of the Pannonian Plain, you are a far cry from the snow-streaked mountains for which Austria is often synonymous – or indeed from many hills of any size. And yet Neusiedler See is one of the country's most breathtaking natural landscapes – a huge, shallow body of water stretching southwards and spilling over the border into Hungary – and one of its finest wine-producing areas. It's a fantastic place to visit whether it's cycling, bird-watching, wine tasting or beach time that grabs your fancy. Schloss Esterházy is an impressive palace in the state capital Eisenstadt, which is inextricably tied to the music and career of the great composer Joseph Haydn.

There are sleepy lakeside towns where storks make their ragged nests on rooftops, as well as watersports, spa resorts and some huge music festivals – from Austria's largest open-air rock festival to the world's largest open-air operetta stage, on the shores of Neusiedler See. Rust and Purbach am See are among the most charming villages on the west side of the lake, while Illmitz on the eastern shore is the main gateway for bird-watching and cycling. Here at Neusiedler See the wines are phenomenal, the welcome in its taverns warm and genuine, and it's hard not to like a place that promises 300 days a year of sunshine.

GETTING AROUND

Neusiedler See and Eisenstadt are easily reached from Vienna by train – Neusiedl am See is just 40 minutes direct from Wien Hauptbahnhof; Eisenstadt just over one hour either direct or via Wiener Neustadt. Bus 280 runs between Neusiedl am See, Purbach and Eisenstadt.

The best way to explore the region is by bicycle, with some wonderful cycle routes and several places to rent bikes and e-bikes locally.

Ferry options across the lake include Illmitz to Mörbisch, and Podersdorf to Rust.

Explore Neusiedler See

Austria's greatest lake

Often called a steppe lake, Neusiedler See is more correctly an endorheic lake, that is, it has no natural outflow – which means it's dried up a few times in recorded history – and it sits amid a great sprawling mosaic of landscapes and habitat types, including wetlands, meadows, dry grasslands, salt ponds and a vast reed belt.

NEUSIEDLER SEE

✓ TOP TIP

While it's also an easy day trip from Vienna, Neusiedler See is an area that lends itself best to slowing down. Hire bicycles, explore the unique landscapes and extraordinary birdlife around the lake, stop at vineyards and *Heurigen* to sample excellent wines and enjoy the region's rich, earthy cuisine.

★ HIGHLIGHTS
1 Schloss Esterházy

● SIGHTS
2 Basilica and Pilgrimage Church of Maria Loretto
3 Bergkirche
4 Breitenbrunn Neuer Strand
5 Jois Lakeside Resort
6 Kellergasse
7 Podersdorf am See Lakeside Recreation Area
8 Weingut Esterházy

● SLEEPING
9 Restaurant & Hotel Braunstein

● EATING
10 Buschenschank Peter Schandl
11 das Fritz
12 Die Sandhofer
see 12 Fossil
13 Gasthaus Zum fröhlichen Arbeiter
14 Gasthaus zur Dankbarkeit
see 12 Gut Purbach
15 Heimlichwirt
16 Im Hofgassl
17 Taubenkogel
18 Weingut-Buschenschank Preschitz

● SHOPPING
19 Haus am Kellerplatz – Leithaberg DAC
20 WeinKulturHaus Gols
21 Weinwerk Burgenland

● INFORMATION
22 National Park Information Centre

● TRANSPORT
23 Fahrräder Bucsis
24 Radhaus Erwin
25 Radsport Waldherr
26 Radverleih Mürner

There are many ways to explore Neusiedler See. You can join a **guided tour** with a national-park ranger, or head off on a cycling or hiking trail. Visit the **National Park Information Centre** at Illmitz to enquire about guided tours. The best way to explore the area around the lake is by bicycle – you can also hire bikes or, better yet, e-bikes (it gets surprisingly windy around the lake) in Illmitz; **Radverleih Mürner** (p160) is the main rental outfit in town. Another great way to get an in-depth experience of the lake is to take a **boat tour** with a ranger, which is really the only way to see the great labyrinth of the reed belt up close.

Birding at Neusiedler See
One of Austria's top birding spots

Neusiedler See is one of Austria's greatest birding hotspots, with over 350 species recorded, and about half of them breeding here. It's a hugely important stopover on winter migration routes, and along with great egrets, purple herons, spoonbills, avocets, stilts and other wading birds, you can spot iconic sea eagles and great bustards (huge birds with a wingspan of over 2m, reckoned to be the world's heaviest flying bird). Also here are bee-eaters, golden orioles, an enormous breeding population of greylag geese and masses of migrating cranes in winter. Much of this area is protected as the **Nationalpark Neusiedler See-Seewinkel** (and continues into Hungary as the Fertő-Hanság National Park); and it's been a UNESCO World Heritage Site since 2001 and a transborder Ramsar site since 2009. Along with all the birdlife here, you can also see breeds of domestic animals, such as Hungarian grey cattle and white donkeys, as well as a few water buffalo.

The **National Park Information Centre** at Illmitz, near Neusiedler See's eastern shore, is the best place to find out more about the lake, its surroundings and amazing birdlife. Tours with a park ranger can be arranged at the National Park Information Centre.

SUP & Swim at Neusiedler See
Enjoy the 'sea'side

If swimming, SUPing in Austria it in Austria it in Austria it in Austria it in Austria, sunbathing or kitesurfing are more your thing, Neusiedler See has you well covered, with several resorts and bathing areas, particularly on the western shore. The shallow depth and gentle gradient make it an excellent

BURGENLAND CARD

If you are staying overnight in Eisenstadt or in towns on the Neusiedler See – or anywhere else in Burgenland for that matter – make sure you get a Burgenland Card, which gives you free use of local bus services as well as free or discounted admission to many sights.

Some hotels issue the card when you check in, others give you a printout of your registration form, which you can take to an issuing office (tourist offices are the easiest), where you'll be given the card.

In either case, the Burgenland Card is free and valid for the entire duration of your stay. See burgenland.info for more information.

EATING & DRINKING AROUND NEUSIEDLER SEE: OUR PICKS

Die Sandhofer: Excellent *Heuriger* on historic Kellergasse in Purbach, with delicious food and wine on a vine-covered terrace. *noon-9pm Wed-Sun* €€

Weingut-Buschenschank Preschitz: Traditional *Heuriger* in the centre of Neusiedl am See. *from 4.30pm Wed-Sat Apr-Sep* €

Buschenschank Peter Schandl: Popular *Heuriger* in Rust with award-winning wines and tables shaded by grape vines. *4-9pm Mon, Thu & Fri, 11.30am-9pm Sat & Sun* €€

das Fritz: Modern restaurant in Weiden am See with a waterfront location and a buzzy atmosphere. *breakfast 9-11am, lunch 11.30am-2pm* €€

NEUSIEDLER SEE BY BICYCLE

Neusiedler See and its surroundings are a dream come true for cyclists, with wonderful landscapes, spectacular wildlife, pretty towns and villages.

START	END	LENGTH
National Park Information Centre	Lange Lacke	50km; 4hrs

Lackenradweg (Lacken Cycle Trail) is the route described here, a 52km relatively flat loop starting from Illmitz that takes you through the heart of the national park; it's the best for birdlife. For a longer route, try the 125km Neusiedler See Radweg. Decide which way to go – clockwise or anticlockwise – based on the wind's direction.

From the ❶ **National Park Information Centre** (p153) in Illmitz, head southwest through the town, passing intermittent salt ponds to the picnic area at ❷ **Sandeck**, a good place to see white donkeys and Hungarian grey cattle. Head north, passing the departure point for the ferry to Mörbisch am See, then bear right through vineyards to reach another picnic area and observation deck at one end of a larger salt pond, ❸ **Zicklacke**. Head left and keep heading north, passing more vineyards and a series of large salt ponds at the charmingly named ❹ **Upper and Lower Stinkersee** – an area known as Hölle (Hell). There's another picnic area, a drinking-water fountain and an observation tower here. Turn right at Podersdorf am See and head southeast to the 3D info point at St Andrä am Zicksee. Then sweep along the southern edge of ❺ **Lange Lacke** and pass two more salt ponds, Darscho and Grosse Neubrucklacke, before turning south again past more vineyards to arrive back in Illmitz.

Zicklacke is one of the distinctive salt ponds which dot the landscape surrounding Neusiedler See, their high salinity creating a highly specialised ecosystem where plants have adapted to the salt content.

Close to the lake, the Sandeck picnic area has an old border watchtower nearby (a relic of the Iron Curtain), and often white donkeys in the vicinity.

The National Park Information Centre is the best place to find information about Neusiedler See.

spot for families. **Podersdorf am See Lakeside Recreation Area** offers 1.4km of supremely accessible waterfront, and is also good for kitesurfing and windsurfing. **Jois Lakeside Resort** has a nice laid-back lakeside meadow for swimming and sunbathing, with boat hire also available. **Breitenbrunn**, on the western shore, has a pebble beach, as well as kitesurfing and windsurfing schools.

Wild, Wild Horses
The Przewalski horse

As well as the Hungarian grey cattle and white donkeys around Neusiedler See, you might be lucky enough to see a Przewalski horse. This little horse, considered by many the last remaining wild horse, was reduced to only 31 surviving animals after WWII. Since then there have been many conservation efforts and reintroductions, though the Przewalski horse is still listed as endangered by the International Union for Conservation of Nature. Around a dozen of them live near the eastern shores of Neusiedler See, where their grazing forms part of the pasture management within the national park. You might spot some of them when following one of the cycling routes in the area.

Neusiedler See Wine Region
Some of Austria's finest wines

The landscape east of Neusiedler See is home to the small but very highly regarded Neusiedler See wine region. The area is noted for its rich, fruity Zweigelt, and has gained Designation of Origin status (Neusiedlersee DAC, introduced from the 2012 vintage). Gols, Frauenkirchen, Mönchhof, Halbturn, Jois and Winden am See are some of the notable places for wine production around the northeast side of the lake. Sticky sweet dessert wines, typically made from Welschriesling, are also a speciality (and were added to the Neusiedlersee DAC in 2020), and Eiswein - sweet dessert wine is produced from grapes which have been frozen - is also made here. Production of these is centred on the area between Podersdorf, Illmitz and Apetlon, with its associated microclimates and sandy soils, and you might have noticed that this is also one of the core areas of the national park. Neusiedler See is a rare thing, a place where small vineyards, salt lakes, fragile ecosystems and epic birdlife all seem able to coexist happily side by side. *Prost* to that.

Weingut Esterházy is one of the vineyards in Burgenland producing Eiswein.

TASTING WINE IN BURGENLAND

Vinothek Burgenland: Wine shop in Deutschkreutz with around 450 top wines from Burgenland.
Haus am Kellerplatz – Leithaberg DAC: Wine shop in Purbach stocking around 350 wines from the Leithaberg DAC at vineyard prices.
WeinKulturHaus Gols: Over 400 wines from almost 100 local winemakers, in a historic cellar in Gols.
Weinwerk Burgenland: In Neusiedl am See, with over 650 wines from Burgenland, and other local products.
Gebietsvinothek Deutschkreutz: In Deutschkreutz in the southern Burgenland wine region – serious Blaufränkisch territory – with over 400 wines from Burgenland.
Vinothek Friedl: Large wine shop on the outskirts of Oberpullendorf, with over 400 wines from Burgenland, Styria and Lower Austria.
weinfachhandel.at

 EATING & DRINKING AROUND NEUSIEDLER SEE: OUR PICKS

Gasthaus zur Dankbarkeit: Landmark traditional restaurant in Podersdorf am See. *11.30am-2pm & 6-9pm Thu & Fri, 11.30am-9pm Sat & Sun* €€

Heimlichwirt: A good value lunchtime menu and an emphasis on local farm produce, in the centre of Gols. *lunch 11.45am-1.15pm Tue-Fri, dinner 4pm-midnight Tue-Sat* €€

Gasthaus Zum fröhlichen Arbeiter: Family-run restaurant in Apetlon, with local dishes. *10am-2pm & 6-11pm Mon & Tue, 6-11pm Fri, 9am-11pm Sat, 9am-9pm Sun* €€

Weingut Braunstein: Family-run restaurant and hotel in Purbach am See, with wines from their 400-year-old vineyard. *11.30am-9pm Mon & Thu-Sat, 11.30am-9pm Sun* €€

HAYDN IN EISENSTADT

Joseph Haydn was employed by the Esterházy family as *Kapellmeister* for around 30 years, then again in his later years, by which time he was the most celebrated composer in Europe.

He wrote some of his best-known works for his Esterházy employers, including his famous Nelson Mass, which Nelson himself probably attended a performance of when he visited Eisenstadt in 1800. The Mass was actually written a couple of years earlier for the Esterházys, but gradually acquired its name following Nelson's victory at the Battle of the Nile.

Initially buried in Vienna, Haydn's remains were later transferred to Eisenstadt, and in 1953 were placed in the Haydn Mausoleum, which forms part of Haydn Church (Bergkirche).

Schloss Esterházy

Get to Know Eisenstadt

Burgenland's small, elegant capital

Eisenstadt, easy to reach by train from Vienna, has some pretty streets in the old town centre, no shortage of good wine and a hugely impressive palace. From 1648 to 1921, Eisenstadt was the seat of the Hungarian noble family, Esterházy, under the Habsburgs and the Dual Monarchy. However, the town is perhaps best known for its most famous former resident, the great 18th-century musician and composer Joseph Haydn, who was *Kapellmeister* to the Esterházys.

The main reason to come to Eisenstadt is to see the extraordinary **Schloss Esterházy** *(esterhazy.at; €19)*, which dominates one side of Esterházyplatz. Originally a castle, the palace received its lavish baroque makeover in the 17th century under Paul I Esterházy; later, in the early 1800s, Nikolaus II Esterházy set about remodelling it in Neoclassical style. However, his planned changes were only partially realised, such as the grandiose entrance built on one side of Haydn Hall – complete with Corinthian columns and overlooking manicured parks and gardens, it was intended as the main entrance. The highlight of the palace is Haydn Hall, the scale and decorations of which are breathtaking, and its acoustics are excellent; look out for concert performances that take place here.

EATING AROUND NEUSIEDLER SEE: FINE DINING

Im Hofgassl: Michelin-listed restaurant in Rust. Traditional, regional dishes with seasonal ingredients and a contemporary twist. *11am-11pm Wed-Sun* €€€

Gut Purbach: Set in a 16th-century farmhouse in Purbach am See, Michelin green-star-awarded Gut Purbach is renowned for its offal dishes. *4-11pm Wed, 11am-11pm Thu-Sat* €€€

Fossil: Set in a traditional old keller in Purbach am See. Awarded a Michelin Bib Gourmand for its excellent quality and good value cuisine. *noon-10pm Wed-Sun* €€€

Taubenkogel: Fine-dining experience at a highly regarded restaurants in Burgenland, near Neusiedler See. *noon-2.30pm & 6-10pm Wed-Sat, noon-3pm & 6-10pm Sun* €€€

Elsewhere in town **Bergkirche** *(Haydn Church; haydnkirche. at)* is worth visiting, and contains the Haydn Mausoleum. You can also visit Haydn House, the composer's baroque residence, which has been beautifully restored.

Dip into Rust
Burgenland's quintessential sleepy lakeside town

Rust, 14km east of Eisenstadt, is one of the most agreeable of the towns that cluster around the western shore of Neusiedler See. Its reed shoreline and hidden boat sheds give it a sleepy, swampy feel on a steamy day, and in the summer months storks glide lazily overhead and clack their beaks from rooftop roosts. Dozens make their homes on chimneys in town, although it's wine, not storks, that has made Rust prosperous. In 1524 the emperor granted local vintners the right to display the letter 'R' (a distinctive insignia as a mark of origin from Rust) on their wine barrels, and today the corks still bear this mark. It's best to sample this history in one of the town's many *Heurigen,* such as Buschenschank Peter Schandl (p153).

Purbach am See's Historic Connections
Visit a historic Kellergasse

The town of Purbach lies around 17km northeast of Eisenstadt, and has some particularly well-preserved old town walls. They were built in 1630, not to protect the town from the Ottomans, but following Hungarian uprisings against the Habsburgs, during which it had a rather hard time. The three gates – the Turk Gate in the west, the Bruck Gate in the northeast and the Rust Gate in the south – are still intact. Keep an eye out for the so-called Turk of Purbach, a bust of a turbaned Ottoman soldier rising above the chimney of a house on Türkenstrasse. However, the most beautiful spot in this wine-producing town is its **Kellergasse**, a street near the town centre lined by some 50 stone cellars, most of them built in the mid-1800s. Many of these are *Heurigen,* with delicious food served along with excellent local wines, such as Die Sandhofer (p153).

Loretto's Pilgrimage Church
Burgenland's greatest pilgrimage site

North of Eisenstadt and less than 2km from Lower Austria, Loretto is a little town with fewer than 500 inhabitants – yet some 200,000 pilgrims make their way to this small community each year. Their object is the **Basilica & Pilgrimage Church of Maria Loretto**, consecrated in 1659 and torched by the Ottomans less than 25 years later. It took 20 years to rebuild it, with the new church being inaugurated in 1707. It's named after the town of Loreto in Italy, and like its namesake the object of veneration is a statue of the Black Madonna. The busiest time of year is around 15 August, when 25,000 or more pilgrims arrive for the Assumption of the Virgin Mary.

MUSIC FESTIVALS IN BURGENLAND

Seefestspiele Mörbisch: Performances at the largest open-air operetta stage in the world, on the shore of Neusiedler See.

Lockenhaus Chamber Music Festival: Created by Gidon Kremer, this festival has intimate performances with an added surprise factor – the programme is announced just 48 hours ahead of the opening.

Opera in the Quarry: Held in a 1st-century Roman quarry with 5000 open-air seats at St Margarethen.

Liszt Festival: In Raiding, the town of Franz Liszt's birth, at a purpose-built modern concert hall.

Nova Rock: Held in Nickelsdorf near the Hungarian border, this is the largest open-air rock festival in Austria.

Beyond Neusiedler See

Music, traditional crafts and more of those excellent Burgenland wines can be found beyond Neusiedler See.

Places

Forchtenstein p158
Raiding p159
Steinberg-Dörfl p160
Weinidylle & Beyond p160

GETTING AROUND

Central and southern Burgenland are covered by a network of bus routes run by Verkehrsbetriebe Burgenland, with connections from Vienna, Wiener Neustadt and Graz, though services are not very frequent.

Vienna to Oberpullendorf (the main transport hub in central Burgenland) by bus takes around two hours.

The best way to get around the wine areas is by bicycle.

Mattersburg is the closest train station to Forchtenstein. Mattersburg is 21 minutes by train from Wiener Neustadt, and 25 minutes by bus from Eisenstadt.

While plenty of people head for Neusiedler See from Vienna, central and southern Burgenland see rather fewer visitors, which is a shame because these areas still have much to offer. There's the wine – in particular the deep, lip-smacking reds made from the Blaufränkisch grape. You can also visit Forchtenstein Castle, with its weapons collection, and Raiding, where the virtuoso pianist and composer Franz Liszt was born.

Several of the villages in central Burgenland are ethnically Croatian, having been settled by Croats who were given land here by Frederick I after fleeing the Ottoman wars in the 1500s. The landscape gets a tad hillier as you progress south, and there are some lovely areas of protected landscape, including the Weinidylle and Raab-Örség-Goričko Nature Parks.

Forchtenstein

Weapons & curiosities

TIME FROM NEUSIEDLER SEE (EISENSTADT): **20MINS**

Burg Forchtenstein *(Forchtenstein Castle; €19, with guided tour €24)* is a vast and imposing fortress on the slopes of Rosaliengebirge, the hills that run along the boundary between Burgenland and Lower Austria. Owned by the Esterházy family since 1626, it was the only castle in the region that was never captured by the Ottomans. It was the repository for the Kunstkammer, or 'cabinet of curiosities', amassed by Prince Paul I Esterházy – a fantastic collection that included precious metalwork, jewellery, textiles, paintings and other items. Access to the collection was through a secret passage requiring two key holders, so it remained remarkably intact – with the exception of nearly 300 objects carted off in 1919 by the Hungarian Republic of Councils to Budapest, where they remain to this day.

The castle houses one of the largest private collections of weapons in central Europe, and hosts a variety of festivals and events. Mattersburg, the closest train station/bus stop, is 5km from Forchtenstein.

Burg Forchtenstein

Wines of Central & Southern Burgenland

If Neusiedler See is noted for its Zweigelt and dessert wines, central Burgenland is Blaufränkisch territory – over 55% of the grapes grown here are of this variety.

Wines from the Mittelburgenland DAC are dark and intense, with a nose of cherries and blackberries. The main wine-producing area lies northeast and east of Oberpullendorf, towards the Hungarian border. **Weingut Silvia Heinrich** *(tastings €25)* in Deutschkreutz is a standout winery in Mittelburgenland, with a focus entirely on Blaufränkisch.

Rosalia is Austria's youngest DAC region, known in particular for its rosé and lying along the hills of western Burgenland, near Burg Forchtenstein.

In southern Burgenland, head for the small Eisenberg DAC wine region, also noted for its Blaufränkisch. This is also the place to try Uhudler – a cuvée with a particularly intense bouquet, reminiscent of strawberries.

Raiding   TIME FROM NEUSIEDLER SEE (EISENSTADT): **50MINS**

Visit Liszt's birthplace

In Raiding, just to the northeast of Oberpullendorf, visit the **Liszt Museum** *(lisztmuseum.at; €10)*, also known as the Liszthaus, where the great composer and pianist Franz Liszt was

SPAS IN BURGENLAND

St Martins, Frauenkirchen: Almost 2000 sq metres of water areas, and a 20-acre bathing lake with its own sandy beach.

Sonnentherme Lutzmannsburg: Family-centric spa offering everything from a baby sauna to a 270m water slide.

AVITA Therme Bad Tatzmannsdorf: Infinity pool, 16 saunas, 2000 sq metres of water areas, grassy sunbathing areas and a serene garden.

Loipersdorf Thermal Baths: Fourteen saunas and pools, relaxing over-16s area for adults, plus plenty of watery outdoor play for kids. In Loipersdorf bei Fürstenfeld.

Allegria Thermal Stegersbach: Over 14 different water pools with temperatures between 26–35°C from Stegersbach thermal spring. The outdoor pool area was renovated in 2025.

EATING & DRINKING IN BURGENLAND: OUR PICKS

Habe d'Ere: Popular tavern in the Oberpullendorf town centre, with friendly service, tasty food and huge portions. *from 7am Mon-Sat, from 8am Sun* €€

Ziegelwerk Gasthaus: Regional dishes plus organic ingredients served in a former brickworks west of Loretto. *4-11pm Mon, Thu & Fri, from 11am Sat, 11am-4pm Sun* €€€

Ratschen: Traditional lunchtime and more elaborate evening menus, set in the Deutsch Schützen-Eisenberg wine region of southern Burgenland. *hours vary* €€

Gasthaus Fuchs: Family-run restaurant near Oberpullendorf and Raiding, with local dishes. *10am-2pm & 5-9pm Wed, Thu & Sat, 11am-2pm & 5.30-9pm Fri, 10am-2pm Sun* €€

BICYCLE HIRE AROUND NEUSIEDLER SEE

While you can bring bikes on the train from Vienna and further afield, it's easy to hire bikes around Neusiedler See.
Radverleih Mürner: Largest bike rental in Illmitz, with e-bikes, touring bikes, kids' bikes and tandems.
Radsport Waldherr: Located in Podersdorf, this bicycle-rental place is well stocked.
Radhaus Erwin: Located in Podersdorf, offering bike servicing and repairs, and bike rentals catering to individuals, families and larger groups.
Fahrräder Bucsis: Conveniently located right outside the train station at Neusiedl am See, with a range of road and trek bikes, e-bikes and tandems.
Nextbike: Set up an account online, then pick up or drop off at any rental point within Burgenland.

Blaudruck (indigo dyeing)

born in 1811. Part of the former Esterházy estate, the house offers multilingual guided tours, and the concert house nearby is home to an outstanding programme of concerts including an excellent music festival held in October.

Steinberg-Dörfl
Traditional indigo dyeing

TIME FROM NEUSIEDLER SEE (EISENSTADT): **35MINS**

Also near Oberpullendorf, in Steinberg-Dörfl, you'll find **Blaudruckerei Koó** *(originalblaudruck.at)* – one of the few workshops in Austria still practising *Blaudruck,* or traditional indigo dyeing. These beautiful textiles are resist-printed by hand with a dye-resistant resin, using wooden blocks, some of which are over 200 years old – before being immersed in vats of traditional indigo dye. The Koós also have a small shop, selling shirts, aprons, hats and more, which make for some of the best Austrian souvenirs you'll find anywhere. *Blaudruck* is inscribed on the UNESCO list of Intangible Cultural Heritage.

Weinidylle & Beyond
Vineyards & nature reserves

TIME FROM NEUSIEDLER SEE (EISENSTADT): **1HR 40MINS**

Weinidylle Nature Park in southern Burgenland has riparian forests and wetlands, where rare plant species thrive, alongside small vineyards and villages with thatched cottages and wine cellars. The **Kellerviertel** in Heiligenbrunn has over 100 listed wine cellars. Spanning the tripartite border between Austria, Hungary and Slovenia is **Raab-Örség-Goričko Nature Park**, a floodplain landscape perfect for exploring by bicycle or canoe.

Places We Love to Stay

€ Budget €€ Midrange €€€ Top End

Wachau Valley

Hotel Unter den Linden €€ Lovely cycle-friendly, family-run hotel, midway between the boats and the train in Krems. Good value.

Hotel Schloss Dürnstein €€€ Opulent rooms in a 17th-century castle – the height of luxury in the Wachau.

Hotel Richard Löwenherz €€€ Beautifully converted from a former medieval convent in Dürnstein, complete with serene monastery garden.

arte Hotel Krems €€ Modern hotel in Krems, near the Kunsthalle opposite the university campus.

Weingut Holzapfel €€€ A 700-year-old pressing house near Weissenkirchen, redesigned in the late 1600s by the Melk Abbey's architect.

Weinquadrat €€ Small, relaxed design hotel in Weissenkirchen, with bicycle hire and a nice garden.

Dream Factory Melk – Green Hostel € Modern hostel with pod-style, bargain-priced dorm beds in Melk.

Rathauskeller Melk €€ Very close to the abbey, in the pedestrianised old town, with its own restaurant.

Hotel-Restaurant Zur Post €€ Family-run hotel in the centre of Melk, right below the abbey, with tastefully decorated rooms.

Wienerwald

Babenbergerhof (p137) **€€** Family-run hotel in Mödling with a good restaurant, making a perfect base for exploring the Wienerwald.

Hotel Gutenbrunn €€ Opulent rooms in Baden bei Wien, in a renovated palace, with direct access to the Römertherme.

Gasthof Gabriele Martinek €€ A small traditional guesthouse and restaurant in Baden.

Wiener Neustadt

Hotel Zentral €€ Conveniently located right on the main square.

The Wiener Alpen

Hotel Looshaus (p143) **€€** Mountain hotel in a historic wooden building designed by modernist architect Adolf Loos.

Payerbacherhof €€ Family-run hotel in Payerbach, with its own restaurant and spa.

Raxalm-Berggasthof €€ Classic mountain guesthouse above the Rax-Seilbahn, with fantastic views and plenty of hiking trails on your doorstep.

Waldviertel & Weinviertel

Loisium Hotel €€ The swankiest place to stay in Langenlois, with its own spa and heated outdoor pool.

Mühlenhof Rooms €€ Stylish rooms in a boutique B&B in Langenlois, with design touches and a big studio space downstairs.

Schloss Hotel Drosendorf €€ Elegant rooms complete with period furniture in a breathtakingly restored historic castle.

Burgenland

Arkadenhof Kroiss €€ Family-run pension in Illmitz, with simple rooms on a traditional Burgenland arcaded courtyard.

Hotel zur Post €€ Clean cosy rooms in a converted former post office in the centre of Illmitz.

Restaurant & Hotel Braunstein (p155) **€€** Family-run hotel in Purbach, with excellent wines from its own 400-year-old vineyard.

Herberge an der Nikolauszeche €€ Historic guesthouse in Purbach, which has been nicely renovated, with plenty of exposed wooden beams and a peaceful garden.

Das Esel – Kleinod in Rust €€ Nicely decorated rooms with a balcony, plus there's a garden and outdoor pool, perfect for cooling off after a day cycling.

Zum Oberjäger €€ Boutique hotel on the grounds of the Esterházy-owned castle in Lackenbach.

Hotel Schlof Guat €€ Good value hotel with smart, comfortable rooms in the centre of Oberpullendorf. Next to and under the same ownership as the excellent Habe d'Ere restaurant.

Ratschen (p159) **€€** Stylish wooden chalets, spa and wellness area and top-notch restaurant set among the vineyards of southern Burgenland.

Hotel Schandl €€ Family-run hotel in the centre of Rust, beside the church. Under same ownership as the excellent Buschenschank Peter Schandl.

Researched by Samantha Priestley

Upper Austria

A LAND OF CONTRADICTIONS

Where traditions hold strong and there's always one and a half feet firmly in the future.

Upper Austria isn't the easiest region of the country to navigate. Physically, mentally and emotionally, it can be tricky. It has an understated beauty about it and most of the area is never trying to play to, or particularly please, visitors. But that's one of the reasons it's so interesting. In authentic alpine villages, among chalet guesthouses, mountains and lakes, you'll be served up dumplings and apple or pear cider, along with the regular feeling of being stuck in time.

There's tradition everywhere, if you want it, but there are also technological displays in museums – reaching to the future of a region that constantly moves forward.

A community-owned brewery sits side by side with ancient castles and baroque cathedrals. And there's modern art and street art, while the majestic Danube (Donau) weaves its way through the diverse landscape as it always has.

In the city of Linz the future is closer, in its many museums and galleries, and a festival of pavement performance brings a pinch of the quirky into the mix, but head out of the more populated areas and you'll find old Austria waiting with open arms.

It's one of the few areas of the country left where you can see the past living and breathing, while the 'here and now' looks to the horizon at the same time. That alone is worth travelling here for.

THE MAIN AREAS

LINZ
Industrial city with an artistic heart.
p166

NATIONALPARK KALKALPEN
A wilderness ripe for exploration.
p176

INNVIERTEL
Nature-rich region with Bavarian heritage.
p181

For places to stay in Upper Austria, see p185

THE GUIDE

UPPER AUSTRIA

Left: Scharding (p182); Above: Nationalpark Kalkalpen (p176)

Find Your Way

Stretching from Lower Austria to the Alps, Upper Austria delivers cities, rural towns and lakes. We've picked the places that best capture the region's character, but each place is a springboard for discovering more.

Linz, p166
The historic regional capital city has two cathedrals, its own unique cake, museums and art galleries, and a street-performance festival.

Nationalpark Kalkalpen, p176
This wild national park is a world away from the cities of Steyr and Wels, bringing an oasis of calm.

CAR
A car is the best option if you want to truly appreciate everything Upper Austria has. Nothing is far away if you have your own wheels and it's the only way to get to smaller villages.

TRAIN & BUS
If you don't have a car it's possible to use the rail links and local buses, though you will have to make changes along the way, especially once you're out of the cities.

Library, Stift Florian (p175)

Plan Your Time

You'll need a day in Linz, at least, to make the most of it, but don't miss out on the surrounding towns and villages.

In Three Days

● Once you've spent time in **Linz** (p166), hitting the markets and museums, get out into the surrounding area. Spend your second day in **Freistadt** (p172), to the north of the city, where the people love their beer. On your third day visit the former concentration camp at **Mauthausen** (p173) and the monastery in **St Florian** (p175) – you can easily travel between them on the same day.

More than a Week

● When you think that **Linz** (p166) and its surrounding towns must be the best of Upper Austria, go south and discover the other two cities of the region, **Steyr** and **Wels** (p177), then head to the **Nationalpark Kalkalpen** (p176). Move on to the west where the border with Germany lies, to the region that still feels Bavarian, heading to **Innviertel** (p181).

SEASONAL HIGHLIGHTS

SPRING
In the spring shoulder season, gardens bloom and towns come to life in the Innviertel region.

SUMMER
The second and third cities of Steyr and Wels are glorious in summer and still much quieter than Linz, which gets busy in high season.

AUTUMN
Hike through the Nationalpark Kalkalpen when the leaves fall and the ground turns to rust; with few visitors, it's a slice of peacefulness.

WINTER
Wrap up warm and visit the Christmas markets in Linz, ski the slopes in the Nationalpark Kalkalpen and enjoy snowy alpine villages.

Linz

ART GALLERIES | MUSEUMS | COFFEE CULTURE

GETTING AROUND

The Blue Danube Airport serves the city, though it's often easier to fly into Vienna and take the train to Linz, due to the lack of direct flights to Linz. The train takes approximately one hour and 15 minutes.

Once in Linz the public transport system is all you need – driving in the centre is slow and usually busy with many one-way streets. Tickets for trams and buses need to be bought in advance, online or from shops or roadside ticket machines.

Linz is also a walkable city. It's possible to wander around and see the city from the rooftops of churches and from the castle on the hill. Then take the tram all the way up a mountain, the Pöstlingberg, to view the city from even higher.

The third-biggest city in Austria and home to the country's second-tallest cathedral, Linz might seem as if it's always lagging behind. But, in fact, for an industrial city that's not on the tourist trail, it comes first in a lot of areas. Built on the banks of the Danube, straddling both sides of the river, Linz has taken its industrial past and created art where there was once functionality, while holding onto its historic heart in its charming old town. The old industrial port-facility buildings are now one big art gallery, featuring murals that visitors can add to.

While still being traditional, serving up authentic Austrian dishes in its restaurants and hosting much fewer tourists in its old town than cities like Vienna, it's a technologically forward-looking city, with many art installations and thought-provoking displays on AI and space travel. Here you can also try the world's oldest cake variety, the *Linzer Torte*, beneath the twin spires of the 17th-century cathedral.

A Foodie Tour of Linz
Mix history with gastronomy

Linzer Torte, a pastry-based cake topped with jam and almonds, is the oldest known cake recipe in the world, and the oldest cake to be named after a city. The recipe was published in a cookbook by Countess Anna Margarita Sagramosa in 1653, though it's doubtful many ordinary people got their hands on a cookbook back then.

Head to the bakery and cafe **k.u.k. Hofbäckerei** (*kuk-hofbaeckerei.at*) for a taste of the oldest cake in the oldest bakery in Linz (it's been here since at least 1371). **Südbahnhofmarkt** (*suedbahnhofmarkt.com*) is an open-air market where fruit and veg stalls, butchers, cheese counters and flower stalls are set up next to cafes and snack bars, so you can wander around the local produce and then nip inside for a coffee.

Later on, after a few beers, seek out **Leberkas Pepi** (*leberkaspepi.at*), makers of Austrian meatloaf. There are a few branches

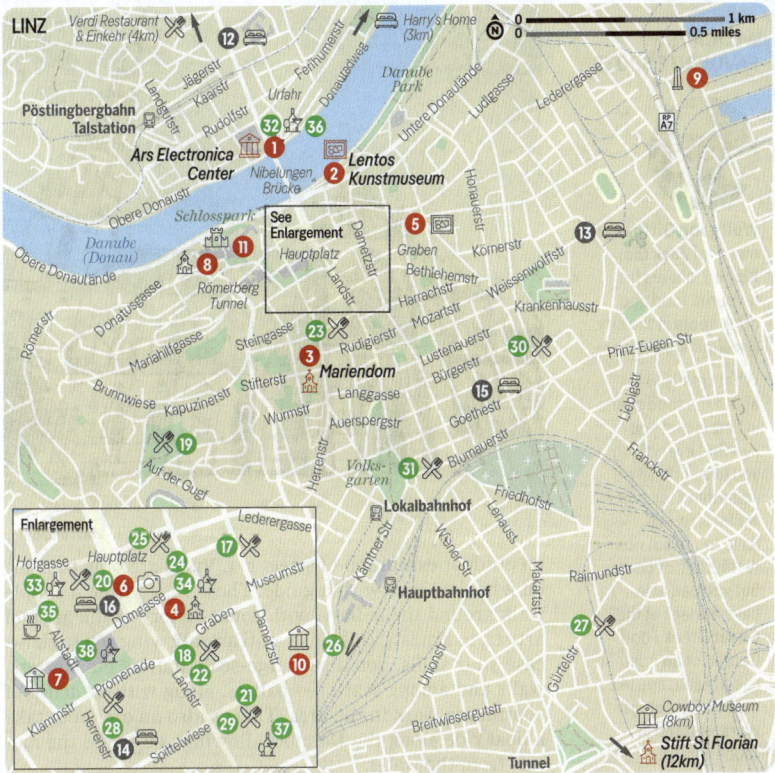

★ HIGHLIGHTS
1 Ars Electronica Center
2 Lentos Kunstmuseum
3 Mariendom

● SIGHTS
4 Alter Dom
5 Francisco Carolinum
6 Hauptplatz
7 Landhaus
8 Martinskirche
9 Mural Harbor
10 Nordico Stadtmuseum
11 Schlossmuseum

● SLEEPING
12 Hotel Goldener Adler
13 Hotel Prielmayrhof
14 Hotel Schwarzer Bär
15 Limehome
16 Wolfinger

● EATING
17 Ängus Downtown
18 Auinger Wurstelstand
19 Café Orchidee
20 Glockenspiel
21 GReat
22 Jack the Ripperl
23 Jindrak
24 k.u.k. Hofbäckerei
25 Leberkas Pepi
26 Maleewan Thai Imbiss
27 Rauner
28 Rooftop 7
29 Skygarden
30 Südbahnhofmarkt
31 Tiktak

● DRINKING & NIGHTLIFE
32 Cafe Strom
33 Frau Dietrich
34 Hemingway's Music Bar
35 Madame Wu
36 Salonschiff Fräulen Florentine
37 Solaris
38 To The Moon

---

of the popular meatloaf house now, but the original at Rathausgasse 3, a former wine bar, and a meatloaf house since 1989, is the most authentic.

Follow the Art

Be part of the scene

Linz has some great art galleries, but as every art lover knows, not all art is in a gallery. The **Mural Harbor** (muralharbor.at) is the industrial harbour area of the city that's become

☑ TOP TIP

Install the Visit Linz app on your phone before you arrive, and you'll have all the addresses and directions you need to make the most of the city. The app has quizzes and games that earn points to be used as discounts on selected partner businesses.

Mariendom

A LOCAL'S FAVOURITE SPOTS

Wolfgang Gittmaier, owner of **Jack the Ripperl**, shares his favourite food and drink spots in the city. *@wolfganggittmaier*

What I really like about the food scene in Linz is that you can find everything you like and there's something for every wallet size. We have the finest ribs restaurant, of course, but you can also have a snack at the **GReat** Greek Food Corner, or an Austrian special sausage like the classic **Auinger Wurstelstand** at Taubenmarkt.

We have two rooftop restaurants – **Skygarden** and **Rooftop 7** – serving steaks and club sandwiches. At Rooftop 7 you have the perfect view to the old Linzer Dom. There are also fine-dining restaurants like Göttfried, Pianino and Essig's.

an outdoor exhibition of street art. Visits are only possible on a booked tour with a guide. These range from a simple walk around the gallery, with some history of the art and artists, to a masterclass in graffiti art, allowing you to showcase your skills. You'll see large-scale murals on shutters, walls and among scattered pallets, along with evidence of continuing work in the area. There's also an option to take a boat ride along the Danube, allowing you to see the murals from the water.

The **Lentos Kunstmuseum** *(lentos.at; adult/child €11/ free)* is a shiny modern building on the banks of the Danube. It looks impressive from the outside, including when lit up in neon colours at night, and inside there's a range of contemporary and modern art on display.

A short walk from the Lentos Kunstmuseum is the **Francisco Carolinum** *(instagram.com/fc_linz; adult/child €6.50/3)*. This gallery also celebrates contemporary art, along with photography and media, but the building itself couldn't be more different to the former gallery. Built in 1895, this stately landmark houses a collection of works by artists from Upper Austria.

CAFES IN LINZ

Jindrak: Historic Linz cafe in the centre of town serving coffee and cakes. *9am-5pm Mon-Sat* €€

Tiktak: Good selection of coffee and a spacious outdoor terrace. Also serves breakfast and lunch. *7am-5pm Tue-Sat* €€

Café Orchidee: Set in the Botanical Gardens, with a wide range of good-quality coffees and a limited food menu. *9.30am-5pm Tue-Sun* €€

Glockenspiel: Traditional coffee house on the main square serving cakes, coffee and an extensive food menu. *8am-11.30pm Mon-Sat, 9am-10pm Sun* €€€

See the City Cathedrals
Delve into the past

There isn't a palpable rivalry between Linz and Vienna today, but back when Linz's **Mariendom** (New Cathedral) was being built, in 1862, a touch of tension entered proceedings. The original plans showed a tower of over 135m, which would have made it higher than Stephansdom in Vienna – something that wasn't allowed. Linz was promptly told to make its shorter, though officials in Vienna didn't seem to pay much attention to the overall size of the two cathedrals. As a result, Vienna's cathedral remains the tallest in Austria, while Linz's new cathedral is still the largest, able to hold 20,000 people.

For a taste of the cathedral hermit life, anyone can sign up to spend a week in the **hermit tower**, where a real recluse used to live permanently, only coming down once a day for meals and prayers, and enjoying absolute solitude for the rest of the time.

But before the impressive Gothic New Cathedral was built, Linz already had a cathedral, which still stands in the City Hall district. **Alter Dom** *(dioezese-linz.at/ignatiuskirche)*, the Old Cathedral, has twin towers and was built in baroque style for the Jesuit order, constructed between 1669 and 1683. There's a world of difference between the two, both outside and in, and seeing both illuminates the changes between the two areas.

Tour the Museums
Look to the future

If you're expecting a traditional castle when you visit the **Schlossmuseum** *(adult/child €6.50/3)*, you might be disappointed. Not much is left of Linz's old castle, and when you arrive at the top of your climb up to the museum, instead of being met with a castle, a modern-looking building (with an even more modern building attached to it) awaits you. There are still some castle walls to see, and the views over Linz are incredible, but this is a museum. Having said that, it's a good one. The exhibits take you back in time to the early Upper Austrians, and there are displays on nature and technology.

Overlooking the Danube on its northern bank, the **Ars Electronica Center** *(ars.electronica.art; adult/child €14/5)* is predominantly a science and technology museum. Many of the displays are interactive and some seem more like art installations than exhibits. Visit at the right time for the 3D

LINZ LIKE A LOCAL

Clarissa Ujvari, from the **Nordico Stadtmuseum** (p171), has lived in Linz for over a decade. She considers a walk along the Danube the ideal opportunity to get to know the Linz vibe in one day.
@clarissauj

Begin with breakfast in the old town: I love the charming tea salon **Madame Wu**. Then cross Hauptplatz and wander to the **Lentos Kunstmuseum** to enjoy an impressive collection of art. Continue along the Danube, where you can wander through the public sculpture park.

Cross the railway bridge to the Urfahr district, with hot spots like **Salonschiff Fräulein Florentine** and **Cafe Strom**.

Finally, venture west to discover one of Linz's urban beaches and relax with a cold drink at one of the taverns directly on the Danube.

 EATING IN LINZ: OUR PICKS

Ängus Downtown: Fine-dining steak bar that also offers some solid vegetarian options. *11am-2pm & 5-11.30pm Mon-Thu, to 1am Fri, 11-1am Sat* €€€

Verdi Restaurant & Einkehr: Traditional Austrian cuisine with a modern slant, plus a well-stocked wine cellar, just north of the city centre. *5pm-1am Tue-Sat* €€

Rauner: Casual dining a short walk from the centre, with Austrian and European dishes including fried breakfasts and burgers. *11am-11pm Mon-Thu* €€

Maleewan Thai Imbiss: Authentic Thai restaurant with an Asian food store attached; it's a popular lunch spot and afternoon hangout. *11am-8pm Mon-Fri, to 3pm Sat* €

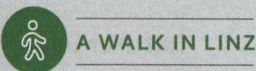

A WALK IN LINZ

Get to know Linz's history better on this cultural sightseeing walking tour of the city, setting out from the main square.

START	END	LENGTH
Hauptplatz	Alter Dom	3.2km; 2hrs

Start at ❶ **Hauptplatz**, where the Holy Trinity column dominates the space. The baroque old city hall and Kirchmayer House are architecturally appealing, but locals mostly come to the square to shop. Head up to the ❷ **Schlossmuseum** (p169). It's a bit of an uphill walk, but with great views. Behind the castle is ❸ **Martinskirche** (St Martin's Church), the oldest original church in Linz.

Walk along the Roman road, through Kinderspieplatz Promenade, a children's park, until you reach ❹ **Landhaus**. Built in 1570, this is the HQ of the government of Upper Austria. Then walk along Herrenstrausse all the way to ❺ **Mariendom** (p169) (New Cathedral). Along the way on this charming old street, pause to see the Bishop's Residence, hop into a few of the small shops or have a coffee in one of the cafes.

Carry on down Herrenstrausse, take a left onto Langasse, and left again onto ❻ **Landstrasse**. This is the most walked street in Linz and the tram runs all the way along it. Apart from the tram, it's pedestrianised, so you can walk around freely. It's where all the high-street shops are, as well as the library and the Martin Luther Church. Along this street, take a moment to view the ❼ **Ursuline Church**, a baroque Roman Catholic church that was built in 1736.

Finish your walk at the end of Landstrasse, at the ❽ **Alter Dom** (p169) (Old Cathedral), and you'll be back near where you started.

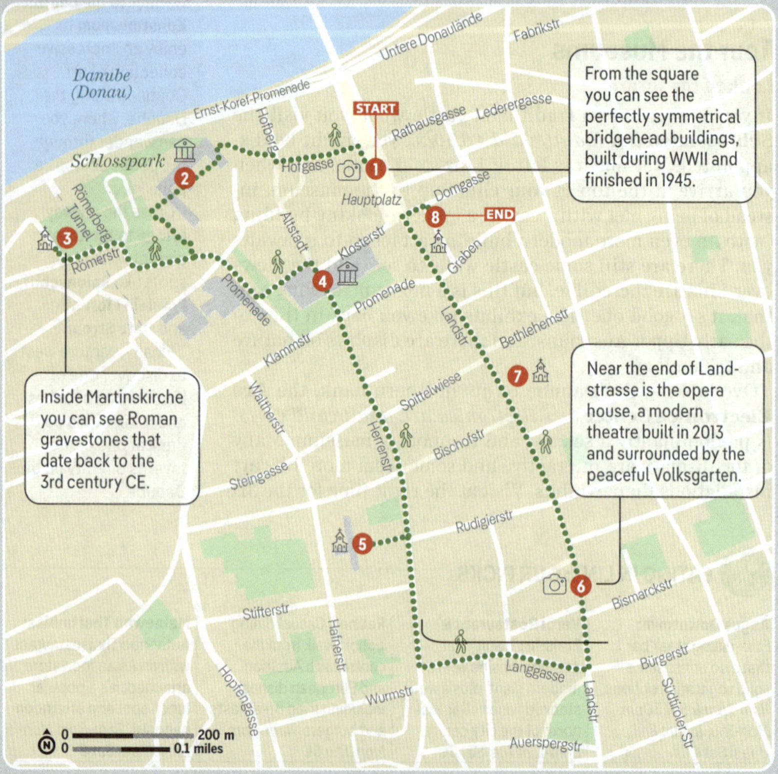

From the square you can see the perfectly symmetrical bridgehead buildings, built during WWII and finished in 1945.

Inside Martinskirche you can see Roman gravestones that date back to the 3rd century CE.

Near the end of Landstrasse is the opera house, a modern theatre built in 2013 and surrounded by the peaceful Volksgarten.

cinema and be sure to check out the AI music and speculations on what AI might mean for us in the future.

For something more offbeat head to the **Cowboy Museum** (*cowboymuseum.at; adult/child €10/5*). As the name suggests this is a museum dedicated to all things cowboy, though it also has displays on Native Americans and serves American beer. It's a little way out of town, a 30-minute drive, or reachable by taking two trains, but it's worth a visit if you're a Wild West fan or just want an unusual experience.

At the **Nordico Stadtmuseum** (*nordico.at; adult/child €8/free*), the focus is on the local life of ordinary Linz people. The exhibition on what life was like for local residents following WWII is especially interesting.

Experience the Pflasterspektakel
The festival on the cobbles

Every year since 1987, for a couple of days during the third week of July, Linz has been transformed into one big stage for street performers during the **Pflasterspektakel** (*pflasterspektakel.at*). Every pavement, alley, square and corner becomes a space for visual and audio art and entertainment. Musicians, jugglers, mime artists, dancers, comedians, magicians and fire performers descend on the city from all over the world to perform on the cobbles.

There's a carnival atmosphere, and you never know what you might see – it's one big street party in the centre of Linz. Apart from some selected acts that are staged, circus style, in tents, all performances take place out in the city streets, and are free to watch. Like any buskers, the performers lay out hats and boxes to collect tips and payments as they're otherwise performing for free. The festival attracts around 200,000 visitors, and if the acts are good those hats can fill up fast. This is one of Linz's busiest times for visitors, so it's best to book your accommodation ahead.

ANTON BRUCKNER

Visit the monastery in the market town of St Florian (p175), where Anton Bruckner is buried. Down in the crypt you'll discover that Bruckner's coffin has some unusual and macabre company.

THE MUSIC LIVES ON

In 1812, while the Old Cathedral was still the only one in the city, Beethoven wrote the *'Three Equals for Four Trombones'* for performance inside this baroque beauty.

From 1856 to 1868 Anton Bruckner was the organist in the old church, while the new church began its life across town. In 1861 Bruckner's seven-part *'Ave Maria'* was performed in the cathedral, and his *Mass No 1* also enjoyed its first-ever performance here.

The **Bruknerfest** (Bruckner Festival) is held in Linz each September to honour its most famous composer. Organised by the Brucknerhaus, the festival has been taking place since 1974, and has been a fixed annual event since 1977.

DRINKING IN LINZ: OUR PICKS

Frau Dietrich: 1920s speakeasy-style bar serving a wide menu of cocktails and spirits in a laid-back atmosphere. *6pm-2am Wed-Sat*

Hemingway's Music Bar: Upstairs bar in the centre of town, with an intimate atmosphere, live music and a good cocktail menu. *5pm-1am Tue-Thu, to 3am Fri & Sat*

To The Moon: Modern, cosy cocktail bar, serving innovative cocktails, with knowledgeable staff who make recommendations. *5pm-midnight Sun, Mon & Thu, to 2am Fri & Sat*

Solaris: Lively bar with DJ. It's a great place for a beer, but it gets very busy at weekends. *5pm-midnight Sun-Thu, to 4am Fri, to 2am Sat*

Beyond Linz

The area surrounding Linz delves into dark history at a former concentration camp and musical moments at a monastery.

Places
Freistadt p172
Mauthausen p173
St Florian p175

GETTING AROUND

It's possible to get around on public transport, though not always easy. Train services are good, but you can't reach everywhere and stations aren't always in the centre of town. The train from Freistadt to Steyr, for example, takes around two hours as there is no direct route. Similarly from Freistadt to Wels by train takes over an hour and requires one change. While there's a good bus network, travelling around can require two or more changes.

A car is advisable if you want to see a lot of the area around Linz. Cycling is a great alternative, with good cycle paths in the area.

Once you get out of the city, things get more rural, but there are still signs of industry and a forward-looking viewpoint in many places. There's an intriguing mix of old and new in the towns and villages around Linz, with a definite pull to the traditional and a yank to the future. A good example is Steyr, which has one of the best preserved old towns in the German-speaking world at 1000 years old. Segways now zip about the market square and uni students amble the streets.

Historic old towns with typical Austrian architecture and rolling landscapes set the scene, while a closer look reveals busy market squares, landscaped public gardens, castles and pretty churches. Walk the spotless streets lined with pastel-painted buildings, nip in and out of small museums and galleries, and stop to try a beer or a coffee as local life goes by.

Freistadt

TIME FROM LINZ: **25MINS**

Tour the brewery

It seems everyone in Freistadt loves beer. Or, at least, everyone has beer, because everyone who owns a house within the city walls also owns a part of the local brewery. This arrangement dates back to 1363 when Duke Rudolf IV gave the citizens of the town the right to brew beer in their own homes. It seems they liked this idea very much, because in 1770 they made it officially legal, with a contract to prove they had this right. In 1780 they built the brewery, **Freistädter Brauhaus** *(freistaedter-bier.at)*, and now every citizen owns a share in this beer-making business because of this contract.

Today this commune is the only one of its kind in Europe, and the brewery is still in operation while also being a museum and an experiential attraction. Freistädter Bier is sold everywhere in Linz, so if you've been there first you've probably already tried it, but there's nothing quite like drinking it at its source.

Brewery tours *(€12)* are available every Thursday at 2pm and there's a beer-tasting dinner on the last Thursday of every month, when visitors can sample a taster menu with pairing beers, including the brewery's lager, brown ale, stout and

Freistadt

CHURCHES BEYOND LINZ

Stadtpfarrkirche: A five-aisled basilica Catholic church in Freistadt. It was built in the 13th-century Romanesque style but Gothicised in the 14th and 15th centuries.

Pfarrkirche Mauthausen: Catholic church built in the 15th-century, late Gothic era. The interior was renovated in the 17th century in baroque style.

Kirche St Johann: Small catholic church by the roadside in St Florian. The black alter inside with marble sculptures is especially worth a look, and the old well outside still produces water.

pilsner. You can even have a go at brewing yourself if you attend one of the live-brewing sessions. There's also a well-stocked bottle shop on-site.

Mauthausen

TIME FROM LINZ: **30MINS**

Contemplate a dark moment in history

Mauthausen Memorial *(mauthausen-memorial.org; free, guided tour adult/child €8/€5)* is a former concentration camp which is today a memorial and museum. It was a quarrying centre before the Nazis turned it into a concentration camp, recognising it as an ideal place to put prisoners to work. Some 190,000 inmates lived and worked at the camp, and around 90,000 of them died here.

Prisoners carried heavy stones up the **Todesstiege** (Stairway of Death) from the quarry. Conditions were particularly bad, with rooms designed for 300 people – a stretch when you see how small the rooms are, and reportedly up to 2000 people slept in them at any one time. Visitors can enter the former gas chamber, disturbingly named 'the killing area', where memorials line the walls and a glass-framed display holds old photos of those murdered here.

There's lots of other macabre rooms to explore, including a dissecting room that was used by training doctors, but for

COFFEE BEYOND LINZ: OUR PICKS

Cafe am Kai: Coffee house overlooking the Danube in Mauthausen. Great coffee, pastries and cakes. *9am-7pm Wed-Fri, to 6pm Sat & Sun* €

Lubinger: Town-centre coffee house in Freistadt with indulgent cakes and ice-cream sundaes. *8am-6pm Thu-Tue* €€

Cafe & Konditorei Kastner: Busy traditional coffee house in Bad Leonfelden, with pavement seating, great cakes and ice cream. *8am-6pm Mon-Sun* €€

Cafe Auszeit: Cosy, intimate cafe in Freistadt, with booths and terrace seating with a casual atmosphere. *9am-10pm Mon-Fri* €€

ST FLORIAN BOYS' CHOIR

The first documented mention of the boys' choir at St Florian's monastery was in 1071, and there's been a boys' choir here ever since. Originally the choir boarded at the monastery and the monks dealt with their schooling, but today the boys attend the local public school, although they do still board.

A lot has changed since the choir was first established and, after first travelling to perform in competitions under the guidance of Professor Hans Bachl, the choir now performs all over the world.

It is still possible to catch a performance at the monastery, although they are few and far between these days.

Mauthausen Memorial (p173)

the most part this is a sombre, though fascinating, museum to wander through, one that holds a palpable sadness. There are information boards and displays of the names of those who were held and died here.

Guided tours are available between May and October; tours in English are available on selected dates in July and August, or you can walk around at your own pace with an audio guide (available in various languages including English). A guided tour lasts around two hours, and to do the whole area justice takes a similar time on your own. Mauthausen can be reached from Linz with a short car ride or the direct 361 bus.

Hiking & history

Starting and ending at the Marktplatz in Mauthausen, you can take a 1½-hour walk in the area, starting by taking a left turn to **Pfarrkirche Mauthausen** (St Nicholas Church), the town's parish church. Step inside this pretty, gothic church, which stands on a hill and overlooks the river, to see the gilded alter, and then continue onto the **Donausteig Trail**, which runs adjacent to the river and is well signposted from here. If you're partway along the trail, the way back to Mauthausen is through a section of forest.

EATING BEYOND LINZ: OUR PICKS

Kraeuterwirt Dunzinger: Traditional restaurant in Freistadt serving authentic national dishes. Austrians travel from surrounding areas just to eat here. *10am-10pm Fri & Sat* €

Freistädter Brauhaus: Classic Austrian dishes in traditional surroundings; part of the brewery, with courtyard outdoor seating. *9am-midnight Mon-Sat, to 3pm Sun* €€

Stiftskeller Sankt Florian: This St Florian restaurant serves big portions of traditional Austrian food and good vegan options. *11.30am-2pm & 6-8pm Mon-Wed, Fri & Sat, 8am-2pm Sun* €€

Moststube Frellerhof: Countryside restaurant in Mauthausen with a kids' playground and generous portions of traditional Austrian food. *3-10pm Tue-Fri, 11am-10pm Sat, 11am-8pm Sun* €€

On this walk you pass the **Schlossmuseum** *(schloss museen-mauthausen.org; €6)*, which includes the **Pharmacy Museum**. This unusual little attraction tells the history of pharmacy in the town, including about the Aichberger family of pharmacists who lived here. The museum is only open between May and October. From here you can carry onto the historic small boat port, which doesn't see a lot of water traffic, but is a nice spot to pause and sit by the little jetty.

For a gentler, more informative walk, join a **nightwatchman tour** *(€6)* from Schlossmuseum, where the costumed nightwatchman takes you on a guided walk around the town by moonlight. The walk starts on a regular street corner at 4310 Mauthausen, and lasts between 1½ and two hours. You'll hear tales of the old Danube market as you make your way through romantic alleyways and past historic townhouses.

St Florian
Find peace in the monastery

TIME FROM LINZ: **30MINS**

The market town of St Florian was named after the Roman officer who converted to Christianity and was drowned in the river for his beliefs. The town itself is pretty and is a nice place to have a wander and stop for a coffee in the square. But most people who come to St Florian are doing so to visit the **Stift St Florian** *(stift-st-florian.at)*. A stunning baroque abbey, the monastery can be seen from many points in town and its dominating twin towers rise above the landscape.

You can't simply walk into the monastery and do your own thing; instead, you need to visit by guided tour. But that's not a bad thing, as there are lots of details you might otherwise miss. The marble hall and the library are highlights, but if you'd like to see something a bit darker, down in the crypt is the coffin of composer Anton Bruckner, positioned in front of a big pile of skulls and bones. These remains are said to be from some of the 6000 Christians who were buried here by the Romans. It seems an odd marriage at first, but Bruckner is purposefully buried here, directly below the Bruckner organ, which you can see in the basilica above.

St Florian is accessible from Linz via bus 410.

TILLYSBURG CASTLE

Schloss Tillysburg *(festspiele-schloss-tillysburg.at)* in St Florian was built between 1633 and 1645, most likely as a fortress but then used as a palace.

The design of the castle, with its four wings and charming inner courtyard, make it perfect for its modern use as an events space. It's popular as a wedding venue, but with a rolling programme of plays and concerts, the castle courtyard is mostly used as a place of entertainment. There's also an 18-hole golf course here.

BAD HALL
If you visit Bad Hall (p180) you can experience the St Florian Boys' Choir at the Bad Hall theatre. The choir performs in the town several times a year.

DRINKING BEYOND LINZ: OUR PICKS

Acanto Bar: A cocktail bar in Freistadt that sells beer too, and has a beach in the beer garden. *6pm-1am Wed & Thu, 7pm-3.30am Fri & Sat*

Café Castello: Cosy bar in Mauthausen with an impressive wine list, run by a friendly couple. *4pm-midnight Tue-Fri, from 6pm Sat*

Rockford Bar: The modest exterior of this bar in Freistadt reflects the prices inside, while the atmosphere makes it a favourite with locals. *8.30pm-4am Fri & Sat*

Latino Freistadt: Come for the cocktails and beer, stay for the pizza, modern bar with pavement seating and upbeat buzz. *6pm-midnight Thu, to 2am Fri & Sat*

Nationalpark Kalkalpen

CLIMBING | WALKING | UNSPOILT NATURE

Places

Steyr p176
Wels p177
Reichraming p178
Sengsengebirge p178
Wilderness Trail Buchensteig p179
Bad Hall p180
Windischgarsten p180
Losenstein p180
Innviertel p181

This sprawling garden of wilderness and forest is young for a national park, established as such in 1997. It's the second-largest in Austria and is widely untouched, containing a large amount of primeval forest species. This kind of old-growth forest can only survive with sufficient numbers of old trees, and is testament to how unspoilt the area is.

You could spend days hiking in the national park, with Hoher Nock, the imposing mountain, offering climbers a challenge and rewarding views. The visitor centre at Molln is where you can book a guided tour, and this is also one of the three entrances to the park. The other two are at Ennstal and Hengstpass. There are some ice caves within the park, but visitors are advised to only attempt exploring them as part of a tour. Lynx numbers are on the rise in the park, though you'll be lucky to catch a glimpse of one. Easier to spot are the park's golden eagles.

Worth noting is that the Hengstpasshütte in Nationalpark Kalkalpen is open between May and October. Staff here can offer tips and advice on routes to take, places to shelter, guided tours, where to stay and where to eat and drink nearby. The hut also has two 10-person dorms.

Close by are the historical cities of Steyr and Wels, both picturesque with pastel buildings and traditional churches overlooking the rivers Steyr and Traun.

Steyr

Walk the city's hills & terraces

About an hour by car from the national park is the small city of **Steyr**. A river town that has long been famous for its manufacturing, Steyr was bombed heavily during WWII. Surprisingly, the city remained more or less unscathed by the bombings because, it once produced weapons in the 19th century and also during both World Wars, Steyr was targeted precisely where its factories were located, at a distance from the city centre. The buildings on the square, apart from the baroque city hall, a 19th-century court house and a turn of the century bank building, are all medieval.

There are numerous levels and terraces in Steyr, so you need a good pair of walking shoes to get around. The Gothic city parish church and the **Palace Lamberg** (*schlosslamberg.at*)

GETTING AROUND

Trains run infrequently from Linz to both Steyr and Wels, but if you time it right the train is a great way to travel between the cities. There's also a rail link from Linz to Nationalpark Kalkalpen, but to reach it by public transport, use the good local bus services.

To really explore the area, you'll need to drive or get active on two wheels and take advantage of the cycle paths.

are all situated on the top terrace of the city and are linked by the romantic Berggasse. The Palace Lamberg is an impressive building, though it is now used as municipal offices and you need to register with the tourist office to be able to visit any of the interior.

The best views over the whole city with views of the Limestone Alps is from the **Taborturm** (Tabor Tower), a restaurant just behind **St Michael's Church** *(dioezese-linz.at/steyr-stmichael)*. You can reach the viewing platform via a panoramic lift or climb the staircase.

Wels

Wander the streets & enjoy the views

Just 45 minutes by car from the national park is the city of **Wels**. At first glance the main square looks similar to Steyr. The soft pastel-painted buildings line the streets, and the square is pretty, though in Wels it is used more for markets and there's a big emphasis on shopping here. But Wels is different. Many of these pretty buildings have hidden courtyards with beautiful gardens that you can visit.

Also, in contrast to Steyr, the **Castle of Wels** *(adult/child €7/€3)* houses a castle museum, and is very much open to the public. The courtyard is often used to host concerts and you can rent out a space within the castle for functions and celebrations.

Walk for around 15 minutes from the town centre up to the tower on the hill climb the steps for panoramic views over Wels and beyond.

A LOCAL'S TOP MUSEUM PICK

Helen Petermandl, a licensed Austrian tourist guide, explains why a visit to the Steyr City Museum is not be missed.

The **Stadtmuseum Steyr** provides a state-of-the art, interesting museum experience, complete with audio and video footage and interactive stations in a light, spacious setting. Housed in two spectacularly preserved and interconnecting Renaissance constructions – a former granary building and the mighty Neutor city gate – the museum was given a major overhaul and redesign in 2021.

There is something for everyone: from time-travelling through the history of the city, visiting an original scythe smithy complete with sound effects, or just admiring the massive 20m-long solid wooden beams of the original 17th-century granary building.

Reichraming

Cycle the forest railway

Following WWII, wood was in short supply and in high demand in Austria, and a series of railways were constructed to run through Nationalpark Kalkalpen so that wood could be taken from its hard-to-reach slopes and moved more easily to where it was needed. These forest railways were vital at the time and during the early part of the 20th century. The last bundle of wood was transported using the forest railway in the park in 1974, but the track has remained.

Today you can take your own bicycle (or hire one) and cycle the route of the old railway track through the forest along the **Hintergebirgsradweg bike trail** (kalkalpen.at/hintergebirgsradweg). It's a unique way to experience the national park, as well as connecting you with a piece of history. The 17 tunnels you'll pass through on the route also make this a thrilling ride through the landscape.

Starting at Reichraming or Unterlaussa/Mooshöhe, this is a circular route that takes around three hours to complete. You can begin at either starting point to cycle it. Mountain bikes and e-bikes can be rented from hire shops and some guesthouses in the region, though not from within the national park itself.

Sengsengebirge

Tackle the pre-Alps

A range of limestone mountains forming part of the 'Pre-Alps', the Sengsengebirge lies within Nationalpark Kalkalpen and is popular with hikers. The 23km hike across four peaks takes most people two days, with an overnight stay in a bivvy hut, the **Hochsengsbiwak** (hochsengsbiwak@gmx.at), which should be booked ahead. The hut is always open, the door never locked, and it can be used for emergency accommodation, but if you're planning to stay here, let them know.

There's no round-trip option, so it's a case of going there and back again. You can do it in one day if you prefer to get home for bed. Cycle all the way to the starting point and leave your bike there for the return journey – it's perfectly safe and lots of hikers do this. Or drive to either Spering or Schillereck car park and follow the yellow hiking signposts. But you do need to be fit to hike and bike in one day, as the hike alone is pretty tough.

SNOWSHOEING

When the snow falls in the Nationalpark Kalkalpen, there's only one way to get around – by snowshoeing. You can join a guided tour if you're not familiar with snowshoeing and don't own your own shoes, or you can take to the snow by yourself.

Basically hiking in snow, snowshoeing gives you a more connected-to-the area way to enjoy the landscape in winter, unlike skiing or snowboarding.

The usual hiking trails in the national park become snowshoe trails when the land is covered in a blanket of white. Snowshoers move relatively slowly through the snow, looking for wildlife and animal tracks, and getting to grips with how the natural habitats and the landscape itself, change in winter.

Snowshoes can be hired at the **Reiraming Visitor Centre** for €15 per day.

 EATING NEAR NATIONALPARK KALKALPEN: OUR PICKS

Knapp am Eck: Classic Austrian tavern in Steyr serving traditional dishes, some with a modern twist. *11am-2pm & 6-11pm Tue-Fri* €€

Adria Fischrestaurant: Modern seafood restaurant in Wels offering fine food and wine in elegant surroundings. *11.30am-2pm & 5.30-10pm Mon-Fri* €€€

Rathausstüberl: Small, rustic diner in Bad Hall serving hearty favourites like burgers and schnitzel. Great value. *3pm-midnight Wed-Fri, 10am-midnight Sat, 10am-9pm Sun* €

Kulinarium Aschauer: Bright and modern restaurant in Bad Hall serving traditional Austrian cuisine and modern classics. *10am-9pm Wed-Mon* €€€

Reichraminger Hintergebirge

The summits you'll reach on the hike are the famous Hohe Nock, the Rohrauer Grosstenberg, Hochsengs and then Schillereck.

Wilderness Trail Buchensteig
Hike the primeval trail

Following one of the longest stretches of intact stream systems in the eastern Alps, the **Reichraminger Hintergebirge** (Wilderness Trail Buchensteig) takes you through one of Austria's largest areas of forest, mostly untouched by human activity – including areas of beech forest, one of only a few in such a condition in Europe. It's this protected beech forest that gives Nationalpark Kalkalpen its UNESCO World Heritage status, which it has held since 2017.

There are old pathways through the forest, left by woodcutters from times gone by, but the stream guides most walkers through here today. Hiking the entire forest in a loop takes around six hours, but that's just pure walking time. For most people, the wildlife and scenery are too good to pass straight by. The alpine longhorn beetle and the white-backed woodpecker, both primeval forest species, can be seen here. With stops or just for a gentle pace, allow closer to eight hours.

TAKE A DIP

For those who like a fresh cold water plunge, the national park has a few natural lakes that are ideal for wild swimming, surrounded by an untamed landscape of mountains and forest.

Edlebach: The small lake at Edlebach is a cool water pool, but right next to a golf course so offering less in the way of wilderness.

Gleinkersee: For something a little more temperate, Lake Gleinker is one of Austria's warmest lakes, reaching temperatures of 25°C. Three wooden jetties give direct access to the water. You can paddleboard or kayak the lake, or sit back and relax on a boat tour.

Elisabethsee: Lake Elisabeth has fewer facilities and isn't as warm, but it makes up for this in wildness. The water is clear and it's a popular camping spot.

CAFES NEAR NATIONALPARK KALKALPEN

Das kleine Schwarze: Modern speciality coffee bar in Steyr with a bright interior and outdoor seating. Buy beans to take home too. *Tue-Sat 9am-6pm Sun 10am-6pm* €

Kaffeeschmiede: A mix of traditional coffee and cake with modern speciality coffees in Steyr, with pavement seating. *8.30am-6pm Mon-Sat, 9.30am-6pm Sun* €€

Cafe Central: Cosy cafe in the centre of Wels, with traditional coffee house vibes and live music on Saturdays. *9am-8pm Mon-Sat* €

Urban Cafe: Established in 1853, this traditional coffee house on Bad Hall's main square serves cakes and great coffee. *9am-6.30pm Wed-Sun* €€

WILDLIFE IN THE NATIONALPARK KALKALPEN

The raw wilderness of this park offers a home to 55 different species of mammals alone. A whopping 17 of these different species are bats.

Otters and deer are easy to spot as you wander the trails, foxes, hares and the elusive lynx maybe less so, but take a closer look at the tiny life going on all around and you can spot some of the 1560 different species of butterflies who call this area home and maybe even the primeval alpine longhorn beetle.

The oldest beech tree here is 525 years old; when these trees die, instead of being cleared away they're left to rot naturally, providing the right conditions for rare animals and plants to thrive.

An old lumberjack hut, which was once used for workers to sleep over in, is now a small cafe serving refreshments to hikers and cyclists. You can follow the stream through the forest, or book onto a guided hike *(€27)*, as part of a group or one-on-one with a ranger.

Bad Hall

Visit a vineyard

A baby in winery terms, the vineyard **Rogl** *(weinbaurogl.at)* has been producing wines in Bad Hall since 2017. Bad Hall is 50 minutes from Nationalpark Kalkalpen by car and the vineyard can be found in the northeast of town. Bad Hall is better known for its natural thermal spa and has been a wellness tourist destination for many years. However, with the arrival of Rogl, its first vineyard, the town is now also gaining recognition for other lifestyle attractions. If you ask us, wine goes perfectly with spas, so this seems like a perfect pairing.

Take a factory tour, have a tasting in a blissful setting right by the vines and get to know their straightforward, fruity wines. Armin Rogl, who owns and runs the vineyard, will also travel to you if there's a special event you'd like a wine tasting for, or you'd just like to be in the comfort of your own accommodation. He'll even bring the wine glasses. As the first winemaker in Bad Hall, Armin might have started something here, and more may follow, but Rogl will always be the original Bad Hall winery.

Windischgarsten

Climb the Panorama Tower Wurbauerkogel

For the best view of the region, taking in the sweeping landscape of peaks and valleys, climb the steps in the glass tower of the **Panorama Tower Wurbauerkogel** *(adult/child €6.60/3.70; closed Nov-Mar)* on the **Wurbauerkogel** mountain at the edge of the Nationalpark Kalkalpen.

As you head up to the top, information displays show the names of the mountains you can view. On the ground floor, there's an exhibition called 'The fascination of rock', where you can learn about the area. If you don't fancy the six flights of stairs, take the lift all the way to the top and enjoy the panoramic views.

Losenstein

Explore Losenstein Castle ruins

Found at the foot of the 1180m Schieferstein mountain at the edge of Nationalpark Kalkalpen, **Burg Losenstein** *(burg losenstein.at)* is one of the oldest castles in Upper Austria. Though it's now a ruin, it was once the seat of the Losenstein dynasty, a powerful family in the region. Information boards dotted around the ruin provide some background to the castle and its inhabitants, and there's an audio description you can

Burg Losenstein

BAD HALL'S IODINE BRINE

A natural spring rich in iodine was first discovered in the city in 777 and today 11 iodine springs have been identified in Bad Hall, making it the most powerful iodine spring in all of central Europe.

Since its discovery these healing waters have been used to treat a variety of ailments and to promote better health, but of all the iodine treatments available in Bad Hall, it's their eye therapies that are the most well-known. Iodine has been found to be effective for dry eye, conjunctivitis, glaucoma and optic nerve disease.

Patients are offered iodine brine eye baths or iodine brine sprays. Iodine brine can also be used as an anti-inflammatory and to promote better blood flow.

download onto your phone. It's free, with entry all year round, making it popular with local families. There's even a fireplace set up, as so many people come here for a campfire in the evenings.

Innviertel

The area of the Innviertel is a walker's paradise, with hills, forests and great blankets of agricultural land. It's still more culturally Bavarian than Austrian, being formally part of Bavaria, and there's a distinct difference in the dialect spoken here. Traditional and historic villages and towns line the River Inn, and rolling hills and valleys sweep the land, where pockets of lakes lie. It's a far cry from the industrial towns of Upper Austria, and is rural like a lot of the region. It's also breathtaking and picture-postcard perfect in its visual appeal.

Cycle by the ancient trade route, sample different types of beer, which is highly important here, and hike through the stunning and lush landscape.

DRINKING IN BAD HALL: WINE

Heuriger Furtmühle: Traditional rustic bar and restaurant, with outdoor benches, gallery seating and a wine tavern. *4-10pm Fri, 11.30am-10pm Sat*

Badhaus: Relax with a glass of wine in the restaurant, where last orders for food are at 8.30pm. *8am-11pm Tue-Sat*

Pup Caprice: Cocktail bar and cafe serving drinks and bar food, with a lively pub atmosphere. *5pm-1am Thu-Sun*

Cafe Da Vinci: Cafe with outdoor seating, specialising in Austrian wines. Also serves prosecco. *8am-10pm Mon-Fri*

Wheat beer, Ried Brewery

MAYR MEDICINE

Born in 1875, Dr Franz Xaver Mayr became a pioneer in fusing traditional medicine with a more modern approach, focusing mainly on how our gut health influences all other areas of our health. He was an early champion of fasting to promote better health.

Today, many spas and specialist health centres across Austria follow the Mayr Cure, a holistic approach to health emphasising improving digestion and intestinal health through diet, fasting and detoxing.

Modern health centres also promote meditation, exercise, mindfulness, rest and better health education. The core idea of Mayr medicine is that good health means better health in the future.

Spas, swims & local medicine

Living life in the great outdoors is important here and there's a big emphasis on nature being something that can improve one's health and create improved wellness. Spas and outdoor swimming aren't only reserved for moments of luxury and 'me time'; they're a part of everyday life in this region.

At the **Geinberg Spa Resort** (*sparesortgeinberg.at*) you can book in for the day and experience the vitality pools, thermal pools, and themed areas like the Caribbean sauna and Oriental World with hammam.

Perfect for families, the **Freibad Ried im Innkreis** on the banks of the river Breitsach is a complex of lane swimming, slides, leisure pool, sun terrace and a volleyball court.

At **Therme Bad Schallerbach** (*eurothermen.at/bad-schallerbach; adult €36-54, child €13.50-27.50*), there's a sauna mountain village with over 40 saunas and pool area, a pirate water adventure world for kids, and Tropicana with palm trees cocktails and its own sandy beach.

Delve a little deeper into your wellness journey and head to **Kurhaus Schärding** (*kurhaus-schaerding.at*) where you can practice yoga by the banks of the river Inn, undergo bowel treatment, take part in fasting, and try Chinese medicine, Indian therapies and traditional Austrian Mayr medicine.

EATING IN INNVIERTEL: OUR PICKS

Bums'n: Traditional Austrian bar and restaurant in Scharding with great beer, a beer garden and extra pavement seating. *8am-midnight Mon-Sat* €€

Seven: Cafe-restaurant in Scharding serving international dishes. Great for people watching. *10am-10pm Sun, Mon & Wed, 9am-10pm Thu, 10am-midnight Fri & Sat* €€

Ernesto: Authentic Italian restaurant in Ried, with good wine pairings and intensely Italian atmosphere. *11am-11pm Mon, 9.30am-11pm Tue-Sat* €€

Steffi's Imbissecke: No-frills bratwurst joint in Ried, with limited seating. Be prepared to queue, as locals love it here. *8am-7pm Mon-Fri, 9am-4.30pm Sat* €

The retreat dates back to the 17th century with a history of therapeutic medicine since 1931. There's a rolling programme of treatment courses, including individually tailored ones for your own needs.

Raise a stein in Ried, the beer city

Once the largest market towns in Austria, **Ried im Innkreis** isn't much visited by tourists today, partly due to its extreme lack of transport connections. If you want to get to Ried you have to either catch the irregular and run down rickety old train, or drive. But most visitors who do make the effort to come to this pretty little town do so for the beer.

Ried is, traditionally, a beer town and once had two busy breweries. One of these, **Ried Brewery**, first opened in 1910 and is still running. A short walk around the town, where buildings are painted in an array of pastel colours, tells you just how important beer is here. Bars in Ried don't only have bartenders and waiters, they have beer sommeliers, and as you wander around you can literally smell beer in the air.

Although most bars and cafes close for much of the winter or only have limited opening hours, come the spring the town leaps into life again. The horse market, held in Horse Market Square, takes place in the spring, with no fixed dates, and signals the beginning of the summer season. Bars and cafes extend their opening hours and the beer begins to flow. There's a very distinct Bavarian feel to the town, where everyone uses any excuse to raise a stein of frothing beer.

Get into history in Braunau am Inn

The quiet town of Braunau am Inn sits right on the border with Germany and has a pretty square of pastel-painted buildings, and a modest clock tower that oversees the town.

The town can't quite escape being the birthplace of Adolf Hitler, and while the house he was born in is still standing, it's certainly not a museum. Outside stands a memorial stone to the victims of the Nazi party and the house itself is currently being renovated and turned into a police station.

Otherwise there's plenty of history in this town, including a carving on **Stadtpfarrkirche St Stephan** (*dioezese-linz. at/braunau-ststephan*) of Hans Steininger, the 16th-century army captain who sported a 6ft-long beard. Head to the **Bezirksmuseum Herzogsburg** (*adult/child €3.60/€2.20*) to see his actual beard in all its glory. The story goes that on

RIED BREWERY

When innkeepers in Ried became frustrated by the supply of beer from other regional breweries in 1908, they got together and decided to form their own brewery.

Maybe it's because innkeepers, who knew more about the business of selling beer than anyone, took this on, or maybe just because Ried loves beer, but the **Ried Brewery** (*rieder-bier. at*) has gone from a small beer making operation, selling its first bottle in 1910, to something much bigger.

Although the brewery is still only medium-sized by comparison to others around the world, it's stood through war and rationing, and today offers tours, tastings and workshops in beer education.

DRINKING IN INNVIERTEL: BEER

Hemingway Bar & Cocktail: Predominantly a cocktail bar, but still a great cosy bar for a beer in Ried. *4pm-2am Mon-Sat*

Bar Auswaerts: Popular, modern bar with outdoor seating in Ried. Gets busy at weekends, but has plenty of seating. *5pm-1am Wed & Thu, to 3pm Fri & Sat*

Zwickl Pub: Looks like offices from the outside but inside it's a traditional tavern in Altheim. *6pm-4am Mon-Sat*

Mike's Music Bar: Quirky bar in Waldzell, serving beer and Austrian dishes, while also running a catering business and sauna. *3pm-2am Wed-Sun*

GETTING AROUND THE INNVIERTEL

It takes an hour and twenty minutes to drive from Linz to the Innviertel region; there are no direct public transport links.

Cycling the route from Linz takes around six hours, and although it's a great way to see the surrounding area, it takes some stamina. The route takes you through Wels, and the small town of Gunskirchen, where St Martin's Church, with its 53m-high tower, dominates the landscape, and then through Ried im Innkreis.

Once in the Innviertel, cycling and hiking takes you from town to town quickly and easily. You can drive in the area, but some roads are old and very narrow.

Stadtpfarrkirche St Stephan (p183)

rushing to put out a fire in the town he tripped on his beard and broke his neck. The museum also features a history of firefighting, sculptures and artefacts through the history of the town and the surrounding region.

The **Local History House with Bell Foundry** (braunau .at/Heimathaus_mit_Glockengiesserei; guided tours 1.30pm Tue-Sat May-Sep, by appointment only) is an old craftsmen's house with a bell foundry workshop dating back to 1385. It's remarkably preserved and feels like a frozen moment in time. Bizarrely, there's a collection of weapons here, which include an ox whip, sledgehammers and clubs labelled as 'fighting tools'.

Lastly, head to the **Historische Badestube Vorderbad** (adult/child €2/1) to see the only viewable bathhouse in town (two others are privately owned) that operated from the 16th to 18th century. It's one of the best preserved bathhouses from this time in the whole of Europe.

Places We Love to Stay

€ Budget €€ Midrange €€€ Top End

Linz

MAP p167

Wolfinger €€ Traditional hotel with lots of character, in a great position overlooking the square.

Harry's Home € Aparthotel in the north of Linz; rooms come with fully equipped kitchens.

Hotel Schwarzer Bär € Modern hotel in a 15th-century building, with a central position and rooftop bar.

Hotel Prielmayerhof € Located in a quiet area, five minutes from town by bus, this comfortable hotel has spacious rooms.

Hotel Goldener Adler €€€ Another comfortable hotel, located in the centre of town with free parking nearby.

Limehome €€ Well-kitted-out apartments with self check-in, just a short walk from the main attractions.

Freistadt

Da Dinghofer Mei Wiaz'Haus €€ Basic but comfortable hotel near Freistadt that's known for its outstanding restaurant.

Hotel Hubertus € Family-run hotel with separate bar and cafe, right in Freistadt's centre.

The owner bakes bread here too.

St Florian

Gästezimmer Brühl €€ Traditional guesthouse with a cute little terrace with seating. Perfectly placed close to the centre of St Florian.

Hotel Florianerhof €€€ This laid-back hotel with spacious rooms is near St Florian's monastery. Many locals eat in the restaurant here.

Mauthausen

Donauhof Mauthausen €€€ A clean, modern hotel with views over the Danube, just 15 minutes from Linz.

Hotel-Restaurant zum Donaueck Mauthausen €€ Minutes from the Mauthausen memorial, this hotel is modern, small and cute, with a secure bike rack.

Steyr

Gasthof Bauer € No-fuss B&B in Steyr with friendly staff, a local vibe and reasonably priced traditional meals.

Hotel Mader €€ Traditional hotel in central Steyr with an impressive wine cellar. Parking is in a nearby long-stay car park.

Stadthotel Styria €€€ Located just 10 minutes from the train station in Steyr, with spacious rooms and a small breakfast buffet.

Wels

Hotel Ploberger €€ Business hotel in the centre of Wels, with the most incredible breakfast spread.

Boutique Hotel Hauser €€ Boutique, central hotel in Wels, with a roof pool, sauna and sun terrace. Self-catering rooms are available.

Amedia Plaza Kremsmunstererhof € This beautiful Wels hotel has a quirky interior design and is extremely good value for money.

Ried

Biergasthof Hotel Riedberg €€ Three-star hotel in Ried that behaves like a four star. There's an impressive beer selection.

Der Kaiserhof Ried €€ A basic four-star hotel with an on-site sauna and small gym.

Gästehäuser Ehrndorfer € Traditional old wooden house turned guesthouse in rural location with a dining room and outdoor seating.

Scharding

Hotel Forstinger €€ Upmarket four-star hotel in a central location, with landscaped gardens and fine food.

Stadthotel Scharding €€ Central hotel with spacious rooms that was once a hospital church and is now beautifully renovated.

Hotel Stiegenwirt € Traditional Austrian guesthouse, family-run and serving hearty dishes. Basic but good value.

Hotel Wolfinger, Linz

For places to stay in Styria, see p213

Above: Vineyards, Styria; Right: Lynx

Researched by Rudolf Abraham

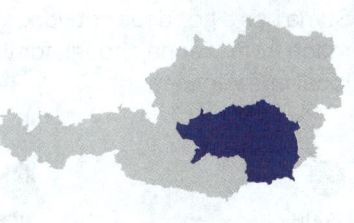

Styria

THE GREEN HEART OF AUSTRIA

Vineyards, mountains, castles, spas, wine roads, exquisitely good food, art and culture – and arguably the coolest city in Austria, the Styrian capital, Graz.

Styria (Steiermark) covers a huge area, and encompasses a vast range of scenery – from snow-streaked mountains and soaring limestone plateaux in the northwest, to the beautiful sweep of the River Mur, and the rolling vineyards and pumpkin fields of Südsteiermark. 'From glacier to wine', reads the Steiermark tourist board's motto – and it's remarkably appropriate.

UNESCO-listed Graz, Austria's second city and definitely one of its most vibrant, reinvented itself as a major centre of the creative arts when it was inaugurated as European Capital of Culture (the first city in Austria to enjoy this accolade) back in 2003.

With its plethora of farmers markets and local produce, Graz is also one of Austria's greatest culinary centres.

Styria is home to some of Austria's best wine-growing regions, in particular Südsteiermark where you'll find the excellent South Styrian Wine Road, and this is also a region famous for its outstandingly good pumpkinseed oil – an area tailor-made for visiting vineyards and stopping at some of the many wonderfully homely *Buschenschenken* (wine taverns), the regional name for *Heuriger*.

There's fabulous hiking around Schladming and on the southern side of the Dachstein, as well as in the lovely Nationalpark Gesäuse – a hot spot of biodiversity and one of the few places in Austria where the lynx has managed to reestablish itself, albeit tentatively. Cycle routes cross the region, and Schladming transforms into a top ski resort in winter.

THE MAIN AREAS

GRAZ	**MARIAZELL**	**SÜDSTEIERMARK**
Cultural capital.	Pilgrimage church.	Wineries and bike rides.
p190	**p205**	**p206**

Find Your Way

Styria has a good rail network, with Graz being particularly easy to reach from Vienna, though for the southwest you'll be more reliant on local bus services.

TRAIN
Graz is well connected by rail with Vienna via the Semmering, and West Styria via Bruck am der Mur, with services continuing beyond Schladming towards Salzburg. Trains head south to Südsteiermark. Graz itself has an excellent tram network.

BICYCLE
Cycling is a great way to explore the wine roads of Südsteiermark and the Sausal, as well as the Mur Valley. There are plenty of places offering bike and e-bike rental in Graz and surrounding areas.

Graz, p190
Austria's UNESCO-listed second city is a vibrant centre for the arts, with a beautifully preserved old town centre, and it's one of the country's greatest foodie hot spots.

Schladming (p211)

Plan Your Time

Styria is Austria's second-largest state, after Lower Austria, and there's an incredible amount to see, but good transport links with Vienna and Salzburg make it easy enough to get around.

Styrian Highlights

● With five days or fewer in hand you should base yourself in **Graz** (p190), exploring the museums and the vibrant culture of Austria's UNESCO-listed second city. You'll also have time to make a couple of day trips – or even better an overnight trip – down to **Südsteiermark** (p206) where you should spend some time on the **South Styrian Wine Road** (p206).

A Week to Explore

● With a week to 10 days, you can see a lot of Styria. Spend the first few days in **Graz** (p190), then in **Südsteiermark** (p206) with its wine roads before going to **Steirisches Vulkanland** (p207) for a spa. Head to West Styria, stopping at **Mariazell** (p205) on the way. Spend time in **Nationalpark Gesäuse** (p209), followed by out-door fun around **Schladming** (p211).

SEASONAL HIGHLIGHTS

SPRING
In spring you'll see wildflowers blooming in the Nationalpark Gesäuse and there are festivals in Graz.

SUMMER
Hiking in Nationalpark Gesäuse and around Schladming, cycling the Styrian wine roads and festivals in Graz.

AUTUMN
Autumn is the season for wine in South Styria, and a great time for cycling along the Mur.

WINTER
In winter you can go skiing in Schladming, or celebrate Advent in Graz.

Graz

CULTURAL CAPITAL | DESIGN CITY | FANTASTIC FOOD

GETTING AROUND

Graz deserves at least a few days if you're going to see even half of what's on offer. It's an easy place to get around – the centre is best explored on foot, and there's also a comprehensive tram network, along with buses beyond the city centre.

Rent a bike and follow the path alongside the River Mur. Graz also makes a convenient base for exploring south and east Styria by public transport – take a bike on the train and set off along the South Styrian Wine Road.

☑ TOP TIP

Available for 24, 48 or 72 hours, the **Graz Card** gets you free use of public transport in the city and free entrance to many museums, including the Kunsthaus, Landeszeughaus, Graz Museum and Schloss Eggenberg, plus a walking tour of the city centre.

Despite often playing second (or third) fiddle to the infinitely more visited Vienna and Salzburg, Graz is a wonderfully vibrant city which is very hard not to fall in love with. As well as having been crowned European Capital of Culture back in 2003, it was named a UNESCO City of Design in 2011, and its historic core is a UNESCO World Heritage Site.

Sitting astride the River Mur, it has museums, galleries, festivals and cultural events aplenty, breathtaking Renaissance, baroque and modern architecture, hidden courtyards, cycle paths, parks and green spaces, cultural flair and a lively student fizz.

And if all that doesn't impress you, come here for the food. Graz has some 300 urban farmers, and lies at the centre of an area famed for its wines and pumpkinseed oil, so you'd do well just to visit for the restaurants, inns and farmers markets.

Art & Architecture at the Friendly Alien   MAP P192
Visit the Kunsthaus Graz

Nothing is more emblematic of modern Graz than the **Kunsthaus**. Opened in 2003 to coincide with the city's stint as European Capital of Culture, it was designed by British architects Peter Cook and Colin Fournier. It's a genuinely dazzling piece of architecture, its biomorphic design and intense blue colouring a complete contradiction to the traditional gabled buildings which surround it, with their red-tiled roofs. Some have likened it to a giant sea slug, others to an oversized baby hippo – but it's the nickname given to it by Fournier which has stuck: the Friendly Alien.

The Kunsthaus stands on the bank of the Mur, its roof bristling with strange, vent-like nozzles, and is attached to the renovated Iron House – a former department store built in 1848, which had a glamorous 1st-floor cafe, and was among the earliest cast-iron buildings in Europe, predating London's Crystal Palace by three years. What was once the Iron House's cafe now forms an exhibition space, Camera Austria,

Hauptplatz

while the ground floor is now the setting for the excellent Kunsthauscafé (p197). The location of the Kunsthaus on the right, hitherto underdeveloped bank of the Mur, led to the surrounding area subsequently becoming one of the hippest neighbourhoods in Graz.

The Kunsthaus has a rolling programme of exhibitions focusing on contemporary and modern art, which have included the work of such luminaries as Sol LeWitt and Ai Weiwei. Make sure you check out the view from the furthest nozzle (the 'naughty nozzle', architect Peter Cook called it) in the upper-floor exhibition space. This one doesn't point towards the sky, but towards that iconic landmark of 'old' Graz, the clocktower, framing it very deliberately.

Markets & Executions

MAP P192

History in the Hauptplatz and town hall

At the corner of Herrengasse and Sporgasse is the city's main square, **Hauptplatz**, where weekly markets (and executions) were held during the Middle Ages. A large, open space, it is surrounded by beautiful old merchants' houses on one side, including the Luegghaus with its elaborate stucco decoration.

continues on p194

SUPER GRAZ FESTIVALS

No surprises here: this university town with a passion for the arts has plenty of festivals, from the International Storytelling Festival (May) to Assembly, the city's Festival of Fashion (September) and Klangnacht, a mesmerising light and sound festival (October).

Elevate: Bills itself as a festival of 'music, arts and political discourse'. Held in March.

Design Month: All of Graz's creative energy condensed into a one-month festival during May.

Springfestival: Live electronic music and art installations. Takes place in late May/early June.

Aufsteiren: Traditional festival with music, dance, handicrafts and good food in September.

Steierischer Herbst: Edgy, contemporary performing-arts festival (September/October), which has been running for over half a century.

EATING IN GRAZ: OUR PICKS

MAP P192

Der Steirer: Styrian tapas, plenty of classic mains and at least a dozen Styrian wines by the glass each month. *11am-midnight* €€

Die Herzl Weinstube: Traditional Styrian inn serving roast pork and other hearty fare as well as vegetarian dishes. *10am-midnight* €€

Die Eschenlaube: Restaurant and cultural space with a beautiful hidden courtyard. Housed in a late 18th-century horse stable. *4pm-1am Mon, noon-1am Tue-Sat* €€

Restaurant Schlossberg: The one with the view. Michelin-listed restaurant on top of the Schlossberg. *5pm-midnight Wed & Thu, 11am-midnight Fri & Sat, 11am-5pm Sun* €€€

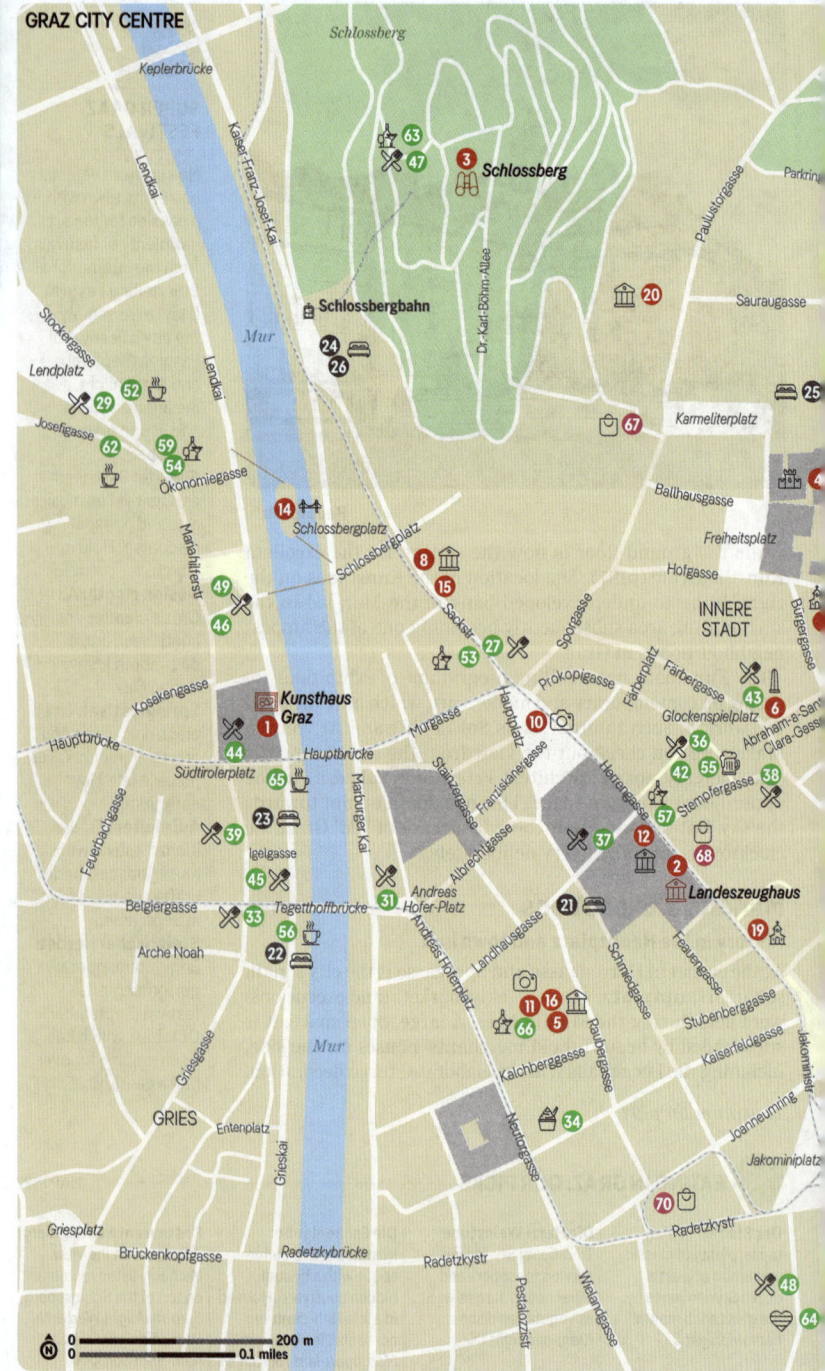

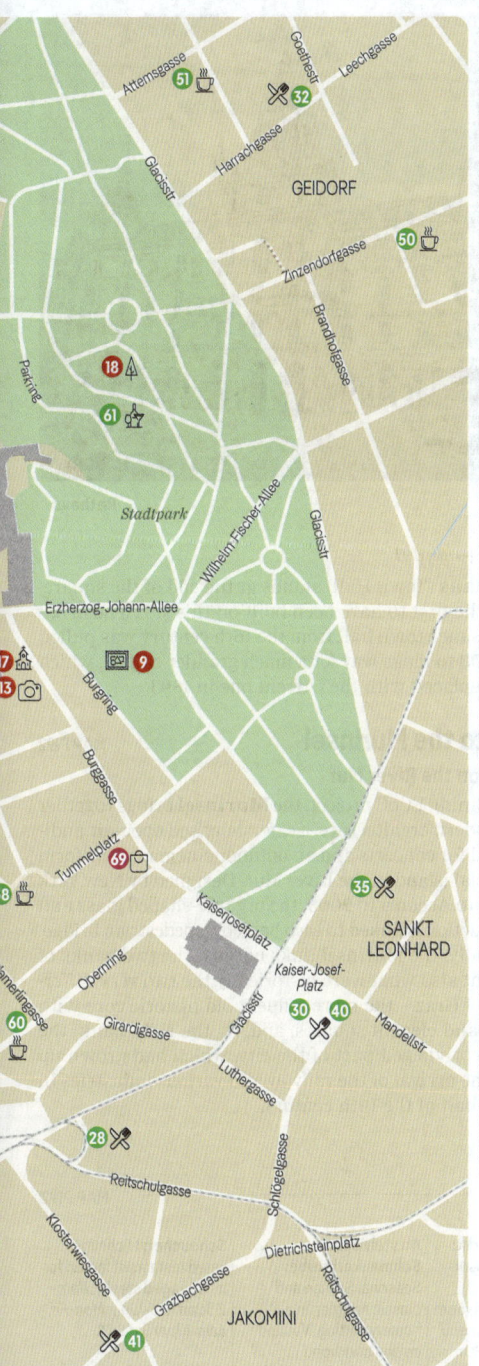

★ HIGHLIGHTS
1. Kunsthaus Graz
2. Landeszeughaus
3. Schlossberg

● SIGHTS
4. Burg
5. COSA Centre for Scientific Activities
6. Glockenspiel
7. Grazer Dom
8. Grazmuseum
9. Halle für Kunst
10. Hauptplatz
11. Joanneumsviertel
12. Landhaus
13. Mausoleum of Ferdinand II
14. Murinsel
15. Museum für Geschichte
16. Naturkundemuseum
17. St Catherine's Church
18. Stadtpark
19. Stadtpfarrkirche
20. Volkskundemuseum

● SLEEPING
21. Aiola Living
22. Das Weitzer
23. Grand Hotel Wiesler
24. KAI 36
25. NH Graz City
26. Schlossberg Hotel

● EATING
27. Altsteirische Schmankerlstube
28. Area 5
29. Bauernmarkt am Lendplatz
30. Bauernmarkt Kaiser-Josef-Platz
31. Cafe Erde
32. Cofeba
33. Der Steirer
34. Die Eisperle
35. Die Eschenlaube
36. Die Herzl Weinstube
37. El Pescador
38. Frankowitsch
39. Gasthaus zur Alten Press
40. Geniesserei am Markt
41. Ginko
42. Ginko Greenhouse
43. Glöckl Bräu
44. Kunsthauscafé
45. Mangolds
46. Mohrenwirt
47. Restaurant Schlossberg
48. Scheucher
49. Speis am Lendhafen

● DRINKING & NIGHTLIFE
50. Beanery
51. Café Futter
52. Die Scherbe
53. Freiblick Tagescafé
54. Ginger
55. Hops Craft Beer Pub Graz
56. Kaffee Weitzer Graz
57. Klapotetz Weinbar
58. Martin Auer Kindercafé
59. Miles Jazz Bar
60. Operncafé
61. Parkhouse
62. Paul & Bohne
63. Skybar
64. Stars
65. Tribeka
66. Viertel 4

● SHOPPING
67. Genussladen Gut Schlossberg
68. s'Fachl
69. Vinothek bei der Oper
70. Wine & Co

WHY I LOVE GRAZ

Rudolf Abraham, Lonely Planet writer

I first visited Graz 25 years ago, when I was living in Zagreb, Croatia. I love the vibrant atmosphere and the informality, the mixture of mind-bogglingly cool modern architecture and design with elegant tradition and student grunge. It oozes history as much as many other cities in Austria, but it always appears to wear it rather lightly.

Along with its fantastic museums, it has a plethora of farmers markets, and the food is wonderful (as is the local wine), from Styrian classics to vibrant bars to excellent vegetarian restaurants – and it has that buzz which only a university city can really capture.

Finally, I love that it's the gateway to Südsteiermark, a region which is rapidly becoming one of my favourite places in Central Europe.

Rathaus

continued from p191

The **Rathaus** (Town Hall) stands at the end of the square, and is not the first to have been built on this site. The original, Renaissance town hall from the 16th century was pulled down in 1803 to make way for a much grander edifice, which itself was replaced with the current one in 1893.

Step onto the Murinsel

MAP P192

The island on the River Mur

Another defining ECoC project, the **Murinsel** brings together striking modern architecture, a cafe, shop, and open-air auditorium used for concerts and an outdoor cinema, in the form of an artificial island in the River Mur. Designed by New York architect Vito Acconci in 2003, the organic-shaped glass and steel construction is linked to each bank by a pedestrian bridge.

Symbolically, the Murinsel links not just the two banks of the river, but also what were historically the two very different halves of Graz – the more affluent old historic core with its palaces and elegant squares, and, on the right bank, the more underprivileged part of the city, which had grown up following the arrival of the railway and various industries in the second half of the 19th century.

 EATING IN GRAZ: OUR PICKS ──────────────────────── MAP P192

Mohrenwirt: Traditional dishes with a contemporary twist, championing organic, seasonal local produce. Michelin Bib Gourmand. *11.30am-11pm Wed-Sat* €€

Geniesserei am Markt: Beside the Kaiser-Josef-Platz farmers market. Come for lunch or the 6pm 10-course seasonal menu (book ahead). *from 9am Tue-Sat* €€€

Altsteirische Schmankerlstube: Seasonal Styrian and classic Austrian in a homely setting. Vaulted ceiling and wood panelling. *10am-11pm* €€

Scheucher: Michelin-listed restaurant famed for its dry-aged steaks. *11am-2.30pm & 6-10pm Mon-Fri, 6am-10pm Sat* €€€

Renaissance Masterwork at the Landhaus MAP P192

A touch of northern Italy

The **Landhaus** (Styria's regional parliament), a beautiful Renaissance palace on Herrengasse dating from the mid-16th century, is the work of northern Italian architect Domenico dell'Allio, who specialised in fortifications and was chief architect to Ferdinand I. Along with his work on the fortifications in Graz, he was responsible for several fortifications in what was then Inner Austria, including those in Klagenfurt and Bad Radkersburg, along with the Lalio Bastion at the Castello di San Giusto in Trieste. He was among the architects summoned to Vienna to improve the fortifications there, which, as had become evident from the first Siege of Vienna, were unlikely to withstand another attack.

The highlight of the Landhaus is its arcaded courtyard, with arches set on three levels, and which is free to enter. Concerts and other events are held in the courtyard throughout the year, and it's here that you'll find the city's ice nativity scene during Advent. Beside the entrance to the Landhaus is the so-called **Rumortafeln** from 1588 – a notice prohibiting the genteel rulers, lords and landowners of Styria from drawing their sword or a knife, or getting into a brawl while inside the building.

The World's Largest Historical Armoury MAP P192

Discover the preserved Styrian armoury

The **Landeszeughaus** (*Styrian Armoury; museum-joanneum .at/landeszeughaus; €12*) is the world's largest preserved historical armoury, with a staggering 32,000 objects on display. Spanning a period from the 15th to the 18th century, the collection ranges from the sabres carried by light cavalry to huge broadswords, delicately inlaid firearms, the halberds and pikes used by foot soldiers, and all the other accoutrements of warfare in between – bullet moulds, powder flasks, bayonets – all beautifully preserved. Among all the items is an early-16th-century horse's armour from Innsbruck.

The reason Graz ended up with such a vast collection of weapons and armour stems partly from its history as a frontier province, and because it actually had three armouries – one for the city, one for its ruler and one for the state. Between the 15th and 17th centuries, Styria was a bulwark against attack from the east, and its armoury grew to enormous proportions.

There are **guided tours** of the armoury in English at 12.30pm daily except Monday (there are others in German); you must

HISTORY OF THE ARMOURY

When Archduke Charles II took up residence in Graz in the 1560s, further weapons were required. The present armoury was built in the 1640s to accommodate these combined stores of weapons, and by 1699 when the Treaty of Karlowitz was signed, and Styria ceased to be a frontier province, the collection stood at around 185,000 pieces.

Reforms under Maria Theresia included a proposal to close the armoury, with outdated weaponry going into scrap – but local estates successfully put forward a petition to keep the armoury intact.

In the 1890s it became part of the museum collection of the Joanneum Universal Museum and, during WWII, the collection had to be shifted to three separate castles across Styria to protect it, returning to the armoury in 1946.

 EATING IN GRAZ: OUR PICKS MAPS P192 & P198

Gasthaus zur Alten Press: Traditional Styrian cuisine in a cosy, friendly setting near the Kunsthaus. Vegetarian dishes too. *11.30am-11pm Mon-Fri, to 3pm Sat* €€

El Pescador: On one side of the Rathaus, this is – as the name implies – the place to eat seafood in Graz. *11.30am-midnight Mon-Sat* €€€

Glöckl Bräu: Typical beer garden fare and tables clustered on atmospheric Glockenspielplatz. *10.30am-11.30pm* €€

Gasthof Sternwirt: Traditional restaurant with a nice garden on the eastern outskirts of the city. *10am-10pm Mon & Thu-Sat, to 7pm Sun* €€

FOUR WAYS UP, FIVE WAYS DOWN

There are four main ways to get to the top of Schlossberg: the Kriegssteig, the steep staircase zigzagging across the cliff face above Schlossbergplatz; the elevator which you'll find inside the left-hand tunnel at the end of Schlossbergplatz; the WWII tunnels, which also start at the end of Schlossbergplatz; and the Schlossbergbahn, which leaves from a little further north along Kaiser-Franz-Josef-Kai. (You can also walk up from Karmeliterplatz around the other side.)

For the descent, you also have the option of the slide – billed as the highest underground slide in the world, 175m long with a vertical descent of 64m, over which you'll reach speeds of up to 30km/h, including a stomach-churning corkscrew in the upper part.

reserve in advance. Alternatively, there are audio guides in several languages. Either option is worth it as the exhibits themselves have fairly minimal labels.

To the Top of the Schlossberg   MAP P192
Graz's unassailable fortified hill

Schlossberg, the city's green hill, stands at 473m high above the left bank of the Mur, an omnipresent landmark and a place to escape and gaze over the city below.

The old medieval castle underwent a complete makeover in the mid-16th century, at the hands of Italian architect Domenico dell'Allio, who turned it into an impregnable Renaissance fortress bristling with bastions. He also dug a 94m deep well (known as the Turkish Well, since Ottoman prisoners are thought to have contributed to the labour), along with a 15m-deep cistern, both of which ensured there was still drinking water during a siege.

So effective were Dell'Allio's fortifications on the Schlossberg that the fortress was never taken – even Napoleon failed to capture it, despite occupying the lower city three times, in 1797, 1805 and 1809. However, following the French victory over Austria and the subsequent Treaty of Schönbrunn, Napoleon stipulated that the fortress at Graz must be dismantled. Only a large sum of money paid by the people of Graz saved the clocktower and the bell tower from destruction. During WWII a system of tunnels was dug beneath the Schlossberg, which were able to shelter up to 40,000 people during air raids, and some of these are now accessible and provide a way up or down from the top.

The best way to approach the Schlossberg is from Schlossbergplatz, from where it towers above you, and a series of steps zigzags upwards – though you also have other less strenuous options, including a glass lift and a funicular, the Schlossbergbahn, which was built in 1894 and has a gradient of 61%.

Up on top of the Schlossberg you'll find the bell tower, complete with its 5-tonne bell (the heaviest in Graz) known as Liesl, as well as the restored casemates (now a stage used for concerts and opera performances), the Schlossberg branch of the Graz Museum which has plenty of information on the hill and its former castle, and the iconic clocktower. But the main thing to do up here is relax and enjoy the view, either in one of the cafes, or in the beautiful garden on the Bürgerbastei – a restored bastion below the clocktower, which has one of the best views out over the rooftops of Graz.

EATING IN GRAZ: VEGETARIAN & VEGAN ———————— MAPS P192 & P198

| **Ginko:** Excellent, good-value vegetarian-vegan restaurant. Laid-back, with self-service dishes priced by weight. *11.30am-9pm Mon-Sat* € | **Cafe Erde:** Small, friendly vegan restaurant with a cosy, bohemian vibe. It's good value and close to the Mur. *11.30am-10pm* € | **Gerüchteküche:** Standout plant-based restaurant with a show-stealer 6.30pm six-course taster menu (reservations essential). *6.30-11.30pm Mon-Fri* €€€ | **Mangolds:** Vegetarian and vegan bowls, burgers, traditional and international dishes, in-house bakery and a huge salad bar. Founded in 1989. *11.30am-5pm Mon-Fri* € |

Clocktower

Uncover 1900 Years in the City
MAP P192

Learn about Graz in its museum

As its name suggests, **Grazmuseum** *(grazmuseum.at; €8)* is the place to come and learn more about the city, through an enormous collection spanning everything from painting and photography to musical instruments.

The permanent exhibition, *360 Graz,* covers the period from 1128 when the city is first recorded, to the opening of ECoC in 2003. It's also now available in an online version, which is worth checking out before arriving in Graz. The museum also has some interesting temporary exhibitions, which in the past have covered themes such as Jewish life in Graz, and the life and films of the iconic Graz-born actress Marissa Mell.

The Graz Museum is on Sackstrasse; there's another branch of the museum on Schlossberg.

Eternity & Reconciliation
MAP P192

The Burg's double staircase

Across the road from Grazer Dom, beside the triple-arched Burgtor (one of the original city gates), is the 15th-century **Burg** – the residential palace built by Frederick III, though it was left to his son Maximilian I to complete. Among the parts

A GRAZ ICON

Schlossberg's clocktower (Uhrturm) is the most recognisable symbol of old Graz. The clocktower dates from the mid-16th century, during the reconstruction of the fortress under Ferdinand I, although a tower is mentioned as standing here as early as the 13th century.

The bell which sounds the hours is the oldest in Graz, dated 1385, and the clock mechanism which dates from 1712 still works, although it has been powered by electricity since the mid-20th century.

The clock face itself has one oddity. The two hands are reversed – the longer hand points to the hours, not the minutes. That's because originally the clock just had one hand to indicate the hours – when a shorter hand was added later, it was decided to leave the original hour hand in its place, and use the newer short hand for minutes.

 CAFES IN GRAZ — MAPS P192 & P198

| **Die Scherbe:** Excellent brunch, with a laid-back vibe, good menu, a lovely garden courtyard and live music downstairs. *9am-1am Mon-Sat, to midnight Sun* € | **Kunsthauscafé:** Coffee, cocktails and excellent food with many vegetarian options, on the ground floor of the 'friendly alien'. *9am-midnight Mon-Sat, to 8pm Sun* € | **Cofeba:** Small, vegetarian-vegan cafe and book exchange. Grab coffee or a bite, and swap a book with one on the shelves. *9am-8pm Mon-Fri* € | **Operncafé:** Landmark cafe which opened its doors back in 1861. Elegant and steeped in coffee-house culture. *8am-11pm Mon-Thu, to midnight Fri & Sat, to 9pm Sun* € |

GREATER GRAZ

★ **HIGHLIGHTS**	● **SLEEPING**
1 Schloss Eggenberg	5 Augarten Art Hotel
● **SIGHTS**	6 Gasthof Lend-Platzl
2 Botanical Garden	7 Harry's Home Graz-Smart City
3 Kunstgarten	8 Hotel Daniel
4 Stadtstrand	9 LEND Hotel
● **EATING**	● **DRINKING & NIGHTLIFE**
10 Gasthof Sternwirt	12 Barista's
11 Gerüchteküche	13 baseMENt_2.0
	14 The FAGtory Club

JOHANN BERNHARD FISCHER VON ERLACH

Architect Johann Bernhard Fischer von Erlach was born in Graz in 1656. His works include such sights as the **Karlskirche** (p95), Stadtpalais (Winter Palace of Prince Eugene; p105) and **Plague Column** (Trinity Column; p135) in Vienna; the Dreifaltigkeitskirche (Holy Trinity Church) and Palais Augarten and Kollegienkirche (Collegiate Church) in Salzburg; and the high altar at the **Basilika Mariazell** (p205) in Styria.

built by Maximilian is the reason you'll be visiting the Burg – a Gothic, double spiral staircase, or *Doppelwendeltreppe*, dating from 1499. The stone stairs part and then rejoin at each floor, leading some to interpret it as a symbol of eternity, while to others it is a symbol of reconciliation.

Traces of the Gothic at Grazer Dom   MAP P192
Visit Graz cathedral

Grazer Dom (*Cathedral of St Giles; Dom St Ägidius*) was built in the mid-15th century on the orders of Frederick III, and originally would have been attached to the adjacent Burg. It was raised to the status of a cathedral in 1786. It received a baroque makeover in the 17th and 18th centuries, including

 CAFES IN GRAZ   MAP P192

Martin Auer Kindercafé: Legendary baker Martin Auer's family-friendly cafe with stunningly good cakes. *7am-6.30pm Mon-Fri, 8am-6pm Sat, 9am-5pm Sun* €

Paul & Bohne: Popular little coffee shop on Lendplatz. Paul & Bohne also run the big, modern-feeling Paul's Kaffeewelt over in Graz Smart City. *8am-6pm Mon-Sat* €

Tribeka: Stylish modern coffee shop across the street from the Kunsthaus; one of four Tribeka branches across Graz. *7am-7pm Mon-Fri, 8am-7pm Sat & Sun* €

Café Fotter: One of the oldest coffee houses in Graz, which opened its doors more than 80 years ago. *8am-3pm Mon-Fri, to 2pm Sat & Sun* €

the marble high altar and the pulpit, but several traces of the original late Gothic church remain. These include the main (west) portal which dates from 1456, its decoration having been enriched by niche sculptures in the late 19th century; and fragments of 15th-century frescos of the interior – one of which shows Frederick III himself in the Styrian ducal crown.

Note the two inlaid chests on either side of the chancel entrance, originally bridal chests of Paola Gonzaga from Mantua, who moved to Tyrol following her marriage to Leonhard of Gorizia. Now used as reliquaries, the chests themselves date from the 15th century and are decorated with scenes from a poem by Petrarch, thought to be the work of the Italian Renaissance painter Andrea Mantegna.

An Emperor's Tomb & St Catherine's Church

MAP P192

Visit an imperial mausoleum

Next to Grazer Dom is one of the most striking buildings in Graz, the **mausoleum of Ferdinand II** – part of **St Catherine's Church** – complete with soaring turquoise domes. Ferdinand had his court artist Giovanni Pietro de Pomis, originally from northern Italy, start work on the mausoleum and church in 1614. However, he was made emperor just five years later and moved to Vienna, so work on the mausoleum ground to a halt – and it was still only half finished when he was laid to rest there in 1637. It was left to his grandson, Leopold I, to finish work on the church and mausoleum. Among the artists whom Leopold commissioned for this was the young, Graz-born Johann Bernhard Fischer von Erlach – who went on to become one of the most influential baroque architects working in Austria.

The rather grand, red-marble sarcophagus in the mausoleum contains the remains of Maria of Bavaria, Ferdinand's mother – the final resting place of Ferdinand himself is simply indicated by a tablet on the wall.

Standing above the gable of the main facade of St Catherine's Church are three statues. The central figure is St Catherine of Alexandria, patron saint of students and philosophers, who is recognisable by the spiked wheel on which she was martyred, and looks to the Priesterseminar (Priest's Seminary) over the road. This was the former Jesuit College, and the original site of Graz University which was founded in 1585.

SHOPPING IN STYRIA: WINE SHOPS

Genussladen Gut Schlossberg: Styrian products such as wine, pumpkinseed oil and locally roasted coffee. Near Karmeliterplatz in Graz.
s'Fachl: Styrian delicacies and local handicrafts in a courtyard off Herrengasse, in Graz.
Wine & Co: Wide selection of Austrian and international wines in Graz, near Jakominiplatz.
Vinothek bei der Oper: The oldest wine shop in central Graz, with Austrian and international wines.
Vinofaktur Genussregal Südsteiermark: Near Ehrenhausen station, making it a perfect Wine Road intro. Big Südsteiermark wine selection.
Vinothek Steiermark: Wide selection of Steiermark wines and a beautiful view from the terrace, in St Anna am Aigen.

 CAFES IN GRAZ — MAP P192

Ginko Greenhouse: An all-vegan cafe with cakes, coffee and juices. Owned by the excellent **Ginko restaurant**. *11.30am-7.30pm Mon-Thu, 9am-7.30pm Fri & Sat €*

Frankowitsch: Landmark place on Stempfergasse serving delicious *Brötchen* (open sandwiches), wine and cakes. *8am-7pm Mon-Fri, 9am-6pm Sat €*

Freiblick Tagescafé: Spritzers, coffee or a bite to eat with super views from the department store's rooftop terrace by the river. *9.30am-6.30pm Mon-Fri, to 6pm Sat €€*

Kaffee Weitzer Graz: The Hotel Weitzer cafe is a lovely place, and a perennial riverside favourite for *Kaffee und Kuchen*. *7.30am-7pm Mon-Fri, 9am-7pm Sat & Sun €*

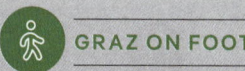

GRAZ ON FOOT

Graz is made for exploring on foot. This walking tour makes a circuit of the city centre, exploring all its main sites and quirky wonders.

START	END	LENGTH
Kunsthaus	Kusthaus	3km; 2 hrs

Start at the ❶ **Kunsthaus** (p190), and go north along Mariahilferstrasse. Since the Kunsthaus opened, this partly pedestrianised street has gone from seedy to very hip, with a succession of upcycling shops, galleries and cool bars. Pass Mariahilferplatz, one of the city's 13 inner city squares, with its view of the Schlossberg, and the Minorite Church, built by a pupil of Palladio.

At ❷ **Lendplatz** (p203), stop to check out the farmers market, then loop back along Stockergasse and left down Ökonomiegasse. Cross the river via the ❸ **Murinsel** (p194), then walk up to Schlossbergplatz. Walk up the steps or take the glass elevator or WWII tunnels to the top of the ❹ **Schlossberg** (p196).

Descend on the eastern side to Karmeliterplatz, turn right on Sporgasse then left along Hofgasse towards the Burgtor city gate. Visit the double spiral staircase in the ❺ **Burg** (p197), ❻ **Grazer Dom** (p198) and the ❼ **Mausoleum & St Catherine's Church** (p199). Head down the steps, left then right down a narrow street to the ❽ **Glockenspiel** (p201), aiming to get there when it chimes. Work your way down to Herrengasse and turn right, calling in to see the Renaissance courtyard at the ❾ **Landhaus** (p195) and the ❿ **Landeszeughaus** (p195) (Styrian Armoury). At the ⓫ **Hauptplatz** (p191) turn left, passing the Franciscan church and crossing the river to arrive back at the Kunsthaus.

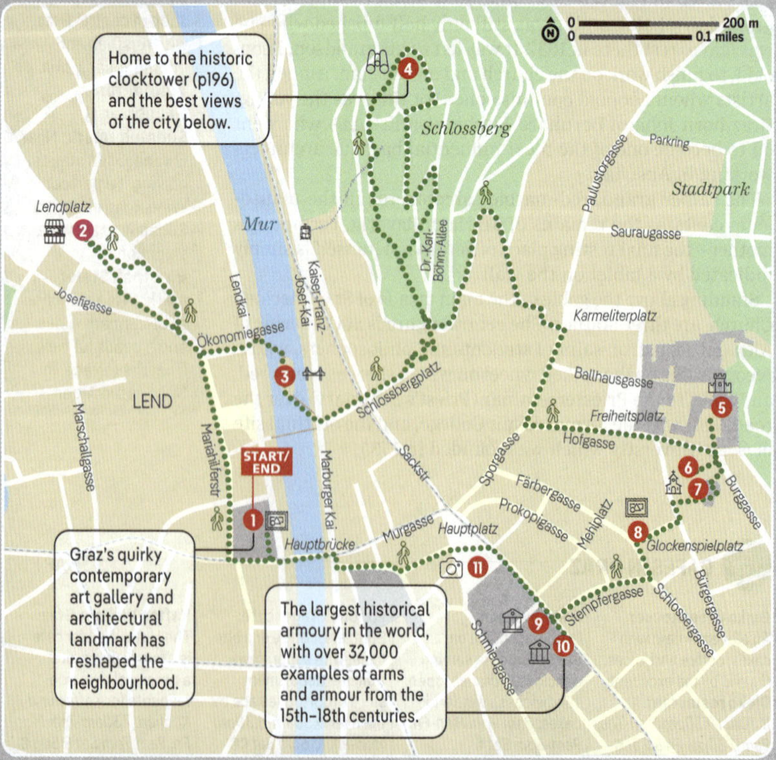

Home to the historic clocktower (p196) and the best views of the city below.

Graz's quirky contemporary art gallery and architectural landmark has reshaped the neighbourhood.

The largest historical armoury in the world, with over 32,000 examples of arms and armour from the 15th–18th centuries.

The City's Beloved Glockenspiel
Historic chimes in Graz

MAP P192

Hidden away down a side street behind the Priest's Seminary is Glockenspielplatz – a lively spot crammed with tables and parasols and surrounded by cafes, restaurants and bars. This is where you'll find Graz's beloved Glockenspiel, installed above the facade of a house by its new owner, one Gottfried Maurer, who had seen a good few carillons on his journeys through northern Germany.

Maurer's Glockenspiel first began chiming on Christmas Eve in 1905, and in 1929 he bequeathed it to the city. The Glockenspiel chimes three times a day, at 11am, 3pm and 6pm, with a pair of figurines in traditional Styrian dress coming out to twirl and dance. The 24 bells play three different melodies – but the positions of the 800 steel pins on the barrel are changed five times a year, meaning these three tunes keep changing throughout.

Graz's New Museum Quarter
Art and science at the Joanneumsviertel

MAP P192

Opened in 2011, the **Joanneumsviertel** *(Joanneum Quarter)* is a major cultural centre in the city's historic core, transformed from a group of historic buildings and now home to several museums. These include the excellent Neue Galerie Graz and Bruseum, with its collection of modern paintings, sculptures, prints and photography from the 19th and 20th centuries. The Bruseum focuses on the work of Styrian-born painter and performance artist Günter Brus.

The Joanneumsviertel also houses the **Naturkundemuseum** *(Natural History Museum; €12)*, with a particularly interesting geology section, and the **COSA Centre for Scientific Activities** *(free)*, which is especially good for kids. It's worth getting a 24-hour ticket *(€18)* which allows entry into all exhibitions at the Universalmuseum Joanneum locations except Schloss Eggenberg.

Surprising Stadtpfarrkirche
Stained glass windows that created a stir

MAP P192

The **Stadtpfarrkirche** (Parish Church) on Herrengasse dates from the 15th century. It's a beautiful building, with traces of Late Gothic vaulting, its appearance subsequently transformed with baroque and neo-Gothic elements. Its more modern

GREEN SPACES IN GRAZ

Graz has plenty of green spaces besides the Schlossberg where you can enjoy a picnic, stroll or swim.
Stadtpark: A well-manicured swathe of green which sweeps around the east side of the city's historic core with broad, winding paths, cafes, old chestnut trees and oodles of space.
Botanical Garden: Northeast of the city centre (tram 1) with modern, cutting-edge glasshouses.
Kunstgarten: Contemporary art in a garden setting, south of the Hauptbahnhof.
Stadtstrand: A city beach on the banks of the Mur, south of the centre; it's easily reached by bike along the river. You can rent SUPs and kayaks here.
Schwarzlsee: A swimming lake and recreation area beside the airport.

CAFES IN GRAZ

MAPS P192 & P198

Speis am Lendhafen: Vegetarian restaurant and coffee house with organic wines. Evening menu highlights local fare. *10am-10pm Mon-Fri, dinner from 4pm* €

Beanery: Speciality coffee and a friendly atmosphere near the Stadtpark. *7.30am-9pm Mon-Fri, 8am-9pm Sat, 9am-9pm Sun* €

Barista's: Coffee, tea, smoothies and more west of the Hauptbahnhof. One of half a dozen branches. *7.30am-9pm Mon-Fri, 8am-6pm Sat, 9am-6pm Sun* €

Die Eisperle: Standout vegan ice-cream shop with several branches across the city. *10am-10pm* €

BÜHNEN GRAZ: DINNER & A SHOW

If you're catching a concert in Graz between October and the end of July, you can take advantage of Bühnen Graz, a scheme offering a pre-performance set menu for a special fixed price (€47 in 2025) at one of 10 restaurants.

Buy your **Bühnen Graz Card** at the ticket centre at Kaiser-Josef-Platz, and make a reservation at a participating restaurant at least one day in advance, and coinciding with the night of the performance you've booked. Let them know when you're making your booking that you want to redeem a Bühnen Graz Gourmet Card. Reservations need to be for between 5pm and 7.30pm.

Participating venues include the Graz Opera, Graz Schauspielhaus, Next Liberty, Orpheum Graz and Dom im Berg. You'll need to show your concert ticket as well.

---

windows created quite a controversy when they were unveiled in the 1950s, after the original Gothic ones had been destroyed by a bomb blast in WWII. The artist responsible for the new windows was Albert Birkle, from Salzburg, and they mainly depict scenes of the Passion and the Resurrection of Christ.

However, look closely and along with the more familiar figures depicted alongside Christ, you'll see the faces of Hitler and Mussolini. Some were outraged by this, but Birkle was in fact having the last laugh – his art had been labelled as degenerate under the Nazis, and here he shows the two fascist dictators among Christ's tormentors.

Baroque & Rococo Masterpiece Palace MAP P198
Pay a visit to Schloss Eggenberg

On the western side of Graz, **Schloss Eggenberg** is a stunning baroque palace, built after 1625 for the Imperial Governor Hans Ulrich von Eggenberg. Backed by wooded hills and set amid beautiful parkland, the palace was designed by the north Italian artist and architect Giovanni Pietro de Pomis, who was court artist to Archduke Ferdinand in Graz. The design includes a wealth of allegorical detail and number symbolism, from the total number of windows (365, in accordance with the days of the year – the Gregorian calendar had only been introduced a few decades earlier, in the 1580s) to the total number of rooms on each floor (31, the maximum number of days in a month).

But it's the palace decoration which really dazzles. The 24 state rooms (those numbers, again) are centred around a large Planetensaal (Planetary Room), and together these are painted with an extraordinary series of ceiling paintings – some 500 of them – by the baroque painter Hans Adam Weissenkircher. The paintings blend Biblical stories with scenes from Greek and Roman mythology, historical events and references to the Eggenbergs themselves, along with astronomical symbolism, including the seven planets known at the time and the 12 signs of the zodiac. In the 1750s the state rooms were lavishly redecorated in rococo style, but the ceiling paintings were left untouched. Since the 18th century, the palace has remained almost perfectly preserved and unaltered.

Along with the palace gardens, with their wandering peacocks, there's a lapidarium with a large Roman collection, an archaeology collection, a coin collection, and the Alte Gallerie which has works from the 15th to the 18th century. In recognition of its value, the UNESCO-designation for the

---

 DRINKING IN GRAZ: BARS & PUBS ———— MAP P192

| **Ginger:** It's in the name – effortlessly cool gin bar and art space on the endlessly vibrant Mariahilferstrasse. *7pm-2am Wed-Sat* | **Miles Jazz Bar:** Jazz, cool vibes and drinks, from Styrian craft beer to single malts and cocktails. On Mariahilferstrasse. *7pm-2am Wed-Sat* | **Area 5:** Bar-restaurant on a rooftop terrace, with views of the Schlossberg. Wine, beer, cocktails, plus burgers, salads and more. *11am-midnight Sun-Thu, to 2am Fri & Sat* | **Klapotetz Weinbar:** Lovely little wine bar on Herrengasse. Top-notch wines, delicious regional products and plenty of atmosphere. *11am-10pm Mon-Fri, to 6pm Sat* |

Schloss Eggenberg

city's old town centre was extended in 2010 to include Schloss Eggenberg.

The easiest way to get here is by tram – take line 1 and get off at the Schloss Eggenberg stop, from where it's a 500m walk down Schlossstrasse beside the park wall.

Fabulous Food & Farmers Markets   MAP P192

Austria's foodie capital

In Styria you'll find one of the country's best and most vibrant food scenes – and nowhere is this more evident than in Graz. Along with its huge range of restaurants, Graz is home to over 300 urban farmers – not to mention all the other farmers, growers and winemakers in surrounding areas, producing everything from exquisite pumpkinseed oil and delicious apples to *Käferbohnen* (scarlet runner beans), world-class hops and superb wine – meaning that fresh, seasonal produce is always on hand, and supplied (among other places) to the city's 14 farmers markets.

The largest farmers market in Graz is on **Kaiser-Josef-Platz**, behind the Opera House, and this – along with the large farmers market on **Lendplatz** with its irresistible

GRAZ MUSEUMS LARGE & SMALL

Graz has plenty of great smaller museums besides its big-hitters.

Museum für Geschichte: Styria's cultural outpouring since the Middle Ages in a huge collection from ceramics to fashion to musical instruments.

Halle für Kunst: This leading contemporary-art exhibition space is in the building which formerly hosted Trigon, a biennial which formed a bridge for cultural exchange during the Cold War.

Volkskundemuseum: The Folk Life Museum spotlights folk culture, including traditional Styrian folk costumes, along with temporary exhibitions.

Arnold Schwarzenegger Museum: The house where the legendary bodybuilder, Hollywood actor and former Governor of California was born in 1947 is now a museum. West of Graz in Thal.

 DRINKING IN GRAZ: BARS   MAP P192

Parkhouse: Beer and music – from live music to late-night DJs to silent disco – in the Stadtpark. *10am-late*

Skybar: Stylish bar and terrace with fabulous views on top of the Schlossberg. *from 5pm Wed & Thu, from 11am Fri & Sat, 11am-8pm Sun*

Viertel 4: Seasonal pop-up bar in the Joanneumsviertel with impeccably made cocktails, deckchairs and beats by local DJs. *May-Sep from 3.15pm Tue-Sat*

Hops Craft Beer Pub Graz: Craft beer hot spot round the corner from Glockenspielplatz with local and international craft beers. *6pm-midnight Mon & Tue, to 1am Wed-Sat*

Farmers market, Kaiser-Josef-Platz (p203)

LGBTIQ+ GRAZ

Tutenball: In February, this is Graz's biggest LGBTIQ+ event – a huge drag ball, which has been running for over 30 years.

CSD Parkfest: Christopher Street Day Parkfest has a parade from the Stadtpark, followed by a festival in the Volksgarten. In June.

STERRRN Fest: Festival founded in 2022 for the promotion of gender equality and elevation of queer-feminist music and art. In June.

Stars: LGBTIQ+ friendly bar-cafe on Schönaugasse. Café Silber on Klosterwiesgasse is another good place.

The FAGtory Club: Monthly queer party venue with an emphasis on being a safe space. Plenty of music and dance.

baseMENt_2.0: Gay club on Brockmanngasse.

food stalls – should be considered an essential part of sightseeing plans in Graz.

Farmers markets are open 6am to 1pm Monday to Saturday, so it's best to go in the morning. Expect to find fresh fruit and vegetables, local cheeses, cured ham and smoked sausages, crusty farmhouse bread, fruit juice and freshly cut flowers. More often than not you'll be buying from the farmers themselves.

In order to factor all this market-browsing and food-buying potential into your stay, aim to include at least one picnic – **Augarten Park** beside the Mur, **Stadtpark** or the nearby **Burggarten** are some of the many good spots for picnicking in the city.

Airplane Parts & Hills

Austrian sculpture park

On the southern edge of Graz next to the airport, lies the huge open-air **Österreichischer Skulpturen Park**, founded in 2003, with 81 large-scale sculptures by Austrian and international artists. The sculptures span a period from the 1940s right up to the present day; sculptors represented include the likes of Chris Burden, Eva & Adele, Nancy Rubins (whose *Airplane Parts and Hills* is one of the highlights), Michael Schuster, Yoko Ono, Peter Weibel, Fritz Wotruba and Erwin Wurm.

Take bus 650 or 671 from the city centre (30-minute journey) and get off at the Schwarzlsee IBC/Skulpturenpark stop.

CAPITAL OF CULTURE

Graz was Austria's first European Capital of Culture in 2003, followed by Linz (p166) in 2009 and the Salzkammergut region (p214) in 2024.

Beyond Graz

Superb wine and winding wine roads, breathtaking mountains, untouched nature, superb food and relaxing spas.

From the vineyards and pumpkin fields of Südsteiermark and the spas of Steirisches Vulkanland south and southeast of Graz respectively, to the baroque pilgrimage church in Mariazell in the north, and the soaring mountains and forests of Nationalpark Gesäuse in the northwest, and the alpine playground of Schladming – Styria offers a huge variety of places to explore beyond Graz. Some of these make for good day trips from Graz; others repay a longer, more immersive experience – such as Südsteiermark, which was literally made for slow travel, and the wilds of Nationalpark Gesäuse. Schladming can be used as a convenient stopover on the way to Salzburg or Tyrol.

Places
Stübing p205
Mariazell p205
Südsteiermark p206
Riegersburg p207
Nationalpark Gesäuse p209
Admont p209
Leoben p210
Murau p210
Schladming p211

Stübing
TIME FROM GRAZ: **35MINS**
Traditional wooden architecture
Stretching along a wooded valley 20km north of Graz, **Österreichisches Freilichtmuseum** *(Austrian Open-Air Museum; €14.50)* is the largest of its kind in Austria. Here you'll find nearly 100 traditional wooden buildings from across Austria – farmhouses, mills, wayside shrines and more – collected in the 1960s, typically when their survival in their existing location was threatened. The wooden buildings were carefully disassembled before being transported to Stübing, then reassembled there using traditional building methods.

Mariazell
TIME FROM GRAZ: **1½HRS**
Austria's greatest pilgrimage site
Situated in the north of Styria, **Basilika Mariazell** is Austria's most important pilgrimage site, and one of Europe's most significant Marian shrines, along with the likes of Lourdes in France and Loreto in Italy. Mariazell itself is a place with only some 2000 inhabitants – but around one million pilgrims flock here each year. It was founded in 1157, with construction of the Romanesque chapel beginning in 1200. The Gothic church, which was later built on the site, was enlarged and given a baroque makeover in the 17th century – this included adding the towers which frame the spire, building the dome, and extending and enlarging the nave. In the 17th century the Habsburgs made Mariazell a national sanctuary.

GETTING AROUND

The best way to explore Südsteiermark is by bike, while Nationalpark Gesäuse and Schladming offer endless possibilities for hiking. Trains run south from Graz to Leibnitz and Ehrenhausen, and there's a handy 'wine taxi' (WEINmobil), which makes getting around the main places on the wine road particularly easy, if you don't fancy cycling or if you're visiting vineyards and (for obvious reasons) don't want to drive.

MARIAZELL PILGRIMAGE ROUTES

The classic way to arrive in Mariazell would of course be on foot, and numerous hiking trails make their way to the shrine from different parts of Austria.

One of the best-known is the 227km **Mariazell Pilgrimage Route 06**, which runs through Styria. The trail begins in Soboth in southern Styria, heads east to Eibiswald, then north up through Graz and the Hohe Veitsch to Mariazell, following a mixture of forest roads, paths and asphalt roads.

St Barbara im Mürztal in the Hohe Veitsch is famous for its Pilgerkreuz – at just over 40m tall, it's the largest accessible wooden cross in the world, with seven separate chambers inside, accessible by stairs.

The object of veneration is a late Romanesque linden wood statue of the Virgin Mary, which according to legend, arrived with a Benedictine monk by the name of Magnus, who was sent here from the monastery of St Lambrecht in southern Styria in the 12th century.

Direct trains from St Pölten to Mariazell take around 2¼ hours. Alternatively, you can travel to Mariazell on the Mariazellerbahn, Austria's longest narrow-gauge railway. Trains from Graz to Kapfenberg and then a bus from there takes around three hours.

Südsteiermark

TIME FROM GRAZ: **45MINS**
TO EHRENHAUSEN

South Styrian Wine Road

Südsteiermark is a rolling succession of steeply pitched hills, covered with a patchwork of vineyards stretching as far as the eye can see – which, as it happens, produce some of the finest wines in Austria. The best way to discover this region and its wines is on one of the Styrian wine roads, in particular the South Styrian Wine Road which runs close to the Slovenian border, sometimes on the border itself, such as at Grenztisch.

Tement is the largest winemaker in the area, but most of the vineyards here are small, with numerous terroirs. They're also steep – almost ridiculously so, meaning that much of the work in the vineyard is done by hand, with tractors only venturing onto the slopes when they are suitably dry. Many of the vineyards are also *Buschenschenken* (wine taverns), offering platters of delicious local food to enjoy over a glass or a bottle of their own wine, and many also offer accommodation *(Winzerzimmer)*. This is the classic way to enjoy the South Styrian Wine Road, or Südsteiermark in general – rent an e-bike, take your time and enjoy what this wonderful region has to offer.

Getting to Südsteiermark is a doddle from Graz – just take e-bikes on the train down to Ehrenhausen, and head off into the hills from there (at which point you'll realise why e-bikes were a good idea). There's also a 'wine taxi' running through the area. A little to the north, the Sausal, Schilcher and Klöcher wine roads are also well worth exploring.

Styrian Pumpkinseed-Oil Trail

If there's one ingredient which defines Styria more than anything else, it's the extraordinarily good pumpkinseed oil – pungent, nutty and intense, with a distinctive deep green colour, and Denomination of Origin status. The main variety is the

 SOUTH STYRIAN WINE ROAD: WEINGÜTER & BUSCHENSCHENKEN

Weingut Kögl: Organic and biodynamic vineyard with superb natural wines (including some wonderful Pet Nats) and delicious food. *seasonal hours* €	**Dreisiebner Stammhaus:** Award-winning vineyard and excellent *Buschenschank*, with rooms and a nice big terrace. *seasonal hours* €	**Oberer Germuth:** Family-run vineyard and *Buschenschank* with a lovely terrace, near Grenztisch. *2-8pm Thu-Sun* €	**Bioweingut Buschenschank Knaus:** The first (and still only) certified organic *Buschenschank* in Styria, since 2005. *Apr-Oct noon-6pm Sat, 2-10pm Sun* €

Styrian oil pumpkins

Styrian oil pumpkin, which has been grown here since 1870. Each yellowish fruit contains around 1000 huskless seeds, which are cleaned and dried before being ground and mixed into a paste with salt and water. This paste is then roasted, before being pressed according to traditional methods – it takes between 2.5kg and 3kg of seeds to produce 1L of oil. As well as being used to drizzle over soups and salads, it's used in a plethora of other dishes, including desserts (if you haven't tried pumpkinseed oil cake in Südsteiermark, you haven't lived).

The **Styrian Pumpkinseed-Oil Trail** (*Styrian Oelspur; steiermark.com*) brings together selected oil mills, restauranteurs and pumpkin farmers across 15 communities in Südsteiermark, including Bad Schwanberg, Deutschlandsberg, Eibiswald, Pölfing-Brunn and Sulmtal, Eibiswald. The best way to explore this network of routes is by bike.

Riegersburg

TIME FROM GRAZ: **50MINS**

Castles, spas & volcanoes

The largest and most imposing castle in Styria, **Burg Riegersburg** (*€23.40, incl falconry display €35.40*) sits atop the stumpy remnants of an ancient volcano – this part of Austria is known as Steirisches Vulkanland (Styrian Volcano Land)

THE WINES OF STYRIA

Styria has three main wine-growing regions – Südsteiermark, Weststeiermark and Vulkanland Steiermark – all of which gained DAC status starting from the 2018 vintage.

Sauvignon Blanc is the most widespread variety in Südsteiermark, both on the South Styrian Wine Road and in the Sausal hills, along with Muskateller. In Weststeiermark you'll find Schilcher, a distinctive rosé, while Traminac is common to the southeast in Vulkanland Steiermark.

Chardonnay (known locally as Morillon) and Pinot Blanc are also grown here, along with the more widespread and regionally typical Welschriesling, with its bouquet of green apples – this one is an acquired taste which tends to divide critics.

 SOUTH STYRIAN WINE ROAD: WEINGÜTER & BUSCHENSCHENKEN

| **Weingut Germuth Stammhaus:** Delicious food and wine, right on the Slovenian border. *from 1pm Wed, Thu, Sat & Sun* € | **Buschenschank Repolusk:** Winery and *Buschenschank* with a particularly nice terrace, home-baked bread and local produce. *from noon Thu-Sun* € | **Weinbau & Buschenschank Legat Tschöggl:** Just north of Leutschach, serving super *Brettljause* with homegrown produce and local game. *seasonal hours* € | **Weingut Peter Grill:** Hilltop setting surrounded by vineyards and forests near Leutschach. *seasonal hours* € |

SPAS IN STEIRISCHES VULKANLAND

Rogner Bad Blumau: Award-winning spa resort with indoor and outdoor water areas including the Vulkania spring fed into a thermal lake.

Thermal Spa Resort Bad Loipersdorf: It has 39 indoor and outdoor pools, 20 saunas, sandy 'baby beach' and kids' adventure spa with 142m double slide.

H20 Hotel-Therme Bad Waltersdorf: Family-oriented with indoor-outdoor pools, adventure park and slides including a 101m double-tube slide.

Die Therme der Ruhe Bad Gleichenberg: Surrounded by parkland, with highly mineralised thermal spa waters bubbling up from 1500m below the surface.

Parktherme Bad Radkersburg: Beside the River Mur, on the Slovenian border, with eight different saunas and kids' adventure area.

Burg Riegersburg (p207)

and is dotted with the remains of a long-extinct belt of volcanoes which were active here around 15 million years ago.

First mentioned in the 12th century, the castle passed between the hands of a succession of noble families over the centuries, gaining its present form in the 17th century under the resolute control of Baroness Elisabeth Katharina Wechsler, better known as 'the Gallerin' and quite a well-known figure in Styrian history. The castle was finally purchased at auction in 1822 by Prince Johann von und zu Liechtenstein, and remains in the possession of the Liechtenstein family to this day.

Of the castle's 100 or so rooms, more than 30 are open to visitors. The castle also houses three museums, the Castle Museum, Weapons Museum and the Witch Museum – the latter focusing on an infamous succession of witch trials in the late 17th century. Audio guides are available in English, and there are tours of the Castle Museum and the Witch Museum on Sundays – it's advisable to book in advance, though these are only in German.

With public transport, take a train to Feldbach (one hour) and then a bus to Riegersburg (25 minutes).

On the apple trail

Styria is Austria's largest apple-growing region – around 80% of the country's apples are grown here, with around 6000 hectares under cultivation – and the main growing region is eastern Styria. As well as being eaten fresh, they're used to make juices and cider, apple wine, apple horseradish sauce and of course, apple strudel. Ten main varieties are grown in Styria, from the international Gala and Braeburn to Kronprinz Rudolf, first planted here in the 1860s, and the increasingly rare Styrian Schafnase, mainly used to make spirits. You can find some of these local varieties at farmers markets.

In eastern Styria, the **Styrian Apple Road** (Steirische Apfelstrasse) begins near Gleisdorf (east from Graz) and stretches north through Puch bei Weiz, with local festivals in September and October.

Nationalpark Gesäuse

TIME FROM GRAZ: 2HRS 40MINS

River deep, mountain high

Established in 2002, Gesäuse is Austria's youngest national park, covering an area of 12,000 hectares in northern Styria, close to Nationalpark Kalkalpen in Upper Austria. The national park centres on the River Enns, which has carved a dramatic gorge through the steep-sided limestone mountains of the Reichenstein, Buchstein and Hochtor groups – a place of rushing water, sheer cliffs, rocky peaks and shadowy forests. The highest peak is the 2369m Hochtor. It's an area of extraordinary biodiversity, with numerous endemic species – 30 endemic species of plants, and 195 endemic species of fauna – along with iconic species like the golden eagle and the elusive lynx.

There are several huts within the national park – Hesshütte and Haindlkarhütte in the Hochtor group, and Buchsteinhaus and Ennstaler-Hütte (the oldest in the region, dating to 1885) in the Buchstein group – along with nearby Admonterhaus, Grabneralm and Mödlingerhütte, and over 500km of hiking trails.

An 80km circuit of the national park, the **Gesäuse-Runde**, can be started in Gstatterboden or Admont and takes five days. Longer trails include the **Luchs Trail** (Lynx Trail), a 210km hiking route through Gesäuse and Kalkalpen national parks and the Dürrenstein Wilderness Area.

The main gateways to Gesäuse are the villages of Gstatterboden by the Enns, and Johnsbach up in the mountains. There are information offices in Gstatterboden, Admont and just across the river from the Johnsbach im Nationalpark train station.

At weekends you can reach the national park (Gesäuse Gstatterboden im Nationalpark) by rail from Vienna's Westbahnhof, with just one change at Amstetten, in just two hours and 40 minutes. Otherwise during the week arrival by public transport usually takes about an hour longer and involves a bus connection at Liezen or similar. From Graz by train to Liezen followed by bus 910 takes two hours and 40 minutes.

Admont

TIME FROM GRAZ: 1½HRS OR 2½HRS VIA LIEZEN

Heavenly volumes at Admont Abbey

On the western side of Nationalpark Gesäuse, the **Benedictine abbey** (€19.50) in Admont houses the largest monastic library in the world. Founded in the 11th century by monks from Salzburg and dedicated to St Blaise, the abbey was remodelled in baroque style in the 1700s, including the creation of the library hall, by the architect Josef Hueber.

The library is an extraordinary place – with 70,000 books on display, in a light-flooded, 70m-long hall awash with white

SCARING THE BIRDS

A *Klapotetz* is a wooden construction which looks something like a rudimentary windmill but is actually a rather ingenious noise-making device used to scare away starlings and other birds from the region's vineyards.

Emblematic of Südsteiermark (they're also found over the border in Slovenia), they're made from specific types of wood, and have been around since at least the late 1700s.

As the sails rotate with the wind, they lift and release a series of hammers which strike a wooden board (usually made of cherry since this produces the best sound), while a 'tail' of birch-twigs turns the sails towards the wind.

The world's largest *Klapotetz* stands on Demmerkogel in the municipality of Sankt Andrä-Höch, and is 17m high.

LEOBEN & THE ERZBERG: A HISTORY OF MINING

Southeast of the bucolic forests of Nationalpark Gesäuse, the industrial town of Leoben is a place defined above all else by its long mining history.

This history is bound inextricably to the nearby Erzberg – a hill sporting a massive open-pit mine, which holds the largest reserves of iron ore in Austria. Surface mining on the Erzberg is recorded as early as the 8th century, with underground mining beginning in the 1500s.

Mining in the surrounding area goes back much further, with evidence of copper ore being mined here in the Bronze Age. Leoben lies at one end of the Steirische Eisenstrasse (Styrian Iron Route), which brings together a dozen separate museums.

and gold. The hall is lit by 48 windows, and the 11m-high vaulted ceiling and central cupola are decorated with allegorical frescos by the baroque painter Bartolomeo Altomonte. There are also wooden sculptures and reliefs by Josef Stammel – including his so-called *The Four Last Things*, painted to look like bronze, and representing death, resurrection, heaven and hell. Also keep an eye out for the 'secret doors', disguised by fake book spines.

The abbey's **Art History Museum** includes paintings, sculptures, textiles and liturgical objects from the Romanesque to the rococo, while its new **Gothic Museum** contains an outstanding group of 85 sculptures, paintings and stained glass, from the Kuno Mayer Collection. The **Museum of Contemporary Art** includes works by around 160 Austrian artists, mostly from the mid-20th century, part of the abbey's 1500-strong collection of modern art. There's also a **Natural History Museum**. Audio guides to the library and museums are available in several languages, and there are guided tours of the library in German.

Leoben
TIME FROM GRAZ: 1HR 🚆 VIA BRUCK AN DER MUR]

Beer & mining

The Erzberg open-pit mine near Leoben, and the huge Voestalpine steel plant in Eisenertz (which makes the longest sections of railway tracks in the world, at 120m), are offset by an attractive main square with elegant 17th-century facades in Leoben itself as well as some good museums. At the **MuseumsCenter Leoben** *(museumscenter-leoben.at; €5)*, the permanent exhibition *Tracks into the Past* presents the history of the city and its surroundings in seven phases, from the Hallstatt culture back around 800 BCE through to the present day.

Here for the beer

Along with its mining heritage, Leoben is the location of the **Gösser Brauerei** *(goesser.at)*, which produces one of Austria's highest-selling beers. The history of Gösser begins with the founding of a nunnery, Göss Abbey, back in the 11th century. The abbey was dissolved in 1782, but in 1860 the young Graz-born master brewer Max Kober took over the building and began brewing here – just as the nuns had been doing since 1459. There are tours *(€11.50)* of the brewery's **Braumuseum**, which includes a tasting session – book tickets online.

Murau
TIME FROM GRAZ: 2HRS 40MINS 🚆

A palace beside the River Mur

Murau has a pretty setting on the banks of the River Mur, some 200km before it reaches Graz. The main thing to see here is the late Renaissance palace, **Schloss Murau** *(€10)*. Built in the mid-13th century by the Liechtenstein family, ownership of the castle passed through marriage to Georg Ludwig zu Schwarzenberg, who had it completely rebuilt in square Renaissance form around a central courtyard between 1628 and 1643. It has remained in the hands of the Schwarzenberg family ever since.

FRESCO CYCLES

Bartolomeo Altomonte was also responsible for the frescoes at St Florian Monastery (p175) and Wilhering Abbey, both in Upper Austria.

Admont Abbey (p209)

From Graz to Murau by train requires changes at Bruck an der Mur and Unzmarkt. Murau also lies on the route of the Murtalbahn, a narrow-gauge railway running between Unzmarkt in Styria and Tamsweg in Salzburgerland.

Cycle the Murradweg

The Murradweg is a 450km cycle trail that follows the course of the River Mur. Starting from Sticklerhütte near the river's source on the edge of the Hohe Tauern National Park in Salzburgerland, the route takes you right across Styria to Bad Radkersburg, in the southeast corner of the state, before continuing into Croatia and its confluence with the Drava at Legrad. The route is typically broken down into eight stages and passes through quite an incredible range of scenery, taking in the mountains of the northwest along with the Styrian capital of Graz and the spa country and vineyards of east Styria.

Schladming
TIME FROM GRAZ: **2HRS 25MINS**
Styria's Alpine playground

Over on the western fringes of Styria, Schladming is a popular ski resort and also the southern gateway to the Dachstein. A former mining town now given over completely to winter and summer tourism, Schladming features 230km of ski slopes, over 400km of cross-country ski trails, 27 bike routes, 30 via ferrata routes and around 1000km of hiking trails. Ski lifts run up to Planai, as well as to the neighbouring Hochwurzen and Reiteralm.

The town and its ski slopes also make up one part of the much larger Schladming-Dachstein region, along with Ramsau am Dachstein, Grimming-Donnersbachtal, Gröbminger Land, Haus-Aich-Gössenberg, Öblarn-Niederöblarn and the Sölktäler Nature Reserve. Ramsau am Dachstein is particularly good for family skiing.

THE LYNX IN AUSTRIA

Once widespread across Europe, the Eurasian lynx became extinct in Austria in 1918, when the last one was shot in Bregenzerwald.

Attempts to reintroduce the lynx in Carinthia in the late 1970s were unsuccessful; however, since 2011 efforts to reestablish the animal in the Northern Limestone Alps – the forested, rocky wilderness on the borders of Styria, Upper and Lower Austria – have met with greater success.

The population is small – just seven individuals according to recent estimates – and the lynx's survival here faces huge challenges, including illegal hunting, and a limited and fragmented habitat.

Lynx have a territorial range of 250 sq km or more, and Gesäuse and Kalkalpen are a crucial corridor linking breeding populations in the Carpathians and Central Europe, ensuring a wider gene pool – another essential criteria for survival.

STYRIAN BREWERIES

Gösser is Styria's largest brewery, and is found across Austria, while Puntigam is a large brewery in Graz. Styria has plenty of microbreweries, making excellent use of the local hops (known as Styrian Golding) for which Styria has long been famous.

Bevog: Distinctive beers from IPA to Helles to smoked porter, as well as limited edition and barrel-aged numbers.
HiFa: Small craft brewery in east Styria.
Murauer: Founded in 1495, with beers from Märzen to Weissbier and a hoppy Murauer 11/11, along with its own lemonades.
Noom Wild Ales: Unique beers made using spontaneous fermentation on wild yeasts (from grapes or other fruit), released in small batches.
Sudhaus: Small brewery and restaurant in Graz.

Dachstein Sky Walk

Hiking the Dachstein's southern slopes

There are some incredibly beautiful hiking trails around Schladming – and no shortage of mountain huts. This is particularly true on the Dachstein's steep southern slopes. For a great half-day hike try the **Silberkarklamm** – a trail which follows a gorge beside a roaring stream, with cliffs and waterfalls, by way of a series of steps and wooden walkways, to the Silberkarhütte.

For something longer, it's easy enough to pick off a couple of stages of the **Dachstein Rundweg** – a well-known, 120km hiking epic which makes a loop of the Dachstein massif.

Schaldming has excellent rail connections with Salzburg (one hour and 35 minutes) and Graz (two hours and 25 minutes).

The Hoher Dachstein

At 2995m, the Hoher Dachstein is the highest mountain in Styria, and divides the sprawling rocky landscape of the Dachstein plateau to the north, from the lush green slopes and summer pastures of the Enns Valley to the south, by way of a stupendous mountain wall.

The **Dachstein Gletscherbahn** *(return €57, incl Sky Walk & Suspension Bridge €60.50)* takes passengers and skiers up to the shoulder of the mountain, where the **Dachstein Sky Walk** and 400m-high **Suspension Bridge** (Austria's highest) offer gob-smacking views that you won't forget in a hurry. The Dachstein's glaciers – the Hallstätter, Gosau and Schladminger – are all shrinking dramatically, and in 2022 it was alarming enough that the whole glacier area was closed for winter skiing.

Places We Love to Stay

€ Budget €€ Midrange €€€ Top End

Graz
MAPS p192 & p198

Das Weitzer €€ Excellent hotel beside the River Mur and near the Kunsthaus, with a popular cafe, rooftop sauna and flower-filled lobby.

Grand Hotel Wiesler €€ Stylish riverside hotel near the Kunsthaus, with seriously nice rooms (one is decorated with reproductions of Banksy's street art) and a fabulous breakfast and bar.

KAI 36 €€ Fabulous little design hotel at the foot of Schlossberg. Plenty of art and a lovely secluded garden.

Lend €€ Smart, modern hotel decorated with plenty of modern art, just north of Lendplatz farmers market.

Schlossberg Hotel €€ Swish art hotel in the former late-16th-century royal carpentry workshops, with an impressive art collection.

Hotel Daniel €€ Quirky, comfortable modern hotel overlooking Europaplatz, near the Hauptbahnhof. Bike and Vespa hire available.

NH Graz City €€ Smart, modern hotel – as you'd expect from NH. Good central location on Karmeliterplatz.

Augarten Art Hotel €€ Beautiful design hotel packed with artworks by the likes of Maria Lassnig, Franz West and Martin Kippenberger, and plenty of designer touches. A pool, sun terrace and views of the Schlossberg complete the picture.

Harry's Home Graz-Smart City €€ Well-designed modern rooms and apartments in Graz's new Smart City neighbourhood. Good value.

Aiola Living €€ Boutique hotel and interior design store, with immaculately stylish, individually designed rooms, just round the corner from the Landhaus.

Gasthof Lend-Platzl €€ Family-run hotel and traditional restaurant in a building dating back to the 17th century.

Gesäuse National Park

Gesäuse-Lodge € Guesthouse with 10 apartments in Gstatterboden, run by a Dutch couple who moved here in 2017.

Gasthof Kölblwirt € Family-run Johnsbach guesthouse with good rooms. Menu features local produce, including from its organic farm.

Gasthof-Pension Ödsteinblick €€ Traditional guesthouse in Johnsbach, with sauna and rustic restaurant.

Admont

Hotel die Traube €€ On the main square in Admont, close to the abbey. Opened as a restaurant back in the 1860s.

Haus ZeitRaum €€ Small, central guesthouse with tasteful rooms and natural light, a bike storage room and breakfasts with local produce.

Mariazell

JUFA Hotel Mariazell €€ Good value, family-friendly hotel set just below the 15th-century Sigmundsberg Chapel, around 3km south of Mariazell.

Hotel zum Heiligen Geist €€ Small, renovated hotel with a very central location – just 400m from the basilica. Somewhat old-style rooms, but clean and welcoming.

Schladming

Falkensteiner Hotel Schladming €€€ Superb hotel with Aquapura Spa, indoor and outdoor pools, good food and pampering.

Hotel Die Barbara €€ Smart, well-placed B&B with rooms and apartments just over the road from the Planaibahn cable car.

JUFA Hotel Schladming €€ Large good-value hotel with a central location near the Planaibahn cable car.

Stadthotel Brunner €€ Stylish, modern hotel with a good restaurant, rooftop sauna and chilled-out teahouse, right on Hauptplatz.

Johann €€€ Hotel and upmarket restaurant serving traditional Styrian dishes prepared with flair.

Ramsau am Dachstein

Bio Hotel Feistererhof €€ Hotel, restaurant and organic farm in a wonderful setting, up in the mountains northeast of Ramsau am Dachstein.

Hotel Annelies €€€ Boutique four-star with smart-looking rooms, high-quality food and half-board, mountain views, sauna and infinity pool.

Researched by Anthony Haywood

The Salzkammergut

MOUNTAINS, LAKES AND SALT MINES

Dramatic peaks, mountain-top restaurants, lake swimming, and trails winding to caves and salt mines – the Salzkammergut packs together magnificent mountain and lakeside beauty, as well as several interesting and eclectic museums on the region's people and history.

The Salzkammergut is a dramatic region of alpine and subalpine lakes, deeply carved valleys, high hills and rugged, steep mountains rising to almost 3000m.

Much of the region is remote wilderness, and even in the heavily visited parts, such as Hallstätter See, Wolfgangsee and Mondsee, you'll always find isolated areas where still, glassy waters provide limitless opportunities for boating, swimming, fishing or just sitting on the shore and skimming stones.

A journey through the region inevitably leads you from one lake to the other and through lakeside towns with an unusual collection of museums and sights. If you prefer to do day trips, the main towns in the region to use as a base are Bad Ischl and Bad Aussee.

As the name suggests, the Salzkammergut was once all about salt, the 'white gold' of the region that was a source of immense wealth for the Habsburg rulers. Salt was mined in Hallstatt as early as 5000 BCE, hacked out of the ground with simple tools or even the antlers of deer. Mining continued during the Iron Age Hallstatt Culture from around 800 BCE to 450 BCE, when Celts inhabited the region; later the Romans inhabited the valley and largely traded in salt until their decline in the region in the 4th century CE. Today the salt mines make for an interesting excursion.

THE MAIN AREAS

BAD ISCHL
Habsburg summer residence and cable car.
p220

HALLSTÄTTER SEE
Spectacular landscape, salt mine and caves.
p224

WOLFGANGSEE & MONDSEE
Lake activities, museums and walks.
p230

BAD AUSSEE & AROUND
Salt mine and lakes.
p235

TRAUNSEE & ATTERSEE
Museums and lakeside explorations.
p239

For places to stay in the Salzkammergut, see p243

THE GUIDE

THE SALZKAMMERGUT

Left: Lake swimming; Above Hallstatt (p225)

Find Your Way

The Salzkammergut is a compact, mountainous region. Bad Ischl and Bad Aussee have convenient transport connections for exploring all lakes and towns if you would prefer to base yourself in just one place.

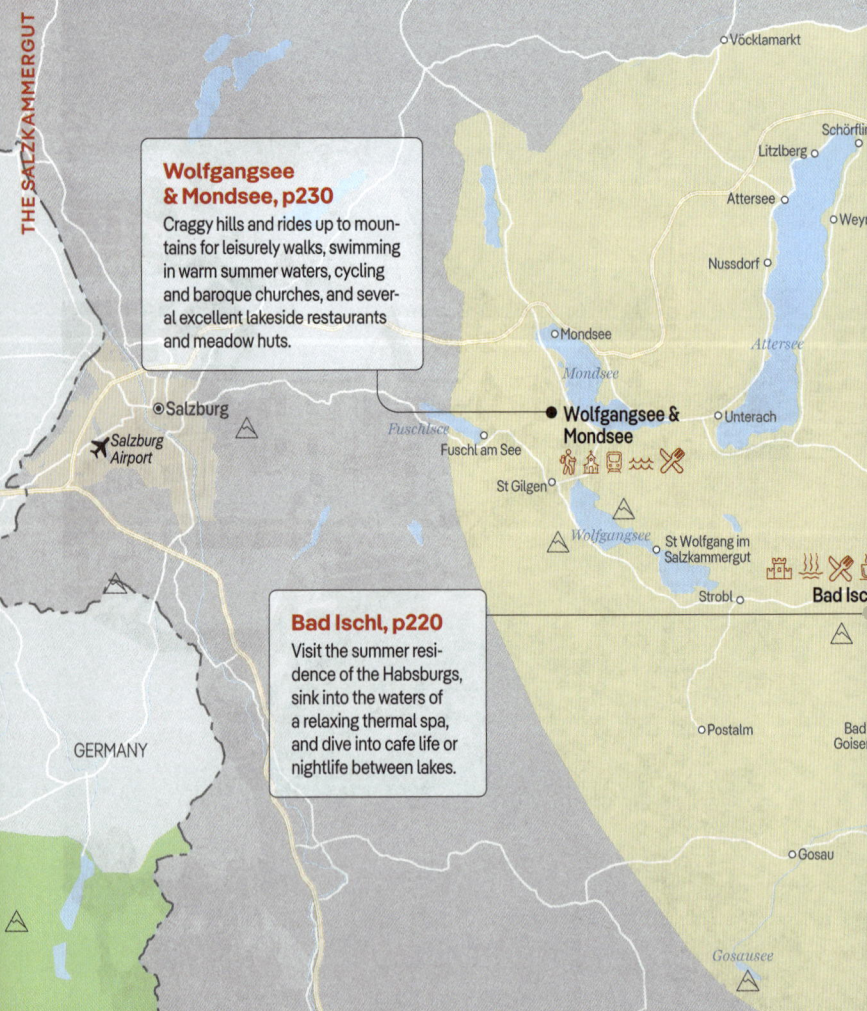

Wolfgangsee & Mondsee, p230
Craggy hills and rides up to mountains for leisurely walks, swimming in warm summer waters, cycling and baroque churches, and several excellent lakeside restaurants and meadow huts.

Bad Ischl, p220
Visit the summer residence of the Habsburgs, sink into the waters of a relaxing thermal spa, and dive into cafe life or nightlife between lakes.

TRAIN
A regional line runs between Bad Ischl and Bad Aussee via Hallstätter See, and another from Bad Ischl along Traunsee, via Traunkirchen. Bad Ischl's train station is close to the town centre.

BUS
Reaching Wolfgangsee, Mondsee and lakes around Bad Aussee requires taking a bus. Buses also complement many train services. Attersee is most easily reached from Mondsee by bus to Unterach or with a change at Sankt Georgen for Kammer-Schörfling.

CAR
Having your own wheels will give you much more freedom to pick and choose, and save you time, especially around Traunsee and Attersee. Hallstatt restricts car traffic and has parking on the edge of town; larger towns have long-term car parks.

THE GUIDE

THE SALZKAMMERGUT

Traunsee & Attersee, p239
A fascinating pulpit in Traunkirchen, the eclectic museum collections of Gmunden on Traunsee, and relaxing lake excursions, boating and swimming.

Bad Aussee & Around, p235
Discover the story of salt at a mine, visit three lakes by boat, dine on lake fish and walk around the Altaussee.

Hallstätter See, p224
A lake with a spectacular Dachstein Mountains backdrop, caves, remote meadows, a fascinating salt-mine tour, amazing lookouts, swimming in summer and winter sports.

217

Plan Your Time

If travelling outside the summer and winter seasons, outdoor activities are limited, so expect the focus to be on vistas of spectacular mountains and lakes, and museums.

Salzwelten salt mines (p225)

A Flying Visit

● If you have just three or perhaps four days, you will need to pick your destinations carefully. If you want to visit the spectacular and picturesque parts, then a good place to start is a visit the salt mine and high mountain valley above **Hallstätter See** (p224).

● After the tour, take a break at **Restaurant Rudolfsturm** (p226) then travel to **Obertraun** (p228) in the afternoon, taking the cable car either to one of the caves or the Five Fingers viewing platform. Return to Hallstatt for an evening meal at one of its restaurants.

● The next day travel on to the picturesque **Wolfgangsee** (p230) and explore the lake towns by boat-hopping, and spend the remaining time in your town of choice or swimming in **Strobl** (p232).

Seasonal Highlights

From skiing in the winter months to hiking, lake swimming or seeing the sights in the warmer months, this region is delightful all year.

JANUARY
Expect a decent snow covering in the winter resorts and downhill skiing above Hallstätter See, or cross-country skiing above the towns. Don't miss the **Glöcklerlauf** (p242) in Ebensee, when the bellringers stage a procession through town.

APRIL
From Easter all museums and major sights are generally open. The salt mines swing into full action from spring, snow is melting on the fields, cable cars come out of their spring maintenance and lakeside hiking is possible.

JUNE
The summer season is hotting up and the warmer lakes like **Wolfgangsee** and **Mondsee** are eminently swimmable. Hiking on the peaks and plateaus is now usually possible and this is the perfect time for a *Brettljause* (cold platter) outdoors.

Up Close in One Week

● Explore the Salzkammergut in two-day chunks. Begin at **Hallstätter See** (p224) and visit the salt mine (p225) on the day you arrive, spending the next day at the caves (p228) and other sights above Obertraun.

● Shift base to **Wolfgangsee** (p230) for the next two days, spending your time cruising the lake, walking a trail or two, and swimming in summer. One of the nicest places to swim is in **Strobl** (p232), but don't miss **St Wolfgang** (p230) and **St Gilgen** (p230).

● For your third leg, choose between the lakes outside **Bad Aussee** (p235) or **Traunsee** (p239). All are beautiful and have lots of trails or spots to swim and walk in summer. For a boat trip, **Grundlsee** (p237) has the most interesting option.

Fresh-air Finds for 10 Days

● Start in **Bad Ischl**, a transport hub, take the Katrin Cable Car up to **Mt Katrin** (p223) and set off on a short hike. Next up, visit **Hallstätter See** (p224) and ride or walk up to the **salt mine** (p225) one day, and the **Five Fingers viewing platform** (p229) the next, exploring the short trails around there.

● For more lakes, travel to **Bad Aussee** (p235) and **Altaussee** (p237), or **Grundlsee** (p237), enjoying a Three-Lake boat tour, before heading to **Wolfgangsee** (p230).

● Travel out to **Strobl** (p232), hire a bike and ride up to Schwarzensee and the **Kienberghütte** (p233) on Eisenaualm for refreshment. Return and get in some Wolfgang-see swimming at Strobl. Spend the last couple of days exploring **Traunsee** (p239) and its surrounds.

AUGUST
The lakes are warm, cable cars are still ferrying visitors up the mountains, the restaurant terraces are full and the **Lehár Festival** (p237) of operas and operettas in Bad Ischl, which starts in July, continues through August.

OCTOBER
A chill is beginning to set in on the mountains and the weather becomes less stable. But in a good year the trees are turning a golden hue in an Indian summer, the crowds are dissolving and lower altitude hiking is still pleasant.

NOVEMBER
Cable cars generally pause for maintenance in preparation for the winter season. November can be cold, grey, blustery – but **St Martin's Day** on 11 November is a highlight, with lots of goose on restaurant menus.

DECEMBER
The winter season begins and the ski season kicks off. Hiking is likely swapped for snowshoeing or cross-country skiing. Many museum attractions have gone into hibernation. **Christmas markets** in towns are great places to visit.

Bad Ischl

ROYAL PALACE | THERMAL SPA | REGIONAL SPRINGBOARD

☑ TOP TIP

Bad Ischl's Kaiservilla and the various museums have limited opening times outside the summer months. You can check these at the city website badischl.salzkammergut. at or drop into **Bad Ischl tourist office** at the Trinkhalle at Auböckplatz 5, on the way from the main train station into the centre.

Nestled in the heart of the Salzkammergut, Bad Ischl is a pleasant town and makes a handy base for visiting the region's major lakes. Its two significant attractions are a spa centre and the Kaiservilla.

This spa town's reputation snowballed after the Habsburg Princess Sophie took a treatment here to cure her infertility in 1828. Within two years she had given birth to Emperor Franz Joseph I; two other sons followed and were nicknamed the Salzprinzen (Salt Princes). Rather in the manner of a salmon returning to where it all began, Franz Joseph made an annual pilgrimage to Bad Ischl, his summer home for the next 60 years, and hauled much of the European aristocracy in his wake.

With a population of around 14,000, Bad Ischl has a good sprinkling of hotels for overnight stays and it offers more nightlife than most other Salzkammergut towns.

GETTING AROUND

Getting around town on foot is straightforward, as the centre is compact, flat and easy to negotiate. Buses from here go to Wolfgangsee, and trains to Obertraun at Hallstätter See and Bad Aussee. Check timetables at fahrplan.salzburg-verkehr.at or oebb.at.

The cable car valley station to Katrin Alm is 2.5km south of the train station. Take bus 551 from the bus/train station to the stop Kaltenbach bei Bad Ischl Katrinseilbahn.

You can rent standard and e-bikes from **Salzkammergut Touristik** *(salzkammergut. co.at; per day standard/e-bike €19/35)*. It also has mountain bike options. Check hours and book on the website.

BAD ISCHL

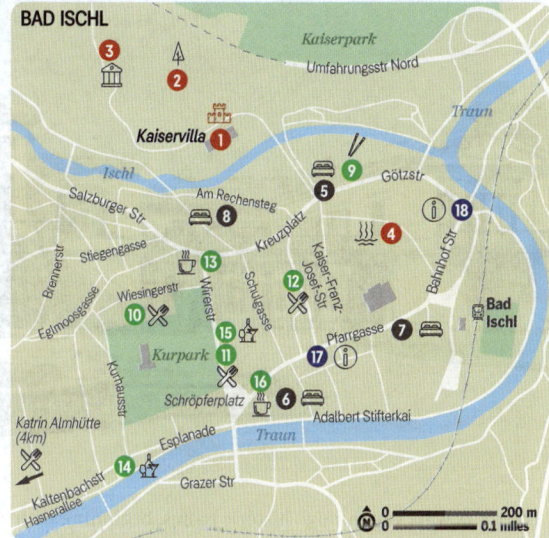

HIGHLIGHTS
1 Kaiservilla

SIGHTS
2 Kaiserpark
3 Marmorschlössl

ACTIVITIES
4 Salzkammergut Therme

SLEEPING
5 Boutique Hotel Hubertushof
6 Goldenes Schiff
7 Hotel Garni Sonnhof
8 Jugendgästehaus

EATING
9 Asia Restaurant
10 Castello
11 k.u.k. Hofwirt
12 Rührwerk

DRINKING & NIGHTLIFE
13 Cafe Boutique Zweitwohnsitz
14 Grand Cafe & Restaurant Esplanade
15 k.u.k. Osteria Miramare
16 Konditorei & Cafe Zauner

INFORMATION
17 Bad Ischl Tourist Office
18 Salzkammergut Touristik

In the Habsburg's Summer Footsteps

The Kaiservilla summer residence

Set in 18-hectare landscaped grounds, the **Kaiservilla** *(kaiser villa.at; park & villa tour adult/child €23.50/10)* was bought as an engagement present for Kaiser Franz Joseph and Princess Elisabeth of Bavaria in 1853 by his mother, Princess Sophie. Kaiserin 'Sisi' Elisabeth was only 15 years old when she accompanied her 19-year-old sister – cousins of Kaiser Franz Joseph – to a party in the villa, ostensibly to celebrate Franz Joseph's 23rd birthday.

His mother hoped to hook up her son with Sisi's sister. Unfortunately it all turned out otherwise. The significantly older Kaiser fell head over heels for Elisabeth, who lacked the confidence to rebuke an emperor, and the couple married in Vienna's Augustinerkirche (p67) some eight months later. It was in this villa that the unhappy couple spent their summers; on the tour you'll discover that the Kaiserin spent hours each day tending her beauty, as well as performing gymnastic exercises and fencing. She was also something of a mountain hiker, which kept her ladies in waiting fit as well.

CAFES IN BAD ISCHL: OUR PICKS

Konditorei & Cafe Zauner: A Bad Ischl institution that has been serving delicious cakes and pastries in elegant surroundings since 1882. *8.30am-6pm*

Grand Cafe & Restaurant Esplanade: Affiliated with Zauner, this riverside spot serves Austrian classics and has outdoor tables in summer. *9.30am-8pm Wed-Sun*

Cafe Boutique Zweitwohnsitz: Looking much like a living room with retro and historic touches, breakfast and brunches. *8am-6pm Thu-Mon*

Rührwerk: Small bakery known for serving the best *Schaumrollen* (cream rolls) in the region. Grab one (or another delicious cake and pastry) with a coffee. *10am-6pm*

SISI – A LEGEND IN HER OWN TIME

The Kaiservilla might be the one attraction Bad Ischl wears on its sleeve today, but Elisabeth loathed the villa and her mother-in-law in equal measure. Nevertheless, the emperor came to love it and this was his permanent summer residence for more than 60 years. His mistress, Katharina Schratt, even lived nearby in a house chosen for her by the Kaiserin.

Sisi became something of a tragic figure who lost her two-year-old daughter a few years into the marriage, and later her son and heir to the throne, Rudolf, who shot his lover before committing suicide.

This was not a happy family. Struggling with depression, and lung and heart problems throughout her life, Sisi acquired legendary status as Europe's most beautiful but also tragic monarch.

The tours walk you through historic rooms, beginning with background on the villa itself. As you progress, you'll learn more about Sisi (and what she did in the rooms), the noble and political greats who came to stay and much about the emperor's passion for hunting – which explains the more than 2000 sets of antlers throughout. Room 13 contains a stuffed chamois, the 2000th of the emperor's unfortunate victims.

So how did this legendary love story made-in-hell end? Here things get rather gory. After much travelling through Europe, in 1898 at the age of 60, Sisi went to Switzerland to take a cure, only to be stabbed by a file-wielding assassin, Luigi Lucheni. Lucheni was sentenced to life in prison in Switzerland, and 12 years later was found hanged in his cell. The assassin's head was promptly preserved in formaldehyde and stored in Vienna in the Narrenturm for some years before being buried in Vienna's Zentralfriedhof.

Guided tours take place daily from April to October (and Tuesday to Saturday in February and March) and last 45 minutes. See the website for the limited times from November to January. Before or after the tour you can stroll through the gardens at leisure and take photographs; however, tours are the only way to see inside the villa, and you can't take photographs once inside. You can also just enter the **Kaiserpark** *(adult/child €6.50/5)* or the park and **Marmorschlössl** *(adult/*

 EATING & DRINKING IN BAD ISCHL

k.u.k. Osteria Miramare: This *Beisl* is a nightspot that also serves Italian dishes. In summer, it's one of several sprawling outdoor areas here. *9-2am* €

k.u.k. Hofwirt: Rambling bistro-pub, part of the k.u.k ensemble, and the top *Beisl* in town. Pub grub and also summer outdoor tables and music. *11am-midnight* €€

Castello: This local mainstay does wood-oven pizza, pasta, beef, lamb and chicken mains, and lots of seafood. Takeaway available. *11am-3pm & 5-11pm* €€

Asia Restaurant: Serving well-priced Chinese, Thai, Japanese and other pan-Asian classic cuisines under one roof. *11.30am-2pm & 5.30-9.30pm Wed-Mon* €€

Kaiservilla (p221)

child €12.50/8), where the imperial couple used to breakfast, and today has been restored and has temporary exhibitions.

Getting above Town

Katrin cable car and walks

One of the most popular excursions around Bad Ischl is with the **Katrin cable car** *(katrinseilbahn.com; return adult/child €26/19)* to nearby Mt Katrin (1542m). From the cable car mountain station, hikes of various difficulty branch out across the meadows and mountains, including a 40-minute hike and climb on a via ferrata to the peak for the experienced with proper gear. Trail 898/895 to the summit is medium difficulty and without the via ferrata, but you will need good shoes and a head for heights.

An easy option is a 1½-hour circuit from the cable car mountain station via Feuerkögerl (1460m), with benches along the way to rest and take in the views. **Katrin Almhütte** *(katrin-almhuette.at)*, just below the cable car mountain station, is one of a couple of huts up here with food, refreshment and great views.

Taking the Cure in Bad Ischl

Soak in a thermal spa

Situated near the railway station – and therefore very convenient if you're returning from a hard day's hiking in the Dachstein Mountains – Bad Ischl's historic **Salzkammergut Therme** *(eurothermen.at/bad-ischl; sauna & thermal baths €37, thermal baths €25)* is today a thoroughly modern operation with a range of salt and freshwater pools, and European spa treatments. The sauna area has everything from steam baths (from 50°C) through to Finnish saunas reaching 90°C for heat-resistant health lovers. Outside you can slip down the 'Lazy River' through a rather tame 'salt grotto'. The sauna area is accessible only with a combined day ticket.

SALZKAMMERGUT SHUTTLE

The Salzkammergut Shuttle is useful when trying to reach places poorly serviced by railway or regular buses, especially at weekends and off-peak times. This is a collective taxi service with fixed routes covering the environs of Bad Ischl, Ausseer Land (Bad Aussee and around), Dachstein (Hallstätter See and around), Traunsee and Almtal, and Mondsee and Irrsee. You need to book the bus at least one hour in advance and name your pick-up and drop-off points.

The easiest way is to choose a trip at buchung.salzkammergutshuttle.at by registering or being a guest. Enter trip details and get a suggestion, which includes a public transport option if available. Give your name and contact number. You can also call +43 50 422 422.

Hallstätter See

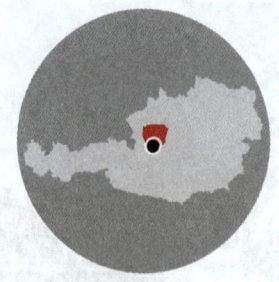

LAKE LOOKOUTS | ICE CAVES | HIKING

☑ TOP TIP

If you want to visit all sights with restaurant stops, plan two to three days. The **Salzkammergut Card** gives up to 25% discounts to many sights and activities, and you can buy advance tickets to the salt mines at salzwelten.at.

Set picturesquely among the sharply rising Dachstein Mountains at an altitude of 508m in the southern Salzkammergut, Hallstätter See is one of the prettiest and most accessible lakes in the region. It offers great summer hiking and swimming, good skiing in winter, and a fascinating insight into the cultural history of the region.

Among its many attractions are the Salzwelten salt mine and a cable car that climbs into the precarious heights of the Dachstein Mountains to two caves, one with permanent ice. Beyond that it goes to scenic lookouts and an isolated alpine meadow hut that invites resting up over drinks and a meal. The most important towns on the lake are the eponymous Hallstatt, the starting point for the trip up to the salt mine, and Obertraun, which is the valley station for the caves and lookouts. The whole Hallstatt-Dachstein region is today a UNESCO World Heritage Site.

 GETTING AROUND

Access to the centre of Hallstatt by car is restricted, so if arriving on four wheels you will need to park outside the boom gates in one of the parking areas. A hotel shuttle bus runs from parking area P1 for overnight guests staying in the restricted area. See hallstatt.net/parking-in-hallstatt for more information.

Trains connect Bad Ischl with Hallstatt train station and Obertraun. **Hallstättersee Schifffahrt** *(hallstattschifffahrt.at)* connects the train station on the eastern shore with the town of Hallstatt year-round, timed with the trains. From May to September it also offers southern-end lake circuits and boat rental. Keep an eye on first and last ferry times.

To get to the caves from Hallstatt, take bus 543 from Hallstatt-Lahn bus terminal to the valley station. From Steeg/Hallstätter See-Gosau, take the train to Obertraun Dachsteinhöhlen station; from there it's a vigorous 30-minute walk to the cable car valley station.

Buses run to Hallstatt-Lahn from Steeg/Hallstätter See Traunbrücke (near the Steeg/Hallstätter See-Gosau train station), and some from the Steeg/Hallstätter See-Gosau train station itself. Some buses connect Bad Ischl and Hallstatt town with a change at Hallstatt Gosaumühle.

HALLSTÄTTER SEE

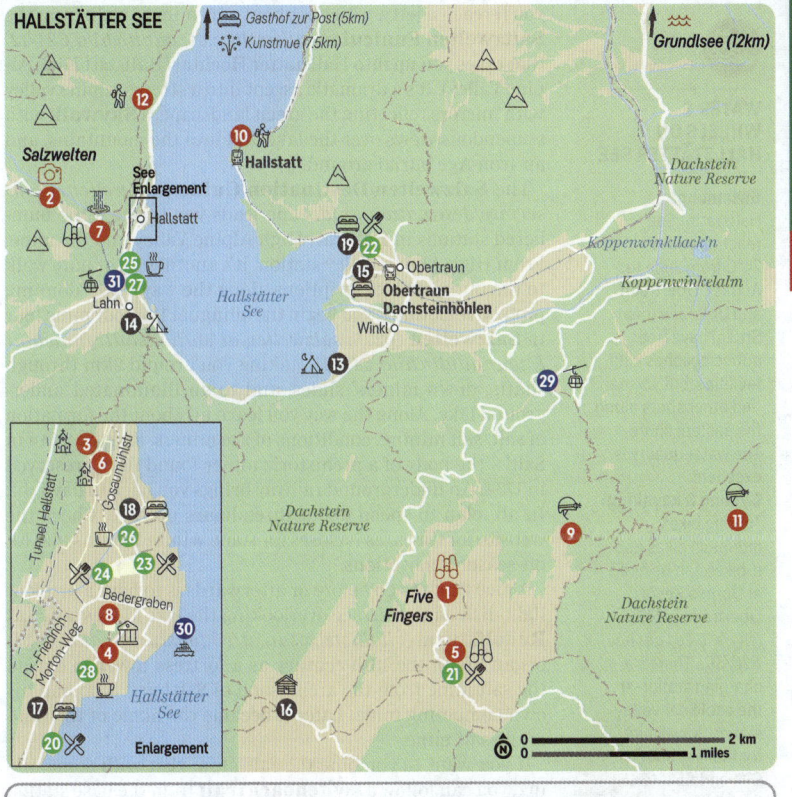

- **HIGHLIGHTS**
  1. Five Fingers
  2. Salzwelten
- **SIGHTS**
  3. Beinhaus
  4. Dachsteinsport Janu
  5. Krippenstein
  6. Pfarrkirche
  7. Skywalk
  8. Welterbemuseum Hallstatt
- **ACTIVITIES**
  9. Mammuthöhle
  10. Ostufer-Wanderweg
  11. Rieseneishöhle
  12. Soleleitungsweg
- **SLEEPING**
  13. Camping am See
  14. Campingplatz Klausner-Höll
  15. Dormio Resort Obertraun
  16. Gjaidalm
  17. Hallstatt Hideaway
  18. Heritage Hotel Hallstatt
  19. Hotel Haus am See
- **EATING**
  see 5 Bergrestaurant Dachstein Krippenstein
  20. Bräugasthof
  21. Lodge am Krippenstein
  22. Pizzeria Kegelbahn
  see 7 Restaurant Rudolfsturm
  23. Restaurant zum Salzbaron
  24. Seewirt Zauner
- **DRINKING & NIGHTLIFE**
  25. Bäckerei und Konditorei Maislinger
  26. Die gemischte Warenhandlung am See
  27. Seecafe Hallstatt
  28. Simple169
- **TRANSPORT**
  29. Cable Car
  30. Hemetsberger Hallstättersee Schifffahrt
  31. Saltzwelten Funicular

Descend into the Salt Mine

Salzwelten tour and mountain valley

Hallstatt township on the western shore of the lake is famous for its salt mine, where mining began over 7000 years ago, and even today miners are still digging white gold out of the earth. If you arrive by train – the most likely approach – you will find yourself at Hallstatt railway station, on the opposite side of the lake from Hallstatt town. After a short ferry ride,

WATER & WHEELS ON HALLSTÄTTER SEE

Swimming: Hallstätter See reaches about 24°C from June to August. Obertraun and Untersee (near Steeg) have free public beaches with facilities, but you can find other spots along the eastern shore. The water quality is excellent.

Cycling & kayaking: Touring bikes, mountain bikes and e-bikes can be hired at Dormio Resort Obertraun (p243) *(city/e-bikes per hour €20/30)*. There's a charging station at the cable car valley station. Kayak hire for the first hour is €10, and €5 after that. Other seasonal bike rental places are signposted in Obertraun.

you'll reach a jetty, which is about a 15-minute walk from the **Saltzwelten Funicular** *(salzwelten.at; adult/child €24/12)* that takes you up into Hallstätter Hochtal (Hallstatt High Alpine Valley). It's a dramatic ascent into a strange alpine valley with mirrors reflecting the green landscape, a **Skywalk** with stupendous views over the lake and into the mountains, and an Iron Age burial ground.

The **Salzwelten Destination Guide** *(salzwelten.at/en/service/destination-guide)* app leads you through the numbered stations in Hallstatt High Alpine Valley and the mine. From High Alpine Valley station, it's another 15-minute walk to the mine, with descriptions along the way. After donning protective clothing, you begin the bilingual 1½-hour mine tour in **Salzwelten** (p225; *salzwelten.at/en/hallstatt; funicular & tour adult/child €43/21*), taking you around 2km through shafts, down miners' slides, and to an illuminated underground lake. Along the way you learn all about the formation of salt, salt mining, conditions of the miners, and the 'Man in Salt' – the body of a prehistoric miner found fully preserved in 1734. An underground railway brings you back to daylight. In all, plan to spend about three hours up here. Check the website for times, as it closes for some winter months and for off-season renovations.

A nice thing to do before or afterwards is to have a drink or light dish on the terrace overlooking the lake at **Restaurant Rudolfsturm** *(vitalhotelgosau.at/rudolfsturm-hallstatt)*. It began life in the 13th century as a fortress tower to defend the salt mine from the archbishop of Salzburg, who had his own competing mine. Later it became the home of the head of the salt mine.

If you want to combine the salt mine visit with some hiking, you can follow a **switchback trail** from the base station of the funicular for about 40 minutes. Signs at the funicular say whether it's open.

Hallstätter See Trails

Walks among history and nature

One of the favourite walks in this region is around Hallstätter See from Obertraun to Hallstatt township. This walk is partly on the **Soleleitungsweg**, a path along the western shore following the historic pipeline carrying brine for processing in Ebensee. The **Ostufer-Wanderweg** (Eastern Shore Hiking Trail) begins in Obertraun, passes Hallstatt train station, and continues along a walkway attached to the rockface at

EATING IN OBERTRAUN & ON THE PEAKS: OUR PICKS

Gjaidalm: Alpine hut (1739m) a short walk from the Gjaidalm cable car station, serving light dishes, casseroles and cold platters. Also rooms. *hours vary* €

Bergrestaurant Dachstein Krippenstein: Restaurant at 2100m alongside Krippenstein cable car station; an easy option to enjoy the great views. *hours vary* €€

Pizzeria Kegelbahn: Convenient location in Obertraun, close to the station, serving simple Italian-oriented dishes. On a warm day the terrace is where to be. *11am-10pm* €€

Lodge am Krippenstein: A short stone's throw from Krippenstein cable car station, with traditional fare in a wood-filled interior. Also overnight stays. *11.30am-7.30pm* €€

Saltzwelten Funicular

the deepest part of the lake, then along a gravel path among riverbank acacias, pines, larch, fir and beech trees to Untersee and Steeg. If you only want to do this very easy section, trains leave Steeg-Gosau train station back to Hallstat. If you continue to the Soleleitungsweg, count on four to five hours for the whole circuit.

Stroll to the Parish Church
Evocative ossuary and frescoes

A short walk north of the centre of Hallstatt to Kirchenweg brings you to the **Beinhaus** (*kath.hallstatt.net/sehenswertes/das-beinhaus-und-die-michaelskapelle; free*). This small ossuary contains rows of neatly stacked skulls, painted with decorative designs and the names of their former owners. Bones have been exhumed from the overcrowded graveyard since 1600, and although the practice waned in the 20th century, the last joined the collection in 1995. It stands in the grounds of the 15th-century Catholic **Pfarrkirche** (Parish Church), which has attractive Gothic frescoes and three winged altars inside.

SALZKAMMERGUT FESTIVALS

Kunstmue: Free two-day music festival held in July each year in Bad Goisern, with alternative rock acts. Festival camping is also free.
Lehár Festival: Bad Ischl stages musical works by operetta composer Franz Lehár and other composers in July and August.
Festwochen Gmünden: A 'year-round' festival framework for events focusing on classical and contemporary music, plus theatre.
Glöcklerlauf: Held on 5 January each year in Ebensee, but these days also at Wolfgangsee and at various towns around the Salzkammergut
Gustav Mahler Festival: The composer and conductor's works is celebrated in early July each year in Steinbach am Attersee.

EATING IN HALLSTATT: OUR PICKS

Restaurant Rudolfsturm: Enjoy a refreshing drink and something to eat with fantastic views in Hallstatt High Alpine Valley. *10am-4pm* €

Seewirt Zauner: Traditional restaurant on Marktplatz serving fresh fish from the lake along with traditional Austrian favourites. *hours vary.* €€

Restaurant zum Salzbaron: The lakeside terrace is the spot to aim for on a summer's day. Traditional Austrian and international dishes. *8-10am & 11.30am-9pm* €€

Bräugasthof: Traditional, long-running favourite on the main lakeside strip, with outdoor seating and regional classics like goulash and lake fish. *11am-8pm* €€

PRACTICALITIES FOR CAVE VISITS & CABLE CAR

Registering for the caves: You pay for everything at the valley station but will need to register for each cave separately at Schönbergalm cable car station. See the first cave, then register again for the second.

Tickets: The Dachstein All in One *(adult/child €66/36)* ticket includes both cave tours and a return trip on all three cable car sections as often as you like on one day.

The Dachstein Höhlenticket *(adult/child €49/27)* is for both caves and the cable car to Schönbergalm.

The Dachstein Panorama Ticket *(adult/child €46/25)* allows a return trip for all three cable car sections (without the caves).

Left-luggage lockers can be found at the valley station.

Welterbemuseum Hallstatt

Digging into Ancient Times
Museum and excavations

A few minutes south of the ferry jetty and about halfway to the tourist office, you reach the **Welterbemuseum Hallstatt** *(museum-hallstatt.at; adult/child €12/8)*, where a multimedia presentation of 26 stations takes you through Hallstatt's history, ranging from geology through to prehistoric salt mining, the proto-Celtic Hallstatt Culture of 800–500 BCE (and the origin of the burial sites in the High Alpine Valley above town), Romans, and aspects of work and everyday life in the region. Explanations are in German and English.

You can also view some fairly low-key excavations from the Celtic era (around 400 BCE) and the Romans (from about 200 BCE) beneath the sports shop **Dachsteinsport Janu** *(dachsteinsport.at; free)*, just around the corner on Seestrasse.

Into Mountains & Caves
Cable car, caves and hut

A good starting point for hikes, **Obertraun** is less crowded and more easygoing than Hallstatt across the lake. This is also the base station for the **cable car** *(dachstein-salzkammergut.com; cable car panorama ticket with all sections adult/child €47/26)* into the **Dachstein Mountains**. Plan on spending a

CAFES IN HALLSTATT: OUR PICKS

Simple169: A modern, quite elegant takeaway (it does a few light dishes) that doubles as a perfect spot to relax over a coffee or drink. *11am-6.30pm Fri-Tue*	**Die Gemischtwarenhandlung am See:** Opposite the church and with outdoor seating, this cafe has sofas and a retro vibe. *10am-1pm & 2-6pm Tue-Fri, 11am-4pm Sat*	**Bäckerei und Konditorei Maislinger:** Cafe and bakery with lots of locations in the region; produces good local bread. *6.30am-6pm*	**Seecafe Hallstatt:** Excellent location on the lake's edge with outdoor seating over the water. Also serves meals. Close to the bus station. *9am-6pm Wed-Sun*

whole day in the mountains if you want to view the two caves and the Five Fingers viewing platform, setting out from the base station at around 10am or earlier. If you decide to go on to Gjaidalm and would like to do some walking, or walk down, two days is much more comfortable. The two caves – Mammuthöhle and Dachstein Rieseneishöhle – take about 15 minutes to reach on foot, each in different directions from Schönbergalm cable car station at 1350m.

If you are visiting both caves, first head to **Mammuthöhle** (*dachstein-salzkammergut.com; cable car all-in-one-ticket incl both caves adult/child €66/36*). This ice-free cave is among the 30 or so deepest and longest in the world. One-hour tours offer insight into its formation, with installations and artworks based on light and shadow to heighten the experience. Expect temperatures of around 3°C and wear warm clothing.

Walk back to the cable car station, register again, and begin your 15-minute walk to **Rieseneishöhle** (*dachstein-salzkammergut.com*), where you will find yourself in a chilly world of ice and subterranean hollows. It's a very chilly -2°C in the cave so, again, be sure to dress warmly. It also gets cold up here (or snowy) outside mid-June to September. You will enter numerous caverns and hear about the origins of the cave, and about the formation of the ice (which is about 600 years old), all intensified by special effects. Entry is only as part of a tour, which you can listen to in seven languages other than German by downloading the app (follow instructions from the website). It's possible to listen anytime you want (useful when the caves are closed in winter).

From Schönbergalm station, the cable car continues to **Krippenstein**, the disembarkation point for the very easy 40-minute walk to the **Five Fingers viewing platform**, which protrudes over a sheer cliff face in five differently shaped platforms (one is reminiscent of a diving board). On a clear day the views from here to the lake are little short of magnificent; a glass floor allows you to peer directly down beyond your feet into a gaping void, either curing your vertigo or turning you into a blathering mess.

The final cable car stretch is to **Gjaidalm**, taking you away from the crowds to an area where walking trails wind across the rocky meadows or lead higher into the mountains. Some of these trails begin at the **Gjaidalm guesthouse** (also a working organic farm), which is situated 10 minutes on foot from **Gjaidalm cable car station** and ideal for a refreshment on the terrace. An 11km downhill ski piste in winter begins at Krippenstein cable car station, passes Gjaidalm cable car station and continues to the valley cable car station. If you walk the section from Krippenstein cable car station to Gjaidalm in summer via the ski piste, plan on it taking about 1½ hours.

HALLSTATT'S CHINESE CLONE

Hallstatt is immensely popular with visitors from China, and for two very good reasons: it is one of the most picturesque and romantic lakeside towns in Austria, and it has a clone deep in the heart of Guangdong province.

Chinese Hallstatt is replete with a copy of the parish church, the fountain and numerous historic houses. This Hallstatt clone was opened with much ado in 2012, and many locals from the original Hallstatt felt flattered by the resulting attention. But it has brought new challenges, as occasionally visitors stroll unwittingly into living rooms, thinking this is a fake museum town, or fly drones over properties.

Another downside of its popularity is that Hallstatt's main strip gets crowded and visitors tend to move in groups.

Wolfgangsee & Mondsee

LAKESIDE TOWNS | SWIMMING | HIKING & CYCLING

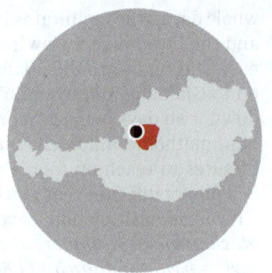

GETTING AROUND

Ferry services ply Wolfgangsee, and buses from Salzburg run to St Gilgen and Strobl, where you can change for St Wolfgang. These continue to Bad Ischl. Direct buses also connect Bad Ischl with St Wolfgang.

Cycling is flat until you leave Wolfgangsee, and although the road from St Gilgen to Mondsee has no dedicated bike path, you can easily ride it. When cycling around Wolfgangsee, you need to take a ferry between Ried and Führberg.

If you are an experienced open-water swimmer tackling this remote but attractive stretch of shoreline, stay within your limits and away from the ferry lane, and pack a suitable swimming buoy.

Named after a local saint, Wolfgangsee is best known for its two very popular resorts, St Wolfgang and St Gilgen. Strobl, another of the lakeside towns, is a less remarkable but pleasant and uncrowded place. All three towns (and several others) are connected by regular ferry.

Wolfgangsee is dominated by the 1783m Schafberg mountain on its northern shore. At the summit you can find a restaurant and hotel with phenomenal 360-degree views over the mountains and Mondsee, Attersee and, of course, Wolfgangsee. A cute historic steam train plies its way to the summit in summer, over lush fields and through dark forests.

In St Gilgen, a cable car rather bizarrely swings across the main road and up to the local Zwölferhorn peak (1520m), where there are more splendid views. Most people come here, though, simply to hang out, walk or hike, cycle and swim in the warm lake waters in summer. Museum attractions are few.

St Gilgen & St Wolfgang by Boat
Museums and mountains

Apart from hiring a bike and cycling the shoreline of Wolfgangsee, the best way to explore the lake is by ferry, which criss-crosses seasonally from April to October (and sporadically at other times) on a route connecting St Gilgen with the two stops in St Wolfgang (St Wolfgang Markt and St Wolfgang Schafbergbahn) and Strobl. The outbound leg takes just over an hour.

St Gilgen has a couple of low-key museums worth visiting, especially in inclement weather. **Musikinstrumenten Museum der Völker** *(hoerart.at; adult/child €6/3)* has a collection of musical instruments from around the world (with live demonstrations). Hours vary considerably, so check opening times on the website. The **Heimatkundliches Museum** *(sanktgilgenmuseum.at)* in St Gilgen is expected to reopen in 2026 following renovations. It is known for its eclectic collection

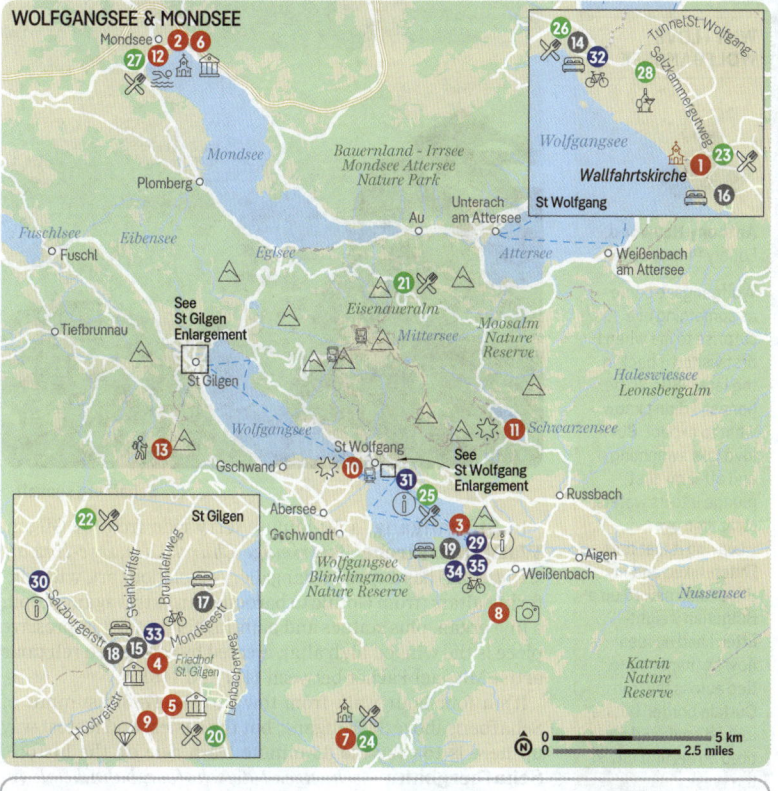

WOLFGANGSEE & MONDSEE

★ HIGHLIGHTS
1 Wallfahrtskirche

● SIGHTS
2 Basilica Minor St Michael
3 Bürglstein
4 Heimatkundliches Museum
5 Musikinstrumenten Museum der Völker
6 Pfahlbau- und Klostermuseum
7 Postalmkapelle
8 Postalmstrasse

● ACTIVITIES
9 Flytandem
10 Schafbergbahn
11 Schwarzensee
12 Segelschule Mondsee
13 Zwölferhorn

● SLEEPING
14 Hotel Cortisen am See
15 Hotel Gasthof zur Post
16 Im Weissen Rössl
17 Jugendgästehaus Schafbergblick
18 Pension Falkensteiner
19 Seehotel Lilly

● EATING
20 Casa M
21 Kienberghütte
22 Lucky's Haus am Hang
23 Paula
see 16 Poll's Kaiserterrasse
24 Postalmhütte
25 Restaurant im Landhaus zu Appesbach
26 See Eck
27 Seegasthof-Hotel Lackner

● DRINKING & NIGHTLIFE
28 13er Haus

● INFORMATION
29 Tourist Office
30 Tourist Office
31 Tourist Office

● TRANSPORT
32 Pro Travel
33 Radhaus Wolfgangsee
34 Schiendorfer
35 Sport Girbl

---

ranging from embroidery – originally manufactured in the building – to religious objects and animal specimens.

In good weather, take St Gilgen's cable car up to the **Zwölferhorn** (*zwoelferhorn.at; return adult/child €35/20*) for spectacular views and easy walks, hiking and tandem paragliding if you would really like to take off. **Flytandem** (*flytandem.at; about 20 mins €179*) offers this year-round. Hiking trails lead back into town (2½ to three hours on a steep, tough track).

☑ TOP TIP

The wolfgangsee.at website is a good source of information. If you stay at a participating hotel, you receive the free Wolfgangsee Card. The discounts are worthwhile especially for e-bike hire.

WHY I LOVE WOLFGANGSEE

Anthony Haywood, Lonely Planet writer

Wolfgangsee came as something of a surprise to me when I first visited it back in the late 1980s. To be honest, I didn't know what to expect. But I love lake swimming, and after my first plunge into its waters, I was won over.

Leaving it that time, I hitch-hiked and my driver also picked up a Bulgarian weightlifter. I had no idea how he managed to flee across the Iron Curtain border, but he looked confused and tired on his first day in the West.

Since then, I've returned many a time, mostly to plunge into the waters and swim a long distance. And I still wonder whatever became of the bemused Olympic weightlifter.

Schafberg summit

In **St Wolfgang**, a 50-minute ferry ride from St Gilgen, **Wallfahrtskirche** *(Pilgrimage Church; dioezese-linz.at/stwolfgang)* has a spectacular gallery of religious art, with glittering altars (from Gothic to baroque), an extravagant pulpit, a fine organ, plus statues and paintings. The most impressive piece is the winged high altar, created by celebrated religious artist Michael Pacher between 1471 and 1481.

It's a four-hour walk from town to the 1783m summit of Schafberg above St Wolfgang, but the easiest and fastest way up here is to take the 35-minute train ride on the historic **Schafbergbahn** *(5schaetze.at/de/schafbergbahn.html; return adult/child €57/17)*, a cute, local icon that passes through beautiful alpine scenery.

Great Outdoors in Strobl & Around
Swimming, walking and cycling

Towns such as St Wolfgang and St Gilgen justifiably attract large numbers of visitors, but to avoid the worst of the crowds, head to **Strobl** at the southern end of Wolfgangsee. From the shoreline in Strobl you can walk northeast along the lake for about 10 minutes towards **Bürglstein**, the high bluff rising above the waters, and a bridge. An easy walk then follows a

---

EATING & DRINKING AT WOLFGANGSEE

13er Haus: Cafe and bar in St Wolfgang with living-room character, open till late from midweek. *6pm-2am Wed-Sun*

Casa M: 'Mediterranean' restaurant and bar by the lake in St Gilgen with garden tables; steaks, pizza, pastas, risottos and salads. *11.30am-2pm & 4.30-10pm Tue-Sat, 11.30am-9pm Sun* €€

See Eck: Smart and friendly Austria-meets-Italy wine bar in St Wolfgang with a small dinner menu it posts on see-eck.at. Wines are mostly Austrian. *5-10.30pm Tue-Sat* €€

Restaurant im Landhaus zu Appesbach: Local fish, steaks and Austrian favourites just a couple of kilometres south along the lake from St Wolfgang. *noon-9pm* €€

path and boardwalks around the bluff to the settlement of Schwarzenbach, and returns to Strobl in a 5km circuit. The swimming is also good at this end of the lake.

Situated 9km from Strobl, **Schwarzensee** is a small, picturesque lake at an altitude of 715m that makes for a good bike tour. It is well signposted from Strobl, and the nicest section of road – which is also the sweatiest – is after the turn-off at Russbach, when you climb a 17% gradient for 800m. Once at Schwarzensee, drop in for a refreshment at one of the lakeside huts with outdoor seating.

If you would like something more isolated, press on to the **Kienberghütte** on Eisenaualm (1015m), following the gravel forestry track along the eastern shore of Schwarzensee and through meadow to this alpine wooden hut serving food and drinks some 9km from the lake. You can reach it in less than an hour by bike from Schwarzensee. Take a local map, check the meadow hut opening times, and keep an eye on weather conditions. From here you can also ride down to Mondsee or reach Attersee on similar track surfaces.

Panoramic Postalm Toll Road
Discover history while you eat

Just under 15km from Strobl, the Postalm alpine plateau (1300m) is reached from Strobl along the private **Postalmstrasse** scenic toll road *(not open all year; postalm.abtenau-info.at; car €13-17)*. Once at Postalm, you will find lots of walking trails branching out over the plateau, which is also a protected area roamed by grazing cattle.

Drop by the historic **Postalmhütte** from 1853, which was built to feed loggers and today will fill you up with *Kaiserschmarrn* (sweet pancake) or a *Brettljause* (cold platter). In 1865, the nearby **Postalmkapelle** (Postalm Chapel) at the hut was built for a visit by Kaiserin Elisabeth (Sisi). You need your own wheels to get up here; a powerful e-mountain bike is one option if you don't have a car.

More than the Sound of Music
Mondsee dining and culture

Stretching along the crescent-shaped lake, the town of **Mondsee** is just 30km from Salzburg and attracts large crowds, especially bus groups. Here you find yourself deep in the throbbing heart of The Sound of Music country. If you are

EQUIPMENT HIRE & TOURS AROUND WOLFGANGSEE

In Strobl, **Sport Girbl** *(girblsport.com)* rents conventional and e-bikes; from Wassbad it has double kayaks and SUP equipment.

Also in Strobl, **Schiendorfer** *(rad-gartentechnik.at)* is another outfit with conventional and e-bikes. The e-mountain bikes are especially useful for reaching Schwarzensee and riding Postalmstrasse. In Strobl the **tourist office** is about 600m from the bus stop.

In St Gilgen, **Radhaus Wolfgangsee** *(radhaus-wolfgangsee.at)* has standard and e-bikes. The **tourist office** in St Gilgen is five minutes by foot from the centre.

In St Wolfgang, **Pro Travel** *(protravel.at)* has bikes and tours. The **tourist office** in St Wolfgang is near the centre. See the website wolfgangsee.at for all tourist office opening times.

EATING AT WOLFGANGSEE & MONDSEE

Paula: Acclaimed restaurant in St Wolfgang's Weisser Bär hotel, with menus strong on lake fish. Wirtshaus in the hotel has traditional fare. *6-10pm Thu-Sat €€€*

Lucky's Haus am Hang: Multi-course seasonal menus skip effortlessly across cuisines at this great spot in St Gilgen. *noon-2.30pm & 6-11pm €€€*

Seegasthof-Hotel Lackner: Inside the hotel at Mondsee, with a wonderful terrace and good gourmet restaurant. *noon-10.30pm Thu-Tue €€€*

Poll's Kaiserterrasse: In St Wolfgang's Im Weissen Rössl hotel, with views over the lake and three seasonal set menus to choose from. *6.30-10pm Wed-Sun €€€*

LIVING OVER THE WATER

Prehistoric pile (stilt) dwellings crop up at many sites throughout the lakes of the Alps, in settlements that date from around 5000 BCE to 500 BCE.

Those around Mondsee (others are on Attersee) were discovered in the late 19th century and are part of the network of just over 100 settlements recognised as UNESCO World Heritage pile dwelling sites. This Neolithic grouping dates from around 3800 BCE to 3500 BCE.

They might have shacked up over the water, but the inhabitants engaged in healthy cultural exchange with their pile dwelling brethren in Italy and elsewhere. They carved tools from stone and bone, worked with copper and ceramics, and kept domesticated animals.

To understand the culture better, drop by the **Pfahlbau- und Klostermuseum** in Mondsee.

Basilica Minor St Michael

allergic to the musical, get out of town – but not so fast, because there is more to Mondsee than Julie Andrews bursting into heartfelt limnological song.

Just 15 minutes on foot from the town centre is one of the region's better food and wine places, part of a pleasant waterfront hotel. **Seegasthof-Hotel Lackner** (p233) is situated right on the lake and has a large terrace on the shorefront, replete with swaying reeds and views into the mountains. The fantastic lakeside location is as much a part of the attraction here as the well-prepared dishes of local whitefish, poultry and other meat, and one of the pleasures is simply enjoying a glass of wine on the terrace.

If after a fine drop you decide to sample *The Sound of Music* and explore the von Trapp sights, head for the 15th-century **Basilica Minor St Michael** *(dioezese-linz.at/mondsee)*, where the von Trapp wedding scenes were filmed. Offset this dose of sweet baroque with the **Pfahlbau- und Klostermuseum** *(Pile Dwelling and Monastery Museum; museum-mondsee.at; adult/child €7/5)*, where you find displays on the pile-dwelling and monastic culture of the region. The museum is open from May to September.

And once the water beckons – which it surely will on a warm day – take to it on a boat or board at **Segelschule Mondsee** *(segelschule-mondsee.at; 1hr SUP or windsurfing €15)*; alternatively, book a sailing, windsurfing or SUP course in advance.

Bad Aussee & Around

LAKE EXPLORATIONS | SALT-MINE TOUR | SPA STAY

Although unprepossessing at first glance, Bad Aussee is blessed with several excellent lakes on its doorstep, and from here you can easily reach Hallstätter See, making it an accommodation alternative to busy Hallstatt or Bad Ischl. You will find the number of sights in town quite limited, but it is a great starting point if you want to hire a bike and explore some of these less-visited lakes in the region.

Like Bad Ischl and Hallstatt, the history of Bad Aussee has been shaped by its nearby salt mine, which began production in the early 14th century. Today is known as the 'Mountain of Treasures', not only because of its valuable salt but because the Nazis used the mine to hide valuable works of art during WWII.

Bad Aussee is a pleasant town, but keep in mind that it is smaller and much quieter than Bad Ischl.

> ☑ **TOP TIP**
> Bus 956 runs to Grundlsee. Get off at Grundlsee Seeklause for the boat dock, or at Gössl if you want to walk straight to Toplitzsee without taking the boat. Walk past the camping ground to reach the pretty forest walking tracks.

Salt & Hidden Treasures

Take a salt mine tour

Situated near Altaussee about 6km north of Bad Aussee, **Salzwelten Altaussee** *(salzwelten.at; adult/child €27/13)*, a working salt mine, is one of three in the 'Salzwelten' network of salt mines open to the public. The other two are in Hallein (outside Salzburg) and in nearby Hallstatt (p224). You can join a 1½-hour English or German tour, which takes

---

 GETTING AROUND

Connecting buses in Bad Aussee meet most arriving trains at the **train station**, dropping you off in the centre. The website verbundlinie.at is useful for planning.

Buses for Altaussee and Grundlsee leave from **Bad Aussee Postamt** in the town centre. No buses run to Salzwelten but you can take the Salzkammergut Shuttle Service by calling +43 50 422 422 one hour ahead. Give your starting point (Bad Aussee Bahnhof) and drop off at Salzwelten Altaussee. The scenic **Loser Panoramastrasse** toll road climbs most of the way to Loser (1838m).

Altaussee is about a 30-minute e-bike ride from Bad Aussee. Various hiking and mountain-biking trails lead around Grundlsee, and the 10km Koppentalweg leads to Hallstätter See from Bad Aussee train station.

BAD AUSSEE & AROUND THE SALZKAMMERGUT

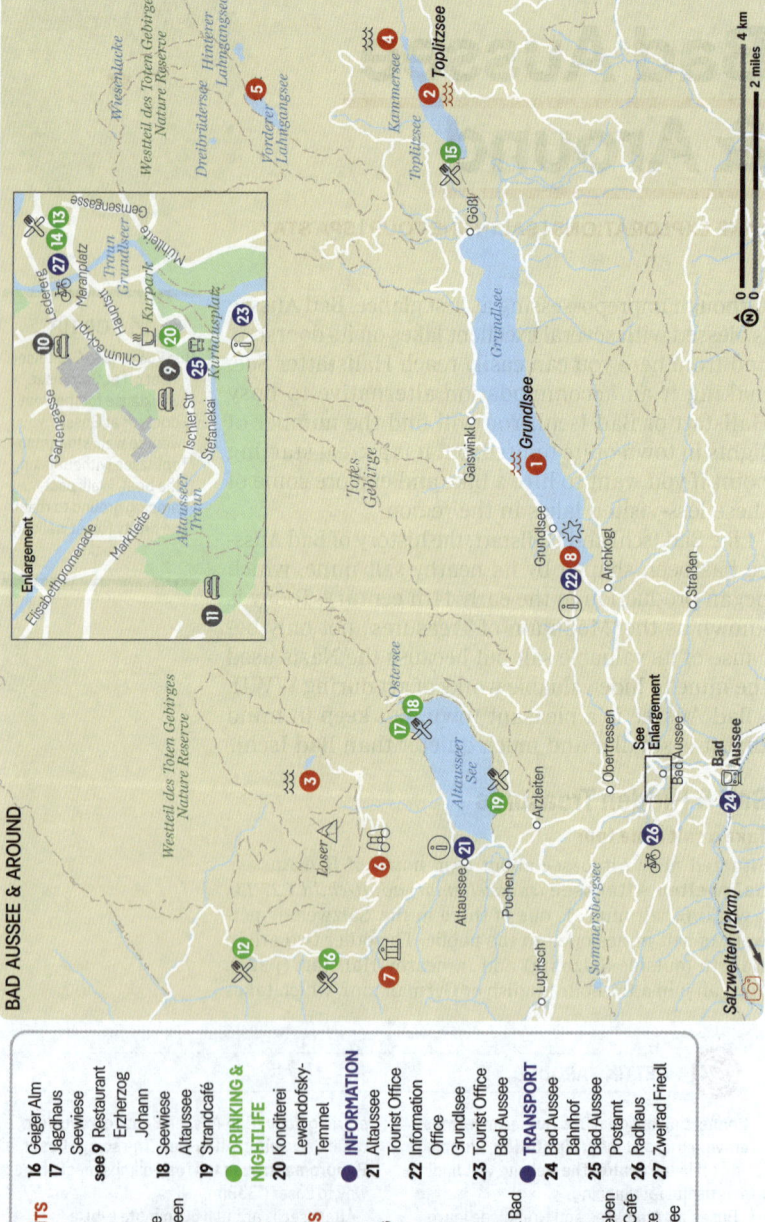

BAD AUSSEE & AROUND

HIGHLIGHTS
1. Grundlsee
2. Toplitzsee

SIGHTS
3. Augstsee
4. Kammersee
5. Lahngangseen
6. Loser Panoramastrasse
7. Salzwelten Altaussee
see 9 Restaurant Erzherzog Johann
18. Seewiese Altaussee
19. Strandcafé

ACTIVITIES
8. Schifffahrt Grundlsee

SLEEPING
9. Erzherzog Johann
10. Frühstückspension Josefinum
11. JUFA Hotel Bad Aussee

EATING
12. Blaa Alm
13. Das gute Leben
14. Das Kleine Cafe
15. Fischerhütte am Toplitzsee
16. Geiger Alm
17. Jagdhaus Seewiese

DRINKING & NIGHTLIFE
20. Konditerei Lewandofsky-Temmel

INFORMATION
21. Altaussee Tourist Office
22. Information Office Grundlsee
23. Tourist Office Bad Aussee

TRANSPORT
24. Bad Aussee Bahnhof
25. Bad Aussee Postamt
26. Radhaus
27. Zweirad Friedl

you through the mine. Along the way, tours explain how the salt was formed and mined, and go literally in-depth into how, during WWII, valuable works of art stolen by the Nazis were stored here. Fearing the precious artefacts would fall into the hands of Allied forces, Hitler had explosives placed in the mine, intending to destroy them. Some of the art was destined for display in his Führermuseum, a monumental construction planned in Linz; it never saw the light of day.

The tour includes two slides and, as in the other mines, you can take the stairs instead. The temperature in the mine is 7–8°C, so dress warmly for a chilly stroll. Check the website for current tour times and months as these vary considerably.

Walking & Exploring Altaussee
Altaussee circuit and eats

The 2.5km-long Altaussee is flanked by high mountains, including the summer and winter hiking and skiing playground, **Loser** (1837m), on its western side. Hiking trails around Loser offer great panoramas, and the 34 pistes (serviced by nine lifts) are popular with skiers and snowboarders in winter.

Arriving at Altaussee from Bad Aussee by bus, disembark at Altaussee Kurhaus and pick up hiking maps from the **Altaussee tourist office**. A leisurely hike around Altaussee itself takes around two hours, with swimming spots on the eastern shoreline. Access to the water is more difficult from the opposite side.

From **Seewiese**, at the northern end of the lake, you have magnificent (in good weather) views to the Dachstein Glacier. Two meadow huts, **Seewiese Altaussee** (p238; *tauroa.at/de/seewiese-altaussee*) and the older **Jagdhaus Seewiese** (p238) (*jagdhaus-seewiese.com*), serve replenishment, and boats also dock here. Check the websites for seasonal opening times.

If you have your own wheels, **Geiger Alm** (*geigeralm.at*), 3km out of town on the way to Loser, is a top restaurant in the region; **Blaa Alm** (*willkommeninaltaussee.at*), at 894m, is 4.5km in the same direction along Blaa-Strasse and popular for its game dishes.

Three-Lake Boat Tour
Grundlsee, Toplitzsee and Kammersee

Travel 5km northeast of Bad Aussee by bike, car or bus and you reach the picturesque **Grundlsee**, a long, thin lake and the first of three lakes separated by narrow strips of land. The other two lakes are **Toplitzsee** and, beyond that, tiny

OUTDOOR TIPS IN THE REGION

Evi Schartel is a biology student and boat guide for Grundlsee and Toplitzsee boat tours. She gives some local hiking tips.

Drei-Seen-Blick (Three Lakes View): This hike of medium difficulty takes about two hours and requires some surefootedness toward the end, but you're rewarded with a superb view of Kammersee, Toplitzsee and Grundlsee.

Lahngangseen: Two crystal-clear mountain lakes and source of one Toplitzsee waterfall. The return hike (medium-difficulty) from Grundlsee to the popular Pühringer Hütte is five hours.

Augstsee: You can reach Lake Augst (a cirque lake) either by cable car or on foot, and also hike (difficult level) to the summit of Loser, with great sunrises and sunsets.

 EATING & DRINKING IN BAD AUSSEE

Das kleine Cafe: Good breakfasts and coffee, along with soup and changing daily dishes, plus pastries in a relaxed atmosphere. *8am-6pm Thu-Sat, 9am-5pm Sun* €

Konditerei Lewandofsky-Temmel: It's hard to miss this cafe, with its summer tables on Kurhausplatz, serving cakes, pastries and also light dishes. *8am-10pm* €

Das gute Leben: This contemporary, cosy and chic wine bar and eatery serves regional dishes, has a good wine selection, and ceramics out the back. *3-10pm Tue-Sat* €€

Restaurant Erzherzog Johann: Fresh, local ingredients in Austrian classics and beyond are served mainly to guests at the spa hotel of the same name. *6-8.30pm* €€

INFORMATION & BIKE HIRE AT BAD AUSSEE

Tourist offices in the region stock hiking and bike trail maps.

You'll find **Tourist Office Bad Aussee** in the centre of town, across a footbridge; when closed it has excellent maps outside on hiking and bike trails.

There's also a small **Information Office Grundlsee** near the boat landing, and an **Altaussee Tourist Office** (p237) at the Kurhaus.

Radhaus *(radhaus-shop.com; per day mountain bike/e-bike €38/63)* rents out conventional and e-powered bikes and mountain bikes, with a range of around 30 different models that will get you up the hills. It's located 1km from the centre.

Alternatively, **Zweirad Friedl** *(zweiradfriedl.at; per day mountain bike/e-bike €18/33)* rents out wheels from its shop in the centre of town and can give you trail tips.

Toplitzsee lake tour

Kammersee. While Grundlsee is a base for water sports, swimming (most beaches are public) and diving, Toplitzsee is the one that has attracted the most attention over the years. The reason is rumoured hidden Nazi treasures, and it has been a problem for the lake due to divers illegally trying their luck in the 103m oxygen-free depths. According to the Österreichische Bundesforste (Austrian National Forests), neither gold nor Swiss bank accounts, nor anything else of value has ever been found here. Nevertheless, printing presses were discovered, as well as counterfeit pound notes intended to destabilise the British economy (though not very cleverly printed on one side).

A better alternative to Nazi treasure-hunting and earning yourself a stiff penalty is to take a three- to four-hour three-lake tour run in season by **Schifffahrt Grundlsee** *(schiff fahrt-grundlsee.at; adult/child €34/21)*, which also involves a 20- to 30-minute walk between Grundlsee and Toplitzsee (or longer on other trails there), a flatboat ride on Toplitzsee past a waterfall and a brief walk to Kammersee. Plan on three to four hours for the entire trip at a leisurely pace.

EATING AROUND BAD AUSSEE: LAKESIDE

Jagdhaus Seewiese: If the fish are biting, expect lots on offer here at the rustic end of the lake, in this rejuvenation of an historic hunting hut. *hours vary* €

Seewiese Altaussee: Modern place – but still in wood – for lake fish and other Austrian favourites, also with vegetarian options. Does boat trips with food. *hours vary* €€

Fischerhütte am Toplitzsee: Forest and craggy cliffs behind you, Toplitzsee at your feet – the place for fish. Famous for local steamed fish. *11am-8pm* €€

Strandcafé: Arrive via an easy 1.5km walking path, along the Altaussee lake shore. Austrian classics plus char and whitefish from the lakes. *seasonal hours* €€

Traunsee & Attersee

ECLECTIC MUSEUMS | STUNNING CHURCH | THEME TRAIL

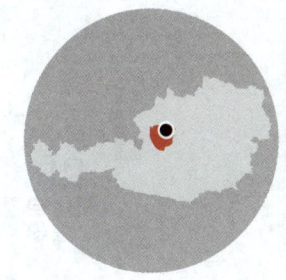

Situated in northern Salzkammergut at just over 400m, Traunsee is the deepest lake in Austria, reaching a depth of 192m. The eastern flank of the lake is dominated by rocky crags, the tallest of which is the imposing Traunstein (1691m). The largest Traunsee town is Gmunden, which exudes a riviera feel with its yacht marina, lakeside square and promenades. The attractive hamlet of Traunkirchen sits on a spit of land about halfway along the western shore of Traunsee and is famous for the wooden Fischerkanzel in the Pfarrkirche.

Attersee is the largest lake in the Salzkammergut and is flanked by hills that gradually become mountains the further south you go. Although its northern reaches make it one of the less scenic of the Salzkammergut lakes, artist Gustav Klimt was drawn to it like a magnet, often spending his summers here. Today it has a theme path dedicated to him.

☑ TOP TIP

The Traunsee resorts are strung along the western shore and are connected by rail to each other and Bad Ischl. Getting around Attersee is more difficult, but direct buses connect Unterach with Nussdorf, continuing on to Litzlberg and Kammer-Schörfling via Attersee.

 GETTING AROUND

The railway station in Gmunden is linked by a tram to the centre (buy tickets on board). The **Traunsee-Almtal tourist office** *(traunsee-almtal.salzkammergut.at)* is located out of the centre in Toscana Park. Get off the tram from the train station at the Gmunden Kuferzweile stop to reach it, and at Rathausplatz for the centre.

Traunkirchen has two railway stations: Traunkirchen Bahnhof is 2km from the centre and has frequent services, but Traunkirchen Ort Bahnhof (in the centre) far fewer, so check whether your train stops at the latter. Getting from Gmunden to Schörfling am Attersee, which takes almost an hour, involves changing trains at Vöcklabruck.

Approaching Attersee from Wolfgangsee and Mondsee is best with your own car or bike. By bike, there's a good track via Schwarzensee (p233) to Attersee.

Ferries ply both Traunsee and Attersee in season. A bus runs from Weissenbach/Attersee Wanderparkplatz to Kammer/Schörfling.

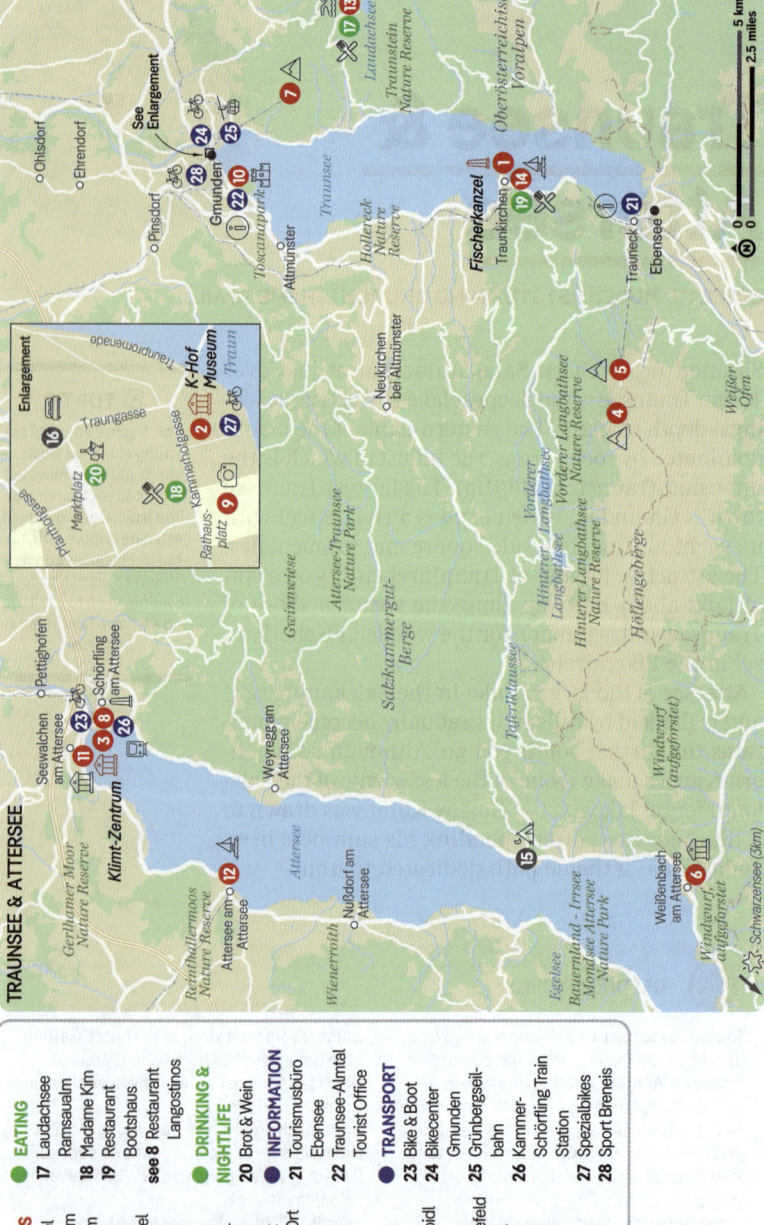

Cultural Gmunden
Museum and lake castle

If you arrive in Gmunden by train, a tram is generally waiting to take you the 2km to **Rathausplatz**, the central square and ferry wharf. From here it's just a short skip towards Traunbrücke (Traun Bridge) to the **K-HofMuseum** *(adult/child €7/2.50)*, five themed museum collections in one building. The most unusual is the **Museum for Sanitary Objects** (Klo & So), where you can admire historic toilets like a padded lavatory from 1836, used by Kaiser Franz Joseph I. Gmunden is famous for ceramics, so there are other ceramics exhibits here, plus sections about salt, fossils and the 15th-century astronomer Johannes von Gmunden, whose theories influenced Copernicus. Another museum section takes in **Bürgerspitalkirche St Jakob** (1340), a former church with a grand interior from 1891–1911. The museum is closed Mondays and Tuesdays.

A 20-minute walk southwest along the lake brings you to **Seeschloss Ort** *(adult/child €5/free, tower €3)*, a castle set just beyond the lake's edge and reached by a walkway. Much of it dates from the 17th century. In the picturesque courtyard is a late-Gothic external staircase and sgraffito from 1578. A small **museum** with German signage and audio tells about the castle and region. You can also reach it by strolling through the Toscanapark nature reserve, a wetland backing onto the castle. The castle is open from mid-April to October.

Up to a Mountain
Cable car and mountain lake

Regular ferries serve the main towns on Traunsee, taking you to **Grünbergseilbahn** *(gruenberg.info; return adult/child €25/14)*, the cable car running up to **Grünberg** (1004m) and walking trails. An easy one leads to the popular **Laudachsee** (894m), swimmable in midsummer, one hour away along a forested track from the cable car mountain station. Once at the lake, drop into the **Laudachsee Ramsaualm** *(laudachsee.com)*, for refreshments, and lake and mountain views from the terrace.

Spectacular Pulpit, Boating & Hiking
Traunkirchen's church and Ebensee explorations

The attractive hamlet of **Traunkirchen** sits on a spit about halfway along Traunsee's western shore. It's chiefly famous for the wooden **Fischerkanzel** in the Pfarrkirche. Carved in 1753, this pulpit depicts the miracle of the fishes from the New

BIKE HIRE & INFORMATION

Bikecenter Gmunden: *(service center.bike/verleih; per day/2 days €60/100)* Fully e-mountain bike rental in Gmunden. No weekend pick-up or drop-off.

Sport Breneis: *(sport-breneis- gmunden.at; per day standard/e-bike €25/45)* City and mountain standard and e-bikes in Gmunden; reserve by email.

Spezialbikes: *(spezialbikes.at)* Conventional city and mountain bikes (per day €20-30) and e-bikes (€30-60) in Gmunden town centre.

Bike & Boot: *(bike-boot.shop; per day trekking/e-mountain bike €25/60)* Good range of child and adult bikes in most variations. Also does SUP rental.

Tourismusbüro Ebensee: *(traunsee-almtal.salzkammergut .at/ebensee.html)* Excellent tourist office in Ebensee with lots of information on activities above town.

 EATING & DRINKING AT TRAUNSEE & ATTERSEE

Brot & Wein: Lunch specials and light dishes to accompany the fine wines, on Marktplatz in Gmunden. *5-10pm Tue-Fri, noon-10pm Sat* €

Madame Kim: This pan-Asian in Gmunden produces some fine flavours in Vietnamese, Chinese and Thai dishes. *11am-3pm & 5-10pm Tue-Sat, to 9pm Sun* €€

Restaurant Langostinos: The lake's top seafood restaurant in Kammer-Schörfling (Attersee). *11.30am-2pm & 6-11pm Mon-Tue & Fri-Sat, 11.30am-2pm Sun* €€

Restaurant Bootshaus: Seasonal dishes from award-winning chef Lukas Nagl in a lake-edge boathouse in Traunkirchen. *6-11pm Thu-Mon, plus noon-2pm Sat & Sun* €€€

EBENSEE'S GLÖCKLERLAUF

On Epiphany eve (5 January), the men of Ebensee – some 300 of them, or more – don giant illuminated headdresses crafted from tissue paper and roam through the streets from dusk in an originally pagan ritual, later Christianised, to drive out evil spirits and win the favour of benevolent ones. It seems a strenuous way of going about it.

The enormous headdresses (called *Glöcklerkappen*) weigh up to 20kg, and the men – dressed in white – wear wide leather belts hung with cow bells or similar.

Although the **Glöcklerlauf** is now performed in some other towns on Traunsee, Ebensee is where it originated; today it is on the UNESCO Intangible Cultural Heritage list.

Testament. It's a rather glam and glowing baroque take on this Bible story that is chiefly about the notion of spiritual plenty but obviously appealed to 18th-century fisherfolk in a more literal manner. Depicting the Apostles standing in a tub-shaped boat and hauling in fish-laden nets, the composition, colours (mostly silver and gold) and detail (even down to wriggling, bug-eyed fish) create a vivid impression.

In good weather in summer, Traunkirchen is also a nice place to take to the water in an e-boat from **Schifffahrt Loidl** *(wassertaxi.at/bootsvermietung; per hour/half-day €25/90)*, which you can hire at the wharf. The lake is narrow enough at this point to cross to the cliffs on the opposite bank in about 20 minutes, with Traunstein towering as a rugged backdrop. If you want to swim from the boat, ask for a free boat ladder.

Further along the lake – or before if you're travelling north – at Ebensee, you can combine a visit to Traunsee with some easy hikes. Take a cable car up to **Feuerkogel** *(1592m; feuerkogel.info; return adult/child €31/17)*, where you'll find walking trails leading across a flattish plateau. In an hour you can walk to **Alberfeldkogel** (1708m), with its fantastic views.

Gustav Klimt on Attersee

Follow the Gustav Klimt artist trail

Gustav Klimt spent many a summer on Attersee from 1900–16, and today the **Gustav Klimt-Themenweg**, an artist theme trail, runs along the lakeshore from the ferry station in Kammer/Schörfling to his summer residence, **Villa Paulick** *(villapaulick.at; tours adult/child €15/free)*, about 1km around the shoreline.

Info boards along the theme trail tell about Klimt's life and his work, some with square holes you look through to form 'picture frames' for the different Klimt motifs. In Schörfling itself, drop into the **Klimt-Zentrum** *(klimt-zentrum.at; adult/child €7/free)*, with exhibitions dedicated to the artist. It's near **Kammer-Schörfling train station** and bus stop.

Explore Attersee & its Shores

Lake adventures and lake-fish dining

To explore more of the lake, you can catch boats to the towns on Attersee's shore with **Attersee Schifffahrt** *(atterseeschifffahrt.at)*. Boats ply the lake from April to October on a one-hour northern circuit *(adult/child €20/10)* between Attersee, Weyregg, Kammer and Seewalchen. The 2½-hour southern circuit *(adult/child €30/15)* takes in Attersee and Weyregg along with a handful of towns south of these, including Steinbach. From July to early September, you can transfer between the northern and southern circuits *(adult/child €37/19)*.

Klimt buffs can visit the **Forsthaus** *(free)* in Weissenbach on the southern shore to see one of the artist's motifs in real life. Mountains rise up closer to the lake along this southern stretch, making it ideal for hiking, with lots of difficult and easy hikes leading off or passing by the Wanderparkplatz bus stop on the fringe of Weissenbach. This is also the stop for the Forsthaus.

Places We Love to Stay

€ Budget €€ Midrange €€€ Top End

Bad Ischl
MAP p221

Jugendgästehaus € Well located in the centre and good value especially out of season for twins, but also offering singles.

Hotel Garni Sonnhof €€ Nestled in a leafy maple glade back from the street, near the train station. Has an on-site sauna and cosy furnishings.

Boutique Hotel Hubertushof €€ Neo-rustic hotel with indoor pool, sauna and steam bath, with free parking and a traditional restaurant.

Goldenes Schiff €€€ Excellent four-star hotel with sleek rooms on the river and wellness facilities; rents e-bikes in summer.

Hallstätter See
MAP p225

Camping am See € Camping, glamping and upmarket wagons in Obertraun; nice lake location with beach and sauna-on-wheels.

Campingplatz Klausner-Höll € Located 800m from the centre in Hallstatt-Lahn, with kitchen and tent sites on a large grassed area.

Gasthof zur Post € In Au (Gosau) close to Steeg/Hallstätter See-Gosau train station, with well-priced rooms and helpful staff. Handy to the caves and other lakes.

Dormio Resort Obertraun €€ Chalet and hotel with resort facilities in Obertraun. An excellent choice especially for small groups and families.

Hotel Haus am See €€ Conveniently next to the boat station and swimming area in Obertraun. No-frills hotel with comfortable rooms with balconies and lake views.

Hallstatt Hideaway €€€ Modern, beautifully textured private suites in the region's most stylish accommodation just back from the lake in Hallstatt. With a sauna, and private garden on the lake itself.

Heritage Hotel Hallstatt €€€ Rooms in this luxury hotel are spread across three buildings, including the atmospheric greystone 500-year-old Stocker House.

Wolfgangsee
MAP p231

Jugendgästehaus Schafbergblick € In St Gilgen, this hostel has a great location close to the lake, with singles and four- to six-bed dorms.

Pension Falkensteiner €€ Well-run, friendly hotel with its own lake access. Rooms are large and all have balconies.

Seehotel Lilly €€€ Located on the water in Strobl. Suites and family rooms, as well as twins and doubles, with views to the lake.

Hotel Cortisen am See €€€ Boutique St Wolfgang hotel with beautiful lakeside lounge area, indoor pool, excellent breakfasts and restaurant. Adults only hotel.

Hotel Gasthof zur Post €€€ Some of the region's most stylish rooms in St Gilgen. Beautifully designed, with a restaurant and elegant terrace.

Im Weissen Rössl €€€ St Wolfgang's most famous hotel is the setting for Ralph Benatzky's operetta; some rooms have a balcony and views.

Mondsee

Hotel Krone €€ Catering to seminar guests, this hotel has large, well-priced rooms in a central location in Mondsee.

Iris Porsche Hotel & Restaurant €€ Modern business hotel with wooden floors, roof terrace and a wellness area in the centre of Mondsee.

Bad Aussee
MAP p236

Jufa Hotel Bad Aussee € Hostel-turned-hotel with wellness facilities, playground and terrace, a 15-minute walk from the centre.

Frühstückspension Josefinum € Located in the centre, this well-priced hotel has clean and comfortable rooms, and a lounge area.

Erzherzog Johann €€ Four-star spa hotel in the centre, with private swimming pool, large sauna and wellness area, and restaurant.

Traunsee & Attersee
MAP p240

Keramikhotel Goldener Brunnen €€ In keeping with Gmunden's tradition in ceramics, wares are everywhere here in this excellent hotel with modern rooms in an historic building.

Camping Seefeld € Run by the Seehotel Föttinger in Steinbach, with bike and SUP hire; bus connection with Kammer-Schörfling and the Wanderparkplatz.

Seehotel Föttinger €€€ Located in Seefeld, part of Steinbach, with private beach, wellness area and restaurant.

Above: Cow, Wildgerlostal, Krimml (p285); Right: Salzburger Marionettentheater (p264)

Researched by Kerry Walker

Salzburg & Salzburgerland

BAROQUE BRILLIANCE AND ALPINE HIGHS

With uplifting Alps and rousing Mozart symphonies, hilltop castles and cultural cachet, this bite-sized region is Austria's scene-stealer.

One of Austria's smallest provinces, Salzburgerland is proof that size really doesn't matter. Well, not when you have Mozart, Maria von Trapp and the 600-year legacy of the prince-archbishops behind you. This is the land that grabbed the world spotlight and shouted 'Austria!' with Julie Andrews skipping joyously down the mountainsides. This is indeed the land of crisp apple strudel, dancing marionettes and high-on-a-hilltop castles. This is the Austria of your wildest childhood dreams.

Spread at the foot of wooded cliffs and along the banks of a turquoise river, Salzburg's baroque-in-overdrive Altstadt rolls back a millennium of history, with its parade of palaces, churches, abbeys and domes, where the prince-archbishops once dreamed big and the horse-drawn carriages clip-clop past evoking the glory days of the Habsburg Empire. Here you're constantly looking up in wonder: at the whopping hilltop fortress, at lavish concert halls where Mozart once performed, and at the mountains ripping across the horizon.

But Salzburg is just the prelude to the region's sensational beauty. Just outside the city, the landscape is etched with deep ravines, glinting ice caves, karst plateaux, mountains of myth and waterfall-splashed cliffs – in short, the kind of alpine gorgeousness that no well-orchestrated symphony or yodelling nun could ever quite capture. Stray deep into the Hohe Tauern National Park for sky-high road trips and over-the-glacier hikes among Austria's big-hitter mountains.

THE MAIN AREAS

SALZBURG
Baroque majesty and Mozart.
p248

ZELL AM SEE
Lakeside action and high-level hikes.
p273

HOHE TAUERN NATIONAL PARK
Nature, trails and mountain views.
p279

FROM LEFT: IMAGEBROKER.COM/ALAMY, JONATHON STOKES/LONELY PLANET

Find Your Way

In Salzburg, it's a cinch to visit most places on foot or by bike, and indeed, the Altstadt is pedestrian-only. Trains journeying deeper into the region are frequent, reliable and scenic, but your own wheels are recommended for reaching Hohe Tauern National Park's remotest corners.

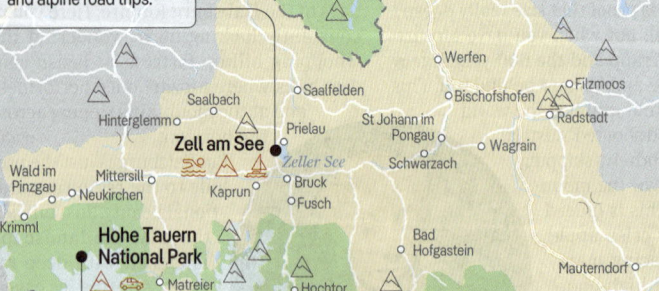

Zell am See, p273
Straddling a bluer-than-blue lake and looking freshly minted for Hollywood, this town is the springboard for water sports, mountain hikes and alpine road trips.

Salzburg, p248
Gazing up to a medieval fortress and the Alps, this visually stunning city bombards you with castles, palaces, abbeys, music and baroque majesty.

Hohe Tauern National Park, p279
Austria's most epic national park is a nature-run-riot spectacle of gnarly peaks, glaciers, trails, wildlife and off-the-chart beauty.

TRAIN
Linking all cities, towns and villages, rail travel here is a delight: **ÖBB** *(Österreiche Bundesbahn, Austrian Federal Railway; oebb.at)* trains are smooth and efficient, and the views are magic. Where trains stop, Postbus services take over.

CAR
The A10 autobahn speeds south of Salzburg and is the road you'll take if you're heading to Werfen, Bad Gastein, Zell am See or Hohe Tauern. E-vehicle charging points are ubiquitous (there's even one in the national park).

Hikers, Hohe Tauern National Park (p279)

Plan Your Time

Salzburgerland looks tiny on the map, but there's a lot of vertical to consider. You can't do it all, so choose wisely, combining a short city break in Salzburg, say, with forays into the great outdoors.

On a Long Weekend

● Stay in **Salzburg** (p248) for castle, palace and gallery visits in the Altstadt, a walk above the city at Mönchsberg, and Mozart and Maria fun. Hitch a cable car up to **Untersberg** (p256) for a shot of the Alps, or waft around regal gardens at **Schloss Hellbrunn** (p267). **Werfen** (p269), with the world's biggest ice caves, and **Hallein** (p268), with mines, are easy day trips.

With a Week or More

● Begin with Salzburg's decorous Altstadt, then **Zell am See** (p273) for lake watersports, Alps walks, and **Kitzsteinhorn** (p277) skiing and glacier hiking. Hit **Grossglockner Road** (p284), through Austria's highest peaks, deep into wild **Hohe Tauern National Park** (p279) and on to the **Krimmler Wasserfälle** (p285) before a thermal bath in **Bad Gastein** (p286).

SEASONAL HIGHLIGHTS

SPRING
Snow on summits but valleys bloom at lower elevations. Salzburg reverberates with music at **Osterfestspiele** (Easter Festival).

SUMMER
Salzburger Festspiele (p262) is in full swing. Music and theatre in Zell am See. Huts open and hikers take to Hohe Tauern's trails.

AUTUMN
Quieter days, colourful foliage and excellent wildlife-spotting in the Alps. It's a terrific time for outdoor activities.

WINTER
Christmas waves a winter wonderland wand, snow draws skiers and **Mozart Week** (p250) pulls in star orchestras.

Salzburg

BAROQUE BRILLIANCE | MOZART'S BIRTHPLACE | ALPINE BACKDROP

☑ TOP TIP

Salzburg has two peak seasons. During the summer holidays (July and August), the city gets swamped. In December, when the city brims with Christmas markets and festival sparkle, it can get busy and expensive, too. To save money, come in spring or autumn for cheaper flights, lower room rates and fewer crowds.

The joke; 'If it's baroque, don't fix it,' could be a perfect maxim for Salzburg: the storybook Altstadt burrowed below steep hills looks much as it did when Mozart lived here 250 years ago. Beside the fast-flowing Salzach River which divides the city in two, your lifted gaze is raised inch by inch to graceful domes and spires, the formidable clifftop fortress and the mountains beyond. It's a backdrop that did the lordly prince-archbishops and Maria proud.

Beyond Salzburg's two biggest money-spinners – Mozart and *The Sound of Music* – hides a city with a burgeoning arts scene, wonderful food, manicured parks, quiet side streets where classical music wafts from open windows, and concert halls that uphold musical tradition 365 days a year. Everywhere you go, the scenery, the skyline, the music and the history send your spirits soaring higher than Julie Andrews' octave-leaping vocals.

GETTING AROUND

Salzburg's sight-packed Altstadt is a joy to explore on foot, and walking is the only way to get a true feel for its pedestrianised backstreets. Unless you're going further afield, you need never set foot in a bus or train.

This is one of Austria's most cycle-friendly cities, with a superb network of bike paths along the river, making the transition from city to mountains seamless. Touring and e-bikes can be rented at **aVelo** (avelosalzburg.com) at Staatsbrücke.

Getting around by public transport (SVV) is quick, easy and inexpensive. It's cheaper to buy tickets online or at the ticket machine than on board. If you're planning on zipping about town, a *Tageskarte* (day pass) is better value than single tickets.

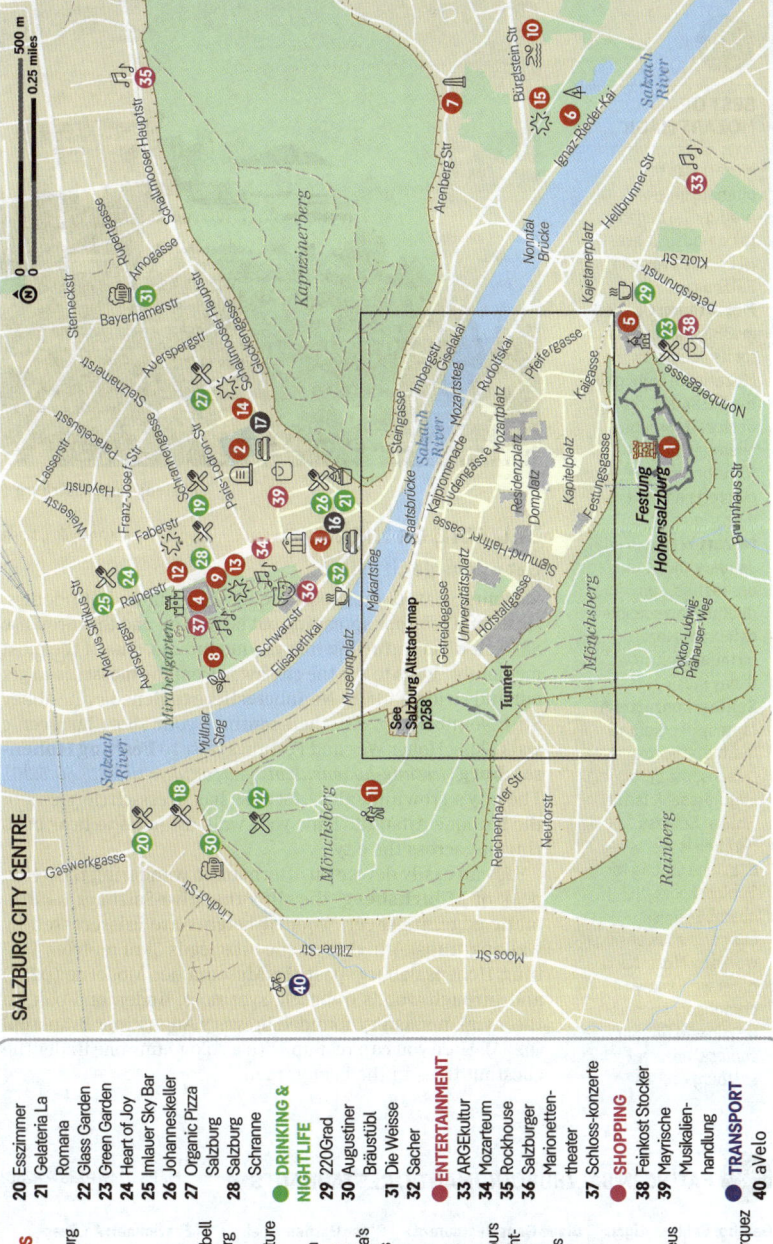

SALZBURG & SALZBURGERLAND SALZBURG

HIGHLIGHTS
1 Festung Hohensalzburg

SIGHTS
2 Friedhof St Sebastian
3 Mozart-Wohnhaus
4 Schloss Mirabell
5 Stift Nonnberg
6 Volksgarten
7 Würth Sculpture Garden
8 Zwerglgarten

ACTIVITIES
9 Fräulein Maria's Bicycle Tours
10 Freibad Volksgarten
11 Mönchsberg
12 Salzburg Panorama Tours
13 Salzburg Sightseeing Tours
14 Segway Tours
15 Spielplatz Volksgarten

SLEEPING
16 Arte Vida
17 Hotel Amadeus

EATING
18 Bärenwirt
19 Bistro de Márquez
20 Esszimmer
21 Gelateria La Romana
22 Glass Garden
23 Green Garden
24 Heart of Joy
25 Imlauer Sky Bar
26 Johanneskeller
27 Organic Pizza Salzburg
28 Salzburg Schranne

DRINKING & NIGHTLIFE
29 220Grad
30 Augustiner Bräustübl
31 Die Weisse
32 Sacher

ENTERTAINMENT
33 ARGEkultur
34 Mozarteum
35 Rockhouse
36 Salzburger Marionettentheater
37 Schloss-konzerte

SHOPPING
38 Feinkost Stocker
39 Mayrische Musikalienhandlung

TRANSPORT
40 aVelo

249

BEST OF MOZART MAGIC

Mozart was the ultimate musical prodigy: he began to compose at five. His works live on in Salzburg.

Mozarteum: Opened in 1880 and revered for its acoustics, the Mozarteum highlights the life and works of Mozart through chamber music (October to June), concerts and opera. *mozarteum.at*

Mozart Week: In late January, much-lauded orchestras, conductors and soloists celebrate Mozart's birthday with an 11-day music fest.

Schlosskonzerte: A fantasy of coloured marble, stucco and frescos, the baroque Marmorsaal (Marble Hall) at Schloss Mirabell is the exquisite setting for Schlosskonzerte, chamber-music concerts showcasing works by Mozart and other well-known composers such as Haydn and Chopin. *schlosskonzerte-salzburg.at*

Festung Hohensalzburg

Salzburg on High
MAPS P249 & P258

Get a ringside city view

Salzburg is at its most entrancing from above, with domes, spires and rooftops spreading out before you and the turquoise Salzach River unfurling into the mountains. One of the most memorable ways to see the city away from the masses is to get out and stride. Puff up Nonnbergstiege to Benedictine abbey Stift Nonnberg (p263), then continue your short but scenic walk along Hoher Weg and Festungsgasse to **Festung Hohensalzburg** *(festung-hohensalzburg.at; adult/child €13.60/5.20)*. The city's crowning-glory fortress has dress-circle views of the baroque Altstadt. Time your walk for noon to hear bells ring out across the city.

You can easily devote an afternoon to wandering the 540m peak of **Mönchsberg**, the cliffs that give Salzburg its dramatic edge. Its sheer, wooded heights are crisscrossed by walking trails. A highly scenic hike leads 3km on from Festung Hohensalzburg, past the Museum der Moderne (p257) and through woods of beech, sycamore, linden and oak, to the jovial monastery-founded brewery Augustiner Bräustübl (p265). Here you can rest up with a cold foamy one under the chestnut trees in the beer garden.

EATING IN SALZBURG: ROMANTIC RESTAURANTS
MAPS P249, P258 & P260

Gasthof Schloss Aigen: This 15th-century country manor does Austrian home cooking with panache. Try the Wiener Melange. *5.30-10pm Thu, 11.30am-10pm Fri-Sun* €€

Blaue Gans Restaurant: In 650-year-old vaults, this restaurant riffs creatively on regional cuisine in seasonal dishes. *noon-midnight Mon-Sat* €€

Glass Garden: Chef Simon Wagner serves food sensations at Hotel Schloss Mönchstein's glass-domed, Michelin-starred restaurant. *noon-10pm Thu-Mon* €€€

Esszimmer: Andreas Kaiblinger puts an innovative spin on market-driven French cuisine at this art-slung, Michelin-starred stunner. *noon-10pm Tue-Sat* €€€

A leap over the river to the Right Bank brings you to the forested, 640m-high hump of **Kapuzinerberg**, which frames the Altstadt like a postcard. Paths twist past Way of the Cross chapels to the Capuchin abbey at the top. Despite the glorious views, it's rarely busy – hence the reason it is still home to a colony of nimble-footed chamois, which you might spot if you're lucky (and quiet).

The Sound of Music Trail
MAPS P249, P258 & P260

The hills are alive

Ever since Hollywood box-office smash *The Sound of Music* hit big screens in 1965, Salzburg has been inseparable from the world's most famous singing nun. Channel your inner Julie Andrews by devising your own self-guided tour of the movie locations.

Start at the very beginning with a cable car ride to the summit of Untersberg (p256), where Maria makes her twirling entrance through blooming alpine pastures and the von Trapp family flee from the Nazis at the end.

At the foot of Mönchsberg's cliffs, the Felsenreitschule (p263) is the dramatic backdrop for the Salzburger Festspiele (Salzburg Festival) in the movie, where the Trapp Family Singers win the audience over with *Edelweiss* and give the Nazis the slip with *So Long, Farewell*. Close by is Residenzplatz (p260), where Maria belts out *I Have Confidence* and playfully splashes the spouting horses of the **Residenzbrunnen** fountain.

Hoof it uphill from here to Benedictine Stift Nonnberg, where the nuns waltzed on their way to mass, including the ever-problematic Maria.

Palaces, you say? Romantically rococo **Schloss Leopoldskron** *(schloss-leopoldskron.com)*, a 15-minute stroll south of the centre, is where the lake scene was filmed. Its Venetian Room was the blueprint for the Trapps' opulent ballroom, where the von Trapp kids bid their heart-melting farewells. Now you can stay the night in its elegant hotel.

Back in town, the Pegasus fountain, gnomes and steps with fortress views in the Schloss Mirabel**l** (p254) gardens might inspire a rendition of *Do-Re-Mi* – especially if there's a drop of golden sun.

BEST PLACES FOR KIDS IN SALZBURG

Haus der Natur: This hands-on museum dives deep into natural history. The clincher is the aquarium, with its clownfish and sharks. See archerfish, moray eels and piranhas being fed at 10.30am.

Spielzeugmuseum: Salzburg's very own toy story, this rambling attic of toys old and new even has 'adult parking areas' where they can hang out while kids play.

Freilichtmuseum: This huge open-air museum whisks you through Austrian farming life, with animals to pet, crafts to explore and a big adventure playground to romp around in.

Schloss Hellbrunn: Kids have a blast splashing in the trick fountains at this fairy-tale palace.

Spielplatz Volksgarten: Let tots burn off excess energy, play with water and dig in the sand at one of the best adventure playgrounds in town.

EATING IN SALZBURG: LUNCH SPOTS
MAPS P249 & P258

Afro Café: Go for fair-trade coffees, lavish brunches and creative day specials at this Afro-chic cafe. *9am-8pm Mon-Sat* €

Green Garden: Tapping into plant power, this vegan cafe rustles up tasty Buddha bowls, brunches and superfood salads. *1-9pm Wed-Fri, 10am-9pm Sat & Sun* €

Heart of Joy: Ayurveda-inspired cafe with an all-vegetarian, part-vegan and mostly organic menu. Bagels, homemade cakes and juices, and daily specials. *8am-7pm* €

Humboldt: Like a blast of nouveau alpine chic, the vibe is cool yet cosy. A good buzz and all-organic, season-driven menu. *10.30am-11pm* €€

SALZBURG IN MOZART'S FOOTSTEPS

Get ready to rock like Amadeus with a spin of the historic centre.

START	END	LENGTH
Schloss Mirabell	Fürst	3.2km; 2 hrs

Begin at baroque ❶ **Schloss Mirabell** (p254), where the Marmorsaal (Marble Hall) is the backdrop for chamber concerts of Mozart's music. Stroll south through fountain-dotted gardens, passing the ❷ **Mozarteum**, a foundation honouring Mozart, and the host of the Mozart Week festival in January/February. Around the corner on Makartplatz is the 17th-century ❸ **Mozart-Wohnhaus** where you can see how the Mozart family lived.

Amble north along Linzer Gasse to ❹ **Friedhof St Sebastian** (p262), the Italianate arcaded cemetery where Wolfgang's father Leopold and his wife Constanze lie buried. Retrace your steps towards the Salzach River, turning left onto medieval Steingasse, then through to Giselakai to cross the ❺ **Mozartsteg** (Mozart Bridge).

On ❻ **Mozartplatz**, a coiffed Mozart is put on a pedestal in bronze. The statue was unveiled in 1842 in the presence of Mozart's sons. Across the way is the ❼ **Residenz** (p260) palace where Mozart gave his first court concert. Beside it is the ❽ **Salzburger Dom** (p263), where Mozart's parents were married in 1747 and little Wolfgang was baptised in 1756; Mozart later composed music here and was the cathedral organist.

Follow Franziskanergasse to the ❾ **Kollegienkirche** on Universitätsplatz, where Mozart's *Mass in D Minor* (K65) premiered in 1769. On Getreidegasse, stop at the bright-yellow townhouse, birthplace of a genius in 1756, at ❿ **Mozarts Geburtshaus** and buy some chocolate *Mozartkugeln* (Mozart balls) at ⓫ **Fürst** (p264).

At what is now Mozarts-Wohnhaus, the prolific Wolfgang composed works such as *The Shepherd King* (K208) and *Idomeneo* (K366).

Highlights at the Mozarts Geburthaus include the mini-violin he played as a toddler, plus a lock of his hair and buttons from his jacket.

At the tender age of just seven, Mozart performed for the prince-archbishop's court at the Residenz.

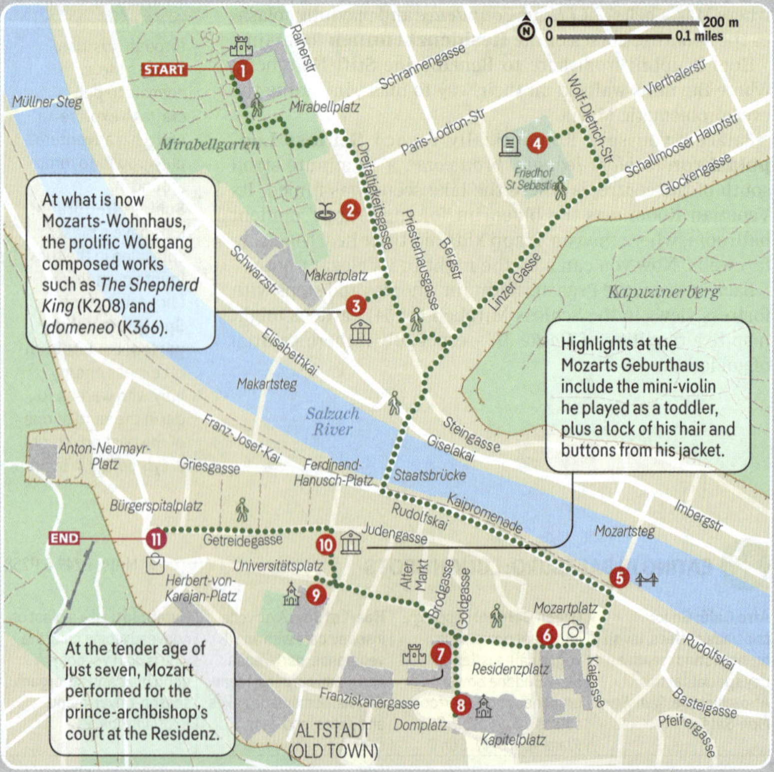

The Sound of Music By Bike
MAP P249,
Sing as you pedal
You don't have to be a die-hard *The Sound of Music* fan or even be able to hit the high notes like Julie Andrews to want to hop onto a bicycle saddle and belt out a few songs as you pedal between the film locations with **Fräulein Maria's Bicycle Tours** (*mariasbicycletours.com; tours adult/child €45/20*). Comfortable cruiser bikes whisk you through key backdrops to the movie, with plenty of fresh air, fun, quirky commentary and uplifting views thrown into the bargain.

Do-Re-Mi, *Sixteen Going on Seventeen*, *So Long, Farewell* – all the classics are in the mix on this half-day bike tour that rolls from palace to plaza, park to abbey. Kicking off at Mirabellplatz (just left of the entrance to the palace), tours run at 9.30am from April to October in all kinds of weather – get in quick in summer as they are crazily popular. From June to August, there are additional tours at 4.30pm if you prefer an early evening pedal.

Kaffeehaus Culture
MAP P258
Full of beans
Swinging open the heavy wooden doors of one of Salzburg's *Kaffeehäuser* (coffee houses) is your ticket to the city's soul. White-pinafored waitresses and bow-tied waiters whirl past with silver platters, the coffee list is long and elaborate, and more folk still chat and rustle newspapers than gaze blankly at smartphones. These unhurried micro-worlds remain largely immune to time and trends.

Vienna claims the coffee-house crown, but Salzburg can rival the Austrian capital with some highly *gemütlich* (cosy) cafes. Rococo and boho, trendy and touristy, grand and grungy – each *Kaffeehaus* has its own distinctive personality.

For full-on nostalgia, head to Alter Markt and **Café Tomaselli** (*tomaselli.at*), founded in 1700. Mozart once frequented this Salzburg institution, where magnificent cakes – including seasonal strudels that flake just so – grace marble-topped tables. Or dig a dainty fork into *Sacher Torte* (dark-chocolate sponge, iced and layered with apricot jam) at chandelier-lit **Café Sacher** (*sacher.com*) by the river. Its artsy neighbour **Café Bazar** (*cafe-bazar.at*) is a 1909 time warp of chandeliers and polished wood. Here locals enjoy the same river views over breakfast, cake and intelligent conversation as Marlene Dietrich did in 1936.

THE TRUTH BEHIND THE MOVIE LEGEND

While *The Sound of Music* is based on the real story of the von Trapps, a singing family with a nun-turned-governess called Maria, fact and fiction blur in the movie, with directors adding a generous pinch of poetic licence.

Did you know that in reality there were 10, not seven, von Trapp children, the eldest of whom was Rupert and that (spoiler alert) there was no Liesl? Or that the captain was not stern and aloof, but rather a gentle, family-loving man?

The real Maria, by contrast, was no soft touch. Unlike playful, warm-hearted Julie Andrews, she was devoutly religious, quick-tempered and strong willed. And during the Nazi annexation of Austria in 1938, the von Trapp family left quietly by train to Italy then flew to the US instead of climbing every mountain to Switzerland.

 EATING IN SALZBURG: ICE CREAM — MAPS P249 & P258

| Icezeit: Grab a cone at this Altstadt parlour, where flavours include salted peanut, caramel and passion fruit. *noon-8pm* € | Fabi's Frozen Yoghurt: Fabi is the whizz behind the frozen yoghurt here, including chocolate and fruit toppings. Organic and delicious. *noon-8pm* € | Eisl Eis: Cool off on Getreidegasse with organic sheep's-milk ice cream made at a 500-year-old farm on Wolfgangsee. *noon-6pm* € | Gelateria La Romana: Freshly made, properly authentic Italian gelato in flavours from cinnamon to blood orange. *11am-9pm Mon-Thu, to 10pm Fri-Sun* € |

There are third-wave newcomers on the scene, naturally. Blink and you'll miss speciality coffee bar **Kaffee Alchemie** (@*kaffeealchemie*). Headed up by a barista trainer, this retro riverfront cafe knows its beans and makes a cracking espresso. A step south of the Altstadt, post-industrial cool **220Grad** (*220grad.com*) wins for its freshly roasted coffee. Its name alludes to the perfect temperature for roasting beans. Its barista-made single-origin espressos and house blends pair brilliantly with delicious breakfasts and cakes.

Down by the River

MAP P258

Fun ways to see the sights

A boat ride along the Salzach River with **Schifffahrt Salzburg** (*schifffahrtsalzburg.at; city cruise adult/child €18/9*) is a leisurely way to pick out Salzburg's sights. Forty-minute cruises depart from Makartsteg bridge, with some of them chugging on to Schloss Hellbrunn. Or swap ordinary boats in favour of **Amphibious Splash Tours** (*amphibious-splash-tours.at; adult/child €41/26*), a novel combination of boat and floating bus. Tours last roughly 1½ hours, with several departures daily.

If you prefer to stay on dry land, guided **Segway Tours** (*segway-salzburg.at; tours from €59*) roll past the big sights by zippy battery-powered scooter. Trundle through the city before heading up to Mönchsberg on a 1½-hour ride, or tick off the trophy sights before speeding across to Schloss Leopoldskron for incredible views of the Altstadt and Alps on a two-hour spin. Kids in tow? Tours are suitable for children aged 12 and over.

Green Salzburg

MAPS P249 & P260

Gardens, lido swims and cycling trails

With the turquoise Salzach River dashing through its heart and Alps hogging the horizon, Salzburg delivers a big hit of nature.

For a central picnic and stroll, head to **Schloss Mirabell** (*salzburg.info; free*). Prince-Archbishop Wolf Dietrich built this lavish baroque palace in 1606 to woo his mistress Salome Alt, but it's the gardens that really shine. Here green-fingered Archbishop Johann Ernst von Thun added fountains, muses, parterres, rose gardens and the *Tänzerin* (dancer) sculpture, perfectly framing the view of high-on-a-hill Festung Hohensalzburg. The gardens seem familiar? Some scenes of *The Sound of Music* were filmed here. Cue the Pegasus statue, the steps and the gnomes of the **Zwerglgarten** (Dwarf Garden), where the von Trapp kids learned to sing *Do-Re-Mi*.

BEST SHOPPING IN SALZBURG: GIFTS

Klosterladen St Peter: This monastery shop has it all from hand-carved angels to gentian syrup and monastic beer.

Salzburger Heimatwerk: This old-school emporium knocks fabric into beautiful *Dirndls*, and does a fine line in handicrafts, books and music.

Lackner: Hand-carved nutcrackers, nativity figurines, filigree Christmas stars and cuckoo clocks are the real deal at this traditional craft shop.

Mayrische Musikalienhandlung: An institution since it opened in the 16th century, this glorious shop stocks a fabulous array of music, sheet music, scores and books.

Wenger: Pick up Lederhosen, *Dirndls*, shawls, scarves and hats at this Getreidegasse classic.

DRINKING IN SALZBURG: SKY-HIGH DRINKS

MAPS P249, P258 & P260

Steinterrasse: See the Altstadt lit up against the fortress at this 7th-floor terrace bar with champagne-sipping socialites. *7am-midnight Sun-Thu, to 1am Fri & Sat*

hu:goes14: The city looks tiny from this 14th-floor glass-walled bar and terrace at the arte Hotel. Get a signature mixed drink or classic cocktail. *4pm-midnight*

Imlauer Sky Bar: Salzburg spreads out in all its glory below this rooftop bar. It's spectacular after dark when the fortress lights up. *9am-1am*

Cool Mama Sky Terrace: Cocktails are served with the coolest of Salzburg views from this skyscraping hotel north of town. *noon-9pm Tue-Sat*

Schloss Leopoldskron

Unfurling from meadow to mountain, the banks of the **Salzach River** are a joy to cycle. Hire a bike or e-bike from **aVelo** *(bike rental per day €25)* at Staatsbrücke to pedal off past the Altstadt's domes and spires, perhaps stopping in the park at the **Volksgarten** for a picnic and swim in the lido **Freibad Volksgarten** *(adult/child €6/3.60)*, or rolling on south to **Waldbad Anif** *(waldbadanif.at; adult/child €9/7)* for a refreshing dip in a forest-rimmed lake. In summer, notch up the action with canoeing, SUPing or wakeboarding.

Make a Splash in the Almkanal   MAP P260
Swim and surf in the city

Flowing through the city since the Middle Ages, Salzburg's Almkanal provides a splash of history, with its network of hidden underground waterways. In summer, you can cycle or walk to **Schloss Leopoldskron** (p251) – the backdrop for the lake scene in *The Sound of Music* – for a bracing swim in the canal's chilly turquoise waters, floating towards the Altstadt before climbing the tree-lined banks and leaping in again.

Should you happen to have a board handy, join surfers to ride the canal's artificial wave, the **Surfwelle am Almkanal**, for free, just north of Weidenstrasse bridge. Year-round it's

SALZBURG'S BEST TOURS

Salzburg City Guides: Pro guides lead insightful walking tours zooming in on everything from architecture to art and the city by night.

Salzburg Panorama Tours: The 'original Sound of Music Tour', ticking off film-set biggies from Schloss Mirabell to Nonnberg, Hellbrunn and Mondsee.

Bob's Special Tours: Minibus tours to *The Sound of Music* locations, the Bavarian Alps and Hallstatt, plus private biking and walking tours.

Rikschatours: See Salzburg by rickshaw with a clued-up guide. Tours range from a 40-minute spin of the historic centre to a three-hour 'Round of Music'.

Salzburg Sightseeing Tours: A multilingual hop-on, hop-off bus tour of the city's trophy sights and *The Sound of Music* locations, plus day trips further afield.

 EATING IN SALZBURG: TRADITIONAL FAVOURITES — MAPS P249 & P258

Zirkelwirt: Jovial tucked-away inn with old-fashioned Austrian grub like schnitzel and dumplings with sauerkraut. *11.30am-11pm* €€

Johanneskeller: Dig into hearty classics like Styrian pork roast on the cosy brick-vaulted cellar or arcaded inner courtyard. *5-11pm Tue-Sat* €€

Bärenwirt: Go for *Bierbraten* (beer roast) with dumplings, locally caught trout or organic wild-boar bratwurst at this rustic tavern, sizzling since 1663. *11am-11pm* €€

Paul Stube: Up the cobbled Herrengasse lies this warm old-world tavern, with a menu full of Austrian classics and a summer beer garden. *5pm-midnight Tue-Sat* €€

OVERTOURISM IN SALZBURG

During peak holiday times (Christmas, Easter and the summer months of July and August), Salzburg is chock-a-block and you can barely move for the crowds pounding the narrow streets of the compact Altstadt, all in search of a little Mozart and Maria magic.

With 3.14 million overnight stays in Salzburg in 2024 (compared with a population of just 153,000), overtourism is a very real issue here, which is why it makes sense, if you can, to dodge the busiest times.

Opt for the calmer shoulder seasons of spring and autumn and you won't have to face such colossal crowds and queues. Other tips for a more sustainable stay: venture out quieter corners of the city beyond the historic centre and plan a longer trip.

With its fantastic public transport network, Salzburg can easily be used as a base for exploring the wider Salzburgerland region.

Paragliding from Untersberg

surfable for all levels, from beginners to experts. Boards are available for hire from **Wuux** *(per half/full day €30/50)*. To reach the wave, take bus 5 to Salzburg Weidenstrasse.

Salzburg's Twin Peaks   MAP P260
Climb ev'ry mountain

Where Austria slams into Germany, the 1973m peak of **Untersberg** *(untersbergbahn.at; cable car return adult/child €34/17)* propels you into the mountains right on the city's southern fringes. A cable car hauls you up the craggy summit, which enthrals with front-row views of Salzburg, the Rositten Valley, and the Austrian and Bavarian Alps. Paragliders launch themselves from the peak in summer (listen for the whoosh), while in winter, there's gentle skiing up here.

From the cable car top station, you can ramble along gentle trails through flower-flecked meadows to lookouts like **Geiereck** (1805m) and **Salzburg Hochthron** (1853m), or hike for a couple of hours across a wild karst plateau to the **Schellenberg Ice Cave** just over the border in Bavaria. Temperatures are significantly cooler up here than down in the valley, so bring a fleece or jacket and solid footwear. To reach the cable car valley station, take bus 25 from Salzburg's Hauptbahnhof or Mirabellplatz.

The rival peak is 1287m **Gaisberg**, puckering up east of the city. Here arresting views of the Salzburg Valley, the Salzkammergut lakes, the limestone Tennengebirge range and neighbouring Bavaria unravel. The best way to appreciate all of this is on the 6km, one to 1½-hour round-the-mountain **circular trail** (route 13a), starting at Zistelalm. Salzburger head up here for mountain biking in summer, cross-country skiing in winter and sunsets that pop year-round. To reach the peak, take bus 151 from Mirabellplatz to Gaisberg.

Modern Art Talking

MAPS P249 & P258

A brush with Salzburg's creative side

Though Salzburg generally moves to a historic beat, the **Museum der Moderne** *(museumdermoderne.at; adult/child €14/free, with lift €16/free)*, perched atop Mönchsberg's cliffs, goes off-piste, pushing boundaries with its engrossing exhibitions of mixed-media 20th- and 21st-century art. The spotlight is on both emerging and established artists. Reached by a lift, the glass-and-white-marble, oblong-shaped gallery is the architectural antithesis to Festung Hohensalzburg on the other side of the hill. While you're up here, pop into **M32** *(m32.at)* for a coffee with a far-reaching view over Salzburg.

In the Altstadt, its sister gallery, covered by the same ticket, is the **Rupertinum**, which zooms in largely on graphic works and photography. Zany Austrian artist Friedensreich Hundertwasser left his mark on the inner courtyard in the form of glittering *Zungenbärte* ('tongue beards').

But art isn't just confined to museums here. Bridging the gap between culture and the outdoors, there is public art sprinkled all over town that won't cost you a cent to admire. Top billing goes to the **Walk of Modern Art**, specially commissioned installations and sculptures that have Salzburg's cultural identity as a common thread. Here attention-grabbers include James Turrell's **Blue Pearl – Skyspace** (go at dawn or at dusk for the full-on bluesy effect) at Mönchsberg; Stephan Balkenhol's giant man-on-a-golden-globe **Sphaera** on Kapitelplatz; and Anselm Kiefer's 4m-high winged book stack, **The Language of Birds**, in Chiemseehof.

In summer, step south of town to **Schloss Arenberg**. Built for the lordly prince-archbishops in the 14th century, the palace's beautiful grounds conceal the **Würth Sculpture Garden**, brimming with contemporary, thought-provoking artworks.

Explore Salzburg's Altstadt

MAP P258

Royal bling and baroque in overdrive

For a city of dinky proportions, Salzburg packs an insane amount of culture into its alley-woven historic centre. For centuries, the ruling prince-archbishops frantically built castles, palaces, churches, domes and abbeys here. And nowhere is the pomp and circumstance of Salzburg more tangible than in the baroque Altstadt, a UNESCO World Heritage Site, with stately squares and museums to keep you absorbed for hours. Rise early to see them at their quiet, crowd-free best.

Begin with an eye-opening spin of Salzburg's baroque heart in the **DomQuartier** *(domquartier.at; adult/child €15/5)*. One ticket covers multiple sights. The showstopper is Salzburger Dom (p263), the lavishly stuccoed and frescoed cathedral where Mozart was baptised.

continues on p260

SALZBURG CARD

If you're planning on doing lots of sightseeing, it's wise to invest in the money-saving **Salzburg Card** *(1-/2-/3-day card €34/41/47)*. The card gets you entry to all of the major sights, galleries, museums and attractions, unlimited use of public transport (including cable cars), and numerous discounts on tours and events. It also allows you to skip the queue at a number of attractions.

The card is half-price for children and €3 cheaper in the low season.

The card can be purchased at the airport, the tourist office and most hotels. Or buy the digital version online at salzburg.info and use it immediately on your smartphone.

MORE SOUND OF MUSIC

Just south of the city, **Schlosspark Hellbrunn** (p268) hides the loved-up pavilion of *Sixteen Going on Seventeen* fame, where you can act out those 'Oh, Liesl'...'Oh, Rolf...' fantasies.

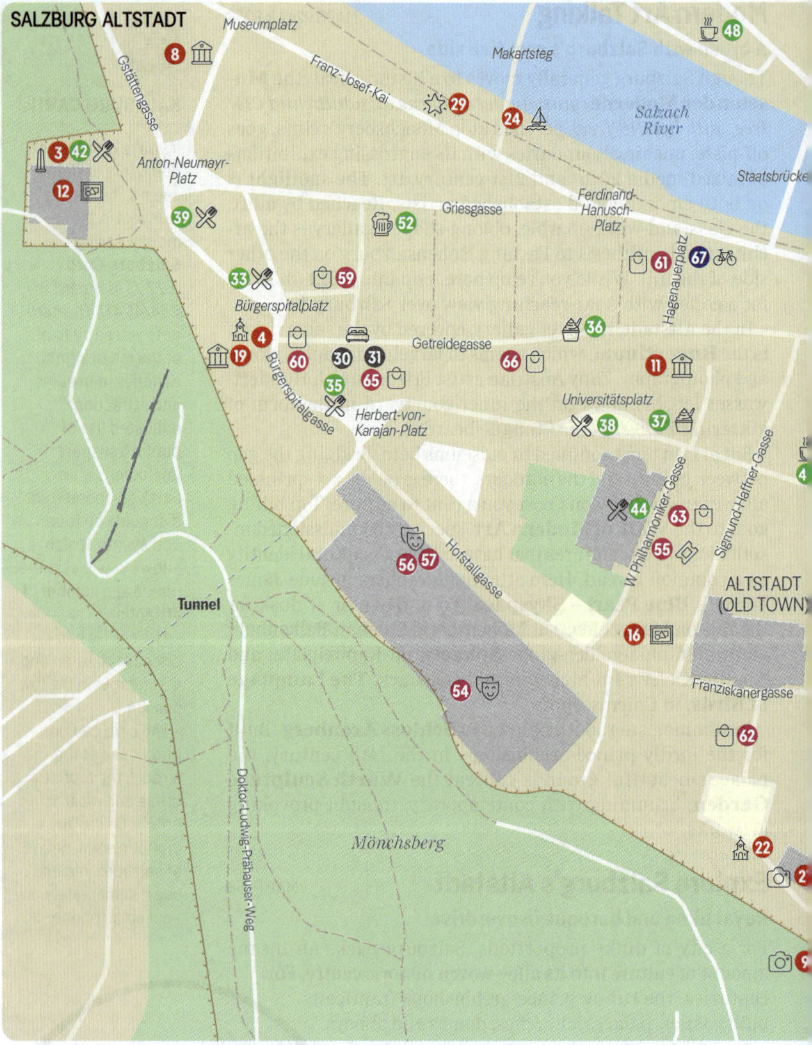

SALZBURG ALTSTADT

★ HIGHLIGHTS
1 DomQuartier
2 Residenz

● SIGHTS
3 Blue Pearl – Skyspace
4 Bürgerspitalskirche St Blasius
5 Christmas Museum
6 Domplatz
7 Friedhof St Peter
8 Haus der Natur
9 Katakomben
10 Mozartplatz
11 Mozarts Geburtshaus
12 Museum der Moderne
13 Plaque to Joseph Mohr
14 Residenzbrunnen
15 Residenzplatz
16 Rupertinum
17 Salzburger Dom
18 Sphaera
19 Spielzeugmuseum
20 Steingasse
21 Stift St Peter
22 Stiftskirche St Peter
23 The Language of Birds

● ACTIVITIES
24 Amphibious Splash Tours
25 Bob's Special Tours
26 Kapuzinerberg
27 Rikschatours
28 Salzburg City Guides
29 Schifffahrt Salzburg

● SLEEPING
30 Arthotel Blaue Gans
31 Goldener Hirsch
32 Hotel am Dom

- **EATING**
- 33 Afro Café
- 34 Bäckerei Holztrattner
- 35 Blaue Gans Restaurant
- 36 Eisl Eis
- 37 Fabi's Frozen Bio Yogurt
- 38 Grünmarkt
- 39 Humboldt
- 40 Icezeit
- 41 Kajetanerplatz
- 42 M32
- 43 Paul Stube
- 44 Salzburger Grill Imbiss
- 45 Stiftsbäckerei St Peter
- 46 Uncle Van
- 47 Zirkelwirt

- **DRINKING & NIGHTLIFE**
- 48 Café Bazar
- 49 Café Tomaselli
- 50 Kaffee Alchemie
- 51 Steinterrasse
- 52 Sternbräu
- 53 StieglKeller

- **ENTERTAINMENT**
- 54 Felsenreitschule
- 55 Festspiele Ticket Office
- 56 Grosses Festspielhaus
- 57 Haus für Mozart
- 58 StageBar

- **SHOPPING**
- 59 Drechslerei Lackner
- 60 Fürst
- 61 Kaslöchl
- 62 Klosterladen St Peter
- 63 Salzburg Salz
- 64 Salzburger Heimatwerk
- 65 Spirituosen Sporer
- 66 Wenger

- **TRANSPORT**
- 67 aVelo

WHY I LOVE SALZBURG

Kerry Walker, Lonely Planet writer

I lost my heart to Salzburg when I first set foot on Austrian soil (well, snow...) more than 20 years ago – and I've been returning ever since as a Lonely Planet author. For me, Salzburg is Austria in microcosm, from the Altstadt, where alleys lead to baroque palaces, domes and a hilltop fortress freshly minted for a Disney fantasy, to the beautifully manicured gardens that unspool along the banks of the Salzach River, grand concert halls pumping out Mozart melodies and the ever-uplifting skyline of Alps.

The city has a unique energy and spirit, bundling together high culture, art and a passion for the outdoors into one neat, beautifully wrapped package. It's a city that never fails to put a spring in my step.

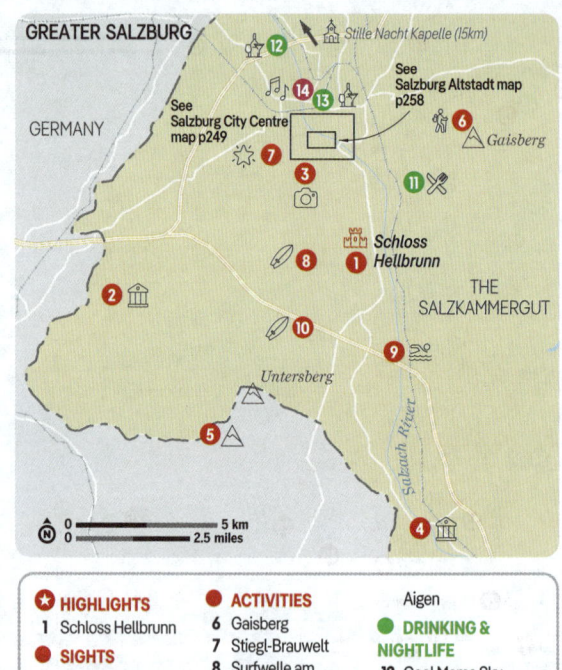

HIGHLIGHTS
1 Schloss Hellbrunn

SIGHTS
2 Freilichtmuseum
3 Schloss Leopoldskron
4 Stille Nacht Museum
5 Untersberg

ACTIVITIES
6 Gaisberg
7 Stiegl-Brauwelt
8 Surfwelle am Almkanal
9 Waldbad Anif
10 Wuux

EATING
11 Gasthof Schloss Aigen

DRINKING & NIGHTLIFE
12 Cool Mama Sky Terrace
13 hu:goes14

ENTERTAINMENT
14 Jazzit

continued from p257

You'll also get entry to the **Residenz** palace. A man of grand designs, Wolf Dietrich von Raitenau, prince-archbishop of Salzburg from 1587 to 1612, gave the go-ahead to plonk this baroque palace on the site of an 11th-century bishop's residence. A tour races through exuberant state rooms adorned with tapestries, Johann Michael Rottmayr frescoes, and its gallery, rammed with Old Master paintings of the Rembrandt and Rubens ilk.

Out front, *Fiaker* (horse-drawn carriages) clip-clop across grand **Residenzplatz**, a late-16th-century vision inspired

 EATING IN SALZBURG: STREET FOOD ─────────── MAPS P249 & P258

Bistro de Márquez: Piedad brings Colombia to this wallet-friendly bistro, with *arepas* (filled maize crêpes) and *pandebono* (cheese bread). *11.30am-7pm Wed-Sat* €

Uncle Van: Hip Vietnamese spot on Steingasse. Authentic takes on ramen noodles, curries, summer rolls and pho. *11.30am-9pm Mon-Fri, noon-9pm Sat & Sun* €

Organic Pizza Salzburg: Good-natured staff, cool music and pizza with super-fresh, organic ingredients. *5-10pm Tue-Fri, noon-10pm Sat, noon-9pm Sun* €

Salzburger Grill Imbiss: Raymond is the wurst whizz at this sausage stand behind Kollegienkirche. Go for a *Bosna* (pork bratwurst). *11am-5pm* €

by Rome and masterminded by Italian architect Vincenzo Scamozzi. Its centrepiece is the **Residenzbrunnen** (p251), an enormous marble fountain ringed by four water-spouting horses and topped by Triton bearing a conch shell.

Christmas in Salzburg
MAP P258
Concerts, carols and markets

Salzburg is a city with Christmas in its bones. It's particularly bewitching in December, when trees twinkle, carollers sing and the cinnamon-clove scent of gingerbread and *Glühwein* drift through the Altstadt's alleyways. The backdrop is a ready-made Christmas card, with the castle-topped baroque skyline lifting the gaze to the snow-dusted Alps.

You'll feel the wide-eyed wonder of a child at the **Christkindlmarkt** *(christkindlmarkt.co.at)* on cathedral-crowned Domplatz and palace-topped Residenzplatz (p260), which shimmer gold from late November to New Year's Day. Here carollers sing angelically, brass bands play and huts sell chestnuts and *Glühwein,* candied almonds and beautifully carved nativity figurines and nutcrackers.

Go for a twirl on the ice rink on nearby **Mozartplatz**, or else head to the insanely romantic Christmas market at Schloss Hellbrunn (p267). The palace is transformed into a giant Advent calendar (with each window representing a door) and its gardens are illuminated by trick fountains and 700 glittering trees.

Music? Christmas brings a flurry of concerts, from carols and Mozart symphonies echoing through the medieval halls of Festung Hohensalzburg (p250) to Advent concerts at the Grosses Festspielhaus (p263).

If you wish it could be Christmas every day, swing on over to Salzburg's **Christmas Museum** *(salzburger-weihnachtsmuseum.at; adult/child €9/5)*. The private collection brings year-round festive sparkle with Advent calendars, hand-carved cribs, baubles and nutcrackers.

All is Calm, All is Bright
Pilgrimage to Oberndorf

Nothing gives you that warm, fuzzy, festive feeling more than making the pilgrimage to **Oberndorf**, a serene town snug against the Bavarian border, a 25-minute train ride northwest from Salzburg. If the flakes fall, pad through the snow to the **Stille Nacht Kapelle**, where Joseph Mohr was

SAVE ON STAYS

Rocking up in peak summer season and expecting to find a deal is wishful thinking in Salzburg.

In high-season months, hotels in the Altstadt can be eye-wateringly expensive, with prices leaping to double what they are in the low season. Note that high-season prices jack up another 10% to 20% during the Salzburg Festival. December is also primetime, with everyone flocking to the city's twinkling Christmas markets.

Finding reasonably priced accommodation is possible, however, if you're willing to go the extra mile, staying in private rooms and simple, family-run B&Bs. There's a cluster of these along Moosstrasse, which can be reached from the city centre in around 15 minutes on bus 21.

If Salzburg is booked solid, consider staying in Hallein or across the border in Bavaria.

SHOPPING IN SALZBURG: PICNIC FIXINGS
MAPS P249 & P258

Grünmarkt: Picnic stop on Universitätsplatz. Stalls laden with regional cheeses, ham, fruit, bread and huge pretzels. *7am-5pm Mon-Fri, 6am-3pm Sat* €

Salzburg Schranne: Farmers set up at 5am Thursday in front of Andräkirche. Produce and flowers from Salzburg and its rural surrounds. *5am-1pm Thu* €

Kajetanerplatz: Locals flock to this organic farmers market on Fridays for fresh produce, meat, cheese and baked treats. *6am-2pm Fri* €

Bäckerei Holztrattner: Pick up fresh-baked loaves, rolls, fruit bread and pastries from this bakery going strong since 1350. *6am-6pm Mon-Fri, to noon Sat* €

ESCAPE THE CROWDS IN SALZBURG

Hildegard Strohmeyer, an official Salzburg city and hiking guide, divulges her favourite spots for giving the crowds the slip. *hildastroh.com*

Friedhof St Sebastian: Mozart's father Leopold and wife Constanze are buried in this cemetery on Linzer Gasse, established in 1600 as an Italian 'campo santo'. Its centrepiece is the mausoleum of Prince-Archbishop Wolf-Dietrich of Raitenau. It's a haven of peace.

Bürgerspitalkirche St Blasius: The civic hospital church near Getreidegasse has an inner courtyard with Renaissance arcades. A Gothic church with 12th-century roots, it impresses with its vault, stained-glass windows and mystical interior.

Waldbad Anif: Rent a bike to pedal south along the Salzach River to this emerald-green lake, perfect in summer. It's like diving into a mountain lake – the water is cool and crystal clear.

Salzburg Christmas market (p261)

once pastor. He penned the six-stanza poem *Silent Night* ('Stille Nacht'), handed it over to parish organist, Franz Xaver Gruber, and asked him to compose the melody. The peaceful carol debuted on 24 December 1818, with the pair singing it in front of the nativity scene. Hearing it sung here on a frosty Christmas Eve, more than two centuries down the line, is spine-tingling stuff.

Translated into 300 different languages, *Silent Night* has become the world's most famous and best-loved carol.

Festival Time

MAP P258

All Salzburg's a stage

When the curtain rises on the **Salzburger Festspiele** *(salzburgerfestspiele.at)* on a summer's evening and locals glide through the baroque streets dressed to the nines in *Tracht* (traditional costume), it's as if the city has been touched by magic. The first stars pinprick a deep-blue sky, the city's domes, churches and castle glow gold, audiences fall silent in squares, and concert halls reverberate with the sound of opera and orchestras.

In 1920, dream trio Hugo von Hofmannsthal, Max Reinhardt and Richard Strauss combined their creative forces, and the Salzburg Festival was born. Opera, drama and classical concerts of the highest calibre have propelled the five-week summer festival to international renown, attracting some of the world's best conductors, directors, orchestras and singers.

Come festival time, Salzburg crackles with excitement, as a quarter of a million visitors descend on the city for some 200 productions. Theatre premieres, avant-garde works and the summer-resident Vienna Philharmonic performing works by Mozart are all in the mix. The **Festival District** on Hofstallgasse has a spectacular backdrop, framed by Mönchsberg's cliffs. Most performances are held in the cavernous **Grosses Festspielhaus**, which accommodates 2179 theatregoers, the **Haus für Mozart** in the former royal stables, and the baroque **Felsenreitschule**.

If you plan to visit the festival, don't leave anything to chance – book flights, hotel and tickets months in advance. Sometimes last-minute tickets are available at the **Festspiele Ticket Office** on Wiener-Philharmoniker-Gasse, but they're like gold dust, especially for the biggest crowd-puller – Hofmannsthal's soul-stirring morality play, *Jedermann* ('Everyman'), on Domplatz.

Spiritual Salzburg

MAPS P249 & P258

In high spirits

Wander Salzburg's baroque Altstadt at the change of hour and fall silent as the city rings with tolling bells and chimes like a giant glockenspiel. It's the most uplifting of sights and sounds.

To tune into Salzburg's spiritual side, begin where the city did: **Stift St Peter** *(stift-stpeter.at)*, the oldest abbey in the German-speaking world, founded by a Frankish missionary named Rupert in 700. Its showpiece is an overwhelmingly baroque church, richly embellished with stucco and altar paintings by Martin Johann Schmidt. Composer Michael Haydn (1737–1806), opera singer Richard Mayr (1877–1935) and renowned Salzburg confectioner Paul Fürst (1856–1941) are buried among the sea of filigree wrought-iron crosses in the **cemetery** here. Most atmospheric of all are the **catacombs** *(adult/child €2/1.50)* – cave-like chapels and crypts carved into the sheer cliff face of Mönchsberg.

Close by, the baroque **Salzburger Dom** *(salzburger-dom.at; adult/child €5/free)* is gracefully crowned by a bulbous copper cupola and twin spires. Bronze portals symbolising faith, hope and charity lead into the cathedral. In the nave, Arsenio Mascagni's ceiling frescoes recounting the Passion of Christ guide the eye to the polychrome dome. To experience the cathedral at its captivating best, catch one of the half-hour lunchtime **organ concerts**, which begin just after the bells ring at 12.04pm.

All the more enchanting for being away from the tourist crowds, Benedictine **Stift Nonnberg** *(nonnberg.at; free)* is a short, stiff uphill hike. Climb up to its rib-vaulted church to glimpse beautifully faded Romanesque frescoes and – if you're an early riser – hear the abbey's nuns singing Gregorian chorales at 6.45am.

MORE SILENT NIGHT

Find a plaque at lyricist Joseph Mohr's former home on **Steingasse** (p264), and in Hallein, visit the **Stille Nacht Museum** (p269), housed in the former residence of the song's composer Franz Xaver Gruber.

CYCLE SALZBURG

There's no better way to see Salzburg than with your backside in a saddle, some say. And right they are. Salzburg is one of Austria's most bike-friendly cities and its vast, 180km-long network of cycling trails, heading off in all directions, including along the banks of the crazily scenic Salzach River, is a two-wheel dream.

Renting a bike or e-bike (for instance from centrally located aVelo) is your backstage pass to a side to the city few get to see. While you can easily piece together your own itinerary, a good starting point is the Instagrammable **Salzburg Cycle Route**, a 23.6km, 10-stop ride beyond the Altstadt, stitching together photogenic churches, palaces, gardens and viewpoints. The website salzburg.info has details or download a self-guided tour at smart-guide.org.

BEST FOOD SHOPPING IN SALZBURG:

Fürst: The pistachio, nougat and dark-chocolate *Mozartkugeln* (Mozart balls) are handmade to the original 1890 recipe.

Kaslöchl: Mouse-sized cheese shop, crammed with creamy alpine varieties, holey Emmenthal and fresh cheese with herbs.

Sporer: In Getreidegasse's narrowest house, Sporer has sold Austrian wines, herbal liqueurs and Vogelbeer schnapps since 1903.

Salzburg Salz: Pop in to this Altstadt emporium to buy pure salt from the Alps of Salzburgerland, salts flavoured with flowers and herbs, and salt chocolate.

Feinkost Stocker: This old butcher's shop in Nonntal is a delight for the finest charcuterie, sausages and wines from the surrounding region.

Daily Bread

MAP P258

Buy a loaf at Salzburg's oldest bakery

A watermill still turns at **Stiftsbäckerei St Peter** (*stifts baeckerei.at*). Part of the historic abbey complex, this vaulted, 700-year-old bakery is still blessed by locals for its daily bread. The bakery churns out Salzburg's finest loaves, lovingly kneaded by hand, made from freshly milled rye and wheat flour and natural sourdough, and baked until crunchy in a wood-fired oven. The bread keeps well, making it perfect for stashing in a backpack for a picnic up in the hills or down by the river. You can also pick up other goodies such as *Gewürzweckerl* (spiced rolls), plaited yeast buns and brioche here, too.

It's all brilliantly sustainable: the bakery is powered with wood from the monastery's forest and its own hydropower from the Almkanal.

Marionette Magic

MAP P249

Like a puppet on a string

Not only children are filled with wonder at the UNESCO World Heritage Site **Salzburger Marionettentheater** (*marionetten.at; tickets adult €33-43, child €15*), where the red curtain has risen on a miniature stage since 1913. The theatre is just as grand and intricate as a full-size one, with stucco embellishments and chandeliers. The level of detail that goes into the costumes and backdrops is extraordinary and the puppeteers are incredibly talented – you'll barely notice the strings as the marionettes dance, swoop and fly through the air.

The repertoire star is *The Sound of Music*, with a life-sized Mother Superior and a marionette-packed finale. Other enchanting productions include Mozart's *The Magic Flute*, Tchaikovsky's *The Nutcracker* and Beethoven's *Fidelio*. Performances (with multilingual subtitles) last around two hours. Or for a taste of the theatre's greatest hits, book the 35-minutes **highlights show** (*adult/child €28/15*).

Silent Nights on Steingasse

Back to the Middle Ages

Slip away from the Altstadt's crowds and back to the Middle Ages on Steingasse. Hugging the banks of the Salzach River, the lane might not look like a major thoroughfare today, but it was once the main north–south route between the city and Italy, its cobbles worn smooth by many a horse's hoof and wagon wheel. Salt from nearby mines was transported from here to Europe and beyond.

The street is a beauty, with a curve of medieval townhouses in soft pastel colours, which are at their photogenic best in the morning sunlight or when lantern-lit in the blue dusk. Look out for the **plaque** at No 9 dedicated to famous past resident Joseph Mohr, who wrote the lyrics to that all-time classic carol *Silent Night* (p262) in 1816, just after the end of the Napoleonic Wars.

Augustiner Bräustübl

Beer Garden Days

MAPS P249 & P258

Salzburg through a beer glass

Bavaria is but a bottle-top-pop away from Salzburg and you can feel it in the city's rollicking, stein-swinging beer halls, traditional breweries and vast beer gardens, where honeyed summer sun trickles through chestnut-tree branches. Seeing Salzburg through the lens of a beer glass is a fun and surprisingly immersive way to experience the city. The first breweries were founded here in the late 14th century and some are still going strong today.

If you can only visit one, make it **Augustiner Bräustübl** (*augustinerbier.at*). Since 1621, this cheery, monastery-run brewery has served potent home brews in beer steins in its vaulted hall and 1400-seat beer garden. Get your tankard filled at the foyer pump and visit the snack stands for hearty, beer-swigging grub including *Stelzen* (ham hock), pork belly and giant pretzels.

For a 365-day taste of Oktoberfest, try the cavernous, Munich-style beer hall **StieglKeller** (*restaurant-stieglkeller.at*) instead, which shares the same architect as Munich's Hofbräuhaus. Perched panoramically above the city and near Festung Hohensalzburg, it has an enormous garden above the rooftops and pairs brews with the likes of pork knuckle and schnitzel. Beer is cheapest from the self-service taps outside.

Though firmly on the tourist trail, the massive beer garden at **Sternbräu** (*sternbrau.at*) remains a lively place to guzzle homebrews and people-watch in the Altstadt. It has been going strong since 1542. Or hop across the river to **Die Weisse** (*dieweisse.at*). The brewpub of the Salzburger Weissbierbrauerei serves cloudy wheat beers in its wood-floored pub and shady beer garden. DJs work the decks in the Sudhaus bar, where you might find locals partying in *Dirndls* and *Lederhosen*.

SALZBURG'S BEST LIVE MUSIC

Jazzit: Regular concerts, from tango to electro, plus workshop, club nights and free Tuesday-night jam sessions in the Jazzit bar.
ARGEkultur: Alternative arts centre. Concerts, cabaret, DJ nights, dance, poetry slams and world music traverse the arts spectrum.
Rockhouse: Salzburg's hottest live-music venue presents first-rate rock, pop, jazz, folk, metal and reggae concerts.
StageBar: B&W photos of music legends plaster the walls of this Altstadt bar, where live music and karaoke are paired with cocktails.
Schloss Mirabell: Internationally renowned soloists and ensembles perform works by Mozart and other well-known composers such as Haydn and Chopin in a sublime palace setting.

Stiegl-Brauwelt

Something's Brewing at Stiegl-Brauwelt

MAP P260

Austria's biggest private brewery

Brewing and bottling since 1492, **Stiegl-Brauwelt** *(audio-guided/guided tour €13.90/19.90)* is heaven to beer lovers. A 1½-hour guided tour whisks you from grain to glass, taking in brewery history in the museum, the different stages of the brewing process and (woohoo!) the world's tallest beer tower, and the brewhouse and bottling plant where 90,000 bottles of Stiegl beer are filled each hour. You'll end, fittingly, with a three-beer tasting. There are tours in English at 1pm daily.

Swing over to the on-site vaulted Stiegl-Bräustüberl, where classic grub like Schweinsbraten (pork roast) drizzled in wheat-beer jus is paired with homebrews like fresh, citrusy Hoppy Hell lager. Or head to the beer garden to fill your own stein from the fountain.

The brewery is 1.5km southwest of the Altstadt; take bus 10 to Bräuhausstrasse.

SALZBURG DIARY DATES

As a high-spirited, music-loving, culture-mad city, Salzburg has a jam-packed events calendar, some of which are free.

Salzburger Festspiele: Can't snag Salzburg Festival tickets? In summer, Kapitelplatz gets crowds into the swing of the Salzburger Festspiele showing opera for free on a big screen.

Sternenkino Movie Nights: Kapitelplatz is also the castle-crowned backdrop for free arthouse movie nights at Sternenkino, held over 10 days from late June to early July. Films begin at 8.30pm. Bring along your own picnic or grab drinks and street food on the square. *sternenkino-salzburg.at*

Jazz & the City: Mid-October brings Jazz & the City, with jazz acts – from rising stars to big names – hitting venues all over the city, from baroque churches to beer halls.

Beyond Salzburg

Salzburg is the curtain-raiser to Alps that will make your heart soar and cinematic backdrops that will prompt you to yodel out loud.

Within minutes of central Salzburg you can be swanning around the fountain-splashed gardens of exuberant baroque summer palace Schloss Hellbrunn, or brushing up on Celtic history and delving deep into medieval salt mines in Hallein.

And the further you venture, the better it gets. For a memorable day trip, take the quick train ride to Werfen, which thrills with a show-stopping medieval castle and the world's biggest ice caves, Eisriesenwelt. Here cliff-skimming trails thread through the rugged peaks of the limestone Tennengebirge, where eagles wheel, winds blow and silence reigns. Further south still, Filzmoos, hemmed in by saw-edged peaks, wings you away from the crowds and back to nature with hiking, skiing and snowshoeing in the Dachstein massif.

Places
Hellbrunn p267
Hallein p268
Werfen p269
Filzmoos p271
Liechtensteinklamm p272

Hellbrunn TIME FROM SALZBURG: 15-20MINS

Stomping ground of the Prince-Archbishops

Many of Salzburg's prince-archbishops were absorbed in matters of a more religious nature, but not Markus Sittikus, Prince-Archbishop of Salzburg from 1612 to 1619. Markus had a frivolous streak, wicked sense of humour and a love of drunken, hedonistic parties. So he had lavish, lemon-fronted Italianate palace **Schloss Hellbrunn** *(hellbrunn.at; adult/child €15/6.50)* built to escape his divine duties, inviting the clergy over to feast, drink and make merry in exotic gardens full of citrus trees, muses and fountains.

While Schloss Hellbrunn's whimsical interior is fabulous, especially the **Chinese Room** and frescoed **Festsaal**, it's the eccentric **Wasserspiele** (trick fountains) that are the big draw in summer. Be prepared to get soaked in the mock Roman theatre, shell-clad Neptune Grotto and the twittering Bird Grotto. No statue here is as it seems, including the emblematic tongue-poking-out Germaul mask (Sittikus' answer to his critics). The tour rounds out at the 18th-century water-powered **Mechanical Theatre**, where 200 limewood figurines depict life in a baroque city.

GETTING AROUND

Much of the region beyond Salzburg is brilliantly accessible by public transport (bus and train), removing the need to hire a car unless you crave the independence of having your own wheels.

There are regional and S-Bahn trains running frequently from Salzburg to Hallein (15 minutes) and Werfen (40 minutes). The two-hour journey to Filzmoos is a little bit trickier, involving a train (to Bischoshofen) and two buses.

ROMAN RULE

In the Holy Roman Empire, prince-archbishops ruled the roost in Salzburg from 1278 to 1803. Markus Sittikus loved pomp and play at Schloss Hellbrunn, but it was his predecessor and successor that made the history books big time.

Wolf Dietrich von Raitenau, prince-archbishop from 1587 to 1612, spearheaded the total baroque makeover of the city, commissioning many of its most beautiful churches, palaces and gardens. He fell from power after losing a fierce dispute over the salt trade with powerful Bavarian rulers, and died a prisoner.

Seizing the reins from Markus Sittikus in 1619 and in power until 1953, Trentino-born Paris von Lodron was stern and ambitious. He founded the Universität Salzburg in 1622 and managed to keep the principality out of the Europe-wide Thirty Years' War.

Don't dash off after seeing the palace. The **gardens** *(free)* are a brilliant spot for a picnic, stroll or run, with tree-shaded avenues, ponds and sculptures. Here you'll find the pavilion of *The Sound of Music Sixteen Going on Seventeen* fame.

To reach Hellbrunn it's a 20-minute bike ride (mostly along the Salzach River) from the city centre, or a 15-minute ride on bus 25, which departs from Mozartsteg/Rudolfskai in the Altstadt.

Ride along the river to Hellbrunn

By far the most scenic way to reach Schloss Hellbrunn from Salzburg is by getting on your bike for the 20-minute roll south. Rent wheels at **aVelo** (p255) *(bike rental per day €25)* at Staatsbrücke and leave the crowds of the Altstadt behind.

You'll pedal through the historic Kaiviertel district and avant-garde Unipark Nonntal before emerging on Mühlbacherhofweg. It's then a straightforward trundle through meadows, passing **Schloss Freisaal**, a dinky medieval castle rimmed by a lake, which backs onto the **Universität Salzburg Botanical Garden** *(salzburg.info; free)*. From here, you'll hook onto Hellbrunner Allee, a grand, straight-as-a-die avenue lined by ancient chestnut trees. Keep an eye out, too, for butter-yellow **Schloss Frohnburg**, a 17th-century summer palace that had a cameo role in *The Sound of Music* as the von Trapp Villa.

Hallein

TIME FROM SALZBURG: **15MINS**

Trip back to medieval times

But a pretzel-throw from Bavaria, the town of Hallein has medieval looks and a riveting mountain backdrop, yet somehow it has managed to dodge the tourist radar. Just a 15-minute train trundle south of Salzburg, it makes a terrific day trip. History here runs deep – in every possible sense of the expression.

During Salzburg's princely heyday, the sale of salt filled its coffers. Dive into the past at cavernous **Salzwelten** *(salzwelten.at; adult child €43/19.50)*, where 'white gold' was mined for 2600 years. Slip into a boiler suit for a tour deep underground, which takes you through a maze of claustrophobic passageways, across an atmospherically lit salt lake, over the border to Germany and down a miner's slide – don't brake, lift your legs and ask the guide to wax the slide for extra speed!

Or tune into Celtic heritage with a romp around the riverside **Keltenmuseum** *(keltenmuseum.at; adult/child €9.50/4.50)*. Overlooking the Salzach, the glass-fronted museum zips chronologically through the region's heritage. The beautifully vaulted rooms showcase a priceless stash of Celtic

 EATING & DRINKING IN HALLEIN: OUR PICKS

| **El'risa:** Vaulted cafe with a relaxed vibe. Creative breakfasts, vegan lunches and Austrian speciality coffees. *9am-2pm Mon-Wed & Fri, to 5pm Sat & Sun* € | **Eckzimmer:** Laid-back cafe for brunch, great coffee, light lunches and to-go picnic boxes. Sit on the garden terrace when the sun's out. *9am-6pm Wed-Sun* € | **Hammerwirt:** Austro-Italian dishes, such as *Backhendl* (crispy breaded chicken), and a chestnut-tree-canopied garden. *5-10pm Wed-Fri, 11.30am-10pm Sat & Sun* €€ | **Aarons Genusskrämerei:** Regional produce is finessed into imaginative dishes served with flair and local wines at the town's oldest inn. *4-11pm Tue-Fri, 10am-11pm Sat* €€ |

Salzwelten

artefacts, from Bronze Age helmets to Celtic gold torques and the 'Mannes im Salz', the mummified remains of a prehistoric salt miner.

Hallein's more festive claim to fame is as the one-time home of Franz Xaver Gruber (1787–1863), who composed the carol *Stille Nacht* ('Silent Night'). Joseph Mohr penned the poem and Gruber, a schoolteacher at the time, came up with the melody on his guitar in 1818. The fabled guitar takes pride of place in the **Stille Nacht Museum** (p263) *(adult/child €5/2.50)*, lodged in Gruber's former residence, which recounts the story of the carol through documents and personal belongings.

Werfen

TIME FROM SALZBURG: **40MINS** **OR 1HR**

Cue the world's biggest ice caves

High above Werfen, the pointed peaks of the Tennengebirge rise like a theatre curtain of solid limestone above the river-woven Salzach Valley. Take the cable car, then hoof it up the steep, scree-strewn trail to **Eisriesenwelt** *(eisriesenwelt.at; adult/child including cable car €42/21)*, the world's biggest accessible ice cave, open from May to October. Stepping through the huge 20m-wide gash in the rock, feeling the frosty blast of 0°C air and seeing the ice twinkle is like pushing through the wardrobe into Narnia.

CENT SAVERS

All ÖBB train stations in the region sell the money-saving **Salt Worlds Salzburg** *(adult/child €38.30/15.50)* ticket. This covers a bus transfer to Bad Dürrnberg, plus entry to the Salzwelten salt mines, the Kelten Erlebnis Berg (Celtic Mountain) themed playground, where kids can take a playful dive into a prehistoric world, the Salina Celtic village, shining a light on the Ice Age settlement, and the Salt Worlds app, which brings Celtic objects to life in 3D.

Stay overnight in Hallein or Bad Dürrnberg and you will automatically receive the **TennengauPLUS-Card** *(tennengau.com)*, which gives you free travel on buses and trains (all the way to Salzburg) and discounted entry to local sights, museums and attractions.

EATING IN WERFEN: OUR PICKS

Pizzeria im Markt: Pizzas fly out of the oven perfectly thin and crisp at this cosy pick in Werfen's heart. *10am-10pm* €

Oedlhaus: At Eisriesenwelt, this 1574m woodsy hut fortifies walkers with grub like *Gröstl* and mountain views. *8am-4pm* €€

Stiege No 1: Venison, asparagus, wild garlic – the menu sings of the seasons. In summer, sit in the lantern-lit garden. *11am-10pm Wed-Sun* €€

Obauer: At this Michelin-starred restaurant, the Obauer brothers make alpine, homegrown and foraged ingredients sing on the plate. *6-9pm Wed, noon-9pm Thu-Sun* €€€

A 1¼-hour guided tour by old-fashioned carbide lamp illuminates your passage through this pitch-black, glittering underworld of frozen tunnels and passageways, where you will be blown away by the scale and beauty of the ice. The clifftop location and elevation at 1641m mean electric lighting has never been installed here, so to walk in these caves today is to feel like an early explorer.

In the soft glow, formations appear from the shadows; there are wavy walls of ice rippled through like marble, frozen waterfalls and stalactites as delicate as cut crystal, and a steep ice mountain that you climb via a flight of wooden steps (watch your footing). Guides hold a flare up to ice sculptures shaped like elephants and polar bears. Most impressive of all, however, is the echoing, cathedral-like **Eispalast** (Ice Palace), with icicles as big as organ pipes and ice-veined walls shimmering from pearl white to sapphire blue.

Passing back through the hole, you emerge in dazzling daylight and back into the mountains that kept these ice caves and their giants a secret for so long.

Big views & birds of prey at Burg Hohenwerfen

Slung high on a wooded clifftop and cowering below the gnarly peaks of the Tennengebirge, **Burg Hohenwerfen** *(burg-hohen werfen.at; adult/child incl lift €17.90/6.10, with guided tour €20.90/7.60)* is visible from afar. For 900 years this turreted beauty of a castle has guarded the Salzach Valley. You'll be mostly captivated by the mountain views from the 16th-century belfry, but the dingy dungeons (displaying the usual nasties such as the iron maiden and thumb screw) are equally worth a look.

Time your visit to catch the stunning **falconry show** (11.15am and 3.15pm daily) in the grounds, where falconers in medieval costume release eagles, owls, falcons and vultures to wheel in front of the ramparts. The brisk walk up from Werfen takes 20 minutes or you can cheat by catching the lift.

Sing like Maria

Werfen looks like something that a romantically inclined film director has dreamed up, with its soaring Tennengebirge rising like fantasy fortifications and whopping medieval castle – and indeed it was the backdrop for the picnic scene in 1965 Hollywood blockbuster *The Sound of Music*. It was here that Julie Andrews (aka Maria the singing nun) played her guitar to teach the von Trapp kids *Do-Re-Mi*.

Unspooling through wildflower-freckled meadows and hills, the 1.4km, hour-long **Sound of Music Trail** follows in the footsteps of the von Trapp family, from the town centre to the Gschwandtanger viewpoint, with cinematic views over the Salzach Valley.

Begin your walk at the Werfen tourist office. The trail is well signposted and information panels along the way give insights into the different film locations. Oh, and don't forget your picnic (or guitar!).

GET A GUIDE

A one-stop shop for outdoor activities, **Filzmoos Aktiv** *(filzmoos-aktiv.at)* arranges everything from themed mountain and glacier hikes to e-bike tours, climbing courses, challenging summit ascents and multiday hut-to-hut treks taking you deeper into the Alps of Salzburgerland, including a three-day trek around the iconic Bischofsmütze.

In winter, slip on snowshoes to crunch through the fresh powder snow and twinkling forests in quiet exhilaration. Guided snowshoeing tours range from a 2½-hour stomp at Rossbrand mountain to a two-day tour at the foot of Bischofsmütze and a heart-pumping five-day snowshoeing expedition on the frozen Dachstein plateau, never lovelier than in its winter mantle of white.

Burg Hohenwerfen

Hut-to-hut hiking on the Salzburger Almenweg

Peak bagging is all well and good, but there's more to Salzburgerland than simply aiming for the cloud-shredding summits. The **Salzburger Almenweg** (Pfarrwerfen to the Gastein Valley) is a mood-lifting, 350km, 25-stage, moderately demanding romp through the region's lush, flower-spotted, cow-nibbled alpine pastures. Many scenes from *The Sound of Music* were shot right here – think Julie Andrews twirling to *The Hills Are Alive*.

Marked with a blue gentian flower and running mostly above the treeline, the hut-to-hut trek starts and ends in Pfarrwerfen at the foot of the Tennengebirge's limestone spires, then climbs up and over meadows and deeply riven valleys to the wild, waterfall-splashed Gastein Valley and beyond. The views of the glacier-capped Hohe Tauern peaks are out of this world. Sections 9 to 11 are particularly striking, diving deep into the Gastein Valley, with its crashing falls, giddy heights and forgotten valleys.

Filzmoos

TIME FROM SALZBURG: 1¼HRS

Long-distance hikes & heady views

The summits of the Dachstein massif fling up like the fortifications of a fantasy fortress above rolling pastures and placid lakes. Crowned by the knobbly Bischofsmütze (Bishop's Mitre), Filzmoos is every inch the mountain dream. And with its tucked-away location, the village has preserved its rural, low-key charm, too.

The tug of the trail is strong here. Bring boots for long-distance stomps like the eight-day, 126km **Dachstein Circuit** (Dachsteinrunde) through the jagged limestone Dachstein range. The walk takes the entire spectrum of alpine landscapes in its stride, from glaciers and lofty mountains to forests, karst plateaux, fast-flowing rivers and pretty meadows.

REACHING EISRIESENWELT

Everyone wants to see Eisriesenwelt, but if you're day tripping from Salzburg or want to tie the ice caves in with a visit to Burg Hohenwerfen, you'll need to get your timings right with careful pre-planning.

Minibuses *(return adult/child €10/8)* run at 8.18am, 10.18am, 12.18pm and 2.18pm from Werfen train station to Eisriesenwelt car park, which is a 20-minute walk from the bottom station of the cable car. Cable cars run at least half hourly and the journey to the top takes just three minutes. The last return bus departs at 5.32pm. Allow roughly three hours for the return trip (including the tour).

You can walk the whole route, but it's a challenging, exposed four-hour ascent, rising 1100m above the village.

THE CHIMNEY EFFECT

Eisriesenwelt is a paradox. Even in the face of climate change, with rapidly retreating glaciers and melting icecaps, ice growth here remains stable. Ironically, recent hot dry summers caused the ice to grow, where rain would have made it melt. Warm winters are bad news, though, as the temperatures need to be cold for the subzero freeze to happen. With ever-warmer winters on the horizon due to global warming, the future of the caves remains uncertain.

Geologically speaking, Eisriesenwelt blows hot and cold – a phenomenon scientifically known as the 'chimney effect'. When temperatures are lower outside than in, warm air rises out of the top of the cave through fissures in the limestone rock, while cold air is drawn in through the entrance, causing the first few kilometres of the cave to freeze and the ice to grow.

Helix, Liechtensteinklamm

For a shorter but no less spectacular walk, hook onto the two-day, 23km **Gosaukamm Circuit**, which dives into the ragged Gosaukamm range, sometimes dubbed 'Salzburg's Dolomites' because they are similar in size and scale. The highlight is the 2012m **Steigl Pass**, an exposed, fixed-cable route that involves some scrambling. Pick up trail maps at the tourist office.

Liechtensteinklamm
TIME FROM SALZBURG: 1HR

A gorge fit for a prince

One of the deepest and longest gorges in the Alps, **Liechtensteinklamm** *(josalzburg.com; adult/child €15/8.50)* near St Johann in Pongau is full-on drama, with vertical 300m-high cliffs thrusting above a foaming turquoise river, rainbow-kissed falls and mossy boulders. The ravine is named after Johann II, Prince of Liechtenstein, who took a fancy to it in 1875 and bankrolled the trail, with bridges, galleries and tunnels hacked into slate cliffs veined with white granite.

Arrive first thing in the morning or in the early evening for the dreamiest light and fewest crowds. Most photogenic of all is the **Helix**, a weathered steel spiral staircase corkscrewing 30m into the depths of the gorge.

Zell am See

LAKE LIFE | ALPINE HIKING | CELEBRITY STYLE

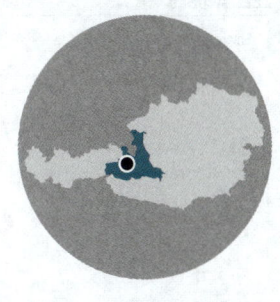

Lifting your gaze steadily to the pearl-white peaks of Hohe Tauern National Park and reflecting its loveliness in the sapphire-blue waters of its eponymous lake, Zell am See is an instant heart-stealer. Pulsing with life in summer, the town is postcard heaven, spinning out around a pedestrian centre of cobbled lanes, brightly coloured chalets and a Romanesque church.

This small town seduces with its phenomenal outdoors. Come here to leap into the lake – swimming, stand-up paddleboarding and windsurfing – cycle its leafy shores, or float up into the mountains on a cable car for some high-level hiking and glacier skiing. Or strike out onto Austria's alpine road trip numero uno: the Grossglockner Road. Every year, more than one million visitors from all around the world – from families to playboys in sports cars – do just that, all in search of the Austrian dream.

Summer on Lake Zell

Action on and around the water

With the water temperatures hovering between 15°C and 23°C in summer, the **Zeller See** (Lake Zell) is an ideal location for an invigorating – if chilly – dip.

For a bit of vertical sightseeing and some sublime Grossglockner views as you swim laps, head to the **Zell am See Lido** in town, which has sunbathing lawns, solar-heated swimming pools and kids' splash areas. Or go for a splash at one of the quieter lidos at **Strandbad Thumersbach** or **Strandbad Seespitz** in Schüttdorf. Entry to all is free with the Zell am See-Kaprun Card.

There are plenty of ways for you to ramp up the adventure on the lake. The stiff breezes, warm summers and crystal-clear waters are ideal conditions for windsurfing or to give paddleboarding a whirl. The **SUP Center** (*board rental per hr €11, 2hr intro course €46*) rents out gear and also offers classes, including a two-hour introductory course and Saturday morning

GETTING AROUND

Spread along the lakeshore, Zell am See's petite, pedestrian-friendly historic centre is nicely compact and easily explored on foot. Upping the resort's ecofriendly credentials and making car-free holidays viable, the **Pinzgau Mobility Card** (available for all overnight guests) gives you free use of all public transport in Zell am See and the wider region.

If you're in town from mid-May to October, ask your hotel or guesthouse for the free **Zell am See-Kaprun Card**, which gives you a boat trip on the lake and one free ride per day on the cable cars that ascend to Schmittenhöhe and Kitzsteinhorn.

ZELL AM SEE

- **ACTIVITIES**
  1. Rundfahrt Schmittenhöhe
  2. Strandbad Seespitz
  3. Strandbad Thumersbach
  4. SUP Center
  5. Zell am See Lido
- **SLEEPING**
  6. Pension Hubertus
  7. Romantik Hotel Zell am See
  8. Schloss Prielau
  9. Seecamp Zell Am See
  10. Steinerwirt
- **EATING**
  11. Deins & Meins
  12. Flos
  13. Kraftwerk
  see 8 Mayer's
- **INFORMATION**
  14. Tourist Office

☑ TOP TIP

The free **Zell Summer Night** festival draws bands, street entertainers and improvised theatre to streets and squares every Wednesday night in July and August.

yoga on the water. Should you wish to channel your chakras and master your downward-facing dog while balancing on a paddleboard, sign up for a Sunday-morning SUP yoga session in July and August.

If you would prefer a more relaxed lake experience, hop in a pedalo or jump aboard the **MS Schmittenhöhe** (*adult/child €23/11.50*) for a panoramic 45-minute round trip of the lake, with cracking mountain views to boot. Alternatively, rent your own set of wheels at **Adventure Service** (*adventureservice. at; e-bike rental per day €45*) to pedal off along the lakeshore under your own steam.

HIKING THE PINZGAUER SPAZIERGANG

Take in tremendous views of the Hohe Tauern range and Kitzbühel Alps from on high on this classic ridge trail, the **Pinzgauer Spaziergang**.

START	END	LENGTH
Schmittenhöhe	Saalbach	17km; 6-7hrs

This is a moderately challenging day hike; bring supplies and consider buying Kompass 1:35,000 map No 30 *Zell am See-Kaprun*.

At ❶ **Schmittenhöhe**, begin a gradual descent from Saalbach/Pinzgauer Spaziergang, enjoying views of Zeller See and the glaciated Hohe Tauern range. The landscape opens up as you wend through wildflower-streaked meadows, and after roughly an hour, contour the rounded summit of ❷ **Maurerkogel**. Make a short, painless ascent to the ❸ **Rohrertörl** saddle. Passing two junctions, follow a balcony trail that contours the base of ❹ **Oberer-Gernkogel** and gently mounts ❺ **Niederer-Gernkogel**. You'll soon reach the foot of ❻ **Zirmkogel**. The rocky trail runs through high meadows and mottled mountains, passing a small hut near a stream.

Around four hours from the trailhead, the path ascends a steepish incline to the ❼ **Klingertörl** saddle, where a sign shows the way to Saalbach. Traverse the base of cliffs that sweep down from ❽ **Hochkogel** and make a short descent to the grassy col of ❾ **Seetörl**. Walk north from here, either climbing over ❿ **Saalbachkogel** or skirting its western slopes. The same option is repeated for ⓫ **Stemmerkogel**. Descend the ridge and continue towards Schattberg, making a final ascent to the ⓬ **Schattberg X-press** gondola and then down to ⓭ **Saalbach**.

At the Rohrertörl saddle, contrast the limestone Kaisergebirge to the north with the icy Hohe Tauern peaks to the south.

Walking from Schmittenhöhe, the ever-narrowing path negotiates an incline and passes through tarn-studded forest, drawing your gaze to shimmering Grossglockner and the Kitzsteinhorn Glacier to the south.

Fancy ramping up the challenge? With will and expertise, the 2215m peak of Zirmkogel can be climbed in little over an hour.

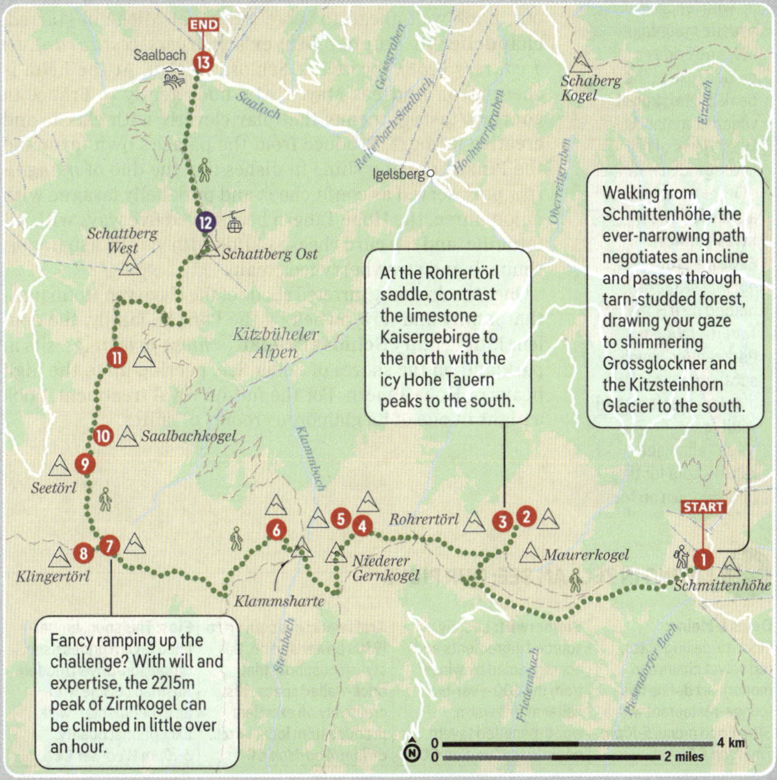

GUIDED WALKS IN ZELL AM SEE-KAPRUN

From mid-June to October, Zell am See-Kaprun **tourist office** arranges guided walks in Zell am See, and the surrounding lakes and mountains, many of which are free with the Zell am See-Kaprun Card.

Among the highlights are Monday's four-hour tour of **Kaprun**, which dives into the waterfall-splashed Sigmund Thun Gorge, winding up with lunch at a rustic mountain hut, and Friday's guided hike at the peak of **Maiskogel**, which commands killer views of the Grossglockner range.

Other tours include a daily four-hour **Kitzsteinhorn Explorer Tour** *(€14, not incl lift ticket)*, guided by a Hohe Tauern National Park ranger, which spotlights the glacier's geology and wildlife.

See zellamsee-kaprun.com for the full lowdown on tours.

Zell am See-Kaprun

A Fancy Night at the Palace
Michelin-starred food with lake views

If it's a special occasion or you just fancy pushing the boat out, book well ahead to score a table at Michelin-starred, chandelier-lit stunner **Mayer's** *(mayers-restaurant.at; 4 courses €168)*, located at Schloss Prielau. At the helm is chef-patron Andreas Mayer, who nods gently to France in gourmet tasting menus that play cleverly with classic and creative flavours. Produce from the palace's own farm and the Pinzgau region shine in dishes like the duo of *mangalitsa* pork served as confit cheek and pork belly lasagne with onion puree, the Hohe Tauern beef served five ways with ratatouille, and the curd cheese soufflé with vanilla asparagus, rhubarb and strawberry ice cream.

Once the dreamily turreted abode of the Hugo von Hofmannsthal family and now owned by the Porsche family, the opulent 15th-century **Schloss Prielau** *(schloss-prielau.at)* sits in parkland on the shores of Zeller See, peering up to the high peaks of Hohe Tauern. For the full-on royal treatment, book a night in one of its glamorous rooms or suites.

 EATING IN ZELL AM SEE: OUR PICKS

Deins & Meins: Floor-to-ceiling glass, red velvet chairs and modern art define this lounge-restaurant with a Slow Food menu. *5–10pm Thu–Mon* €€

Steinerwirt: Locally sourced ingredients and accompanied by wines from the 600-year-old cellar at this warm, wood-panelled tavern. *noon–10pm Tue–Sun* €€

Kraftwerk: In a converted 1930s power station, this stylish postindustrial, brick-walled space riffs creatively on excellent produce from local farms. *6–11pm Wed–Mon* €€

Flos: This snug, timber-lined tavern prides itself on season-driven modern Austrian cuisine with an experimental twist. Exceptional quality. *6–10pm Wed–Sat* €€

Beyond Zell am See

Mountains rise above Zell am See like a natural amphitheatre, with the Kitzbühel Alps puckering up to the north and the Hohe Tauern range ripping south.

Heading north you'll find fast-paced mountain biking and some of the country's finest and most extensive skiing in the rugged, gorge-riven peaks of Saalbach-Hinterglemm, host of the FIS Alpine World Ski Championships 2025. A snowball-throw away from the Tyrolean border, the resort has 270km of slopes to play on. Shuffle south instead and you reach Kaprun, Zell am See's smaller, quieter, environmentally conscious sister. Topped off by a 12th-century castle, the town is the gateway to the dazzling Kitzsteinhorn Glacier, reached by tri-cable gondola K-onnection, which wings you from 768m to 3029m and from summer to winter in a matter of minutes.

Places
Kitzsteinhorn Glacier p277
Saalbach-Hinterglemm p278

Kitzsteinhorn Glacier
Embrace the eternal ice

TIME FROM ZELL AM SEE: 45MINS

At an ear-popping 3000m above sea level, Kitzsteinhorn Glacier offers top-of-the-beanstalk views of the icy peaks of the Hohe Tauern Alps. Snow or shine, there's enough powder up here for glacier skiing for 10 months of the year. In summer, you can swim in Lake Zell in the morning and whoosh down the slopes here in the afternoon.

A cable car glides up to the top-station **Gipfelwelt 3000** *(kitzsteinhorn.at; adult/child €59/29.50)* at 3029m, where you'll be floored by the grandstand views of the Hohe Tauern National Park's mountains rising in great waves, including highest-of-the-high: 3798m Grossglockner. From mid-May to mid-September, park rangers lead free hour-long **guided tours** at 10.30am and 1pm daily, covering the Hohe Tauern's glaciers, crystal formations, wildlife and plant life. Tours depart from the **National Park Gallery**, at the top station, where you can also learn about local geology.

In summer, short, gentle walks head off to jewel-coloured glacier lakes and a tougher scramble leads to the 3203m summit of **Kitzsteinhorn**, with astonishing views of three-thousanders and the Steinernes Meer ('Rocky Sea'). Free hiking maps are available at the information desk in the **Alpincenter**, close to the Gipfelbahn cable car station at 2450m. Mountain bikers are in their element here, with three freeride trails and the 12km **3K K-onnection** tour linking up the peaks of Maiskogel and Kitzsteinhorn, and heading through high-alpine

GETTING AROUND

Buses run twice hourly from Zell am See Bahnhof to Kaprun, a 25-minute ride away. In Kaprun, jump on the state-of-the-art, tri-cable gondola K-onnection, which whisks you above the summits on a 12km ride right up to the glacier at 3029m.

En route to Kitzsteinhorn, stop off at Maiskogel for a heart-pumping ride on the Maisi Flitzer, a year-round toboggan negotiating jumps, spins and picking up speeds of up to 40km/h.

SUSTAINABLE SNOW

When the flakes fall in winter, Zell am See and its sister town Kaprun provide access to 408km of slopes straddling three resorts, all covered by a single ski pass, the **Ski Alpin Card** *(1-/3-/6-day pass €79/231/425, child half price)*. The two must-ski biggies are Schmittenhöhe (1965m) and the Kitzsteinhorn Glacier (3203m). The terrain is more tree-lined and scenic than hair-raising, but there are a couple of steep black pistes for experts and some fabulous freeriding in the backcountry.

You can also ski here with a clean conscious as Zell am See and Kaprun are upping their green credentials big-time, including high-elevation recultivation projects, lifts running on 100% ecologically generated energy and free ski buses.

Kitzsteinhorn (p277)

terrain. Otherwise, check out the deckchair-clad snow beach, toboggans and slides at the **Ice Arena**.

In winter, the glacier is ski-touring, boarding, freeriding and snowshoeing heaven. Slide over to the **Ice Camp** where you'll find a spectacularly lit igloo bar, lounge and sundeck for cocktails and mellow beats after a hard day on the slopes.

Saalbach-Hinterglemm

TIME FROM ZELL AM SEE: 20MINS

Go forest bathing

Light trickles through the canopy in the tall spruce forests of Saalbach-Hinterglemm. The air is pine-fresh. All is silent but for twittering birds and the sound of your own heartbeat. Rooted in the Japanese practice of *shinrin-yoku*, forest bathing comes into its own in the high woods of the Alps. They are the ultimate hourglass of the seasons – from spring's first buds to summer's honeyed light and bilberries, autumn rains to winter snows. Walking in the woods is a moment of pure mindfulness, where all the senses are on high alert. The crackle of a leaf, the babble of a brook – here you can shut out the world and be fully present.

Take the cable car up from Hinterglemm to the 1810m **Reiterkogel** for a deep forest dive on the **CO2 Wellness Trail**, which leads into the green wilds of a 200-year-old spruce forest. Allow two to three hours for the full forest-bathing experience, stopping off to swing on a hammock, browse books in the forest library, kick back on a wooden lounger beneath the lofty trees, stretch out on a yoga mat, or stop off at panorama points where the woods crack open to reveal views reaching far into the valley. Picnic baskets stuffed with local goodies and wild herb smoothies can be pre-ordered at the **Reiteralm** *(reiteralm.at)* at least two hours in advance.

Hohe Tauern National Park

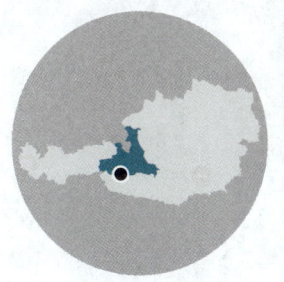

TOWERING MOUNTAINS | GRANDIOSE GLACIERS | RAGING WATERFALLS

If you thought Mother Nature pulled out all the stops in the Austrian Alps, Hohe Tauern National Park is her finest moment. Welcome to Austria's outdoor wonderland and one of Europe's largest nature reserves (1786 sq km), which straddles Tyrol, Carinthia and Salzburgerland, and is overshadowed by the 3798m hump of Grossglockner, the country's highest peak.

Try as we might, no amount of hyperbole about towering snow-clad mountains, shimmering glaciers, impossibly turquoise lakes and raging waterfalls can do this park justice. These mountains are eyes-on-stalks beautiful, whether you're cresting a lonely peak in quiet exhilaration, crunching across a glacier or witnessing a fiery sunset from a splintery mountain hut. Go see it for yourself.

If you only have time for one road trip, make it the unmissable Grossglockner Road, which serves up 48km (30 miles) of stomach-flipping hairpin bends, glaciers, crashing waterfalls and sapphire-blue lakes.

Epic Climbs in Hohe Tauern National Park
Hitting the heights

One look at the ragged, snow-streaked peaks flinging above the high meadows and flower-carpeted plateaux of Hohe Tauern and you'll be itching to whack on hiking boots or grab a karabiner and rope. It isn't until you strike out on foot or grapple with rock that you realise just how beautiful this national park really is. Popular hikes include the tough-but-unforgettable two-day ascent of the eternally icecapped, 3666m **Grossvenediger**, flanked by glaciers. The closest you can get by road is the 1512m-high alpine chalet **Matreier Tauernhaus** *(matreier-tauernhaus.com; s/d from €75/130)*, a rustic chalet with more comfort than most and astonishing views of the three-thousanders. Here you can get a meal and good night's kip before embarking on the 31km out-and-back trek. Glacier equipment is needed for the final stretch and a mountain guide is highly recommended.

GETTING AROUND

Grossglockner Road is technically open from early May to early November, but check the forecast before setting out as conditions can change rapidly and you won't see much in bad weather.

For the remoter reaches of the national park, you will need your own wheels. Otherwise, hop on the ecofriendly **Glocknerbus** *(adult/child €44.50/26.50)*, which departs Zell am See at 9am Tuesday from late May to September (and also every Thursday in July and August), returning at 3pm. The journey is accompanied by a park ranger.

☑ TOP TIP

With 9% gradients and 36 tight bends, you'll need to be a confident driver to negotiate Grossglockner Road. Leave at dawn to beat the worst of the traffic.

HOHE TAUERN NATIONAL PARK SALZBURG & SALZBURGERLAND

HOHE TAUERN NATIONAL PARK

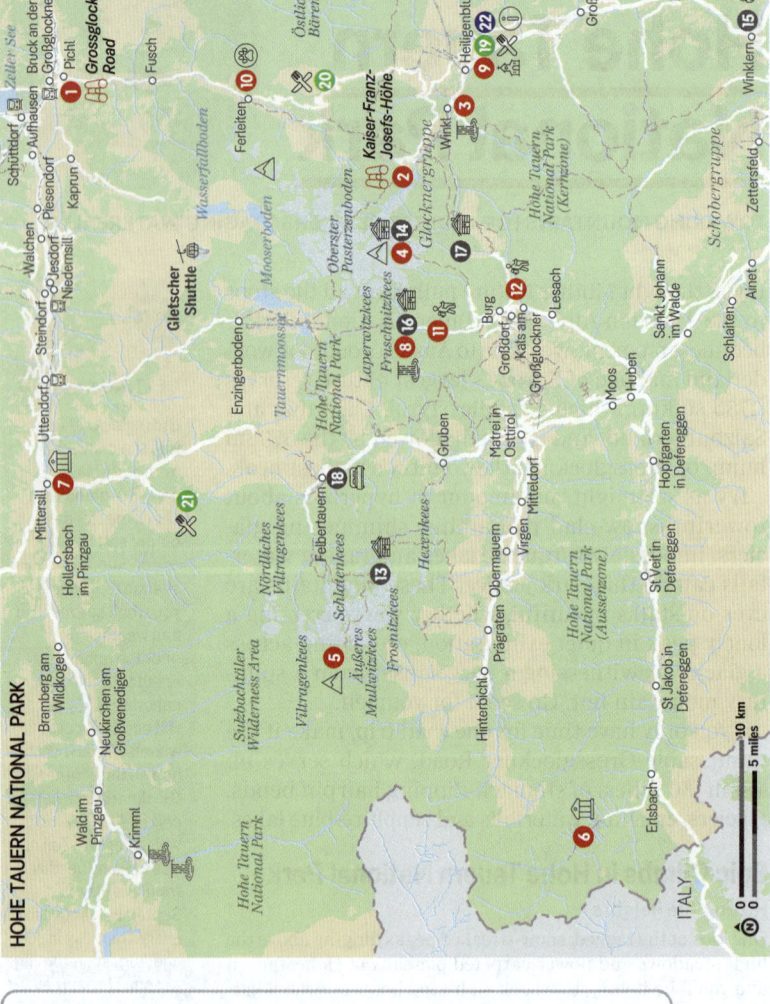

★ HIGHLIGHTS
1. Grossglockner Road
2. Kaiser-Franz-Josefs-Höhe

● SIGHTS
3. Gössnitz Falls
4. Grossglockner
5. Grossvenediger
6. Jagdhausalmen
7. National Park Worlds
8. Stotzbachfall
9. Wallfahrtskirche St Vinzenz
10. Wildpark Ferleiten

● ACTIVITIES
11. Kalser Dorfertal
12. Ködnitztal

● SLEEPING
13. Badener Hütte
14. Erzherzog-Johann-Hütte
15. Hotel Tauernstern
16. Kalser Tauernhaus
17. Lucknerhütte
18. Matreier Tauernhaus

● EATING
19. Dorfstub'm Café
20. Edelweisshütte
21. Meilingeralm

● INFORMATION
22. Tourist Office

For a shorter, moderately challenging hike, just walk the first leg: the 9.4km **Innergschlöss Glacier Trail**. One of the most spectacular half-day hikes in the park, it kicks off at the Matreier Tauernhaus. From here, it's a 1½-hour trudge to the dramatically crevassed Innergschlöss Glacier. Involving 500m of ascent, the challenging four- to five-hour circuit heads through a sublime alpine valley and past shimmering glacial lakes. Keep an eye out for bearded vultures.

With climbing experience under your belt and a reasonable level of fitness, you can climb the mighty **Grossglockner** (3798m) via the 'normal' route, though again, a guide is recommended. The main trail begins at the **Erzherzog-Johann-Hütte**, a four- to five-hour hike from Heiligenblut. From here, the roughly two-hour route crosses ice and rocks, following a steel cable over a narrow snow ridge, to the cross at the summit.

Nature Escapes in Hohe Tauern National Park

A walk on the wild side

Everyone raves about the Grossglockner Road – and rightly so – but to see a quieter side to the national park, you need to go off-piste. A quick glimpse of the map reveals forgotten valleys, where you can be at one with nature, up your chances of spotting wildlife and revel in the pin-drop peace of Austria's most beautiful mountainscapes.

For a taste of these Alps before the tourists rocked up, explore **Kalser Dorfertal**, a remote valley unfurling at the foot of Grossglockner. Here a trail slips through a rugged, river-woven gorge to pastures that erupt with alpine flowers in spring. Eventually you'll emerge at the **Stotzbachfall** waterfall, crashing over cliffs and through forest. Rest up at the idyllic, ecofriendly **Kalser Tauernhaus** (kalser-tauernhaus.de; dm €27) at 1755m, or retrace your steps (it's a 12km, four- to five-hour round trip).

One valley over in **Ködnitztal**, the great snowy summit of Grossglockner feels close enough to reach out and touch. Fin-shaped peaks sweep above flowery pastures, streams, and larch and stone pine forests in this unscathed valley. Precious few crowds make it a wildlife hot spot – keep your eyes peeled for ibex, marmots and golden eagles. Starting at Lucknerhaus car park, the 4.8km, two-hour trudge up to the 2241m **Lucknerhütte** (lucknerhuette.at; r from €64) shows

PLANNING YOUR ASCENT

Hohe Tauern has treks to suit every level of ability, from day walks to extreme expeditions.

Freytag & Berndt (freytagberndt.com) produces detailed 1:50,000 walking maps covering the national park and surrounding areas, available online, at the visitor centre **National Park Worlds** (nationalpark zentrum.at) in Mittersill or in bookshops.

When planning a major trek, it's worth booking overnight stops in advance, as accommodation can be sparse the higher you go; local tourist offices can advise.

Most trails open from mid-June to September. It's essential to have the proper equipment (maps, ropes, crampons, etc) and to check weather conditions before setting out. For mountain guides, contact the **tourist office** in Heiligenblut or check the options with **Bergführer Kals** (bergfuehrer-kals.at).

EATING IN HOHE TAUERN NATIONAL PARK: OUR PICKS

| **Dorfstub'm Café:** Heiligenblut fave, with B&W mountaineering photos and menu classics like goulash and dumplings. *8.30am-11pm Mon-Fri, 1-11pm Sat* € | **Meilingeralm:** South of Mitersill, this pretty Alpine hut rolls out home-cooked schnitzel, noodles and desserts and glorious Hohe Tauern views. *9am-7pm* € | **Lucknerhütte:** In the dramatic Ködnitztal, this venue at 224lm wows with Grossglocker views and dishes using ingredients from their own organic farm. *7am-10pm* €€ | **Edelweisshütte:** On the Grossglockner High Alpine Road at 2571m, this mountain tavern doles out Pinzgau specialities like cheesy dumplings and strudel. *9am-6.30pm* €€ |

RANGER HIKES

You can go it alone, but to get more out of Hohe Tauern National Park, consider signing up for one of the guided walks led by clued-up park rangers.

On weekdays from July to September, these hikes cover everything from herb-discovery trails to high-altitude treks, around-the-glacier tours, gorge climbing, waterfall rambles and wildlife watching. In early autumn, bring binoculars for 'big five' safaris where you head out to spot ibex, chamois, marmots, golden eagles and bearded vultures in the wild. Most of the walks cost between €10 and €20, and last between a couple of hours and half a day. For ranger hikes at a glance, visit hohetauern.at.

off the valley from its loveliest angles. Stop for lunch, or spend a cosy, starlit night up here in a timber-clad room.

Brilliant for families is the gentler 4km, two-hour nature path to the wispy plume of the **Gössnitz Falls**. The loop trail from the car park in Winkl-Heiligenblut is an up-close encounter with a highland moor formed by the retreating Pasterze Glacier.

An Alpine Idyll: Heiligenblut
The legend of the Holy Blood

One of the single-most striking images on the Grossglockner Road is of Heiligenblut, the needle-thin spire of its 15th-century pilgrimage church framed by the glaciated summit of Grossglockner. The village's iconic scenery and easily accessible mountains lure skiers, hikers and camera-toting tourists. The compact centre is stacked with wooden chalets, and despite an overload of yodelling-kitsch souvenirs, retains some traditional charm.

As though cupped in celestial hands and held up to the mighty Alps, the village's late-Gothic **Wallfahrtskirche St Vinzenz** *(heiligenblut.at)* lifts gazes – and spirits. Inside is a tabernacle, which purportedly contains a tiny phial of Christ's blood, hence the village name (Heiligenblut means 'holy blood'). Legend has it that the phial was discovered by a saint named Briccius in 914 CE, who was buried in an avalanche on this spot more than a thousand years ago.

Life at the Top: Kaiser-Franz-Josefs-Höhe
Sunrise chasers and ice breakers

The wow never leaves your lips on the Grossglockner Road, especially at its crowning glory viewpoint, the 2369m-high, flag-bedecked **Kaiser-Franz-Josefs-Höhe**, named after the mountain-loving Austrian emperor who stopped by with Empress Elisabeth ('Sisi') in 1856. It commands astonishing ringside views of the mighty Grossglockner and the snaking Pasterze Glacier. The interactive visitor centre spills the beans on the geography and geology of the mountains and eternal ice.

Like a perfectly cut crystal, the **Wilhelm Swarovski Observatory** frames the view of the pearl-white, bell-shaped peak of 3798m Grossglockner and a ripple of other peaks. You can also get shots of marmots and ibex, which have their home near the observation tower.

From the visitor centre, strike out on the 5.6km, two-hour out-and-back **Gamsgrubenweg**. The trail sheds light on the origins of the 8.4km-long, rapidly retreating Pasterze, the largest glacier in Austria and the Eastern Alps, and provides photogenic angles of its deeply crevassed, ethereally blue ice. A longer 7.4km circular route takes you even closer to its icy tongue. If you'd prefer to get out on the ice with crampons and a harness, enquire about guided glacier hikes at the visitor centre.

Kaiser-Franz-Josefs-Höhe

Reach for the Stars
Go on a cosmic adventure

On crystal-clear, moonless nights, Hohe Tauern National Park is heaven on earth for budding astronomers. Far removed from any light pollution and with dramatic backdrops perfect for astrophotography, the park's wildly mountainous heart peers up to some of Europe's darkest night skies, which glitter with an eternity of stars, distant planets, nebulae and meteor showers. It makes for riveting viewing and there's no need for fancy equipment – rock up with a head torch and you can often identify constellations and admire the silvery swirl of the Milky Way with the naked eye alone or the simplest pair of binoculars. For more insight into what you are looking at, download the Stellarium star app before heading out.

For twinkling night skies once the lights flick off, stay in one of the park's high, remote huts, or base yourself in a mountain village like Heiligenblut. Stargazing is at its spectacular best at **Jagdhausalmen** at the far end of East Tyrol's Defereggental valley. Perched at 2009m above sea level, this time-lost cluster of historic stone huts has been used by herders and farmers for centuries. In a gloriously secluded spot among ancient stone pine forests, grassy meadows and rocks, it is dubbed 'Klein Tibet' (Little Tibet).

If you would prefer to reach for the stars in the company of experts, **Osttirol Tourismus** *(osttirol.com)* arranges three-night stargazing packages from late May to early September, including a choice of accommodation, guided hikes with national park rangers and headlamp rental.

EXPLORING HOHE TAUERN

Ekkehard Heider is a Hohe Tauern National Park ranger.

Favourite day tour: I like biking into the Habach Valley, hiking to the Neue Thüringer Hütte, then continuing to the rocky 3017m summit of the Larmkogel for breathtaking views above 3000m. Mountain boots, surefootedness and a head for heights are essential.

Wildlife hot spot: One of the best places for wildlife is Krumltal near Rauris village. With luck, you'll spot golden eagles, bearded vultures, griffon vultures, marmots, wall creepers, alpine salamanders, ibex, chamois, black vultures and more. Please stay on the tracks!

Sunrise and sunset: One of the best and easiest-to-reach points for an amazing sunrise or sunset is the 2571m Edelweiss Spitze lookout in Fusch on Grossglockner Road, reachable by car. Magnificent national park views are guaranteed!

DRIVING THE GROSSGLOCKNER ROAD

Buckle up for a head-spinning, glacier-gawping, sky-high alpine drive along the **Grossglockner Road**, getting up close and personal with the Austrian Alps.

START	END	LENGTH
Bruck	Heiligenblut	48km; 5-6hrs

Leaving ❶ **Bruck**, enter the mountainous Fuschertal, passing Fusch and ❷ **Wildpark Ferleiten**. Once through the tollgate, the road climbs steeply to ❸ **Hochmais** (1850m), where glaciated peaks like Grosses Wiesbachhorn (3564m) crowd the horizon. The road zigzags up to ❹ **Haus Alpine Naturschau** (2260m), which spotlights local flora and fauna.

A 2km side road heads to ❺ **Edelweiss Spitze** (2571m), the road's highest viewpoint. Refuel with coffee and strudel on the hut's terrace. Get your camera handy for ❻ **Fuscher Törl** (2428m), with smashing views, and ❼ **Fuscher Lacke** (2262m) nearby. Here is a small exhibition on the road's construction, built by 3000 men in five years during the Great Depression, 1930–35. The road goes through high meadows to ❽ **Hochtor** (2504m), the top of the pass.

Next there's a steady descent to ❾ **Schöneck**. Branch off west onto the 9km Gletscherstrasse, passing waterfalls and *Achtung Murmeltiere* (Beware of Marmots) signs. The Grossglockner massif slides into view on the approach to flag-dotted ❿ **Kaiser-Franz-Josefs-Höhe** (p282; 2369m), with views of Grossglockner (3798m) and the Pasterze Glacier. Allow time for the glacier-themed exhibition at the visitor centre and the Wilhelm-Swarovski observatory. Round out your road trip in ⓫ **Heiligenblut**, where a 15th-century pilgrimage church lifts gazes to Grossglocker.

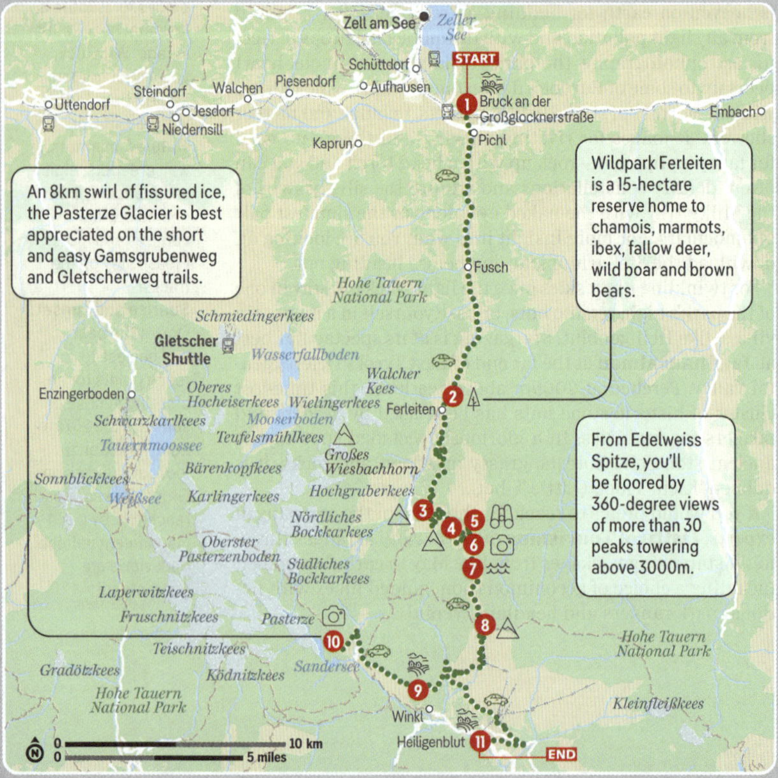

An 8km swirl of fissured ice, the Pasterze Glacier is best appreciated on the short and easy Gamsgrubenweg and Gletscherweg trails.

Wildpark Ferleiten is a 15-hectare reserve home to chamois, marmots, ibex, fallow deer, wild boar and brown bears.

From Edelweiss Spitze, you'll be floored by 360-degree views of more than 30 peaks towering above 3000m.

Beyond Hohe Tauern National Park

Waterfalls, giddy peaks and one magical valley after the next – this region looks as if it was touched by a godly hand, especially when you deviate from the beaten track.

More heavenly alpine landscapes await as you stray beyond the national park borders, deep into the surrounding valleys and high over wild, wind-beaten mountain passes, with views of snowcapped, 3666m Grossvenediger and other Hohe Tauern peaks crowding your rear-view mirror. Moving west of Zell am See, it's an hour's drive to the boulder-smashing, rainbow-kissed Krimmler Wasserfälle, Europe highest waterfall, the centrepiece of the charmingly time-lost, timber-clad village of Krimml.

Edge east instead for off-the-radar hiking, skiing and ziplining in the Gasteinertal. Here the fairest village of the lot is Bad Gastein, with belle-époque villas clinging to forest-cloaked cliffs, thunderous falls and hot springs still hailed for their miraculous healing properties.

Places
Krimml p285
Bad Gastein p286

GETTING AROUND

While having your own wheels opens more possibilities, you can see a fair bit with public transport if you plan ahead. Buses run year-round from Zell am See to Krimml (1½ hours) and there are frequent train connections to Bad Gastein (roughly equidistant). A car is advisable for remoter regions like the Lungau.

Pick up the **Gastein Card** for free use of local buses and guided half- and full-day hikes. It also yields great discounts on spas, bike tours and concerts.

Krimml   TIME FROM HOHE TAUERN NATIONAL PARK: 1HR

Feel the force: Krimml Falls

You can hear its roar for miles around as it smashes boulders and thunders over thickly forested cliffs. The 380m-high, three-tier **Krimmler Wasserfälle** *(wasserfaelle-krimml.at; adult/child €9/4.50)*, Europe's highest waterfall (and the fifth highest in the world), is a real crash-bang spectacle. Tucked into a remote pocket of Salzburgerland, where glinting glaciers and the 3666m-high peak of Grossvenediger guard the horizon, these falls make for compulsive viewing, whether veiled in mist, rainbow kissed or iced over in winter's big freeze.

Many visitors just climb up to the first viewpoint for the obligatory selfie or Instagram shot – but don't. These falls really work their magic when you stomp up the **Wasserfallweg** (Waterfall Trail), which starts at the ticket office and twists gently uphill through mixed forest, where picnic areas and observation platforms crack open the view and provide astonishing close-ups of the falls.

CYCLE THE TAUERNRADWEG

If you have the will and the stamina, this is a great region to explore by bike. Well-marked cycling and hiking trails fan out from Krimml into the surrounding Alps.

The moderately challenging **Tauernradweg** (Tauern Cycle Path) is a 310km bike route through the mind-blowing mountain scenery of the Hohe Tauern National Park. Starting in Krimml, the route shadows the Salzach River downstream to Salzburg via Zell am See, St Johann, Werfen and Hallein, before pushing on north to the fortress-topped baroque city of Passau over the border in Bavaria, Germany.

Brace yourself for plenty of highs: the path covers some high-altitude stretches and demands a good level of fitness. The Krimmler Wasserfälle Trail begins near the Tauernradweg's starting point.

While you're up here, breathe deeply. These falls are now used as the backdrop for waterfall therapy. Charged with negative ions, the air up here is said to work wonders on the immune system and respiratory conditions.

It's about a two-hour walk to the top of the falls and back, or double that if you want to stride on to the Achental, where a brook burbles through a beautiful glacial valley to **Hölzlahneralm** *(hoelzlahner.at)* and a silent world far removed from the day-tripping crowds. This cosily rustic, timber-clad hut has stirring views of boulder-strewn pastures and mountains punching above 3000m in the Hohe Tauern National Park. Put your feet up on the terrace and order a *Brettljause* (snack board), piled high with local cured meats, cheeses, bread and pickles.

Bad Gastein
Waterfalls & hot springs

TIME FROM HOHE TAUERN NATIONAL PARK: **50MINS**

What a backdrop for a *Wasserkur* (water cure). Snuggled away in a wildly romantic valley and rimmed by the glacier-capped Hohe Tauern mountains, the spa town is a looker, with belle-époque villas clinging to sheer, forested slopes. The minute you arrive, you hear the roar of the 341m **Gasteiner Falls**, dashed into mist as they nosedive over rugged cliffs and rage through forest to tumble into three turquoise pools. The **Wasserfallweg** trail shadows the magnificent cataract and provides great photo ops. Or for a sky-high view of the falls, whoosh above it on the **Flying Waters** *(adult/child €20/15)* zipline, linking Villa Solitude to the thermal park below.

Hotel spas and public baths tap into the rejuvenating waters. Take a private bath and within minutes you'll notice a deep inner heat begin to unknot tension. More atmospheric is a float at the grotto-like **Felsentherme** *(felsentherme.com; adult/child €32.50/17)*, where you can dunk in an indoor pool carved out of prehistoric rock and open-air hot springs with front-row views of the peaks.

Or splash in the architecturally innovative **Alpentherme** *(alpentherme.com; day ticket adult/child €48.50/27)* spa in nearby Bad Hofgastein. Here you can float in radon-rich thermal baths and sweat it out in red-hot saunas and brine grottoes before cooling off in the glacier ice lounge. The family area is a surefire hit with kids, with its slides, flumes, lazy river and swim-in saltwater aquarium.

Bathe in a cave: Gasteiner Heilstollen

In the alpine village of Böckstein, just outside Bad Gastein, the **Gasteiner Heilstollen** *(gasteiner-heilstollen.com; intro session with/without Gastein Card €75/94)* is like nowhere you've ever visited before. After a brief health check, you board a little yellow train to chug 2km into the humid 38°C depths of Böckstein's medieval gold mine. The lights dim and hush falls as spa-goers ditch bathrobes to recline on beds and absorb the powerful radon vapours. The product of 3000 years of geological forces, the radon rays release mild alpha rays in the body, which stimulate cell repair, activate healing and

Stubnerkogel

are purported to cure everything from asthma to arthritis and fibromyalgia.

You can get a taster with a one-off session. Allow around four hours for the experience, which includes an initial medical examination and post-cave relaxation time. But for the radon to have a lasting effect, 10 to 12 sessions over a three-week period are recommended.

Outdoor thrills in Bad Gastein

Setting a wobbly foot on the 140m-long bridge that floats giddily from peak to peak at 2246m **Stubnerkogel** is like walking on air. Take the **cable car** *(return ticket adult/child €38.50/17.50)* up from Bad Gastein on a calm, dazzlingly clear day for a heart-stopping stroll across Europe's highest suspension bridge for out-of-this-world views of the Hohe Tauern mountains.

More highs, you say? Hook onto the **Rock Trail**, which skims cliff and crag to afford uplifting perspectives of the Alps, or gasp at the view from **Talblick**, a lookout platform jutting above the abyss and peering deep into the valley. For an arresting view of 3798m Grossglockner, swing over to **Grossglocknerblick platform**, which perfectly frames Austria's highest peak.

CELEBRITY SPRINGS

'Only sick bones I thought of bringing, where mystically your hot water springs...' So wrote an enraptured Empress Elisabeth of Bad Gastein's healing waters in her 1886 poem.

These radon-laced waters and their health-boosting properties have been feted for 2000 years: first extolled by the beauty-conscious Romans, then – during the imperial boom – beloved of the rich, royal and famous likes of Kaiser Wilhelm, composers Franz Schubert and Johann Strauss, and a paintbrush-wielding Gustav Klimt, who captured the town on canvas in 1917.

Thomas Mann, Albert Einstein, Sigmund Freud, the Shah of Iran, Hollywood stars such as Liza Minelli and Anita Ekberg, and the Churchills were hot on their heels in the 20th century.

 EATING IN BAD GASTEIN: OUR PICKS

Betty's Bistro: Snug, central pick, with fusion cooking. Go for spot-on tarte flambée or Asian tapas like chilli-infused edamame. *6-10.30pm Tue-Sat* €

Jägerhäusl: Opening onto a terrace, this villa serves pizza and Austrian faves like schnitzel. Live folk music in summer. *4-10pm Mon & Tue, noon-10pm Wed-Sun* €€

Valeriehaus: This alpine hut in Sportgastein wows with mountain views and a menu with Austrian classics like *Kasnocken* (cheese dumplings) and strudel. *10am-5pm* €€

Almgasthof Windischgrätzhöhe: At the foot of Graukogel, this traditional hut has views and faves such as fondue. *3-9pm Wed-Fri, noon-9pm Sat & Sun* €€

SUPER & FREE GUIDED HIKES

From May to November, the Bad Gastein tourist office organises fantastic guided half- and full day hikes in the Gastein Valley, many of which are free with the **Gastein Card**, which you receive digitally before your arrival.

Bookable online in advance at gastein. com, hikes range in scope and difficulty, swinging from gentle three-hour rambles into Kötschachtal to see alphorn players at a mountain hut, to geology-themed hikes focusing on minerals, rocks and crystals at Sportgastein and a summit trek up to 2467m Gamskarkogel.

There's a terrific line-up of walks for families, too, including a survival in nature one in Dorfgastein, where kids get to build a fire pit and learn how to light a fire.

For some themed walks, such as alpaca walks and alpine herb hikes, there is a nominal charge.

Full moon dinner

The glitter of snow, mountains glowing pearl white as if lit from within in the inky blue of dusk, lanterns flickering the length of a long communal table draped in white linen, the hum of chatter and chink of mulled wine mugs. From December to April, the full moon dinners held under a canopy of stars at Sportgastein are the hottest ticket in town. Touched with winter magic, the backdrop is pure magic, with peaks grazing 3000m above a snow-frosted valley.

But as wild as the setting is, the five-course menu is a spectacular showcase of the regional produce, changing each month in tandem with the seasons and matched with Austrian wines. With torches burning bright, the table is laid in front of the rustic timber **Valeriehaus** *(valeriehaus.com)*, with dinner beginning at 8pm and the night only ending as the moon finally rises above the summits. Wrap up warm and bring extra layers as it can get cold outside. It costs €138 per person.

Wild Swimming

If you're into wild swimming and can brave shockingly icy waters, Bad Gastein is the dream, with thundering falls, crystal-clear streams, babbling brooks, Alpine tarns and looking-glass lakes where you can take a life-affirming dip.

You'll have seriously earned a refreshing swim if you take on the steep 10km, 3½-hour hike from Sportgastein to the Bockhartsee lakes in a valley where gold was mined in the Middle Ages, heading up and over scree fields, rocky passes and wildflower-flecked pastures where marmots whistle and cows jangle their heavy bells. Of the two, the higher, jewel-like **Upper Bockhartsee** is the most dazzling, clasped between mountains at 2000m, and with water so cold you'll gasp out loud (bring a towel and layers to warm up). On the descent, stop at the lakefront **Bockhartseehütte** *(bockhartseehuette. at)* for sublime views and a bowl of venison stew.

Other memorable spots for a swim include the **Palfnersee**, which can be reached on a 9km, 2½-return hike from Graukogel summit through an ancient stone pine forest. Mirroring the ragged peaks around it, the teal-green lake is a remote beauty for an invigorating dip. Bring your own picnic.

For minimum effort and maximum reward, there's nothing like rising with the first light and paddling – or, if you dare, immersing yourself completely – in the tinglingly cold waters of the Gasteiner Ache. Prime bathing spots include **Kötschachtal**, an idyllic, silent, lushly wooded valley on Bad Gastein's fringes, where the river flows into pools and over smooth boulders. Take care after heavy rain when the water is too wild for swimming.

Alpine asanas: mountain yoga

The soft pink light of dawn illuminating the summits of the Hohe Tauern National Park one by one is enough to make you want to reach up high to the heavens – or perhaps perform some impressive sun salutations. Bad Gastein has carved out a niche as one of the hottest places in the Austrian Alps for

Upper Bockhartsee

yoga. Here it's all about practising at your peak, whether you're mastering *asanas* (poses) on a platform in the forest within earshot of the waterfall, or finding your own spot to stretch in a quiet pasture or on a mountaintop like Stubnerkogel (p287).

In summer, the tourist office offers yoga sessions in beautiful, nature-immersed settings, which are free with the local guest card. More mindful still are the **Yoga Spring** and **Yoga Autumn**, 10-day yoga events that bringing together some of the world's best yoga teachers and a jam-packed programme of nature-embracing classes and workshops. Simply reserve your spot and roll out your mat. See gastein.com for more information.

The perfect yoga base? Alpine-chic chalet **Haus Hirt** is yogi heaven, with its soul-soaring views, daily yoga classes, and breathwork and yoga retreats.

Take a detour to Burg Mauterndorf

Tucked into Salzburgerland's remote southeastern pocket, medieval **Burg Mauterndorf** *(burg-mauterndorf.at; adult/child €14/5.20)*, built in the 13th century by the archbishops of Salzburg on the site of a Roman fort, looks every inch the fairy-tale castle with its setting atop a rocky outcrop and sturdy towers.

If you're driving the Radstädter Tauern Pass in the wonderfully forgotten Lungau region, look out for the Roman milestones along the road. Emperor Claudius built the first route over the mountains here 2000 years ago. Running for 38km from Mauterndorf to Radstadt, it's now sensational road-trip material, swinging up to 1738m, opening up views of the Radstädter Tauern Alps and with steep gradients of up to 15% to negotiate.

HEALING WATERS

There's something in the water in Bad Gastein: radon. Dip into the hot spring-fed baths and the aches, pains and years miraculously slip away, leaving you glowing with good health.

Five million litres of radon-rich waters bubble up through the rocks at temperatures of around 46°C, gushing forth at 16 different springs at the foot of Graukogel. They are said to cure rheumatism, respiratory and inflammatory conditions, boost circulation and stabilise the immune system.

Bad Gastein made its fortune from these healing waters, as the belle époque villas clinging to its forest-cloaked cliffs reveal.

Its marble-clad, chandelier-lit hotels are more Vienna than the Alps.

For decades, the *Kur* (spa cure) fell out of fashion and the town had an air of faded grandeur. But now it's shining once again with a new breed of luxe hotels, including the stylishly restored Straubinger Grand and cōmodo design hotel, tapping into the waters 21st-century style.

HELP ME PICK:

Outdoor Activities

With the Alps whooshing up above river-woven valleys and flower-flecked, trail-woven meadows, and one of Europe's biggest national parks at its heart, Salzburgerland is a sensational backdrop for pretty much every activity you care to mention. From hut-to-hut hikes to multiday mountain bike rides, stand-up paddleboarding across glassy alpine lakes to glacier skiing and epic climbs – this region has the lot. And with Salzburg as the gateway, you can race from city to slopes in no time.

Where to Go if You Love...

Alpine Hikes

Pinzgauer Spaziergang (p275) Above Zell am See, this high-level day hike enthrals with views of the Hohe Tauern and Kitzbühel Alps.

Salzburger Almenweg Skip through flowery Almen (meadows) on this epic hut-to-hut, 31-stage trek from Pfarrwerfen to the Gastein Valley, with mesmerising views of the glacier-capped Hohe Tauern peaks.

Dachstein Circuit (p271) Hike deep into the ragged limestone turrets of the Dachstein range on this eight-day, 126km stomp from forest to glacier.

Family Faves

Krimmler Wasserfälle (p285) Feel the colossal force of the 380m-high, rainbow-kissed Krimml Falls, Europe's highest, on the trail running alongside them.

The Sound of Music Trail (p270) Twirl like Julie Andrews and belt out *Do-Re-Mi* on this hour-long trail above Werfen, where the picnic scene in the movie was filmed.

Stubnerkogel (p287) Marvel at the ravishing views of the Hohe Tauern mountains from Stubnerkogel's head-spinning, 140m-long suspension bridge swinging high above Bad Gastein.

Watersports

Zeller See Eyeball the snow-dusted peaks of the Hohe Tauern as you swim, windsurf or stand-up paddleboard on this cobalt-blue alpine lake.

Almkanal (p255) You might not have Salzburg down as a surfing hub, but you can have a blast surfing this canal's artificial wave.

Cycling & Mountain Biking

Salzkammergut Trail The views make your heart sing as you roll around the glittering, mountain-rimmed lakes of the Salzkammergut on this 345km trail.

Tauernradweg (p286) (Tauern Cycle Path) The sky-scraping Hohe Tauern Alps form the backdrop to this 310km pulse-raising ride from Krimml to Passau.

Kitzsteinhorn (p277) Bikers find thrills on freeride trails and a 12km, peak-to-peak tour at glacier-capped Kitzsteinhorn.

Salzburger Almentour Pedal in quiet exhilaration through flower-flecked mountain pastures on this 146km route from Annaberg to Edtalm via Wolfgangsee.

Dachstein Circuit Mountain biking heaven, this exhilarating three-day, 182km route powers through the rivetingly beautiful Dachstein massif.

Mountain Highs

Kitzsteinhorn (p277) Soar above the peaks in a cable car to 3000m for a summer glacier ski with exhilarating views of the Hohe Tauern Alps.

Grossglockner (p281) If you have climbing experience under your belt, hook up with a guide to surmount Austria's highest-of-the-high Grossglockner (3798m).

Grossvenediger (p279) Take a deep breath for the two-day scramble up to the 3666m, glacier-capped summit of Grossvenediger.

- **SIGHTS**
1. Pinzgauer Spaziergang
2. Salzburger Almenweg
3. Dachstein Circuit
4. Krimmler Wasserfälle
5. Sound of Music World Trail
6. Stubnerkogel
7. Zeller See
8. Surfwelle am Almkanal
9. Salzkammergut Trail
10. Tauern Trail
11. Kitzsteinhorn
12. Salzburger Almentour
13. Dachstein Runde
14. Kitzsteinhorn Glacier
15. Grossglockner
16. Grossvenediger

HOW TO

When to Go
With longer, lighter, warmer days, summer (June to September) is ideal for hiking, biking, water- and adventure sports. For snow, hit the slopes from December to early April.

Book Ahead
Prebooking activities during peak months is wise. Ski hire and lift passes can be arranged in advance. Most towns and villages have an Intersport where you can rent equipment.

Getting Around
Salzburgerland is well connected by public transport, so base yourself in one place and strike out from there.

Budget
Discovering the region's great outdoors doesn't have to cost much, whether you want to hike, cycle or wild swim. Alpine huts are affordable and immerse you properly in nature.

DIY or Guided Tour?

While many high-level day hikes are doable solo, you'll benefit from a decent topographical map (1:25,000), compass and route book (Cicerone produce a reliable range). Many of the mountain huts run by the Austrian Alpine Club *(oav.at)* make high-level treks accessible and affordable, but be sure to book in high season. Hiring equipment on the ground often makes more sense than bringing it with you. At an Intersport *(intersportrent.at)*, you can rent everything from skis and snowboards to bikes and climbing gear. On lakes like Zeller See, boats, kayaks and stand-up paddleboards can be hired.

Prefer to join a group? Stay overnight in many towns and villages in the region and you'll be given a guest pass with free or heftily discounted outdoor activities, from full-day guided hikes and mountain bike tours to ski safaris and snowshoeing. Hohe Tauern National Park dives deep into the wilderness of the Alps. With mountains above 3000m, it's wise to enlist the services of pro guides for peak-bagging ascents, such as those in Heiligenblut *(grossglockner-bergfuehrer.at)*. For hikes at lower elevations, check out the national park's guided ranger tours, which vary from wildlife-watching rambles to glacier hikes. Most tend to cost around €22.

Places We Love to Stay

€ Budget €€ Midrange €€€ Top End

Salzburg Altstadt MAP P258

Hotel am Dom €€ Antique meets boutique at an Altstadt hotel in an 800-year-old building. Original vaults and beams contrast with sharp design.

Arte Vida €€ With the boho-chic feel of a Moroccan riad, this colourful pick has generously sized apartments big enough to accommodate families.

Hotel Amadeus €€ Centrally situated on the right bank, this 500-year-old hotel has a boutique feel, with bespoke touches such as chandeliers and a four-poster bed.

Arthotel Blaue Gans €€€ Welcoming folks since 1350, this art hotel blends avant-garde design with original vaulting, beams and floors.

Goldener Hirsch €€€ A skylight illuminates the arcaded inner courtyard of this 600-year-old Altstadt pile, where famous past guests include Queen Elizabeth II and Pavarotti.

Beyond Salzburg Altstadt

YoHo € Backpacker dream: comfy bunks, cheap beer and *The Sound of Music* movie screenings daily at 8pm. Staff can arrange bike hire.

A&O Salzburg Hauptbahnhof € Modern hostel in a revamped factory near the Hauptbahnhof. Airy dorms and rooms among the city's cheapest.

Haus am Moos € An alpine-style chalet offering a slice of rural calm. Rooms have gorgeous mountain views and there's an outdoor pool.

Hotel & Villa Auersperg €€ Fuses late-19th-century flair with the contemporary. Relax in the vine-swaddled garden or rooftop spa with Kapuzinerberg views.

Cool Mama €€ This ultra-modern skyscraper is a burst of urban cool near the Salzburg Exhibition Centre. Glass-walled rooms perfectly frame views of the city and Alps.

Hotel Rosenvilla €€ This bijou hotel goes the extra mile with its sharp-styled contemporary rooms, faultless service and incredible breakfasts.

Schloss Mönchstein €€€ On a fairy-tale perch atop Mönchsberg and set in hectares of wooded grounds, this 16th-century castle is honeymoon (and second mortgage) material.

Hallein

Kranzbichlhof €€ In serene gardens, this Bad Dürrnberg chalet has spacious rooms, a natural pool and a spa with ayurvedic treatments.

Pension Sommerauer €€ Housed in a 300-year-old farmhouse on the fringes of Hallein, this welcoming guesthouse has rustic rooms, a heated pool and a kids' playground.

Werfen

Weisses Rössl € In the village centre, this good-value pension has great views of the fortress and the Tennengebirge from its rooftop terrace.

Landgasthof Reitsamerhof €€ Rousing views of the Tennengebirge peaks at a sunny yellow, geranium-bedecked chalet just south of Werfen.

Söldenhütte € Above Werfen, this woody 1531m hut is a cracking base for Tennengebirge hiking. The restaurant rolls out hearty dumplings, goulash and homemade cakes.

Filzmoos

Naturhotel Hammerhof €€ Ecofriendly hotel in a 400-year-old farmhouse in Filzmoos with light-bathed rooms, a herbal bath and horses to saddle.

Hotel Alpenblick €€ Right on the doorstep of the slopes and hiking trails, this smart chalet has a petite spa, restaurant, sun terrace and kids' playground.

Zell am See MAP P274

Seecamp Zell am See € Camp out at this tree-shaded campground on the lakeshore to wake up to views of the snowcapped Kitzsteinhorn mountain.

Steinerwirt €€ This 500-year-old chalet has alpine-cool rooms, a rooftop whirlpool tub and mountain-facing sauna, as well as a much-fêted dark-wood-panelled restaurant.

Pension Hubertus €€ Expect a heartfelt welcome, organic breakfasts and country-style rooms at this eco-savvy chalet opposite the cityXpress gondola to Schmittenhöhe.

Romantik Hotel Zell am See €€ This 500-year-old dark-wood chalet has cosy, antique-slung rooms, a solar-heated pool with mountain views and a small spa.

Schloss Prielau (p276) €€€
This swanky 16th-century castle was once the haunt of Bavarian prince-bishops. It's luxury all the way with a private beach, spa and Michelin-starred restaurant.

Hohe Tauern National Park   MAP P280

Badener Hütte € In the Venediger peaks, this 2608m hut hovers above the romantic Frossnitztal valley. Simple dorms perfect for hikers.

Erzherzog-Johann-Hütte (p281) € The number-one base for Grossglockner climbs and Austria's highest hut at 3454m. Out-of-this-world views.

Matreier Tauernhaus (p279) €€ In the shadow of Austria's highest peaks, this rustic spot at 1512m is a great base for Grossvenediger ascents.

Hotel Tauernstern €€ Sweeping valley views extend from the balconies of this mountain-set beauty in Winklern, with a spa and gourmet restaurant bigging up farm-fresh produce.

Heiligenblut

Nationalpark Camping Grossglockner € Year-round Heiligenblut site with table tennis, playground and stellar Grossglockner views.

Bauernhof Stempf € Working farm with snug rooms, gorgeous views, ponies to ride, fresh eggs in the morning and a warm family welcome.

Nationalpark Lodge €€ Alpine-chic lodge with views, panoramic spa and restaurant with regional ingredients like Hohe Tauern venison.

Krimml

Burgeck Panorama Hotel €€ Perched above the village with waterfall views. Its restaurant has local, organic ingredients and homegrown herbs.

Nationalpark Hotel Klockerhaus €€ Spacious rooms with waterfall views, a lounge with open fire, and great post-hike or -ski spa and pool.

Hotel Krimml €€ Central pick sending the alpine chalet winging into the 21st century with sleek rooms, fitness centre and sauna.

Bad Gastein

Gamskarkogelhütte € High above Bad Gastein, this cloud-grazing 2467m hut has simple digs for hikers and surreal sunrises and sunsets.

Kur-Camping Erlengrund € Close to a natural lake, this campground has shady pitches and, in summer, a heated pool is available.

Haus Hirt (p289) €€ High on a perch above Bad Gastein, this alpine-chic chalet entices with modern-rustic, art-slung rooms, slopes and trails on the doorstep, outstanding food and a peak-gazing spa.

Hotel Miramonte €€ Hill-hugging design hotel with forest and mountain views, yoga, thermal spa treatments and understated glam rooms.

Alpenblick €€ Panoramically perched hotel at the foot of Graukogel ski slope. Slickly traditional rooms, spa, pool and smashing views.

Grand Hotel Straubinger €€€ Combining history with modern luxury, this grand hotel by the waterfall bears the imprint of BWM architects.

Schloss Mönchstein

Researched by Anthony Haywood

Carinthia

DRAMATIC LANDSCAPES AND MEDIEVAL HISTORY

Rugged mountains, pristine lakes, and flamboyant, eclectic and medieval towns – Carinthia brings it all together.

Few regions in Europe match Carinthia for its rugged beauty. Travelling through it is often a serpentine journey through carved valleys, between soaring mountains and along the shores of glistening lakes. Its best-known lake is Wörthersee – situated just a few kilometres from the centre of flamboyant Klagenfurt and warmed by hot springs that make it a comfortable swimming temperature in mild weather, and a tepid 25°C or more during the hottest months of a sizzling summer.

In contrast, other parts of Carinthia often feel remote, especially once you ascend to mountain meadows, where you also find excellent walking, skiing and mountain-bike trails.

The deep medieval heritage of Carinthia is celebrated in picturesque walled villages such as Friesach and Gmünd, and impressive castles like the hilltop fortress of Hochosterwitz. In winter, the region turns into a ski paradise around towns such as Hermagor and Lienz.

The province's proximity to Slovenia (the border between Austria and Slovenia has been redrawn several times over the centuries) means that many of the place names are of Slavic origin and Slavic surnames are common among the local inhabitants. Villach holds an annual summer festival with folk-music groups and bands of roving performers often coming from neighbouring Italy and Slovenia to play alongside locals. Carinthia is a place to unwind and really get away from it all.

THE MAIN AREAS

KLAGENFURT & WÖRTHERSEE
Flamboyant capital and lakeside living.
p298

VILLACH
Multicultural Villach and alpine borderland.
p303

CENTRAL CARINTHIA
Medieval towns and offbeat explorations.
p307

MILLSTÄTTER SEE
Superb swimming and Romanesque abbey.
p310

LIENZ & THE DOLOMITES
Alpine bike trip and cultural delights.
p318

For places to stay in Carinthia see p321

THE GUIDE

CARINTHIA

Left: Villacher Kirchtag (p304); Above: Burg Hochosterwitz (p308)

Find Your Way

Carinthia has some beautiful and remote parts, especially as you travel further west. Take your time to visit a few mountain meadow huts and the magnificent lakes, while also exploring its popular medieval towns.

Millstätter See, p310
Wild lake swimming, kayaking, a wonderful Romanesque abbey and some great high-country hikes above Weissensee, plus art in Gmünd.

Central Carinthia, p307
A Romanesque abbey in Gurk, the walled town of Friesach, a nod to 'Tibet' in eccentric Hüttenberg, and a medieval castle all await.

Lienz & the Dolomites, p318
Lienz has plenty of local city flair while the dramatic peaks of the Dolomites around town offer alpine adventures.

Villach, p303
Music fills the streets of Villach in summer, local lakes are perfect for a dip, and mountains offer hiking or mountain biking. In winter it's all about skiing.

Klagenfurt & Wörthersee, p298
Carinthia's relaxed capital lures with art while the shores of Wörthersee tempt with cycling, dining and swimming.

TRAIN
Rail connections are excellent in Carinthia. The useful S1 regional line links Friesach with Lienz, via St Veit an der Glan, Klagenfurt, Villach and Spittal an der Drau. Hotel-issued local discount cards include free S-Bahn train travel.

BUS
Buses usually leave from the main train stations, winding out of the valleys into the hills and mountains, and are essential for reaching Millstätter See (from Spittal an der Drau) and Weissensee (from Greifenburg or Hermagor).

Klagenfurt (p298)

Plan Your Time

With its rugged mountains, alpine meadows, lakes and deep valleys, Carinthia is all about the great outdoors, but you will also feel medieval Carinthia tugging at your sleeve.

If You Have Three Days

● The contrast of city and spectacular country landscapes is what makes Carinthia so fascinating. If you only have a few days, spend two exploring **Klagenfurt** (p298) and perhaps riding around **Wörthersee** (p298) and swimming. On the third day, head into the mountains on a day trip, such as to **Hermagor** (p305) or the Dolomitenhütte outside **Lienz** (p318). In winter, go skiing.

Two Weeks in Summer

● Combine cultural highlights with hiking and cycling. Visit medieval **Friesach** (p309) or **Burg Hochosterwitz** (p308), spend a few days in **Klagenfurt** (p298) and around **Wörthersee** (p298), check out **Villach** (p303) and **Hermagor** (p305). Then on to **Millstätter See** (p310) and **Weissensee** (p316). Wrap up with **Lienz** (p318) and the **Dolomitenhütte** (p318).

SEASONAL HIGHLIGHTS

SPRING
Cable cars pause for maintenance but valley hiking is possible. Cultural sights in small towns reopen from Easter.

SUMMER
From June most mountain and outdoor activities are possible. Villach has festivals like **Kirchtag** (p303), late July to August.

AUTUMN
Cable cars pause before the ski season. In early September some meadow huts are still open. Wörthersee is about 16°C.

WINTER
Snow activities at mountain huts; Hermagor and Lienz attract winter-sports fans. Museums in larger towns stay open.

Klagenfurt & Wörthersee

ART MUSEUMS | LAKE SWIMMING | RENAISSANCE ARCHITECTURE

GETTING AROUND

You can hire bikes (not mountain bikes) at stations in the region, including at the Klagenfurt tourist office. Boats for destinations around Wörthersee leave from a quay just north of **Strandbad Klagenfurt**; check times at woerther seeschifffahrt.at. To reach Wörthersee from Klagenfurt, follow the Lendkanal for 3km, or take bus No 10 or 20 from Heiligengeistplatz.

If you have the Wörthersee Plus Card and register with nextbike at/de/ klagenfurt, you get free use of a bike for 24 hours.

☑ TOP TIP

Klagenfurt tourist office *(visitklagenfurt.at)* on Neuer Platz is a pick-up and drop-off point for city bike rental from **Papin Sport** *(papinsport.com)*, which has an excellent network across Carinthia.

Vibrant and sunny in summer, and with a compact centre, Klagenfurt walks a fine line between being a provincial capital and a salubrious playground. It is an enjoyable city with several good art museums, pleasant Renaissance courtyards, alleyways and arcades, and a highly unusual electric-keyboard museum.

Excellent transport links and bike-hire facilities make it a perfect base for exploring the immediate region. In that case, the first port of call is the large Wörthersee, just a few kilometres from Klagenfurt, with great swimming in summer along its 16km or so length – open-water swimmers love its placid, tepid waters – and a 40km bike route around the entire shoreline.

Both Klagenfurt and Wörthersee offer plenty of places to eat, drink and be entertained, bringing together the urban and the outdoors in a relatively compact space. Its excellent rail connections also mean you can easily take day trips far and wide to other places.

History & Architecture in Klagenfurt

Evocative architecture and altar painting

Klagenfurt's cultural highlights are mostly in the compact centre. The city's central square, **Neuer Platz**, is dominated by the 16th-century **Dragon Fountain**. This blank-eyed statue is modelled on the Lindwurm (dragon) of legend, said to have resided in a swamp here long ago – sporting a wriggly pig-like tail, and devouring cattle and virgins.

Directly along from Neuer Platz on the north side and adjoining Landhauspark, the Renaissance **Landhaus** (State Parliament) dates from the late 16th century and is still the centre of political power today. If you take the stairs on the right (facing the portico), you reach the **Grosser Wappensaal**

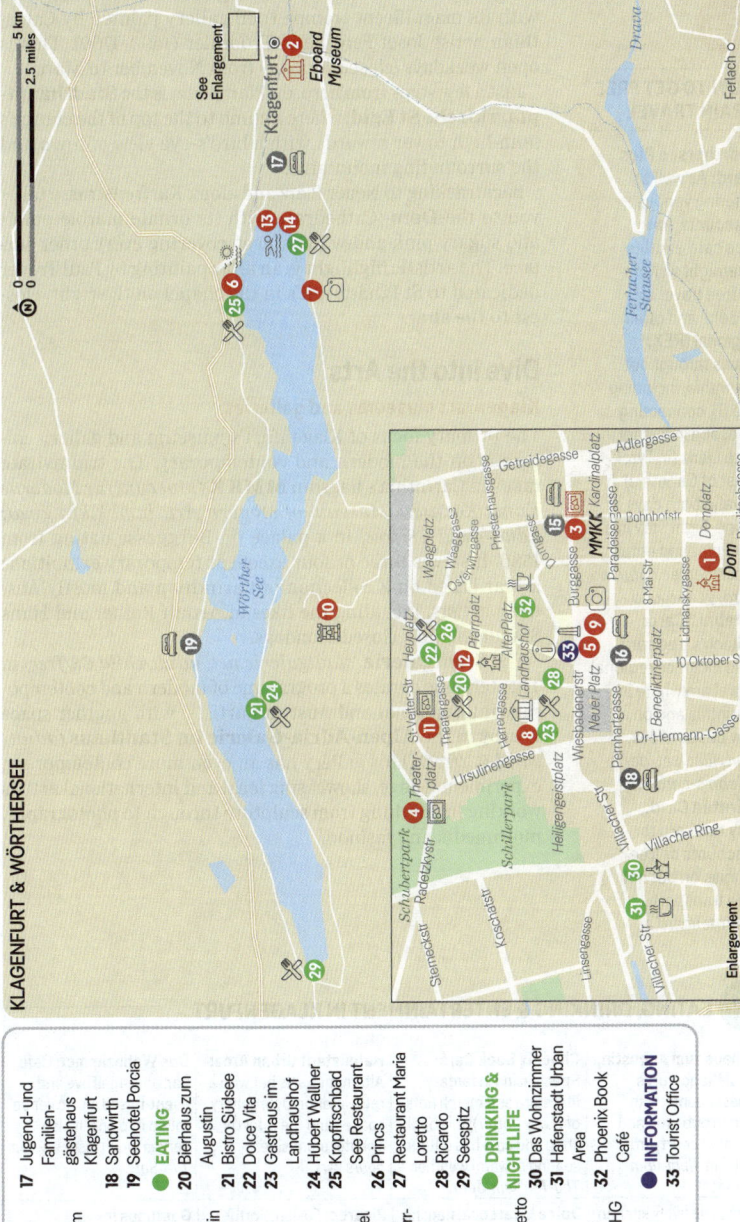

KLAGENFURT & WÖRTHERSEE

★ **HIGHLIGHTS**
1 Dom
2 Eboard Museum
3 MMKK

● **SIGHTS**
4 Alpen-Adria-Galerie im Stadthaus
5 Dragon Fountain
6 Duttinger Park
7 Gustav Mahler Composer's House
8 Landhaus
9 Neuer Platz
10 Pyramidenkogel
11 Stadtgalerie
12 Stadthauptpfarrkirche St Egid

● **ACTIVITIES**
13 Strandbad Klagenfurt
14 Strandbad Loretto

● **SLEEPING**
15 Garner Hotel Moser Verdino Klagenfurt by IHG
16 Hotel Palais Porcia

17 Jugend- und Familiengästehaus Klagenfurt
18 Sandwirth
19 Seehotel Porcia

● **EATING**
20 Bierhaus zum Augustin
21 Bistro Südsee
22 Dolce Vita
23 Gasthaus im Landhaushof
24 Hubert Wallner
25 Kropfitschbad See Restaurant
26 Princs
27 Restaurant Maria Loretto
28 Ricardo
29 Seespitz

● **DRINKING & NIGHTLIFE**
30 Das Wohnzimmer
31 Hafenstadt Urban Area
32 Phoenix Book Café

● **INFORMATION**
33 Tourist Office

(*Heraldic Hall; landesmuseum.ktn.gv.at; adult/child €7/free*), with its magnificent trompe l'oeil gallery painted by Carinthian artist Josef Ferdinand Fromiller (1693–1760). This is open weekdays (closed Monday from November to March).

Just a few steps from here, on Pfarrplatz, is the **Stadthauptpfarrkirche St Egid**, where a climb to the top of the church's 90m-high tower rewards with a bird's-eye view of town and the surrounding mountains.

Backtracking to Neuer Platz and along Karfreitstrasse takes you to the **Dom** (Cathedral), with its ornate marble pulpit and sugary pink-and-white stucco covering every other surface. The artistic highlight is an altar painting by Paul Troger dedicated to St Ignatius; it's in the chapel on the right, closest to the altar.

Dive into the Arts

Klagenfurt museums and galleries

The primary focus of Klagenfurt's museum and gallery culture is on the modern and contemporary. The triumvirate takes in Carinthia's flagship **MMKK** (*Museum für Moderne Kunst Kärnten, Museum of Modern Art; mmkk.ktn.gv.at; adult/child €8/free*) in a palace on Burggasse dating from 1586. It stages three or four excellent temporary exhibitions a year based on a collection of Carinthian and mostly Austrian artists, including the likes of Arnulf Rainer and Hans Staudacher. It's closed Mondays.

The **Stadtgalerie** (*stadtgalerie.net; adult/child €8/free*) in Theatergasse curates a programme of modern and contemporary international and Austrian artists, with another space nearby in the **Alpen-Adria-Galerie im Stadthaus** (*adult/child €3/free*). This gallery has an even more contemporary, experimental edge, showcasing local and international artists working in anything from sculpture through to photography, multimedia and fashion.

HOW TO GET FREE TRAIN TRAVEL

Wörthersee Plus Card: As well as offering various discounts, this free card entitles overnight visitors to free travel on S-Bahn and other regional (REX) trains throughout Carinthia, including the S1, connecting Friesach in the north with Lienz (in Tyrol, west of Carinthia). It is valid both days of a one-night stay in a participating hotel. *woerthersee.com/card; year-round*

Erlebnis Card: Villach's free card also includes regional travel anywhere in Carinthia and on a few bus services. *visitvillach.at/de/erlebnis-card.html*

Kärnten Card: Buy this card for discounts or free admission but not free transport. *kaerntencard.at*

 EATING, DRINKING & ENTERTAINMENT IN KLAGENFURT

Bierhaus zum Augustin: One of Klagenfurt's liveliest haunts, with Austrian pub grub and a cobbled courtyard for dining. *11am-11pm Mon-Sat*	**Phoenix Book Café:** Specialising in fantasy literature and merch (lots of *Harry Potter*), this book shop and cafe has outdoor seating in warm weather. *Thu-Tue 9am-6pm*	**Hafenstadt Urban Area:** Alternative arts bar with a retro interior, Deli, gallery spaces and the Dock04_ Theater alongside. *hours vary*	**Das Wohnzimmer:** Cafe, bar, and small live and event-based music venue rolled into one. It also serves lunch dishes. *9-1am Tue-Sat*
Princs: The lively kitchen sends out endless pizzas, pasta and street food. Kitchen closes at 9pm. Also with a popular bar. *10am-midnight Mon-Thu, to 2am Fri & Sat* €€	**Dolce Vita:** Local flagship restaurant-bistretto with northern Italian cuisine and a local seasonal menu. *11.30am-3pm & 6.30-10pm Mon-Fri* €€	**Ricardo:** Fusion, Portuguese, tapas, vegetarian (and vegan) dishes and steaks, with outdoor seating. *11.30am-2pm & 6-11.30 Tue-Sat, 6-11.30pm Mon* €€	**Gasthaus im Landhaushof:** Classic Austrian cuisine, with outdoor seating in the yard and all-day kitchen. *11am-9pm Mon-Sat, to 3pm Sun* €€

WÖRTHERSEE CYCLING & SWIMMING

The R4 bike track winds 40km around Wörthersee on an easy, well-marked ride. Stop off along the way for food, refreshment and swimming in summer.

START	END	LENGTH
Klagenfurt (Lendkanal)	Maria Loretto	40km; 3hrs

To reach the R4 bike track, follow the bike path along the Lendkanal (Lend Canal) from ❶ **Klagenfurt** for 3km. Cycling anti-clockwise for about 10 minutes, you come to the first swimming spot at ❷ **Dultinger Park**. The nearby ❸ **Kropfitschbad See Restaurant** is next to a pay-for-entry beach and bar. Beyond this is the resort of ❹ **Pörtschach**, and then the nightlife hub of ❺ **Velden**, where the Strandclub (strand club.com) offers paragliding and water-skiing.

Keep close to the lake and you'll find yourself on Velden's illustrious ❻ **Seecorso**, packed with bars and restaurants. The bike route from here is mostly along the relatively quiet Süduferstrasse via ❼ **Schiefling** (free swimming) and ❽ **Oberdellach** to ❾ **Maria Wörth**, and just beyond that, ❿ **St Anna**, 13km from Velden.

For a detour, walking trails (plan on at least 1½ hours each way) lead up to the ⓫ **Pyramidenkogel**, a hill topped by a 71m tower made of steel, with wooden beams spiralling up its exterior. Climb the 441 steps, or take the glass panorama lift and return via Europe's longest slide. Without the detour (7km each way), just carry on along the lake to ⓬ **Restaurant Maria Loretto** (p302).

If you only want to ride (or ride and hike) to the Pyramidenkogel, set off clockwise to St Anna along Süduferstrasse. The road up is relatively flat until Keutschach, after which it climbs about 300m in altitude over the next 5km.

In 1900 Gustav Mahler commissioned his so-called **Gustav Mahler Composer's House** on the banks of Wörthersee, where he wrote some of his major musical compositions.

Wörthersee reaches about 25°C in midsummer. It's one of the warmest lakes because of its protected location against wind and the fact that few watercourses flow out of it.

You can't enter the water from Restaurant Maria Loretto, but the **Strandbad Loretto** (Loretto Swimming Beach) is a great alternative to the more-crowded Klagenfurt Strandbad.

FESTIVALS & EVENTS

Klagenfurter Altstadtzauber: For three days in August, Klagenfurt's old town comes to life with music, theatrical acts, and food and drink stands. *stadtrichter.at/altstadtzauber*

Klagenfurt Festival: Held over about six weeks in May and June, this festival features a diverse offering of concerts, readings, discussion events, dance and more. *klagenfurtfestival.com*

Wörthersee Classics Festival: A series of classical music concerts held in Klagenfurt over a few days in late June or July. *woertherseeclassics.com*

Pink Lake LGBTQ Festival: Held in late August at various locations around the Wörthersee. Very tongue in cheek, especially if the event's signature drag queen Klara Mydia is doing their highly entertaining thing. *woerthersee.com/pinklake*

Eboard Museum

World's Largest Electric Keyboard Collection

Analogue instruments in the Eboard Museum

For Gert Prix, it all began back in the late 1980s, when digital instruments were making dramatic inroads and analogue e-keyboards were losing their allure. 'The digital instruments are fantastic and have huge advantages, but the gentler tones more compatible with the human ear come from analogue instruments', he says. Walk into Gert Prix's **Eboard Museum** (*eboardmuseum.com; €15*) on Florian Gröger Strasse and you can't help being overwhelmed by these analogue creations, including rarities like the Model A Hammond from 1934.

Ask Gert to take you around and he will strike up iconic riffs from classics, and you can play many of the instruments yourself. Gert has only ever sold one – an Eko Sensor piano, the first instrument he used when playing live in a band – with the serial number 0549. And he's been trying to find it again ever since. Regular live events bring the instruments into action onstage; see the website for the programme. It's closed Mondays and Tuesdays from November to March.

 EATING & DRINKING AT WÖRTHERSEE: MOSTLY LAKESIDE

Restaurant Maria Loretto: Italian-Austrian dishes and drinks, with a traditional vibe indoors, and outdoor seating in warm weather. *11am-11pm Wed-Sun* €€

Seespitz: Directly on the water in Velden, with slow food menu and vegan variant of this, as well as upmarket Austrian classics. *noon-5pm & 6-8.30pm* €€

Bistro Südsee: Top dining from chef Hubert Wallner and team in Dellach-Maria Wörth, with Austro-Italian flavours. *noon-3pm & 6-9pm Wed-Sun May, Jun & Sep, daily Jul & Aug* €€

Hubert Wallner: Austro-Mediterranean menus and prime location on the lake in Dellach-Maria Wörth, with a fair-weather terrace. See *hubertwallner.com*. *hours vary* €€€

Villach

HIKING & BIKING | WINTER SPORTS | VIBRANT CENTRE

Wedged between the Karawanken (Karawanks) on the border with Slovenia along Austria's southern flank, and the Nockberge (Nock Mountains) in the northwest, this part of Carinthia is a scenic and serene region of small towns and villages, high mountains and gouged valleys.

Travelling west from Klagenfurt, Villach is the first major town. It is a small, outward-looking city with a lively, multicultural atmosphere. Although actual sights are rather limited in Villach itself, it is the kick-off point for activities in the region immediately beyond in the Gail Valley and above it. This and lots of music events make Villach a good base for exploring the region. But you don't need to travel far to get active. Some local lakes just a few kilometres from town provide plenty of opportunities for camping, boating and swimming. Of these, Faaker See can be easily reached by train or bus, and is a good place to rent a kayak and paddle to your heart's content.

Explore Villach Old Town

Historic town centre

Arriving by train – as is likely – one of your first impressions of Villach will be as you walk across the bridge into the old town, with the Drau whishing below your feet and snow-capped or shimmering mountains rising up in the distance. Off to the right after the bridge, Lederergasse is the former street of leatherworkers and today has a smattering of bars, eateries and boutiques.

In the centre of Villach at the top of the pedestrian Hauptplatz, the **Stadtpfarrturm** *(adult/child €5/4)* rises up from the Stadtpfarrkirche St Jakob. The tower is closed Sundays, and from November to April. The attractive church interior changes from ochre-coloured ribbing and soaring Gothic pillars to attractive frescoes above the altar, culminating in a vast rococo altar in gold leaf, bedecked with fresh flowers. Some of the walls are studded with the ornate memorial plaques of the region's noble families. From the tower you have spectacular views over the countryside.

GETTING AROUND

Villach is easy to walk around, but it's also the best place to hire a bike. **Papin Sport** *(papinsport.com)* has pick-up and drop-off points in Carinthia and a full range on offer in Villach; make reservations online.

If you are based in Villach and staying at one of the places offering the free **Erlebnis Card** (p300), you can travel on regional trains for free anywhere in Carinthia.

Faaker See is easily reached by bike or public transport. Bus 5194 from the bus station (at Villach railway station) takes you to Drobollach on Faaker See, and the S5 train to Faak am See.

☑ TOP TIP

Villacher Kirchtag *(villacherkirchtag.at)* is the biggest folklore bash in the region. Catch it from late July to early August.

SUMMER MUSIC IN VILLACH

Each summer Villach hosts many events, especially music-based ones. Various free theatre, opera and street artist performances are also hallmarks of a Villach summer. See visitvillach.at for event listings.

Rookie Music Year: In 2025 Villach staged the inaugural Rookie Music Year, with rookie musicians and bands appearing in free concerts each Friday afternoon from late June to early September.

Villach Unplugged: A regular busker event over two days around mid-July or early August. *gemma.cc/termine*

DRAUpuls: On Wednesday and Friday evenings in July and August, the town puts on the DRAUpuls fountain show, with music, from 9.30pm.

Villacher Kirchtag: The biggest event for traditional folk. There are also street markets with French, Italian and Catalan foods.

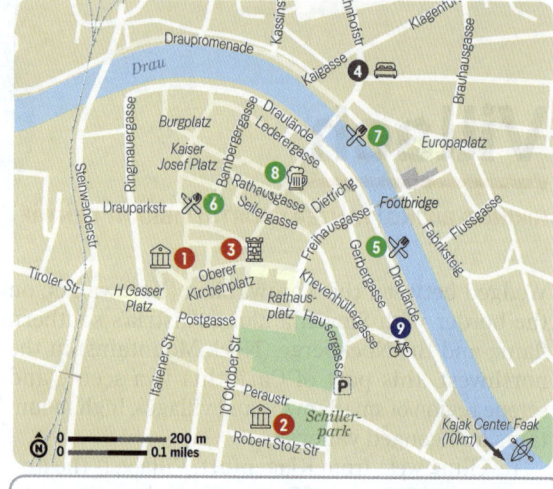

SIGHTS
1 Museum der Stadt Villach
2 Relief Von Kärnten
3 Stadtpfarrturm

SLEEPING
4 Hotel Mosser

EATING
5 Alexander's
6 Aurea
7 Lagana

DRINKING & NIGHTLIFE
8 McMullen's

TRANSPORT
9 Papin Sport

Local History & Landscape

City museum and Schillerpark

A visit to the **Museum der Stadt Villach** *(adult/child €6/5)* provides you with local history, archaeology and medieval art. Meanwhile, the **Relief von Kärnten** *(free)*, about 400m south of the centre in Peraustrasse, is a huge relief model of Carinthia housed in Schillerpark. It covers 182 sq m and depicts the province at a scale of 1:10,000 (1:5000 vertically, to exaggerate the mountains). Multimedia effects heighten the experience.

Dip into a Local Lake

Faaker See

Faaker See is within easy reach of Villach by train and a pleasant spot for cooling off in hot weather. One way of navigating the lake is by kayak, canoe or SUP from **Kajak Center Faak** *(kajak-faak.com)*, located across from Faak am See in Neuegg at **Sunset Beach**, which can be reached with bus 5194 from Villach. You also have to pay €5 beach admission to rent.

EATING & DRINKING IN VILLACH

Lagana: Austrian classics and a business lunch inside the Voco Villach hotel. There's a hotel bar too. *6-9pm Tue-Sat, business lunch 11.30am-1.30pm Mon-Fri* €€

Aurea: This small and casual restaurant serves excellent multi-course menus, including a vegetarian option, using seasonal ingredients. *6-10pm Wed-Sat* €€

Alexander's: Large restaurant with pizza, pasta and Italian classics, and a vinothek with a good selection of wine. *11am-3pm & 5-9pm Mon-Fri* €€

McMullen's: Popular Irish pub in a yard, back from the main pedestrian street, with occasional low-key live music and outside tables in summer. *5pm-1am*

Beyond Villach

Hike and mountain bike high in the Alps in summer, or explore a picturesque gorge, replete with a gurgling mountain stream.

Situated around 50km west of Villach, Hermagor is a lively base for skiing and a popular summer hot spot for hikers and mountain bikers. When the weather plays along, one of the most interesting hikes in the region is through the Garnitzenklamm gorge. Another good reason to travel out here is to ride the Millennium-Express cable car in its three stages to the Madritsche mountain station, in an area bursting with mountain bike trails of varying levels of difficulty. Families will also find lots of opportunities for summer fun. The bike season runs from early June to late September. Plan on spending two full days here to hike the Garnitzenklamm gorge and ride the cable car.

Places
Hermagor p305
Tröpolach p306
Dreiländereck p306

Hermagor

TIME FROM VILLACH: 1HR

Entering a gorge
Around 3km outside the town of Hermagor, **Garnitzenklamm** is a spectacular gorge open from late May or early June to mid-September. You need quite a good head for heights, decent hiking shoes and sure-footedness (cross bridges one at a time), but the first two sections are moderate in difficulty. You can find out if it's for you at garnitzenklamm.at and download excellent maps of the four sections (see 'Touren' in the menu). The **tourist office** at Wulfeniaplatz 1 in Hermagor can also give you information on the hike and current conditions.

From an information stand at the Klammwirt (p306) restaurant, set out on section 1, which leads around a weir and waterfall. In the early stages of section 2, which begins after **Idawarte**, there are some pretty rock formations, spectacular cascades and narrow, bubbling pools flanked with lush vegetation. From Idawarte the trail climbs steeply and leads past more waterfalls to **Franzenswarte**. Some parts here have a chain you can hold onto, while others run along natural ledges. Shortly before the end of section 2, cross the bridge and follow **Steinwender Weg** (trail No 485) for about 1km until it joins the forestry road (still trail No 485). While descending the forestry road, take trail No 410 to the right where trail No 410 and No 116 cross. Nearby is a cross (and a bloody kneed Jesus), and about 500m from here **St Urbani Chapel** is set picturesquely in the woods. From St Urbani you can follow a path and rejoin the forestry track back to the start.

GETTING AROUND

From Hermagor Gasserplatz take bus 5059 or walk 3km to Möderndorf and just beyond to the Garnitzenklamm gorge. Reaching the Millennium-Express valley station just outside Töpolach involves changing to bus 5058 at Hermagor train station. From the Töpolach Feuerwehr stop it's a five-minute walk.

Take the S4 to Arnoldstein and bus to Seltschach for the Dreiländereck chair lift.

Hermagor is also one of two train stations where you can change to bus to reach Weissensee (p316).

BIKE RENTAL BEYOND VILLACH

If you want to cycle this part of Carinthia, Papin Sport in Villach is the best place to pick up bikes. You can drop these off at other points.

Bikeparadies Härle Rents out a full range from its location on the edge of Hermagor, with e-bikes and conventional trekking and mountain bikes. This rental place is especially useful if you want to ride out to the Garnitzenklamm gorge (p305), or to Techendorf am Weissensee (p316), about 25km by road from Hermagor. *bikeparadies.at*

Sölle Sport Full range of conventional and e-bikes at the Millennium-Express cable car in Tröpolach. These can be transported on the cable car with a lift ticket. Cycle back down. *soelle.at*

Dreiländereck

Tröpolach

TIME FROM VILLACH: 1½HRS

Cable car to walks & mountain biking

Tröpolach, 8km west of Hermagor, is the valley station for the **Millennium-Express cable car** *(nassfeld.at; all sections return adult/child €36/22)*, taking you up to the skiing, hiking and mountain-biking area on the Italian border, with high alpine lakes and spectacular scenery. Hire a mountain bike at the valley station or in Hermagor and take the cable car to the top, where trails of varying difficulty branch out and an easy 12km asphalt and gravel track leads back down to Gmanberg station, the middle section.

Dreiländereck

TIME FROM VILLACH: 45MINS

Explore the borderlands

Villach is situated below the Dreiländereck, or 'three country corner', where Austria, Italy and Slovenia meet at around 1600m, with views to the mountains. A summer **chairlift** *(3laendereck.at; return adult/child €23/12)* leaves the valley station in Seltschach, 3km from Arnoldstein. Medium-difficulty hiking trails lead up from Arnoldstein if you want to walk to the views. One of the routes is a section of the GRENZgenial-GRENZgänger trail, starting from the parking area of the valley station and taking about four hours to reach Dreiländereck.

EATING & DRINKING BEYOND VILLACH

Klammwirt: Traditional restaurant at the Garnitzenklamm gorge, with outdoor seating and all the food you need before the hike. *9am-6pm May-late-Oct* €€

Mari e Monti: In Hermagor, this Italian restaurant serves the classics, including vegan and vegetarian options. *10am-10pm Wed-Mon, from 9am Sun* €€

Bärenwirt: Austrian cuisine in Hermagor, with multi-course menus as well as a classic selection of individual dishes. *noon-2pm & 6-8pm Thu-Mon* €€

Gasthof Tressdorfer Alm: Located at 1600m and near the Millennium-Express cable car station, with cold platters, soups and more, as well as a few rooms. *hours vary* €€

Central Carinthia

MEDIEVAL TOWN | ROMANESQUE CATHEDRAL | SPECTACULAR FORTRESS

Extending north of Klagenfurt and dissolving into Styria, central Carinthia (Mittelkärnten) is a region predominantly of high hills, patchwork fields and forest. Its most important towns are nestled in the snaking valleys between alpine ranges extending around its fringes.

Travelling north from Klagenfurt, you first reach St Veit an der Glan, which is a major town in the region and has a pretty town square. In the far north of this region, a popular destination is Friesach, with its impressive medieval town wall and fortifications.

East of Friesach is Hüttenberg, a small mining village now famous for being the birthplace of Heinrich Harrer, mountaineer and Himalayan explorer.

West of the main north–south rail artery, in the Gurk Valley, the town of Gurk is famous for its Romanesque cathedral. In all, this is a varied, interesting and eccentric region culturally.

Explore St Veit an der Glan

Baroque town square and Rathaus

Just 20 minutes north of Klagenfurt by train, St Veit an der Glan was historically important as the seat of the dukes of Carinthia from 1170 until 1518, and today is best known for its lovely baroque town square, **Plague Column** and **Rathaus** *(Town Hall; sv.or.at; free)*. The latter dates from the 15th century and was modified over the following three centuries. The highlight is its beautifully symmetrical interior courtyard and arcades with Tuscan pillars and sgraffito.

GETTING AROUND

To reach Burg Hochosterwitz from St Veit an der Glan, take bus 5373. The trip takes around 45 minutes. An S1 rail and bus connection is faster. From Launsdorf-Hochosterwitz station, it's a 3km walk or taxi ride to the castle.

Regular buses run to Hüttenberg from Klagenfurt with a change at Göschitztal Vierlinden. These are augmented by trains from Klagenfurt that connect with buses at Treibach-Althofen, which is also where you change if you are coming from Friesach.

A bus and train connection serves Gurk with a change at Treibach-Althofen.

★ HIGHLIGHTS
1 Dom zu Gurk

● SIGHTS
2 Burg Hochosterwitz
3 Diözesanmuseum
4 Heinrich Harrer Museum
5 Lingkor
6 Petersberg Fortress
7 Peterskirche
8 Plague Column
9 Rathaus
10 Rotturm
11 St Bartholomew Church
12 Virgilienberg

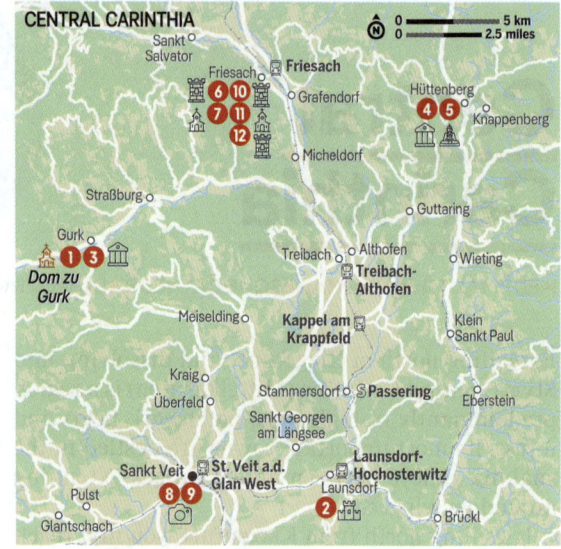

☑ TOP TIP
This part of Carinthia is fairly low-key and quiet, with most places 'folding up their footpaths' at sunset. But its proximity to Klagenfurt and good transport connections mean you can easily visit on day trips.

To a Hilltop Fortress
Hochosterwitz Castle and exhibitions

From St Veit it's a 15- to 30-minute trip by bus or rail and bus connection to **Burg Hochosterwitz** *(burg-hochosterwitz.com; adult/child €18/11)*, located 10km east of town, so you could easily visit both in one day from Klagenfurt. This fairy-tale fortress claims to be the inspiration for the castle in *Sleeping Beauty* and drapes itself around the slopes of a hill, with 14 gate towers on the path up to the final bastion. These were built between 1570 and 1586 by its former owner, Georg Khevenhüller, to ward off invading Turks. There's a lift, and an armoury inside has lots of medieval exhibits. It's closed in winter and Mondays in shoulder seasons.

Gurk's Religious Pedigree
Romanesque cathedral and museum

Just over an hour from Klagenfurt by train and bus, the small town of Gurk (Krka in Slovenian) is famous for its **Dom zu Gurk**, built in the 12th century and Austria's foremost church from the Romanesque epoch; it also has Gothic, baroque and rococo elements. The remarkable crypt *(€2.50)*, dating from 1174, is supported by 100 pillars and contains the Tomb of St Hemma of Gurk. The complex's early-baroque high altar has an astounding 72 statues and 82 angel heads, whereas the frescoes in the Bischofskapelle (dating from around 1200) are all the more beautiful for the use of raw colours.

The **Schatzkammer** *(treasury; adult/child €10/5)* in the neighbouring **Diözesanmuseum** (Diocesan Museum) contains treasures spanning the Romanesque period to the baroque. It's open May to October and closed Mondays.

Hüttenberg Meets Himalaya
Heinrich Harrer Museum and walkway

Step off the bus in the tiny former mining village of Hüttenberg and you might be forgiven for thinking you've stumbled into the Himalayas. The fluttering prayer flags rising up the cliff are somewhat unexpected. Hüttenberg is the birthplace of Heinrich Harrer, famous mountaineer (he was in the party that made the first ascent of the Eiger's fearsome North Face in Switzerland) and Himalayan explorer. The **Heinrich Harrer Museum** *(huettenberg.at; adult/child €15/9)* is packed with items shipped back from Harrer's expeditions to various corners of the world, with a section devoted to Harrer himself. It's open May to October from Thursdays to Sundays (daily in July and August).

Across the road from the museum is a Buddhist **Lingkor** *(€2)*. The metal staircases cling to the side of a sheer cliff (it's not for vertigo sufferers) and pass prayer wheels and rock paintings.

Back to the Middle Ages
Visit medieval Friesach

Situated one hour by train north of Klagenfurt near the border of Styria, sleepy **Friesach** is Carinthia's oldest town. The ruins of four fortresses punctuate the hilltops above town, while the centre is flanked by a moat and imposing greystone walls.

If you have time, you can walk between all four fortress ruins along picturesque paths, although the nicest sections are also the easiest to explore: **Petersberg** and **Rotturm** (Red Tower), directly above the centre. There are lovely views from **Peterskirche** *(kath-kirche-kaernten.at)*, a pretty village church you can reach by following a path from the Gothic **St Bartholomew Church** *(kath-kirche-kaernten.at)*. Just south of Rotturm are the ruins of the fourth fortress, **Virgilienberg**. Plan on about two hours without stops to walk to all of these.

FRIESACH'S FAMOUS FESTIVAL

Friesach is a sleepy, rather remote town, but it comes to life on the last Saturday in July during its **Spectaculum festival** *(spectaculum-friesach.at)*. On these two days every two years, the town gates are locked and everyone dresses up in medieval costumes.

Friesach reenacts its history, with jesters, princesses and knights strolling around the town juggling, fire-eating and staging jousting tournaments and duels. Friesach even reverts to the currency that made it famous, with medieval meals from street stalls being paid for with Friesach pennies. It is this medieval throwback feel that makes it a place worth visiting.

The years 2026 and 2028 are the ones to watch out for it.

Millstätter See

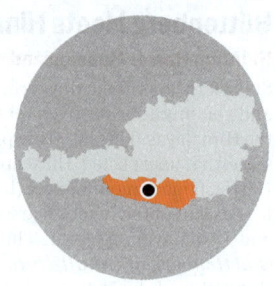

HIKING & BIKING | HISTORIC ABBEY | SWIMMING

GETTING AROUND

Frequent buses run from outside the train station in Spittal an der Drau to the Millstätter See, going first to Seeboden and continuing on to Millstatt and Döbriach. The trip to Millstatt only takes about 20 minutes.

A relatively easy 30km bike path runs around the lake, which links Millstatt, Seeboden and Döbriach, with places to stop off for refreshment along the way.

Boats operated by **Millstätter See Schifffahrt** *(millstaetterseeschifffahrt.at)* also serve the lake from May to October, with eight stops taking in the main towns. The complete lake circuit takes 2½ hours, and the panorama section between Millstatt and Döbriach 1½ hours. The towns themselves are relatively flat and easy to walk around.

Located just outside Spittal an der Drau at an altitude of almost 600m, Millstätter See is one of Carinthia's finest lakes. It extends for just under 12km and is less than 2km wide at its widest point. The main towns on the lake are Millstatt, with its magnificent Romanesque abbey, and the more functional Seeboden, both on the northeast shoreline. This side of the lake is largely developed along the shore, whereas across the lake is a large expanse of forest where development is restricted.

A cycle path and walking tracks run around the perimeter, and there's equipment hire aplenty in Millstatt. Leave the shoreline and you find yourself in mountains, accessible from Millstatt by a toll road and leading to some good hikes, fantastic views and a couple of good meadow huts where you can satisfy an appetite or thirst. If you are into open-water swimming, the southwest shoreline is a good place to set out from.

Millstatt's Romanesque Abbey
Visit historic Stift Millstatt

Nestled just above Lake Millstatt in the eponymous town of Millstatt is a magnificent and atmospheric Romanesque **Benedictine abbey**. It was founded in 1077 and, as then, is Millstatt's cultural epicentre today. The beautiful complex consists of the moderately interesting **Stiftsmuseum** *(stiftsmuseum.at; adult/child €7/3.50)*, an attractive 11th-century abbey church, a graveyard and abbey buildings south of the church with lovely yards and arcades.

On the main approach to the church you pass a **1000-year-old lime tree**, today on private property in a small yard just off the access path. The abbey grounds, and especially the arcades and cloisters, exude tranquillity through their age and symmetry. You will also find works of contemporary art

MILLSTÄTTER SEE

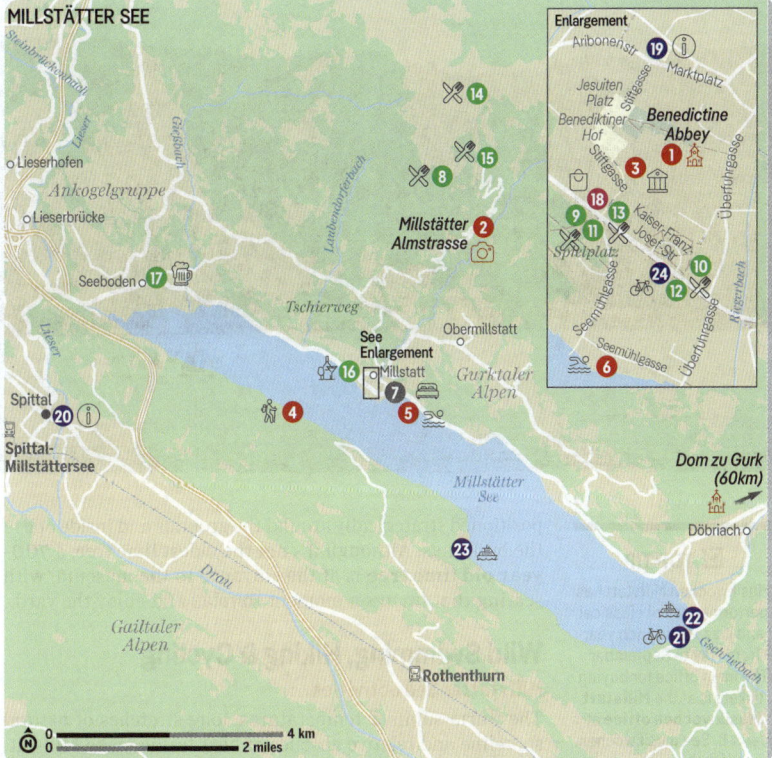

- **HIGHLIGHTS**
  1. Benedictine Abbey
  2. Millstätter Almstrasse
- **SIGHTS**
  3. Stiftsmuseum
- **ACTIVITIES**
  4. Slow Trail Südufer
  5. Surf und Segelschule Millstatt
  6. Wassersport Strobl
- **SLEEPING**
  7. Hotel See-Villa
- **EATING**
  8. Alexanderhütte
  9. Butcher's Steakhaus
  10. Columbia
  11. Due Cuori e Prosciutto
  12. Fisch-Häusl Stark
  13. Lindenhof
  14. Millstätterhütte
  15. Schwaigerhütte
- **DRINKING & NIGHTLIFE**
  16. Kap 4613
  17. Weinzeit
- **SHOPPING**
  18. Souvenir Shop
- **INFORMATION**
  19. Millstatt Musikwochen Office
  20. Tourist Office
- **TRANSPORT**
  21. Charly's Seelounge
  22. Döbriach-Glanz Ferry Jetty
  23. Laggerhof Ferry Jetty
  24. Mountainbike Station Thomas Graf

TOP TIP

Musikwochen Millstatt has performances of classical and jazz music each year from May to September. The main office for buying tickets is at the **Millstatt Musikwochen office** at Markt 8. See musikwochen.com for the programme. Millstatt also has the best places to eat, drink and relax.

positioned strategically around the grounds and inside one of the buildings. Although it's not the oldest lime tree, a **700-year old lime tree** is at the entrance to the museum, with seating that invites a moment to relax and enjoy the yard.

Wild Swimming, Hiking & Cycling
Millstätter See activities

The warm summer temperatures, long stretches of natural shoreline and relative absence of boat traffic make Millstätter See ideal for **wild swimming**. Situated at an altitude of 558m, the lake often reaches a summer temperature of 25°C. A couple of times a year in July and August the local lifesaving association organises a 1km group swim to Grossegg, directly across from Millstatt township, which is a fun swim if you're a keen group swimmer. Doing it independently is also possible for experienced open-water enthusiasts. See 'Events' at millstaettersee.com.

An excellent section of the 12km-long lake is on the southern shore. The roughly 5km stretch from Grossegg to Seeboden is mostly adjacent to mixed deciduous and conifer forest without roads nearby. To combine it with walking and

EATING IN MILLSTATT: OUR PICKS

Fisch-Häusl Stark: (Millstatt) Takeaway and pavement stand-up place for fresh Millstätter See and Weissensee fish. *hours vary* €

Due Cuori e Prosciutto: Italian restaurant serving light dishes and Neapolitan pizza, plus hams, hence the name 'two hearts and ham'. *11.30am-10pm Mon & Wed-Sun* €€

Butcher's Steakhaus: Serves a range of steaks plus polenta and grilled vegetable dish for non-meat eaters. Opposite the abbey. *5-9pm Mon-Tue & Fri-Sat, noon-8pm Sun* €€

Hotel See-Villa: The historic hotel restaurant, located on the lake, serves dishes drawing on lake fish, game, seasonal vegetables and fine wines. *noon-1.45pm & 6-9pm* €€€

Millstätter See

ferry transport, take the **ferry** from Millstatt and follow the mountain-bike trail uphill (cyclists with mountain bikes can follow this **Millstätter Radweg** back to Millstatt or do a complete 28km circuit of the lake) until the so-called **Slow Trail Südufer** for walkers veers off after about 20 minutes. This pleasant, gnarly rooted serpentine hiking track winds 4.7km to Seeboden.

A few hundred metres into it you find some decent entry points to start swimming, and it's easy to get out elsewhere, combining the swim with a hike. Kayakers and SUP-ers can do the same from the water, but because getting back is less of a problem, you could also easily go off in the other direction towards **Döbriach-Glanz ferry jetty**.

Swimmers have the option of returning from Seeboden by frequent bus or infrequent ferry; if swimming eastwards, there's also a ferry from **Laggerhof ferry jetty**, along with buses from Döbriach-Glanz. Keep within your limits and experience for whatever activity you decide to do, especially if swimming early or late in the season when the water may get chilly.

WHERE TO RENT EQUIPMENT

Souvenir shop: For equipment, the souvenir-type shop alongside Stift Millstatt usually gets a delivery of dry bags each summer (but it is best to pack your own swimming buoy).

Wassersport Strobl: On the shore at Seemühlgasse, this sports hotel has all manner of vessels that float on water, such as kayaks, SUPs, row boats and yachts. *pensionstrobl.at/bootsverleih*

Surf und Segelschule Millstatt: Alongside Villa Verdin, with a range of sailing boats, SUPs and kayaks. *segelschulemillstatt.at*

Mountainbike Station Thomas Graf: Conventional and e-bikes for hire in Millstatt. *mountainbikestation.at*

Papin Sport: Has drop-off and pick-up points at Spittal an der Drau (at the tourist office (p315) and in Döbriach at **Charly's Seelounge**.

DRINKING AT MILLSTÄTTER SEE

Weinzeit: This wine bar in Seeboden is the perfect spot for a fine Austrian drop on a warm day in summer or indoors in winter. *2-10pm Mon & Tue, 9am-10pm Wed-Sat*

Kap 4613: (Millstatt) Atrium with a deck area and a beach bar extending over the water, with breakfasts and a healthy buffet lunch. *8.30am-8pm Tue-Sat, to 6pm Sun*

Columbia: (Millstatt) On the main square, Columbia is part of a constellation of restaurant, cafe, pastry shop and a cinema that also has music. *hours vary* €€

Lindenhof: Also a restaurant serving Austrian classics, it does light dishes and quenches a thirst in the outdoor terrace section. *11am-11pm* €€

HEMMA PILGRIM'S WAY

All roads may lead to Rome, but eight pilgrim's ways lead to the **cathedral** (p308) in Gurk, where St Hemma of Gurk (Ema Krška in Slovenian) lies in the magnificent cathedral crypt.

One picturesque section runs from the abbey in Millstatt to Kleinkirchheim, 26km away, from where it continues to Gurk (85km in all).

According to legend, the pilgrimage to Gurk dates back to the 11th century, when Hemma wished to found a church in Škofja Loka (Slovenia). Inhabitants opposed her and drove her out. After their harvests failed, they resolved to make a pilgrimage to seek forgiveness in Gurk, where Hemma had founded the Benedictine monastery in 1036.

Dom zu Gurk (p308)

Millstätter Almstrasse
Panorama road and hikes

Starting in Tschierweg, 3km north of Millstatt, **Millstätter Almstrasse** *(seeundberg.at/wandern/panoramastrassen; car/bike €9/free)* is a narrow, winding toll road that from May to October takes you high above the lake on asphalt and gravel to the **Schwaigerhütte** (1625m), from where you can set off on easy walks to other meadow huts.

From the 1786m **Alexanderhütte** *(alexanderalm.at)*, 30 minutes from the Schwaigerhütte by foot, you can pick up the **Sentiero dell'Amore** (Love Trail) on an easy 6.5km walk to Granattor, an artificial granite gate that frames stupendous views over the lake. Plan about three to four hours each way for the walk. You'll pass **Millstätterhütte** *(millstaetterhuette.at)*, at 1880m, and some poetic surprises along the way.

Pick up the free bilingual (German and English) **Wander-Zeit Westkarte** from a tourist office to plan your connecting walks. See **Nockmobil** *(nockmobil.at)* for the call bus and prices for the huts.

Beyond Millstätter See

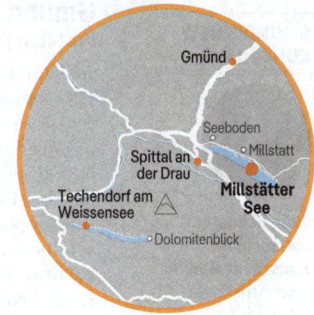

Dip a toe into the fine arts in the medieval artists' town of Gmünd before plunging into Austria's highest swimmable alpine lake.

While Millstätter See is the beating heart of this part of Carinthia, most travellers will pass through Spittal an der Drau to reach it. It is a pleasant and friendly town but one low on sights except for a regional folk museum. North of this, and also reached by bus from 'Spittal', is the beautiful artists' community of Gmünd, an intact medieval walled town with galleries and an excellent art museum. Travel west of Millstätter See and you reach Austria's highest swimmable alpine lake, Weissensee, and magnificent high-country walks, cycling, mountain biking and swimming in crystal clear waters. Those who take the pace off their journey are well rewarded here with spectacular landscapes and fine outdoor activities.

Places
Spittal an der Drau p315
Gmünd p316
Techendorf am Weissensee p316

GETTING AROUND

You can reach Techendorf on Weissensee two ways. From Hermagor take bus 5066 from Gasserplatz, and change to a nature park bus (marked NPB on timetables) at Kreuzberg bei Weissensee (Hotel Kreuzwirt) for Techendorf. From Spittal/Drau-Millstätter See Bahnhof, take the train to Greifenburg-Weissensee Bahnhof and pick up bus 5068 to Techendorf, or to Kreuzberg bei Weissensee and get the nature park bus. The NPB runs around the lake.

Regular buses run from Spittal an der Drau to Gmünd.

Spittal an der Drau

Lake springboard & museum

TIME FROM MILLSTÄTTER SEE: **20MINS**

Lacking the lure of the lake, Spittal an der Drau is a town you will most likely use as your springboard to Millstätter See, Gmünd or further north to Bad Gastein (p286). If you're based here or have time, drop by **Schloss Porcia**, with its eye-catching Renaissance edifice and **Museum für Volkskultur** (Heritage Museum; museum-spittal.com; adult/child €10/5). The museum has 3D infotainment exhibits on Carinthia's landscape, and a focus on local artisans, mining, skiing and mountain climbing. The **tourist office** in Spittal is in the same building as the museum, and is a pick-up and drop-off point for Papin Sport bike rental.

Spittal an der Drau is also a good base for visiting the **Nockberge Biosphere Reserve** (biosphaerenparknockberge.at), a high-country cultural landscape of Swiss pines, larch trees and meadows north of Millstätter See, with a very good sprinkling of alpine flora and fauna.

GMÜND'S NEW KUNSTHAUS

Julia Schuster is curator of the **Kunsthaus Gmünd**. @kuenstlerstadt_gmuend

The Kunsthaus Gmünd sees itself as a place for vibrant encounters with international art. We've deliberately placed our focus on international printmaking, which offers a direct way to experience the artistic signature of great masters – it is experimental, versatile, technically demanding and yet very accessible.

Over nearly three decades, Gmünd has earned an excellent reputation in this field. Architecturally, the Kunsthaus Gmünd brings together history and the present day into a whole, contrasting historical elements like stucco ceilings and original box windows with a minimalist, contemporary wall design.

Gmünd
TIME FROM SPITTAL/DRAU-MILLSTÄTTER SEE: **25MINS**

Water, light & sound

Just 15km north of Millstätter See, Gmünd is an attractive 11th-century town with a delightful walled centre and 14th-century hilltop castle. It fell to ruins after the Hungarians occupied the town for seven years from 1480, using it as their base to plunder the region.

Today, life here is noticeably quieter and the castle is a setting for plays and musical events. Gmünd has an abundance of artists' ateliers, as well as the offbeat and fascinating **Pankratium** *(pankratium.at; adult/child €14/7)*, an extraordinary space bringing together water, light and sound in hands-on pieces designed for the senses. You can bring sound gadgets and all manner of instruments to life on a tour that includes bubble-blowing in the yard. It's a sure-fire winner with kids, but an intriguing excursion into a universe of the senses for anyone. It is open from May to October, but closed Mondays. Book ahead to be sure of a spot.

International printmaking

While ducking into the atmospheric backstreets streets of Gmünd or simply strolling along its main street, you quickly realise how much this medieval city is today built on art. **Kunsthaus Gmünd** *(kuenstlerstadt-gmuend.at; adult/child €15/6)* is the latest addition to the scene, housed in an historic building that makes clever use of its protected status to create a fascinating artistic space for printmaking. It kicked off its opening year in 2025 with an unusual exhibition of printmaking by David Hockney. As you move through the 10 rooms, you not only appreciate the works of art but also the eye-catching features of the space itself. The 400-year old tiled oven in the men's bathroom is just one of these. The gallery is open daily late May to early October.

Techendorf am Weissensee
TIME FROM SPITTAL/DRAU-MILLSTÄTTER SEE: **1½HRS**

Swimming, alpine meadows & huts

Wedged within a glacial cleft in the Gailtal Alps with mountain ridges flanking its northern and southern shores, **Weissensee** *(weissensee.com)* is Carinthia's highest swimmable glacial lake, the least developed of Carinthia's large lakes, and a spectacular and peaceful nature reserve. It stretches as a

EATING & DRINKING IN SPITTAL AN DER DRAU & GMÜND

Juicy Lucy: Breakfast, brunch and daytime menu including delicious salads, pasta, homemade lemonade and more in Spittal an der Drau. *8am-9pm Wed-Sat* €€

El Venado: Mexican and Tex-Mex restaurant and bar in Spittal's Hotel Ertl, with a lovely outdoor verandah, doubling as a cocktail bar. *from 5pm Tue-Sat* €€

The Satisfactory: Part of the Hotel Erlebnis Post in Spittal, with different elements: microbrewery, bar, Thai food, Austrian food in Zellot and pizza. *hours vary* €€

Alte Burg: Traditional Austrian cuisine, mostly from locally sourced ingredients. Nestled above town in the former fortress. *noon-8pm Wed-Sat* €€

Weissensee

turquoise-and-deep-blue slither for almost 12km and in most parts is about 1km wide. Because it's at an altitude of 930m, the water is cooler than Wörthersee's, but in July and August you can expect temperatures of above 20°C in most parts.

From the southern edge of Techendorf, the main town on Weissensee, **Bergbahn Weissensee** *(single adult/child €16/10, return €23.50/14)* swings up the mountainside on a 12-minute chairlift ride to a mountain station near **Naggler Nock** (1324m), from where it's a 10-minute walk to **Naggler Alm** *(naggleralm.at)*, a popular meadow hut and the starting point for walks, more difficult hikes and mountain biking. In winter, the chairlift serves skiing and snowshoeing enthusiasts. From Naggler Alm the walk to **Kohlröslhütte** *(kohlroesl.at)* takes 1½ hours (4km), mostly across meadows with views into the lake valley, passing the working homestead Jadersdorfer Ochsenalm.

The views from Kohlrösslhütte are stupendous: deep into the Gitsch Valley to Sankt Lorenz and the Alps in three countries from an altitude of 1534m. Along the way, stop at one or more **meadow huts** for a delicious cold platter and refreshment. Check varying opening times on the websites.

A nice trail for mountain bikers or walkers – the Naggler Alm path is not an official mountain-bike trail – starts from **Paterzipf** (near the town of Naggl) and leads to **Hermagorer Bodenalm** *(hermagorer-bodenalm.at)*, at 1231m, through forest on a broad track for much of the 4km from Naggl. Sitting very prettily in an alpine meadow, this 'hut' makes its own cheese and cured meats to sustain hikers and mountain bikers during the day and, like Kohlrösslhütte, feeds and puts up hikers for the night. Several fully fledged mountain bike trails are signposted from Naggler Alm.

TOLL ROAD PRACTICALITIES

The main access road into the Nockberge Biosphere Reserve is eponymous **Nockalmstrasse** *(nockalmstrasse.at)*, a 34km summer toll road. It is generally open from May to late October, and is weather-dependent. Motorbikes are not allowed on it from 6pm to 8am.

If you're heading north to Bad Gastein (p286) from Spittal an der Drau, you'll need to use the **Autoschleuse Tauernbahn** *(Railway Car Shuttle Service; gasteinertal.com/autoschleuse)* through the 8370m-long tunnel from Mallnitz to Böckstein. Trains depart every hour.

You drive onto the wagon at the loading point (apply the handbrake and make sure the vehicle is in first gear) and then take your seat in a panorama carriage. It takes 12 minutes to get through the tunnel.

Lienz & the Dolomites

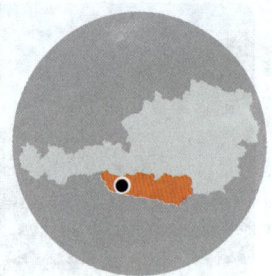

HIKING | CYCLING | SKIING

GETTING AROUND

The S1 and intercity trains will deliver you from Spittal an der Drau in an hour or less (the S1 is free if you have a valid guest card for regional trains; p296). The main train station in Lienz is just a couple of minutes on foot from the centre of town, whereas Schloss Bruck (the museum) is a stiff 30-minute walk from the station, or a 20-minute bus ride and uphill walk.

To get to the Aguntum museum and ruins, take bus 940/941 to Strebach. Summer buses leave half-hourly to Tristacher See from the bus station (at the train station). Papin Sport, behind the train station, is mainly a drop-off point for rented bikes, but does rentals as well. Book ahead to be sure of getting one in midsummer.

Rising up like a beautiful amphitheatre, the Dolomites are the defining feature of this small but rugged region situated in Tyrol, just a few kilometres from the border to Carinthia. At its heart is Lienz, a town of around 12,000 inhabitants with a strong Italian influence, straddling the Drau River as this gurgles north from its mountain source in Italy's Alto Adige (South Tyrol). The Drau is joined by the Isel River at a confluence close to the centre of town.

In winter Lienz is a hub for skiing on the pistes around Zettersfeld, and Hochstein just west of Lienz. In summer, it's a fantastic place to get on your bike – preferably an e-bike unless you're into sweaty ascents – and cycle into the Dolomites to the Dolomitenhütte and around, a mountain restaurant hut with views over the Dolomites. Along the way you can cool off in a lake, and before or afterwards check out a couple of Lienz's historical highlights.

Cycle to Dolomitenhütte Outside Lienz
Dramatic alpine restaurant

The Dolomites exert a magnetic force for the outdoors inclined, and there is no better way to succumb to this force in summer than on a 12km bike ride to the spectacular alpine restaurant **Dolomitenhütte** *(dolomitenresort.at)* near Lienz, with mesmerising views from the terrace. Throw yourself into a mountain lake on the way up or down and you have the makings of an invigorating day. From behind the train station at Lienz, cycle across the bridge, turn left and follow Tristacher Strasse. Signs later point the way to Dolomitenhütte. After the turn-offs, the hard stuff begins and you climb a continuously steep gradient through deciduous mixed forest and past a turn-off to Tristacher See (6km), at an altitude of 821m, with an almost vertical cliff-face on one side and excellent swimming along its almost 500m length.

LIENZ & THE DOLOMITES

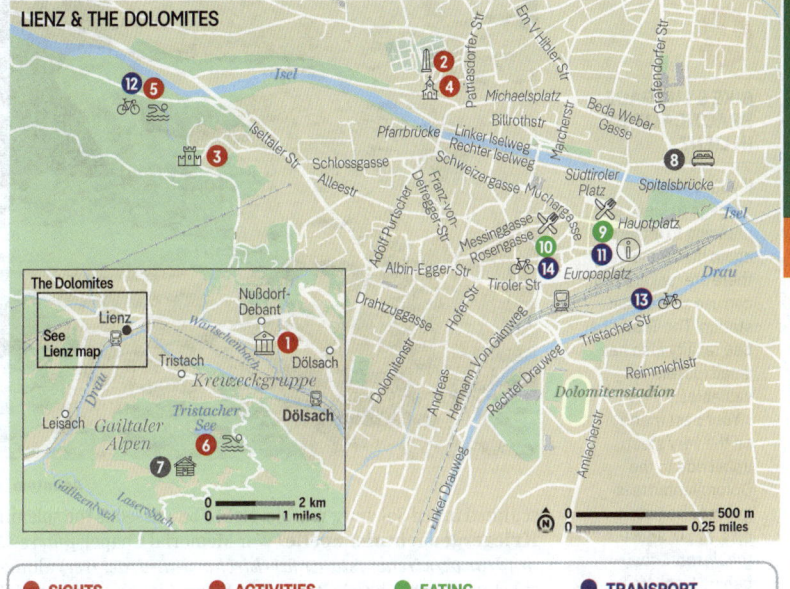

- **SIGHTS**
  1. Aguntum
  2. Kriegergedächtniskapelle
  3. Schloss Bruck
  4. Stadtpfarrkirche St Andrä
- **ACTIVITIES**
  5. Cool's
  6. Tristacher See
- **SLEEPING**
  7. Dolomitenhütte
  8. Grand Hotel Lienz
- **EATING**
  9. Da Leonardo
  see 7 Dolomitenhütte
  10. Himmelblau
- **INFORMATION**
  11. Tourist Office
- **TRANSPORT**
  12. Bikerent24
  13. Papin Sport
  14. Probike Lienz

As the climb continues, you leave the deciduous tree line, pass through attractive meadows and finally reach the hut, which clings to a 1600m clifftop like an eagle's nest. It is watched over by the bare faces of the Dolomites and its dramatic peaks. Trails ranging from easy to difficult lead out from the hut. To top up with mountain-pure water, follow the track off to the left of the hut for a couple of minutes to a wooden **drinking trough** and flowing water. After enjoying the views and home cooking on the terrace, consider soothing aching muscles in the cool waters of **Tristacher See** (dolomitenbad.at; adult/child €7/3.50) again on the way down.

Cultural Lienz

Museums, church and excavations

Lienz's major cultural attraction is **Schloss Bruck**, with its **Egger-Lienz-Galerie** (museum-schlossbruck.at; adult/child €10/2.50) devoted to the emotive works of painter Albin Egger-Lienz. It's open from June to October, but closed Mondays; check summer opening times.

Another of the city's cultural highlights is **Stadtpfarrkirche St Andrä** (pfarre-st-andrae.at), which has a startling baroque altar, 14th-century frescoes and a pair of unusual tombstones

☑ TOP TIP

Winter skiing and summer hiking action takes place above town, serviced by a cable car and lifts. Check out lienzer-bergbahnen.at for more. The **tourist office** (osttirol.com) in Lienz stocks lots of hiking maps and can give suggestions.

BIKE & LUGGAGE PRACTICALITIES IN LIENZ

If you're taking luggage to Lienz and planning to move on again that same day, there are lockers you can use at the train station. The Tristacher See facility also has small lockers for valuables.

Your best friend on the very steep, uphill ride to the Dolomitenhütte is going to be your bike. **Papin Sport** *(papinsport.com)* behind Lienz train station has excellent conventional and e-bikes, including sufficiently powerful e-mountain bikes that will easily cover the distance to the hut for the average cyclist. Renting from Papin Sport in Villach is another option.

Two other bike rental places in town are **Probike Lienz** *(probike-lienz.at)* and **Bikerent24**, which also organises e-bike tours and works with **Cool's** *(cools-lienz.at)*. Cool's also offers rafting and canyoning.

Agluntum

sculpted in red Salzburg marble. Not to be missed is the solemn **Kriegergedächtniskapelle** (War Memorial Chapel; *pfarre-st-andrae.at/kirchen/stadtpfarrkirche-st-andrae; free*) alongside the church. This shelters Albin Egger-Lienz's controversial frescoes, one depicting an emaciated Jesus post-resurrection, which in 1925 so scandalised the Vatican that religious activity was banned here for the next 60-odd years. If it's closed, pick up keys from the Kirchenwirt restaurant nearby.

The Romans came to the region about 2000 years ago, and inevitably vanished again – though not without trace, for it was here that they built Aguntum, a bustling centre of trade and culture. Today, the museum **Aguntum** *(aguntum.at; adult/child €7/4)* in Dölsach, 4km outside Lienz, lets you to explore everything Roman through artefacts, tools and frescoes before their decline from the 3rd century. You can take a stroll through the archaeological park while you're here.

EATING & DRINKING IN LIENZ & THE DOLOMITES

Dolomitenhütte: Order a hearty goulash and other simple fare here and enjoy it with stupendous views over the Dolomites from the terrace. *11.30am-8.30pm* €

Himmelblau: This popular restaurant in Lienz walks a broad culinary line from Mexican omelette and tapas to chicken on skewers and steaks. *5-10pm Tue-Sat* €€

Da Leonardo: Large restaurant on the main square serving delicious pizza and pasta dishes with genuine Italian flavours, also with outdoor tables. *9am-10.30pm* €€

Laite: In Sappada (Italy), with seasonal Italian cuisine in this historic homestead. See ristorantelaite.com to book. *noon-2pm & 7-9pm Fri-Tue* €€€

Places We Love to Stay

€ Budget   €€ Midrange   €€€ Top End

Klagenfurt & Wörthersee   MAP p299

Jugend- und Familien-gästehaus Klagenfurt € Close to Wörthersee, this modern hostel has double rooms that can be booked as singles and dorms, with ground-floor wheelchair access.

Sandwirth €€ Contemporary, comfortable and central. Apartments ideal for families.

Hotel Palais Porcia €€ Faux-classical statues and ornate furnishings. In the heart of town.

Garner Hotel Moser Verdino Klagenfurt by IHG €€ Located in the centre of town in an historic building, with quiet, contemporary rooms, good breakfasts and rooftop bar.

Seehotel Porcia €€€ In Pörtschach and on Wörthersee, with a private beach, free private parking and elegantly decorated rooms in antique styles, some with lake views.

Villach   MAP P304

Hotel Mosser €€ The cheapest singles are small, but otherwise this central hotel has excellent rooms, including doubles and suites with whirlpool. Friendly cafe downstairs.

Hermagor

Villa Blumegg €€ Located on a hill about 10 minutes' walk to the centre, with comfortable rooms, some with balconies. Outdoor pool.

Hüttenberg

Schloss Süssenstein €€ Just up from the museum, this castle has large rooms with antique furnishings.

Friesach

Metnitztalerhof €€ At the top of the main square, this four-star hotel has contemporary rooms, views to the hills or town, and a restaurant.

St Veit an der Glan

Kunsthotel Fuchspalast €€ The eccentric exterior and lobby and mystical symbolism in this historic Ernst Fuchs design hotel give way to modern rooms.

Hotel Taggenbrunn €€ Hotel, restaurant and vineyard 4km east of St Veit at the foot of Burg Taggenbrunn, with activities and panorama lift nearby.

Gurk

Kronenwirt € Across from the cathedral, this historic hotel has rooms with balconies and mountain or garden views, and does a good breakfast.

Jufa Hotel Stift Gurk €€ Alongside the cathedral, this hotel-hostel retreat has attractively furnished rooms, ayurveda health centre, sauna and a quiet, green setting.

Millstatt   MAP P311

Hotel See-Villa €€ Turn-of-the-20th-century hotel with a terrace restaurant, private sauna and swimming jetty.

Villa Verdin €€ Sought-after 19th-century lakeshore villa-hotel with retro furnishings, beach bar and restaurant on the shoreline. LGBTIQ+ friendly.

Spittal an der Drau

Hotel Ertl €€ Located across from the station, with comfortable rooms, large outdoor pool, and the on-site **El Venado** (p316) Tex-Mex restaurant.

Hotel Erlebnis Post €€ Themed or business rooms in this Spittal an der Drau hotel, with the Zellot restaurant and **The Satisfactory** (p316) microbrewery and bar.

Gmünd

Gasthof Kohlmayr €€ Cosy rooms with private bathrooms in a 400-year-old building in the heart of town. Free parking.

Hotel Restaurant Platzer €€ Located across the river from the old town but still central, with modern rooms. It has mountain views.

Weissensee

Hermagorer Bodenalm (p317) **€€** Above the lake, this historic meadow hut has simple rooms, milking cows and half-board if you wish.

Kohlröslhütte (p317) **€€** Free transfer is available to this meadow hut if you book the half-board minimum of three nights. Otherwise, enjoy the hike here for simple rooms and an outdoor swimming pool.

Strandhotel am Weissensee €€€ Located in Neusach, this wellness hotel stands out for its rooms with lake views, quality cuisine, a beach cafe, private beach and spa treatments.

Lienz   p319

Dolomitenhütte €€ The six panorama rooms are on the edge of the abyss, with views into the Dolomites.

Grand Hotel Lienz €€€ Five-star hotel with spa and pool. Terrace dining overlooks the Isel River and the Dolomites.

THE GUIDE

TYROL & VORARLBERG

For places to stay in Tyrol & Vorarlberg, see p378

Above: Innsbruck (p328); Right: Golden Eagle

THE MAIN AREAS

INNSBRUCK
Cultured capital with soaring views.
p328

THE ZILLERTAL
Year-round action in the Alps.
p340

KITZBÜHEL
Ritzy slopes of Olympic legend.
p348

Researched by Kerry Walker

Tyrol & Vorarlberg

ALPINE VISTAS AND FOLK TRADITIONS

Willkommen to the most Austrian of states, where regal palaces, cloud-grazing Alps and pinch-yourself-pretty villages will send your soul spiralling as high as the region's famous golden eagles.

There's no place like Tyrol for the 'wow, I'm in Austria' feeling. Nowhere else in the country is the downhill skiing as exhilarating, the après-ski as pumping, the wooden chalets as chocolate boxy, the food as hearty. Whether you're schussing down the legendary slopes of Kitzbühel, cycling the Zillertal or hiking in the Alps with a flawlessly blue sky overhead, the sublime scenery here makes you glad to be alive.

Welcome to a place where snowboarders brag under the low beams of a medieval tavern about awesome descents, where *Dirndls* and *Lederhosen* have street cred, and where *Volksmusik* (folk music) features on club playlists.

While you can find pulse-quickening outdoor pursuits in any given corner of the Austrian Alps, Tyrol has the year-round edge – whether you want to glacier ski, hike above the treeline over crags from hut to alpine hut at eye level with eagles and ibex, drift above the summits paragliding or throw yourself into a foaming turquoise river for some white-water rafting. Nature here is wholly embraced.

The Arlberg Alps give way to rolling dairy country in pleasingly low-key Vorarlberg. Spilling east to the glittering expanse of Bodensee (Lake Constance), this eastern pocket of the country swings happily between ecofriendly architecture on the cutting edge of design and deeply traditional hamlets with more cows than people.

THE ÖTZTAL
Big wilderness and prehistory.
p356

ST ANTON AM ARLBERG
Outdoor thrills, scary slopes and après-ski.
p362

BREGENZ
Festival-loving city by the lake.
p369

Find Your Way

Snuggled in among some of the country's highest Alps, Tyrol and Vorarlberg are way bigger than they look on paper. Choose your base and strike out from there. Public transport will get you pretty much everywhere.

Bregenz, p369
On the shimmering shores of Bodensee, this petite city delivers a big hit of culture, with avant-garde architecture, arts and a mammoth summer opera festival.

St Anton am Arlberg, p362
The snow doesn't get hotter than in St Anton am Arlberg, where the first ski club in the Alps was born and people party as hard as they ski.

The Ötztal, p356
You'll be struck by the wild beauty of this alpine valley, whether soaking in a spa, pounding the slopes, white-water rafting or exploring the Neolithic world of Ötzi, the ice man.

CAR
Shadowing the Inn River, the east–west Inntal Autobahn (A12) cuts the province into almost equal halves, entering from Germany near Kufstein and exiting west of St Anton in Vorarlberg. The A13 connects Tyrol with Italy, crossing the Brenner Pass directly south of Innsbruck.

TRAIN
The main route in and out of Tyrol follows the Inntal (Inn Valley). ÖBB *(oebb.at)* trains operate a frequent, efficient and inexpensive service to most destinations and journey times are short: it takes just over an hour to get from Innsbruck to Kitzbühel or St Anton am Arlberg.

BUS
Regional transport, covering buses, trams and trains, is run by the Verkehrsverbund Tirol *(vvt.at)*. Buses join the dots to smaller villages and towns embedded deep in alpine valleys that do not have train stations.

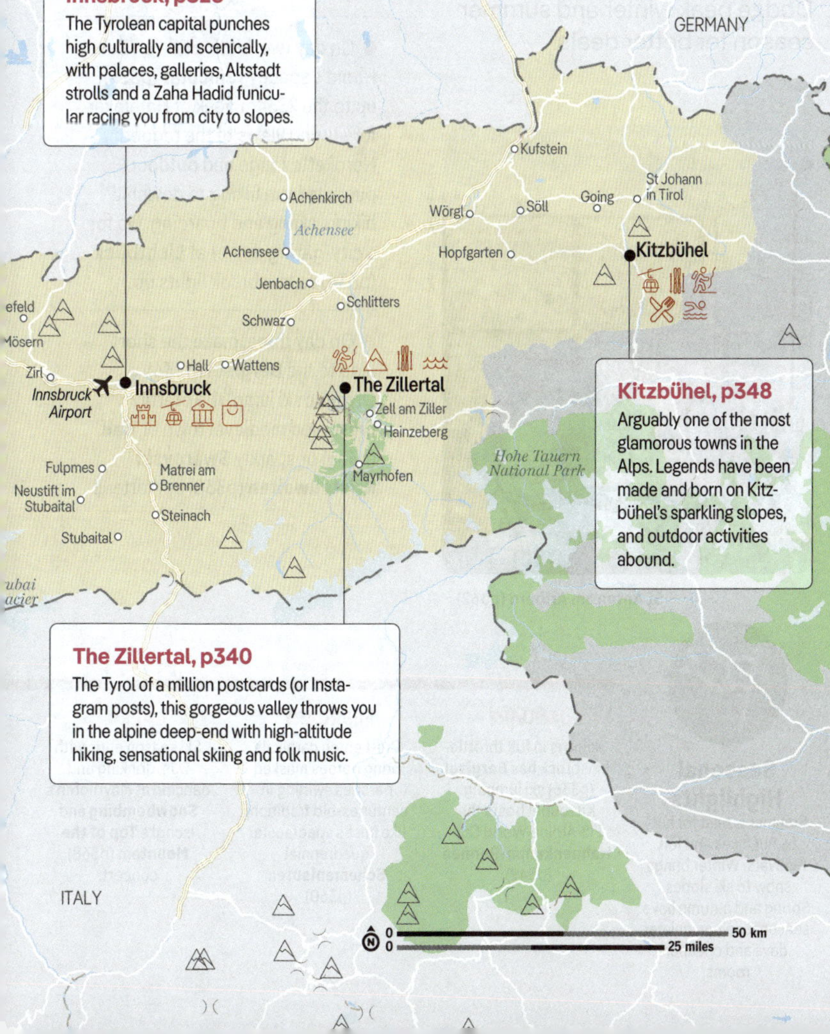

Innsbruck, p328
The Tyrolean capital punches high culturally and scenically, with palaces, galleries, Altstadt strolls and a Zaha Hadid funicular racing you from city to slopes.

Kitzbühel, p348
Arguably one of the most glamorous towns in the Alps. Legends have been made and born on Kitzbühel's sparkling slopes, and outdoor activities abound.

The Zillertal, p340
The Tyrol of a million postcards (or Instagram posts), this gorgeous valley throws you in the alpine deep-end with high-altitude hiking, sensational skiing and folk music.

Plan Your Time

Tyrol is too big for just one bite. Plan your time wisely, combining a day or two in Innsbruck with a few days in the mountains. Dodge peak winter and summer season for better deals.

St Anton am Arlberg (p362)

A Long Weekend

● Base yourself in cultured, Alp-rimmed **Innsbruck** (p328), beginning with a historic romp of the Altstadt and its most distinctive landmark **Goldenes Dachl** (p332), domed **Stadtturm** (p334), lavish imperial palace **Hofburg** (p328) and royal court church **Hofkirche** (p328).

● On day two, hitch a ride on Zaha Hadid's spacey **funicular** (p329) up to the 2334m peak of Hafelekar for stirring views of the ragged Nordkette range and outdoor pursuits from hiking to downhill biking, skiing and boarding. Go for a city-gazing dinner at **Lichtblick** (p334) as Innsbruck lights up.

● On day three, make the short leap to the **Bergisel** (p336) Olympic ski jump, the prettily preserved medieval town of **Hall** (p336) or sparkly **Swarovski Kristallwelten** (p338) in Wattens.

Seasonal Highlights

Summer is best for hut-to-hut hikes and folk festivals. Winter brings snow to ski slopes. Spring and autumn have seasonal colour, quieter days and cheaper rooms.

JANUARY
Skiing is in full throttle. Innsbruck has **Bergisel** (p336) ski jumping. Kitzbühel hosts the FIS Alpine World Cup **Hahnenkamm-Rennen** (p349).

FEBRUARY
Pre-Lenten carnivals bring riotous masked parades swirling in centuries-old tradition, like Imst's spectacular quadrennial **Schemenlaufen** (p360).

APRIL
Ski season ends with DJs, drinking and dancing at Mayrhofen's **Snowbombing** and Ischgl's **Top of the Mountain** (p368) concert.

A Week in Hand

- Kick off with a day in Innsbruck, then dip into the Tyrolean Alps for a pinch of culture and outdoor action. Go west to **Stift Stams** (p360), a baroque stunner of a Cistercian abbey.

- From here, dive into the **Ötztal** (p356), a heavenly alpine valley, with adventure thrills at **Area 47** (p358), an exhilarating trip back to the neolithic past at **Ötzi Dorf** (p356) and peak-gazing swims in thermal waters at space-age spa **Aqua Dome** (p357).

- Next, stop off in **Imst** (p359) to hike the phenomenally wild **Rosengartenschlucht** (p359) ravine and distillery village **Stanz** (p361) to taste plum schnapps at its source. Wind out the week with a couple of action-packed days hiking, skiing or partying in **St Anton am Arlberg** (p362).

Two-Week Tour

- Ease yourself in with the long-weekend itinerary, then make your way gradually east, stopping for a spin of the medieval silver mines in **Schwaz** (p337) before catching the train into the **Zillertal** (p340), one of Tyrol's most ravishing alpine valleys.

- **Zell am Ziller** (p340) and **Mayrhofen** (p343) deliver folk music, gorgeous views and action – rafting, biking, hiking and skiing – but it's the nature-run wild backcountry around the **Schlegeisspeicher** (p342) reservoir and **Naturpark Zillertaler Alpen** (p346) that really charm.

- Divide your final week between **Kufstein** (p353), with its cliff-hugging **castle**, storybook Altstadt and trail-woven Kaisergebirge peaks, and glitzy **Kitzbühel** (p348) for rave-worthy trekking and skiing.

THE GUIDE

TYROL & VORARLBERG

MAY
Snow is thawing, blossom sprinkles meadows. Zell am Ziller gets folksy at **Gauderfest** (p343) with beer, feasting, parades and alpine wrestling.

JULY
Hear opera echo across Bodensee at summer's unmissable **Bregenzer Festspiele** (p370) in Bregenz.

SEPTEMBER
Golden days bring the **Mountain Yoga Festival** (p366) to St Anton am Arlberg and folksy cattle drives to alpine valleys like the Zillertal.

DECEMBER
Krampus tears through villages on St Nicholas Eve, Christmas markets twinkle in Innsbruck and the first proper snow lures skiers.

Innsbruck

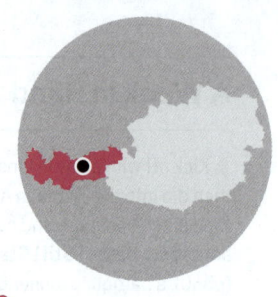

LIVING HISTORY | HABSBURG CULTURE | HIGH ALPS

GETTING AROUND

Innsbruck's compact, pedestrianised, alley-woven Altstadt is a pleasure to explore on foot. Most trophy sights are huddled here, and ultra-modern funiculars race you up into the mountains.

For outlying sights such as Bergisel and Schloss Ambras, hop on one of the local IVB *(ivb.at)* buses; for multiple journeys, invest in a 24-hour ticket. Public transport is free with summer's Welcome Card (p334), the free guest card you receive with stays of more than two nights.

☑ TOP TIP

Tourist centres on Burggraben, at the Stadtturm and the Hauptbahnhof are handy first port of calls for maps, tickets, ski passes and information.

Tyrol's capital is a sight to behold. Rising like a theatre curtain above the city, the jagged rock spires of the Nordkette range are so breathtakingly close that when you fly here, you'll feel as though you're going to smash right into them. It isn't just an illusion: within minutes you can whizz from the city's stately heart to more than 2000m above sea level and be up among crags where alpine choughs glide and cowbells tinkle.

Summer and winter activities abound, and it's understandable why some visitors only take a peek at Innsbruck proper before heading for the hills. But to do so is a shame, for Innsbruck is in many ways Austria in microcosm: its late-medieval Altstadt (old town) is picture-book stuff, presided over by a grand Habsburg palace and baroque cathedral, while its Olympic ski jump with big mountain views makes a spectacular leap between the urban and the outdoors.

Palace of Dreams

Imperial Innsbruck

Grabbing attention with its pearl-white facade and cupolas, the **Hofburg** *(burghauptmannschaft.at; adult/child €9.50/free)* imperial palace was built for Archduke Sigmund the Rich in the 15th century, expanded by Emperor Maximilian I in the 16th century and given a baroque makeover by Empress Maria Theresia in the 18th century.

Take a romp around the lavish rococo state apartments and you'll be gobsmacked by the 31m-long **Riesensaal** (Giant's Hall), a feast of frescoes, weighty chandeliers and Habsburg portraits. Particularly unmissable are the full-length ones of Maria Theresia and her 16 children (including Marie Antoinette), who look strangely identical – maybe the artist was intent on avoiding royal wrath arising from sibling rivalry in the beauty stakes.

Right opposite is the **Hofkirche** *(tiroler-landesmuseen.at; adult/child €14/free)*, one of Europe's finest royal court

Hofkirche

churches. It was commissioned in 1553 by Ferdinand I, who enlisted the top artists of the age. Top billing goes to the ornate black-marble tomb of Emperor Maximilian I (1459–1519), a masterpiece of German Renaissance sculpture, embellished with Alexander Colins' white marble reliefs based on Dürer's *Ehrenpforte* (Triumphal Arch) woodcuts, depicting victorious scenes from Maximilian's life such as the Siege of Kufstein (1504).

The twin rows of 28 giant **bronze figures** that guard the sarcophagus include Dürer's legendary King Arthur, who was apparently Emperor Maximilian's biggest idol. You're now forbidden to touch the statues, but numerous inquisitive hands have already polished parts of the dull bronze, including Kaiser Rudolf's codpiece!

Innsbruck on High: Nordkette

From city to slopes

You'll be itching to head up into the humungous mountains on Innsbruck's doorstep, so perfectly etched they almost look like a cardboard cut-out in the sharp light of winter. Iraqi-British architect Zaha Hadid's space-age funicular **Nordkettenbahnen** (nordkette.com; Top of Innsbruck return ticket adult/child

continues on p333

BEST SHOPS IN INNSBRUCK

Acqua Alpes: This vaulted perfumery bottles the scent of the Alps, with fragrances inspired by the meadows, crisp air and wildflowers.

Culinarium: Stop by this deli for a tempting array of regional oils, salts, honeys, meats, cheeses and wines.

Tiroler Heimatwerk: Find traditional Tyrolean handicrafts, from *Dirndls* to hand-carved nativity figurines, stained glass and puppets.

Swarovski Crystal Worlds: Swarovski's flagship store in Innsbruck sparkles with crystal trinkets and jewellery. The showstopper is Berlin-based light artist Susanne Rottenbacher's two-tier, 80,000-crystal lily landscape.

Speckeria: Pick up quality *Speck* (bacon), smoked sausages, Alpine cheese and schnapps at this vaulted cubby-hole on Hofgasse.

 EATING IN INNSBRUCK: OUR PICKS

Olive: Vegetarians and vegans are in their element at this cute bistro with vintage furniture. Book – it gets busy. *5-11pm Mon-Sat* €

Die Wilderin: A modern hunter-gatherer restaurant, where season-spun menus play up farm-fresh and foraged ingredients. *5pm-midnight Tue-Sun* €€

Il Convento: Tucked into the old city walls, this Italian job has dishes like clam linguine and braised veal, plus a well-stocked cellar. *11.30am-midnight Mon-Sat* €€

Oniriq: Explosive Austrian flavours are given a foraged twist in ingredient-led tasting menus at this stylishly monochrome pick. *6-11pm Wed-Sat* €€€

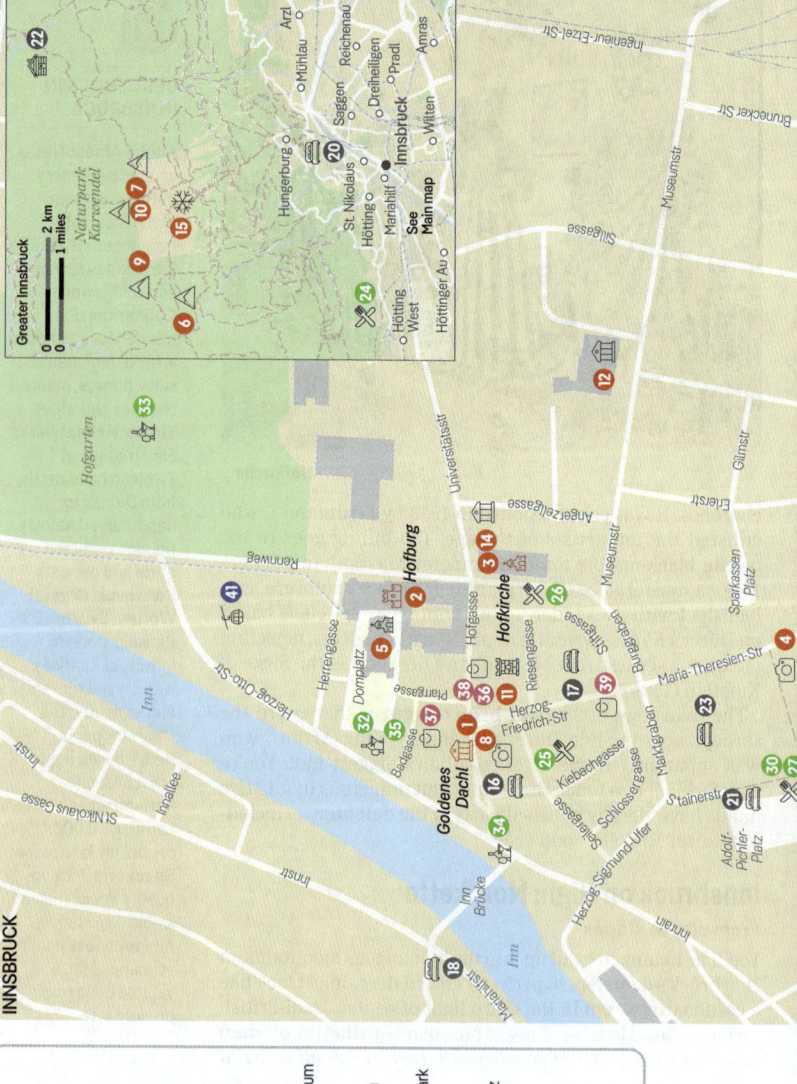

INNSBRUCK

★ HIGHLIGHTS
1. Goldenes Dachl
2. Hofburg
3. Hofkirche

● SIGHTS
4. Annasäule
5. Dom St Jakob
6. Frau-Hitt-Sattel
7. Hafelekarspitze
8. Helblinghaus
9. Kemacher
10. Seegrube
11. Stadtturm
12. Tiroler Landesmuseum Ferdinandeum
13. Triumphpforte
14. Volkskunst Museum

● ACTIVITIES
15. Nordkette Skylinepark

● SLEEPING
16. Goldener Adler
17. Hotel Weisses Kreuz
18. Mondschein
19. Nala
20. Pension Paula
21. Penz Hotel
22. Pfeishütte
23. Stage 12

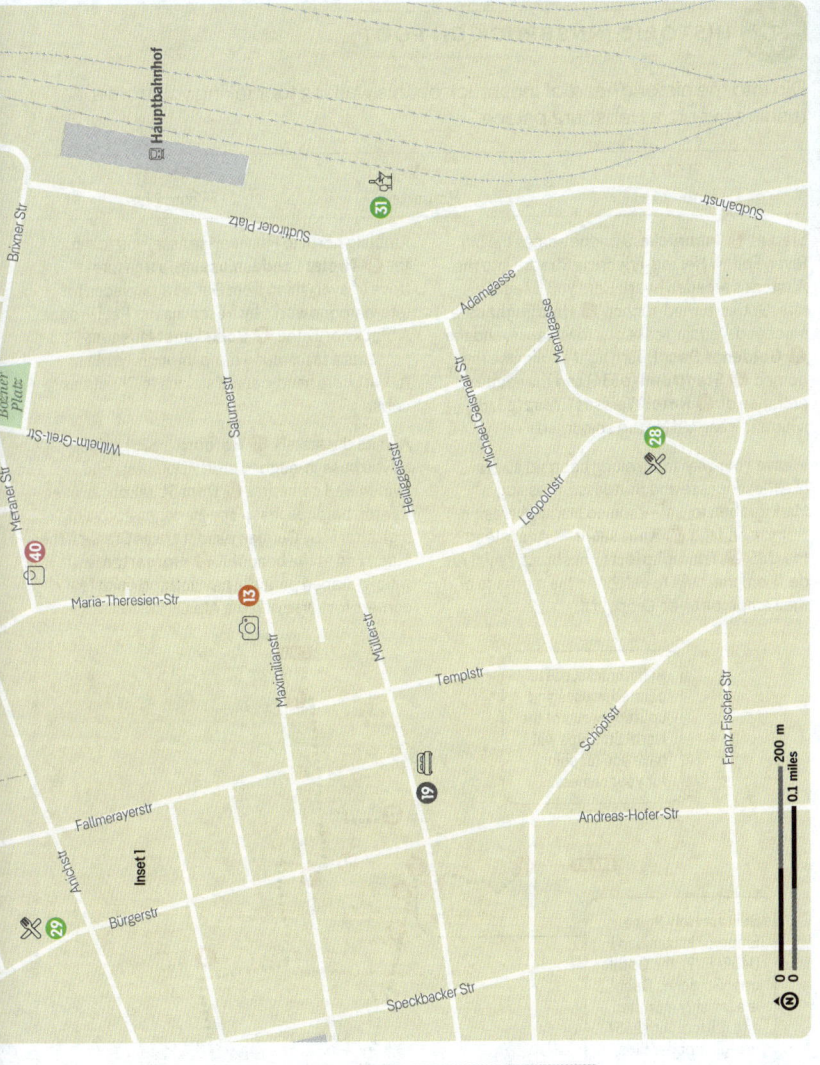

- **EATING**
- 24 Buzihütte
- 25 Die Wilderin
- 26 Il Convento
- 27 Lichtblick
- 28 Olive
- 29 Oniriq
- **DRINKING & NIGHTLIFE**
- see 27 360°
- 31 Cloud One
- 32 Fuchs & Hase
- 33 Hofgarten
- 34 In Vinum
- 35 Moustache
- **SHOPPING**
- 36 Acqua Alpes
- 37 Culinarium
- 38 Speckeria
- 39 Swarovski Crystal Worlds
- 40 Tiroler Heimatwerk
- **TRANSPORT**
- 41 Nordkettenbahnen

HISTORIC INNSBRUCK ON FOOT

Dip into the historic heart of Innsbruck on this walking tour taking you from a rushing river to a Habsburg palace.

START	END	LENGTH
Innbrücke	Hofgarten	2km; 2 hrs

Start at ❶ **Innbrücke**, a bridge across the Inn River. Follow Herzog-Friedrich-Strasse into the Altstadt's arcaded heart. Here you'll see the late-Gothic-turned-rococo ❷ **Helblinghaus**, a stuccoed wedding cake of a townhouse, and the ❸ **Goldenes Dachl**. Turn right to glimpse the domed ❹ **Stadtturm** (p334) and the vaulted entrance of ❺ **Hotel Weisses Kreuz** (p378), where 13-year-old Mozart sojourned.

Weave your way south along cobbled alleys like Riesengasse and Stiftsgasse, crossing Marktgraben to, cafe-rimmed Maria-Theresien-Strasse and the ❻ **Annasäule**. Further along is the 1765 ❼ **Triumphpforte**, Innsbruck's mini Arc de Triomphe, built to celebrate the marriage of then emperor-to-be Leopold II.

Ambling north to Museumsstrasse, you reach the ❽ **Tiroler Landesmuseum**, a treasure-trove of everything from Gothic altarpieces to late-baroque works by fresco master Paul Troger. A block north, the ❾ **Volkskunst Museum** presents a fascinating romp through Tyrolean folk art from hand-carved sleighs to Christmas cribs.

Admire the stately ❿ **Hofburg** (p328) palace as you pass through to pretty Domplatz and twin-spired cathedral ⓫ **Dom St Jakob**, an over-the-top baroque feast. The Madonna above the high altar is by German painter Lukas Cranach the Elder. End at the beautiful ⓬ **Hofgarten**, with willow-draped ponds, a pavilion and quiet leafy corners for surveying the Alps.

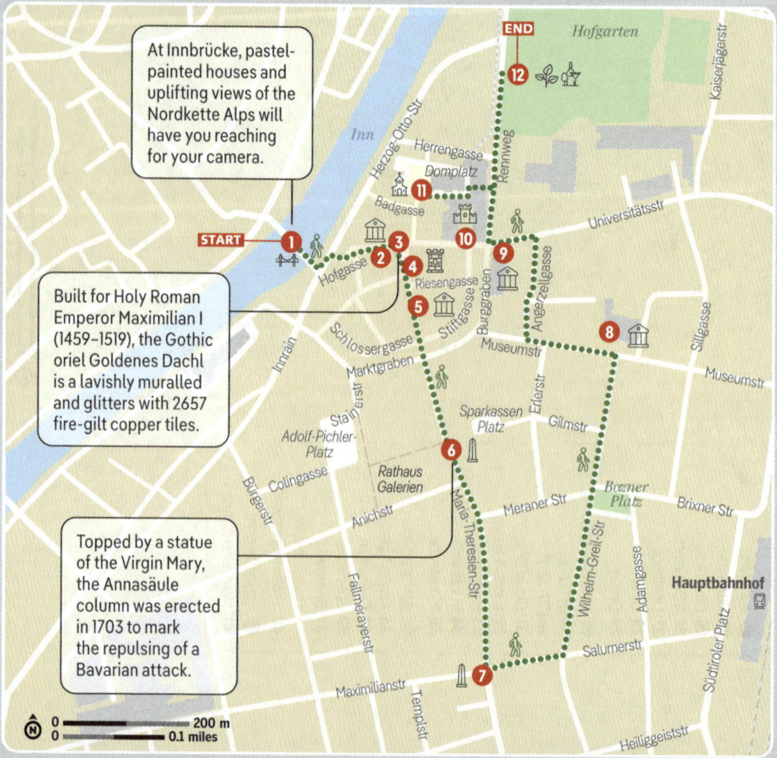

At Innbrücke, pastel-painted houses and uplifting views of the Nordkette Alps will have you reaching for your camera.

Built for Holy Roman Emperor Maximilian I (1459–1519), the Gothic oriel Goldenes Dachl is a lavishly muralled and glitters with 2657 fire-gilt copper tiles.

Topped by a statue of the Virgin Mary, the Annasäule column was erected in 1703 to mark the repulsing of a Bavarian attack.

continued from p329

€52/31.20) wings you from the Congress Centre to the slopes in no time, stopping at Hungerburg, where you switch to a cable car to Seegrube and, finally, 2256m Hafelekar.

A 15-minute uphill trudge brings you to 2334m **Hafelekarspitze**, where alpine choughs ride the breeze, gnarly limestone mountains rise in great waves, and Innsbruck is reduced to a speck in the valley below. The views are riveting, reaching all the way to 3798m Grossglockner when it's clear.

On the southern rim of the Karwendel Nature Park, the ragged Nordkette range is where the Innsbrucker come to play. Walking trails head off in all directions from **Hungerburg** and **Seegrube**, but for more of a challenge, out-of-this-world views and chance encounters with wildlife such as eagles, chamois and marmots, hike the ridgetop **Goethe Trail**, leading through meadows and mountain pines to the **Pfeishütte**. It's a 10km, five-hour, out-and-back stomp.

The very steep, technically demanding **Nordkette Single Trail** is a magnet for hardcore downhill mountain bikers and starts 200m below Seegrube.

In winter, the most central place to pound powder is the Nordpark. Boarders are in their element at the **Nordkette Skylinepark**, with its quarter-pipe, kickers and boxes, while fearless skiers ride the **Hafelekar Run**, one of Europe's steepest runs with a 70% gradient.

Get an Alpine Fix
Innsbruck's via ferrata

With a click of a karabiner, you're on. Rising to the challenge of Innsbruck's *Klettersteig* (via ferrata) is a day you (and your muscles) won't forget in a hurry. Kicking off near **Hafelekarspitze** and taking between five and seven hours as it clambers over seven mountains, this fixed-rope route teeters high above the rooftops, domes and spires of Innsbruck, toytown tiny in the river-woven Inn Valley far below, while cracking open views of the wild, jagged peaks of the Stubai and Karwendel Alps.

Not for novices, the exposed route covers steep, rocky terrain and divides into two sections. With a difficulty rating of C, the first section is marginally easier (though you'll still need experience under your belt), ticking off the peaks of 2350m **Seegrube** and 2480m **Kemacher** on the ridge to Lange Sattel. You can descend after this or continue, if you dare, on the trickier, D-rated next leg to 2270m **Frau-Hitt-Sattel**, where you'll need to negotiate notches, turrets, chimneys and steep

BACK-TO-NATURE HIKES

Innsbruck guide **Monika Unterholzner** shares her top recommendations for stepping back to nature in Innsbruck.

Mühlauer Klamm: North of Innsbruck, this mystical gorge is steeped in legends of witches. A great hike begins at Schweinsbrücke, leading along a steep forest path past waterfalls to a huge avalanche breaker.

Innsbruck Botanical Garden: A short walk from the historic centre, these tranquil gardens brim with 7000 species, from mountain and medicinal plants to spices. Come at noon for a free concert.

Goldbichl: Rising above Igls, this magical place has an archaeology trail that taps into 4000 years of history. Hiking in the footsteps of our ancestors, you'll pass prehistoric Brandopferplatz (a ritual place for burning offerings).

 DRINKING IN INNSBRUCK: OUR PICKS

Fuchs & Hase: On Domplatz, this vaulted bar is a mellow pick for an expertly mixed cocktail, proper coffee or a glass of wine. *5pm-1am Tue-Sat*

Stage 12: This backlit, gold-kissed bar at Stage 12 has a terrace for summer imbibing and mixologists who know their stuff. *noon-midnight Sun-Thu, to 1am Fri & Sat*

Moustache: Play Spot-the-Moustache at this spot, with a terrace overlooking Domplatz. Go for cocktails and craft beers. *10am-2am Tue-Sun, 4pm-2am Mon*

In Vinum: This snug Altstadt wine bar is a relaxed choice to sample Austria's finest wines. *11am-midnight Mon-Sat, 4-10pm Sun*

INNSBRUCK CARD

Innsbruck Card: *(24/48/72-hour €69/79/89, child half price)* Money-saving card allowing one visit to Innsbruck's main sights and attractions, a return journey with any cable car or funicular, a guided city walk and unlimited use of public transport that includes the Sightseer and Kristallwelten shuttle bus. Plus numerous discounts on tours and activities.

Welcome Card: Stay at least two nights in Innsbruck from May to October and you'll receive a Welcome Card, giving discounts on transport and activities, entry to a number of pools and lidos. It also allows you to join the tourist office's free activity programme (including e-bike tours, sunrise hikes, family walks) in summer. The winter version covers free or discounted lift rides and activities such as guided snowshoe tours.

---

walls. Loosen your grip briefly for a must-have shot from the hanging bridge.

Usually tackled from east to west, the via ferrata requires forward planning. You'll need some climbing experience, plus a good head for heights and surefootedness. Check weather conditions before setting out as you'll need a fine, thunderstorm-free day. Rent gear *(per day €25)* including safety harnesses and helmets in advance online from the sports shop at Seegrube. Bring your own gloves.

Moving On Up
Romantic views and roof terraces

With the Nordkette Alps as skyscrapers, Innsbruck forces you to gawp and gasp – and never more than when sunrise touches the summits like a caress or skies blaze at sunset. Lookouts, rooftop bars and restaurants rev up the drama, providing Instagram-worthy views, snow or shine.

The onion-domed **Stadtturm** *(innsbruck.info; adult/child €4.50/2)* pops up in the heart of the Altstadt. Guards once kept watch over the city from this medieval tower. Puff up 133 steps and you'll be rewarded with 360-degree views of Innsbruck's rooftops, spires and the surrounding mountains.

Beyond this, there's a wave of bars and restaurants where you can swoon over front-row views of the cityscape and Alps. Head up to **360°** for a knockout view of the skyline from the balcony that skirts this spherical bar. It's a chilled spot for a coffee or sundowner.

As the city twinkles in the blues of dusk, stay for dinner at **Lichtblick** *(restaurant-lichtblick.at)*, a slickly minimalist, backlit, glass-walled restaurant that serves Italian-inflected cuisine and takes in the entire sweep of city and its mountain backdrop.

Also in town, **Cloud One** *(motel-one.com)* on the 13th floor of Motel One floats above the city like froth on a cappuccino. The glamorously alpine, glass-fronted bar is an uplifting spot for an evening drink. Play at mixologist with a 'shake your own' cocktail or go for a signature pomegranate margarita.

For cracking views of Innsbruck from on high, the **Buzihütte** *(buzihuette.at)*, a 3km hike northwest of town or a five-minute taxi ride, is a woodsy alpine hut, with a peak-gazing terrace for summer dining. The menu bigs up traditional faves like *Spinatknödel* (spinach dumplings) and *Käsespätzle* (cheese noodles).

Beyond Innsbruck

Glittering crystal worlds and glaciers, medieval time warps and Olympic marvels are all just a whisper away from Innsbruck.

Those lofty mountains in Innsbruck? They're just a taste of what's out there. Easy, memorable hops from the centre include resplendent Renaissance castle Schloss Ambras, Zaha Hadid's peak-gazing Bergisel ski jump and the Olympic bob run in Igls. A 10-minute train ride from Innsbruck, Hall, built high on the silver minted at its castle in the Middle Ages, is an atmospheric romp back in time. And within half an hour you can be dazzled by fantasy crystal bling bearing the hallmark of designers and artists at Swarovski Kristallwelten.

And when the flakes fall, the city is but a short ski shuffle away from the slopes. Whether it's boarding at nearby Patscherkofel or cruising at the Stubai Glacier, free ski buses make getting there a breeze.

Places
Schloss Ambras p335
Bergisel p336
Igls p336
Hall in Tirol p336
Schwaz p337
Wattens p338
Seefeld p338
Stubai Glacier p339

Schloss Ambras TIME FROM INNSBRUCK: 10MINS

A palace of grand proportions

Picturesquely perched on a hill, the fortified **Schloss Ambras** *(schlossambras-innsbruck.at; adult/child €18/free)*, 4km south of the city centre, bears the whimsical Renaissance touch of Archduke Ferdinand II, then ruler of Tyrol. Its showstopper is the **Spanische Saal** (Spanish Hall), a 43m-long banquet hall with a wooden inlaid ceiling and Tyrolean nobles gazing from the walls.

Wonders in the **Heldenrüstkammer** (Armour Collection) include the archduke's wedding armour – specially shaped to fit his bulging midriff! – and the 2.6m suit created for giant Bartlmä Bon. The **Kunst und Wunderkammer** is crammed with curiosities, from a petrified shark to the *Fangstuhl* – a chair designed to trap drunken guests at Ferdinand's raucous parties.

Titian, Velázquez and Van Dyck originals hang in the **Portraitgalerie**. Maria Anna of Spain (No 126, Room 22) wins the prize for the most ludicrous hairstyle. When Habsburg portraits begin to pall, you can stroll or picnic in the extensive gardens, home to strutting peacocks, myth-inspired grottoes and medicinal herbs.

GETTING AROUND

There's no need to hire a car unless you want the freedom of the open road. The region surrounding Innsbruck is connected by public buses, trams and trains. Distances are generally short and fares inexpensive. Many connections are covered by free guest cards you receive locally, so check this before shelling out on tickets.

In winter, Innsbruck's money-saving **Ski Plus City Pass** wraps up 346km of pistes in 12 ski areas around Innsbruck and the Stubaital, and opens the doors to 22 sights and attractions.

WITH A REBEL YELL

Nobody epitomises the proud, resilient spirit of Tyrol quite like rabble-rousing hero **Andreas Hofer** (1767–1810). An innkeeper and horse dealer, Hofer was an imposing bearded figure of a man and a staunch patriot.

In 1809 he led a local revolt against Napoleon's Franco-Bavarian forces and was initially successful, winning the Battle of Bergisel and reclaiming Innsbruck. But his victory was short-lived: in January 1810 Hofer's neighbour Franz Raffl was bribed to betray his hideout in the Passeiertal. That February, Hofer was shot by firing squad in Mantua and proved brave to the last, telling his executioner to 'shoot straight'.

Today he lies buried in Innsbruck's **Hofkirche** (p328), and the Tyrolean anthem *Zu Mantua in Banden* recounts his tragic fate.

Bergisel

TIME FROM INNSBRUCK: **5MINS**

Skyline views & ski jumping

Rising above Innsbruck like a celestial staircase, the glass-and-steel **Bergisel** *(bergisel.info; adult/child €11/5.50)* ski jump was designed by much-lauded Iraqi-British architect Zaha Hadid. It's 455 steps or a two-minute funicular ride to the 50m-high viewing platform, with a breathtaking panorama of the Nordkette range, Inntal and Innsbruck.

From May to July, fans pile in to see athletes train, while preparations step up a gear in early January for the World Cup Four Hills Tournament. Year-round you can get giddy on the astonishing views of Innsbruck spread out at your feet and the snow-tipped Alps from the **SKY** restaurant. Tram 1 trundles here from central Innsbruck.

Igls

TIME FROM INNSBRUCK: **10MINS**

Life in the fast lane

For a minute in the life of an Olympic bobsleigh racer, ride the **Olympia Bob** *(knauseder-event.at; bobsleigh ride summer/winter €55/120, skeleton €65)* at the foot of Patscherkofel mountain in Igls, built for the 1976 Winter Olympics. Zipping around 14 curves and picking up speeds of up to 120km/h, the 1.3km bob run is a single minute of pure hair-raising action and it's all over in the blink of an eye.

From December to March, you can either join a four-person bobsleigh driven by a professional or throw yourself head-first down the run on a skeleton. Otherwise, join a pro-bobsled driver from April to October for the summer version. See the website for dates, times and bookings. To reach the bob run, take Bus J from the Landesmuseum to Igls Olympiaexpress.

Hall in Tirol

TIME FROM INNSBRUCK: **10MINS**

Back to the Middle Ages

Stepping through the cobbled streets of Hall in Tirol by night is pure enchantment. As blue dusk creeps in, the town's web of winding lanes falls silent and glows softly by lantern light. Peering up to stout stone houses and pastel facades, the centuries slip away. A 10-minute train ride from Innsbruck, this handsome medieval town grew fat on the riches of salt in the 13th century and now features on the tentative list of UNESCO World Heritage Sites.

All streets in Hall lead to the **Oberer Stadtplatz**, bookended by the **Rathaus**, Hall's 15th-century town hall, with its distinctive courtyard, complete with crenellated edges and mosaic crests. Across the way is the Gothic, onion-domed **Pfarrkirche St Nikolaus** *(pfarre-hall.at)*, swirling with frescoes by Viennese court painter Adam Mölk, and with a high altar designed by Erasmus Quellinus, a gifted protégé of Rubens. In the northern side aisle, the **Waldaufkapelle** showcases treasures bequeathed by famous 16th-century knight Florian Waldauf, notably his grisly collection of skulls and bones,

Burg Hasegg

picked from the remains of minor saints. Each rests on an embroidered cushion, capped with a veil and elaborate headdress, reminiscent of a spiked halo.

On the southern fringes of town is **Burg Hasegg** *(muenzehall.at; adult/child €13/9)*, where a staircase spirals up to the 5th floor for expansive views over Hall and the Inntal. The castle had a 300-year career as a mint for silver thalers (the origin of the modern word 'dollar'), and this history is spelled out in the **Münze Hall**, which presents water-driven and hammer-striking techniques. Audio guides are included in the price and you can have a go at minting your own coin.

Schwaz

TIME FROM INNSBRUCK: **25MINS**

Schwaz silver

For the inside scoop on the region's rich silver-mining heritage, take a scenic train ride east of Innsbruck to Schwaz. What is today a sleepy little town with pastel-washed houses and winding streets was once, believe it or not, Austria's second-largest city after Vienna. Schwaz wielded clout in the Middle Ages when its eyes shone brightly with silver (85% of the world's silver was mined here 500 years ago).

You can relive the town's glittering past glories by going underground at the silver mine **Silberbergwerk** *(silberbergwerk.at; adult/child €23/15)*. A spin begins with a train ride taking you down 800m into the bowels of the silver mine. From here, you follow in the footsteps of the miners, with guides telling fascinating tales of the hard life they endured. The water wheel, installed in 1556 to raise the mine water, was a marvel of engineering of its time.

FESTIVAL TIME

With its medieval looks and time-honoured traditions, Hall in Tirol puts on a cracking line-up of events. February jumpstarts the year with pre-Lenten *Fasnacht* (carnival), banishing winter, with folk music, handcrafted masks, flamboyant costumes and parades at **Absamer Matschgererumzug**.

Spring signals **Palm Sunday** processions and the two-week **Tyrol Easter Festival**, which brings high-calibre music, dance, performance, film and literature to stages in Hall and Innsbruck.

Summer notches up a gear with folk music taking to the medieval cobbled streets and courtyards of the Altstadt at **Klangstadt**, while autumn brings bountiful farmers markets. Hall slides into winter in December with a glittering **Christmas market**, an advent calendar projected in lights onto the town's historic facades, crafts, choirs and brass bands.

ONWARDS TO ITALY: BRENNER PASS

Just south of Innsbruck, the 190m high **Europabrücke**, beloved of bungee jumpers, makes a spectacular leap over the milky blue Sill River. Continuing south of here brings you to the remote, mountainous, wooded **Wipptal**, an under-the-radar valley leading to the Brenner Pass, where the A13 leaps over from Austria into Italy. Drive the length of this valley and you can go from Innsbruck to Italy in less than an hour. By rail, high-speed trains breeze from Innsbruck to the pass in just 35 minutes.

Linking north to south, the **Brenner Pass** has been a strategic crossing point since Roman times, linking Germany to the Po Valley, Munich to Verona. Open year-round, it is one of the lowest passes in the Alps at 1375m.

Wattens

TIME FROM INNSBRUCK: **30MINS**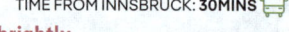

Where Swarovski twinkles brightly

The quaint village of Wattens has but one claim to fame (albeit an impressive one): it's the glittering heart of the Swarovski crystal empire. Call them kitsch or classy, but there is no doubting the pulling power of these crystals at the fantastical **Swarovski Kristallwelten** (*kristallwelten.swarovski.com; adult/child €26/8*), one of Austria's most-visited attractions.

Stepping into the fantasy world, you'll spy an ivy-swathed giant's head spouting water in the garden, where there are contemporary art and sound installations to explore. There's more sparkle about the **Crystal Cloud**, which floats above a mirrorlike pool and is bejewelled with 800,000 crystals that glitter like stars in the night sky.

Artists and designers from all over the world have pooled their creativity into the **Chambers of Wonder**, which showcases the likes of Alexander McQueen's wintry **Silent Light**, the Eden crystal forest where a waterfall flows and South Korean artist Lee Bul's perspective-bending **Into Lattice Sun**, a kind of crystal utopia. **Pulse Voronoi**, designed by Mexican-Canadian media artist Rafael Lozano-Hemmer, is the largest chamber of all. It's a light fantastic walk through 7000 shards of crystal inspired by a Big Bang–style blast.

The crystal fun continues outdoors for families, with a crystalline play tower designed by Norwegian starchitects Snøhetta, a giant hand-shaped maze by Austrian artist André Heller and a stunning modernist, black-and-white carousel glimmering with 15 million crystals by Spanish designer Jaime Hayon.

The quickest and easiest way to reach Kristallwelten is by hopping on one of the five daily **shuttle buses** (*round trip adult/child €12/8, free with Innsbruck Welcome Card*) from Innsbruck's Hauptbahnhof or Congress Centre. It's a 30-minute ride.

Seefeld

TIME FROM INNSBRUCK: **30MINS**

Going Nordic

The gentle swish of skis on empty tracks. The glitter of snow falling from spruce trees as you glide in silent wonder through forests at daybreak. A timber hut at the end of a remote valley. A frozen waterfall that makes you catch your breath with its beauty. Downhill skiing gets all the fuss, but as many *Langlauf* (cross-country) fans will confess, the real joy of slipping on skis isn't in the rush, it's in exploring the backcountry in quiet slow motion, with those alpine landscapes all to your lucky self.

 EATING BEYOND INNSBRUCK: TYROLEAN FLAVOURS

Smokerei Wattens: Local Tyrolean beef burgers are elevated to a whole new gourmet level at this cool, neo-rustic restaurant. *5.30-11pm Tue-Sat* €€

Goldener Löwe: This historic tavern in Hall dishes up Austrian comfort food like *Tafelspitz* (boiled beef with horseradish). *5pm-midnight Tue-Sat* €€

Gasthaus Vogelsberg: Above Wattens, this mountain hut dishes up schnitzel and dumplings. There's a floodlit toboggan run in winter. *10am-8pm Wed-Sat, to 5pm Sun* €€

Centrale: This elegant Italian takes you from morning espresso to evening pizza. There's terrace seating when it's warm. *8am-10pm Mon-Sat, to 6pm Sun* €€

Swarovski Kristallwelten

Whether you stick to the prepared *Loipe* (trail) or prefer to go off-piste skating like a pro, the village of Seefeld, half an hour northwest of Innsbruck, is the Nordic dream. High on a south-facing plateau and ringed by the fearsome limestone peaks of the Wetterstein and Karwendel Alps, the resort is laced with 245km of well-marked trails in winter and hosted the FIS Nordic World Ski Championships in 2019.

Cross-country skiing is the village's raison d'être and you can give it a whirl by hooking onto trails at 1200m, such as the beautiful 5.5km one that zips across the shimmering, forest-fringed plateau to **Mösern**, where there are fine views of the Inn River and the peaks beyond. And you can do so with a clean conscious as cross-country is significantly lower impact than downhill skiing. Day tickets cost €11/15 with/without a guest card and cross-country gear can be rented at all local sport shops.

Stubai Glacier

TIME FROM INNSBRUCK: 1¼HRS

Summer skiing

It's a bizarre feeling to slip out of sandals and into skis in midsummer, but that's precisely what draws people to the **Stubai Glacier** *(stubaier-gletscher.com; cable car return adult/child €39.10/19.60)*, a snowball-throw south of Innsbruck. The glacier is a year-round skiing magnet with guaranteed snow from October to May and more than 110km of wide, snow-sure pistes that are great for cruising and intermediate skiing. Summer skiing is limited to between 2900m and 3300m. And the views? Just wow. Here the panorama reaches over the ripple of 109 three-thousanders.

From December to April a ski bus (free with the Innsbruck Welcome Card) runs daily between Innsbruck and the glacier, making it a viable day trip.

THE MIRACLE OF ST OSWALD

If you love miracles, Seefeld's is a good one. Beyond the village's cross-country slopes, the big cultural draw is the late-Gothic parish church, **Pfarrkirche St Oswald**, the supposed location of a Eucharistic miracle.

The story goes that Oswald Milser, a gallant knight from Schlossberg fortress, gobbled a wafer reserved for the clergy at Easter communion here in 1384. After almost being swallowed up by the floor (you can see his handprint in the stone to this day), the greedy layman repented. But the wafer was streaked with blood – not from foolish Oswald but from Christ, naturally.

You can view the **Blutskapelle** (Chapel of the Holy Blood), which held the original wafer, by climbing the church stairway.

The Zillertal

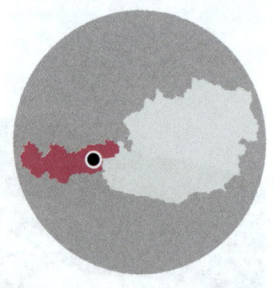

HIKING | SLOPES | NATURE ESCAPES

GETTING AROUND

Private railway Zillertalbahn *(zillertalbahn.at)*, which travels the 32km from Jenbach to Mayrhofen every half-hour, services the Zillertal. There's a *Dampfzug* (steam train) along the valley, which runs at 10.44am from Jenbach to Mayrhofen and at 1.35pm from Mayrhofen to Jenbach.

Bikes and e-bikes can be rented at ÖBB train stations in the valley. Buses take you deeper into the region (to Ginzling, for instance), but you'll need a car to venture off-piste on the Gerlos Alpine Road.

Squished between the Tuxer and the Kitzbühel Alps, the Zillertal (Ziller Valley) is like something out of a kids' bedtime story. Chuffing through the broad valley from Jenbach to Mayrhofen, you'll be glued to the window as the train unzips velvety, flower-stippled pastures and wooded mountains, affording snatched glimpses of snow-polished peaks, dark-timber chalets and the fast-flowing, milky turquoise Ziller River. It's all absurdly lovely, especially in winter when snow transforms every casual smartphone shot into a ready-made Christmas card.

This valley gets you up and out, with a zillion ways to make hearts pound: from rafting and paragliding in quaint, folksy Zell am Ziller to mountain biking, hardcore skiing and snowboarding in party-mad Mayrhofen. And when (phew!), you tire of that, you'll find glaciers, back-to-nature escapes and over-the-mountains road trips that take you even deeper into this stupendously wild pocket of Tyrol.

Outdoor Action in Zell am Ziller
Gateway to the Zillertal Alps

Peering up to the 3303m dagger of Reichenspitze, the folksy little village of Zell am Ziller has carved out a name for itself as one of Austria's hottest outdoor-adventure bases. In summer, hiking trails vein the landscape, scrambling up to reservoirs, ridges, flower-freckled meadows and dark-timber huts serving cheese-rich grub and sensational views. Memorable rambles include the 8km round hike to **Zellberg** via the Talbach falls, three hours of fairy-tale woods and wispy waters, and the tougher 14km, five-hour stomp up to the 2558m-high, cross-topped summit of **Kreuzjoch**, the highest peak in the Kitzbühel Alps.

Mountain bikers and road cyclists are equally in their element in this spectacularly rugged terrain. Unspooling from Strass to Mayrhofen, the 30km **Zillertal Radweg** is brilliant for freewheeling, heading along forest paths, shadowing the river and delivering mountain views on repeat. For more of a challenge, puff up the 35km **Zillertaler Höhenstrasse**, a long, steep, full day of a mountain climb, with breathtaking

✅ TOP TIP

If you're planning on spending a week or more here between late May and October, the value-for-money **Zillertal Activecard** covers public transport, one journey per day on any of the Zillertal cable cars and swimming-pool entry. Buy it at tourist offices and train stations.

THE ZILLERTAL

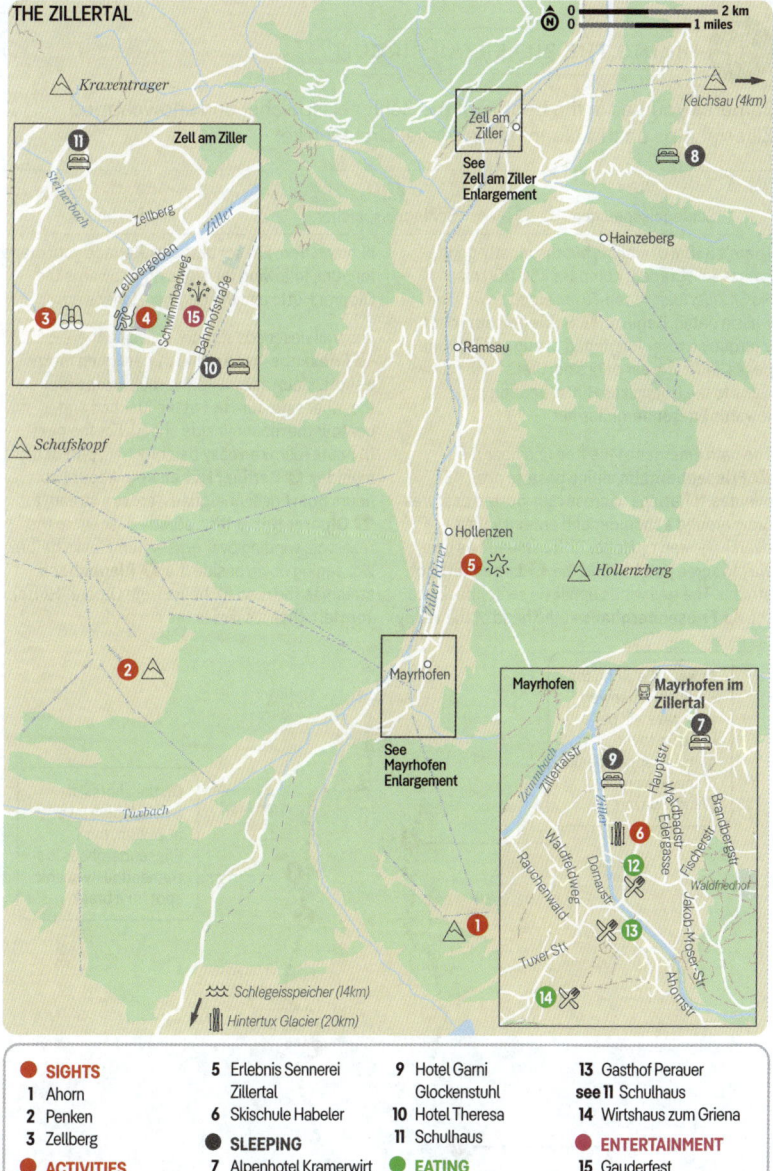

- **SIGHTS**
  - 1 Ahorn
  - 2 Penken
  - 3 Zellberg
- **ACTIVITIES**
  - 4 Aktivzentrum Zillertal
- 5 Erlebnis Sennerei Zillertal
- 6 Skischule Habeler
- **SLEEPING**
  - 7 Alpenhotel Kramerwirt
  - 8 Enzianhof
- 9 Hotel Garni Glockenstuhl
- 10 Hotel Theresa
- 11 Schulhaus
- **EATING**
  - 12 Gasser
- 13 Gasthof Perauer
- see 11 Schulhaus
- 14 Wirtshaus zum Griena
- **ENTERTAINMENT**
  - 15 Gauderfest

views of the Tux and Zillertal Alps. Topping out at 2020m, the high-altitude road was built in the 1960s to help farmers manage their pastures. If you prefer the downhill buzz to the uphill slog, ride the Wiesenalm single trail, which snakes through forest from Rosenalmbahn midway station. Bike rental is available at the train station.

HIKING THE ZILLERTAL CIRCUIT

Immerse yourself in the beauty of the Schlegeisspeicher and snowcapped Zillertal Alps on this stunning high-level circular hike.

START	END	LENGTH
Schlegeisspeicher	Schlegeisspeicher	11km; 5-6 hours

There's 850m of incline, but the mostly gentle path is well graded. Kompass 1:50,000 map No 37 *Zillertaler Alpen-Tuxer Alpen* covers the walk in detail. Begin at ❶ **Schlegeisspeicher**, a turquoise reservoir ringed by rugged 3000m peaks. From the car park's northeast end follow signs to the Dominikus Hütte, bearing right towards Friesenberghaus hut.

The path emerges at the tree line near the ❷ **Friesenbergalm** alpine pasture after 45 minutes. It flattens to cross tarn-dotted pastures. Sidle around a shoulder and enter a valley overshadowed by Hoher Riffler. Meadows give way to scree patches and the ❸ **Lapenkarbach** stream. The trail winds uphill via switchbacks, to the ❹ **Friesenberghaus** at the head of the valley 1½ hours from Friesenbergalm. Retrace your steps for 50m, following the signs right towards the Olperer Hütte and the Berliner Höhenweg.

The trail descends slightly, crossing the ❺ **Friesenbergsee** outlet stream, then makes a short, steep ascent up the rocky slope on the other side. Turn left at the junction and contour the mountainside ahead. For the next 1½ hours follow an easy balcony trail, part of the multiday ❻ **Berliner Höhenweg**. About two hours from Friesenberghaus, cross a stream to ❼ **Olperer Hütte**. It's a steady descent to the reservoir, winding over grassy hummocks before zigzagging down beside the ❽ **Riepenbach** stream to the road (1½ hours from Olperer Hütte). Turn left, then it's 1km to the car park.

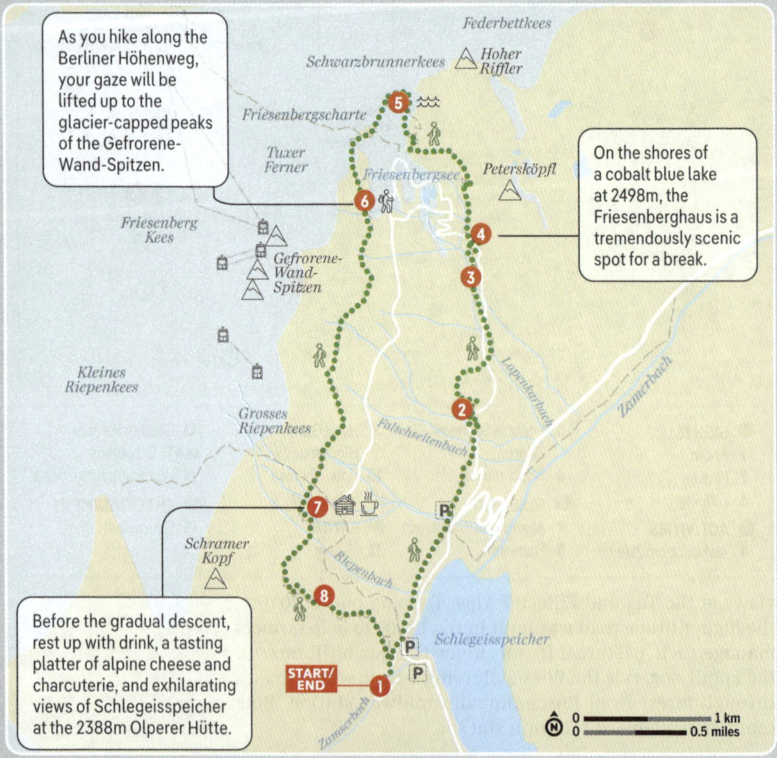

As you hike along the Berliner Höhenweg, your gaze will be lifted up to the glacier-capped peaks of the Gefrorene-Wand-Spitzen.

On the shores of a cobalt blue lake at 2498m, the Friesenberghaus is a tremendously scenic spot for a break.

Before the gradual descent, rest up with drink, a tasting platter of alpine cheese and charcuterie, and exhilarating views of Schlegeisspeicher at the 2388m Olperer Hütte.

For even bigger thrills, the **Aktivzentrum** *(aktivzentrum-zillertal.at)* is a one-stop shop for adventure sports, whether you want to clip onto a via ferrata to flirt with mountaineering, catch thermals tandem paragliding above the summits, go white-water rafting or river bugging in raging waters or try your hand grass-skiing and mountain-boarding (yes, really). With the first flurry of snow in winter, the activities switch to snowshoeing tours, ski touring and tobogganing in Zell's backyard.

Pound the Powder in Mayrhofen
The ultimate downhill dash

When the snow falls in winter, there's outstanding skiing in the Zillertal, but Mayrhofen, right at the head of the valley, has the edge. The peaks soaring above town pull in skiers with slopes largely channelling confident intermediates, as well as terrific off-piste.

Mayrhofen is the showpiece of **Zillertal 3000**, which unites 204km of well-groomed slopes and 65 lifts (some pretty high-tech). Families and beginners play on the wide, sunny pistes of **Ahorn** *(cable car return adult/child €39/16.50)*, while thrill-seekers rave about the slopes of **Penken** *(cable car return adult/child €39/16.50)*. If you're a boarder or freestyler, take your daring self to the rails, jumps, obstacles and half-pipe of **PenkenPark**, one of Europe's best terrain parks. One ticket covers the lot: the **Zillertal Superskipass** *(zillertal.at; adult/child €79/35.50)*.

Fast and furious, you say? Follow swishing tracks on Penken to Austria's steepest piste, the knee-trembling **Harakiri**. With a 78% gradient, this is half diving, half carving; a heart-stopping, hell-for-leather descent that leaves even pro skiers quaking in their ski boots. Only super-fit, experienced skiers with perfect (think Bond) body control should consider tackling this monster of a run. Check piste conditions before heading out as ice renders the slope treacherous. For bragging rights in the après-ski bars, you can pick up 'survivor' souvenirs in the shop at the base of the Ahornbahn.

Even if snow lies thin in the valley, it's guaranteed at the nearby, snow-sure **Hintertux Glacier** *(hintertuxergletscher.at; cable car return adult/child €53.50/32.50)*. The cable car is an attraction in itself, sheering above jagged cliff faces and peaks to the tip of the ice-blue glacier. The sundeck at 3250m affords phenomenal views of the Tuxer Alps and, on clear days, Grossglockner, the Dolomites and Zugspitze.

THE GAUDERFEST

On the first weekend in May, Zell am Ziller plays host to the **Gauderfest** *(gauderfest.at)*, Austria's biggest spring folk festival. The festival opens with the beer tapping of super-strong Gauderbier (reputedly over 10% alcohol), brewed specially for this shindig. This slides into a village-wide party, with copious eating, dancing and drinking, *Volksmusik* (folk music) bands and alpine wrestling.

The big parade is on the Sunday, with horse- and oxen-driven historic carriages and more than 2000 folk from across the Alps showing off their *Tracht* (traditional costume).

With 15th-century origins, its history is long and fascinating. Historically, it was a coming together of people from remote alpine communities, with a cattle market dancing, merry-making and marriage matchmaking.

EATING IN THE ZILLERTAL: OUR PICKS

Gasser: Grab a snack on the way down from the slopes at this award-winning butcher in Mayrhofen. *7am-6pm Mon-Fri, 8am-noon Sat* €

Wirtshaus zum Griena: Faves like *Schlutzkrapfen* (cheese-filled pasta) and *Speckknödel* (bacon dumplings) at a 400-year-old chalet in Mayrhofen. *3-11pm Mon & Thu-Sun* €€

Schulhaus: Perched above Zell am Ziller, this old schoolhouse has sublime views and a Tyrolean menu that swings with the seasons. *6-11pm Fri* €€

Gasthof Perauer: This *Gasthöfe* in Mayrhofen brims with Tyrolean good cheer. Dishes include specials from the family butchery like venison goulash. *11am-10pm* €€

THE COMING HOME OF THE COWS

In autumn, the Zillertaler celebrate the **Almabtrieb**, or coming home of the cows from their summer pastures to their winter digs in cosy barns. It's a proper taste of the rural Alps to see the cows strut down from the mountains adorned with heavy and elaborate floral headdresses and jangling giant bells.

The centuries-old event is a valley-wide party with feasting, *Volksmusik* (folk music) with the jaunty melody of accordions and yodelling, locals dressed in *Tracht* (traditional dress), and schnapps before another harsh, long, snowbound winter.

Some of the best celebrations are held in the villages of Fügen, Gattererberg, Hart and Gerlos from mid-September to early October.

PenkenPark (p343)

For private and small-group ski lessons, check out the highly personal **Ski School Habeler** *(skimayrhofen.com; group lessons per day €120)* run by Chris Habeler, son of famous mountaineer Peter Habeler.

Behind the Scenes at the Dairy

The big cheese

For a fly-on-the-wall tour of a working dairy, head to the **Erlebnis Sennerei Zillertal** *(erlebnissennerei-zillertal.at; adult/child €17.90/8.90)*, where audio guides in six languages whisk you through the butter, yoghurt and cheese-making processes, from delivery to culturing in copper vats and mould ripening. The final products are huge wheels of *Tilsiter*, *Bergkäse* and *Graukäse*, a grey cheese that is virtually fat-free.

You'll get to sample plenty of dairy goodies with your entry ticket, including hay milk, creamy yoghurts and cow, sheep and goat's milk cheeses from the *Käsomat* (automatic cheese dispenser). If you're here with kids, take them to the farmyard, where they can meet doe-eyed Tyrol grey cows, chickens, pigs and goats, jump into sweet-scented hay, ride the mini tractor course, and check out the natural pond and beehive.

If you're having fun, stay for lunch. The working dairy restaurant whips up rich specialities from pungent *Graukäsesuppe* (grey cheese soup) to gooey *Käsespätzle* (cheese spaetzle). And if this whets your appetite for more, stock up at the shop, where you can buy the whole gamut of cheeses including varieties laced with hay flowers, herbs, truffles and wild garlic.

In autumn, the dairy pairs cheese tours and tastings with live *Volksmusik*. Dust of your *Dirndl* and *Lederhosen* and get your groove on at the Friday afternoon Cheese with Music sessions, at the two-day **Funky Autumn Festival** in late September, and at the three-day **Hoo-Ruck Festival** in early October. See the website for booking details.

Beyond The Zillertal

The real wild show begins right on the Zillertal's doorstep, with giddy peaks, glaciers and exhilarating alpine road trips.

The Zillertal is the overture for one of the most outrageously lovely reaches of Tyrol, where the glacier-encrusted Zillertal Alps, capped off by the great 3510m fin of Hochpfeiler, razor south towards Italy. The beauty here is off the charts, whether you're stomping in quiet exhilaration through Ginzling's valley-braided nature reserve, gasping at ink-blue lakes and eagles wheeling overhead, witnessing blazing sunsets from an above-the-clouds mountain hut on a long-distance trail, or helter-skeltering over the heights on the epically scenic Gerlos Alpine Road to the booming Krimml Falls.

And if you fancy a summer ski, Mayrhofen is just a half-hour hop from the 3250m Hintertux Glacier, which surveys a vast swathe of the Alps from on high.

Places

Gerlos Alpine Road p345
Ginzling p346
Achensee p346

GETTING AROUND

Regular buses run from Mayrhofen to Ginzling (the jumping-off point for hikes in Hochgebirgs-Naturpark Zillertaler Alpen) and Hintertux, where you can switch to a cable car to the Hintertux Glacier. But if you want to venture beyond, realistically you're going to need your own wheels: car, bike or e-bike.

The Gerlos Alpine Road is open year-round.

Gerlos Alpine Road TIME FROM THE ZILLERTAL: 50MINS

An Alpine road trip to remember

Open year-round, the phenomenally scenic **Gerlos Alpine Road** *(gerlosstrasse.at; 1-/8-day ticket €12.50/27.50)* linking the Zell am Ziller in Tyrol to Krimml in Salzburgerland is one immensely impressive drive. With seductive views on every hairpin bend, the 37km road untwists like a ribbon through high moors and spruce forest, topping out at 1630m. The lookout above the startlingly turquoise **Stausee Durlassboden** reservoir is a great picnic stop, with a tremendous vista of the Alps.

If you've ever felt the urge to burst into song Julie Andrews–style as you skip through meadows ablaze with wildflowers, you'll love the **Jodel Wanderweg** *(Yodel Trail; zillertalarena.com)* in Königsleiten. You can hit the high notes at huts with giant cowbells, alpine horns and listen-repeat audio clippings. For a deeper dive, hook onto one of the free guided hikes where you can learn how to yodel like a pro. These are held every two weeks on a Wednesday from July to mid-September.

On the approach to Krimml near Schönmoosalm, there are bird's-eye views of the thundering **Krimmler Wasserfälle** (Krimml Falls).

WHAT'S COOKING?

Remote, rural and deeply rooted in alpine farming traditions, the region unfurling beyond the Zillertal is superb for dipping into hearty Tyrolean food, whether it's to be dinner in a woodsy, fire-warmed *Stube* (inn parlour) or lunch in a mountain hut with soaring peaks and cowbells as a backdrop.

Cheese is a staple, especially *Heumilchkäse* (hay-milk cheese), made from pure milk from summer pastures; you'll find often find it on a sharing platter together with speck, ham and mountain sausage.

Other hearty menu faves include *Gröstl* (pan-fried potatoes, pork and onions topped with a fried egg), *Kaspressknödel* (bread dumplings with cheese, onions and egg) and *Griesnockerl* (semolina dumplings in a clear, flavoursome broth).

Cheese pops up again in *Käsespätzle* (egg pasta topped with cheese and caramelised onions) and *Schlutzkrapfen*, a Tyrolean take on ravioli.

Ginzling

TIME FROM THE ZILLERTAL: **15MINS** OR

Hike in an Alpine wonderland

Idyllically embosomed in the Zemmtal Valley, the cute-as-a-button hamlet of Ginzling is the off-grid alpine dream, with its sprinkling of dark-timber chalets, rushing stream and colossal mountain backdrop. And, hear that? Silence.

You don't come here for sights, you come here for nature – and you'll find plenty of it in the **Naturpark Zillertaler Alpen** *(naturpark-zillertal.at)*, a 422-sq-km pristine wilderness of deep valleys and glaciated peaks.

The highlight for hikers is the hut-to-hut Berliner Höhenweg. The **Naturparkhaus** *(naturpark-zillertal.at)* in Ginzling runs 200 excellent themed guided hikes from May to October. The extensive programme includes everything from glacier tours to sunrise photo excursions, herb walks, forest bathing, wildlife-spotting rambles and high-alpine hikes. Most cost around €15. You'll need to register online at myzillertal.at by 8pm the day before the tour.

This off-grid corner of Tyrol is ideal for sidestepping crowds at an at-one-with-nature alpine hut. Most open from mid-June to September; book well ahead.

Trek the Berliner Höhenweg

If you have a week and want to nail a proper alpine hike, dust off your boots for the tough, 85km **Berliner Höhenweg** (Berlin High Trail) through the heart of the Naturpark Zillertaler Alpen. You need to be fit and have mountain experience under your belt for this eight-day, hut-to-hut traverse of the ravishing Zillertal and Tux Alps. The brutal ascents and thigh-burning descents sure are worth it, however, for the top-of-the-world views of peaks and glaciers that await. You'll often share these remote, rocky heights with just the odd ibex, chamois or golden eagle.

Beginning in Finkenberg, just north of Ginzling, and ending in Mayrhofen, the hike wows with the dazzling Schlegeisspeicher reservoir, glimpses of snow-iced mountaineering magnets like 3509m Hochfeiler and 3476m Olperer, and overnight stays at back-of-beyond mountain huts, including the namesake **Berliner Hütte** *(berlinerhuette.at; dorm €24-40)* at 2042m. Book well ahead in summer.

Achensee

TIME FROM THE ZILLERTAL: **20MINS**

One lake beyond

Scything between the Karwendel and Brandenburg Alps, fjord-like **Achensee** *(achensee.com)* is Tyrol's largest lake and one of its loveliest – a turquoise splash necklaced by beaches and flanked by thickly wooded peaks that shoot straight above its shores. Mountain rivers and snow meltwater flow into its glassy depths, making for a refreshing dip, with water temperature highs of 22°C. The lake's beauty has long been eulogised – Emperor Maximilian I used to summer at his hunting lodge in Pertisau 500 years ago.

Achensee

On its southern shore, Maurach is now a fine base for adventure and watersports. The **Rofanseilbahn** *(rofanseilbahn.at; adult/child €29.50/18)* cable car floats up to 2040m Gschöllkopf, a great fang of rock and the region's very own Sugarloaf Mountain. It's crowned by the **Adlerhorst** (Eagle's Nest), an eyrie-inspired viewing platform with enthralling 360-degree views of the lake, Karwendel mountains and Zillertal Alps. From Gschöllkopf, you can up the thrill factor by testing out the **Air-rofan Skyglider** *(adult/child €17.50/12)*, whooshing above the mountainscape like an eagle at speeds of 80km/h.

Back at lake level, **Atoll Achensee** *(atoll-achensee.com; day ticket lake lido adult/child €7.50/5.50, 2hr panorama bath €14.40/9.40)* is a terrific place to spend a sunny day swimming and resting by the lake. Head to the panorama bath for indoor and outdoor pools, water playgrounds, slides and mountain-facing bubble loungers. Or slide over to the lake lido for beach fun, sundecks, bathing platforms where you can launch yourself into the water, and activities from wing foiling to SUP-ing.

You can reach Maurach from Jenbach easily by bus, but for a shot of nostalgia board the **Achenseebahn** *(achenseebahn.at; adult/child round trip €45/23)*, a cogwheel steam train that's been puffing to the lake since 1889.

DEVIL IN DISGUISE: KRAMPUS

Deep in the villages and valleys of Tyrol, in late November or around St Nicholas Day, all hell literally breaks loose with the arrival of the horned, hairy **Krampus** (half goat, half demon). Wearing shaggy sheep or goat skins and menacing wooden masks, these ghoulish creatures pound the streets, clattering chains, banging drums and threatening to carry naughty children off to the pits of hell.

A mix of pagan solstice, and Christian traditions and alpine folklore, the Krampus is there to drive away winter and you can see him in action in and around the Zillertal, with parades in Jenbach, Gerlos, Kundl and Rattenberg.

In January the bell-clattering **Perchten** take over around Epiphany (6 January), banishing winter and bringing good fortune. Look out for the masked figures in Mayrhofen-Hippach.

EATING BEYOND THE ZILLERTAL: OUR PICKS

Helmut's Fischerhütte: Fresh trout, Austrian classics and views at this tavern on the shores of Schlegeisspeicher south of Ginzling. *9.30am-6pm* €€

Tristenbachalm: This warm, woody hut above Ginzling is alpine fantasy stuff. Go for cheesy Zillertal specialities and homemade cakes. *10am-6pm Mon & Wed-Sun* €€

Wein Zeit: Excellent wines paired with regional, seasonal cooking with a pinch of Italian flair at this chalet in Königsleiten on the Gerlos Alpine Road. *4-10pm Wed-Sun* €€

Almstuberl Rofan: Mountain views wow at this hut next to the top station of the Rofanseilbahn in Maurach. Try the house specialities. *8.30am-5.30pm* €€

Kitzbühel

LEGENDARY SLOPES | ALPINE CHIC | MOUNTAIN ADVENTURE

GETTING AROUND

Kitzbühel's petite historic centre is pedestrian only and a real pleasure to explore on foot with its parade of pastel-hued facades. The only traffic here is the odd horse-drawn carriage and getting from one side of town to the other takes just minutes. Beyond, cable cars wing you up to the surrounding heights.

Taking you to neighbouring villages like Wörgl, Kirchberg and St Johann in Tirol, buses and regional trains are free when you stay overnight.

The Kitzbüheler Alpen Card gives you free and unlimited use of public transport (including local trains, but not IC, EC and Railjet services) as well as discounts on cable cars.

Ask an Austrian to rattle off the top ski resorts in the country, and Kitzbühel invariably comes out on top. Ever since Franz Reisch hoofed up 1996m Kitzbüheler Horn, slipped on skis and blasted down the slopes to the valley back in 1893, so christening the first alpine ski run in Austria, Kitzbühel has carved out its sterling reputation as one of Europe's foremost ski resorts. Legends have been made and born on these pistes, not least three-time Olympic medallist Toni Sailer.

Kitzbühel began life in the 16th century as a silver- and copper-mining town, and today preserves a charming medieval centre despite its other persona as a posh resort. It's renowned for the white-knuckled Hahnenkamm-Rennen downhill ski race in January, the excellence of its slopes in winter and scenery straight out of an Alfons Walde landscape painting. Come summer, these mountains move with hikers, bikers and adventure-hungry thrill-seekers.

Snow Legends in Kitzbühel
World Cup winter wonderland

Winter sparkles brightly in Kitzbühel, which is right up there among the world's best ski resorts. When falling flakes blanket the landscape, skiers hit the slopes for 233km of downhill – from sweeping runs through forest glades to the kind of vast, high, wondrously white backcountry that sends off-piste fans into raptures. **Hahnenkamm** *(bergwelt-hahnenkamm.at)* is intermediate heaven, **Kitzbüheler Horn** (p350; *kitzski.at*) is much loved by novices, while boarders slide over to **Snowpark Kitzbühel** at **Hanglalm**, with its rails, kickers, boxes, tubes and obstacles. The **KitzSki Pass** *(2-day pass adult/child €125.50/63)* covers all lifts.

But with so much snow, where do you begin? Well, if you're a confident intermediate up for a challenge, tackle the tremendously scenic, hut-to-hut, lift-to-lift, 35km **Ski Safari**,

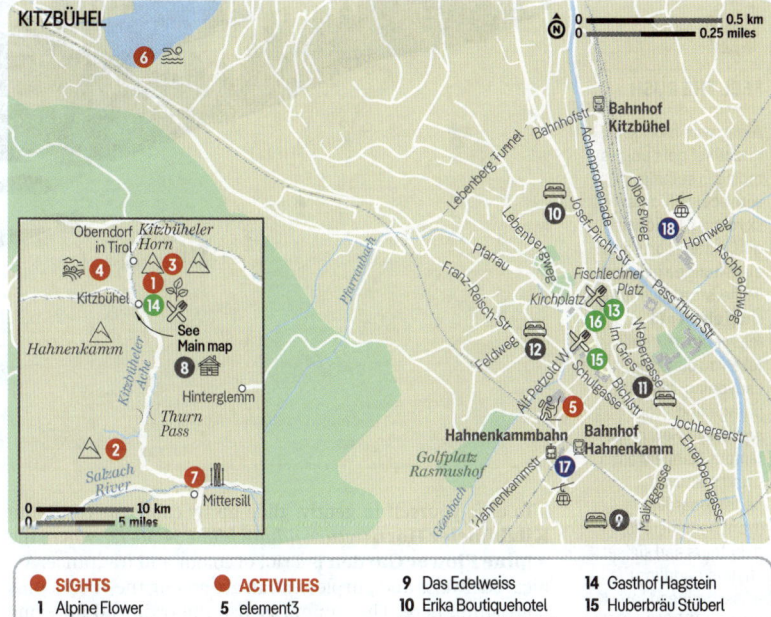

- **SIGHTS**
  1. Alpine Flower Garden
  2. Hanglalm
  3. Harschbichl
  4. Reith bei Kitzbühel
- **ACTIVITIES**
  5. element3
  6. Schwarzsee
  7. Snowpark Kitzbühel
- **SLEEPING**
  8. Bochumerhütte
  9. Das Edelweiss
  10. Erika Boutiquehotel
  11. Snowbunny's Hostel
  12. Villa Licht
- **EATING**
  13. First Lobster
  14. Gasthof Hagstein
  15. Huberbräu Stüberl
  16. Simple Food
- **TRANSPORT**
  17. Hahnenkammbahn
  18. Kitzbüheler Hornbahn

linking the Hahnenkamm to Pass Thurn and covering 6000m of vertical. Marked by elephant signs, the full-day alpine tour is a cracking overview to the entire ski area and a free ski bus takes you back to Kitzbühel at the end.

If you want more, let your daring self loose on the heart-stopping **Streif** at Hahnenkamm. The mind-bogglingly sheer, breathtakingly fast downhill course is a badge of honour for hardcore skiers. Even experts feel their hearts do somersaults on the Mausefalle ('mousetrap'), a notoriously steep section with an 85% gradient. Jumps reach up to 80m and speeds can top 145km/h, which is sheer insanity on skis. One of the most terrifying World Cup courses at January's **Hahnenkamm-Rennen**, it's the stuff of true legend.

If you're not quite ready for that yet, sign yourself up for some lessons or get a free ride guide at element3 (p350).

Hit the Trail

Summer in the Kitzbühel Alps

The pull of the Kitzbühel Alps is just as irresistible in summer as winter. The peaks aren't as high as in some regions of Austria, granted, but they are stupendously wild and diligently waymarked trails make them hiking nirvana.

☑ **TOP TIP**

Stay in Kitzbühel and you'll automatically receive the **Kitzbüheler Alpen Card** (kitzbueheler-alpen. com), which entitles you to a number of discounts on local attractions and activities, free use of public transport and free guided hikes, from summer summit treks to winter snowshoeing tours.

FEEL THE RUSH

Along with hiking, Kitzbühel gets pulses racing in summer with scenic flights, skydiving, ballooning, golf, watersports and even bungee jumping.

One-stop adventure shop **element3** *(element3.at)* can take you climbing, canyoning, tandem paragliding – for a bird's-eye view of the famous Hahnenkamm – and stand-up paddleboarding (from beginners to river tours and sunset chillout paddling).

As a trailhead for the epic 1000km, 32-stage **Bike Trail Tirol**, Kitzbühel is also mountain-biking central. Whether you want to pedal gently through the valley or zoom downhill on the **Gaisberg Trail** – a 2km rattle through forested terrain, over roots, jumps and raised timber trails for experts only.

The tourist office's **KitzAlpBike** cycling map is an excellent reference, showing all routes in the area.

To ease yourself in gently, glide up by cable car to 1996m **Kitzbüheler Horn** *(return adult/child €34.50/12)*, where the **Alpine Flower Garden** is a riot of colour and fragrance. Arnica, edelweiss and purple gentian are among the 400 blooms flourishing here. The summit is also the trailhead for some beautiful walks, which deliver a big hit of alpine splendour with minimal exertion. Among them is the geologically fascinating **Karstweg**, a 2.4km, two-hour circular route diving into karst landscapes pockmarked with sinkholes and honeycombed with caves that have been around since before dinosaurs walked the earth.

For slightly more of a challenge, hook onto the 6.2km, 3½-hour round **Horn Summit Trail**. Kicking off at **Harschbichl** *(cable car return adult/child €29/15)* top station, the steep and at times exposed trek commands grandstand views of the sawtooth, pale-limestone peaks of the Wilder Kaiser range and, on cloudless days, glacier-capped, 3798m-high Grossglockner, Austria's highest peak.

To make a day of it, pack a picnic and strike out on the 15km, six-hour **Kaiserblickweg**. Beginning in **Reith bei Kitzbühel**, this exhilarating hike skips through wildflower meadows, over streams and cross-topped summits, with front-row views of the Kaisergebirge massif.

EATING IN KITZBÜHEL: OUR PICKS

Simple Food: No-frills cafe serving breakfasts, superfood salads, smoothies and burgers that deserve the credit they are given locally. *11am-8pm Mon-Fri* €

Huberbräu Stüberl: Old-world haunt with vaults and pine benches, delivering Austrian classics like schnitzel, goulash and dumplings. *9am-11pm* €€

First Lobster: Oyster shells mounted on brick walls are a nod to the terrific fish and seafood on the menu at this slick, bistro-style restaurant. *4-11pm Mon-Sat* €€

Gasthof Hagstein: In the mountains above Kitzbühel, this rustic hut enthrals with sensational views and regional faves from Tyrolean barley soup with speck. *10am-10pm* €€

Kitzbühel (p348)

Or rise with the pink dawn to tackle the tough but phenomenally scenic **9 Summit Experience**. Starting and ending at **Bochumerhütte** car park, the 11-hour, 17.7km trek involves 1447m of ascent and clambers all the way up to 2174m.

Summer Swims at Schwarzsee

Plunge into a moorland lake

In the hush and still of morning, barely a ripple breaks the surface of the **Schwarzsee** (Black Lake), an enchanting moorland lake 3km north of Kitzbühel. There's a particular thrill about being at this forest-rimmed lake at this early hour, its glassy emerald surface holding up a mirror to the jagged peaks of Wilder Kaiser. Time it right and you can go for a silent swim before others arrive.

Carved by raw glacial forces during the last Ice Age some 10,000 years ago, the lake has been famed for the healing properties of its boggy waters for centuries. A nature reserve unfurls along its shores, stippled with rare flowering plants like bog rosemary, marsh calla (swamp lily), common cranberry and carnivorous sundew. If you walk the circular trail, keep an eye out for beaver dams and gnawed logs on the northern shores of the lake.

Heating up to 27°C in summer, the lake has some of the warmest waters in the region for a swim and a **lido** *(adult/child €5.50/3)* open from May to September. Kids are in their element here, with a diving tower, water slide, playground, beach volleyball, and boat and paddleboard rental letting you head off to explore. Or you can channel your chakras with SUP yoga. Visit discoverkitz.com for times and prices.

EMBRACE THE OUTDOORS IN KITZBÜHEL

David Kreiner *(david-kreiner.at)*, born in Kitzbühel, Nordic combined skier, Winter Olympics gold-medal winner and mountain guide.

Sonnspitze: South of Kitzbühel, this 2062m peak is my paradise, with vast green slopes and steep rocky walls. Start hiking early to spot wildlife like marmots, deer and chamois.

Weisskopfkogel: In the Aurach Graben, this summit is brilliant for ski touring. Once you're on top, follow your ascending tracks or enjoy steeper variations.

Wilder Kaiser: Every climber has tried to leave a mark on these wild peaks. There are many inspiring routes but you'll need a local guide to find the best fit.

Torsee: Never overcrowded, this stunning lake, 2000m above sea level, is best approached by e-bike. After a refreshing dip, summiting Gamshag is much easier.

Beyond Kitzbühel

Kitzbühel's surrounds invite slow travel, with glittering lakes, castle-topped towns and soul-stirring villages peeking up to the Wilder Kaiser.

Places
Going am Wilden Kaiser p352
Kufstein p353
Hinterthiersee p354

GETTING AROUND

A 40-minute drive from Kitzbühel on the B173, Kufstein has speedy connections to the rest of Tyrol, as well as to Bavaria over the border in Germany (Munich is just an hour away by high-speed train). Kufstein is on the main Innsbruck–Salzburg train route and the 50-minute journey from Kitzbühel requires a change at Wörgl. Buses leave from outside the train station.

Green is the word in this region, with guest cards, free when you stay overnight, enabling you to explore by public transport without spending a cent.

Kitzbühel is a limelight stealer, but snuggled at the foot of the Wilder Kaiser massif are equally lovely, church-topped villages that receive far less tourist traffic, among them Kirchdorf, Going am Wilden Kaiser and Ellmau. They move to a more mellow beat, yet still have first-class hiking and skiing in their backyards.

These prelude the heavenly vision that is Kufstein: much feted in the Germanic world, lesser known beyond its borders. Presided over by a cliff-hanger of a medieval fortress and with cobbled lanes lined with frescoed houses, the town is pure film-set stuff. And that's even before you wild swim in its jewel-like lakes or zip up to the heights in a treetop-skimming vintage cable car.

Going am Wilden Kaiser
Dine in a barn

TIME FROM KITZBÜHEL:
15MINS

Alpine dining is elevated to a whole new authentic level at **Gasthof Stanglwirt** *(stanglwirt.com)* in Going am Wilden Kaiser, where the ragged limestone pinnacles of the Kaisergebirge punch high above flower-flecked pastures. This gorgeous vision of a 400-year-old Tyrolean inn has been converted into a luxe spa hotel without losing a jot of its original character. But the real reason to come here is to eat, with seasonal menus showcasing freshest produce from their own organic farm, including milk, butter, yoghurt cheese, bread and beef from their own butchery

With heavy, creaking timber beams and candlelight, the Cowshed is the top table, where windows peek through to the stables where the farm's happy, well-looked-after cows graze. The Cowshed might look rustic, but the menu is anything but. Dig into specialities from gooey cheese fondue to meltingly soft Tyrolean Black Angus beef chateaubriand and magnificent steak tartare garnished with quail egg, black garlic mayonnaise and wild herbs.

Kufstein

After lunch with the cows, a wander up into the mountains is irresistible. Dust off your hiking boots for a scenic 12km, four-hour circular stomp from the village up to **Astbergsee**, a glassy mountain lake at 1267m, which perfectly frames the reflection of the Wilder Kaiser. The silver-pink sunsets up here are something else.

Kufstein
The Pearl of Tyrol

TIME FROM KITZBÜHEL: **40MINS**

In the 1970s, Karl Ganzer eulogised Kufstein in his hit yodelling melody *Perle Tirols* (The Pearl of Tyrol) and rightly so. Resting at the foot of the mighty limestone Kaisergebirge, Kufstein is medieval fantasy stuff – and never more so than when you're sauntering along gingerbready **Römerhofgasse**, a reconstructed medieval lane that is bedtime story material with its overhanging arches, oriel windows, lanterns and frescoed facades.

Perched high on a rocky crag surveying the Alps that surround it, the turreted **Festung Kufstein** *(festung.kufstein. at; adult/child €14.50/8.50)* takes a gripping look at the town's turbulent past. The fortress dates from 1205 (when Kufstein was part of Bavaria) and was a pivotal point of defence for

SWEET DEALS

Check into a hotel in Kufstein and you'll automatically receive the **Kufsteiner- landCard** *(kufstein. com)*, which has some fantastic benefits, including use of the green and efficient public transport network, including hiking and ski buses.

The card also gets you free entry to the fortress, a return trip on the Kaiserlift and entry to the Riedel Kufstein glassworks, plus activities and guided tours and, in winter, use of the cross-country ski trails.

Covering a quartet of beautiful villages (Going, Ellmau, Scheffau and Söll), the digital guest card of the **Wilder Kaiser** *(wilderkaiser.info)* region is also a sweet deal. You'll get free use of the KaiserJet shuttle, linking up trails, lidos, lakes and ski slopes. The card also covers a number of activities, from torchlight hikes to brass band concerts and farm animal meet-and-greets.

EATING IN KUFSTEIN: OUR PICKS

Auracher Löchl: Going strong for 600 years, this tavern rolls out Tyrol dishes like *Kaspressknödel* (cheesy dumplings). *5-11pm Mon-Fri, noon-11pm Sat & Sun* €€

Bräustüberl: Traditional brewpub; its freshly tapped brews pair nicely with Tyrol grub, from schnitzels to goulash and bratwurst. *10am-11pm Mon-Sat* €€

Purlepaus: With a vaulted interior and chestnut tree-shaded terrace, this popular choice skips from tarte flambée to Tyrolean grub. *11am-11pm Wed-Mon* €€

Minute's: Chef Umberto riffs imaginatively on Italian and Tyrolean flavours in menus that wow at this vintage-chic restaurant. *11.30am-10pm Tue-Fri, 6-10pm Sat* €€€

LAKE SWIMS NEAR KUFSTEIN

Kufstein's surrounds are rich with gorgeous alpine lakes. By summer waters warm up to around 24°C. If you come for a dip at dawn or sunset, you'll most likely have the jewel-like waters all to your lucky self.

Hechtsee: *(lido adult/child €6/3)* If you fancy a swim, sneak down to the shores of dazzling turquoise, mountain-rimmed, forest-flanked Hechtsee, 4.5km north of town.

Thiersee: *(lido adult/child €5/2.50)* Head 7km west of Kufstein to bottle-green Thiersee, perched on a sunny plateau and with uplifting views of the Brandenberg Alps. If you want to explore further, rent out a rowboat, pedal boat or stand-up paddleboard for €10 per hour.

Stimmersee: *(lido adult/child €3.50/2.20)* Just 2.5km south of Kufstein is quiet Stimmersee. Hailed for having some of Austria's cleanest waters, this glassy green lake is fed by mountain streams, and skirted by forest and ragged mountain peaks.

both Bavaria and Tyrol during the struggles. The round **Kaiserturm** (Emperor's Tower) is a 1522 addition.

Take the lift to the top for views rippling across Kufstein to the craggy mountains beyond. The small but imaginatively presented **Heimatmuseum** distills history, with everything from Bronze Age urns to folk costumes and folk hero Andreas Hofer's shoe.

Below the Kaiserturm is the **Heldenorgel**, the world's largest open-air organ, with 4948 pipes, 46 organ stops and a 100m gap between the keyboard and the tip of the pipes; the delay in the sounding of the notes makes playing it a tricky business. Catch recitals at noon and, in July and August, 6pm. The organ is so loud, it can be heard for miles around.

When the fortress is closed in the evening, you can walk up the path in under 15 minutes, and roam the ramparts and the grounds free of charge.

Up, up to Brentenjoch

Few rides are more memorable than the **Kaiserlift** *(return €23.50/12)* to 1256m Brentenjoch. As you float above Kufstein and the forested valley in this wonderfully nostalgic single-seat vintage chairlift, the treetops are almost close enough to tickle your toes and karst mountains fling up all around you. At the top, you can pause over soul-soaring panoramas at the **Eagle's View** and **Sky View** lookouts. But these views are just a taste of what's out there.

From the bottom station of the Kaiser Lift, the 13.8km, 6½-hour, moderately challenging hike to **Brentenjochalm** passes through meadows, forest and gorges up to a beautiful mountain hut where you can revive with homemade nut cake, strudel or *Kiachl* (fried pastries) with fresh jam.

Hinterthiersee

Ayurveda in the Alps

TIME FROM KITZBÜHEL: **55MINS** OR 1¼HRS

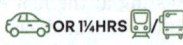

Walking around the serene, divinely pretty shores of Hinterthiersee lake, a 15-minute drive west of Kufstein, you wouldn't expect to find a slice of India. Yet **Ayurveda Resort Sonnhof** *(sonnhof-ayurveda.at; single per night incl full board €220)* has exported the 5000-year-old science and ancient wisdom of ayurveda to the heart of the Tyrolean Alps, adding its own distinctive touch. Cue soul-stirring mountain views, a Garden of Five Elements where you can stroll among roses, Buddha statues and ponds, and cooking spices, garden herbs and produce from the Mauracher family's farm. In tune with nature and its rhythms, the plateau-perched hotel has chakra-cleansing vibes: arrive, breathe in the incense, cocoon yourself in the

Festung Kufstein (p353)

spa, sip a tea matched to your *dosha* (constitutional type) and feel stress instantly lift.

The Sonnhof has carved out a unique niche as one of Europe's foremost centres for ayurvedic medicine, therapy and detox, setting the benchmark high with an outstanding team of experts. Hailing from India, there are doctors specialising in acupuncture, manual medicine and kinesiology and near-psychic experts who determine *doshas* (vata, pitta and kapha) and energy levels by measuring the pulse.

Each guest receives an individual diagnosis and therapy plan, so no two stays are alike. But incredibly relaxing treatments might include detoxifying, balancing *vishesh* (deep-tissue massage), purifying, energy-boosting Himalayan salt scrubs and hypnotically soothing *shirodhara* – where warm herbal oil is poured across the forehead. Between treatments, you are free to rest in the candlelit **Ayurveda Centre**, with its moon and sun saunas, indoor pool, infrared cabins, dosha-inspired steam chambers and meditation rooms, or with classes from mindful spirit yoga to qigong. Even a few nights here can have a profound, life-altering effect.

SLIPPERY SLOPE: HORN SLEDGE RACING

For centuries, folk from Tyrol and over-the-mountains Bavaria have been making a mad dash down the mountains on *Hornschlitten*, traditional and staggeringly weighty wooden sledges, with curved runners like the horns of a chamois.

What began many moons ago as a means of mountain farmers transporting hay and felled trees from high alpine pastures to the valley below evolved into a crazy sport, full of bumps, jumps and snowy tumbles. Innsbruck hosted its first races as far back as the 18th century.

In a few small pockets of the Alps, huge crowds still gather to watch sledgers pick up speeds of up to 100km/h as they hurtle down frozen slopes in winter.

Oberndorf in Tirol, just a couple of miles north of Kitzbühel, hosts *Hornschlitten-Rennen* races in mid-March, when you can see daring young farmers in hell-for-leather action.

The Ötztal

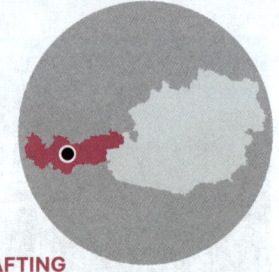

PREHISTORY | GLACIER SKIING | WHITE-WATER RAFTING

GETTING AROUND

Trains from Innsbruck arrive at Ötztal Bahnhof at the head of the valley, the jumping-off point for exploring. A car gives you greater freedom and lets you stray into the Ötztal's less-visited corners. You should be able to get at least as far as Hochgurgl year-round, but the road beyond into Italy via the high-alpine 2509m Timmelsjoch Pass is often blocked by snow in winter.

Buses are frequent, cheap and efficient and link up villages like Umhausen, Längenfeld and Sölden. Bikes and e-bikes be rented at local sport shops, including Intersport in Längenfeld. Bring boots as 1600km of signed hiking trails lace the valley.

☑ TOP TIP

Stay overnight and you're entitled to the **Ötztal Guest Card**, which gets you free use of local buses, discounts and activities.

Over millennia, the Ötztal has been shaped into rugged splendour by grinding glaciers and raw elemental forces. But this is no empty wilderness: civilisation took root here in Neolithic times, as the Stone Age remains of Ötzi, the ice man, the best-preserved mummy in the world, attest. And people have been coming ever since for the kind of big, in-your-face nature only this corner of the Austrian Alps can deliver.

Nudging the Italian border and bookended by Tyrol's highest peak, 3774m Wildspitze, this dramatic valley runs north of the Ötztaler Alpen to drain into the Inn River. And whether you've come to glacier ski, snowshoe through twinkling white forests, raft the rapids of the Ötztaler Ache, climb its granite summits or hike on 1600km of diligently signposted trails through meadows, along ridges and up to wood-smoke-filled huts, this valley really is the Tyrolean dream.

Rewind to Neolithic Times

Enter the world of the Ötzi, the ice man

For a blast of the prehistoric past, you can race back to Neolithic times at the open-air museum **Ötzi Dorf** (*oetzi-dorf. at; adult/child €12/6*), embedded in the woods in Umhausen. At this brilliantly reconstructed Copper Age village, you can take a deep dive into how life would have been for Ötzi before he was buried, frozen and mummified deep in the ice of the Similaun Glacier.

Arrive at the village when it opens at 9am to experience it at its silent and most atmospheric best. With light softly filtering through the treetops, you can picture how life might have been more than 5000 years ago. A visit takes in traditional thatched huts, herb gardens, craft displays and enclosures where wild horses and goats, mangalitza pigs, rare-breed Soay sheep and oxen roam.

If you have kids in tow, they'll love the caveman-like activities, from shooting with a yew bow to making a flint knife. You can also get active yourself, making fire with stones, giving archery a whirl, fur tanning and baking flatbread according to Neolithic recipes. For more insight into what you are seeing, join one of the free guided tours at 10am, noon, 1pm and 3.30pm.

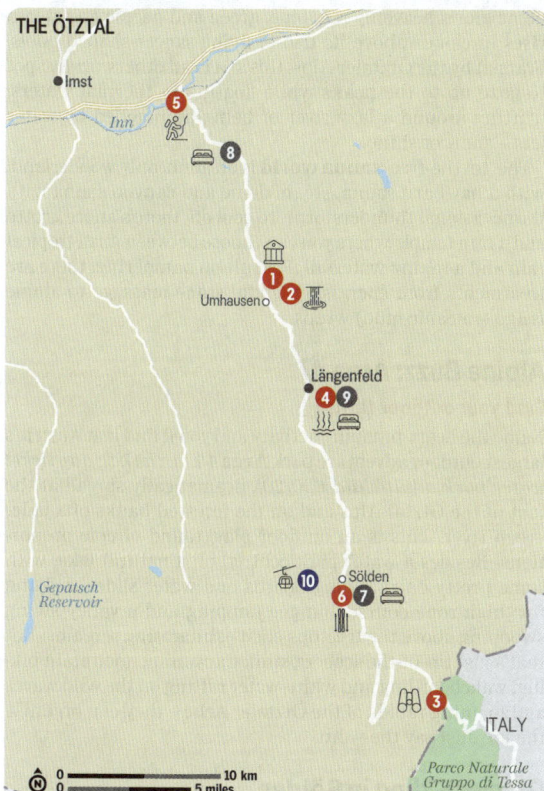

THE ÖTZTAL

- **SIGHTS**
  1. Ötzi Dorf
  2. Stuibenfall
  3. Timmelsjoch Pass
- **ACTIVITIES**
  4. Aqua Dome
  5. Area 47
  6. Sölden
- **SLEEPING**
  7. Die Berge
  8. feelfree Nature Resort
  9. Hotel Rita
- **TRANSPORT**
  10. Giggijochbahn

SUMMER SAVINGS

If you're staying in the Ötztal in summer, it's worth investing in the all-inclusive **Summer Card** *(oetztal.com; adult 3/5/7/10 days €87/125/156/199, child 3/5/7/10 days €52/75/94/119)* in addition to the guest card that you automatically receive when staying overnight.

Valid from early June to mid-October, the card covers public transport, toll roads and cable cars in the valley, attractions such as Ötzi Dorf, activities from lidos and swimming lakes to bike rental and guided hikes, plus one free entry to Aqua Dome and Area 47. Visit the website for a full list of all the card's benefits and savings.

Feel the Force
Marvel at Tyrol's highest falls

From Ötzi Dorf, it's a beautiful 20-minute forest walk to Tyrol's longest waterfall, the wispy **Stuibenfall**, crashing 159m over slate cliffs and moss-covered boulders. You can continue for another 40 minutes up to the top viewing platform and hanging bridge. A thrilling 450m *Klettersteig* (via ferrata) takes you right over the waterfall; bring your own karabiner and helmet.

If you want to brush up your climbing skills – and frankly there's no better place in Tyrol to do just that – take a course with the experts at the adventure centre **Alpinzeit** *(alpinzeit.tirol; lantern hike/via ferrata tour €10/80)*, which range from guided via ferrata tours of the Stuibenfall to highly atmospheric lantern-lit hikes of the falls as the stars begin to glitter in night skies.

Otherworldly Bathing: Aqua Dome
Chilling in a space-age spa

Arrive at **Aqua Dome** *(aqua-dome.at; day ticket adult/child €54/28)* in the ethereal pink-blue glow of sunset and you might think you've been teleported to another planet, as its crystalline

ICE, ICE ÖTZI

In 1991 German hiker Helmut Simon came across the body of a man preserved within the Similaun Glacier in the Ötztaler Alpen, some 90m within Italy. Police and forensic scientists were summoned to the scene.

Carbon dating revealed that the ice man, nicknamed 'Ötzi', was nearly 5400 years old, placing him in the late Stone Age and making him the oldest and best-preserved mummy in the world.

Ötzi became big news, more so because his state of preservation was remarkable; even the pores of his skin were visible. In addition, Ötzi had been found with 70 artefacts, including a copper axe, bow and arrows, charcoal and clothing.

Physiologically he was found to be no different from modern humans. X-rays showed he had suffered from arthritis, frostbite and broken ribs. Ötzi was relinquished to the Italians to become the centrepiece of a museum in Bolzano in 1998.

---

dome glows heavenly red, blue, green and purple and steam rises in clouds above its trio of flying-saucer-shaped pools. Framed by the Ötztaler Alps, this spa is an otherworldly spot to gaze up to the peaks while floating in thermal waters, drifting around a lazy river or being pummelled by water jets – snow or shine.

The 'textile-free' **sauna world** is an adult-only wonderland, with a hay-barn sauna, steam dome and canyon sauna with the occasional thunderstorm. To cool off, there's an ice grotto and a rain temple where you can choose between mist, tropical rain and a raging waterfall. For full-on pampering, there are treatments from energising Ötztal stone massage to alpine fango (volcanic mud) wraps.

Alpine Buzz: Area 47
Find your outdoor thrill

Name the heart-pumping activity and you'll find it at Austria's largest outdoor adventure park **Area 47** *(area47.at; day ticket water park adult/child €30/20)*, dramatically spread at the foot of the Ötztal Alps and on the forested banks of a jade-green river. This is an outdoor playground of epic proportions. Besides a water park centred on a natural lake, with some pretty hairy diving boards and water slides, a flying fox, high-rope course, bungee jumping and a valley swing swooping above the treetops elicit exhilarating screams. But that's just tip-of-the-iceberg stuff. Canyoning, mountain biking, wakeboarding and white-water rafting on the wild waves and foaming rapids of the Ötztaler Ache – they can organise the lot. Just say the word.

Glacier Skiing in Sölden
Slalom into summer

Alpine Ski World Cup venue **Sölden** *(soelden.com)* has one of the longest seasons in the Tyrolean Alps with snow from October to May. Spread between 1350m and 3340m, the resort's slopes draw intermediates and are complemented by glacier skiing at Rettenbach and Tiefenbach. Up for a challenge? Ski the 50km four-hour downhill **Big 3 Rally**. It begins at the mountain station of **Giggijochbahn** *(return adult/child €25/14)* and takes in a trio of 3000m peaks.

A Sky-High Drive
The scenic road to South Tyrol

If you'd rather get behind the wheel, Sölden is the gateway to the dramatic **Timmelsjoch High Alpine Road** *(timmelsjoch.com; car one-way/return €20/28)*. Nicknamed the 'secret pass to the south', this little-driven but beautiful pass road wiggles from the Ötztal and the Passeier Valley in the Italian South Tyrol. Known since the Stone Age, the route attracted traders and smugglers in the Middle Ages. Negotiating 30 hairpin bends, it crests the highest point at 2509m, where a tavern awaits.

Beyond The Ötztal

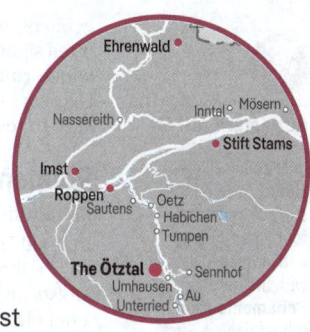

Nature works on a grand scale in Tyrol's west, with the Inn River flowing swiftly past the limestone crags of the Lechtal Alps.

Ötzal is just a skip away from Imst, where the ferny fantasy of the Rosengartenschlucht gorge and its falls await. Culturally, the town enthrals with its riotous pre-Lenten, UNESCO World Heritage Schemenlaufen, a parade held every four years and engagingly brought to life in the local museum. Roads slip like thread veins south into remote, under-the-radar valleys such as Pitztal, Kaunertal and Inntal, where snow-sure, crowd-free slopes beckon skiers who have ventured this far. West still is Landeck, with an impressively intact medieval castle astride a hill and outdoor activities galore. Its orchard-rimmed neighbour, Stanz, heaves with distilleries producing some of Austria's most potent plum schnapps.

Imst
TIME FROM THE ÖTZTAL: **20MINS** 🚗 OR **30MINS** 🚌

Fairy-tale ravine & Roman caverns

Near-vertical walls of dolomite punch above the turbulent falls of the Schinderbach and mossy, fern-flecked forests where you can imagine sprites frolicking at Imst's showpiece **Rosengartenschlucht** *(imst.at)*. You can admire the ravine's rugged splendour from the bottom bridge, but to really feel nature pulling out all the stops (quite literally), strike out on the gentle 2½-hour loop trail that threads through this wild and dramatic gorge. Starting and ending in Imst, the 4.6km ramble teeters along boarded walkways blasted into the rock, ducks into small tunnels and gently ascends on a footpath that shows off the waterfall from every photo-worthy, mist-wisped angle.

When you reach the top, the trail meanders through sun-dappled woodland, with the trees occasionally drawing back to give glimpses of the Lechtaler Alps. When you see a dazzling shimmer of cerulean-blue water, you know you've reached the **Blaue Grotte**, formed by Romans mining these caves for silver-rich galena millennia ago. Push on and you'll reach Hoch Imst and the kid-pleasing **Alpine Coaster** *(adult/child €11.60/8.40)*. Billed as the 'world's longest alpine roller coaster', it's a whizzy, exhilarating, 40km/h, 3.5km dash down the mountains in a track-mounted bobsleigh.

The trailhead for the Rosengartenschlucht is the **tourist office** on Johannesplatz in Imst, which stocks maps of the walk. It's easy to go it alone, but for more insight on the local

Places
Imst p359
Roppen p360
Stift Stams p360
Ehrwald p361

GETTING AROUND

The east-west A12 motorway from Innsbruck to Landeck speeds things up if you're driving, but zipping about by public transport is pretty easy, with relatively short distances, quick, efficient connections, and buses and trains joining the dots.

If you want to dip further into the region's remoter valleys, which stretch their fingers south to Italy, you'll need a car (bear in mind some roads are blocked by snow in winter).

Bike and e-bike rental are available locally, including at some ÖBB train stations.

SCHEMENLAUFEN

Imst seems like a sleepy town on the surface, but every four years it leaps and jangles to life with the riotous **Schemenlaufen** (ghost dance). First documented in 1597, this UNESCO-listed, pre-Lenten festival is a sight to behold.

The unmissable part is the parade, where 900 locals (10% of the population) don spectacularly intricate costumes, hand-carved masks and locally forged bells. The main characters are Roller (jumpers) and Scheller (ringers), with cowbells that weight 35kg attached to their hips, who engage in an elaborate dance of jumps and bows.

Bears, shrieking, broom-wielding Hexen (witches), bag-swinging Sackner, water-squirting Spritzer and masked chimney-sweeps also storm the streets.

Even if you can't make the Schemenlaufen (next held in February 2028), you can get the inside scoop on its centuries-old heritage in Imst's **Haus der Fasnacht** *(fasnacht.at).*

geology, plant and wildlife (the red-winged wallcreeper is often sighted here), join one of the tourist office's guided hikes, which run every Monday from 2pm to 5.30pm from May to October. These are free with the Imst holiday pass, but be sure to reserve your spot ahead and bring sturdy footwear.

Roppen

TIME FROM THE ÖTZTAL: **10MINS**

Behold the Earth Pyramids

In Wald-Hohenegg in the Inntal, 11km south of Imst, set out on a 4.2km circular march through beautiful waterfall-laced forests and the steep-sided Innschlucht (Inn Gorge). You'll do a double take when you eventually clap eyes on the **Erdpyramiden** (earth pyramids). Slender and stone-capped, these geologically fascinating spires of rock – also known as fairy chimneys or hoodoos – have been eroded into bizarre formations over millennia. Created from moraine left over when glaciers melted, they are remnants of the last Ice Age. The moderately challenging walk to the viewing platform begins at a small car park in front of an information board, just after the hamlet of Waldele on the narrow road to Wald im Pitztal. Allow around two hours for the return hike.

Stift Stams

TIME FROM THE ÖTZTAL: **15MINS**

An opulent abbey

As if cupped in celestial hands, **Stift Stams** *(stiftstams.at; museum adult/child €8/5, with guided tour €13.50/7)* lifts your gaze to the great rocky summits of the Alps. One of Tyrol's true architectural and spiritual treasures, the Cistercian abbey was founded in 1273 by Count Meinhard II of Görz-Tirol and his wife Elisabeth of Bavaria, mother of Konradin, the last of the Hohenstaufens. Today it's still the centrepiece of a thriving monastic community. Reclining in beautifully manicured gardens, the monumental, ochre-and-white facade stretches 80m and is easily recognised by its pair of silver cupolas at the front, added as a final flourish when the abbey was revamped in baroque style in the 17th century.

The abbey's pride and joy is its astonishingly elaborate **basilica** dominated by the **high altar**: the intertwining branches of this 19m-high 'tree of life' ensnare 84 saintly figures surrounding an image of the Virgin. Near the entrance is the **rose grille**, an exquisite iron screen studded with 80 roses, fashioned in 1716 by Tyrolean metalsmith Bernhard Bachnetzer. Look up to the heavens to admire the ceiling adorned with rich stuccowork, gold swirls and elaborate frescoes by Georg Wolker.

Join one of the hourly **guided tours** in summer and you can also take a peek in **St Bernard's Hall**, lavishly frescoed with scenes form the life of St Bernard of Clairvaux, the founder of the Cistercian Order. The vaulted **Holy Blood Chapel** contains relics that came to Stams from France in the 14th century, which are paraded through the village on the first Sunday in May.

Before heading off, pop into the **abbey shop** for marmalade, juice, honey, liqueurs, ciders and schnapps made on the Stift Stams premises, plus bread that's freshly baked here on Friday.

Stift Stams

Ehrwald

TIME FROM THE ÖTZTAL: **50MINS**

Surmounting Zugspitze

Nudging the German border, the bijou town of Ehrwald is dwarfed by colossal peaks, including the craggy limestone peaks of the Wetterstein range. In summer, the town has cross-border hiking trails to make your heart sing, many of which thread high to waterfall-laced mountains and through sheer-sided gorges stippled with spruce trees and pounded by aquamarine rivers.

Ehrwald's crowning glory is the glaciated 2962m **Zugspitze** *(zugspitze.at; cable car one-way/return adult €41.50/63.50, child €25/38.50)*, Germany's highest peak, straddling the Austro-German border. From the crest there's a magnificent panorama of the main Tyrolean mountain ranges, as well as the Bavarian Alps and Mt Säntis in Switzerland.

Riveting views aside, you can dive into the history of the peak, mountaineering legends and first ascents at the **Adventure museum**, marvel at the snow-draped landscape from the hexagonal, glass-and-steel **Snow Crystal visitor centre** and get a free summit tour by downloading the Hearonymus app. For added drama, visit the summit just as the first rays illuminate the peaks with a sunrise ticket.

While you can glide from Ehrwald to the top by panoramic cable car in just 10 minutes, striking out on foot gives you a true flavour of these wild heights. A five-hour hike from the summit to the mountain station of the Almenbahn throws you in at the Alpine deep end, clambering over the Gatterl saddle and taking you through the dramatic karst landscape of the Zugspitze plateau. The trek is moderately challenging, so you need to be surefooted and have a good head for heights.

THE STANZ DISTILLERIES

Heading west along the Inn Valley, you reach the town of Landeck, visible from afar with its medieval cake-topper of a castle. Lifted above the valley on a plateau, tiny Stanz, 3km away, is home to some of Europe's highest apple and plum orchards.

The village has 150 houses and 53 schnapps distilleries. There are a number of rustic huts where you can kick back and taste the local firewater before rolling back down to the valley.

In early September, Stanz hosts **Stanz Brennt**, a distillery festival with plenty of the local schnapps, live music, food stalls and a farmers market selling fruit-based goodies.

St Anton am Arlberg

SENSATIONAL SKIING | HARDCORE PARTYING | SUMMER TRAILS

Once upon a time St Anton was a sleepy village on the Rosanna River, defined by the falling and melting of snow, and the coming and going of cattle, until one day the locals beheld the virgin powder on their doorstep and discovered their happy-ever-after… In 1901, the resort founded the first ski club in the Alps and downhill skiing was born.

If ever the ski bug is going to bite it will surely be here. Whether you're flying down a black piste with the Lechtal Alps across the horizon or swishing through the great white backcountry, St Anton is up there on the podium with Europe's hottest ski resorts. In summer, the focus flicks to high-altitude hikes, mountain biking, white-water rafting and lazy lunches at meadow-rimmed alpine huts to the backbeat of cowbells. Two very different dreams. Choose yours.

Action Stations: St Anton

Born to be wild

You can find heart-racing activities all over the Austrian Alps, but wild child St Anton has the edge. With serrated, snow-frosted mountains ripping across the horizon and glassy rivers smashing their way through dark spruce forests, these untamed landscapes are like Canada minus the bears, some say. But why imagine yourself elsewhere?

Thrill-seekers have flocked to St Anton for more than a century – but not only skiers get a buzz. In summer, those same black pistes test nerves with rough, rocky mountain biking – try the bone-rattling, 4.5km **Galzig Trail** if you dare, or master tricks on the tracks and natural obstacles at **EldoRADo Bike Park** *(dirt bike rental per hr/half day €5/15)*. If you're hungry for more, road-biking routes clamber over the mountains into neighbouring valleys such as Paznauntal and Montafon, while others twist into the immediate heights – a phenomenally scenic one being the 39km return, half-day tour to the 2320m **Neue Heilbronner Hütte** *(dav-heilbronn.de)*, involving a sweaty 1600m of ascent.

GETTING AROUND

Central St Anton is compact, pedestrian-friendly and easily explored on foot.

Right in the heart of town, ultra-modern cable cars haul you up to the heights and over the mountains to the neighbouring resorts of Lech and Zürs. Free local buses go to outlying parts of the resort, such as St Jakob, which is a five-minute bus journey or a 40-minute walk. You can rent mountain and e-bikes at Intersport Arlberg on central Dorfstrasse.

Taxis and shuttles can be shared between up to eight people. Contact the **tourist office** *(stantonamarlberg.com)* for information.

☑ TOP TIP

The best accommodation fills up in a flash in winter, so book well ahead. For cheaper pensions, try Nasserein and St Jakob.

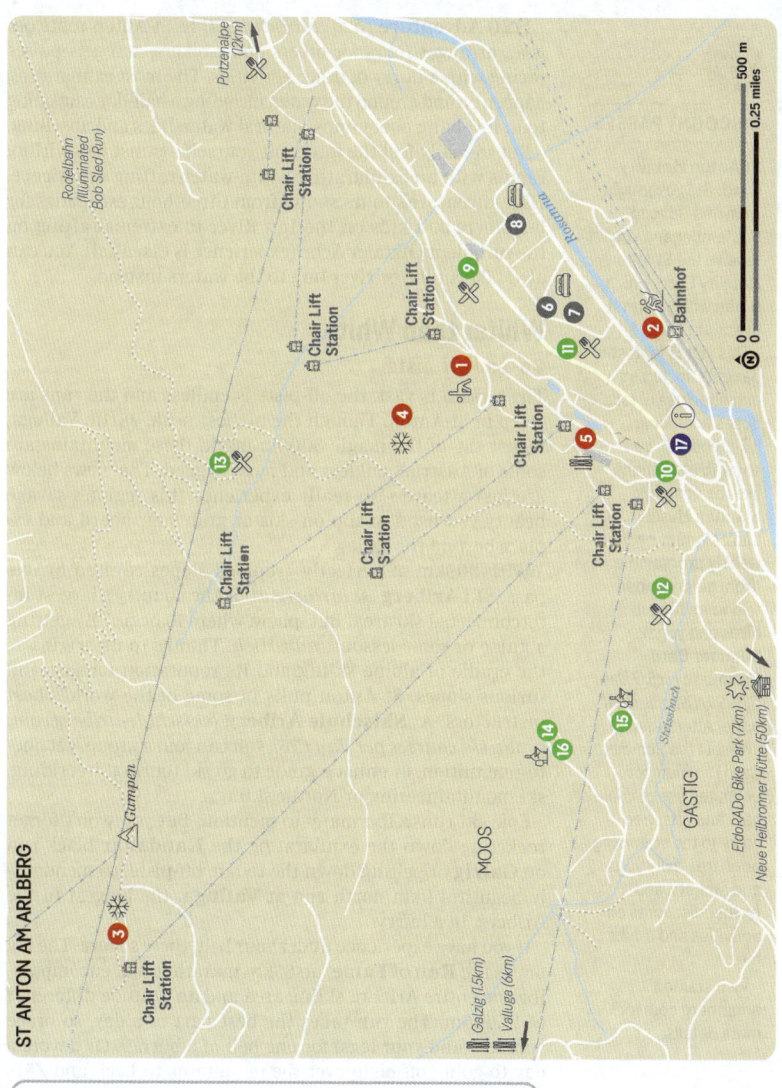

DISCOUNT PASSES

St Anton Mobility Card: Stay overnight from mid-June to September and you'll receive the St Anton Mobility Card, which is free with your first overnight stay.

This yields fantastic benefits, including unlimited use of local buses (including hiking buses), free entry to attractions like the nostalgic St Anton Museum, and activities on the weekly programme (from guided mountain tours to herb hikes and yoga).

Summer Card Premium: *(3/5/7 days €79/99/119, child half price)* Alternatively invest in the Summer Card Premium for unlimited use of cable cars and lifts, free entry to the swimming pool, free daily yoga and archery, and further discounts on activities and e-bike hire.

Visit stantonamarlberg.com for more details.

H2O Adventure *(h2o-adventure.at)* in St Anton rents out gear, arranges tours for bikers and e-bikers, and gets pulses racing with a flurry of other activities. The most exhilarating happen on and around the water, including a half-day canyoning tour, involving pool jumps, natural waterslides and abseiling.

But to really feel the force, pit yourself against its swirling rapids with an exhilarating white-water-rafting experience. H2O Adventure's tours swing from three-hour escapades for beginners and kids on the Inn River to extreme rafting on the turbulent Ötztaler Ache (experience is essential). You can also take a tube or river bug to the waters instead.

Whiter than White
On- and off-piste

The terrain is vast, the off-piste is endless and the runs are steep in St Anton. Though the highest peak, 2811m Valluga, is just shy of the magic 3000m mark, these mountains are some of Austria's wildest and most rugged. The views below are just a tease – to really experience this region's savage beauty you need to slip on skis or grab your board and explore beyond the valley.

With 308km of perfectly groomed slopes covered by one pass, **Ski Arlberg** *(skiarlberg.at)* is the country's largest interconnected ski area. But, phew, where to begin? By getting a guide or some lessons, *natürlich*. Thanks to its origins as the cradle of alpine skiing and its reputation for fast and furious slopes, St Anton pulls in some of the world's best instructors. At **Skischule Arlberg** *(skischule-arlberg.com; group ski courses per day €76)*, you can join a group, get one-to-one tuition, or enlist a guide to go ski touring, freeriding, ski mountaineering or Nordic skiing.

Epic ski runs? Too many to mention. But you won't forget rocketing down the exhilarating the **Kandahar** black run on **Galzig** or pelting down the tough, off-piste, tremendously beautiful 9km north run at **Valluga**, the longest in the Arlberg, in a hurry.

If you have experience under your belt, there's more. The big one is the **Run of Fame**, an 85km marathon ski, encompassing the entire Arlberg skiing area and an altitude difference of 18,000m. The run takes the best part of a day, so brace yourself (and your legs) for one hell of a burner. Or devote a day to going off-piste over the mountains to Lech and Zürs on the spectacular (and spectacularly challenging) **Great Arlberg Tour**.

EATING IN ST ANTON: OUR PICKS

Galzig Bistrobar: Seasonal Austrian meets globetrotting faves from pasta to Thai curry at this modern bistro at the base of the slopes. *10am-11pm* €€

Museum Restaurant: Succulent Tyrolean beef and trout fresh from the pond land on your plate at this gorgeous rustic restaurant. *noon-6pm Tue-Sun* €€

Endlich: Intimate restaurant with a social dining ethos where fresh ingredients get a slice of Nordic finesse. Book ahead. *7-11pm Mon-Sat* €€€

Hazienda: This slickly contemporary restaurant at m3 Hotel bigs up seasonal ingredients in fresh-faced dishes that sing of Tyrol. *6pm-midnight Tue-Sun* €€€

Mooserwirt

Party On
Après-ski in overdrive

When the flakes fall in winter, St Anton am Arlberg is a cross between a ski bum's Shangri La and Ibiza in fast-forward mode – the terrain fierce, the nightlife hedonistic. The town is Austria's unrivalled après-ski king. Dancing on tables, *Schlager* sing-alongs, Jägermeister shots – it's just an average night out in St Anton, where people party as hard as they ski. Pace yourself.

You're bound to find your own fun, but rollicking bars to shake in your snow-boots include pumping, piste-side **Taps** *(taps-stanton.com)*, with its huge terrace and ice bar, and its neighbour, loud, fun and jam-packed **Krazy Kanguruh** *(krazykanguruh.com)*, where DJs whip the crowd into action from 3pm. But best (or maddest) of the lot, is **Mooserwirt** *(mooserwirt.at)*, heaving with skiers guzzling beer (the place sells around 5000L a day), dancing to Eurotrash and sweating in their salopettes.

Hike the Eagle's Way
The ultimate Tyrol trail

Right up there with Austria's finest hikes, the hut-to-hut **Adlerweg** (Eagle's Way) sends spirits soaring as high as the region's beloved eagles. The 324km, 24-stage, near month-long trek takes Tyrol in its stride, leading from St Johann in Tyrol to St Anton am Arlberg and dropping you in some of the country's most compelling alpine landscapes. Thundering falls, gorges, ice caves, pine forests, fast-flowing rivers and glaciers unfold as you stomp along paths through the limestone peaks of the Kaiser and Karwendel massifs, the Inn Valley and Lechtaler Alps.

FATHER OF MODERN SKIING: HANNES SCHNEIDER

St Anton owes much to Hannes Schneider (1890–1955) for – quite literally – carving out its stellar reputation as the cradle of alpine skiing. Born and raised in the Arlberg, Hannes was a whizz on skis as a kid.

The son of a dairy farmer, he quickly realised that the telemark style, which was popular at the time, wasn't the best way to tackle the region's steep slopes – it was too unstable, leading to wobbles and falls in the high-alpine terrain.

A pioneering Hannes began experimenting with his own revolutionary way of skiing – the Arlberg technique – crouching and shifting his weight forward to lower his centre of gravity to improve balance and stability, and moving weight one ski to another to elegantly control the turns.

In 1921, he founded the first ski club in St Anton, triggering a boom in ski tourism to the region. To this day he is revered as a local hero.

STRIKE A POSE

Sun salutations take on a whole new meaning as dawn creeps over the Arlberg Alps and you reach up to the summits to embrace the day.

St Anton has carved out an unexpected niche as one of Austria's yoga meccas. But here it's about more than mastering the *asanas* (poses) – it's about tuning into nature, hearing the wind rush through wildflower meadows and the hypnotic beat of cowbells in the distance and feeling the soul-calming silence of these mountains.

Early September brings the four-day **Mountain Yoga Festival** *(mountainyogafestivalstanton.at)*, with world-class instructors leading al fresco yoga sessions, meditation and workshops.

Year-round, you can channel your chakras at **arlflow** *(arlflow.at)*, with a roster of classes, including rooftop ones with mountain views when it's warm.

The good news: it isn't as tough as it sounds. The trail is diligently waymarked, following established tracks, and villages, towns and mountain huts offer respite at the end of each stage. Hike it from late June to mid-September when the huts are open and the passes snow-free, and take Cicerone's *The Adlerweg* as your companion.

A Downhill Dash
The glitter of snow and stars

You'll whoop out loud with childish joy as you negotiate bends, bump over snowdrifts and dash through snow-daubed forests, with pearl-white peaks glowering down, on Gampen's 4km **Rodelbahn** (toboggan run), reached by taking the gondola from Nasserein up to 1850m. It's terrific fun, especially when floodlit on Tuesday and Thursday nights in winter.

Rent your sledge at halfway hut **Thony's Barn** *(anthonys.at)*, and pop in there afterwards, with glowing face and frosty fingers, to warm up with schnapps and a big plate of *Schweinshaxe* (pork knuckles), *Gröstl* (Tyrolean potato, egg, bacon and onion fry-up) or cheese fondue. An open fire keeps things toasty in the pine-panelled interior.

Until the Cows Come Home
Head to pastures high

In summer, St Anton moves to a more mellow, nature-focused beat, with meadow paths twisting up to timber huts and high-mountain pastures cloaked in wildflowers from purple gentian and hot-pink alpine rhododendrons.

For a heart-warming taste of alpine life, take an 8km hike up to **Putzenalpe**, a mountain hut nestled in a tranquil meadow, where you can often spot marmots if you look carefully. It does a great *Brettljause* (tasting platter), featuring the cheese from its 50 cows, which you can, incidentally, see coming down from the pastures around 5pm, their clanging bells resonating through the valley.

In mid-September, the cows come home from their summer pastures in their floral finery at St Anton's **Almabtrieb**, a village-wide excuse for a party.

Beyond St Anton am Arlberg

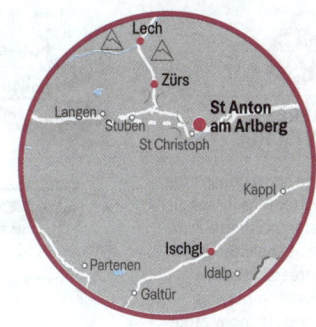

St Anton's surrounds will bowl you over with their wild alpine beauty. Grab skis or boots and head on up.

St Anton is merely the overture for the fiercely beautiful Arlberg region, where the remote backcountry delivers some of Austria's finest hiking and skiing. Cable cars swing over the mountains from St Anton to Lech and Zürs, a pair of ritzy, chocolate-box pretty resorts, where you'll share the slopes with piste-bashing celebs and royals. Grazing the Swiss border, Paznauntal (Paznaun Valley) is a dramatic landscape overshadowed by the pearly white peaks of the Silvretta range. The villages are sleepy in summer but for hikers trotting up into the heights and mountain bikers dashing down them. This lull is broken in winter when skiers descend on party-hearty resorts such as Ischgl.

Lech & Zürs
Snowflakes & silver screens

TIME FROM ST ANTON AM ARLBERG: **20-30MINS**

Rugged mountains huddle conspiratorially above the fabled slopes of **Lech** (1450m) and its smaller twin **Zürs** (1716m), a gorgeous pair 6km south of St Anton. Their paparazzi-free pistes have attracted a flurry of celebs and royals over the years, with a discreet, low-key vibe, fine looks and all the trappings that go with their cachet: a blizzard of five-star digs and a flurry of gourmet restaurants. Forget designer boutiques, however – the atmosphere here is old-school posh, not flashy.

The duo had their starring moment on the silver screen, too. Remember Bridget Jones hurtling backwards down the mountain on skis in *The Edge of Reason?* That was filmed on Lech's scenic, forest-streaked runs.

You can have your own Bridget moment on a vast 300km network of slopes, with a nice mix of cruisy pistes taking you up and down to neighbouring villages and phenomenal off-piste powder when you stray into expert terrain. For a challenge, tackle **Der Weisse Ring** (The White Ring), an epic, half-day 22km ski that will leave you breathless – both because of the 5500m of ascent and descent involved, and the views.

For a taste of the high life, stay like a star at the all-suite **Severins – The Alpine Retreat** *(severins-lech.at)*.

Places
Lech & Zürs p367
Ischgl p368

GETTING AROUND

You can easily reach Zürs and Lech by bus from St Anton am Arlberg. For Ischgl, you'll need to take a train to Landeck and then a bus. The Flexen Pass (1773m), 1km south of Zürs, is occasionally blocked by winter snow, after which the road splits: the western fork leads to Stuben (1407m), the eastern to St Anton am Arlberg.

From mid-June to early October, pick up the money-saving **Lech Card** *(2/4/7 days €45/69/99)* for the use of all buses and cable cars, plus themed guided hikes and e-bike rides and entry to the forest swimming pool and alpine water park.

APRÈS-SKI IN ISCHGL

The snow doesn't get hotter than in Ischgl, famous Europe-wide for its boisterous après-ski scene. Oompah-playing barns, raunchy table-dancing bars and glitzy clubs with DJs and dancing shake the resort. Here folk music and techno happily coexist.

Most places go with the snow and open in winter only. Pumping post-slope bars include Hexenküche, Kuhstall, Trofana Alm, Niki's Stadl and Schatzi.

The big ticket for party-mad skiers is the **Top of the Mountain** winter-season opening and closing concerts in late November and early May respectively. In recent years, these have brought a host of stars to the stage, including the Black Eyed Peas, Ellie Goulding and OneRepublic.

Ischgl, Silvretta Arena

Ischgl   TIME FROM ST ANTON AM ARLBERG: 1HR 20MINS

Skiing the Silvretta Arena

Ischgl in the Patznauntal is the centrepiece of the vast **Silvretta Arena** *(ischgl.com)*, offering fabulous skiing on 239km of groomed slopes, ultramodern lifts (heated seats and all) and few queues. Suited to all except absolute beginners, the resort has great intermediate runs around **Idalp**, tough black descents at **Greitspitz** and **Paznauer Taya**, and plenty of off-piste powder to challenge experts. Skiing to **Samnaun** in Switzerland for lunch adds the novelty factor. Boarders can play on the half-pipe, jumps, rails and boarder-cross at two snow parks. The **Silvretta Ski Pass** *(1/4/6 days €76/286/408)* covers all 75 lifts in the region.

Summertime biking in Ischg

Summer in Ischgl is decidedly more chilled in the resort, but just as heart-pumping on the slopes as skis are swapped for mountain bikes. Straddling the Austrian-Swiss border the vast **Silvretta Bike Arena** features 100km of bikeable terrain, ranging from downhill tracks to circular trails. The **Silvretta Bike Academy** *(silvretta-bikeacademy.at; tours/bike rental €51/48)* offers freeride day tours, technique training and fat-bike rental.

In early August, things turn up a notch at the two-day **Ironbike** *(ischgl.com)*, where super-fit mountain bikers compete in a race, involving steep climbs and exhilarating descents in the Silvretta massif. The extreme route is 70km and follows the old smugglers' route from Ischgl to Samnaun and back. But it's not just for pros – there are races for all ages and levels.

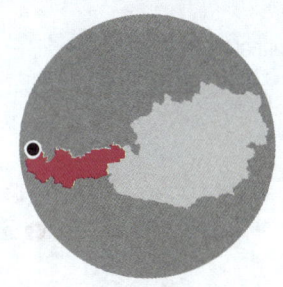

Bregenz

CUTTING-EDGE ARCHITECTURE | FESTIVAL SPIRIT | RELAXED LAKE LIFE

In Austria's wild west, Vorarlberg is where mountains and high-alpine meadows abruptly give way to the mellow weather, flowery shores and open vistas of Bodensee and Bregenz, the region's cultured, charismatic, high-spirited capital.

What a backdrop. Bregenz has the loveliest of views: before you Bodensee (Lake Constance), Europe's third-largest lake, spreads out like a liquid mirror; behind you the Pfänder (1064m) climbs to the Alps; to the right you see Germany, to the left the faint outline of Switzerland.

Whether contemplating avant-garde art and architecture by the new harbour, sauntering along the promenade on a summer's evening, swimming from a *Strandbad* (lake lido) or watching opera under the stars at the much-lauded Festspiele, you can't help but think – clichéd though it sounds – that Vorarlberg's pocket-sized capital has almost got it all.

Culture Club

Art by the lake

You can easily devote half a day to dipping into the high-calibre galleries and museums in Bregenz. Designed by Swiss architect Peter Zumthor, the striking glass-and-steel cube of Bregenz's **Kunsthaus** *(kunsthaus-bregenz.at; adult/child €14/free)* resembles a lamp, reflecting the changing light of the sky and lake. The stark, open-plan interior is perfect for rotating exhibitions of contemporary art, which swing from the abstract to the avant-garde, with artists hailing from Austria and beyond. Entry is free on the first Thursday evening of the month.

One of Bregenz's most eye-catching landmarks is the white, cubic **Vorarlberg Museum** *(vorarlbergmuseum.at; adult/child €10/free)*, emblazoned with what appears to be 16,656 flowers (actually PET bottle bases imprinted in concrete). The gallery homes in on Vorarlberg's history, art and architecture in its permanent exhibitions, including one on the

GETTING AROUND

A scenic promenade running along the flower-fringed shores of Bodensee and a compact, pedestrian-friendly historic centre make Bregenz a delight to explore on foot or by bicycle.

If you want to venture further around or across the lake, regular **Vorarlberg Lines** *(vorarlberg-lines.at)* boats breeze across the water to pretty towns in Germany such as Lindau, Meersburg, Friedrichshafen and Konstanz – all of which make excellent over-the-border day trips.

In a pavilion right on the lakefront, **Ewald Bikes** rents out city, mountain and e-bikes. With your own two wheels, you can easily whizz over to neighbouring Germany or Switzerland for an hour or two on the Bodensee Radweg.

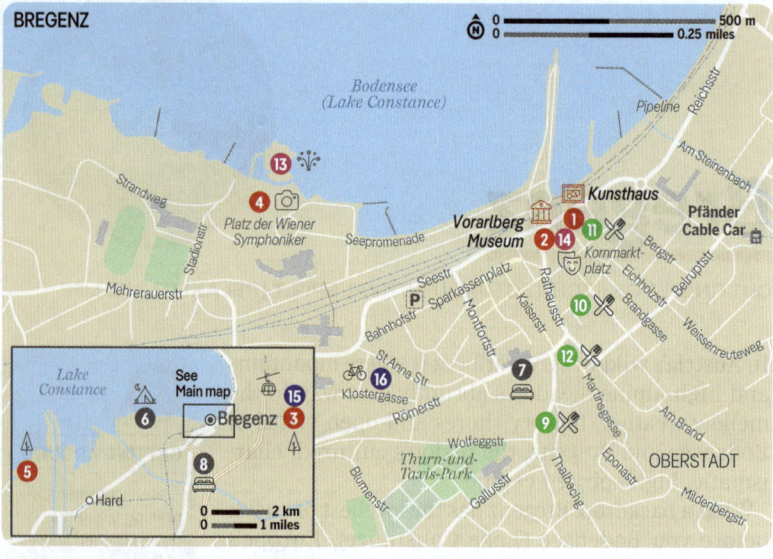

- **HIGHLIGHTS**
  1. Kunsthaus
  2. Vorarlberg Museum
- **SIGHTS**
  3. Alpine Game Park Pfänder
  4. Festspielhaus
  5. Rheindelta
- **SLEEPING**
  6. Camping Mexico
  7. Hotel Weisses Kreuz
  8. Schwärzler
- **EATING**
  9. BAHI
  10. Cafesito
  11. Kornmesser
  12. Küchentanz in der Ilge
- **ENTERTAINMENT**
  13. Bregenzer Festspiele
  14. Vorarlberger Landestheater
- **TRANSPORT**
  15. Pfänderbahn
  16. Radverleih

☑ TOP TIP

Many hotels in Bregenz are of the nondescript chain variety, but there are a few charming historic exceptions, plus an appealing hostel and a campsite. Prices soar and beds are at a premium during the Bregenzer Festspiele; book ahead. If Bregenz is booked solid, consider hopping over the border to Lindau in Germany, 9km away.

Roman archaeological finds of Brigantium. It also stages rotating exhibitions that provide insight into the region's cultural heritage.

Festival Time

Operatic highs on the lake

Hearing opera reverberate across Bodensee on a balmy summer evening is spine-tingling stuff. With one of Austria's romantic backdrops, the **Bregenzer Festspiele** (*bregenzer festspiele.com; tickets €30-440*), held each year from mid-July to mid-August, punches high on a world scale. Spectacularly choreographed operas, orchestral works and other highly imaginative productions are staged on the open-air, semicircular **Seebühne**, a floating stage on the lake, in the **Festspielhaus** (*festspielhausbregenz.com*) and at the **Vorarlberger Landestheater** (*landestheater.org*). Information and tickets are up for grabs about nine months before the festival.

Even if you can't bag tickets, the Festspielhaus is a must-see. All tinted glass, smooth concrete and sharp angles, this is one of Bregenz's most visible icons.

Cycling Bodensee
One lake, two wheels, three countries

When the sun's out, there's no finer way to see Bodensee (Lake Constance) than with your backside in a saddle. The well-marked **Bodensee Radweg** *(bodensee-radweg.com)* makes a 273km loop of the lake, taking in vineyards, meadows, orchards, wetlands, historic towns and small beaches where you can stop for a refreshing dip. Bikes and e-bikes can be rented at **Radverleih** *(radverleih-bregenz.at; per day bike/e-bike rental €29/39)* in Bregenz, then you're free to explore at your own steam. The entire cycle route takes around a week, but trains and Vorarlberg Lines boats make it possible to cover shorter chunks.

There are memorable rides even if you have just a couple of hours at hand. Roll 9km south of Bregenz to the **Rheindelta** nature reserve, where the River Rhine flows into the Bodensee. The mossy marshes, reeds and mixed woodlands attract more than 300 bird species, including curlews, grey herons and rare black-tailed godwits. Or pedal the same distance north to **Lindau** in Germany, a pretty island town, with lavishly frescoed houses, a palm-speckled island and a harbour watched over by a lighthouse and Bavarian lion.

Going up: Pfänder
A taste of the Alps

The lake shrinks and the mountains unfurl in all their glory as you float by cable car from the historic centre of Bregenz up to the modest 1064m peak of the **Pfänder** *(pfaenderbahn.at; cable car return adult/child €18/9)* – a journey that passes in the blink of an eye. Rearing above Bregenz, this wooded peak commands dress-circle views of Bodensee and 240 summits in the not-so-distant Alps in Austria, Switzerland and Germany.

At the top of the Pfänder, a 30-minute circular trail brings you close to deer, mouflon, wild boar, ibex and whistling marmots at the year-round **Alpine Game Park Pfänder** *(free)*. Longer hikes and mountain climbs also head off into the heights from here, while in winter you can stomp through the snow on marked tracks or dash along icy runs tobogganing.

ARCHITECTURAL TRAILBLAZER

Vorarlberg is among the world's most progressive places for architecture. It started in the mid-1980s when a group of forward-thinking architects began calling themselves *Baukünstler* (building artists).

Today, Vorarlberg is at the forefront of design when it comes to simplicity and sustainability, and almost everywhere you look – private homes, hotels, office blocks, supermarkets – you'll find cutting-edge buildings.

Some, like **Inatura** science centre in Dornbirn and the **Kunsthaus** (p369) in Bregenz, make urban-design statements; others, like the **Silvretta-Haus** at the Bielerhöhe Pass, integrate seamlessly into the natural environment and have impeccable eco credentials.

For more insight, hook onto one of the region's **Architecture Trails** *(vorarlberg.travel)*.

EATING IN BREGENZ: OUR PICKS

Cafesito: This artsy cafe in the Altstadt serves freshly roasted coffee, bagels, brownies and smoothies. *7.45am-6.30pm Mon-Fri, 8am-1pm Sat* €

BAHI: Relaxed cafe, yoga studio and co-working space with great coffee, homemade cakes and tasty lunch mains like curries and falafel. *9am-6pm* €

Kornmesser: Dine on local faves such as pork knuckle with bread dumplings and roast local trout in the vaulted interior or beer garden of this baroque *Gästehaus*. €€

Küchentanz in der Ilge: This rustic-chic, wood-panelled, candlelit space wows with global tasting menus that big up regional ingredients. *5-10pm Tue-Sat* €€€

Beyond Bregenz

Medieval towns, cheese-focused road trips and mountains galore – the region beyond Bregenz is little-visited and ripe for exploring.

Places
Feldkirch p372
Bludenz p373
Schwarzenberg p375
Montafon p375

Edging west of Bregenz, the rural, deeply traditional Bregenzerwald is a storybook vision of limestone peaks, with velvety pastures, cheese dairies and wood-shingle-tiled farms festooned with red geraniums. It's a silent region for unplugging and spending time in nature. One lungful of that good clean air and you'll want to grab your boots, slip into your skis or get on your bike. Moving south of Bregenz, you're in for a treat in towns like Bludenz, home to Milka chocolate and an arcaded old town, and medieval knockout Feldkirch, with its hilltop castle, historic fortifications and cobbled lanes lined with pavement cafes. But all of this is just the curtain-raiser for Montafon, one of the most enchanting valleys in Austria, where the snowy Alps slip quietly and unobserved into Switzerland.

GETTING AROUND

With time, you can get around the Bregenzerwald and Montafon on public transport, though both are tremendous road-trip material, allowing you to stop in off-the-map locations, take in views in back-of-beyond beauty spots and explore at your own steam. Taking you up to 2032m, hairpin-bend-riddled Silvretta-Hochalpenstrasse is quite some drive. The toll road opens early June to late October.

Stay three nights or more between May and October, and the **Bregenzerwald Guest Card** provides free use of local buses, cable cars and outdoor pools.

Feldkirch
TIME FROM BREGENZ: **30MINS**
Back to the Middle Ages

Nudging the Swiss border, hemmed in by steeply wooded slopes and vineyards, and hugging the banks of the milky turquoise Ill River, Feldkirch is a looker. With an Altstadt that's a joy to explore on foot, this time-capsule of a town, just south of Bregenz, wings you back to the Middle Ages, with lanes unfurling past arcades and step-gabled houses in bright pastel shades. In summer, the town fizzes to life with pavement cafes, markets and open-air festivals such as the July **Gauklerfestival** (Juggler Festival), where jugglers, fire-eaters and clowns entertain crowds at an enormous street party.

The best way to drop yourself right into Feldkirch's medieval past is by taking a serendipitous stroll of the Altstadt, where the cobbles have been worn smooth by centuries of shoe leather. The towers surviving from the old fortifications include the step-gabled **Churertor**, once the gateway to the bridge that was used to transport salt across the Ill River to Switzerland. Keep an eye out for the **Mühletor**, or Sautor, where the pig market was held in the Middle Ages. Part of the original town walls, the 40m-high **Katzenturm**, built in 1507, is where Vorarlberg's biggest bell, weighing 7500kg, still dongs. Built high and mighty by the Dukes of Montfort in 1200, **Schattenburg** (schattenburg.at; adult/child €8/4) with its riot of towers and creeping vines presides over the town from a wooded hilltop perch. It's

Feldkirch

a steep climb up to the ramparts, which command far-reaching views over Feldkirch's rooftops. Once the seat of the counts of Montfort, the castle now harbours a museum spelling out the town's past in religious art, costumes and weaponry.

Bludenz

TIME FROM BREGENZ: **50MINS**

Seeing purple cows

The Alps provide a spectacular backdrop to Bludenz, a 15-minute train ride east of Feldkirch. Pretty looks aside, this is the only town in Austria – perhaps the world – that can lay claim to having purple cows; the Milka chocolate churned out from the Mondelēz International factory. To learn about the making and the history of the purple cow (spoiler alert: she's called Lila and has been around since 1972), stop by the interactive **Milka Lädele** (milka.at) experience shop on Fohrenburgerstrasse.

Bludenz's Old Town

Gorging on chocolate aside, Bludenz's arcaded old town takes you back to its heyday as the seat of the Habsburg governors from 1418 to 1806. For stellar views over the town's rooftops to the Alps beyond, climb the covered staircase to Gothic parish church **St Laurentiuskirche**, dominated by an octagonal onion-domed spire.

CHEESE PRIMER

The wooded limestone peaks, cow-nibbled pastures and bucolic villages of the Bregenzerwald unfold to the south of Bregenz. This rural region entices with its mellow vibe, rambling farmhouses and – best of all – cheese-tasting in alpine dairies.

If you like cheese, you're in for a treat. You can fill your boots (and bags) with local cheeses made with *Heumilch* (hay milk), including hard, smooth, nutty *Bergkäse* (mountain cheese) to summer-only *Alpkäse* made from milk produced on high pastures, herby *Kräuterkäse* with aromas of hay and thyme, and tangy *Rässkäse*.

Many guesthouses double as restaurants, dishing up satisfying regional specialities like *Bregenzerwälder Käsknöpfle*, egg pasta served with cheese, fried onions, potato salad and apple sauce.

EATING IN FELDKIRCH: OUR PICKS

Wirtschaft zum Schützenhaus: Lederhosen-clad staff and a beer garden with castle views. *5pm-midnight Mon, Thu & Fri, 10am-midnight Sat, 10am-10pm Sun* €€

Dogana: Sky-blue Altstadt fave with a fine-weather terrace. Bistro-style menu with Austrian classics and spot-on steaks. *8.30am-midnight Tue-Sat* €€

Magma: In a minimalist space Magma places the accent on top-quality ingredients in lunches like goulash, poke bowls and salads. *9am-4pm Mon-Sat, 10am-4pm Sun* €€

Gutwinski: Regional ingredients shine in seasonal dishes like venison with porcini ravioli and chestnut gravy at this chandelier-lit number. *noon-11pm Tue-Sat* €€€

THE BIG CHEESE: BREGENZERWALD KÄSESTRASSE

This road trip threads through quaint villages and stops for silo-free milk and cheese at local Sennereien (dairy farms). Spring to autumn is the best time to visit.

START	END	LENGTH
Käsekeller Lingenau	Bergkäserei Schoppernau	40km; 4-5 hours

First are the huge cellars of ultramodern ❶ **Käsekeller Lingenau**. Pop in to see how cheese is matured, and taste flavoursome *Bergkäse* (mountain cheese) with a glass of wine. Hit the pretty, church-topped village of ❷ **Egg**, where the Bregenzerach river flows swiftly and, slightly west, ❸ **Käse-Molke Metzler**, an avant-garde dairy and farmhouse duo.

Veer southwest to the pretty village of ❹ **Schwarzenberg** (p375), where stout farmhouses tiled with wood shingles and bursting with scarlet geraniums crowd narrow streets. Contemplate art in the ❺ **Angelika Kauffmann Museum** (p375) before lunching on cheese-topped *Käsespätzle* (egg noodles) in the wood-panelled parlour or garden at ❻ **Hotel Hirschen** (p375).

The narrow country lane now wends its way gently to ❼ **Bezau**, 7km southeast. The village has shops where you can buy cheese, honey, herbs and schnapps. Continue southeast towards the Arlberg and mountainous ❽ **Mellau**. Drive southeast to peaceful ❾ **Au**, with sweeping valley views, lovely on a golden autumn day. Round out your tour with total cheese immersion at the ❿ **Bergkäserei Schoppernau,** where you can nibble pungent, nutty *Bergkäse*.

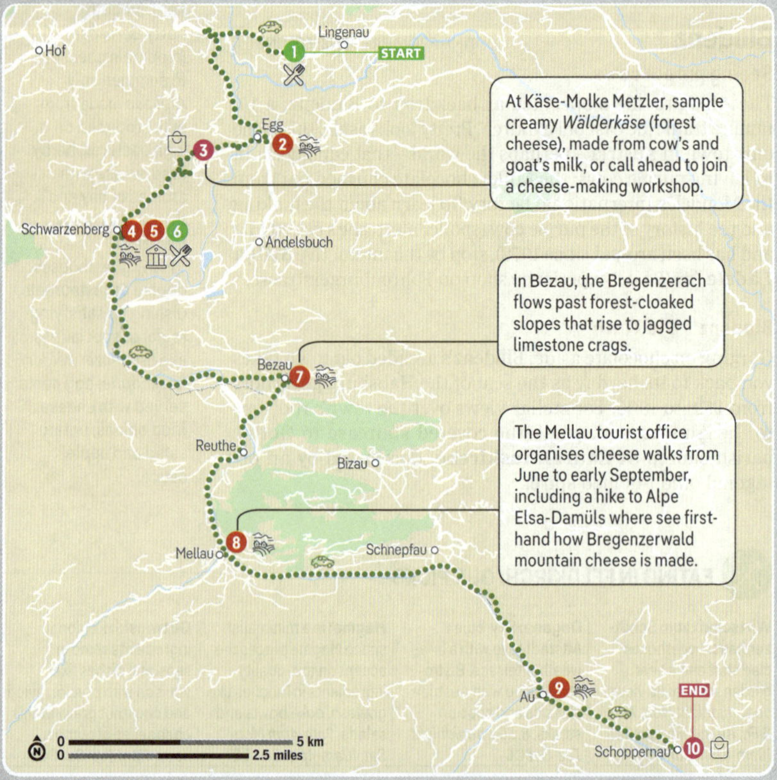
Hof
Lingenau
START
At Käse-Molke Metzler, sample creamy *Wälderkäse* (forest cheese), made from cow's and goat's milk, or call ahead to join a cheese-making workshop.
Egg
Schwarzenberg
Andelsbuch
In Bezau, the Bregenzerach flows past forest-cloaked slopes that rise to jagged limestone crags.
Bezau
Reuthe
Bizau
The Mellau tourist office organises cheese walks from June to early September, including a hike to Alpe Elsa-Damüls where see first-hand how Bregenzerwald mountain cheese is made.
Mellau
Schnepfau
Au
END
Schoppernau
0 5 km
0 2.5 miles

Schwarzenberg

TIME FROM BREGENZ: **30MINS**

Picture-perfect village

Surrounded by buttercup-cloaked pastures that rise to mountains, the village of Schwarzenberg with its cluster of historic chalets is as pretty as a picture. No wonder, then, that it inspired the paintbrush of Swiss-Austrian neoclassical painter Angelika Kauffmann, whose father was born locally. Angelika spent much of her childhood and later years here.

To view her striking work, visit the **Angelika Kauffmann Museum** *(angelika-kauffmann.com; adult/child €9.50/free)*, which hosts rotating exhibitions from May to October. A ticket covers entry to the neighbouring **Heimat Museum** (Heritage Museum), a pristine alpine chalet. Displays of traditional painted furniture, extraordinary headwear, hunting paraphernalia and filigree iron crosses zoom in on rural 19th-century life.

Round out your visit with a superb lunch or a blissfully peaceful night at **Hotel Hirschen** *(hotel-hirschen-bregenzerwald.at)*, a 270-year-old dream of a *Gasthof*. The wood-shingle facade is festooned with geraniums, while inside low-ceilinged corridors lead to antique-filled nooks, individually designed rooms and an appealing spa with a bathhouse and gardens. The restaurant elevates regional produce to fine-dining heights, with seasonal dishes like venison tartare with chanterelles, herb salad, shallots and spruce tips.

Montafon

TIME FROM BREGENZ: **50MINS**

Into the wilds of Montafon

Silhouetted by the glaciated Silvretta range, Montafon still feels wild and forgotten, its tiny villages touched by a timeless magic. Giving you a glimpse of the Alps before the tourists arrived, the valley remains one of the most serene and pristine in the Austrian Alps. In winter, this is beautifully unspoilt terrain for low-key skiing, snowshoeing and ski touring. **Silvretta-Montafon** *(silvretta-montafon.at; 1-day ski pass adult/child €61.50/35.50)* has 140km of slopes and a snow park to play on, as well as off-piste fun from sledding to winter hiking.

Summer is road trip season. **Partenen** marks the start of the serpentine 23km **Silvretta-Hochalpenstrasse** *(silvretta-bielerhoehe.at)*, the Silvretta High Alpine Road, which wends its way under peaks rising to well over 2500m before climbing over the 2036m **Bielerhöhe Pass** via 34 white-knuckle switchbacks. At the top of the pass is the **Silvretta Stausee**. Glittering at a giddy 2030m above sea level, this startlingly aquamarine reservoir mirrors the snowcapped diamond of 3312m **Piz Buin** on bright mornings.

The lake is the start and end point of the unmissable – if challenging – **Radsattel Circuit**, a five- to six-hour, 15km hike, best tackled in July or August, which takes you high into the realms of 3000m mountains and glaciers, and traverses the Radsattel at 2652m, crossing from one valley to another. The Alpenvereinskarte 1:25,000 map *No 26 Silvrettagruppe* covers the trail in detail.

HEMINGWAY IN MONTAFON

Montafon's savage beauty and fiery schnapps had Ernest Hemingway in raptures when he wintered in a country inn in the village of Schruns in 1924 and 1925. Then a young man as strong as an ox, he shouldered his skis, climbed high into the blizzard-ripped mountains and raced down them in blissful solitude, the snow so dazzling it hurt his eyes. Hemingway loved speed.

There were no funiculars back then, just logging and cattle trails. And when the snow was too deep, he slipped seal skins to the bottom of his skis.

His memories of those happy, carefree winters are evocatively captured in his 1964 memoir *A Moveable Feast*.

HELP ME PICK:

Snow Sports

Tyrol is Austria's original winter wonderland and has carved its name out as one of the best places in Europe for skiing ever since Franz Reisch dashed down the Kitzbüheler Horn in 1893, nailing the first alpine ski run, and a pioneering Hannes Schneider mastered the Arlberg technique in the 1920s, revolutionising downhill skiing. Legends have been made and born on these slopes for more than a century. And when the flakes fall, you'll find the country's most exhilarating snow sports right here.

Where to Head if You Love...

Epic Ski Safaris

Kitzbühel Ski Safari Swish joyously from peak to peak and hut to hut on this full-day 35km ski marathon from Hahnenkamm to Pass Thurn.

Arlberg Run of Fame This 85km ride takes the whole Arlberg region in its stride, covering a whopping 18,000m of vertical. Psyche yourself up for a challenge.

Der Weisse Ring (The White Ring) Few half-day rides can match the phenomenally scenic, 22km ski around the postcard villages of Lech and Zürs.

Big 3 Rally (p358) Conquer three 3000m mountains and 10,000m of altitude in a day on this 50km ride in Sölden.

Hairy Black Runs

Hafelekar Run Famed for its breathtakingly sheer couloirs, this Nordkette black run is one of Europe's steepest runs with a 70% gradient.

Harakiri Feel your heart thump in your chest as you leap into the void on this heart-pumping black run with a 78% gradient on the peak of Penken in Mayrhofen.

Streif Pluck up the nerve to ski this gravity-defying World Cup run on Kitzbühel's Hahnenkamm. The Mausefalle ('mousetrap') section is insanely steep, with an 85% gradient.

Kandahar This World Cup black run on Galzig in St Anton is an absolute beast. Ski it if you dare.

Snowboarding

PenkenPark (p343) Boarders and freestylers hit the rails, jumps, obstacles and half-pipe at this rave-worthy terrain park in Mayrhofen.

Snowpark Kitzbühel (p348) Boarders are in their element at Hanglalm, mastering the rails, kickers, boxes, tubes and obstacles.

Glacier Skiing

Stubai Glacier (p339) Just south of Innsbruck, this glacier has snow from October to May and summer skiing between 2900m and 3300m. And the view over a sea of three-thousanders is magic.

Hintertuxer Glacier (p343) Glide above ragged cliffs and peaks to this shimmering glacier for a ski with views of the Tuxer Alps and, on cloud-free days, mighty Grossglockner.

Sölden (p358) This FIS Ski World Cup resort has one of the longest seasons in the Tyrolean Alps, with glacier skiing at sky-high Rettenbach and Tiefenbach.

Family Snow Fun

St Anton Rodelbahn Dash through snowy forests under starry skies on this 4km floodlight toboggan run from Gampen, pausing at a chalet to warm up over a pot of gooey fondue.

HOW TO

When to Go
Go with the snow. Generally the flakes fall from December to early April, but glaciers have a longer ski season (October to May). Avoid school holidays for cheaper deals.

Book Ahead
Prebook ski hire to speed things up on the ground. Most towns and villages have an Intersport where you can rent equipment.

Choose Your Slope
You'll find piste maps at the valley stations of ski lifts; runs are colour-coded according to difficulty. Blue runs are easy and for beginners; red are steeper, narrower and for intermediates; black are for experts.

Ski Passes
Lift passes cost roughly €400 for six days, less in under-the-radar resorts. Children usually pay half price.

Choose Your Resort

Even the tiniest speck of a village on the map has access to ski slopes in Tyrol, so the question isn't *if* you can ski but *how* and *where*. For variety and a vast piste network, you could go for one of the big-name resorts like ritzy Kitzbühel *(p348; kitzbuehel.com)*, host of January's hell-for-leather World Cup Hahnenkamm Race, where you'll find 233km of well-groomed snow-sure pistes to pound (including some exhilarating black runs and a snowboarding terrain park) and some outstanding off-piste powder in the backcountry.

Its main rival in scope is wildly beautiful St Anton am Arlberg *(p362; stantonamarlberg.com)*, with 308km of immaculately groomed slopes to play on, highly regarded ski schools and a pumping après-ski scene. An ultra-modern gondola swings over the mountain to the posh twinned resorts of Lech and Zürs *(lechzuers.com)*, whose standout looks have attracted the rich and famous, from British royals to a hapless and hilarious Bridget Jones in the 2004 film *The Edge of Reason*.

In Paznauntal south of St Anton, Ischgl *(p368; ischgl.com)* rocks with skiers and boarders, who flock here for challenging descents, dreamy off-piste powder and hardcore partying.

Places We Love to Stay

€ Budget €€ Midrange €€€ Top End

Innsbruck MAP p328

Pension Paula € Up the hill towards Alpenzoo, this alpine chalet has super-clean, homely rooms with great views across the city.

Hotel Weisses Kreuz €€ This 500-year-old hotel oozes history with creaking beams, wood-panelled parlours and twisting staircase.

Goldener Adler €€ Opened in 1390, this elegant pile has welcomed queens and Salzburg's biggest exports: Mozart and Mrs von Trapp.

Mondschein €€ In a 15th-century riverside fisher's house. Bright rooms give way to marble bathrooms glittering with Swarovski crystals.

Stage 12 €€ Design-driven pick lodged in a 16th-century Altstadt townhouse, with slick mountain-view rooms, a 6th-floor spa and an upbeat cocktail bar.

Nala €€ From oriental to naturalistic, the bijou rooms here reveal a razor-sharp eye for design and suites have terraces with entrancing mountain views.

Penz Hotel €€€ Behind a sheer wall of glass, this contemporary design hotel next to the Rathaus Galerien has minimalist-chic rooms and a rooftop bar for sunset cocktail sipping.

Hall

Gasthof Badl €€ Family-friendly guesthouse in a converted 17th-century bathhouse, a dash across the Inn River from the Altstadt.

Kontor €€ In a restored 1450 townhouse, this boutique number has bags of personality. Breakfast is in the baroque hall.

Parkhotel €€ The mountains seem close enough to touch in the curvy glass-walled rooms of this strikingly avant-garde hotel, with a terrific spa to boot.

Wattens

Pension Clara €€ This sweet B&B in the heart of Wattens wings alpine design into the 21st century.

DION Hotel €€ This cubic, glass-walled, design-minded hotel has super-stylish rooms and a prime location right opposite Swarovski Kristallwelten.

Schwaz

Gasthof Einhorn Schaller €€ This super-central, family-friendly inn has modern rooms and a wood-panelled restaurant dishing up cheese-rich regional grub.

Schloss Mitterhart €€ This turreted 17th-century castle has knockout views of the turquoise Inn River and Karwendel mountains.

The Zillertal MAP p340

Schulhaus €€ Charismatic schoolhouse on a panoramic perch above Zell am Ziller. Rustic rooms, mountain views and a menu championing Slow Food.

Enzianhof €€ Farmhouse on a 1272m hill above Zell, with rooms and a wood-beamed restaurant. It makes gentian schnapps and smokes ham.

Alpenhotel Kramerwirt €€ Big on alpine flair and bedecked with geraniums in summer, this rambling 500-year-old chalet in Mayrhofen has warm-hued rooms and a rooftop spa with saunas and hot tub.

Hotel Garni Glockenstuhl €€ Good old-fashioned Austrian hospitality, dreamy alpine views, free bike rental and a relaxing spa make this Mayrhofen chalet stand out.

Hotel Theresa €€€ Spa hotel in Zell am Ziller blending tradition with style with Alps views from jetted outdoor pools. Seasonal, region-focused food.

Kitzbühel MAP p348

Snowbunny's Hostel € This friendly, laid-back hostel is a bunny-hop from the slopes.

Das Edelweiss €€ Oozing Tyrolean charm with green surrounds, alpine views, sauna and cosy interiors. Near the Hahnenkammbahn.

Villa Licht €€ Pretty gardens, modern apartments with pine trappings, balconies with mountain views, peace – this charming Tyrolean chalet has the lot.

Erika Boutiquehotel €€€ Turreted Art Nouveau villa with high ceilings and a rose garden. Unwind with an alpine herb massage in the spa.

Kufstein

Hotel Kufsteinerhof €€ One of Kufstein's best central picks. Contemporary rooms and substantial breakfasts a short toddle from the castle.

Träumerei #8 €€ No two rooms are alike at this boutique hotel in a stylishly converted 600-year-old guesthouse between Römerhofgasse and the Inn River.

The Ötztal MAP p356

feelfree Nature Resort €€ Riverside retreat in Ötz with eco-chic chalet rooms in sustainable pine, a spa and activities like bike tours and rafting.

Hotel Rita €€ Set in gardens with mountain views, this handsome chalet in Längenfeld gives you unlimited access to Aqua Dome in summer.

Die Berge €€ Contemporary mountain lodge in Sölden with light-drenched, alpine-style rooms, big views, rooftop Sky Spa and infinity pool.

Imst & Landeck

Hotel Hirschen €€ Inviting pick in Imst with pine-clad rooms, a spa for a post-hike unwind and a rustic restaurant serving venison ragout.

Tramserhof €€ Calm retreat among trees in Landeck with alpine-style rooms, a spa and natural swimming lake. Organic produce for breakfast.

St Anton am Arlberg MAP p362

Piltriquitron Lodging € This super-central, Nordic-cool base is for outdoor lovers. Owner Jacob is a keen mountaineer and font of Alps knowledge.

Altes Thönihaus €€ A listed 1465 wooden chalet oozing alpine charm. Fleecy rugs and pine in cosy rooms with mountain-facing balcony.

Himmlhof €€€ *Himmlisch* (heavenly) chalet with open fire. The cosy spa with grotto-like plunge pool beckon after a day's skiing.

Lech & Zürs

Lavendel €€ You'll receive a heartfelt family welcome at this super-cosy chalet next to the ski lifts in Lech.

Severins – The Alpine Retreat (p367) €€ Luxe ski retreat with just nine suites and a fabulous spa.

Ischgl

Gletscherblick €€ Contemporary, wood-and-stone-built B&B with boutique flair, nouveau-alpine rooms and a spa for a post-ski steam.

AlpVita Piz Tasna €€ Set on a slope, Piz Tasna gets rave reviews for its welcome, big, comfy rooms with mountain views, superb food and relaxing spa.

Bregenz MAP p369

Camping Mexico € In summer, pitch up at this eco-labelled lakeside campground, with leafy pitches and a restaurant serving organic food.

Hotel Weisses Kreuz €€ In the Altstadt, this historic pile has a cocktail bar and a vaulted restaurant rustling up season-spun Austrian fare.

Schwärzler €€€ Turreted, ivy-clad place with contemporary rooms and spa. Regional organic-farm produce features on the breakfast buffet.

Montafon

Silvretta-Haus (p371) €€ Stay in this architecturally innovative hotel at Bielerhöhe for its bright, contemporary rooms and bewitching mountain views.

Posthotel Rössle €€ Ernest Hemingway once stayed in this 200-year-old chalet. It has well-kept rooms, a superb wood-panelled restaurant and spa, as well as indoor and outdoor pools.

Goldener Adler

TOOLKIT

TOOLKIT

The chapters in this section cover the most important topics you'll need to know about in Austria. They're full of nuts-and-bolts information and valuable insights to help you understand and navigate Austria, and get the most out of your trip.

Arriving
p382

Getting Around
p383

Train Travel
p384

Money
p385

Accommodation
p386

Family Travel
p387

Food, Drink & Nightlife
p388

Responsible Travel
p390

Health & Safe Travel
p392

LGBTIQ+ Travellers
p393

Accessible Travel
p394

Nuts & Bolts
p395

Language
p396

Cycling, Tannheimer Tal, Tyrol (p323)
WESTEND61/GETTY IMAGES

Arriving

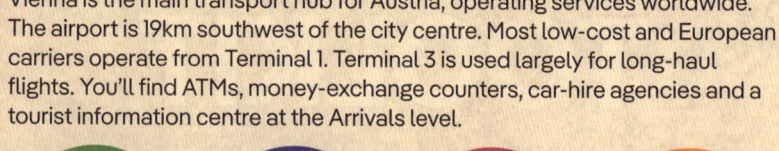

Vienna is the main transport hub for Austria, operating services worldwide. The airport is 19km southwest of the city centre. Most low-cost and European carriers operate from Terminal 1. Terminal 3 is used largely for long-haul flights. You'll find ATMs, money-exchange counters, car-hire agencies and a tourist information centre at the Arrivals level.

Visas
Austria is part of the Schengen Agreement. Citizens of the EU, Eastern Europe, USA, Canada, Central and South America, Japan, Korea, Malaysia, Singapore, Australia and New Zealand don't need visas for stays of up to three months.

SIM Cards
SIM cards for unlocked phones can be purchased at the SIM Local shop at Vienna International Airport.

Border Crossing
There are numerous entry points by road from Germany, Czechia, Slovakia, Hungary, Slovenia, Italy and Switzerland. All border crossing points are open 24 hours.

Wi-Fi
There is free wi-fi available in all areas of the airport. At Gates B and C, seats are equipped with power outlets and USB charging ports.

Airport to City Centre

	Vienna	Salzburg	Innsbruck
TAXI	25min €40–60	15min €20–25	15min €15
BUS	25min €11	23min €3	20min €2.80
S-BAHN	25min €4.50	N/A	N/A

FAST TRACK TO THE SLOPES

Austria is so well-facilitated that you can reach the slopes within minutes of touching down. Salzburg and Innsbruck have small, minimal-fuss airports, where you can often clear passport control, pick up your bags and be on your way within minutes, maximising snow time.

With the Nordkette on its doorstep and the Stubai Glacier half an hour away, Innsbruck is so close to the mountains you can base yourself there and use free ski buses to nearby resorts. Salzburg is a *Katzensprung* (short hop) from resorts like Filzmoos, Bad Gastein and Zell am See.

There's no need for pricey taxi transfers either: public transport is swift, reasonably priced and efficient.

Getting Around

Austria's public-transport network is a dream, with swift, reasonably priced trains linking towns, and cities and buses filling the gaps. Car hire gives you greater freedom to explore the country's remotest corners.

TRAVEL COSTS

Car rental
Per day from €60

Petrol
Per litre approx €1.50

EV charging
From €0.45/kWh

Train ticket from Vienna to Salzburg
€65

Hiring a Car

It's often cheaper to prebook a car than hire one on arrival. You'll find all the major car-hire companies at airports, including Sixt, Hertz and Enterprise. The minimum age for hiring small cars is 19; for prestige models, 25 years. A valid licence issued at least one year prior is necessary.

Road Conditions

The *autobahn* (motorways) are well maintained. You can only drive on them with a *Vignette* (motorway tax), available at border crossings and petrol stations. Be prepared for exposed, sharply twisting roads in the Alps. Many of the mountain roads and tunnels levy an additional toll.

TIP
The ÖBB app is the easiest way to book tickets. Use the price filter to find the cheapest deals. See oebb.at.

GET ON YOUR BIKE

Austria is cycling heaven. Thousands of miles of well-signposted trails shadow rivers and lakeshores, and twist up the Alps. There's challenging terrain, but also flat, gentle routes through valleys like the Danube, Enns and Mur. Bike and e-bike rental is ubiquitous and many ÖBB stations rent wheels. Most regional trains will transport bikes in the baggage car (you'll need a bicycle ticket). On long-distance trains, reserve online or use the ÖBB app.

DRIVING ESSENTIALS

Drive on the right

All passengers must wear seatbelts

Winter tyres are obligatory from November to mid-April

.05
Blood alcohol limit is 0.05%

Train

The rail system is inexpensive with a discount card. **Österreiche Bundesbahn** (*ÖBB, Austrian Federal Railway;* oebb.at) is the main operator. The best deals are *Sparschiene*, heavily discounted tickets sold online up to six months ahead. For more on train travel, see p384.

Bus

Rail routes are often complemented by **Postbus** (postbus.at) services, which are useful in inaccessible mountainous regions. Buses are fairly reliable, and usually depart from train stations. Aim for weekday travel; services are reduced or nonexistent on weekends.

Mountain Railways

When trains stop in the Alps, the only way up is on a *Seilbahn* (funicular) or *Bergbahn* (cable car). Costs quickly mount, meaning it's often cheaper to buy a weekly pass (a ski pass in winter) or use a discount card. Some guest cards get you a free ride.

Train Travel

Whisking you from valley to peak, city to slope and far beyond the borders, Austria's smooth, extensive, reasonably priced rail network is a traveller's delight. Book well in advance for the best bargains.

GLOSSARY

Abfahrt Departure
Ankunft Arrival
Bahnhof (Bf) Station
Bahnsteig Platform (the platform number)
Einfache Fahrt ('hin') Single
Erste Klasse 1st class
Fahrkarte (Fahrausweis) Ticket
Gleis Platform
Hauptbahnhof (Hbf) Main station
Retour Return
Speisewagen Dining carriage
Täglich Daily
Umsteigen Change of trains
Wagen Carriage
Zweite Klasse 2nd class

Tickets & Timetables

Österreiche Bundesbahn *(ÖBB, Austrian Federal Railway)* is Austria's main rail operator, supplemented by a handful of private lines. The easiest way to buy ÖBB tickets and check timetables is online at oebb.at. You can also get your tickets via the ÖBB app. Alternatively, tickets can be purchased by calling the 24-hour hotline (+43 05 1717); you'll be given a 12-digit collection code for printing the ticket at a machine or at the service desk.

Train Types & Reservations

Express trains are EC (EuroCity; serving international routes) or IC (InterCity; serving national routes). RailJet national and international train services are faster still. Extra charges can apply on fast trains and international trains, and it's a good idea (and sometimes obligatory) to make seat reservations for peak times and on certain lines. Reservations are recommended for weekend and peak season travel and cost from €3 for 2nd-class express services within Austria.

Discounts & Rail Passes

If you plan on travelling a lot by train, a rail pass is a no-brainer. Valid for 12 months, the **ÖBB Vorteilscard** gives a discount of 50% on standard fares and costs €71 for adults (it's even cheaper for youths, seniors and families). You'll need to show photo ID on the train. Other handy passes for European residents include InterRail's **One-Country Pass Austria**. Adult 2nd-class costs €165/196/223/292 for three/four/five/eight days within a month.

ÖBB's **Sparschiene** tickets can also be brilliant value. These are the cheapest available tickets. Book them well in advance online or via the app as they are popular and sell out quickly. They are valid for a specific date and time, and are non-refundable.

The Night Train

If you fancy going to bed in Innsbruck, Graz or Vienna and waking up in Rome, Berlin or Paris, consider hopping on the excellent **ÖBB Nightjet** *(nightjet.com)*, linking the country to 25 European cities. Overnight trains usually offer a choice between a *Liegewagen* (couchette) or a pricier *Schlafwagen* (sleeping car) and have a dining car or snacks available. Tickets can be booked up to six months in advance.

THE JOURNEY BEYOND

- Bordering eight countries, Austria's super-central location makes international rail travel a breeze. Vienna is an hour from Bratislava, Innsbruck is 3½ hours from Verona, Linz is four hours from Prague. You get the idea – Europe really is your oyster here.
- The **European Rail Timetable** *(europeanrailtimetable.eu)* is an invaluable resource for planning a trip, with all train schedules, supplements and reservations information. The **Man in Seat 61** *(seat61.com)* also has helpful tips and details on booking trains across Europe. You don't need to disembark at borders, but make sure you have your passport/ID and any necessary visas.

Money

CURRENCY: **EURO (€)**

Credit Cards
Visa and Mastercard (EuroCard) are more widely accepted than Amex and Diners Club. Upmarket shops, hotels, restaurants and many train stations accept cards. You can get cash advances on ATMs and over-the-counter at most banks with a credit card.

Digital Payment
Most shops accept contactless payments by debit or credit card, smartphone or smartwatch. Tap and pay is common, though some places insist on cash (check ahead).

Taxes & Refunds
Mehrwertsteuer (VAT) in Austria is typically 20%. Look for the Global Refund Tax Free Shopping sticker to reclaim about 13% on single purchases over €75 (by non-EU citizens/residents); see globalrefund.com. Refund desks are at major department stores, as well as Vienna and Salzburg airports.

Tipping
Bars About 5% at the bar and 10% at a table.
Hotels One or two euros per suitcase for porters and valet parking in top-end hotels.
Restaurants About 10% (unless service is poor).
Taxis About 10%.

HOW MUCH FOR A...

single ticket on a bus/U-Bahn
€3

10-day motorway Vignette
€12.40

museum entry
€12

Tagesteller (lunch special)
€10–15

HOW TO... Tip Like an Austrian

Some restaurants automatically add a service charge (around 12.5%) to your bill, so check before tipping. Austrians tend to tip 5% to 15%, so 10% is a good bet.

For bar and cafe bills, round up to the nearest euro or two. Don't leave a tip on the table. Hand it over when paying and say *'Stimmt so'* ('keep the change').

LOCAL TIP
Always keep some change handy, especially in rural areas. There are still shops, mountain huts and restaurants that insist on *Bargeld* (cash).

CENT SAVERS

Travelling in low season often means you can get cheaper rooms – avoid peak summer and winter season and school holidays, when rates soar. Look out for ÖBB *Sparschiene* (discounted train tickets) online in advance. Local guest cards often provide free use of public transport and many other discounts.

Want to eat out for less than €15? Make lunch your main meal and go for the *Tagesteller* (day special) or *Mittagsmenü* (set lunch).

CLOCKWISE FROM TOP LEFT: JULIA MOUNTAIN PHOTO/SHUTTERSTOCK, RUSTAM SHIGAPOV/SHUTTERSTOCK, SASHKIN/SHUTTERSTOCK

Accommodation

Romantic Hotels

Hotels in Austria come in all shapes, sizes, stars and budgets, but to ramp up the romance, check out the **Romantik Hotels** *(romantikhotels.com)*, which often come with a scene-stealing location, spa and generous pinch of luxury. Romantik hotels are often nestled on lakeshores or up in the *Alm* (alpine meadows) and mountains. Some are converted palaces and castles.

Eco Hotels

For a stay with green credentials, check out Austria's *Bio-* or *Öko-* ('eco') hotels. Most are attractively set in the countryside or mountains, many with spa facilities, menus playing up locally sourced, health-conscious ingredients, and with easy access to winter skiing and other outdoor activities. Generally, you'll need own wheels – car or bike – to reach these. **Bio Hotels** *(biohotels.info)* has a list.

Farm Stays

Bauernhöfe (farmhouses) are great for a slice of rural life, with serene views and often very welcoming hosts. Many are ideal for families, with animals to pet, farm-fresh eggs, plenty of fresh air, and hiking and cycling trails on the doorstep. Most rent out apartments for a minimum of three nights. You'll often need your own transport to reach them. Browse **Urlaub am Bauernhof** *(urlaubambauernhof.at)* for ideas.

Camping

Camping is a brilliant way to explore Austria inexpensively. Campgrounds are often well-maintained and scenically located near national parks, reserves and beauty spots. Most close in winter. Wild camping is officially not permitted, but bivouacking is often overlooked, especially above the tree line. To search for a campground, **Österreichischen Camping Club** *(campingclub.at)* is a handy resource.

HOW MUCH FOR A NIGHT IN...

an alpine hut
€50

a pitch for two in a campground
€30

a Romantik Hotel
from €150

Alpine Huts

Hikers can trek to one of over 400 Austrian Alps huts, which open roughly mid-June to early October (booking essential). Maintained by the **Österreichischer Alpenverein** *(Austrian Alpine Club; alpenverein.at)* and the **German Alpine Club** *(DAV; alpenverein.de)*, they're often a simple dorm *(Mehrbettzimmer)* or bunkhouse *(Matratzenlager)*. Meals and cooking facilities are often available. Membership yields a discount.

HIGH SEASON & TOURIST TAX

High season in Austria goes with the sun and snow, spiking price-wise around the summer holidays (July and August) across the country and in winter (especially Christmas) in the Alps. Outside peak periods, there are better deals on flights and rooms, especially in shoulder season. On top of the room rate, you'll pay an *Ortstax* (local tax), roughly 3.2% of the accommodation cost. But, before you grumble, this often goes towards paying for the invaluable *Gästekarte* (guest card), which usually covers local public transport and offers discounts on things such as cable cars and museum admission.

Family Travel

With castles, palaces and gardens fit for a Disney princess, gentle trails twisting through alpine meadows where doe-eyed cows graze, crystal-clear lakes beckon and cable cars whirl to villages that are a *Frozen* fantasy in winter, Austria is a surefire kid-pleaser.

Facilities

Most parks have a *Kinderspielplatz* (kids' playground) and you'll find marked buggy (stroller) and pram trails in the Alps. Many hotels have family or interconnecting rooms, or will squeeze in an extra bed or cot (you might need to book ahead). Nappies, toiletries and other essentials are available at chemists and *Apotheken* (pharmacies).

Sights

Many big-hitter museums and galleries have dedicated exhibitions, workshops and activities for kids. Children aged six to 15 get heavily discounted (at least half-price) entry, while tots aged four and under nearly always go free. Vienna, in particular, has great kids' attractions, including the Zoom Kindermuseum and Haus der Musik.

Getting Around with Kids

Rental car companies can arrange child and booster seats. Newer public transport, such as trams and buses in Vienna, are accessible for buggies and prams. Children under six usually travel free on public transport, or half-price up to 15 years.

Eating

Dumplings, schnitzel, colossal cakes and gelato – Austria has a lot to please little appetites. Most midrange restaurants have high chairs and a *Kindermenü* (children's menu) or will prepare smaller portions if you ask. Some have a play area.

KID-FRIENDLY PICKS

Eisriesenwelt (p269)

Find a real-life Narnia at the world's largest accessible ice caves.

Wörthersee (p298)

Splash in the safe waters of this lake, with boats, beaches and playgrounds.

Salzwelten Hallstatt (p225)

Slide into the salt mines in the village that inspired Disney's *Frozen*.

Haus der Musik (p71)

Get into the groove at this musical museum in Vienna with interactive lab and melodic staircase.

H20 Hotel-Therme Bad Waltersdorf (p208)

Enjoy baby swimming and water slides at a family spa resort.

ACTION STATIONS

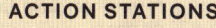

Austria makes it easy for families to embrace the great outdoors. Just about every tourist office in the Alps can point out family-friendly hikes – from nature rambles to wildlife-spotting trails and paths through fairy-tale gorges.

Austria Info *(austria.info)* has a dedicated page on hiking with kids. In winter, the country is a snowy wonderland, with resorts offering ski lessons for children (generally aged four and up), plus slope-side fun from snowshoeing to tobogganing.

In summer find a lake with supervised beach area, with kids' splash areas, slides and games. Even cities have lidos with activities like table tennis, volleyball and slides.

Food, Drink & Nightlife

When to Eat

Frühstuck (7am–10am) Breakfast is substantial, with fruits, cereal, yoghurt, eggs, bread, cold cuts and plentiful coffee.

Mittagessen (noon–2pm) Lunch – usually soup or salad followed by a main course.

Kaffee und Kuchen (3pm–4pm) The exception to not snacking between meals is 3pm coffee and cake.

Abendessen (7pm–9pm) Time for dinner.

Where to Eat & Drink

Beisln/Gasthäuser Rural inns with *Gutbürgerliche Küche* (home cooking).

Brauereien Microbreweries and brewpubs, often with beer gardens.

Cafes Bakery-cafes, organic delis and *Eiscafés* (ice-cream parlours).

Heurigen Wine taverns.

Imbiss Snacks or takeaway, the most famous being the *Würstelstand* (sausage stand).

Kaffeehäuser Coffee houses; many also serve food.

Konditoreien Traditional cake-shop cafes.

Neo-Beisln New-wave *Beisln* (small tavern or restaurant) often with a market-fresh take on classics.

Restaurants Pizzerias to Michelin-starred finery.

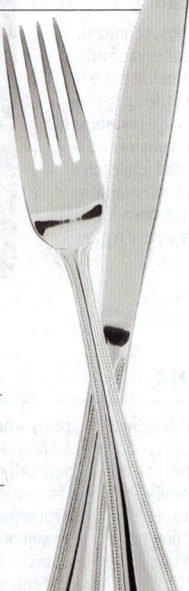

MENU DECODER

Degustationsmenü Gourmet tasting menu.

Hauptspeise Main course – fish, meat or *vegetarisch* (vegetarian).

Beilage(n) Side dish(es).

Kindermenü Two- or three-course kids' menu.

Laktosefrei/Glutenfrei Lactose-free/gluten-free.

Mittagstisch/Mittagsmenü Fixed lunch menu; usually two courses – soup or salad and a main.

Nachtisch Dessert sometimes with coffee or schnapps.

Speisekarte À la carte menu.

Tagesteller Good-value dish of the day; generally only at lunch.

Vorspeise Starter, appetiser.

Gruss aus der Küche Amuse-bouche (single, bite-sized hors d'oeuvre). Literally 'greeting from the chef'.

Weinkarte Wine list.

Weisswein White wine.

Rotwein Red Wine.

Sekt/Perlwein Sparkling wine (white or rosé).

Restaurant Etiquette

Reservations Booking is best at popular and top-end restaurants, especially in peak season. Call a week ahead.

Menus English menus are not a given, though you'll often find them in city hot spots like Salzburg and Vienna, and in ski resorts. If in doubt, waitstaff can usually translate.

Bon appétit Dining with Austrians? It's polite to wish them *guten Appetit* or *Mahlzeit* before digging in.

Cheers Raise a toast by saying Prost, Prosit or zum Wohl, clink glasses and make eye contact.

Water Asking for free *Leitungswasser* (tap water) is not the done thing, especially in upmarket places. Order *stilles* (still) or *prickelndes* (sparkling) *Mineralwasser* (mineral water).

Dress Smart casual in fancier places, where the locals dress up for dinner. In more relaxed places, jeans, sneakers and T-shirts are fine.

Paying *Zahlen, bitte* or *die Rechnung, bitte* to get the bill.

HOW MUCH FOR A...

Kaffee und Kuchen
€8–12

wurst at a sausage stand
€4–6

scoop of ice cream
€2–3

lunch special
€10–15

gourmet dinner
€50–100

glass of wine
€4–8

beer
€3.50–6

cocktail
€12–15

HOW TO... Order Coffee in Austria

Swing open the heavy wooden door of one of Vienna's *Kaffeehäuser* (coffee houses) and it's as though the clocks stopped in 1910. The waiters are just as aloof, the menu still baffles and newspapers outnumber smartphones. The story of their evolution from the Turkish siege of Vienna to today is an interesting one sprinkled with not just a few grains of fiction.

You'll need to know your *Mokka* from your *Brauner* to order Viennese style. A quick glance at a menu will uncover a long list of choices, so brush up on the ones below. A good coffee house will serve the cup of java on a silver platter accompanied by a glass of water and a small sweet.

Brauner Black, served with a splash of milk; comes in *Gross* (large) or *Klein* (small).
Einspänner With whipped cream, served in a glass.
Fiaker *Verlängerter* with rum and whipped cream.
Kapuziner With a splash of milk and perhaps a sprinkling of grated chocolate.
Maria Theresia With orange liqueur and whipped cream.
Masagran, Mazagran Cold coffee with ice and Maraschino liqueur.
Melange Viennese classic; served with milk, and maybe whipped cream, too; similar to a cappuccino.
Mocca, Mokka, Schwarzer Black coffee.
Pharisäer Strong *Mocca* topped with whipped cream, served with rum.
Türkische In a copper pot with coffee grounds and sugar.
Verlängerter Brauner Weakened with hot water.
Wiener Eiskaffee Cold coffee with vanilla ice cream and whipped cream.

Coffee-House Style

Wait to be seated in formal places, take your pick of the tables in casual coffee houses. You're welcome to linger over a cup if you wish; the waiter shouldn't move you on until you ask for the *Rechnung* (bill).

AUSTRIAN WINE

Austrian wine hails from 17 wine-growing areas, mostly situated in Lower Austria and Burgenland (known as the Weinland Österreich region), Styria and the vine-strewn fringes of Vienna.

A wine that is typical of the region is labelled DAC (Districtus Austriae Controllatus), which is similar to the French AOC and the Italian DOC or DOCG, and if it is labelled 'reserve' then the wine has been made for cellaring. Well-known varieties to look out for include crisp Grüner Veltliner and *Weissburgunder* (Pinot Blanc) whites, fruity *Blauburgunder* (Pinot Noir) and full-bodied *Zweigelt* reds, and sweet *Eiswein*, made from grapes that have frozen on the vines.

In winegrowing regions, many vintners open their doors for tasting and rustic *Heurigen* (wine taverns) pair wine with hearty grub like roast pork, blood sausage and pickled vegetables. Often identified by a *Busch'n* (green wreath or branch) hanging over the door, these simple establishments date back to the Middle Ages and have the right to sell their wine directly from their own premises in wine-growing regions.

Because they are seasonal and are open on a roster, the easiest thing to do when in a wine-growing region is to pick up the local *Heurigenkalendar* (Heurigen calendar) from the tourist office. September to mid-October, following the harvest, is when the new wines are sold, and this is the time to indulge in *Sturm* (literally 'storm' for its cloudy appearance and chaotic effects on drinkers).

Responsible Travel

Climate Change & Travel

It's impossible to ignore the impact we have when travelling; Lonely Planet urges all travellers to engage with their travel carbon footprint, which will mainly come from air travel. While there often isn't an alternative, travellers can look to minimise the number of flights they take, opt for newer aircrafts and use cleaner ground transport, such as trains.

One proposed solution — purchasing carbon offsets — unfortunately does not cancel out the impact of individual flights. While most destinations will depend on air travel for the foreseeable future, for now, pursuing ground-based travel where possible is the best course of action.

The **UN Carbon Offset Calculator** shows how flying impacts a household's emissions

The **ICAO's carbon emissions calculator** allows visitors to analyse the CO2 generated by point-to-point journeys

Support Local

Take the lead from the Austrians and stay, eat and buy local. Swap the chains for independent B&Bs and guesthouses, pick up freshest seasonal produce (including picnic fixings) at *Bauernmärkte* (farmers markets) and look for Slow Food label restaurants.

Go in Low Season

Mountain resorts that get swamped for a few months of the year and then deserted for the rest are increasingly becoming things of the past. Think sustainably and visit in the low or shoulder seasons.

Rising Snow

As the planet warms, the snow levels in Austria are rising more rapidly than ever. 'Snow-sure' is becoming more wishful thinking in resorts at lower elevations, with a decline in natural snow and shorter seasons.

Austria has the lion's share of the Alps (28.7%) and around 60% of the country is mountainous. In the face of climate change, the country's greatest challenge is protecting this fragile alpine environment.

With luck, patience and a keen, binocular-trained eye, marmots, golden eagles, chamois and ibex can be spotted in the Alps, especially above the treeline at around 2000m. Head to the national parks for best chances.

CHOOSE WISELY

Responsible tourism means casting the net wider than the usual crowded hot spots. In peak season, eschew places like Vienna, Salzburg and Hallstatt in favour of less-visited beauties like Graz, the Waldviertel and Silvretta Alps.

ECO SNOW

To offset the impact of skiing, many resorts now have ecofriendly policies. Among then are Lech in Vorarlberg with its biomass plant, Zell am See-Kaprun with renewable energy powering cable cars, and St Anton am Arlberg using chemical-free artificial snow.

Take the Train
Run by ÖBB, Austria's public transport network is on track to becoming CO_2-neutral, operating almost entirely on renewable energy like hydroelectric power, wind power and photovoltaics.

Slow Food
Bordering Italy and Slovenia, Carinthia is the birthplace of Austria's Slow Food movement. Villages play up the delights of seasonal, regional, farm-to-fork produce and bring the experience to life with behind-the-scenes insights into cheesemaking, bread baking, beer brewing and honey making.

Walk this Way
Want to lower your carbon footprint? Bring boots. Waymarked hiking trails cross almost every inch of Austria. Long-distance, hut-to-hut, nature-immersive trails – from Tyrol's Adlerweg (Eagle Way) to the Salzburger Almenweg – create ambassadors for the country's delicate environment.

Low Impact Activities
Skiing and artificial snow can cause erosion, disturb wildlife and increase emissions. Look for winter resorts diversifying their offer with low-impact activities like cross-country skiing, snowshoeing, winter hiking and tobogganing.

Hohe Tauern is the biggest national park in the Alps (1856 sq km), topped off by the country's highest peak, 3798m Grossglockner.

You can find out about and volunteer for citizen science projects from mushroom spotting to bumblebee monitoring by visiting citizen-science.at.

Melting Ice
There's a red alert for Austria's glaciers. Dry, hot summers mean they're melting at unprecedented levels. In Hohe Tauern National Park, the Pasterze Glacier has shrunk to half its size over the past 150 years and is predicted to disappear by 2075.

RESOURCES

umweltbundesamt.at
Environment Agency Austria for information on Austria's landscape, flora and fauna.

birdlife.at
Twitching heaven with the lowdown on species, bird trips, apps and podcasts.

wwf.at
WWF's Austrian website, with the scoop on nature, climate change and wildlife.

Health & Safe Travel

VACCINATIONS

The World Health Organization (WHO) recommends that, regardless of their destination, all travellers should be covered for diphtheria, tetanus, measles, mumps, rubella, polio and hepatitis B. A vaccination for tick-borne encephalitis is also highly advisable.

Insurance

For EU citizens, a UK Global Health Insurance Card (GHIC) or European Health Insurance Card (EHIC) from your healthcare provider covers most emergency medical care in Austria. This is no substitute for good insurance. Many standard policies don't cover outdoor activities (especially higher risk activities like skiing). You'll need to pay a premium for winter sports and adventure sports.

Health Care

Health care in Austria isn't cheap, and treatment for a skiing injury, for instance, can quickly amount to thousands, so ensure that you have adequate travel health insurance before travelling. Expect to pay anything from €40 to €75 for a straightforward, non-urgent consultation with a doctor.

WASPS & MOSQUITOES

Wasps can be a problem in midsummer but are only dangerous for those with an allergy or if you get stung in the throat. When outdoors, look before you take a sip from a sweet drink. Mosquitoes can be a nuisance around lakes.

SKI SAFELY

Blue Beginner to intermediate runs that are well-groomed.

Red Intermediate runs that are narrower, steeper and require more technical skill.

Black Expert-level runs that are steep and very difficult, with short drops and possibly moguls.

Orange/yellow Ungroomed, off-piste terrain – more difficult than black.

Yellow triangle Warning – danger of avalanches.

Infectious Diseases

Ticks can carry Lyme disease (*Borreliose* in German) and encephalitis (TBE). They are usually found below 1200m, in undergrowth at the forest edge and long grass. Long trousers tucked into boots or socks and a DEET-based insect repellent is the best prevention. If a tick is found attached to the skin, press down around the tick's head with tweezers, grab the tick and rotate until the tick releases itself.

MOUNTAIN SAFETY

Every year people die from landslides and avalanches in the Alps. Always check weather conditions before heading out; consider hiring a guide when skiing off-piste. Before going on challenging hikes, ensure you have the proper equipment and fitness. Inform someone at your accommodation where you're going and when you intend to return.

LGBTIQ+ Travellers

Progressive and diverse, Vienna is home to the country's biggest gay community. Positive change is afoot elsewhere, too, though there is still some discrimination, especially in staunchly conservative, Catholic pockets of the country. But events like Sölden's Winter Pride (Europe's highest) in Tyrol's Ötztaler Alpen give hope that minds are opening beyond the capital.

Oh, Vienna

With its open-minded spirit, party-loving soul and unmissable events from summer's Pride to winter's **Rainbow Ball** *(regenbogenball.at)*, Vienna is light years ahead of much of Austria on the LGBTIQ+ scene. A squat for gay activists in the 1980s, boldly painted **Türkis Rosa Lila Villa** *(dievilla.at)* is now the beating heart of the capital's queer community. It houses **Vida Café** *(villavida.at)*, runs Queer Base (welcoming and supporting LGBTIQ+ refugees and asylum seekers) and hosts the popular Queens Brunch international drag brunch show.

PARTIES & PARADES

Beyond Vienna, diary dates for LGBTIQ+ travellers in other cities include February's **Tuntenball** *(tuntenball.at)*, a huge drag ball, and June's **CSD Parade & Park Festival** *(csd-graz.at)* in Graz, October's **Perlen Pride** *(pride.tirol)* in Kufstein, Tyrol, and **Linz Pride** *(linzpride.at)* in June. In late August, Wörthersee hosts the **Pink Lake Festival**, with beach clubs, costume parties and boat cruises across the lake.

Bars & Cafes

There's plenty of queer nightlife in Vienna, but fewer options elsewhere. In the capital, hit **Village Bar** and the **Hive**, central and lively gay-owned watering holes, or **Cafe Savoy**, for the queer coffee-house experience. Graz has bar-cafe **Stars**, while in Linz **FortyNine**, **Blue Heaven** and **Musikcafe Sax** are popular.

TOURS

Gaily Tour *(gailytour.com)* runs insightful tours of the Austrian capital, giving the inside scoop on its queer history and taking you to hidden corners you'd probably otherwise overlook. Tours include Queer Secrets, shedding light on famous past queer residents, and a tour of the city's gay nightlife.

Vienna Pride

Never does the rainbow flag fly higher than at **Vienna Pride** *(viennapride.at)*, which takes Vienna's stately Ringstrasse boulevard by storm the first two weeks in June. The highlight is the Rainbow Parade, which attracts a 200,000-strong crowd and features parties, presentations, fun runs and beach days.

RESOURCES

Check out the **Rainbow Cities Network** *(rainbowcities.com)*, **Queer Base** *(queerbase.at)*, **Trans X** *(transx.at)* and **Travelgay** *(travelgay.com)* for the lowdown on the LGBTIQ+ scene in Austria. The **Spartacus International Gay Guide** *(spartacus.gayguide.travel)* is a good international directory of LGBTIQ+ entertainment venues worldwide (mainly for men). For a self-guided spin of queer Vienna, download the LGBTIQ+ guide for the Ivie app from wien.info.

Accessible Travel

Austria scores highly with accessible travel, but a trip still requires careful planning. Ramps into buildings are common but not universal; most U-Bahn stations have wheelchair lifts but on buses and trams you'll often have to negotiate gaps and steps.

Cobbled Streets

Austria's historic city centres are often paved with cobblestones and lanes that can be narrow and difficult to navigate in a wheelchair, particularly when crowded in the peak summer season.

Airport

Airports in Vienna, Salzburg and Innsbruck have on-the-ground staff who can assist passengers with reduced mobility. Services range from barrier-free shopping to parking and transfers from terminal to plane. Notify your airline for assistance at least 48 hours before departure.

Accommodation

Small guesthouses and B&Bs (especially those in historic buildings) are often unable to provide services for guests with reduced mobility. Larger, more expensive hotels (four-star or above, usually) have facilities tailored to travellers with disabilities.

RESOURCES

Austria Info *(austria.info)* Has a fantastic page on accessible travel in Austria, with at-a-glance information on everything from travelling without limits to cultural experiences, leisure activities and holidays in the mountains.

Wien Info *(wien.info)* Provides the inside scoop on barrier-free travel in Vienna, with information on accessible sights, museums, hotels, transport and tour guides.

CRUISING THE DANUBE

DDSG Blue Danube *(ddsg-blue-danube.at)* accessible river cruises, catering to people with special needs. Walking aids and rollators are available, but wheelchair users should book at least a week ahead.

Public Transport

ÖBB *(oebb.at)* has a barrier-free travelling webpage. Call 05 171 75 for mobility assistance (at least 24 hours ahead). Staff at stations will help with boarding and alighting. Passengers with disabilities get 50% discount off the usual ticket price.

Parking

If you have an EU-issued disability parking permit, you're allowed to park in no-stop zones and on yellow lines. Loading wheelchairs and mobility aids is also permitted in pedestrian zones. Disabled parking spaces are marked with a wheelchair symbol.

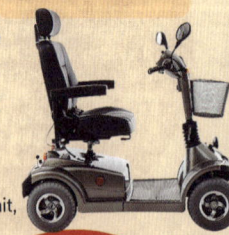

MUSEUM ACCESS

Many museums are accessible for visitors in wheelchairs, with ramps, lifts and well-spaced exhibitions. Great accessible choices include Vienna's Schloss Schönbrunn, Hallein's Celtic Museum and Salzburg's DomQuartier.

Gallery Days

Kunsthaus Graz is designed to be completely accessible. Lentos gallery in Linz offers guided tours in sign language. Vienna's Kunsthistorisches Museum has viewing sessions for the visually or cognitively impaired.

Nuts & Bolts

OPENING HOURS

Opening hours vary through the year and can differ between cities and small villages.

Banks 9am–3pm Monday to Friday

Cafes 8am–11pm

Post offices 8am–noon and 2–6pm Monday to Friday

Pubs & bars 5.30pm–midnight

Restaurants 11am–2.30pm & 6–11pm

Shops 9am–6.30pm Monday to Friday, to 5pm Saturday

Supermarkets 8am–8pm Monday to Friday, to 5pm Saturday

Toilets

Public toilets are widely available at major stations and attractions, but you'll need a €0.50 or €1 coin. Bars and cafes don't take kindly to passers-by using their facilities without buying a drink at least.

Smoking

Smoking is not allowed in restaurants in theory, but in practice controls can be lax. It's legal to smoke anywhere on outdoor terrace

Weights & Measurements

Austria uses the metric system.

GOOD TO KNOW

Time zone
CET (UTC/GMT+1)

Country code
+43

Emergency number
112

Population
8.96 million

Electricity
220V/50Hz

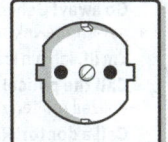

PUBLIC HOLIDAYS

There are 13 public holidays in Austria. Some non-essential businesses may close.

New Year's Day (Neujahr) 1 January

Epiphany (Heilige Drei Könige) 6 January

Easter Monday (Ostermontag) March/April

Labour Day (Tag der Arbeit) 1 May

Whit Monday (Pfingstmontag) 6th Monday after Easter

Ascension Day (Christi Himmelfahrt) 6th Thursday after Easter

Corpus Christi (Fronleichnam) 2nd Thursday after Whitsunday

Assumption (Mariä Himmelfahrt) 15 August

National Day (Nationalfeiertag) 26 October

All Saints' Day (Allerheiligen) 1 November

Immaculate Conception (Mariä Empfängnis) 8 December

Christmas Day (Christfest) 25 December

St Stephen's Day (Stephanitag) 26 December

Language

The national language of Austria is German. Let's get to grips with the basics here.

Basics

Hello. Servus. *ser*-vus
Hello. Grüss Gott. *grewss*-got
Good morning. Moagn. *mwah*-gen
Goodbye. Auf Wiedersehen. owf *vee*-der-zay-en
Bye. Tschüss./ Tschau. chüs/chow
Yes. Ja. yah
No. Nein. nain
Please. Bitte. *bi*-te
Thank you. Danke. *dang*-ke
Excuse me. Entschuldigung. ent·*shul*·di·gung
Sorry. Entschuldigung. ent·*shul*·di·gung
What's your name?
Wie ist Ihr Name? (pol) vee ist eer *nah*·me
Wie heißt du? (inf) vee haist doo
My name is ...
Mein Name ist ... (pol) main *nah*·me ist ...
Ich heiße ... (inf) ikh *hai*·se ...
Do you speak English?
Sprechen Sie Englisch? (pol) *shpre*·khen zee *eng*·lish
Sprichst du Englisch? (inf) shprikhst doo *eng*·lish
I don't understand. Ich verstehe nicht. ikh fer·*shtay*·e nikht

Directions

Where's (the station)?
Wo ist (der Bahnhof). vo ist (der *bahn*·hawf)
What's the address?
Wie ist die Adresse? vee ist dee a·*dre*·se
Could you please write it down?
Könnten Sie das bitte aufschreiben? *kern*·ten zee das *bi*·te *owf*·shrai·ben

Can you show me (on the map)?
Können Sie es mir (auf der Karte) zeigen *ker*·nen zee es meer (owf dair *kar*·te) *tsai*·gen

Signs

Ausgang Exit
Eingang Entrance
Damen Women
Herren Men
Heiß Hot
Kalt Cold
Offen Open
Geschlossen Closed
Kein Zutritt No Entry
Rauchen Verboten No Smoking
Verboten Prohibited

Time

What time is it? Wie spät ist es? vee shpayt ist es
It's (10) o'clock. Es ist (zehn) Uhr. es ist (tsayn) oor
morning Morgen *mor*·gen
afternoon Nachmittag *nahkh*·mi·tahk
evening Abend *ah*·bent
yesterday gestern *ges*·tern
today heute *hoy*·te
tomorrow morgen *mor*·gen

Emergencies

Help! Hilfe! *hil*·fe
Go away! Gehen Sie weg! *gay*·en zee vek
I'm ill. Ich bin krank. ikh bin krangk
Call the police! Rufen Sie die Polizei! *roo*·fen zee dee po·li·*tsai*
Call a doctor! Rufen Sie einen Arzt! *roo*·fen zee *ai*·nen artst

NUMBERS

1 eins *ains*
2 zwei *tsvai*
3 drei *drai*
4 vier *feer*
5 fünf *fünf*
6 sechs *zeks*
7 sieben *zee*·ben
8 acht *akht*
9 neun *noyn*
10 zehn *tsayn*

ESZETT & THE UMLAUTS

In German, the ß character is called eszett. Look out for it in words like *Straße*, meaning street. It's often transliterated as 'ss' (which is used in this book). The two dots that sometimes appear above the vowels a, o and u are called umlauts and affect how words are pronounced. You'll see them in words like *Bäckerei* (bakery), *Löffel* (spoon) and *Frühstück* (breakfast).

Speak Like a Local

Hey! Hey! hei
Great! Toll! tol
Cool! Spitze! *shpi*·tse
No problem. Kein Problem. kain pro·*blaym*
Sure. Klar! klahr
Maybe. Vielleicht. fi·*laikht*
No way! Auf keinen Fall! owf *kai*·nen fal
It's OK. Alles klar. a·les klahr
What a pity! Schade! *shah*·de
Doesn't matter. Macht nichts. makht nikhts

False Friends

Warning: many German words look like English words but have a different meaning altogether, eg *Chef* shef is boss, not chef (which is *Koch* in German). Tipp tip is 'advance information' (not 'bonus payment', which is Trinkgeld *trink*·gelt); komisch *kaw*·mish is 'strange' (not 'comical', which is lustig *lus*·tikh); and blank blank is shiny (not 'blank', which is leer leer).

Must-know Sounds

Note that kh sounds like the 'ch' in 'Bach' or in the Scottish loch (pronounced at the back of the throat), r is also pronounced at the back of the throat, and ü as the 'ee' in 'see' but with rounded lips.

Vowels

Vowels are pronounced crisply and cleanly, with your mouth tenser than in English, eg *Tee* is pronounced tay, not tay·ee.

It is estimated that about **90 million** people speak German as their first language

9 million Austrians speak German as their first language

Long Words

Don't be intimidated by the length of some German words. Unlike English, which often uses a number of separate words to express a single notion, German tends to join words together. After a while you'll start to recognise parts of words and find it easy to understand longer words. For example, haupt howpt means 'main', so Hauptpost *howpt*·post means 'main post office', and Hauptstadt *howpt*·shtat is 'main city', ie 'capital'. Also keep in mind that nouns start with a capital letter in German, making it very easy to recognise them.

Formalities

German has a formal and informal word for 'you' (Sie zee and du doo respectively). When talking to someone familiar or younger than you, use the informal du form.

WHO SPEAKS GERMAN?

German is the official or co-official language of Austria, Germany, Liechtenstein, Belgium, Switzerland and Luxembourg, and a recognised language in Namibia.

THE AUSTRIA
STORYBOOK

Our writers delve deep into different aspects of Austrian life

A History of Austria in 15 Places
Discover its past through the buildings, landscape and people
Kerry Walker
p400

Meet the Austrians
An introduction to the people and their passions
Viktoria Urbanek
p404

The Green City: Capital of a Green Nation
Vienna's eco credentials and the inspiration behind them
Becki Enright
p406

Austria's Coffee House Culture
How coffee made its mark on Austrian society
Samantha Priestley
p408

From Falco to Mozart
Global legacy of two iconic musical giants
Anthony Haywood
p412

Mountain Highs: Hiking in Austria
The beauty of Europe's greatest mountain range
Rudolf Abraham
p414

Mountains of the Mind
Spiritual and mythical sides to the amazing Austrian Alps
Kerry Walker
p417

Boat to Hallstatt (p401)
WILLIAN JUSTEN DE VASCONCELLOS/UNSPLASH

A HISTORY OF AUSTRIA IN
15 PLACES

Austria's history makes a rollicking read. Neolithic ice men, proto-Celts on horseback, stampeding Romans, medieval dukes and margraves, Cistercian monks, saints, prince-archbishops and Habsburg emperors with riches, artistic inclinations and ambition all burst forth from the pages of a book so engrossing, it's impossible to put down. By Kerry Walker

AS THE ICE Age got a grip, so too did civilisation in the Danube Valley in Lower Austria. Venus figurines excavated here testify that Austria has been inhabited for at least 30,000 years – probably longer. Some 5000 years ago, folk were building pile dwellings on the shores of Mondsee in Salzkammergut (dive under water and you can still splash past prehistoric remains). Then came the late Bronze Age and early Iron Age Hallstattkultur (Hallstatt culture), where settlers worked in salt mines. Around 450 BCE Celts arrived in the region and built on this flourishing culture.

Romans started to muscle into Austria around 200 BCE, building Carnuntum, centre of the fortifications along the Danube, and later, around 80 CE, Vindobona, forerunner of Vienna's Innere Stadt. In their hobnail-booted footsteps came the powerful Babenbergs (962–1246), a medieval dynasty of dukes and margraves. Hot at their heels were the Habsburgs (1282–1918), who ruled a mighty empire that spanned continents and was once at the very pinnacle of politics and high culture. Despite having to battle Ottomans, Prussians and Napoleon, they left behind an extraordinary legacy that still reverberates in palaces, castles, abbeys, cathedrals and galleries today.

The 20th century brought cultural explosion, Austro-fascism, Nazi occupation and, finally, stable democracy.

1. Naturhistorisches Museum
VENUS IS HER NAME

Austria's alpine regions were bitterly cold and inhospitable during the last Ice Age 30,000 years ago – virtually impenetrable for human and beast. While mammoths were lumbering across a frozen landscape, civilisation began to sprout up in the warmer, flatter Danube Valley. Archaeological remnants from this period include ancient Venus figurines housed inside Vienna's Naturhistorisches Museum. The starlet is the Venus of Willendorf, discovered in 1908 in the Wachau region of the Danube Valley. The plump, buxom beauty, measuring just 11cm, is made of limestone and estimated to be around 25,000 years old. Her rival is the 30,000-year-old Venus of Galgenberg (aka Dancing Fanny).

For more on the Naturhistorisches Museum, see page 77

2. Ötzi Dorf
THE ICE MAN

Tyrol's Ötztal is another pretty alpine valley on the face of things, but its history is special. In 1991, a German hiker stumbled across the body of a man preserved in the Similaun Glacier in the Ötztal Alps. The forensics were called in and carbon data showed that the ice man, nicknamed 'Ötzi', was nearly 5400 years old. He'd been in the deep freeze since the late Stone Age, making him one of the oldest and best-preserved mummies on the planet. Ötzi Dorf gives a snapshot of Ötzi's Neolithic world, with traditional thatched huts, crafts and rare-breed animals.

For more on Ötzi Dorf, see page 356

3. Hallstatt
BACK TO THE BRONZE AGE

With its glass-blue lake and lofty, forested mountains lifting your gaze to postcard heaven, Hallstatt in the Salzkammergut is prime fodder for Instagrammers. But its history runs deep. For it was here that a proto-Celtic civilisation – the Hallstatt culture – took root in the region in the late Bronze Age around 800 BCE, centring on burial sites in the high alpine valley above town. These proto-Celts mined salt and traded with the Mediterranean. A spin of the cavernous Salzwelten salt mines, which are the world's oldest, and a visit to the Weltkulturerbe Museum, wing you through Hallstatt's long and fascinating history.

For more on Hallstatt, see page 224

4. Carnuntum
ALL ROADS LEAD TO ROME

East of Vienna and but a catapult-shot away from Slovakia, Carnuntum is the centrepiece

Carnuntum (p150)

of the 360km-long Austrian section of the UNESCO World Heritage Danube Limes, once the dividing line between the Roman Empire and tribal areas of Germania. Once a metropolis home to 50,000 and protected by a legionary camp, Carnuntum now presents a romp through Roman times, with its impressively reconstructed amphitheatres, Roman quarter and museum of archaeological finds. Among 3300 Roman treasures is the Tanzende Mänade (Dancing Maenad), a marble figure with a most perfect backside. September's Roman Festival brings legions, barbarians and gladiators to the fore.

For more on Carnuntum, see page 150

5. Stift Heiligenkreuz
BABENBERG BEAUTY

Embosomed in the forested Wienerwald, this medieval monastery is a knockout. It's both the second-oldest Cistercian monastery in the world, and the oldest continuously inhabited and active one. A visit pings you back to Austria in the Middle Ages, as you roam the vaulted Romanesque nave, founded in 1133 by Margrave Leopold III, a member of the House of Babenberg, patron saint of Austria and Vienna. Look out for the tomb of Leopold V – Richard the Lionheart's kidnapper. The chapter house is the final resting place of most of the Babenberg dynasty, which ruled Austria from 962 to 1246.

For more on Stift Heiligenkreuz, see page 139

6. Dürnstein Castle
A FAIRY-TALE FORT

Medieval castles guard many a hilltop in Austria, but few have such a gripping past as Dürnstein, whose rocky ruins cling to a steeply forested crag in the Wachau. An open-air exhibition among the ruins gallivants back to the Middle Ages. Richard the Lionheart was incarcerated here from 1192 to 1193. His crime was insulting Leopold V; his misfortune was to be recognised when journeying through Austria on his way home from the Holy Lands. His liberty was granted only upon payment of an enormous ransom of 35,000kg of silver (this sum partly funded the building of Wiener Neustadt).

For more on Dürnstein Castle, see page 133

7. Hofburg
PALACE OF HABSBURG DREAMS

Imagine what you could do with unlimited riches and Austria's top architects at hand for 640 years and you'll have the Vienna of the Habsburgs. The crown jewel is the Hofburg, HQ of the Habsburgs from 1273 to 1918, with a flabbergasting stash of cultural and art treasures. The oldest section is the 13th-century Schweizerhof (Swiss Courtyard), named after the Swiss guards who protected its precincts. Feel the weight of the empire marvelling at the treasury's imperial crowns and precious religious relics, the equine ballet of snow-white Lipizzaner stallions at the Spanische Hofreitschule and the chandelier-lit apartments fit for a rather fussy Empress Elisabeth.

For more on the Hofburg, see page 64

8. Schloss Ambras
RENAISSANCE RICHES

Nowhere captures the marvels of Renaissance Austria better than Innsbruck's Schloss Ambras, which harbours one of the world's oldest museums. In 1564, Archduke Ferdinand II, then ruler of Tyrol, transformed it from fortress to palace, complete with a magnificent banquet hall. He was a passionate collector of art and the palace is full of treasures – many still displayed in their original location – from a 2.6m suit created for giant Bartlmä Bon in the armour collection to wonderful oddities in the curiosity cabinet, and Titian, Velázquez and Van Dyck in the portrait gallery.

For more on Schloss Ambras, see page 335

9. Salzburg Altstadt
BAROQUE AND ROLL

Set against the backdrop of the Alps, Salzburg has long been a city of grand designs. But it was Wolf Dietrich von Raitenau, prince-archbishop of Salzburg from 1587 to 1612, that gave the Altstadt its magic baroque touch, enlisting famous Italian architects of the age including Santino Solari and Vincenzo Scamozzi. The UNESCO World Heritage historic centre dazzles with brilliance: from the copper-domed, twin-spired Dom, a masterpiece of baroque art, to the Residenz, a stately baroque palace on the site of an 11th-century bishop's residence, and the resplendent, fountain-adorned Residenzplatz.

For more on Salzburg Altstadt, see page 248

10. Semmeringbahn
TIMELESS TRACKS

If the Semmeringbahn (Semmering Railway) seems impressive today, imagine how jaws must have dropped when it was built between 1848 and 1854. Some 20,000 workers toiled to create the railway, a pioneering alpine first, in a feat of 19th-century engineering that is now a UNESCO World Heritage Site. Today it's a panoramic journey through the eastern Alps and a nostalgic trip back to early rail travel. Though steam has been replaced by electricity, you can imagine the wonder of the first passengers as the train curves around 16 viaducts, burrows through 15 tunnels and glides across 100 stone bridges.

For more on the Semmeringbahn, see page 142

11. Ringstrasse
GET IN THE RING

If you like it then you should put a ring on it. So thought a bold and extravagant Emperor Franz Joseph I, as he raided imperial coffers in 1857 to build a boulevard to out-pomp them all: Vienna's Ringstrasse. Wrapping up the historic treasures of the capital's 1st district Innere Stadt and flaunting the power of the empire, this 5.3km masterpiece was 50 years in the making. Explore it on foot or by tram or bike, ticking off grand 19th-century hotels, coffee houses and landmarks like the Gothic-revival Rathaus, the neoclassical Parliament and the neo-Renaissance Wiener Staatsoper (Vienna State Opera), where waltz king Strauss once conducted.

For more on the Ringstrasse, see page 76

12. Café Central
COFFEE-HOUSE CULTURE

Step into Café Central and you will be wowed by the grandeur of soaring columns, marble polished to a sheen and black-vested waiters. In the epoch-defining times of the late 19th and early 20th centuries, artists, writers, poets, thinkers and political big players flocked to this palatial

Burgtheater (p77), Ringstrasse, Vienna

Kaffeehaus. Sigmund Freud, architect Adolf Loos, writer Stefan Zweig, poet Peter Altenberg, Hitler and Stalin once sipped coffee below its high-vaulted ceiling, while Trotsky came here to plot his next move – in chess and the Russian Revolution. Take a moment to contemplate this while digging a fork into a slice of chocolate-truffle Altenbergtorte.

For more on Café Central, see page 72

13. Secession
IT STARTED WITH A KISS

In 1897, a group of rebels, including Gustav Klimt, Otto Wagner, Joseph Olbrich and Josef Hoffmann, swam away from the mainstream artistic establishment to form the Vienna Secession. Olbrich designed this exhibition centre, which combined sparse functionality with stylistic motifs and the decorative flourish of a gold dome, intertwined with leaves. Its scene-stealer is Klimt's sumptuously gilded *Beethoven Frieze*. Klimt's fascination with women and use of gold-leaf and mosaic-like detail is typical of his golden period, inspired by the Byzantine imagery he saw in Venice. The frieze is as resonant and alluring today as when he sent ripples of scandal through fin-de-siècle Vienna, with his exotic, erotic style.

For more on the Secession, see page 97

14. Mauthausen Memorial
REMEMBERING THE HOLOCAUST

The Holocaust of WWII saw thousands of Austrian Jews perish in concentration camps. At KZ Mauthausen, prisoners were forced into slave labour in the granite quarry and many died on the Todesstiege (stairway of death) leading from quarry to camp. Some 100,000 prisoners died or were executed here between 1938 and 1945.

The camp has been turned into this memorial, where you can see the remaining living quarters and gas chambers. The former Sick Quarters now shelters most of the camp's harrowing material – charts, artefacts and photos of both prisoners and their SS guards.

It is a stark and incredibly moving reminder of human cruelty.

For more on Mauthausen Memorial, see page 173

15. Linz
FUTURE FOCUSED

'In Linz beginnt's' ('It begins in Linz') goes the Austrian saying – and it's bang on. While much of Austria celebrates the past, Linz, capital of Upper Austria, steams into the future.

A UNESCO City of Media Arts, it has its finger firmly on the pulse of new technology, science, media art, digital culture and the creative economy.

Plug its progressive groove with a tour of the colour-changing Ars Electronica Centre – whizzing you through subjects like AI and music, neurobionics, deep space and global warming – catch a cutting-edge exhibition at architecturally striking Lentos, or glimpse street art at Mural Harbour.

For more on Linz, see page 170

MEET THE AUSTRIANS

Austrians love the Alps, and winter sports in particular, religiously. Even if you speak some German, be prepared to not be able to follow conversations. Viktoria Urbanek introduces her people.

MANY AUSTRIANS PROUDLY claim that they first learned to ski and only then learned to walk. I am certainly one of them – and do take some pride in it. Skiing and winter sports in general are a huge part of Austria's identity. The most challenging downhill race in the world takes place each January in posh Kitzbühel, in Tyrol, and is known as Die Streif. For an entire weekend, ski enthusiasts flock from all parts of the country and beyond. It's an international spectacle and a great testimony to our sports attitude.

Identifying the Homo austriacus and pinning down specific personality traits is no easy undertaking. Even though it's a relatively small country, there are nine states that not only differ culturally but also language-wise.

Our dialects play a significant role in our everyday lives. While it is still German that we speak, we tend to pronounce it differently and have our own words for certain things. Apple juice in German is *Apfelsaft*, in Austria we'd pronounce it *Opflsoft*. To express content or describe a cool situation or person, you may refer to it or them as *'leiwand'*. If you want to emphasise something, use *'ur'*. You may even combine the last two to describe something as being beyond awesome by saying *'ur leiwand'*.

A somewhat good listener can determine where the other person grew up and will mostly likely start a conversation about their home. Some regions are easier to get than others, and some dialects vary from valley to valley. The Carinthian is very melodic, the Viennese rather snobbish, and while the Tyrolean can be hard to understand, the dialect in Vorarlberg remains a big mystery to the rest of us Austrians. This is a huge challenge for someone who moves to Austria and then learns the language. Yet, if mastered, it's the key to a more in-depth understanding of Austria and its inhabitants.

Austrians are an interesting folk to get to know, but a hard one to truly understand. You'll stumble upon smaller and bigger controversies as you travel around. One of my all-time favourites is that Vienna has been named both the most liveable city and the most unfriendly one at the same time.

We are a content and proud nation, yet we are grumpy, too. If there was a world championship in complaining, we'd easily win it. We love *sudern* (*'sudern'* is a very Austrian term for the practice of complaining about minor inconveniences, serving both as a form of social bonding and an outlet for daily frustrations), and as soon as we're done talking about what teeny-weeny thing happened on our commute or in the neighbourhood, it's a thing of the past. Don't take it personally, that's just how and who we are – and we don't really mean it anyhow.

> **WHO & HOW MANY**
>
> In 2023, Austria surpassed the nine million inhabitants mark. Of these, almost two million live in Vienna. Burgenland is the least inhabited state of all nine. While German is the official language, Croatian, Slovenian and Hungarian are also considered official in some parts of the country.

THE AUSTRIA(N) AFICIONADO

My parents, who were both ski instructors during their time at university, moved around a lot in their younger years. This resulted in me being born in Carinthia and my sister in Tyrol. After a few years, we eventually moved back to my parents' hometown of Leoben in Styria. There, I grew up in a multi-generational household of nine. To me, this was paradise. There was always someone to play cards with or some story that my grandma hadn't shared with me about her childhood yet.

Maybe it was this togetherness that kept me there until the age of 23 before I moved to Upper Austria where I now call the oldest city in the country, Enns, my home.

When someone asks me about my favourite country, I always answer promptly, despite or because of having travelled to more than 70 countries: Austria. Such a tiny country and yet so rich in culture, history and – my favourite – weird and random places.

THE GREEN CITY: CAPITAL OF A GREEN NATION

It may be a bricolage of epochs and architecture, but Vienna's green credentials are as widespread as its historical layers are deep. By Becki Enright

SURE, VIENNA IS a metropolis, but half the city is green space: predominantly the esplanade public grounds of Augarten and Stadtpark; the landscaped Schönbrunn and Belvedere, and lawns of Burggarten and Volksgarten; the green Prater expanse and Lainzer Tiergarten biosphere; the circumambient Vienna Woods and city vineyards; and the stretching Danube wetlands. And 14 city hiking trails forge paths through it all.

Vienna's Greenest Residents

Within this blanket of recreation are some 800 urban farms and community gardens. The 4000-sq-metre City Farm in the Augarten grows the most extensive collection of tomato varieties, which complements the

Pictured clockwise from top left: Alpine marmot; Kaiser-Josef-Plat farmers market (p203); Heiligenstadt vineyard (p119); Hundertwasserhaus (p87) in April

'cucumber capital' – Vienna's fruition is more than all the remaining eight Austrian states combined. Around 700 hectares of vineyards cultivate a city wine-growing culture, and traditional snail farming continues at Wiener Schnecken Manufaktur Gugumuck, in the south of Vienna. The farm-to-table offering is ripe with choice.

The greenest residents are the bees, with 456 species across 6000 city beehives. There are 130 species documented in the Botanical Garden of the University of Vienna in the Belvedere Garden alone – Empress Maria Theresia founded the world's first beekeeping school in Vienna in 1769. While you flit between sites, the bees are busy on the rooftops of the Kunsthistorisches Museum, the University of Vienna, the State Opera, the Secession and the Rathaus, to name a few. Hotel rooftops like Hotel Daniel, 25hours Hotel Wien and Hotel InterContinental are abuzz, too.

Eco-warrior Hundertwasser ignited change with his eco-housing project in the 3rd district, and hotels are following. Hotel Gilbert's noise-reducing and air-purifying green facade is also a bird home. At the same time, Boutiquehotel Stadthalle operates with a 'zero energy balance' using photovoltaics solar power on its lavender garden roof. Others like Magdas put upcycling at the core of their design.

Vienna fights the heat waves from climate change. Streets are climate-adapted with more trees and water features – Zieglergasse in the 7th district was the city's first 'Cool Mile', completed in 2019. The city's 1300 drinking fountains and glorious 175 mist showers bring the fresh mountain spring water from the Lower Austrian-Styrian Alps to the streets.

Streets are spotless thanks to the legendary rubbish collectors, and converting waste to energy is an artwork at the Hundertwasser incinerator. Streets are phasing out car spaces – 74% of residents walk, use public transport or cycle. Visitors can use affordable public transport – a single ticket for trams, buses and metro costs €3. And you can access over 1660km of cycle paths with the WienMobile bike-hire network, including between Prater Park and the city centre on Vienna's 1st Mega Cycle Highway – the 7km-long, 4m-wide, two-way cycle path connecting the far suburbs to the centre.

Initiatives Throughout the Nation

Vienna is the capital of a green nation. Austria's second-biggest city, Graz, reserves 60% of its urban spread for green spaces. Wander between its car-free historical UNESCO centre and trendy cross-river neighbourhoods and find a host of zero-waste, upcycling and social-impact outlets, farm-to-table eateries, and farmers markets like those on Kaiser-Josef-Platz and Lendplatz. In Burgenland, the city of Güssing is a prime example of energy self-sufficiency – using biomass, photovoltaics and wind power for its entire energy needs. Skiing completes the seasonal sustainability cycle, especially regarding cable cars. The Gastein Valley uses 100% certified green electricity. Tyrol's largest connected ski area, SkiWelt Wilder Kaiser – Brixental, produces 100% hydropower and is home to the world's first solar-energy-powered lift, the Brixen Sonnenlift (sun lift).

From the grassy prairies of the east to the jagged Alps in the west, nearly half of Austria's nature is under special protection, preserving rare plant and animal species. Hohe Tauern National Park, Austria's oldest and biggest national park stretching across three states, is home to half the country's total animal species, counting marmots as some of its most famous residents alongside golden eagles. It declares itself an 'open-air laboratory' with scientists cataloguing thousands of animal and plant species and recording the impact of climate change.

Pastured, lakeside Neusiedler See–Seewinkel National Park in Burgenland is a migratory bird sanctuary and breeding ground. It's also Austria's only grassy steppe national park, declared a World Heritage site in 2001. Stretching from Vienna to Lower Austria, the wild 96-sq-km wetland of Donau-Auen National Park is the last remaining of its kind in Central Europe.

There's a lot of green ground to cover, but with a national ÖBB train network powering you from Vienna to the westernmost state of Vorarlberg in little over seven hours, a 50/50 chance you will encounter nature, and a nationwide farm-to-table food culture that runs to the seasons, a visit to the capital and beyond is environmentally conscious, by default.

Café Central (p72), Vienna

AUSTRIA'S COFFEE HOUSE CULTURE

Austria's coffee houses have been many things over time, but time, and how it's used, is at the heart of this cultural affair. By Samantha Priestley

AUSTRIA MIGHT NOT be the first place in the world to have opened coffee houses, but they are certainly the best at it. The first coffee house in Europe opened in Venice in 1647. Long before that, as far back as the 12th century, coffee houses were a regular thing in Mecca. In England coffee houses began opening their doors in 1650. Austria didn't open their first coffee house until 1683. So, why is it such a big deal here?

History

It's no coincidence that the opening of the first coffee house in Austria coincided with the end of the Siege of Vienna. And it all started with one man. Jerzy Franciszek Kulczycki was a translator for the Austrian Oriental Company. He was living in Vienna at the time of the siege and he was the only one to bravely offer to leave the city undercover to get help. He's hailed as a local hero by Austrians for this act of heroism and there's a statue of him in Vienna. And he wasn't even Austrian.

Jerzy Franciszek Kulczycki was born in Kulczyce, which is in modern-day Ukraine, but back in Jerzy's day was part of the Polish-Lithuanian commonwealth. It was his skills as a translator that got him safely out of Vienna that day. He took his servant with him and he crossed enemy lines cheerfully singing Ottoman songs. And no one batted an eyelid.

When it was all over the people of Vienna awarded Jerzy a large amount of cash and a house. Oh, and some coffee beans the Ottomans had left behind. Following these events Jerzy was given the first licence to serve coffee in Austria. However, there's no evidence that he attempted to open a coffee house at this time. For that we have to look to Johannes Diodato, an Armenian spy living in Vienna.

Johannes had skills Jerzy didn't yet have. He knew how to make great coffee from those beans. He was also already familiar with coffee houses. But what he really wanted was a secret meeting place where people could pass and gather information. So, he opened a kind of speakeasy coffee house. It was hidden behind a false shopfront and you had to know the password to gain entry.

No one knows why, but after only a few years of being open, this coffee house was suddenly closed. Given Johannes' work as a spy and his love of secrecy we can only speculate on what happened. But this did leave the arena open for Jerzy to step back into the spotlight. Jerzy had been working hard to perfect his coffee-making skills. Sadly, by all accounts, his coffee was never that good, but he did open a coffee house shortly before he died.

A New Age
The coffee houses we see in Austria today have the upper classes to thank for their grandeur. Coffee was expensive in Austria, which led the wealthy to begin drinking it. After all, if it costs a lot it must be something you want, right?

Coffee wasn't something ordinary people in Austria could afford and the first coffee houses were opulent and stylish, as they are today, to cater to those upper classes. The owners soon found that the lower classes were coming into the coffee house because it was warm and they could read a newspaper, which were first laid out for free in 1720, but they weren't spending much money. Instead, they were lounging about all day in rooms they didn't have to pay to heat, taking their sweet time over one highly priced cup of coffee.

In the mid-19th century the price of coffee came down dramatically and everyone could afford to enjoy a cup in one of the now many coffee houses in Austria. But that old tradition of taking your time over one cup, reading a newspaper and relaxing in the warmth of an opulent coffee house, stuck. This was how Austria's coffee-house culture was shaped.

In 1856, women were allowed into the coffee houses. Until that point a woman could only enter a coffee house if she had a job there. Although the waiters were always men and still largely are, the cashiers were often women. But now women could sit quietly and enjoy a cup of coffee in the grand surroundings along with the men.

Writers & Artists
It was in 1890 that a coffee house in Vienna became the unofficial meeting place for a young group of Austrian writers. Soon the writers began to branch out and try other coffee houses and before long artists were also frequenting the coffee houses. These writers and artists would spend all day in the coffee houses, going from one to another, sitting and sketching, scribbling, some even took their typewriters with them, and all sipping slowly on one coffee. Just like the poor people of Austria before them who just wanted to keep warm.

Part of the reason the writers and artists loved the coffee house so much was the space it gave them. Most of them lived in small apartments and in the coffee houses they could stretch out and do some work in comfort, and they had each other to socialise with at the same time. At this point, the coffee itself wasn't the draw. That would come later.

Postwar Changes
WWII was disastrous for the coffee houses. Many of them were owned by Jews and were destroyed and the ones that weren't suffered a serious decline. After the war,

Vienna *Kaffeehaus* (coffee house; p72)

in the 1950s, Italian espresso bars arrived in the cities of Austria and the young people turned their backs on their own heritage and instead began queuing up for a cappuccino. But it could be this that saved the coffee houses in the end, and cemented their place as an Austrian tradition.

The people were being exposed to some wonderful new types of coffee from Italy and the coffee houses saw that if they incorporated these, and other coffees into their menus, they could become something no espresso bar could ever be.

They expanded their menus and began serving food and alcohol, but they kept the grand furniture, the chandeliers and the chic decor. They kept the stern waiters in waistcoats and tails. They kept the free newspapers on stands or laid out on tables. They moved on with the times but they kept their heart. And new generations began to discover the authenticity of a real Austrian coffee house.

In 2011, UNESCO included Viennese coffee culture in its national inventory of tangible cultural heritage. Today these coffee houses are many things. They are an experience in Austrian culture. They are a place where anyone can spend as long as they like over a coffee, in fact, taking your time is encouraged as good coffee is not to be rushed. They are somewhere you can go to relax, an extension of your living room at home where you can enjoy a coffee and some cake while slowly reading a newspaper. They are a place of perpetual Sunday mornings, but they open from early morning till midnight. You can eat breakfast there, lunch, dinner or supper. But most of all, you drink coffee there.

IN 2011, UNESCO INCLUDED VIENNESE COFFEE CULTURE IN ITS NATIONAL INVENTORY OF TANGIBLE CULTURAL HERITAGE.

Café Korb (p72), Vienna
MOJMIR FOTOGRAFIE/SHUTTERSTOCK

The coffee menus in today's coffee houses are extensive. It's unlikely you've heard of many of these coffees, unless you're a connoisseur, but whatever you choose, it's good coffee. Each cup of coffee is served with a glass of fresh alpine water, which complements the coffee and brings out the intense flavours. The water is there to cleanse the palate between sips and to allow your taste buds to experience the coffee each time you drink.

More Than Great Coffee

Over time the coffee house has been many things. Spy house, opulent cafe for the rich, a place to keep warm for the poor, a meeting place for writers and artists, and a proud symbol of Austria's heritage. Today the grand coffee houses are living museums and a place for Austrians and visitors to settle into a soft sofa, spread out a newspaper and sip a speciality coffee. And today, at last, the coffee itself is what defines a coffee house.

Are you now wondering where to sample a super coffee? Turn to the Help Me Pick: Coffee Houses article on p72.

FROM FALCO
TO MOZART

These two Austrian musical figures have more than a few things in common – and their legacies live on. By Anthony Haywood

WHEN THE END came, it was sudden and made the headlines worldwide, even if the musician himself had become something of a backbeat in the meantime. He died too early, at the age of 40 years in 1998 – the Austrian rock musician Falco. Just over 200 years earlier, another famous Austrian composer, Wolfgang Amadeus Mozart, died at the even less timely age of 35. Falco and Mozart. Two very different people and lives, and yet it is difficult to imagine Austrian music today without them.

Falco – It Ended in a Wreck
If we are to believe the portrayal of his life in the film, *Falco – Verdammt, wir leben noch!* ('Falco – Damn we're still alive!' 2008), before colliding fatally with a bus in the Dominican Republic, he spent the last hour of his life alone inside his car in a disco car park.

From his modest beginnings as Hans Hölzel (his real name), growing up in Vienna's 5th district of Margareten and starting his career in the oddly named Austropop rock-punk group Drahdiwaberl in the 1970s, Falco brought together the coolness of New Wave rock in the 1980s in songs that often switched back and forth effortlessly between German and English. Frequently, he delivered the lyrics in chants in the Viennese dialect and rather priggish English,

Pictured clockwise from top left: Mozart statue, Mozartplatz, St Gilgen (p230); Mozartkugel (p264); Mozart Wohnhaus (p252), Salzburg: Falco's grave, Zentralfriedhof, Vienna (p50)

earning the reputation of being the German-speaking world's first rapper.

Although *The Kommissar* was a hit in Europe, his big international breakthrough came with *Rock me Amadeus*, which topped the music singles charts in the UK, USA and elsewhere. Fatalism was in there somewhere; drugs and alcohol crept into his musical style. Legendary songs like *Ganz Wien* (Total Vienna), about heroine abuse, and *Jeanny* and *Junge Römer* (Young Romans) played with the chill of human life on the edge of a precipice.

On the Shoulders of Giants

Falco was a stroke of musical luck for contemporary Austria. And before he shook up the scene, you could be forgiven for feeling Austria was still slumped in the comfortable armchair of mid- and late-18th-century Vienna Classic, if briefly tickled out of it by the likes of Franz Liszt (1811–86), Johannes Brahms (1833–97) and Anton Bruckner (1824–96) in the 19th century.

The earliest of the great Austrian composers was Joseph Haydn (1732–1809), whose nickname was 'Papa Haydn'. He earned the monikers 'Father of the Symphony' and 'Father of the String Quartet'. Franz Schubert (1797–1828) followed and achieved fame composing vocal works, operas, chamber music and symphonies, above all his 'Symphony No 9 in C Major', which was first performed publicly only after his death. Something of a good socialiser, he was known for his 'Schubertiades', which were intimate house parties where guests gathered to hear his works. Although he was yet another Austrian musical great in a rush to his grave (only 31 when he died), his influence on classical music was enormous.

Less well-known is the 'blind virtuoso' Maria Theresia von Paradis (1759–1824), who received voice training from the Italian composer Antonio Salieri (1750–1825), and this is where the Mozart plot thickens: the supposed rivalry between Salieri and the genius who inspired Falco's biggest hit, Wolfgang Amadeus Mozart (1756–91).

Mozart & the 'Poison' Rumours

Mozart was born in Salzburg – among his sweetest local legacies are the so-called 'Mozart Balls' (Mozartkugeln) of chocolate, pistachio, marzipan and nougat – and began tinkling his way to fame on the piano at the age of four, earning a reputation as a Wunderkind.

After Mozart's meteoric rise, Salieri was appointed by the Habsburgs to head Italian opera at the royal court. Rumours that Mozart was poisoned surfaced soon after he died. However, if this sounds like an envious court appointee slipping a shot of mercury to an adult Wunderkind with fame, fortune, looks to kill and a glamorous wife by his side, a dip into a 1983 article in the Journal of the Royal Society of Medicine entitled 'Mozart's illness and death' paints a very different picture.

The author describes Mozart as obsessed and immature, a child plagued by numerous illnesses (the article lists where and when he came down with them), 5ft tall, scarred by smallpox and sporting a large honker, with a wife who suffered greatly during her pregnancies (only two of their six children survived childhood), disorganised and unable to make ends meet, borrowing money to send his wife to spas to improve her health, suffering from melancholia, snubbed by the aristocracy in Vienna after initial success, living in 11 different apartments in Vienna in less than 10 years of married life, and so it goes on. The things going for him were an enduring fondness for his wife and rather acute hearing. And he also happened to be a revolutionary genius in musical composition.

Mozart's great works include *Symphony No 40*, *The Magic Flute*, *Eine kleine Nachtmusik*, *Requiem* and *Piano Concerto No 21*. Along with musical cousins such as Bach and Beethoven, he was a tour de force in Western classical music. The poisoning rumour kept its traction when Alexander Pushkin wrote a play *Mozart and Salieri* (1830), and another Russian, Nikolay Rimsky-Korsakov, wrote the opera *Mozart et Salieri* in 1898. Fires were rekindled in 1980 when Peter Shaffer wrote the play *Amadeus*, which became the basis for Miloš Forman's film of the same name in 1984. One year later, Falco burst through the doors pleading with Amadeus to rock us, in his glottal rap-like style, describing our Wunderkind as a drinking, indebted superstar. And indeed he was.

Hiking, the Zillertal (p340)

KASAKPHOTO/SHUTTERSTOCK

MOUNTAIN HIGHS:
HIKING IN AUSTRIA

Incredible scenery, unforgettable hospitality – Austria is one of the most spectacular and rewarding hiking destinations on the planet. By Rudolf Abraham

RUN YOUR FINGER across a map of Austria, and you'll effectively trace a line through more than half the length and breadth of Europe's greatest mountain range: the Alps. Perhaps not surprisingly, this goes more than a little way towards making Austria one of the world's best hiking destinations. The scope for hiking here is virtually limitless. There are literally thousands upon thousands of kilometres of hiking trails, both in the mountains and beyond – don't forget that along with all those high peaks, alpine passes, crinkled ridges and glacier-scoured valleys, Austria also has a whole slew of other landscapes to explore, from the forested hills south of Vienna to the sprawling wetlands of Neusiedler See.

These trails come in an enormous range of shapes and sizes – from broad and level enough to take a pushchair on, to narrow, twisting mountain paths with sweeping views, and airy, vertigo-inducing ridges secured with cables – and pretty much everything in between. So whether you're after a leisurely half-day stroll beside an idyllic lake, or a challenging long-distance trail stretching several hundred kilometres, it's pretty much guaranteed that Austria has you covered.

Trails are exceptionally well maintained, and routes are clearly marked with a uniform system of red- and white-trail blazes. Some are simply numbered paths which you're unlikely to have heard of outside Austria; others are legendary. The Adlerweg (Eagle Walk) comes under the latter category, following the spine of the eastern Alps across Tyrol, in a spine-tingling three- or four-week mountain adventure; the Alpe Adria Trail is a 750km epic from the foot of the Grossglockner to the shores of the Adriatic, wonderfully accessible yet still packed with enough mind-bogglingly impressive views to last a lifetime.

Hiking at Its Most Scenic

So what is it that makes hiking in Austria so special? Well, there's all that scenery for a start. Giant glaciers spew from the foot of vertical walls of rock, and jagged peaks pierce the skyline in the Hohe Tauern. Rivers slice through a steeply pitched wilderness of rock and forest in the Gesäuse, while the rounded, more ancient tops of the Nockberge paint a completely different picture.

The lake-studded, chocolate-box landscape of the Salzkammergut is bordered by the Dachstein, Totes Gebirge and Höllengebirge – enormous limestone plateaux, where trails snake their way through a sprawling wilderness of shattered rock pitted with sinkholes and, somewhere below your feet, a labyrinth of cave systems.

Wildlife & Wildflowers

There's also a huge amount of wildlife to see. Hiking through the mountains of Austria, you'll likely spot chamois and possibly ibex wandering the high, rocky slopes or pausing on almost imperceptible ledges, marmots pottering about beside their burrows, perhaps a golden eagle or a bearded vulture soaring overhead.

In spring, you can wade through meadows carpeted with wildflowers, as clouds of butterflies fill the air around, while wandering across the rock-strewn landscape of the Höllengebirge you might see the tiny, fragile outline of an alpine salamander, making its slow way across your path.

Austria's national parks and protected areas are also home to more elusive species such as the lynx, along with precious habitats including riparian forest, reed beds and salt lakes.

Where to Meet Local Hikers

And everywhere you go, there are the *Hütten* (mountain huts), which go a long way towards making hiking in Austria such an enormous pleasure. Ultimately it's not just the scenery which makes a hiking trip here so memorable – Austria certainly isn't the only place with breathtaking mountains and plenty of mountain huts – it's also the people, and the wonderful tradition of alpine hospitality for which the country is synonymous.

Mountain huts tend to be more than just a bed for the night and a hot meal (not to mention a cold beer, or a bottle of Zweigelt) – they are also a place to meet local hikers. There's often something of a shared camaraderie, at least or especially in those huts you have to hike to, rather than arriving by car or by cable car – and Austria certainly has no shortage of either.

There are few places where I've felt so happy to arrive, and so genuinely welcomed, as a mountain hut at the end of a long day's hike across the Austrian Alps. And the food, however simple, is likely to taste exceptionally good – think warm, freshly made Kaiserschmarrn (sweet pancake) at a remote hut on the Dachstein plateau.

Magical Themed Trails for Children

Austria is an amazing place for hiking with kids. When my daughter was seven, I took her to Austria to walk her first hut-to-hut trail – a few days on the Salzburger Almenweg, which winds in a giant loop through Salzburgerland, between the Dachstein and the Hohe Tauern. Over the next two years we went on a succession of half a dozen hiking trips to Salzkammergut together.

Austria has plenty of themed trails for families with young children – a 'fairy trail' here, a 'discovery trail' there – but you'll probably find that just the experience of hiking through stupendous scenery and stopping at rustic mountain huts is more than captivating enough. It's where a child might first drink from an icy-cold mountain spring, or first see chamois skittering across a scree slope through veils of mist, and it will come with the memory of watching the sunset from the terrace of a mountain hut, and waking to the clang of cattle bells.

As a parent, these shared experiences have made for some of the most rewarding and memorable trips I've ever done.

Join the Locals

Hiking is hugely popular in Austria – the Austrian Alpine club has a membership of well over half a million, making it one of the largest organisations of its kind (the German Alpine Club is generally reckoned to be the largest, with around a million).

Spazieren (going for a stroll) or *Wandern* (going for a hike) are simply a big part of what makes Austria what it is – so don't forget to bring those hiking boots.

Wildflowers, the Zillertal (p340)
TUNATURA/SHUTTERSTOCK

MOUNTAINS
OF THE MIND

With peaks that challenge the body and vistas that expand the mind, the Austrian Alps have long been a place of myths, artistic inspiration, spiritual enlightenment and psychological rebirth.
By Kerry Walker

HOME TO GHOSTS, witches, monsters and giants, the Austrian Alps were feared for centuries by valley-dwelling residents. They brought ferocious storms and blizzards, livelihood destroying landslides and avalanches. Their realms were dangerous and unknown; their summits hostile, lonely and insurmountable. Better to keep a respectful distance. Better not to stir malevolent spirits. Better not to risk life and limb to climb them.

And yet folk still did. Brave souls first tramped across these wild, snowbound heights and settled in these mountains 5000 years ago, as the neolithic mummy of Ötzi the 'Ice Man' in Tyrol's Ötztal reveals. The Romans followed in their footsteps on the Via Claudia Augusta, one of the main routes between south and north, which rippled over foreboding summits into that most alpine of lands: Austria.

Why? Just look around you. Still today the Austrian Alps are more than a pretty Instagram post – they symbolise the bigger picture, the notion that there is more up there than we will ever see, know or understand, the jostle between freedom and restraint. With their ever-changing light, storms and open horizons, they are a reminder of nature's unerring constancy and its sudden, brilliant unpredictability.

Myths & Legends

Since time immemorial, Austria's jagged peaks have swirled with myths and legends, which have been handed down from generation to generation and enshrined in folklore. Every rock tells a story. Rising above Innsbruck in the Nordkette range is Frau Hitt, a prominent needle of limestone resembling a petrified giant. Lore has it she gave a beggar woman a stone to eat, who then cursed her and turned her to stone. For centuries, no local would set a foot in the ice caves of Eisriesenwelt, perched high in the Tennengebirge mountains of Salzburgerland, as it was believed to be the gateway to hell.

Even today, ancient customs survive in the Austrian Alps that nod to a spookier, more sinister past. Pagan winter solstice traditions live on at the Krampuslauf, where the horned, hairy Krampus (half goat, half demon) scares kids silly with rusty chains, birch rods and baskets to carry naughty little children off to the pits of hell on the eve of St Nicholas (5 December).

In January, it's the turn of the Perchten, similarly nightmarish, bell-clattering figures who exorcise winter, drive away evil spirits and bring good fortune.

Adventurers & Alpinists

With the dawn of the Age of Enlightenment in the 17th and 18th centuries, fear of the Alps became curiosity, as natural scientists, researchers, intellectuals and philosophers changed the way we measured and understood the world.

Maps, waymarked trails, mountain shelter, guides and equipment were scant, but lack of resources couldn't quell their burning desire to conquer these foreboding peaks.

STORYBOOK

As tough as hobnail boots and often perilously ill equipped, the first alpinists were hot on their trail, with the first ascent of mighty 3798m Grossglockner via the Adlersruhe on 28 July 1800, where the intrepid five mountaineers planted a cross at the top. Many followed and the Austrian Alps became fertile ground for mountaineers limbering up for bigger things, with Austria birthing such illustrious climbers as Peter Habeler who, together with Reinhold Messner, became the first to ascend Mt Everest without supplemental oxygen in 1978.

Inspiring Heights

The sensations of the Alps in winter – the bitter cold, the shining snow, the physical challenge of stomping up to a summit and the thrill of racing down it on seal-skin-soled wooden skis stirred great emotion in writers during the 1920s.

Hemingway raved about the beauty, solitude and wilderness of the Montafon in Vorarlberg. The American novelist spent two refreshing off-the-radar winters in Schruns in 1924 and 1925, eloquently evoked in his 1964 memoir *A Moveable Feast*. British writer Ian Fleming preferred the glitzy slopes of Kitzbühel when he wintered here from 1927 to 1930, and it is rumoured that its mountains inspired many a Bond-like skiing stunt.

Here writers found space to breathe and think, reconnect with nature – let inspiration flow. And they weren't the only ones. In the summer of 1893, Sigmund Freud broke free from the muggy streets of Vienna and headed into the Hohe Tauern mountains. As he hiked in the cool, quiet heights, feeling mentally refreshed, he made an extraordinary breakthrough in his work on neurosis. Over many years, his visits to these alpine landscapes are believed to have shaped his psychoanalytical theories.

Painting the Peaks

A cradle of alpine skiing, Kitzbühel is feted for its winter sports, but it will also forever be synonymous with the work of Alfons Walde (1891–1958), Austria's 'Painter of Snow'. Wintry landscapes, scenes of rural life and skiers dashing down slopes epitomise the silent beauty, majesty, romance and adventurous spirit of life in the Austrian Alps in a way no other Austrian artist has achieved.

Gustav Klimt (1862–1918) felt rested and revived on the glittering shores of Attersee in the Salzkammergut. Over the course of many summers, the Vienna Secessionist fervently painted the lake in all its changing lights and moods. These were landscapes he loved well.

Hills Are Alive

But it was Hollywood that really propelled the Austrian Alps onto the world stage. When blockbuster movie *The Sound of Music* (1965) hit screens, with singing nun Julie Andrews (Maria) twirling through meadows against the spectacular mountain backdrop of Salzburg and the Salzkammergut lakes, it said 'visit Austria' like never before. These were views to send vocals and spirits soaring. The Rodgers and Hammerstein favourite lives on today in tours of the film locations.

Today these hills (well, mountains) are still alive with alpine traditions. Come summer, valleys like the Zillertal in Tyrol reverberate with Alpenländische Volksmusik (alpine folk music), whose origins can be traced back to 18th-century travelling Tyrolean singers.

Brimming with love for the Heimat (homeland), these jaunty melodies bring in yodelling and instruments like the accordion, violin, contraguitar and zither. Locals turn out at festivals and in beer gardens dressed in *Tracht* (traditional costume), which might be *Lederhosen* and an embroidered woollen waistcoat for men, a flowing *Dirndl* for women.

With 60% of Austria given over to the Alps, mountain life is still an integral part of what makes this country tick, and age-old traditions like the Almabtrieb, the cattle drive down from the Alps in September, with cows ornately decorated with bells and floral wreaths, are fiercely protected and celebrated.

Montafon (p375), Vorarlberg

INDEX

A

abbeys 12-13
 Admont Abbey 209-10
 Göttweig Abbey 133
 Heiligenkreuzerhof 63
 Stift Dürnstein 134
 Stift Göttweig 128
 Stift Heiligenkreuz 139, 401
 Stift Melk 128
 Stift Millstatt 310
 Stift Nonnberg 250, 251, 263
 Stift St Florian 175
 Stift St Peter 263
 Stift Stams 360
 Stift Zwettl 146
accessible travel 394
accommodation 30, 43-4, 366, see also individual locations
activities 40-7, see also individual activities
Admont 209-10
Aggsbach 129-30
airports 382
Airrofan Skyglider 347
Aktivzentrum 343
Alpine Coaster 359
Alpine Game Park Pfänder 371
alpine huts 386
Alpinzeit 357
animals, see wildlife
architecture
 Graz 190-1, 198
 Payerbach 298
 Lower Austria 143
 Vienna 87, 90, 95, 99, 103
 Vorarlberg 371
Area 47 358
art 15, see also museums & galleries
 Art Nouveau trail 97-8

Map Pages **000**

Danube Canal 104-5
Forum Frohner 127
Grosser Wappensaal 298
Hundertwasser Village 87
Hundertwasserhaus 87
Kunsthaus Graz 190-1
Mural Harbor 167-8
Österreichischer Skulpturen Park 204
Otto Wagner Pavillon Karlsplatz 95
Secession 97, 403
Walk of Modern Art 257
Würth Sculpture Garden 257
Attersee 239-42, **240**
 accommodation 243
 drinking 242
 food 242
 travel within Attersee 239
Augarten Porcelain Manufactory 83
Austrian Alpine Club 43-4
Austrian Parliament 77
Austro-Hungarian strike 141
Ayurveda Resort Sonnhof 354-5

B

Bad Aussee 235-8, **236**
 accommodation 243
 drinking 237
 food 237, 238
 travel within Bad Aussee 235
Bad Gastein 286-7
 accommodation 293
Bad Ischl 220-3, **221**
 accommodation 243
 drinking 221, 222
 food 222
 travel within Bad Ischl 220
Baden bei Wien 139-40
ballooning 350
bathrooms 395
beaches 86, 89, 304
beer 35
bees 88
Beethoven 75, 139
Beinhaus 227
Belvedere 90-2, **91**

Bergbahn Weissensee 317
Bergisel 336
bicycle hire 131, 160
bicycle travel, see cycling, mountain biking
Bielerhöhe Pass 375
birdwatching 153
Bludenz 373
boat trips
 Attersee 242
 Grundlsee 238
 Millstatt See 313
 Neusiedler See 153
 Salzach River 254
 Salzburg 254
 Traunkirchen 242
 Wachau Valley 127
 Wolfgangsee 230-1
 Zell am See 274
bobsleighing 336
Böckstein 286
books 33
border crossings 382
Brandoferplatz 333
Braunau am Inn 183
Bregenz 369-71
 beyond Bregenz 372-5
 food 371
 travel within Bregenz 369
Brenner Pass 338
breweries 11
 Augustiner Bräustübl 250, 265
 Bevog 212
 Die Weisse 265
 Freistädter Brauhaus 172
 Gösser 212
 Gösser Brauerei 210
 HiFa 212
 Noom Wild Ales 212
 Ottakringer Brauerei 118
 Ried Brewery 183
 Sternbräu 265
 Stiegl-Brauwelt 266
 Sudhaus 212
Bruckner, Anton 171
budget 385, see also costs
bungee jumping 338, 350, 358
Burgenland 123-61, **124**
 accommodation 161
 events 125
 festivals 125
 itineraries 125

 navigation 124
 travel seasons 125
 travel within Burgenland 124
Bürglstein 232-3
bus travel 383
business hours 395

C

cable cars
 Dachstein Gletscherbahn 212
 Ehrwald 361
 Feuerkogel 242
 Gipfelwelt 3000 277
 Gjaidalm 229
 Grünbergseilbahn 241
 Harschbichl 350
 Hungerburg 333
 Katrin 223
 Kitzbüheler Horn 350
 Millennium-Express 306
 Obertraun 228
 Penken 343
 Pfänder 371
 Rax-Seilbahn 143
 Reiterkogel 278
 Rofanseilbahn 347
 St Gilgen 231
 Stubnerkogel 287
 Untersberg 251
 Untersbergbahn 256
 Zugspitze 361
Café Central 72, 402
Café Sacher 72
cakes 36
camping 386
canyoning 41
car travel 383
Carinthia 294-321, **296**
 accommodation 321
 festivals 297
 itineraries 297
 navigation 296
 travel seasons 297
 travel within Carinthia 296
castles & fortresses 12-13
 Burg Aggstein 130
 Burg Forchtenstein 158
 Burg Hasegg 337
 Burg Hochosterwitz 308
 Burg Hohenwerfen 270

420

Burg Losenstein 180-1
Burg Mauterndorf 289
Burg Riegersburg 207-8
Burgruine Mödling 139
Castle of Wels 177
Drosendorf castle 147
Dürnstein Castle 139, 401
Festung Hohensalzburg 250
Festung Kufstein 353
Gmünd 316
Kartause Aggsbach 129
Kuenringerburg 133
Neue Burg 65, 76
Petersberg 309
Rotturm 309
Schattenburg 372-3
Schloss Freisaal 268
Schloss Rosenburg 146, 146-7
Schloss Tillysburg 175
Schloss Waldreichs 146
Schloss Wilhelminenberg 119
Seeschloss Ort 241
Virgilienberg 309
cathedrals, see churches & cathedrals
caves 16-17
Blaue Grotte 359
Eisriesenwelt 41, 269-70
Gasteiner Heilstollen 286
Mammuthöhle 229
Rieseneishöhle 229
Schellenberg Ice Cave 256
Carnuntum 150, 401
cemeteries
Friedhof St Sebastian 262
Hietzinger Friedhof 115
Stift St Peter 263
Central Carinthia 307-9, **308**
travel within Central Carinthia 307
chairlifts
Bergbahn Weissensee 317
Dreiländereck 306
Kaiserlift 354
children, travel with 41, 251
Chinese Hallstatt 229
Christmas markets 99
Vienna 31, 78-9, 99
churches & cathedrals
Alter Dom 169
Augustinerkirche 67
Basilica Minor St Michael 234
Basilica & Pilgrimage Church of Maria Loretto 157
Basilika Mariazell 205
Bergkirche 157

Blutskapelle 339
Bürgerspitalkirche St Blasius 262
Bürgerspitalkirche St Jakob 241
Cathedral of St George 141
Church of St Othmar 139
Dom zu Gurk 308
Grazer Dom 198-9
Heiligenblut 282
Hofkirche 328-9
Karlskirche 95
Kirche am Steinhof 118
Kirche St Johan 173
Klangenfurt Dom 300
Kriegergedächtniskapelle 320
Maria Treu Kirche 108
Mariendom 169
Michaelerkirche 67
Minoritenkirche 127
Peterskirche 309
Pfarrkirche (Hallstätter See) 227
Pfarrkirche (Spitz an der Donau) 130-1
Pfarrkirche (Traunkirchen) 241-2
Pfarrkirche Mauthausen 173, 174
Pfarrkirche St Nikolaus 336
Pfarrkirche St Oswald 339
Postalmkapelle 233
Ruprechtskirche 63
Salzburger Dom 257, 263
Schottenkirche 61
St Bartholomew Church 309
St Catherine's Church 199
St Laurentiuskirche 373
St Michael's Church 177
St Pölten cathedral 135
St Urbani Chapel 305
Stadthauptpfarrkirche St Egid 300
Stadtpfarrkirche 173
Stadtpfarrkirche St Andrä 319-20
Stadtpfarrkirche St Stephan 183
Stadtpfarrturm 303
Stephansdom 56-7
Votinkirche 109
Wallfahrtskirche 232
Wallfahrtskirche St Vinzenz 282
Wehrkirche St Michael 131-2
Weissenkirchen 133
Wiener Neustadt cathedral 141

cider 35, 137
climate 30-1
clothes 32
coffee 35, 389
coffee houses 389, 408-11
Salzburg 253
Vienna 72-3
costs 385
accommodation 386
food & drinks 389
travel 383
credit cards 385
culture 18
Austrian Alp 419
Austrians 404-5
Blaudruckerei Koó 160
Kunsthaus Gmünd 316
WUK 107
currency 385
cycling 10, 42, 46-7, 383
cycling tours & trails
Bike Trail Tirol 350
Bodensee Radweg 371
Danube Cycle Path 134
Dolomitenhütte 318
EldoRADo Bike Park 362
Gaisberg Trail 350
Hallstätter See 226
Hintergebirgsradweg bike trail 178
Ischg 368
Kitzsteinhorn 290
Murradweg 211
Neusiedler See 154, **154**
Salzach River 255
Salzburg 253
Salzburger Almentour 290
Salzkammergut Trail 290
Schloss Hellbrunn 268
Silvretta Bike Arena 368
Sound of Music, the 253
Tauernradweg 286, 290
Wachau Valley 132
Wörthersee 301, **301**

Dachstein Sky Walk 212
Dachstein Suspension Bridge 212
Danube 127, 131, 150
Danube Canal 83
disabilities, travellers with 394
discount cards 43-4
discounts 55
Dolomites, the 318-20, **319**
Donau Turm 55
doughnuts 36
Dreiländereck 306
drinking 388 see also individual locations
drinks, see beer, cider, coffee, schnapps, wine

driving 383
driving tours 10
Bregenzerwald Käsestrasse 374, **374**
Gerlos Alpine Road 345
Grossglockner Road 284, **284**
Postalmstrasse toll road 233
Ringstrasse 76-7, 402, **77**
Silvretta-Hochalpenstrasse 375
Timmelsjoch High Alpine Road 358
Drosendorf 147
Dürnstein 133-4

earth pyramids 360
Edge of Reason, The 367
Ehrenwald 361
Eisenstadt 156
EldoRADo Bike Park 362
electricity 395
emergencies
language 396
number 395
Erdpyramiden 360
Erlebnis Sennerei Zillertal 344
Europabrücke 338
events, see festivals & events

Falco 33, 412-13
falconry 270
falconry displays 146
family travel 41, 387
Salzburg 251
farm stays 386
Feldkirch 372-3
festivals & events 30-1
Almabtrieb 344, 366
Art Advent 98
Aufsteiren 35
Bregenzer Festspiele 31, 370
Bruknerfest 171
Buskers Festival 98
Calle Libre festival 54, 104-5
Donauinselfest 31, 75
DRAUpuls 304
Ebensee's Glöcklerlauf 242
Elevate 31, 191
Fasnacht 337
Festspielhaus 370
Festwochen Gmünden 227
Funky Autumn Festival 344

festivals & events continued
Gauderfest 343
Gauklerfestival 372
Glöcklerlauf 227
Gustav Mahler Festival 227
Hoo-Ruck Festival 344
Jazz & the City 266
Klagenfurt Festival 302
Klagenfurter Altstadtzauber 302
Kunstmue 227
Lehár Festival 227
Liszt Festival 157
Lockenhaus Chamber Music Festival 157
Mozart Week: 250
Nova Rock 157
Opera in the Quarry 157
Ottakringer Bierfest 35, 118
Perchten 347
Pflasterspektakel 171
Pink Lake LGBTQ Festival 302
Popfest 98
Rookie Music Year 304
Salzburger Festspiele 31, 251, 262, 266
Schemenlaufen 31, 360
Seefestspiele Mörbisch 157
Spectaculum 31, 309
Stanz Brennt 35, 361
Steirischer Apfelfeste 35
Steirischer Herbst 31
Sternenkino Movie Nights 266
Summer Night Concert 54
Top of the Mountain 368
Villach Unplugged 304
Villacher Kirchtag 304
Wiener Weinwandertag 35, 119
Wörthersee Classics Festival 302
film locations 8-9
films 33
Before Sunrise 95
Sound of Music, The 233-4, 251, 270, 419
Third Man, The 33, 98

Filzmoos 271-2
accommodation 292
food 34-6, 388-9, *see also individual locations*
apricots 133
cheese 344, 373, 374
poppy seeds 147
pumpkinseed oil 206-7
sausages 36, 104
Slow Food 391
Forchtenstein 158-9
forest bathing 278
Forsthaus 242
fortresses, *see* castles & fortresses
Freistadt 172
Freud, Sigmund 106-7
Friesach 309
funiculars
Bergisel 336
Nordkettenbahnen 329
Saltzwelten Funicular 226

gardens, *see* parks & gardens
gay travellers, *see* LGBTIQ+ travellers
Garnitzenklamm 305
Gerlos Alpine Road 345
Ginzling 346
Gjaidalm 229
Glockenspiel 201
Gmünd 316-17
Going am Wilden Kaiser 352-3
gold mines 286
golf 350
Graz 190-204, **192-3, 198**
accommodation 213
beyond Graz 205-12, *see also individual locations*
drinking 197
entertainment 292
festivals 191
food 191, 196
green city 407
history 191, 197
itineraries 28-9, **29**
LGBTIQ+ 203
shopping 199, 203
travel within Graz 190
walking tour 200, **200**
green cities 406-7
Grossglockner Road 284, **284**

H

Hall in Tirol 336
Hallein 268-9
accommodation 292

Hallstatt 225-6, 401
Hallstätter See 224-9, **225**
accommodation 243
drinking 228
food 226, 227
history 228
travel within Hallstätter See 224
walking tours 226-7
Haydn, Joseph 75, 156
health 392
health & wellness retreats
Ayurveda Resort Sonnhof 354
Kurhaus Schärding 182-3
Heiligenblut 282
accommodation 293
Heldenorgel 354
Helix 272
Hellbrunn 267-8
Hemingway, Ernest 375
Hermagor 305
highlights 8-19
hiking 19, 40-1, 42, 43-5, 46-7, 414-16
9 Summit Experience 351
Adlerweg 365
Alps 43
Augstsee 237
Berliner Höhenweg 346
Brentenjochalm 354
Dachstein Circuit 271, 290
Dachstein Rundweg 212
Donausteig Trail 174
Drei-Seen-Blick 237
Garnitzenklamm 305
Gesäuse-Runde 209
Goethe Trail 333
Goldbichl 333
Gosaukamm Circuit 272
Grossglockner 281
Grossvenediger 279
Hagenbachklamm 138
Hemma Pilgrim's Way 314
Hermannskogel 138
Hoher Lindkogel 138
Höllental 143
Innergschlöss Glacier Trail 281
Kaiserblickweg 350
Kitzsteinhorn 277
Lahngangseen 237
Loser 237
Luchs Trail 209
Lucknerhütte 281
Mühlauer Klamm 333
Obertraun 228-9
Orth Circular Trail 150
Pinzgauer Spaziergang 275, 290, **275**
Putzenalpe 366
Radsattel Circuit 375
Raxalpe 143

Reichraminger Hintergebirge 179
Salzburger Almenweg 271, 290
Schneeberg 143
Schönau Danube Trail 150
Semmering 142
Sengsengebirge 178-9
Silberkarklamm 212
Sonnspitze 351
Steigl Pass 272
Wasserwunderweg 55a 146
Wien Stadtwanderwege 85
Zellberg 340
Zillertal Circuit 342
Zillertaler Höhenstrasse 340-1
hiking equipment 43-5
Hinterthiersee 354-5
history, *see also* Jewish history, Middle Ages, Stone Age
Café Central 402
Carnuntum 401
Dürnstein Castle 401
Hallstatt 401
Hofburg 402
Linz 403
Mauthausen Memorial 403
Naturhistorisches Museum 400
Ötzi Dorf 400
Ringstrasse 402
Salzburg Altstadt 402
Schloss Ambras 402
Secession 403
Semmeringbahn 402
Stift Heiligenkreuz 401
Hitler, Adolf 183
Hofburg 64-7, 402, **66**
Hohe Tauern National Park 31, 40, 41, 279-84, 402, **280**
accommodation 293
beyond Hohe Tauern National Park 285-9, *see also individual locations*
food 281
travel within Hohe Tauern National Park 279
holidays 395
horn sledge racing 355
hotels 386
Hüttenberg 309

ice man 358
ice rinks 261

Igls 336
iodine springs 181
Imst 359-60
Innsbruck 41, 328-34, **330-1**
 accommodation 378
 beyond Innsbruck 335-9, *see also individual locations*
 drinking 333
 food 329
 itineraries 24-5, **25**
 shopping 329
 travel within Innsbruck 328
 walking tour 332, **332**
insurance, health 392
Innviertel 181
 drinking 183
 food 182
Ischgl 368
itineraries 22-9, **22-3**, **25**, **27**, **29**, *see also individual locations*

Jewish history 57, 61, 83

Kalser Dorfertal 281
Kamptal Reservoirs 145-6
Karl-Marx-Hof 119
Kitzbühel 348-51, **349**
 accommodation 378
 beyond Kitzbühel 352-5, *see also individual locations*
 food 350
 travel within Kitzbühel 348
Kitzsteinhorn Glacier 277-8
Klagenfurt 298-302, **299**
 accommodation 321
 food 300
 travel within Klagenfurt 298
Klimt, Gustav 97-8, 115, 242
Kokoschka, Oskar 143
Krampus 347
Krems an der Donau 126-8
 drinking 128, 129
 food 128, 129
Krimml 285-6
 accommodation 293
Krippenstein 229
Kufstein 353-4
Kunsthaus Graz 190-1
Kunsthistorisches Museum Vienna 68-70, **69**

lakes 14, 16-17
 Achensee 346
 Astbergsee 353
 Atoll Achensee 347
 Bodensee 370, 371
 Edlebach 179
 Faaker See 304
 Grundlsee 237
 Hechtsee 354
 Kammersee 238
 Lake Elisabethsee 179
 Lake Gleinkersee 179
 Laudachsee 241
 Palfnersee 288
 Schwarzensee 233
 Schwarzsee 351
 Segelschule Mondsee 234
 Silvretta Stausee 375
 Stausee Durlassboden 345
 Stimmersee 354
 Thiersee 354
 Toplitzsee 237
 Torsee 351
 Upper Bockhartsee 288
 Waldbad Anif 262
 Zeller See 273
Landhaus 298
landscapes 16-17
Langenlois 147
language 33, 396-7
Lech 367
 accommodation 379
legends 417
Leoben 210
LGBTIQ+ travellers 393
 Graz 203
 Vienna 97
Liechtensteinklamm 272
Lienz 318-20, **319**
 accommodation 321
 travel within Lienz 318
Lindau 371
Lingkor 309
Linz 166-71, 403, **167**
 accommodation 185
 beyond Linz 172-5, *see also individual locations*
 drinking 168, 171
 food 166-7, 168, 169
 travel within Linz 166
 walking tour 170, **170**
Lipizzaner horses 65, 66
Liszt, Franz 159-60
Looshaus 143
Loretto 157
Losenstein 180
Lower Austria 123-61, **124**
 events 125
 festivals 125
 itineraries 125
 navigation 124
 travel seasons 125
 travel within Lower Austria 124
Lower Austrian Falconry & Bird of Prey Centre 146

Mariazell 205
markets, *see also* Christmas markets
 Brunnenmarkt 117
 Graz 203
 Karmelitermarkt 83
 Naschmarkt 96
 Rochusmarkt 88
 Südbahnhofmarkt 166
 Weihnachtsmarkt am Spittelberg 99
Mauthausen 173-5
Mauthausen Memorial 173, 403
Mayr Cure 182
measures 395
Melk 128
Middle Ages
 Feldkirch 372
 Friesach 309
 Innere Stadt 61
Militärakademie 141
Millstätter See 310-14, **311**
 beyond Millstätter See 315-17
 drinking 313
 food 312
 itineraries 28-9, **29**
 travel within Millstätter See 310
Mödling 139
Mohr, Joseph 264
Mönchsberg 250
Mondsee 230-4, **231**
 accommodation 243
 food 233
 travel within Mondsee 230
money 385
Montafon 375
Mösern 339
Mostviertel 137
mountain biking 46-7
 Dachstein Circuit 290
 Galzig Trail 362
 Ironbike 368
 Millstätter Radweg 313
 Nordkette Single Trail 333
 Paterzipf 317
 Zillertal Radweg 340
mountains 19, 414-16, 417-19
 Brentenjoch 354
 Dachstein Mountains 228-9
 Grossglockner 281, 290
 Grossvenediger 279, 290
 Grünberg 241
 Gschöllkopf 347
 Hafelekarspitze 333
 Hoher Dachstein 212
 Karwendel 347
 Kemacher 333
 Kitzbüheler Horn 350
 Kitzsteinhorn 277, 290
 Ködnitztal 281
 Kreuzjoch 340
 Mt Katrin 223
 Nordkette Alps 334
 Ötztal Alps 358
 Patscherkofel 336
 Piz Buin 375
 Seegrube 333
 Stubnerkogel 287
 Untersberg 256
 Wurbauerkogel 180
 Zillertal Alps 347
 Zugspitze 361
Mozart, Wolfgang Amadeus 33, 71, 74, 250, 257, 412-13
Murau 210
Murinsel 194
museums & galleries
 Adventure museum 361
 Aguntum 320
 Albertina 67
 Alpen-Adria-Galerie im Stadthaus 300
 Angelika Kauffmann Museum 375
 Architekturzentrum Wien 103
 Arnulf Rainer Museum 140
 Ars Electronica Center 169-70
 Austrian Folk Museum 109
 Beethoven Pasqualatihaus 75
 Beethovenhaus 139
 Belvedere 90-2
 Bezirksmuseum Herzogsburg 183-4
 Carthusuan Museum 129
 Christmas Museum 261
 Condomi Museum 96
 COSA Centre for Scientific Activities 201
 Cowboy Museum 171
 Diözesanmuseum 308
 Eboard Museum 302
 Egon Schiele Birthplace 136
 Egon Schiele Museum 136

museums continued
Ephesos Museum 66
Falconry Museum 146
Fälschermuseum 96
Francisco Carolinum 168
Freilichtmuseum 251
Funeral Museum 96
Grazmuseum p197
Haus der Geschichte Österreich 66
Haus der Natur 251
Haydnhaus 75
Heimatkundliches Museum 230-1
Heimat Museum 375
Heimatmuseum 354
Heinrich Harrer Museum 309
Hermesvilla 110-11
Historische Badestube Vorderbad 184
Hofburg 64-7, 402, **66**
House of Strauss 74-5
Jüdisches Museum 57
Kaiserliche Schatzkammer Wien 65
Karikaturmuseum 126-7
Keltenmuseum 268-9
K-Hof Museum 241
Klimt Villa 115
Klimt-Zentrum 242
Kunsthalle Krems 127
Kunsthalle Wien 103
Kunsthaus 369
KunstHausWien Museum Hundertwasser 88
Kunsthistorisches Museum Vienna 68-70, **69**
Landesgalerie Niederösterreich 127
Landeszeughaus 195
Lentos Kunstmuseum 168
Leopold Museum 102-3
Liszt Museum 159-60
Local History House with Bell Foundry 184
Mauthausen Memorial 173, 403
MMKK 300
Mozarthaus Vienna 74
MQ Freiraum 103
mumok 103
Museum der Moderne 250, 257

Museum der Stadt Villach 304
Museum for Sanitary Objects 241
Museum für angewandte Kunst (MAK) 76
Museum für Volkskultur 315
MuseumsCenter Leoben 210
MuseumsQuartier 102-3
Musikinstrumenten Museum der Völker 230
Naturhistorisches Museum 77, 400
Naturkundemuseum 201
Nordico Stadtmuseum 171
Oldtimer Museum 141
Ötzi Dorf 356, 400
Pfahlbau- und Klostermuseum 234
Pharmacy Museum 175
Pharma und Drogistenmuseum 96
Portraitgalerie 335
Österreichisches Freilichtmuseum 205
Relief von Kärnten 304
Rollett Museum 140
Römermuseum 61
Rupertinum 257
Schatzkammer 308
Schifffahrts Museum 131
Schlossmuseum 169, 175
Schubert Geburtshaus 75
Schubert Sterbewohnung 75
Sigmund Freud Museum 106-7
Sisi Museum 64
Spielzeugmuseum 251
St Pölten Stadtmuseum 135
Stadtgalerie 300
Stadtmuseum Steyr 177
Stiftsmuseum 310
Stille Nacht Museum 269
Teisenhoferhof Wachaumuseum 133
Third Man Museum 98
Treasury of the Teutonic Order 57
Uhrenmuseum 96
Venusium 128
Vorarlberg Museum 369-70
Welterbemuseum Hallstatt 228
Weltmuseum 65-6
Wheel of History 84
Wien Museum 93-5
MuseumsQuartier 102-3
music 15, 33, 412-13
Haus der Musik 71

Mozarteum 250
Musikverein 71
Salzburg 265
Schloss Mirabell 265
Schlosskonzerte 250
St Florian Boys' Choir 174
Vienna Boys' Choir 81
Vienna State Opera 76, 80
music locations 8
myths 417

national parks & nature reserves 46-7
Hohe Tauern National Park 31, 40, 41, 279-84, **280**
Nationalpark Donau-Auen 149-50
Nationalpark Gesäuse 209
Nationalpark Kalkalpen 176-84, **177**
Nationalpark Neusiedler See-Seewinkel 153
Nationalpark Thayatal 144-5
Nockberge Biosphere Reserve 315
Ötscher Tormäuer Nature Park 136-7
Rheindelta nature reserve 371
Nationalpark Kalkalpen 176-84, **177**
accommodation 185
drinking 179
food 178
health & wellness 182-3
travel within Nationalpark Kalkalpen 176
Neolithic relics 356
Neusiedler See 151-7, **152**
beyond Neusiedler See 158-60, *see also individual locations*
cycling tour 154, **154**
drinking 153, 155, 156
food 153, 155, 156
travel wtihin Neusiedler See 151
nightlife 300, *see also individual locations*
Nockalmstrasse 317

Oberndorf 261
Olympia Bob 336
opening hours 395
Österreichische Postsparkasse 76

Ötzi 358
Ötztal 356-8, **357**
accommodation 379
beyond the Ötztal 359-61, *see also individual locations*
travel within Ötztal 356

palaces 12-13
Am Hof 61
Hofburg (Innsbruck) 328
Hofburg (Vienna) 64-7, 402, **66**
Kaiservilla 221
Palace Lamberg 177
Palais Coburg 61
Palais Liechtenstein 105
Residenz 260
Schloss Ambras 335, 402
Schloss Arenberg 257
Schloss Bruck 319
Schloss Eggenberg 202
Schloss Esterházy 156
Schloss Frohnburg 268
Schloss Hellbrunn 251, 267
Schloss Leopoldskron 251
Schloss Mirabell 251, 254
Schloss Porcia 315
Schloss Prielau 276
Schloss Schönbrunn 112-14
Palmenhaus 65
Pankratium 316
paragliding 40, 231
parks & gardens
Alpine Flower Garden 350
Arenbergpark 89
Augarten 81
Belvedere Gardens 92
Burggarten 65
Doblhoff Park 140
Heidenreichstein Nature Park 142
Hohe Wand Nature Park 142
Innsbruck Botanical Garden 333
Kamptal-Schönberg Nature Park 142
Karwendel Nature Park 333
Kurpark 140
Lainzer Tiergarten 110
Naturpark Zillertaler Alpen 346
Nordwald Nature Park 142
Ötscher-Tormäuer Nature Park 142
Prater Park 84-5, **84**

Raab-Örség-Goricko Nature Park 160
Schloss Mirabell 254
Schloss Schönbrunn Park 113
Schweizergarten 88
Stadtpark 89
Universität Salzburg Botanical Garden 268
Volksgarten 65
Weinidylle Nature Park 160
Zwerglgarten 254
Payerbach 143
people 404-5
Pfänder 371
pile dwellings 234
plague column 307
planning
 alpine hikes 43
 Austria basics 32-3
 clothes 32
 etiquette 32
population 395, 404
Prater Park 84-5
printmaking 316
Przewalski horses 155
public holidays 395
Puchberg am Schneeberg 143
Purbach am See' 157
purple cows 373

Raiding 159-60
Raimund, Ferdinand 96
Red Vienna 119
Reichraming 178
Reichraminger Hintergebirge 179-80
Reith bei Kitzbühel 350
responsible travel 390-1
Ried im Innkreis 183
Riegersburg 207
rock climbing 40, 41
 Hafelekarspitze 333
 Peilstein Klettersteig 138
 Wilder Kaiser 351
Rodelbahn 366
Roman relics
 Aguntum 320
 Brigantium 370
 Michaelerplatz 61
Rosenburg am Kamp 146-7
Rosengartenschlucht 41, 359
Rust 157

Saalbach-Hinterglemm 278
safe travel 392
salt mines 41, 225-6, 235, 268

Salzburg 30, 245-66, 402 **249**
 accommodation 261, 292
 beyond Salzburg 267-72, see also individual locations
 coffee houses 253
 cycling tours 253
 drinking 254, 265, 266
 festivals & events 247, 262-3, 266
 food 250, 251, 253, 255, 260, 264
 itineraries 22-3, 26-7, 247, **22-3, 27**
 shopping 254, 261, 264
 Sound of Music, The 251
 theatre 264
 tours 255
 travel seasons 247
 travel within Salzburg 246, 248
 walking tour 252, **252**
Salzburgerland 245-93, **246**
 festivals & events 247
 itineraries 247
 navigation 246
 outdoor activities 290-1
 travel seasons 247
 travel within Salzburgerland 246
Salzkammergut 214-43, **216-17**
 activities 218-19
 festivals & events 218-19, 227
 itineraries 218-19
 navigation 216-17
 travel seasons 218-19
 travel within Salzkammergut 217, 223
Salzwelten (Hallein) 268
Salzwelten (Hallstätter See) 225-6, 268
Salzwelten Altaussee 235
scenic railways 10
 Achenseebahn 347
 Lilliputian Locomotive 85
 Mariazellerbahn 136
 Schafbergbahn 232
 Schneebergbahn 143
 Schwaz 337
 Semmeringbahn 142, **402**
Schiele, Egon 136
Schladming 211
Schloss Ambras 335
Schloss Schönbrun 112-14
Schlossberg p196
Schmetterlinghaus 65
Schmidt, Martin Johann 128
schnapps 11, 35, 361
Schneider, Hannes 365
schnitzels 36

Schoenberg, Arnold 139
Schönbrunn Zoo 113
Schubert, Franz 75, 139, 413
Schwarzenberg 375-7
Schwaz 337
Secession 97-8,403
Seefeld 338
Semmering 142
Sengsengebirge 178-9
Silberbergwerk 337
Silent Night 264
silver mines 359
silver mining 337
Ski Arlberg 38, 364
skiing & snowboarding 19, 37-9, 46-7, 392
 Ahorn 343
 Bad Gastein 39
 Big 3 Rally 358
 Der Weisse Ring 367
 Galzig 364
 Great Arlberg Tour 364
 Greitspitz 368
 Hafelekar Run 333
 Hahnenkamm 348
 Hahnenkamm-Rennen 349
 Harakiri 343
 Hintertux Glacier 39, 343
 Idalp 368
 Ischgl 368
 Kandahar 364
 Kitzbühel 38, 348
 Kitzbüheler Horn 348
 Kitzsteinhorn Glacier 39, 277
 Lech 367
 Mausefalle 349
 Mayrhofen 343
 Montafon 375
 Nordkette Skylinepark 333
 Paznauer Taya 368
 Penken 343
 Run of Fame 364
 Samnaun 368
 Schladming 211
 Seefeld in Tyrol 39, 338
 Silvretta Arena 368
 Silvretta-Montafon 375
 Ski Amadé 38
 Ski Arlberg 38, 364
 Snowpark Kitzbühel 348
 Sölden 358
 St Anton am Arlberg 364
 Streif 349
 Stubai Glacier 39, 339
 Weisskopfkogel 351
 Valluga 364
 Zell am See-Kaprun 38, 39
 Zillertal 38, 340
 Zillertal 3000 343
 Zürs 367

skydiving 350
smoking 395
snow 31
snow sports 376-7
snowshoeing 39, 41, 178
Spanische Hofreitschule 65
spas & thermal baths
 Allegria Thermal Stegersbach 159
 Aqua Dome 357-8
 AVITA Therme Bad Tatzmannsdorf 159
 Bad Gastein 289
 Baden bei Wien 139
 Die Therme der Ruhe Bad Gleichenberg 208
 Felsentherme 286
 Freibad Ried im Innkreis 182
 Gasteiner Heilstollen 286
 Geinberg Spa Resort 182
 H20 Hotel-Therme Bad Waltersdorf 208
 Loipersdorf Thermal Bath 159
 Parktherme Bad Radkersburg 208
 Rogner Bad Blumau 208
 Römertherme 139-40
 Salzkammergut Therme 223
 Sonnentherme Lutzmannsburg 159
 St Martins, Frauen-kirchen 159
 Thermal Spa Resort Bad Loipersdorf 208
 Thermalstrandbad 139-40
 Therme Bad Schallerbach 182
Spittal an der Drau 315
Spittelau Incinerator 107
Spitz an der Donau 130-3
St Anton am Arlberg 40, 362-6, **363**
 accommodation 379
 beyond St Anton am Arlberg 367-8, see also individual locations
 food 364
 nightlife 365
 travel within St Anton am Arlberg 362
St Florian 175
St Gilgen 230-1
St Pölten 135-6
St Veit an der Glan 307
St Wolfgang 232
Stanz 361
stargazing 283
Steinberg-Dörfl 160
Steyr 176

425

Index

S

StieglKeller 265
Stone Age 358
Strauss, Johann 74-5
Strobl 232-3
Strudlhofstiege 109
Stubnerkogel 290
Stübing 205
Styria 186-212, **188**
  itineraries 189
  navigation 188
  travel seasons 189
  travel within Styria 188
Südsteiermark 206
suspension bridges 287
Swarovski Kristallwelten 338
swimming 354, see also wild swimming
synagogues
  Stadttempel 61

T

taxes 385, 386
Techendorf am Weissensee 316-17
theatres
  Mechanical Theatre 267
  Salzburger Marionettentheater 264
  Theater in der Josefstadt 108
  Theatre am Spittelberg 99
  Vorarlberger Landestheater 370
thermal baths, see spas & thermal baths
time 395
tipping 385
train travel 383, 384, see also scenic railways
toboggan runs 366
toilets 395
traditional indigo dyeing 160
traditions 18
Traunkirchen 241-2
Traunsee 239-42, **240**
  accommodation 243
  drinking 242
  food 242
  travel within Traunsee 239

Map Pages **000**

travel seasons 30-1, 386, see also individual locations
travel to/from Austria 382
travel within Austria 383-4
travelling with kids 41, 251
trekking, see hiking
Tröpolach 306
Tulln 136
Tyrol 323-79, **324-5**
  events 326-7
  festivals 326-7
  itineraries 24-5, 326-7, **25**
  navigation 324
  travel seasons 326-7
  travel within Tyrol 325

U

University of Vienna 77, 109
Upper Austria 162-85, **164**
  activities 165
  itineraries 165
  navigation 164
  travel seasons 165
  travel within Upper Austria 164

V

via ferrata 41
Vienna 50-121, **52-3**, **57**
  15th district 116, **117**
  accommodation 120-1
  Alsergrund 99-109, **100-1**
  coffee 71, 95
  coffee houses 72-3
  drinking 74, 104, 105, 106, 111, 118, 119
  driving tours 76-7, **77**
  festivals & events 54-5, 75, 98, 104-5
  food 61, 71, 83, 86, 88, 95, 97, 104, 105, 106, 111, 116, 118, 119
  green city 406-7
  Hietzing 110-15, **111**
  history 61, 83, 115
  Innere Stadt 56-80, **57**, **58-9**, **60**
  itineraries 22-3, 54-5, **22-3**
  Josefstadt 99-109, **100-1**
  Landstrasse 87-92, **89**
  Leopoldstadt 81-6, **82**
  LGBTIQ+ 97
  Mariahilf 93-8, **94**
  music 71, 74-5, 80
  navigation 52-3
  Neubau 99-109, **100-1**
  nightlife 89, 96, 104, 107
  Ottakring 117
  Outer Districts 116-19, **117**

shopping 74, 83, 86, 88, 96, 104, 107, 116, 117
tours 63, 98
travel within Vienna 52-3, 56, 81, 87, 93, 99, 110, 116
walking tours 62, 63, 108-9, 119, **63**, **109**
Wieden 93-8, **94**
Vienna City Card 67
Vienna Peace Pagoda 85
Vienna Philharmonic 114
Vienna State Opera 80
viewpoints
  360° 334
  Adlerhorst 347
  Alberfeldkogel 242
  Buzihütte 334
  Cloud One 334
  Eagle's View 354
  Five Fingers viewing platform 229
  Gaisberg 256
  Geiereck 256
  Gloriette 114
  Grossglocknerblick platform 287
  Kaiser-Franz-Josefs-Höhe 282
  Panorama Tower Wurbauerkogel 180
  Salzburg Hochthron 256
  Sky View 354
  Skywalk 226
  Stadtturm 334
  Talblick 287
  Überstieg viewpoint 144
  Wienerblick 111
Villach 303-4, **304**
  accommodation 321
  beyond Villach 305, see also individual locations
  drinking 304
  food 304
  travel within Villach 303
visas 382
Vollpension 95
Vorarlberg 323-79 **324-5**,
  events 326
  festivals 326
  itineraries 326
  navigation 324-5
  travel seasons 326
  travel within Vorarlberg 325

W

Wachau Valley 126-34, **127**
  accommodation 161
  beyond the Wachau Valley 135-43, see also individual locations

cycling tours 132, 134
drinking 130, 131
food 130, 131
shopping 130
travel within the Wachau Valley 126
Wagner, Otto 76, 95, 98, 118
Waldreichs 146-7
Waldviertel 144-8, **145**
  accommodation 161
  beyond Weinviertel 149-50, see also individual locations
  boat trips 127
  drinking 145
  food 145
  travel within Waldviertel 144
walking, see hiking
walking tours
  Gamsgrubenweg 282
  Graz 200, **200**
  Gustav Klimt-Themenweg 242
  Hallstätter See 226-7
  Horn Summit Trail 350
  Hungerburg 333
  Innsbruck 332, **332**
  Innviertel 181
  Jodel Wanderweg 345
  Karstweg 350
  Kohlröslhütte 317
  Linz 170, **170**
  Neubau to Alsergrund 108-9, **109**
  Paterzipf 317
  Rosengartenschlucht 359
  Salzburg in Mozart's footsteps 252
  Seegrube 333
  Sentiero dell'Amore 314
  Sewer Tour 98
  Slow Trail Südufer 313
  Sound of Music Trail 270, 290
  Third Man Walking Tour 98
  Vienna 62, 63, 108-9, 119, **62**, **109**
  Wasserfallweg 285
  Zell am See-Kaprun 276
water parks 358
  Area 47 41
waterfalls 16-17
  Gasteiner Fall 286
  Gössnitz Falls 282
  Krimmler Wasserfälle 285-6, 290, 345
  Stotzbachfall 281
  Stuibenfall 357

426

watersports 14, 41
Almkanal 290
Faaker See 304
Hallstätter See 226
Kamptal Reservoirs 145
Kitzbühel 350
Millstätter See 312-13
Salzburg 255-6
Zeller See 273, 290
Wattens 338
weather 30-1
weights 395
Weinviertel 144, 148, **145**
 accommodation 161
 beyond Weinviertel 149-50, see also individual locations
 travel within Weinviertel 144
Weissenkirchen 133
Wells 177
wellness, see health & wellness retreats, spas & thermal baths, yoga
Weltmuseum 65-6
Werfen 269-71
 accommodation 292
Wiener Neustadt 140
Wiener Philharmoniker 71
Wiener Rathaus 77
Wienerwald 137-40
 accommodation 161
wildlife 16, 41, 180, 282, 371, see also bees, birdwatching
wild swimming 288, 312
Willendorf 128
Windischgarsten 180
winds 30
wine 35, 389
wine regions 11
 Eisenberg 159
 Kamptal 147
 Mittelburgenland 159
 Neusiedler See 155
 Purbach am See' 157
 Rosalia 159
 Südsteiermark 206
 Vienna 118
 Weinviertel 148
wine taverns 138
wineries
 10er Marie 54
 Kellergasse 157
 Kellerviertel 160
 LOISIUM WeinWel 147
 Rogl 180
 Ursin Haus 145
 Weingut Brandl 145
 Weingut Bründlmayer 145
 Weingut Esterházy 155
 Weingut Hirsch 145
 Weingut Schloss Gobelsburg 145
 Weingut Silvia Heinrich 159
Wolfgangsee 230-4, **231**
 accommodation 243
 boat trips 230-1
 drinking 232
 food 232, 233
 travel within Wolfgangsee 230
Wörthersee 298-302, **299**
 accommodation 321
 cycling tour 301, **301**
 drinking 302
 food 302
 travel within Wörthersee 298
Wurstelprater 84

yoga 40, 182, 289, 366

Zell am See 273-6, **274**
 accommodation 292
 beyond Zell am See 277-8
 food 276
 hiking tour 275, **275**
 itineraries 26-7, **27**
 travel within Zell am See 273
Zell am Ziller 40
Zillertal 41, 340-4, **341**
 accommodation 378
 beyond Zillertal 345-7, see also individual locations
 food 343
 itineraries 24-5, **25**
 travel within Zillertal 340
ziplines 286
zoos 113
Zürs 367
 accommodation 379
Zwettl 146
Zwölferhorn 231

NOTES

NOTES

NOTES

"Dining alfresco by lantern light as the full moon rose above the Alps of Sportgastein (p288) on a crisp, snowy evening was pure magic."

KERRY WALKER

"The first time I entered 'the killing area' at Mauthausen Concentration Camp (p173), was one of the few times I've cried in public."

SAMANTHA PRIESTLEY

"On my first visit to Vienna, I tried to help a waiter with my coffee cup in a traditional coffee house (p72). Rookie error; never intervene!"

BECKI ENRIGHT

"Staring at the Fairlight synthesizer in Klagenfurt's Eboard Museum (p302), I thought, 'This was how it began, the progenesis of sampling'."

ANTHONY HAYWOOD

All rights reserved. No part of this publication may be copied, stored in a retrieval system, or transmitted in any form by any means, electronic, mechanical, recording or otherwise, except brief extracts for the purpose of review, and no part of this publication may be sold or hired, without the written permission of the publisher. Lonely Planet and the Lonely Planet logo are trademarks of Lonely Planet and are registered in the US Patent and Trademark Office and in other countries. Lonely Planet does not allow its name or logo to be appropriated by commercial establishments, such as retailers, restaurants or hotels. Please let us know of any misuses: lonelyplanet.com/legal/intellectual-property.

Mapping data sources:
© Lonely Planet
© OpenStreetMap openstreetmap.org/copyright

LEFT: GIANNIS PAPANIKOS/SHUTTERSTOCK. RIGHT: ABB PHOTO/SHUTTERSTOCK

THIS BOOK

Destination Editor
Sandie Kestell

Coordinating Editor
Gabrielle Innes

Production Editor
Sarah Farrell

Image Editor
Carol Farrell

Cartographer
Dorothy Davidson

Assisting Editor
Peterjon Cresswell

Cover Researcher
Katelyn Perry

Thanks Alison Killilea, Kate Mathews, Charlotte Orr

MIX
Paper | Supporting responsible forestry
FSC™ C021741

Paper in this book is certified against the Forest Stewardship Council™ standards. FSC™ promotes environmentally responsible, socially beneficial and economically viable management of the world's forests.

Published by Lonely Planet Global Limited
CRN 554153
12th edition – Apr 2026
ISBN 978 1 83869 674 0
© Lonely Planet 2026 Photographs © as indicated 2026
10 9 8 7 6 5 4 3 2 1
Printed in China